HEADLINE

HOLLYWOOD

A CENTURY OF

FILM SCANDAL

HEADLINE HOLLYWOOD

EDITED BY

ADRIENNE L. McLEAN

AND DAVID A. COOK

RUTGERS UNIVERSITY PRESS

NEW BRUNSWICK, NEW JERSEY, AND LONDON

Library of Congress Cataloging-in-Publication Data

Headline Hollywood : a century of film scandal / edited by Adrienne L. McLean and David A. Cook
      p.   cm. — (Communications, media, and culture)
   Includes bibliographical references and index.
   ISBN 0-8135-2885-2 (cloth : alk. paper) — ISBN 0-8145-2886-0 (pbk. : alk. paper)
    1. Motion pictures—California—Los Angeles—Biography. 2. Motion picture industry—California—Los Angeles—Anecdotes. 3. Scandals—Calfifornia—Los Angeles. I. McLean, Adrienne L. II. Cook, David A. III. Series

   PN1993.5.U65 H39 2001
384'.8'0979494—DC21   00-039040

British Cataloging-in-Publication data for this book is available from the British Library.

This collection copyright © 2001 by Rutgers, The State University.
Individual chapters copyright © 2001 in the names of their authors.
Lucy Fischer's essay was originally published in another form in *Women and Performance* 6, no. 2 (1993): 27–40. Copyright © 1993 by New York University Press.
Adrienne L. McLean's essay was originally published in another form as "The Cinderella Princess and the Instrument of Evil: Surveying the Limits of Female Transgression in Two Postwar Hollywood Scandals" in *Cinema Journal* 34, no. 3 (spring 1995): 36–56. Copyright © 1995 by the University of Texas Press, P.O. Box 7819, Austin, TX 78713-7819.

Manufactured in the United States of America

Contents

ACKNOWLEDGMENTS

*T*his collection began as a series of discussions about how useful Hollywood scandal seemed to have been, and remains still, in providing a locus for the wide debate of difficult and unwieldy questions about identity politics and what constitutes right and moral behavior both individually and collectively, in public and in private. It took shape, however, with the discovery that our own interests in the history and theory of Hollywood scandal were shared by a large number of our colleagues in film studies. This collection rests on their efforts, and we want first to thank the contributors for their exemplary work, their good humor, and their (usually) astonishing cooperation in the matter of deadlines. We would also like to thank Dean Dennis Kratz and Associate Dean Michael Wilson at the University of Texas at Dallas for their support, and Larry Thomas for knowing more weird stuff than anyone in the world. Finally, we offer our deepest thanks to everyone at Rutgers University Press, especially Joe Abbott, for his thorough and expert copyediting; Marilyn Campbell, for her logistical help and for patiently dealing with hundreds of more or less frantic questions; George Custen, our series editor, whose comments and suggestions improved this book in innumerable ways; and Leslie Mitchner, for her wisdom, energy, optimism, and enthusiastic support of this project, and her ultimate guidance in making its preparation so smooth and rewarding an experience.

HEADLINE HOLLYWOOD

INTRODUCTION

ADRIENNE L. MCLEAN

Hollywood is a synonym for wealth and glamour; it has also become a synonym for sin. As a symbol of sin, it should be noted, Hollywood is a scapegoat for traditional hostilities, the embodiment of Bohemia to all the Philistines on the face of the globe.

LEO ROSTEN, 1941[1]

Artist shall perform the services herein contracted for in a manner that shall be conducive to the best interests of Producer, and to the best interests of the motion picture industry generally, and if Artist shall at any time . . . either while rendering services hereunder or in Artist's private life, commit an offense involving moral turpitude under federal, state, or local laws or ordinances, or if Artist's conduct shall offend against decency, morality, or social proprieties, or shall cause Artist to be held in public ridicule, scorn or contempt, or cause public scandal, then . . . Producer may suspend the payment of compensation to Artist . . . [or] may terminate this agreement at any time after the happening of such event.[2]

ollywood has had a long association with scandal—with covering it up, with managing its effects, in some cases with creating and directing it. Of the wide range of memoirs and biographies that make up the lore of Hollywood and its stars, some are little more than strings of anecdotes, presented in greater or lesser detail and with greater or lesser fidelity to basic accuracy, about who did what with whom (or with what), and how these actions were kept secret— or leaked, divulged, laid bare—and to what effect.[3] But despite its extraordinary ubiquity as a term, *scandal* has received relatively little attention in regard to the often contradictory ways it has functioned across time in American film and culture.

In fact, one of the reasons that we initiated this project was our curiosity about why many famous scandals of Hollywood's past would now, in a new millennium, scarcely raise a ripple of widespread public interest. What makes one era's scandals seem tame to succeeding generations, the response of the condemnatory public bewildering or ludicrous, the treatment of the participants unjust? Conversely, discussions among ourselves and our colleagues about what makes a scandal a scandal—to determine the parameters of moral turpitude—always ended in polite discord. For although we all agreed that scandals are, to borrow from Erving Goffman, "deeds, not mere events," we knew that deeds we thought innocuous could be comprehended as offensive or shocking by groups surveying them through social frameworks, in Goffman's terms, different from our own.[4]

Goffman reminds us that in any situation "many different things are happening simultaneously" and that the meaning of any action that involves human agency does not attach to the action alone but also to its presentation (or representation, in the case of a mass-mediated scandal) in multiple frameworks.[5] Scandals arise from the collision of deed, intention, context, and perspective and are therefore much more complex than their usual rendering as anecdote would suggest.

However, another recurring feature of our conversations about scandal was their tendency to devolve into gossip sessions, in that our attempts to establish the limits of scandalous behavior by recounting anecdotes ourselves about Hollywood and its stars would inevitably be met at some point with an astonished "I didn't know that!" We are also interested, therefore, in how we learn about scandalous deeds, where our information comes from and when, and who controls the terms of our knowledge. Even the most canonical Hollywood scandals, if one may call them that—Roscoe "Fatty" Arbuckle's arrest for his involvement in the death of starlet Virginia Rappe in 1921; the unsolved murder of director William Desmond Taylor in 1922; matinee idol Wallace Reid's death from the effects of morphine addiction in 1923; the publication of sexually explicit excerpts from Mary Astor's diary in 1935; Errol Flynn's trial for the statutory rape of two teenaged girls in 1942; Robert Mitchum's arrest and incarceration in 1948 for possession of marijuana; the extramarital affairs of Rita Hayworth and Ingrid Bergman in 1949, and the birth of Bergman's "love child" in 1950; the death of Lana Turner's mob boyfriend Johnny Stompanato, apparently stabbed in the stomach by Turner's daughter Cheryl in 1958; among many possible examples—have acquired different inflections now than they appear to have had in the past, at least in certain frameworks. Instead of being a morality tale about debauchery, licentiousness, and the arrogance of unearned wealth, Arbuckle's story is now more often employed in film scholarship, for instance, as exemplary of Hollywood's hypocrisy. In this version the subject has become Hollywood's ability to mobilize public outrage to its own ends—the way it scapegoated Arbuckle and defined him as deviant[6] in order to stave off government censorship and ultimately to consolidate studio power over exhibitors, the film product, and industry workers alike for thirty-odd years.[7] Scandals are thus always discursive constructions as well as events, and it matters who controls the selection and omission of their narrative details. Rather than the result of knowing too much, a scandal may result from the public's being told too much about some things and too little about others.

Finally, we wanted to participate in an ongoing scholarly dialogue about how scandal *should* be defined. As Herman Gray has argued in his work on scandal and race, the standard use of the word associates it with personal or individual transgression against the "dominant social and moral order"; yet that order also names what and who is outside its own boundaries and thus can define as transgressive whatever is marginal to its concerns or does not submit to its power.[8] Gray differentiates the word and its associated forms diacritically in his discussion of how what we are told is "scandalous" often "hides and glosses" what is truly *scandalous*. Miscegenation, then, explicitly prohibited in Hollywood films between 1934 and 1952 by the terms of the Production Code, may have been "scandalous," but this designation covers the truly *scandalous* institutionalized racism on which miscegenation, as a deed, depends. What *scandals*, in short, might even the most famous Hollywood "scandals" cover up? And what is the relationship of Hollywood to the "culture of scandal" that we are told by so many we live in today?

Anyone who picks up a paper, reads a magazine, or watches television would have to agree with the first sentence of James Lull and Stephen Hinerman's 1997 anthology *Media Scandals*: "Scandals are pervasive today."[9] Scandal is now a commodity with proven market value, a dominant feature of contemporary journalism and even the most "respectable" forms of mass media, as well as of supermarket tabloids, gossip magazines, "trash television" talk shows and celebrity exposés, and chat parlors in cyberspace. Over the past couple of decades there have been sensational scandals involving professional sports figures, "televangelists," the music industry, banking and finance, and ordinary people; presidential politics have certainly been intermittently but spectacularly scandal-ridden since Watergate in 1974.[10] Hollywood is still the locus of occasional scandals, but it is arguably no longer the predominant one (indeed, Lull and Hinerman bypass it almost entirely). We need to be reminded, therefore, that it once was, and that movies themselves, as Robert Sklar writes in *Movie-Made America*, "have historically been and still remain vital components in the network of cultural communication, and the nature of their content and control helps to shape the character and direction of American culture as a whole."[11]

In her 1998 book *Scorpion Tongues: Gossip, Celebrity, and American Politics*, Gail Collins locates the roots of celebrity scandal in the nineteenth century, with the "incredible uproar" produced by Harriet Beecher Stowe's public revelation that the "brooding poet Lord Byron . . . had slept with his own half sister." The "class of entertainment celebrities that we know today," however, began to be created around the 1880s as a result of increased urbanization and leisure time, and the concomitant development of tabloids and other media forms that relied on "visual appeal." Although political scandals — beginning with the "Washington gossip wars" that pitted "profligate" John Quincy Adams against the "adulterer" Andrew Jackson in the 1828 presidential election — are the major focus of her book, Collins points to a number of Hollywood scandals in her account of how movies, theater, sports, and radio displaced politics as the "main provider of celebrities to talk about."[12] From the 1920s on, Collins writes, "Except in times of national crisis, the nation would never again be as interested in politicians as in movie stars."[13]

Scandal has a *history*, in other words, and in America, throughout the twentieth century, that history was often Hollywood's as well. All of the scholars whose work appears here believe that Hollywood scandal has generated enormously potent and diverse historical, cultural, and ideological meanings in relation to American film as an industry, as a mass medium, and as an art form. It has done so in the past, and it is doing so now. Any attempt to establish the truth value of a Hollywood scandal by using newer, "better" sources (like insider autobiographies) or reinterpreting old ones (whether media reports or archival studio documents) runs the risk of replacing one kind of rumor with another; nonetheless, we believe that this risk is worth taking because of the demonstrable inaccuracy of many stories that have, over time, acquired the opaque status of "common knowledge." [14] Although the melancholy fact remains that we can seldom tease apart all of the diachronic processes by which rumor or misinformation solidifies into "fact," we are able sometimes to elucidate in whose interests an entertaining, appalling, or titillating story is chosen over a more dependable rendering of "what is going on here." [15] The first essay begins virtually at the beginning, with the 1906 star scandal of Evelyn Nesbit that occurred at cinema's moment of consolidation in America into a medium of mass appeal and controversy. The last brings us up to the postmodern star text of Bill Clinton, reminding us that rumor and scandal still often take rhetorical precedent over more difficult renderings of motivations and actions (chapter topics are described in more detail in a separate section at the end of this introduction).

But despite the broad range of its subject matter, this collection is not a comprehensive guide to film-related scandals, a footnoted version of those ur-texts of our fascination with movies and their stars, Kenneth Anger's *Hollywood Babylon* series. [16] Many of the essays do center on well-known star scandals of the sort pictured so luridly in Anger's books, but others consider less familiar topics precisely as a means to explore how the fear of scandal's effects and, conversely, scandalmongering were used in Hollywood to repress information or as a means of control over insubordinate or intransigent employees. Thus, we use the word *headline* in our title with some irony because not all of the situations covered here made headlines, and sometimes headlines were generated in order to deflect attention from the truly *scandalous*, the historical and structural inequities and prejudices that made some more vulnerable than others as targets of rumor, gossip, and innuendo.

Although Hollywood always feared scandal's potential effects on box office returns and careers, and plotted continually to dodge threats of localized boycotts and censorship, it frequently participated in generating, creating, and manipulating scandal and innuendo for its own purposes. Spurious "leaks" to the press about a star's bad behavior, usually in terms that made that star look lazy, arrogant, or ungrateful to fans, were a common means of keeping recalcitrant or demanding employees in line. Stars and studio heads invested heavily in maintaining relationships with nationally syndicated gossip columnists like Louella Parsons and Hedda Hopper not only to keep discrepant reality under wraps but because mass-mediated gossip was one of the ways Hollywood set the limits for what was good, bad, transgressive, acceptable. [17] Hollywood lost that ability to regulate the terms of its own representation in the 1950s, when the studio system began to break down and tabloids like *Confidential* and *Inside Story*, and new media like television, openly valorized revelation over concealment.[18] Today, with private lives "sold" to the media on a daily basis, as David Ehrenstein puts it in his study of gay and lesbian life in Hollywood, *secrecy* has become the location of the scandalous.[19] The question is no longer *whether* scandals will occur but at what point they will be made public.

Yet at the same time we believe that Hollywood scandal has often produced effects more salutary, and certainly more ambiguous, than its common association with moral lapse would suggest. As William Cohen writes in his work on sexual scandal and Victorian fiction, "However pious and disciplinary the public narrative scandal produces about private sexual transgression . . . its effects cannot be predicted according to formulas for ideological containment. While it inculcates an understanding of normative behavior in its audience, scandal also provides the opportunity to formulate questions, discuss previously unimagined possibilities, and forge new alliances." The fates of scandal's victims may mean to teach what Cohen calls "punitive lessons, often deliberately intended to induce conformity in [their] audience," but the fact remains that scandal's "thrilling terrors always pose the danger of inciting disobedience to the norms they advertise."[20] Rather than being simply that which upsets the status quo temporarily, scandal can thus function as what sociologists call a "wedge-driver,"[21] a type of disturbance that reveals the vulnerability of the many "primary social frameworks" that together make up what we so often refer to as dominant ideology.[22]

Dominant ideology—or the dominant fiction, to use Jacques Rancière's appealing term—comprises the rules, regulations, lore, and laws (which mass media circulate and reproduce) that organize and anoint as such the natural, the normal, the commonsensical (as well as what is properly public or properly private).[23] A Hollywood scandal, the publicized and mediated violation of these rules, can challenge our very notions and definitions of what is conventional or acceptable in private behavior, public conduct, gender roles, family relationships, and film art. For marginalized groups or subcultures whose conduct has historically been limited by the dominant fiction—women, ethnic and racial minorities, gays and lesbians—certain events may not be perceived as shameful, or in need of punitive action, but as liberating: a star who was "outed" in the 1950s did not signify to gay or closeted audiences as scandalous, or not *only* as scandalous.[24] (As Cohen points out, the media often insist that the public is outraged simply because they assume that it is.)[25] John B. Thompson maintains that, although the consequences of media scandals are not always deleterious, "scandals can have a corrosive impact on the forms of trust which underpin social relations and institutions."[26] Yet the history of Hollywood scandal shows that forms of *deception* have also supported the same relations and institutions; as we shall see, scandal may help to erode those forms as well.

In fact, Hollywood's scandals, and the industry's normalization of milder forms of scandalmongering in fan magazines and gossip columns, are at least partly responsible for one prominent feature of today's "culture of scandal": scandal's omnipresence in, or as, "harmless" mainstream entertainment. The primary framework for scandal has been transformed— "rekeyed," in Goffman's terms— from one in which scandal represents a serious threat or shock to "universal" standards of morality and correct social conduct to one of "play."[27] Although some organs of public opinion continue to bemoan the destigmatization of acts or conditions once labeled "shameful," the very ubiquity of scandal combined with the relative lack of widespread dismay provoked by its omnipresence seems to suggest that scandal has been substantially rekeyed into an amusement, *patterned* on the sensations generated by traumatic ruptures to the dominant fiction but understood by its participants and audience to be "something quite else." Yet for many of its players power inequities and imbalances have made, and continue to make, the game one-sided or corrupt.

So, one of our main points is that any scandal potentially means different things to different people because of the variety of even primary frameworks that are employed to "locate, perceive, identify, and label" experience.[28] We remain wary of defining scandal categorically as good or bad in its effects and believe that ambivalence is the only reasonable stance to take toward most, if not all, of the complex situations described and explored in the twelve essays that follow. Nevertheless, other scholars have labored to characterize the structural components of mass-mediated scandal, to name its consistent features and parameters. We lay out some of this work below before attempting a bit of small-scale theorizing of our own. In 1996 it was possible for William Cohen to lament the fact that there had been "remarkably few attempts to theorize scandal."[29] Only a few years later, however, this is no longer the case.

• • •

Lull and Hinerman and other contributors to *Media Scandals* (of which Herman Gray is one) theorize the modern media scandal as a generalized phenomenon with distinct locatable features.[30] To paraphrase their work, a media scandal occurs when the *intentional* or *reckless personal actions* of *specific persons*, who can be *identified* as perpetrators of those actions, *disgrace or offend the idealized, dominant morality of a social community*. The actions and events must have *differential consequences for those involved* (perpetrators must be seen to benefit from their actions, in contrast to the suffering of their victims). And the revelations of the actions or events must be *widely circulated* by mass media, *effectively narrativized* into a story, and inspire *widespread interest and discussion*. Media scandals, in other words, are *made*; they have to be responded to by relatively large groups (as John B. Thompson writes, "no responses, no scandal"), and they must circulate as what Thompson calls *fixed* information in a "relatively durable medium," like print, film, or video.[31]

Moreover, Lull and Hinerman provide a "typology" of media scandals:[32] A *star scandal* "erupts" when the mass media reveal "how the desires of famous people overrule social expectations, norms, and practices" and when the individual star's private behavior "enters the public arena under circumstances that are outside that star's control." An *institutional scandal* involves a "bureaucratic matrix" and an institution's reputation, with the institution being "personalized" and held publicly responsible for a scandalous act. A *psychodrama scandal* turns "ordinary people" into stars on the basis of their transgressive actions and "strong stories."

We find these criteria useful for understanding *some* Hollywood scandals or rather some *parts* of them. There are certainly Hollywood scandals that seem to involve clear perpetrators and victims—Arbuckle and Virginia Rappe, for example—yet few scandals that are not also complicated by the industry's handling of them. And Hollywood as an institution was itself frequently held to be responsible for scandalous acts, including any number of suicides by its factory "workers."[33] Yet we feel the key terms in these sorts of definitions raise as many questions as they answer. First, film studies has devoted much attention to what makes stars famous, how and why audiences make them into people whose "desires," normal or otherwise, matter.[34] The broad range of identificatory positions available to the spectator of the film text are brought to bear on the star as well: stars may be formally appreciated, impersonally admired from a distance, or fetishized, adored, and fantasized about in ways that arguably make them psychically as close to us as are some friends and family members. This psychic bond to movie stars may be qualitatively different than even the strongest regard for politicians who hold public office, for example, and will be explored further below.

Second, for the purposes of understanding the partial and fragmented nature of scandal, its imbrication in relationships of power and control, then we want to know whose dominant morality, whose social community, who benefits, how reckless behavior is defined and by whom, and who controls a star's image. Although in Lull and Hinerman's structural terms Arbuckle *is* obviously the perpetrator and Rappe the victim, and the scandal is a star scandal, we have noted that this initial construction gave way over time to a sort of "second-order," *institutional* scandal: Hollywood's scapegoating of Arbuckle and its bowing to certain segments of the public who wanted to continue to vilify him even in the face of his acquittal and his demonstrated innocence of the official charges against him. In many, if not most, of the essays in this collection, the "deed" that provokes a scandal of Lull and Hinerman's definition is shown to be less *scandalous*, and hence less interesting, than the subsequent attempts, whether by Hollywood or others, to censor, to appease, to punish, to exploit.[35] Lull and Hinerman claim that media scandals make their perpetrators "shameful" and "humiliate the 'guilty' party as an essential programmatic ingredient in the process." Questions of who *should* be ashamed need to be asked as well, and these return us to the issue of why so many acts or conditions once labeled shameful have been rendered benign, harmless, even healthy.[36] And, of course, we must ask why the careers of large numbers of unrepentant and unashamed individuals flourished in spite of their scandalous acts.[37]

Even the most apparently cut-and-dried star scandal therefore invokes the need to understand context, the cultural horizon against which any action or condition stands out as offensive, and on whose terms. Nevertheless, we would like briefly to perform some metatheorizing ourselves about Hollywood scandal—to investigate some of the psychic mechanisms by which reported deeds might provoke emotional responses that could, if sufficiently strongly felt, lead to punitive thoughts or actions. We use as our example a fan's potential reaction to the wide disclosure of a scandal—manufactured or otherwise—involving a favorite star. How and why would this scandal evoke unappealing emotions like disgust, humiliation, shame, and embarrassment? Scandal "always hangs upon a name," according to Cohen, "since reputation itself is about maintaining a good name, and keeping one's name out of the mouths of others is the principal goal of avoiding scandal."[38] Yet in a profound sense Hollywood is Hollywood because it is full of stars and because their names are always in the mouths of others. What is even more to the point, stars may be stars precisely because we attach *our* good name to *theirs*.

•   •   •

As Richard deCordova writes in his landmark work on early film stardom, "scandal was from the beginning the repressed underside of the movie star's existence. Indeed even the earliest writing on the stars' private lives referred fairly frequently to the potential for scandal, if only to deny it as a reality."[39] Yet, deCordova also points out, the "only scenario that offers the promise of a full and satisfying disclosure of [any] star's identity" is the sexual scandal, the "primal scene of all star discourse."[40] To be a fan, in other words, is to want to know what is hidden about one's object of admiration, and the model for what is hidden in our culture *is* "the truth of sexuality."

This is not to say that we may not be disgusted or that careers may not be ruined by nonsexual behavior as well. But the dynamic of "secrecy and confession, concealment and revelation" that constructs star discourse also, in deCordova's words, "engages us in the very processes through which our society constitutes sexuality as an object of knowledge and fascination." To investigate, as well as to suppress, to repress, to conceal, invokes the well-known Freudian or Foucauldian figure by which we are forced to acknowledge and police the very practices and identities that we want not to imagine or know. Certainly the Hollywood scandals of the early 1920s demonstrated to studio heads how closely they needed to watch, how quickly and carefully events needed to be managed in order to prevent the sorts of "disclosures" that turned Arbuckle into a murderer rather than a murder suspect and Hollywood itself into a vile cesspool in which other depravities lurked beneath the smiling surfaces of films and publicity photos. Despite Arbuckle's acquittal of the charge of manslaughter in the death of Virginia Rappe, his image remained tainted, his ruined career and the loss of the money invested in him serving as Hollywood's originary lesson about "psychological contamination," the enduring power of the secret, the hidden, the sexual to become confused with the authentic.[41]

Stars, as celebrities, are thus a construction of many discourses that enable them to function as what David Marshall calls "site[s] of intense work on the meaning of both individuality and collective identity in contemporary culture."[42] A star "contains" its public's desires, fantasies, longings, and so forth. What accomplishes the work at the site of the star text, however, is the star's connection to an "affective economy" of identification that is always paradoxical.[43] As Edgar Morin, Richard Dyer, John Ellis, and a host of others have pointed out, stars become stars because they are considered unusually talented in some way, but we are equally attracted to them because they are also ordinary and "just like us."[44] And, as many studies over the years have shown, identification — particularly what Jackie Stacey describes as "extra-cinematic" identification (with material circulated about a star's "real" or "private" life) — is often based on similarity rather than difference.[45] These studies indicate that we attach ourselves most easily to those with whom we share particular attributes — age, gender, class, nationality — or whose attributes we would most like to share. If we identify so closely with stars as public personalities (rather than as roles they play on the screen), then any humiliation or shame their acts might occasion is in some sense "ours" as well. A scandalous act is always *vain* because it suggests a disregard for the opinion of others.

William Ian Miller, whose thoughtful ruminations on the unpleasant we find particularly useful in pondering this issue, suggests that although vanity, generally speaking, "begs for humiliation," it is rarely our own humiliation that we desire.[46] Rather, humiliation (or the fear of it) "is perhaps the key emotion that supports our self-esteem and self-respect."[47] The "work" of humiliation "is deflation of pretension. Shaming operates by stripping someone of a status she had some right to before [a] particular failing, whereas humiliation destroys the illusion of having belonged at all."[48]

If one thinks of the Hollywood star as embodying or containing the self-images and "ego stereotypes" (a term used as far back as Henry Forman's alarmist *Our Movie Made Children* in 1933 and invoked countless times since) of many different audience groups, then the shamefulness of a star's scandalous actions or behaviors sets up the possibility for an unpleasant, and often ire-inducing, deflation of what Miller refers to as the "norms whose validity we accept."[49] If the interest we have in stars is equally curiosity about ourselves and our own actions, then we are upset by "inappropriate" behavior because it suggests that we, too, are not who we think we are. If scandal makes the hidden visible, it also forces us to acknowledge that something *is* hidden (which we thought did not exist, or did not know was there) or that something is true that we do not have the psychic equipment to understand or do not want to believe. To identify with a star means to accept the pretense that he or she is worth identifying with; to be shamed by that star's behavior is to have one's own status degraded as well. The social terms of stigmatization bear this out. Anyone who — like Fatty Arbuckle — is stigmatized "variously generate[s] alarm, disgust, contempt, embarrassment, concern, pity, or fear" — but so do these emotions in turn "confirm the stigmatized person as one who is properly stigmatized."[50] The stigmatized individual must be expelled, indeed deserves to be expelled, because he or she generates what feels too much like self-disgust, self-contempt, self-pity, and so on.

Of course, there are many ways to identify with Hollywood films and their stars. Often stars represent what Stacey calls the "bad object" whose "transgressive or rebellious character" is one that a spectator admires but dares not emulate.[51] And, beyond certain prohibitions (against murder, for example) that constrain all of us, there are a few stars (and a few presidents) who seem immune to at least some forms of scandal. Certainly anything written above can have its obverse as well *because* of the aforementioned uncontainability of scandal's "thrilling terrors." As Miller writes in reference to disgust, "Societies, like individuals, learn to modify and suspend the range and subject of certain disgust rules once acquired . . . It is rather remarkable how much variation in disgust norms we learn to accommodate over the course of a lifetime, with more or less shock and resistance."[52]

Again, Cohen suggests that scandal assumes "its modern form" only when "several conditions are met: that news media are national and accessible; that they distance the subjects of their stories from their audience enough to effect a divide between the exposed private life and the anonymous public reading about it; and that the audience itself is conceived in terms sufficiently capacious to encompass a wide range of class, gender, and geographical positions."[53] Although we have argued that the divide between Hollywood and its audience is potentially psychically quite close and that this makes scandal even more significant and powerful, we would not all be able to discuss the same scandals were it not for the mass media. Scandal *is* everywhere now; it has been commodified; it is something we expect to find, to see, to hear about. But the stigmatized individuals whom scandal creates and attempts to punish are also frequently the victims of racism, sexism, and class biases of all kinds. Although gossip itself has acquired new respect as what Ralph Rosnow and Gary Fine call "the dramaturgical format of the novel, the motion picture, and the play" and as the means by which we speak a world we want to live in, we also use gossip, rumor, and scandal to separate, to cast out.[54] For Rosnow and Fine, the question we need to ask is "how people know what they know. Belief in a certain rumor can alter one's perception of the world and create a new semblance of reality. The classical sociological dictum states that if situations are defined as real, they will be real in their consequences."[55] Thus, although we agree emphatically that a Hollywood scandal cannot be identified as such until it is represented, or understood *through* representation, to be a serious or outrageous disruption of some sort of existing social framework, we are equally interested in what, and when, and to whose benefit those frameworks were put into place.

• • •

The essays that follow are organized chronologically, as determined by the rough dates of their precipitating "acts," rather than in arbitrarily designated groupings. That is, although three of the essays share some features that would fit under a rubric like "scandal and politics" (namely the essays of Cynthia Baron on the shutting down of the Actors' Lab in Hollywood by Hedda Hopper and the Tenney Committee; Susan McLeland on "Hanoi Jane" Fonda; and James Castonguay on Bill Clinton, *Wag the Dog*, and contemporary media culture), one of these (McLeland's) is also a detailed study of a star scandal. And Sam Stoloff's essay on Fatty Arbuckle centers on perhaps the most famous star scandal in Hollywood's history, but the political and legislative ramifications of that scandal are among the essay's most important points. The same may be said of Mary Desjardins's essay about *Confidential* magazine and star scandals of the 1950s. And so on. We do note significant links between and among essays in the summaries below, but we hope that readers will produce their own new meanings from pondering the patterns and points of convergence and difference that these and other scandals produce across the passage of time.

Lee Grieveson's essay considers one of the first film scandals, the furor provoked by the film *The Unwritten Law: A Thrilling Drama Based on the Thaw-White Case* (Lubin, 1907). *The Unwritten Law* was produced and exhibited when the first trial of Pittsburgh millionaire Harry Thaw for the 1906 murder of architect Stanford White was coming to a close in 1907. Completed, apparently, after Evelyn Nesbit Thaw's sensational testimony about her rape by Stanford White (presumably the motive for the murder), *The Unwritten Law* enacts a number of key scenes from her testimony before moving forward in time to show Thaw's acquittal on the grounds of an "unwritten law" that gives men the right to defend their property, including wives and children. The film was insistently pointed to in 1907 as a sensational example of the immorality of moving pictures and nickel theaters, and it became a lightning rod for an emerging reform consensus. Its exhibition was frequently challenged by reform groups and police forces, and it was singled out in an influential crusade by the *Chicago Tribune* against nickel theaters. The intense reform concern raised by *The Unwritten Law* emerged at a critical moment of cultural contestation in urban America; first centered on the scandal itself, this concern rippled outward to the film made about it and from there to the scandal of cinema more generally.

Grieveson traces the outlines of the initial scandal as it emerged from the sensational press and through textual analysis of its filmic articulation in *The Unwritten Law*. He concludes that the issues that animated the scandal became central to the way cinema itself was discussed and defined, and he argues that to understand fully the emergence of reform concern about moving pictures and nickel theatres at this precise historical moment means to inscribe cinema into the context of a broader regulatory space. Cinema by 1907 had become one element among other regulatory issues subject to public decisions, discussions, and legislative interventions. The Thaw-White scandal is thus a productive place from which to begin excavating the precise discursive contexts within which cinema and scandal (including Evelyn Nesbit's subsequent show-business capitalization on her own role in the scandal) emerged as a problem of morality and governance.

The issue of governance also organizes Sam Stoloff's exploration of the "Black Sox" World Series scandal of 1919–1921 and the Fatty Arbuckle scandal of 1921–1922. Although the two scandals are, in phenomenal terms, only indirectly linked, Stoloff shows that both are best understood in terms of the politically charged aftermath of World War I and as episodes in the oligopolistic consolidation of emerging culture industries during this period. In response to increased but disparate and often competing pressures for regulation on community and state levels, professional baseball and Hollywood had begun moving toward the creation of some kind of trade or regulatory agencies by the end of the teens. But the specific form those associations took, Stoloff argues, was largely determined by the scandals themselves—and the scandals, in turn, occurred not as isolated instances of egregious behavior by a few individuals but as objects of public dispute within the same moment of social, political, and economic history.

Both the Arbuckle and the Black Sox scandals were significantly influenced by postwar paranoid movements (particularly the Red Scare and anti-Semitism) and ideological conflicts concerning nationalism, ethnicity, gender roles and masculinity, labor organization, and social class. Most important, they were both interpreted within this framework of interrelated anxieties. As a result of this wider cultural context, professional baseball and the American film industry created highly visible public agencies, headed by men drawn from the government who became "czars." Under the aegis of the Baseball Commissioner's Office and the Hays Office, respectively, the major leagues and the major studios were able to maintain a virtually unchallenged dominance in their industries for a generation, and in the process shifted away from their origins as urban, lower-class amusements and toward their status as solidly middle-class and respectable cultural institutions.

As Stoloff's essay traces particular historical issues relating to paranoia and Arbuckle's troubled (and troubling) masculinity, so does Mark Lynn Anderson analyze Wallace Reid's drug addiction and 1923 death in the context of changing attitudes about addiction and the demographics of the "junkie" in the period immediately following World War I. As a star, Reid was a model of rugged, healthy, virile, and all-American (white) masculinity. His death became the occasion for a social reform effort that sought to teach the public about the social basis of drug addiction and to replace both clinical and popular notions of the "dope fiend" as a moral degenerate with a more "modern" understanding of drug addiction as disease.

The circumstances of Reid's death presented problems for Hollywood, which was already having to confront and ameliorate growing demands for state and local censorship legislation. Anderson shows how the industry made Reid's use of narcotics conform to his earlier star image through a set of discourses that purportedly sought to extend public knowledge about the causes of drug addiction. The idea that an open discussion of Reid's addiction would serve the public good allowed the film industry to use the scandal to its own advantage. Anderson thus details the specific strategies of the industry's media coverage, among them the use of Reid's wife of nine years, actress Dorothy Davenport (after Reid's death referred to invariably as "Mrs. Wallace Reid"), as the major yet mutable interpreter of Reid's identity. The postmortem reconstruction of Reid's stardom produced a persona, Anderson suggests, that was not only susceptible to but determined by a set of demands entailed by mass culture. Although the studio was portrayed as exploiting Reid's popularity with grueling work schedules, his death was also represented as a consequence of an excessive popular demand by an adoring audience for whom Reid sacrificed himself and his family. Yet the "deviant excesses" of Reid's fans were by no means censured or proscribed by the posthumous publicity. Reid had "killed himself" with kindness to his public, and thus his death became an object lesson about the simultaneous emotional proximity of the motion picture star to his or her "adoring" fans and the alienated nature of mass communication itself.

The first three essays all show how the scandalous acts of famous individuals could serve figuratively to personify massive and widespread civic concern about the expansion, pervasiveness, and ultimate "meaning" of mass-mediated culture in periods of bewildering change. Although the connection of the events of 1907 and of 1919–1923 to emerging social problems made their eruption all the more spectacular, the scandals named above were also the result of *behaviors* whose discovery upset the dynamic of concealment and revelation that Richard deCordova has found at the base of our fascination with public figures and movie stars. All three of the film scandals led to demands for increased reform and censorship and created new strategies for the regulation of film-industry personnel and publicity: morality clauses became standard in most Hollywood contracts after 1921, and studios fostered economic ties to the press and local law enforcement agencies in order to exert greater control over the types of information the public was allowed to know.

Nancy Cook's essay shifts attention to Hollywood's reaction to the threat of scandal and the meaning of the term itself. Employing Herman Gray's work on scandal and racialized discourse,[56] and on how the designation of scandal has historically been used to maintain the American moral and social order by designating and controlling those who, like African Americans, are "marked and discursively positioned" outside of it, Cook's subject is Chief Buffalo Child Long Lance, born Sylvester Long, who starred in an "authentic documentary" about Native Americans, *The Silent Enemy*, released by Paramount in 1930. Something of a celebrity in Jazz Age America, Long Lance was frequently cited as an example of the realized potential of American Indians: by the end of the 1920s he had published a popular autobiography and a book on General Custer, had worked as a newspaperman, was a member of the prestigious Explorer's Club, and had become enormously popular with the New York social set. Yet during the production of *The Silent Enemy* in 1929, Long Lance was revealed to be a "fraud," a black man trying to "pass." His former intimates subsequently deserted him, and he died, under suspicious circumstances, in 1932.

Cook's use of the term *scandal* thus describes the way this information was discovered, negotiated, and then suppressed by the producers of *The Silent Enemy* to avoid a "national scandal over the racial identity of their star." Yet Long Lance was a tremendous success in *The Silent Enemy*, and the producers did not hesitate to use his performance to proclaim the film's authenticity. Cook thus also employs scandal, as Gray does, as a means by which to understand the "scandal of race" exemplified by Long's treatment by his contemporaries and subsequently by scholars who have used his race as "the signifier of transgression." The "forgotten scandal" of Long Lance gives us insight into the ways Hollywood imagined both Native American identity and the audience for its films and provides another way of examining the social construction of racial identity and prejudice in film and in film scholarship.

Gray's and Cook's work foregrounds the discursive mechanisms by which the dominant social order at once censors and polices the identities of those whom it designates as transgressive and designates as transgressive and in need of censoring and policing anyone outside the dominant social order. Lucy Fischer's essay about Hedy Lamarr's performance in the 1933 Czechoslovakian film *Ecstasy* (*Extase*) shows that a scandalous film text can provoke not only censorship of particular images or scenes but of the notion that a film narrative might center on an active female sexuality, the "simple *acknowledgment* of female sexual pleasure." Lamarr's stardom in America was forever inflected by her association with the scandalous text of *Ecstasy* (in which she appeared nude), and her image (like

Ecstasy itself) was manipulated and altered over time — for example, by a focus on maternity — in attempts to "inoculate" Lamarr's public "against her scandalous aura." Yet Lamarr's performance of sexual pleasure, so convincing on the screen, was the result of physical pain inflicted by her director and thus was derived from familiar patterns of patriarchal subjugation, Fischer explains. And throughout her life the "performance" of sexual pleasure of the "Ecstasy girl" was repeatedly problematized by Lamarr's own statements and actions, particularly the publication in 1966 of her sexually explicit "autobiography," whose authenticity she disavowed and which she claimed was "false, vulgar and scandalous." Rather than being (scandalously) an agent and subject of female sexual pleasure as she had been in the 1930s, Lamarr became (scandalously) a ludicrous figure, a figure shamed, defamed, and libeled by her own book, which glorified the pleasures of female sexuality.

As all of the essays described above imply in some way, libelous or defamatory statements can be used by what sociologists call "claimsmakers" or "moral entrepreneurs" to cause disgrace to others, the loss of their reputations and good names.[57] The essays also draw attention to the fact that the perceived threat posed by scandal tends to be greater during periods of national paranoia, change, and uncertainty. The techniques of fomenting, extorting, and circulating rumor and innuendo were famously deployed in Hollywood during the cold war and the HUAC investigations beginning in 1947. Cynthia Baron's essay traces the history of the Actors' Laboratory, founded in Hollywood in 1941 by Richard Fiske (a Columbia contract player) and former members of the Group Theatre. The Actors' Lab was soon an extremely active component of the Hollywood system through its actor training, and it maintained a close and mutually beneficial relationship to several Hollywood studios. By 1948 the Lab had 250 members and several thousand audience-sponsors from the Hollywood community. Yet by 1949 it was gone, its source of income cut off and its key members blacklisted.

Building on charges circulated by Hedda Hopper and columnists at the *Hollywood Reporter,* the Tenney Committee (the California State Senate Fact-Finding Committee on Un-American Activities) effectively shut the Actors' Lab down. The fact that the Lab is rarely, if ever, mentioned in studies of American cinema shows just how successful scandalmongering can be. Even though Actors' Lab members had served in the armed forces during World War II and had gone out on U.S.O. and hospital tours, the sympathy of members toward unions, Jews, and African Americans would make them the target of cold-war conservatives. Baron examines the activities of the Actors' Lab in the context of cold-war politics — particularly the complex interaction of the Lab with Hollywood, the Veterans Administration, and desegregation and labor politics — to reveal how the process of establishing guilt by association, pioneered by U.S. Representative Martin Dies in his tenure as chairman of HUAC from 1938 to 1945, was central to the scandalmongering approach employed by Hollywood columnists and members of the Tenney Committee. What their use of the strategy reveals is that putatively scandalous behavior worked to further the interests of certain figures and factions within the studio system and within California governor Earl Warren's administration and against the interests of "undesirable" craftspeople, who were therefore expendable as well.

Sociologists also tell us that a succession of scandals or a rash of transgressive behaviors can cause a "moral panic," a widespread but amorphous sense that the social conventions of ordinary life are breaking down.[58] Certainly the cold war was a time in which many institutions of American culture appeared to be threatened from within and without, and Baron's research reminds us of the extent to which individuals attempting to confront and ameliorate the structural inequities of American society are too easily transmuted into traitors, agitators, and troublemakers. The extramarital affairs of Rita Hayworth and Ingrid Bergman with, respectively, Aly Khan and Roberto Rossellini also took place in the context of cold-war paranoia. And although they are not, strictly speaking, political scandals, the women's transgressions against traditional gender roles were put to use by politicians as "signs" of the moral breakdown and decay of American society.

Hayworth's and Bergman's affairs occurred from the end of 1949 through 1950 and are usually cited as evidence that scandal affects star careers in proportion to the compatibility of the transgressive activity with the star's popular image. According to conventional wisdom, Bergman's Hollywood career was badly damaged by scandal because her image was "pure" and domestic, whereas Hayworth's career was enhanced because her image already contained elements of exoticism and eroticism. Differences in Bergman's and Hayworth's star images do account for some of the public response to the affairs, chiefly in their early stages. But, as Adrienne McLean's essay shows, the reception of the Bergman and Hayworth scandals, particularly the way they were symbolized by and for the American public, is also responsible for the difference in our view of the outcomes. The fame of the two stars not only accounted for the public's interest in their behavior but also allowed others — for example, Senator Edwin Johnson of Colorado — to use the scandals to further their own careers. Johnson's exploitation of Bergman and Hayworth, whom he called "apostles of degradation" on the floor of Congress in 1950, certainly helped to "scandalize" their images and their subsequent film careers. To an America in the grip of anticommunist witch-hunts, blacklisting, spy scandals, the nuclear threat, and crises of containment, the domino effect of Hayworth's and Bergman's affairs, in conjunction with others that had recently occurred, made what appeared to be the flagrant flouting of women's traditional domestic roles seem all the more heinous. But, McLean argues, Senator Johnson's own ostentation and self-aggrandizing exploitation of the two stars' transgressions connects his actions, as well as the HUAC investigations of Hollywood generally, with Washington's *scandalous* attempts to divert public attention from its own corruption.

Erik Hedling's essay continues the exploration of Bergman's liaison with Roberto Rossellini but through the effects, heretofore undocumented, of the Swedish
star's exploits on Swedish sexual politics and cultural struggles. In fact, Bergman
was very roughly treated by the conservative Swedish press and, when she returned to Sweden for the first time since the scandal to perform in the Honegger-
Claudel oratorium *Joan of Arc at the Stake* in 1955, the attacks became even
more vituperative but on different terms. Rather than being someone whose immoral actions had "tainted the Swedish flag," Bergman was now accused of being
unable to recognize that she was not an artist but a hack whose only interest was
money. Rossellini, too, was treated viciously, often in ethnically inflected terms,
as a commercial "Hollywood" filmmaker—thus obviating his well-known contributions to Italian neorealism as a reaction against Hollywood-style filmmaking.
Bergman's and Rossellini's previous transgressions became the peg on which was
hung a cultural struggle between masculinized "high art" and feminized "low
art" in 1950s Sweden. Yet Bergman's strong defense of herself in the face of
the attacks also triggered a kind of radical feminist discourse, which evolved in
women's weeklies, with Ingrid Bergman cast as a female hero. Drawing on and
translating Swedish press materials from the period, Hedling explores this development as well, taking specific account of how the phenomenon of Hollywood
scandal itself is circulated and considered in a small and basically ethnocentric
European cultural economy like Sweden.

The Bergman-Rossellini scandal occurred near the end of the "studio years"
of Hollywood, when the power of the studios was being weakened by assaults
from the federal government, from theater owners, from television, and from new
forms of popular and overtly scandalous discourse aimed at fans. Mary Desjardins's essay explores this critical juncture in American film history. For three
decades the studio system's legal power over stars (exclusive contracts, morality
clauses) and mass production of material about stars (photos, press releases,
orchestrated appearances, not to mention films themselves) were meant to intrigue audiences with the promise of revelations about star identity but also to
prevent the "actualization" or disclosure of actualizations of the star's transgressions of social and/or sexual norms that might result in the studios' loss of symbolic or economic power. Although there were, of course, scandals after these
studio "controls" were put in place in the 1920s, the general mass media's contribution to the disclosure of star transgression was oriented toward short-term profit
and gain.

The mass media behaved this way, that is, until the scandal magazines of the
1950s rivaled the studios' mass production of star stories with their own "scandal
narratives" about stars that appeared in monthly or bimonthly issues sold at newsstands. Desjardins examines these scandal magazines, particularly *Confidential*,
to begin a historical inquiry into the development of media that produce star
scandal for profit. Even when scholars write histories of the tabloid press and

scandal publications, they tend to start with broadsheets and the penny press of several hundred years ago, skipping entirely over the 1950s and its important debates about privacy, obscenity, and sexuality. Examining the 1950s scandal magazines not only contributes to the filling of gaps in journalism histories but extends our knowledge of 1950s Hollywood and stardom as well. Desjardins explores the dynamic relationship between the Hollywood film industry, the state (both in the abstract and specifically the state of California), and the magazine publishing industry, focusing on three stories published by *Confidential* between 1955 and 1957—one "outing" Liberace, one alleging that Maureen O'Hara had sex in Grauman's Chinese Theatre, and one revealing the criminal past of Rory Calhoun—and the motion picture *Slander*, which was Hollywood's response to Calhoun's story. This detailed focus also establishes a framework for understanding how social knowledge was circulated by the powerful institutions of Hollywood, publishing, and the law through, specifically, star scandal.

By the 1960s and 1970s, then, knowledge about stars circulated in a much wider and more unpredictable discursive realm. Although some scholars have argued that television gave stars the ability to present themselves "directly" to the public and to control more precisely the terms of their own representation,[59] Susan McLeland's essay suggests that, especially for women stars, cultural proscriptions and rules for public behavior continued to hold sway and to make women who spoke for themselves, much less about the masculinized concern of international politics, not only transgressive but offensive. Jane Fonda was not the only American antiwar activist to visit North Vietnam in the early 1970s, but contemporary press reports depict her visit as *the* one that outraged the American people and their elected officials. When Fonda made a series of radio broadcasts to U.S. troops in South Vietnam, asking them to reconsider their orders and stop their raids on North Vietnam, responses back in the United States were swift and angry—in part, McLeland shows, because on radio Fonda's voice could be heard on its own terms, away from the spectacle of her body. Fonda became the subject of film boycotts and treason investigations, her speeches were cancelled, and she was pelted with red paint at an antiwar rally. Yet Fonda's transformation from the innocent sexual plaything of *Barbarella* (1968) to the treasonous "Hanoi Jane" was not as instantaneous as the reaction to the broadcasts would suggest, and McLeland maps the transformation, as well as the various ways that Hollywood and Fonda herself subsequently sought to return her image to public favor by emplotting her within a narrative of feminine rage unleashed, then rehabilitating her by a return to marriage, reconciliation with her father, Henry Fonda (America's patriarch), and maternity. Her recuperation lay, in part, in her reembodiment as an American woman who could be known and contained through her physical being rather than her intellect, in the process establishing a tradition of attractive celebrity spokeswomen for even the most mundane issues as women increasingly entered mass-mediated public life in the late twentieth century.

Ironically, anyone who watches television or who reads *People, Entertainment Weekly, Vanity Fair,* or other magazines of their ilk knows that, now, celebrities *must* speak "politically," in terms of their sexuality, class, race, ethnicity, and nationality — if only to target the most potent demographic group for the "products" their images are used to sell or to deny or render ambiguous any aspects of identity that are perceived to reduce the commercial potency of a given celebrity image. Yet gossip and rumor continue to function, as they always have, to "reorder" the official record, especially with respect to a public figure's sexual orientation. Within the gay and lesbian community, for example, the posing and answering of questions about sexual orientation positions gay spectators and fans to "get" the gay subtext of movies and television programs. Identifying individuals as gay, and implicitly speaking to them, is important to such a reception context. Peter Lehman and William Luhr examine the issue of Blake Edwards's rumored homosexuality (and, by implication, that of his wife Julie Andrews) in relation to critical analyses of his work. The ways that Edwards's films question dominant cultural notions of masculinity and sexuality disturb some heterosexuals, who want to "blame" that disturbance on something: homosexuality can be that something. In such cases labeling Edwards a homosexual is a reactionary tactic designed to explain potentially disturbing elements in his films. If there is something "wrong" with his films, then there must be something "wrong" with the filmmaker.

But a disclosure that Edwards *is* gay would also produce complex effects: what has appeared to critics as a courageous honesty about the anxieties and insecurities of masculinity would suddenly become a smokescreen to hide behind. Far from being honest, Edwards would be using his films to hide the truth. In examining the relationship between rumor and biographical responsibility, Lehman and Luhr show how the same rumor can function in entirely different ways when applied to different people by different audiences and the extent to which what is scandalous to some (for example, audiences who admire Edwards and Andrews as a monogamous heterosexual couple and Andrews for her wholesome image) is not, or may be no longer, scandalous to others. They also address the responsibilities of critics and biographers in relation to rumor and scandal.

The final essay in the anthology again confirms Herman Gray's notion that what we are told is "scandalous" — for example, sexual misconduct — is often not as pornographic or as *scandalous* as the "secret" abuses of power that the misconduct hides. Since the end of the studio era, since *Confidential,* since Watergate and the spread of the investigative mode of reporting to mainstream news and entertainment practices, we have come to expect scandal from our public figures; it is no longer the repressed underside of their existence. Nor are we sure any longer about what properly separates a star from a celebrity from a politician because stars can become politicians and politicians are de facto stars in the new "system" of celebrity known as postmodernity. James Castonguay's essay examines several of the limit-texts of this discursive regime of scandalous "revelation," namely Bill Clinton, Monica Lewinsky, and the film *Wag the Dog* (Barry Levinson, 1997). Drawing from print media, as well as from television and Internet texts, Castonguay explores the ways that *Wag the Dog* became inextricably bound to "Zippergate" (also known as "Monicagate," "Lewinskygate," and "Clinterngate") through a remarkable blurring of boundaries between the fictive and real, entertainment and news, gossip and facts, sexual politics and military politics. Although these generic, aesthetic, and political boundaries have long been conflated in film history and accounts of star scandals, the degree and intensity of the mediation of the last White House sex scandal of the past millennium amounts to a difference in kind, making it the first truly postmodern political scandal.

While still in theatrical release, *Wag the Dog* received a flurry of media attention for anticipating the Clinton/Lewinsky sex scandal. One reporter even referred to the film during a February 1998 press briefing when she asked the White House press secretary if the current "showdown with Saddam" amounted to a "real-life *Wag the Dog* scenario." Jean Baudrillard has claimed that "the Gulf War did not take place" because its version of reality was constructed for American audiences by television, which, for all intents and purposes, gave us no images of the actual war; but *Wag the Dog* creates the even more disturbing possibility that future wars might be fabricated whole out of Hollywood cloth. *Wag the Dog*'s fascination with (or fetishization of) faking visuals continues on a Web-site tie-in for the film that allows users to construct their own virtual war and victim and to partake in a long tradition of mass-mediated war simulation. Given the rise in Clinton's approval ratings immediately following initial revelations of the scandal, *Wag the Dog* also posits that, in addition to war being faked to cover up scandal, scandal may be fabricated to deflect attention away from the real *scandals* of politics like "military actions" and unethical foreign policy. *Wag the Dog*'s representation of scandal — and the film's intertextual presence in the journalistic reporting of Clinterngate et al. — is used to address larger methodological questions surrounding theoretical and critical complicity in the process of social and political hyperrealization and to ponder what activities or representations of them actually might still be considered scandalous.

• • •

The essays collected in *Headline Hollywood* go far toward addressing many of the critical, historical, and theoretical concerns we have described in this introduction. But in the process they have raised new questions and laid out new areas for research into the relationship of film, scandal, and American culture. Although some pundits have suggested that what we name the rekeying of scandal into entertainment indicates a disarticulation between transgression and "real" moral turpitude, this does not mean that, in the words of Gail Collins, "there are no rules left that matter."[60] Whether or not the culture of scandal persists in the same form in the new millennium, we hope that others will join us in working to understand scandal, the scandalous, and the scandalized. As long as there are powerful people to make them and break them, there will always be rules that matter.

NOTES

1. Leo C. Rosten, *Hollywood: The Movie Colony, the Movie Makers* (New York: Harcourt, Brace and Company, 1941), 109.

2. The standard "morality clause" from a Hollywood contract, in this case one securing the services of actress Lizabeth Scott for producer Hal Wallis (contract dated July 9, 1946). From the Hal Wallis Collection, Academy of Motion Picture Arts and Sciences, Los Angeles.

3. Many of these memoirs and biographies are listed in the first section of the bibliography at the back of this collection. It has been our experience, however, that virtually any book about Hollywood's past and its personalities will make some reference to a scandal or scandals.

4. Goffman poses natural frameworks (e.g., the sun coming up) against social ones (e.g., lowering the blind to block out the sun's glare); and although some events seem to be interpretable through a single "chiefly relevant" framework, designating any framework as "primary" is difficult, Goffman warns, because of the "embarrassing fact" that, during "any one moment of activity, an individual is likely to apply several frameworks." Erving Goffman, *Frame Analysis: An Essay on the Organization of Experience* (Cambridge: Harvard University Press, 1974), 22–26.

5. Ibid., 9.

6. Scandals represent an activity that is deviant from a sociological standpoint, particularly the interactionist perspective from which an "alleged behavior or condition [becomes] 'deviant' if people say it is." Earl Rubington and Martin S. Weinberg, eds., *Deviance: The Interactionist Perspective* (Boston: Allyn and Bacon, 1999), xiii. This obviously jibes with our use of the term, as does Erving Goffman's definition of *stigma* as "the situation of the individual who is disqualified from full social acceptance." Erving Goffman, *Stigma: Notes on the Management of Spoiled Identity* (New York: Jason Aronson, 1974), n.p.

7. Virtually all histories of Hollywood and censorship link the 1920s scandals, particularly Arbuckle's, to the formation of the Hays Office. In addition to works about Arbuckle and film and censorship listed in the bibliography see Ruth Vasey, *The World According to Hollywood, 1918–1939* (Madison: University of Wisconsin Press, 1977), 16–32; and Sam Stoloff's essay in this volume. In regard to Arbuckle's deviance these studies also show that Arbuckle's accusers repressed the iniquitous backgrounds of both Virginia Rappe and the main "witnesses" to the crime during the trial.

8. Herman Gray, "Anxiety, Desire, and Conflict in the American Racial Imagination," in James Lull and Stephen Hinerman, eds., *Media Scandals: Morality and Desire in the Popular Culture Marketplace* (New York: Columbia University Press, 1997), 85–98. All other quotations in this paragraph are from these pages. The etymology of the word *scandal*, from the Greek noun and verb forms of *trap* and *snare*, is similarly doubled: traps and snares are things one is caught by and also things that one may set out, or do, in order to catch something or someone else.

9. James Lull and Stephen Hinerman, "The Search for Scandal," in Lull and Hinerman, *Media Scandals*, 1. For more on the culture of scandal in America see Gail Collins, *Scorpion Tongues: Gossip, Celebrity, and American Politics* (New York: William Morrow, 1998), and Neal Gabler's similarly subtitled *Winchell: Gossip, Power, and the Culture of Celebrity* (New York: Alfred A. Knopf, 1995). Interestingly, Gabler's massive study of reporter and journalist Walter Winchell makes his legacy the motivating force behind our ingrained belief in "our entitlement to know everything about our public figures" (553); although Collins's book explores the same "ingrained belief," Winchell is never so much as mentioned. Both Collins and Gabler do, however, name Hollywood as a "pervasive vehicle," in Gabler's words, in the development of a culture of celebrity "in which the famous always have something to hide" (Gabler, 553).

10. See Lull and Hinerman, *Media Scandals*, for information on recent non-Hollywood scandals. For more on the history of political scandals in America see also Collins, *Scorpion Tongues*, and Michael Schudson, *Watergate in American Memory: How We Remember, Forget, and Reconstruct the Past* (New York: Basic Books, 1992).

11. Robert Sklar, *Movie-Made America: A Cultural History of American Movies*, 2d ed. (New York: Vintage Books, 1994), x.

12. Collins, *Scorpion Tongues*, 16–18, 30–40.

13. Ibid., 137. The exception, according to Collins, would be the Kennedy family, "whose genius was to appear to be movie stars impersonating politicians."

14. The "Special Collector's Edition" of the tabloid *National Examiner* (December 29, 1999) featured a story on the "Top 100 Scandals of the Century," in which it names Arbuckle a murderer and rapist, illustrating the story with a photo of the "hotel room where Fatty Arbuckle murdered Vivian [*sic*] Rappe" (23). (The same story also includes as scandals the sinking of the *Titanic*, the Lindbergh baby kidnapping, the death of Princess Grace [Kelly] in an automobile accident, and the disappearance of Jimmy Hoffa.) Although supermarket tabloids are well known for their sensationalism and concocted stories, research shows that readers often take them seriously as sources of information, particularly about the past. See, e.g., S. Elizabeth Bird, "What a Story! Understanding the Audience for Scandal," in Lull and Hinerman, *Media Scandals*, 99–121, and *For Enquiring Minds: A Cultural Study of Supermarket Tabloids* (Knoxville: University of Tennessee Press, 1992).

15. Although sensational rumors may have long lives and continue to shape our attitudes about the past, academic scholarship is also an important major "vehicle," in Michael Schudson's terms, of "collective memory" (Schudson, *Watergate in American Memory*, 5, 65).

16. Kenneth Anger, *Hollywood Babylon* (San Francisco: Straight Arrow Books, 1975) and *Hollywood Babylon II* (New York: Dutton, 1984). Matthew Tinkcom explores Anger's gay camp perspective on Hollywood and use of "gossip-driven fan accounts to rethink the status of Hollywood as a purveyor of purportedly 'wholesome' entertainment" in "Scandalous! Kenneth Anger and the Prohibitions of Hollywood History," in Ellis Hanson, ed., *Out Takes: Essays on Queer Theory and Film* (Durham, N.C.: Duke University Press, 1999), 271–287.

17. References to Hedda Hopper and Louella Parsons dot any studio-era star biography or history. William Mann writes that by the end of 1934, when the Production Code was being "strictly adhered to," the "gossip columnists and fan-magazine writers realized their full potential," and the "level of acrimony in the columns increased a hundredfold," with Hopper and Parsons now able to say to the studios,

"You do things our way or you'll see some stories you don't like." *Wisecracker: The Life and Times of William Haines, Hollywood's First Openly Gay Star* (New York: Viking, 1998), 228–229. Others, however, maintain that Hopper and Parsons were, in the words of Neal Gabler, "toothless" because they were "part of Hollywood's social order, not antagonistic to it" (*Winchell*, 254), an opinion shared by Gail Collins (*Scorpion Tongues*, 17–18). See also Amy Fine Collins, "Idol Gossips," *Vanity Fair*, April 1997, 358–375. Hopper and Parsons each wrote two autobiographies, as did many Hollywood columnists; for references to these see the bibliography.

18. For more on tabloids of the 1950s see Alan Betrock, *Unseen America: The Greatest Cult Exploitation Magazines, 1950–1966* (New York: Shake Books, 1990), and Mary Desjardins's essay in this volume. For more on tabloids generally see Bird, *For Enquiring Minds*, and Gabler, *Winchell*.

19. David Ehrenstein, *Open Secret: Gay Hollywood, 1928–1998* (New York: William Morrow and Company, 1998). Ehrenstein recounts how the "local knowledge" of Hollywood insiders—e.g., about a star's closeted gay or lesbian identity—intersected with and differed from the studios' "official" discourse, which included that produced by studio-affiliated gossip columnists like Parsons and Hopper. These "open secrets," Ehrenstein claims, are now themselves part of fan discourse. See also the essay by Peter Lehman and William Luhr in this volume.

20. William A. Cohen, *Sex Scandal: The Private Parts of Victorian Fiction* (Durham, N.C.: Duke University Press, 1996), 4–5.

21. Ralph L. Rosnow and Gary Alan Fine, *Rumor and Gossip: The Social Psychology of Hearsay* (New York: Elsevier, 1976), 23–31.

22. Goffman, *Frame Analysis*, chap. 2. Goffman never uses the phrase "dominant ideology," but he characterizes "primary social frameworks" (see note 4) in quite familiar terms: as structures that have "no apparent articulated shape, providing only a lore of understanding, an approach, a perspective"; each framework "allows its user to [understand] a seemingly infinite number of concrete occurrences defined in its terms," and "He [*sic*] is likely to be unaware of such organized features as the framework has and unable to describe [it], yet these handicaps are no bar to his easily and fully applying it" (21).

23. Jacques Rancière, "Interview: The Image of Brotherhood," trans. Kari Hanet, *Edinburgh Magazine*, no. 2 (1977): 26–31. See also Kaja Silverman's use of the term in relation to Hollywood film in *Male Subjectivity at the Margins* (New York: Routledge, 1992), 15–51.

24. See Ehrenstein, *Open Secret*. See also William Mann's account in *Wisecracker* (especially chaps. 4, 5, and 6) of how attitudes about gay and lesbian behavior fluctuated in Hollywood in the 1920s and 1930s. As Mann points out, William Haines and other stars were frequently referred to in public discourse in the 1920s with terms that quite explicitly rendered them gay. In addition, stars of sufficiently high box office clout, like Haines, were often able to have morality clauses removed from their contracts. Those same stars were subsequently closeted—e.g., by studio-arranged marriages—during the more restrictive 1930s (with Haines's refusal to disavow his sexual identity contributing to the cancellation of his MGM contract).

25. Cohen, *Sex Scandal*, 2.

26. John B. Thompson, "Scandal and Social Theory," in Lull and Hinerman, *Media Scandals*, 59. He repeats this statement twice on the same page.

27. This and all subsequent quotations in this paragraph are from Goffman, *Frame Analysis*, chap. 3. As Goffman shows, social frameworks are "vulnerable" to

rekeying from repetition and parody, deception and fabrication, through discrediting, through the entry of doubt or boredom, or suspicion that one is being tricked or duped, etc. The convulsive upsets that Hollywood scandals have seemed to cause since the early twentieth century may mutate so quickly into the acceptable or the normative because of this vulnerability.

28. Ibid., 21.

29. Cohen, *Sex Scandal*, 2.

30. Unless otherwise noted, all quotations in this paragraph come from Lull and Hinerman's introduction, "The Search for Scandal," to *Media Scandals*. Italics are theirs and indicate direct quotation. For further theorizing on the meaning and parameters of scandal see Gray, "Anxiety, Desire, and Conflict," and Thompson, "Scandal and Social Theory."

31. Thompson, "Scandal and Social Theory," 44, 52.

32. All quotations in this paragraph are from Lull and Hinerman, "The Search for Scandal," 19–25.

33. Suicide presents an interesting case in relation to scandal. Among the famous suicides Kenneth Anger lists are those of stars Olive Thomas in 1920, Barbara La Marr in 1926, Alma Rubens in 1931, Paul Bern in 1932, Thelma Todd and Lou Tellegan in 1935, Lupe Velez in 1944, Carole Landis in 1948. Judy Garland began attempting suicide in 1950; her death in 1969, like Marilyn Monroe's in 1962, was the result of an "incautious self-dosage," in the coroner's words, of sleeping pills. In most of these cases the suicides were framed by Hollywood at the time as the result of unrequited love, mental instability, or accident—so that Hollywood could seem to be the "victim" rather than an institutional source of some of the psychic pain and suffering that contributed to the suicides in the first place.

34. See, for example, Judith Mayne, *Cinema and Spectatorship* (New York: Routledge, 1993); Richard Dyer, *Stars* (London: BFI, 1979/1998); Richard deCordova, *Picture Personalities: The Emergence of the Star System in America* (Urbana: University of Illinois Press, 1990); Jackie Stacey, *Star Gazing: Hollywood Cinema and Female Spectatorship* (London: Routledge, 1994).

35. Besides reflecting the mutability of the scandalous, second-order scandals can also occur when someone appears to be trying to profit from the scandalous past of another, as happened to Esther Williams when *Vanity Fair* published an excerpt from Williams's autobiography in September 1999 in which she "outed" B-movie star Jeff Chandler's "desire to wear women's clothing." *All* of the letters to the editor published in subsequent issues castigated both Esther Williams for her questionable ethics ("Shame on you, Esther!") and *Vanity Fair* for invading Chandler's privacy "in this pointless way, 38 years after his death" and tarnishing his reputation with such "an off-putting, but harmless, aberration." Continues one letter, "I am not outraged by Mr. Chandler's red wig; I *am* by Ms. Williams's *big mouth*." *Vanity Fair*, November 1999, 94, 96.

36. Sociologist Joseph Gusfield has labeled such a process "moral passage": i.e., the rejection of the designation of being "outside" society or marked as a victim by conditions or features once held to be deviant or to produce a stigma (e.g., racial identity, homosexuality, physical disabilities, prostitution), and in turn embracing and advocating the same condition, often as an activist. See Joseph Gusfield, "Moral Passage: The Symbolic Process in Public Designation of Deviance," *Social Problems* 15 (1967): 175–188; John I. Kitsuse, "Coming Out All Over" (1980), in Rubington and Weinberg, *Deviance*, 21–29.

37. Among the most notorious scandalous acts survived by their perpetrators were Charles Chaplin's "shotgun marriage" to underage and pregnant Lita Grey in 1924, the extramarital sexual affair with George S. Kaufman detailed in Mary Astor's diary in 1935, Errol Flynn's statutory rape trial in 1942, Robert Mitchum's 1948 marijuana "bust," and Lana Turner's involvement with the death of Johnny Stompanato. For more on the survivability of celebrity scandals since the studio era see Lull and Hinerman, *Media Scandals.*

38. Cohen, *Sex Scandal*, 22.

39. DeCordova, *Picture Personalities*, 118.

40. Ibid., 141.

41. Psychological contamination results when an *idea* of something disgusting profoundly affects anything that is not, properly speaking, disgusting in itself. Thus, as Carroll E. Izard describes it in *The Psychology of Emotions* (New York: Plenum Press, 1991), "Orange juice served from a new and perfectly sterile bedpan would be disgusting to most people" (260–261). Arbuckle was thus "contaminated" by his demonstrable proximity to disturbing acts.

42. P. David Marshall, *Celebrity and Power: Fame in Contemporary Culture* (Minneapolis: University of Minnesota Press, 1997), 241.

43. Ibid., 247. See also Leo Braudy, *The Frenzy of Renown: Fame and Its History* (New York: Oxford University Press, 1986).

44. See, for example, Edgar Morin, *The Stars*, trans. Richard Howard (New York: Grove Press, 1961); Dyer, *Stars*; John Ellis, "Stars as a Cinematic Phenomenon," *Visible Fictions: Cinema, Television, Video* (London: Routledge and Kegan Paul, 1982), 91–108.

45. Stacey, *Star Gazing.*

46. William Ian Miller, *Humiliation and Other Essays on Honor, Social Discomfort, and Violence* (Ithaca: Cornell University Press, 1993), 137. See also the sections on shame, disgust, anger, and humiliation in Izard, *Psychology of Emotions.*

47. Miller, *Humiliation*, x.

48. Ibid., 157.

49. Henry James Forman, *Our Movie Made Children* (New York: Macmillan, 1933), 4; Miller, *Humiliation*, 127; see also Stacey, *Star Gazing.*

50. William Ian Miller, *The Anatomy of Disgust* (Cambridge: Harvard University Press, 1997), 199. See also Izard, *Psychology of Emotions*; and Goffman, *Stigma.*

51. Stacey, *Star Gazing*, 230.

52. Miller, *Anatomy of Disgust*, 177.

53. Cohen, *Sex Scandal*, 6–7.

54. Rosnow and Fine, *Rumor and Gossip*, 99.

55. Ibid., 78.

56. Gray, "Anxiety, Desire, and Conflict."

57. For more on these terms, see Gary Alan Fine, "Scandal, Social Conditions, and the Creation of Public Attention: Fatty Arbuckle and the 'Problem of Hollywood,'" *Social Problems* 44 (August 1997): 297–334.

58. For discussion of "moral panic" see Erich Goode and Nachman Ben-Yehuda, *Moral Panics: The Social Construction of Deviance* (Oxford: Blackwell, 1994), and Kenneth Thompson, *Moral Panics* (London: Routledge, 1998).

59. There is no consensus about how television affected celebrities and scandal. In *Scorpion Tongues* Collins writes that television forced "entertainers and politicians" to "market themselves directly to the public—a process that involved

embarrassment and ruined careers on both sides" (18). Gabler, however, claims that television provided celebrities with a "means of bypassing the mediator and directly facing their public" so that television was "usurping one of the primary functions of the gossip columnist: rendering judgments on personalities" (*Winchell*, 503); and Alan Betrock contends that tabloids like *Confidential* arose *because* the "growing home television market placed both [movies and magazines] on the defensive." Magazines fought back with sex, violence, and scandal, weapons "television chose not to use" (*Unseen America*, 3). Subscription television services like cable have, of course, always fought with these "weapons," with network television now not far behind.

60. Collins, *Scorpion Tongues*, 270.

THE THAW-WHITE SCANDAL, THE UNWRITTEN LAW, AND THE SCANDAL OF CINEMA

LEE GRIEVESON

On June 25, 1906, Harry K. Thaw shot and killed the prominent architect Stanford White at the opening of a new musical review at Madison Square Garden, New York City, allegedly claiming as he did so, "He ruined my wife."[1] "The flash of that pistol," the *New York Evening Journal* wrote four days later, "lighted up the depths of degradation, an abyss of moral turpitude."[2] The intense press interest in the scandal continued this process of illumination, fastening on details of immorality, debauchery, and perversity in endless pages of detail from 1906 through 1908, when Thaw was finally committed to the Matteawan insane asylum.[3] The story of immorality and degradation lit up by the press was briefly this: the well-known architect Stanford White had pursued the sixteen-year-old model and chorus girl Evelyn Nesbit after seeing her on stage as part of the *Floradora* chorus in 1901. One night during their brief relationship Nesbit visited White's apartment and was allegedly drugged and raped. In 1903 Nesbit married millionaire Harry Thaw, and three years later Thaw shot and killed White. These details were seized on by the press, who were increasingly linking sexual concerns to national and class concerns and constituting them as news, and shaped into a melodrama: the event was enfolded into a narrative of the "ruination" of an innocent lower-class girl by a sexually rapacious male villain — coded by class, for elements of the press made much of White's elevated social status and of what the *New York Times* called "the doings of the fast set" — and the subsequent rescue of the girl by the chivalric hero.[4] Melodrama, as Peter Brooks has suggested, provided the nineteenth century with a "fiction[al] system for making sense of experience," a system that for Brooks frequently "express[ed] an anxiety brought by a frightening new world in which the traditional patterns of moral order no longer provide[d] the necessary social glue."[5] The shaping of the scandal as melodrama in the press responded to broader contestations over transformations in moral order that were at this moment linked to concerns about consumerism, class, sexuality, and changing gender relations. Historians have suggested that such concerns were central to this conflicted and contested moment in American history.[6] Scandal is in many ways perfectly suited to melodrama, for they both function by personalizing broader moral questions and by mediating between the specific and the general;[7] in this sense the Thaw-White scandal effectively instantiated broader moral questions, providing a symbolic terrain on which the terms and boundaries of public morality were negotiated in early-twentieth-century America.

The Thaw-White scandal was literally turned into melodrama in late 1906, with the production of a play based on it, and in early 1907, with the production of the film *The Unwritten Law: A Thrilling Drama Based on the Thaw-White Case* (Lubin, 1907), produced and exhibited while the first trial of Thaw was still going on.[8] Popular culture intervened in intriguing ways in the representation of the scandalous event, shaping it in a particular direction consistent with norms (or developing norms) of representation and, with the film at least, shifting the representation of the event to a relatively new forum of mediated visibility (accessible, it is worth noting, to those who might not read the press). The filmic intervention into topicality and scandal in turn became central to the emergence of a series of regulatory contestations over cinema in 1907. These controversies had profound effects on the shaping of cinema at this formative moment, when nickelodeons began to proliferate and thus when "cinema" as we know it emerged.[9] *The Unwritten Law*, cinema historian Charles Musser suggests, was "the most controversial film produced prior to the establishment of the Board of Censorship in 1909";[10] its exhibition was frequently challenged by various reform groups, and it became central to an influential *Chicago Tribune* "crusade" against moving pictures and nickelodeons in early 1907 that culminated with the establishment of the first municipal censorship ordinance in the United States in Chicago in November 1907.[11] The recently formed trade journal *Moving Picture World* commented: "The exhibition of this one film alone has been the cause of more adverse press criticism than all the films manufactured before, put together, have done. It has the police active in trying to put down the nickelodeon. It has been the cause of action by church, childrens [*sic*], purity and other societies and these societies have branded all alike, taking the old saying, 'Birds of a feather flock together.'"[12] *The Unwritten Law* was increasingly singled out as metonymic for the alleged immorality of cinema itself in a fashion similar to the way the scandal had been read as symptomatic of the broader immorality of the age. *The*

Unwritten Law merits attention, then, because it was effectively the first film in the United States to become widely scandalous in itself and because it became embroiled in a series of important formative debates and decisions about both the boundaries of what could be seen on cinema screens and the boundaries of what cinema could be used for and how it could intervene in real-life events.

Scholars have suggested that scandals are frequently intertextual and serial in nature, and my contention is that *The Unwritten Law* became a dense transfer point between the Thaw-White scandal and the production of a "moral panic" about cinema that had far-reaching implications for the shaping of cinema at this moment when what cinema would become was malleable and up for grabs.[13] Scandals and moral panics work to enforce regulation. This is to suggest also — borrowing from the structure of melodrama and scandal — that there is both something specific about the Thaw-White scandal and *The Unwritten Law* but also something more general, that the events outlined here are part of a wider contestation over moral norms and part of what I will term a broader "regulatory space" at this precise historical moment, when cinema emerged as an incredibly popular leisure practice.[14] Cinema was, then, inscribed into a regulatory space that transcended it, a space glimpsed in the highly visible Thaw-White scandal. Accordingly, my account of this specific and general process follows a clear narrative thread, beginning with an outline of the issues animating the reporting of the Thaw-White scandal, moving on to detail the filmic reenactment of the scandal, and concluding with a description of the reform concern about that film and about cinema more generally in early 1907.

"AN ABYSS OF MORAL TURPITUDE"

For cultural historian Lewis Erenberg, the Thaw-White scandal "provided the most dramatic evidence that urban life was changing," evidencing a "reorientation away from the confinement, restrictions, and conventions of urban industrial society and the code of gentility" and toward what historian Kevin White terms more generally a "new moral code" epitomized by a heterosocial leisure world increasingly geared toward youth and vitality.[15] Such a transformation was viewed with considerable suspicion by various reform and elite groups, and a constellation of concerns about gentility, respectability, moral codes, and heterosocial leisure spaces clearly informed the reporting of the Thaw-White case. This was figured in the press through three main issues: concerns about *pleasure* superseding traditions of self-restraint, hard work, and respectability; concerns about sexual immorality and *perversity*; and anxieties about the vulnerability of women in the public sphere of commercialized leisure (and, more generally, about transformations in the roles of women).[16] These three threads of concern underpinned the melodrama of the Thaw-White case and would return in various ways to reform concerns about the film of the scandal and about cinema more generally.

The issue of pleasure and respectability was central. Many of the initial press reports focused on Stanford White's alleged immorality and debauchery, producing what *Harper's Weekly* termed a "postmortem defamation" by a "trial by newspapers" that included details of White's alleged relationships with young actresses,[17] his role in bachelor parties where naked women emerged from cakes, and the exoticism of his apartment at Madison Square Garden that he himself had designed (there was a red velvet swing in his lounge and a bedroom lined with one hundred mirrors).[18] Much of this commentary counterpoised White to prevailing notions and traditions of "character" that were, historians Kevin White and Gail Bederman suggest, an "essential component of bourgeois manhood," involving above all else "the cultivation of morals."[19] Such cultivation was apparently absent in what *Harper's Weekly* termed White's "pursuit of pleasure," which was "sacrificing the lasting and the far removed good to some slight and momentary gratification."[20] Likewise, a Reverend Samuel C. Deans asserted that the case exposed the "utter degeneracy which exists among a large class of our richest Americans. The revolting indulgence in vice is the direct result of the American habit of worshipping gold instead of character."[21] This stance suggested that the pursuit of pleasure in the leisure world of New York City was profoundly troublesome to traditions of morality, a stance that was certainly more widespread in this period, with, for example, one group of purity reformers arguing that "the commercialization of practically every human interest in the past thirty years has completely transformed daily life. . . . Prior to 1880 the . . . main business of life was living. . . . The main business of life now is pleasure."[22] White became a highly visible symbol of this broader transformation on the eve of cinema's emergence as the principal forum of commercialized leisure in the urban spaces of the United States.

White's "pursuit of pleasure" was also, it should be noted, positioned as problematic to notions of domesticity that were central to prevailing structures of moral order and class alignment.[23] White's apartment in the city was separated from the home he shared with his wife and son and was a part of the leisure environment of the city, literally inside Madison Square Garden. The *New York World* hinted that the apartment had been known as his *"pleasure house"* (a theater manager observed that White's "playhouse was the playhouse"): the conjunction of pleasure, play, and house was significant.[24] Pleasure in the leisure spaces of the musical theater and restaurants congregated around Broadway was clearly positioned in much of this discourse as opposed to notions of character and to structures of domesticity.

Such a stance on pleasure, respectability, and domesticity informed the rhetoric at the first trial of Thaw in early 1907 (the trial ran from February 4, 1907, to April 12, 1907, and concluded with a hung jury; Thaw was retried in early 1908 and pronounced insane). The defense attorneys for Thaw sought to position White as immoral and perverse in order to justify Thaw's actions. Much of this focused on the age disparity between White and the sixteen-year-old Evelyn Nesbit. Chief defense attorney Delphin Delmas claimed, "He [White] established himself in a paternal attitude to the family . . . this man old enough and more than old enough to be her father. He was a man whose wife and son awaited him at home at that hour. Is it necessary for me to recite the details of that night? The child was plied with drugs and became the victim of the man who had posed as her protector."[25] Such a stance cleared the grounds for the representation of Harry Thaw as a chivalric avenger of children and, more generally, the domestic upholder of the code of gentility that White contravened. Delmas suggested then that Thaw "struck as the tigress strikes the invader who comes to rob her of her young. He struck for the purity of the home."[26] This rhetoric culminated in Delmas's famous closing address to the jury, in which he suggested that Thaw suffered from a species of insanity he labeled *dementia Americana*, "that species of insanity which makes every home sacred. It is that species of insanity which makes a man believe that the honour of his wife is sacred; it is that species of insanity which makes him believe that whoever invades the sanctity of that home, whoever brings pollution upon that daughter, whoever stains the virtue of that wife, has forfeited the protection of human laws and must look to the eternal justice and mercy of God."[27] This stance rhymed with a legal tradition of an "unwritten law" defense, which had proliferated throughout the nineteenth century, that justified an outraged husband, father, or brother in killing the alleged libertine who had been sexually intimate with the defendant's wife, daughter, or sister.[28] The broader currency of this stance on respectability and the sanctity of the domestic sphere was visible, for example, in a poll in the *New York Evening Journal* between the end of June and August 1906, which asked readers whether Thaw was justified, and therefore innocent, or guilty. The final count favored Thaw: 2,054 thought him guilty, 5,119 innocent.[29]

Such a representation of Thaw as chivalric man of character was contested, both at his trial and, more widely, in the press. It emerged fairly quickly after the murder that he too had previously engaged in acts the *New York Times* deemed "of a character unfit to describe" (before they went on to note that Thaw had bought a dog whip and "lashed [a woman] into submission").[30] The *New York World*, a tabloid that was invariably first with this kind of story, had the headline "Thaw a Drug Fiend and Degenerate" just two days after the shooting. Further details of Thaw's immorality and "perversity" emerged in the press, even more so at his second trial in early 1908 and in the autobiographies written by Evelyn Nesbit Thaw in 1914 and 1934.[31] District Attorney William Travers Jerome mockingly referred to Thaw as a "veritable Sir Galahad" in response to Delmas's rhetoric, undercutting the discourse of character and chivalry that underpinned the defense strategy.[32]

For many commentators, therefore, Thaw too was immoral and perverse, and this became closely linked to his social status. Thaw was an extremely wealthy socialite who had inherited his money from his father's industrial enterprises. The *New York World* commented scornfully that Thaw "had nothing to do with his life but devise ways of spending money of his father's that he did not earn," his life "unbridled from the cradle to the cell."[33] A German doctor lecturing on Thaw the day before the verdict in the first trial outlined Thaw's condition as one where will and reason had been weakened by wealth and hereditary nervous disorders, asserting, "Idleness in the children of the rich, the lack of proper education, the gratification of every desire for whatever can be purchased are powerful factors in producing criminality."[34]

Both Thaw and White, then, emerged in the glare of press interest as perverted subjects, their perversions closely linked to class alignment (White was part of what the *New York World* termed "the high flying bohemian set").[35] Such a labeling of perversity may perhaps figure as a footnote to the broader process delineated by Michel Foucault, as the perversities of the two men were presented as "the kind of deviation by which sexuality was ceaselessly threatened" and they were produced as other to that broader hegemonic constellation of economic, familial, social, and political relations that were articulated by, and as, the dominance of the middle class.[36] Melodrama was in many ways the clearest means of articulating this process of class definition via discourses of sexuality and perversity, for the insistent moral legibility of melodrama frequently plays a cultural role in mediating sociopolitical change and is often associated with the self-definition of a middle class against a decadent upper class (although, as we shall see, the parameters of this reading can certainly change: the central issue is the self-definition of a moral middle class).[37] The rhetoric of the press, reformers, and attorneys at the trial thus sought to delineate moral norms through outlining the characters and actions of these two men, using them to mark off the boundaries of acceptable behavior in a structure of melodrama that quite clearly responded to anxieties about the transformations of moral norms, about pleasure superseding character and domesticity, and about perversity and class.

• • •

The figure of Evelyn Nesbit Thaw was also critical to the proliferation of discourse around the scandal. A picture of Nesbit drawn by Charles Dana Gibson when she was an artists' model, entitled "The Eternal Question" and in which Nesbit's hair is arranged as a question mark, was widely reproduced during the scandal, offering an embodiment of the confusion that circulated around the figure of Nesbit. Gibson's pictures, Kevin White has noted more generally, "broke away ever more decisively from the restraints of the cult of True Womanhood and of Victorianism in general."[38] Nesbit was a visible figure in this movement, emerging in mid-1906 as a critical contested site around which debates about gender roles and about the positioning of women in the emergent heterosocial sphere of leisure practices were waged. Such a contestation over the figure of

Figure 1. Postcard of Evelyn Nesbit, printed and distributed at the time of the first trial of Harry Thaw in early 1907. Courtesy of the Bill Douglas Centre for the History of Cinema and Popular Culture, University of Exeter.

Nesbit was critical to the press coverage of the scandal, which insistently speculated on her role in the scandal and effectively argued either that she was a "ruined" innocent "girl" (much play was made of her age) or that she was in fact a corrupt "public woman" who had brought the scandal on herself because of her role in the public eye (as artists' model and chorus girl).

Such a division in the construction of the role and meaning of Nesbit was visible most clearly at the first trial of Thaw in early 1907. "The schoolgirlish appearing wife," the *New York Times* reported on the day after Delmas's plea of dementia Americana, had been "depicted under cross examination as a typical member of the Tenderloin colony of New York" but now "saw herself depicted in a halo of virtue."[39] (See fig. 1.) Delmas's strategy was quite clear: he attempted to present Nesbit as virtuous in order to bolster his suggestion that Thaw's actions were a tolerable protection of his wife and of domesticity more generally. His summation initially centered on another telling of Nesbit's life story, a story told countless times in the immediate aftermath of the murder and again in detail

Figure 2. Composite photograph of Evelyn Nesbit Thaw and Harry Thaw, distributed as a postcard in early 1907. Nesbit is sexualized in a way that is consistent with much of the discourse that circulated around her at the time of the scandal and the subsequent trials. Courtesy of the Bill Douglas Centre for the History of Cinema and Popular Culture, University of Exeter.

when Nesbit testified at the trial. Here as elsewhere the narrative began with the death of Nesbit's father and the dissolution of an idyllic domestic past that plunged the family into poverty and forced Nesbit to work outside the home to protect that home. "She drudged," Delmas claimed, "giving her scant dollars to the support of her mother and brother."[40] Her life as a model and chorus girl was protective, not destructive, of the domestic. This aimed to counter a widely held suspicion that, as one of the jurors at the trial would subsequently remark in an interview, a career on the stage could be seen "as an expression of revolt against the enforced routine of home life."[41] District Attorney Jerome emphasized this position, representing Nesbit as a typical immoral member of the Tenderloin, the vice district of New York City. Jerome produced a diary Nesbit had written after she had met White. She had written of other girls: "they will never be anything except, perhaps, good wives and mothers," and next to this had drawn a picture of a nun with three exclamation marks. "This child," Jerome remarked, "[had] no desire to be a good wife or mother."[42] (See fig. 2.) Jerome's strategy in relation to Delmas's was summed up by a comment in the English paper the *Daily Telegraph*: "Public conscience may condone private vengeance for such acts, but the hearth that has been violated must have been kept tolerably clean before."[43]

Nesbit as a performer inhabited a commercial world in which the breakdown of class- and sex-segregated entertainments of the nineteenth century enabled the emergence of women as consumers. She stands at the threshold of this transformation, her discursive positioning prefiguring debates about the pleasures and dangers of female consumption that would come to center on the new nickelodeons proliferating in urban space from late 1906. The debates about Nesbit chimed also with the emergence of the "white slavery" scandal from around 1907 in the United States (a concern that women were being abducted into prostitution) and also prefigured the emergence of the middle-class "New Woman" in the 1910s and 1920s.[44] Nesbit would maintain a visibility through the teens, going on to become a vaudeville and cinema star. She was perhaps—as E. L. Doctorow's novel *Ragtime* suggests—America's first sex symbol, certainly a visible part of that broader shift in the representation of women from, in historian Joanne Meyerowitz's words, "Victorian angel to sexy starlet."[45] Such a shift was represented, contested, and negotiated in relation to Nesbit and the Thaw-White scandal and would become increasingly central to cinematic representation and to contestations over film texts and the space of cinema. It is toward these issues that I now turn, first detailing the controversial filmic rendering of the Thaw-White case and its negotiation of the cultural locale—asking, how did the film construct the scandal? how did it intervene in the broader public scandal?—before moving on to detail the reform concern about that film and about cinema more generally.

"THIS FAKED UP REPRESENTATION"

The Millionaire's Revenge, a play based on the Thaw-White case, was produced in September 1906. Described in an advertisement as a "play true to life founded on the New York Madison Square Garden tragedy" and as a "sensational melodrama, depicting the life of the chorus girl and rich clubmen of New York,"[46] the play featured three main characters—Harold Daw, Emiline Hudspeth Daw, and Stanford Black (a heavily overdetermined shift from White to Black)—and documented several lurid episodes in the life of Black that seem loosely based on tales of White's debauchery. The villainous Black is introduced in a scene in which he brutally knocks down a blind old man who was begging to know what had become of his young daughter.

There is some suggestion that Harry Thaw's mother had financed the play.[47] The *New York World* commented that it certainly seemed to have been created for the "purpose of making public sympathy for Thaw." "Throughout the melodrama," the paper went on, "the sentence 'The unwritten law will prevail!' is repeated,"[48] and at the close of the play Daw declares from his cell: "No jury on earth will send me to the chair, no matter what I have done or what I have been, for killing the man who defamed my wife. That is the unwritten law made by men themselves, and upon its virtue I will stake my life." [49] The play would seem to be part of the tradition of sensational melodramas, which were frequently based on topical subjects. From what can be gathered from the few remaining descriptions of the play, it appears that it followed the episodic structure of such theater, linking together a number of key scenes to create a succession of arresting highlights. [50]

The film *The Unwritten Law*, produced in early 1907, had much in common with this play. The character of Stanford White is also called "Black"; the refrain "the unwritten law" forms the title of the film, and Thaw is released at the close on the basis of such a law; and the structure of the film leans toward the episodic in representing a succession of "attractions" drawn from the sensational reporting of the scandal. This linkage suggests a specific intertextual source but also the broader intertextual legacy of sensational melodrama for film and, perhaps, for wider social and cultural representations that, a number of scholars have suggested, frequently fastened in this period on the "sensational" and that, as we have seen, utilized melodrama to articulate complex sociopolitical change. [51]

The melodramatic intertext for the film was made more explicit by the timing of the film's production and release. Copyrighted on March 4, 1907, the text was probably conceived and produced in the wake of Nesbit's testimony at the trial of Thaw on February 7 and 8. In a brief review of the film *Variety* commented: "The record of the trial has been combed over with an eye to its *sensational* points and these have been strung along into a fairly complete exposition of Mrs. Harry Thaw's testimony." [52] Fred Balshofer's memories of working with Sigmund Lubin, the producer of the film, also suggest this. Recalling Lubin's practice of reenacting boxing films by reading out summaries of the rounds for stand-in boxers to enact, Balshofer wrote: "We then sold the picture as the actual championship fight with real boxers—we even made a one reel picture portraying the shooting of Stanford White by Harry Thaw." [53] The specific timing of the film thus suggests that it was the image of the *ruination*, or *fall*, of Nesbit at the hands of the villainous White, central to Nesbit's testimony, that was critical to the filming of the scandal. [54] The scene of the rape of Nesbit was thus central to the film and in turn became central to reform concerns about the film and about filmic representation of immorality.

The Unwritten Law begins with Nesbit, accompanied by her mother, posing for an artist as White/Black enters. This scene shifts to one of Nesbit learning to dance, then to a scene in a cafe where Thaw strikes Black, and from there to a scene in Black's apartment. After a title, "The Velvet Swing," Nesbit is swung up and down by Black on the swing in the lounge of his apartment, ultimately puncturing a parasol Black had placed in the door frame. Nesbit and Black then leave to go upstairs, emerging in what the title refers to as "The Boudoir with 100 Mirrors." Both scenes were highly charged moments in the testimony of Nesbit and were singled out in the press as images of a secret, decadent, and perverse other world. Their representation in the film would become central also to the reform concern generated around it and to a series of debates about the boundaries of what could be seen on cinema screens. The *Chicago Tribune*, for example, noted that "the stairway scene . . . is made the most of in this faked up representation"; at some exhibitions of the film it was suggested that these scenes be removed.[55] In the film, as Nesbit examines the pictures on the back wall of the boudoir, Black is seen in the foreground drugging her drink, after which she collapses, he places a screen around her prone body, and the shot ends.

The scene of rape was a central and contested issue at the trial of Thaw. Delmas, Thaw's chief defense attorney, introduced it to demonize White and to gain sympathy for Thaw's actions. District Attorney Jerome attempted to stop Delmas from introducing this information, arguing that it was irrelevant to the murder. After a complex series of negotiations, details of the alleged rape were allowed as evidence on the grounds that Nesbit had allegedly told Thaw about it. That is to say, in the words of the judge, "whether the acts took place or did not take place, is an immaterial matter";[56] what was relevant was that Thaw believed it to be true and thus acted accordingly. Jerome directed the jury that this testimony was admissible "purely to show that the mind of this defendant was affected by the narration of these facts by the witness, and . . . the rules of evidence do not permit the District Attorney to controvert the facts as ever having occurred."[57] Jerome's obvious frustration at this resulted in numerous interjections during Nesbit's testimony and a series of arguments about the distinctions between narrative and truth, fiction and reality, and the effects of narrative that would perhaps not be out of place in the pages of an article on literary or film theory. The debate on how we are influenced to commit criminal acts by stories we believe to be true will return later to cinema itself, in the proliferation of concerns about narrative, realism, and effect in early 1907 discussed below.

The film follows Nesbit's testimony, depicts the rape as fact, and in so doing engages the audience in the act in a way that prefigures Thaw's (alleged) engagement that would lead to his murder of White. The audience is invited to become emotionally involved in these events, setting up a structure of "allegiance" with Thaw.[58] Such a structure becomes more apparent as the film continues. After an intertitle reading "After the marriage and the invitation to the roof garden," a party of four leave what appears to be a church, with the next shot showing Nesbit and Thaw in a room (Nesbit looks at her hand as if at a wedding ring, which suggests that the two shots are temporally connected). A man enters and the three leave in a car and arrive at the roof garden where, after Black enters behind them pointing and laughing at Thaw, Thaw gets up and shoots him. This sequence of four shots maintains a sense of continuity unusual at this moment in film history, although it certainly deviates from the reality of events, telescoping the wedding with the night of the murder — temporally gluing together events in reality separated by years — as the text shifts away from a narrative entirely reliant on audience foreknowledge to a self-sufficient and partly fictionalized one. Such a compression of events offers up a cause-effect justification, as the film makes Thaw's actions more believable and sympathetic and thus enhances the structure of allegiance. In the film, it seems, he married Nesbit, discovers her ruination, and kills Black. In reality, or let us say in the versions of reality surfacing in the press and at the trial, Nesbit told him about the rape before they were married, and three years later he killed White.

From this point the film shows Thaw in prison and in the courtroom. After a title, "The Tombs Prison," Thaw is seen in a cell and is visited by Nesbit and a woman whom I take to represent his mother. They leave, and he falls asleep, dreams of the murder, is woken, and enters the courtroom. After a fairly lengthy and difficult-to-follow courtroom scene, in which Nesbit is on the witness stand, Thaw is acquitted and walks down the center of the courtroom, arm in arm with his mother and Nesbit in a shot that seems almost to suggest the reaffirmation of Nesbit and Thaw's marriage. Produced and exhibited while Thaw was on trial, the film thus closes with Thaw walking free, acquitted on the basis of the "un-written law" of the film's title. This goes further than *The Millionaire's Revenge* in actually representing Thaw's acquittal. The film thus moves over into a self-sufficient narrative that engages the viewer through suspense and surprise and intervenes as "propaganda" on Thaw's behalf. A month later Delmas invoked a similar defense in his closing address to the jury.

The film thus followed the melodramatic structure of much of the press re-porting, of the defense rhetoric at the trial, and of the play *The Millionaire's Re-venge*, demonizing White as immoral and perverse and presenting Thaw as a chivalric avenger. In the process, of course, the film could show immorality in action and thus have it both ways, an early example of the balancing of morality and immorality that would become increasingly central to American films and to production strategies that at times sought to suggest scandalous content while staying within the confines of respectability. Nevertheless, at this moment the engagement of the film in topical and scandalous subject matter became deeply problematic and central to a series of attempts to figure out what was appropriate entertainment for a mass audience. The following section works to elucidate the contestations over this film and over cinema more generally.

IMPERILING MORALS

The Unwritten Law was quickly singled out by the trade press, reform groups, the general press, and police forces as an unacceptable representation. The trade journal *Moving Picture World* had spoken out against the film as early as March 16, 1907, just twelve days after it was copyrighted. Underneath a brief note announcing the film—which would "show the entire tragic story from the time Evelyn Nesbit was a young girl to the thrilling episodes in the court room" — there was a bracketed paragraph from the editor asserting, "Surely there is enough rubbish on the market, without inflicting the public with such nauseous films. We hope the better elements of the public will express their disapproval, and that legal steps will be taken to prevent such exhibitions."[59] Once exhibited, the film ran into further difficulties. An exhibition of the film was stopped by police in Houston on April 6. The exhibitor, *Moving Picture World* reported, offered to cut out the "mirrored bedroom scene," but the authorities would not allow any of the film to be seen, and "[a]n audience of several hundred got their money back."[60] The film was stopped also by police in Worcester and in Superior, Wisconsin.[61] In the latter instance the local branch of the Women's Christian Temperance Union (WCTU) had asked the police to stop the film, and as it began the chief of police walked on stage and "dramatically stopped the show." The audience, *Moving Picture World* noted, was two-thirds women. In April and May 1907 the Children's Society raided two New York City nickelodeons that had been showing films of the Thaw-White case, including *The Unwritten Law*.[62] The exhibitors were taken to court and convicted of, respectively, "imperilling the morals of young boys" and "impairing the morals of young children."[63] They were fined $100.

The film effectively became a symbol of what was seen as the wider immorality of cinema at this moment, a time when a series of reports and investigations were emerging about the recent proliferation of nickelodeons and about the effects of films on audiences and on standards of morality.[64] Such concerns about cinema drew on the wider regulatory space instantiated for a time by the Thaw-White case. The pivot of reform concern from the scandal, to the film, to cinema more generally is perhaps most immediately visible in the *Chicago Tribune*'s influential "crusade" against nickelodeons in early 1907. On April 10, 1907, the *Tribune* discussed at length Delmas's famous closing address outlining the condition of dementia Americana. In the same edition an editorial entitled "The Five Cent Theatres" began the "crusade" by castigating nickel theaters, which "minister to the lowest passions of childhood. They make schools of crime where murders, robberies and holdups are illustrated. The outlaw life they portray in their cheap plays lends to the encouragement of wickedness. They manufacture criminals to the city streets."[65] Three days later the paper extended this crusade against the nickel theaters, in an article entitled "Nickel Theatres, Crime Breeders," on the same day that it reported a hung jury in the Thaw trial (the circulation of newspapers was highest on days when verdicts in big murder trials were announced). Nickel theaters, the paper argued, destroy the sanctity of the home in two ways. First, because the films in them are "suggestive" (and, furthermore, many of them are of "Parisian design").[66] Here the *Tribune*'s list of titles was seen to speak for itself, including *Beware, My Husband Comes*; *The Bigamist*; *Gaieties of Divorce*; and so on. Second, nickel theaters destroy the sanctity of the home because the space of the theaters directly opposes that of the domestic space and because they have furthermore "invaded" the "residence districts," with their "tawdry facades" and "screaming ragtime" standing alongside the "harassed householder."[67]

The corruption of childhood innocence, the encouragement of criminality, the immorality of commercialized amusements and the pursuit of pleasure, the desecration of the domestic were familiar themes indeed to those readers engaged in the rhetoric of the Thaw trial. In a move that seems to highlight this coalescence of reform concerns, *The Unwritten Law* came to occupy a central place in the *Tribune's* crusade. After describing the film at some length, singling out the scenes in White's apartment for particular condemnation, the paper reported on audiences watching the film:

> It was noticed that after 4 o'clock the audiences were composed largely of schoolgirls, who came in with books or music rolls under their arms. The interest these girls in short dresses took in the production may be gathered from the fact that they remained sometimes for two or three views of the pictures. . . . A good many grown women got up and went out before the completion of the series. It shocked them. But the girls remained. Around 6 o'clock or just before that hour the character of the audiences . . . shifted again. This time they were composed largely of girls from the big department stores, who came in with bundles under their arms. . . . [T]hey frequently are found talking with men of mature years, whom they could not have met before going to the theatres.[68]

Both the schoolgirls and the young working women had something in common with Nesbit, and both collectives were threatened here by the representation of a perverse male desire or by its actual presence within the space of the nickel theater (those men of mature years mirroring Stanford White's "perversity"). These young women were inscribed into a narrative of sexual danger similar to that visible on the screen and in the initial scandal.

Much of the reform concern about cinema at this moment would in fact focus on these anxieties about women in the public space of commercialized amusements. There was, for example, a concern that nickelodeons were sites that white slavers targeted, and stories of nickelodeon managers seducing children proliferated. (The *Tribune* ran a story about a fifteen-year-old running away from home with a manager of a "tawdry" nickelodeon; the Chicago Vice Commission reported on a case in which "a proprietor of one of these nickel theatres assaulted fourteen young girls.")[69] The Thaw-White scandal was a particularly important intertext for these concerns about women and children in public space, about the dangerous immorality of "men of mature years," and about the ability of moving pictures to impair morals (the court cases against the two exhibitors showing *The Unwritten Law* were brought by the Children's Society in order to protect the morality of children). The scandal provided one of the dominant ways of encoding the "dangerous" spaces of heterosocial leisure. The developing critique of moving pictures and nickel theaters thus borrowed from the melodramatic narrative constructed from the Thaw-White case, inscribing cinema into a melodrama of concern focused on pleasure beyond the domestic sphere, perversity, and the place of women and children in the public sphere of leisure.

Moral panics are, as Jeffrey Weeks has suggested, "fundamentally *serial,*" assuming an "infinite variety of tone and posture."[70] Concerns about cinema certainly borrowed from and extended the rhetoric that proliferated around the Thaw-White case, but there were also important transformations at work here, for the developing regulatory concern about cinema came to focus almost exclusively on concerns about the effects of moving pictures and the space of nickelodeons on lower-class and immigrant audiences. Such audiences were perceived as both vulnerable and, perhaps more important, dangerous; these audiences threatened structures of morality, either in terms of criminality or in terms of sexual immorality, and the cinema was seen to encourage this through representations such as *The Unwritten Law* (which "impaired morals" and represented both sexual immorality and unpunished criminality) and through the provision of an ill-lit space beyond familial regulation. In effect, then, the concerns about morality, governance, and pleasure that animated the Thaw-White scandal spread outward from the decadent upper classes and "high flying bohemian set" to include those lower-class and immigrant audiences who had for the first time begun to participate in commercialized leisure activities (and those primarily immigrant entrepreneurs who ran production companies and exhibition outlets). The central factor in this pivot of concern from an upper-class perversity to a lower-class and immigrant immorality and delinquency was the delineation of a moral middle class.

I have argued elsewhere that the emergence and proliferation of anxieties about ethnically coded lower-class audiences was linked to broader concerns about regulating and governing populations.[71] Such a process of regulation was particularly important at this moment because of the combined forces of industrialization, immigration, and urbanization and attendant reorganizations of the configuration of public and private space. In this context the regulation of morality was central and the Thaw-White scandal provided a site on which moral norms could be dissected, disseminated, and contested, a role continued by the scandal over the film and the broader culture wars over cinema from 1907 onward. Contestations over film texts are one of the principal forums for discussions of moral norms, of how people are to live—a particularly pressing question in the United States in the early years of the twentieth century.

The scandal of *The Unwritten Law* also provided a site for the intensification of regulatory concern and pressure about cinema. For reform groups like the WCTU and the Children's Society, and for newspapers such as the *Tribune,* the film was singled out as a symptom of the broader immorality of cinema—this was a specific case, the argument ran, that was part of a more general problem (the principle, as *Moving Picture World* had phrased it, that "birds of a feather flock together.") Such rhetoric helped establish the first municipal censorship ordinance in the United States in Chicago in November 1907. For the film industry, anxious to establish the respectability of cinema to assuage reform and governmental concern, *The Unwritten Law* was deeply problematic. *Moving Picture World* ultimately countered the gathering reform concern by suggesting that the film was just one bad case. "The exhibition of this one film alone," the journal argued, "has been the cause of more adverse press criticism than all the films manufactured before, put together, have done. . . . There is nothing to elevate, nothing to entertain, or any good lesson to be gained in its exhibition."[72] Such a stance sought to block the metonymic slippage central to the reform concern about the film and to single out individual bad films rather than cinema more generally as the object of regulatory concern. *The Unwritten Law* was produced as "other" to a respectable and moral cinema. This position would lead to support for self-regulatory censorship bodies that could police the morality of individual films and also to the emergence of a narrative configuration that was, Tom Gunning suggests, closely imbricated with moral discourse and that was in turn a critical precursor to the establishment of the norms of classical Hollywood cinema.[73] The self-regulatory National Board of Censorship emerged in early 1909 also and set about standardizing formulas of acceptable content and narrative development ("unwritten law" themes, it is worth noting, were consistently singled out for condemnation by the board).[74] The contestation over cinema from early 1907, focused so intensely on *The Unwritten Law*, had profound effects on the shaping of textuality, on the regulation of cinema, and thus in effect on the medium of cinema.

One final point here. *Moving Picture World* criticized the film because it was not "elevating" or "entertaining" — it was not educational in a way that documentary films can be, and it was not simply entertaining.[75] Such a distinction was important at this moment in figuring out what was appropriate entertainment for a mass audience. On the one hand, films could be elevating (principally nonfiction), whereas on the other hand they could be simply entertaining (entertainment was principally associated with fiction). *The Unwritten Law* seems particularly troublesome in this context, blending a certain form of nonfiction with fiction and intervening in real-life events as they actually took place (the subtitle of the film seems to speak to this disjuncture: a *thrilling drama* that is *based on the real*). Distinctions between fiction and nonfiction were certainly less fixed in early cinema but would become increasingly distinct through the teens and ultimately central to the definition of cinema as "harmless entertainment" and to its positioning beyond the sphere of the political.[76] The filmic engagement with real-life controversial events would become increasingly muted in the following years. One of the eight standards listed by the chairman of the National Board of

Censorship in 1914 stated: "The Board prohibits anything obviously or wantonly libelous in films, anything calculated to cause injury to persons or interests from an obviously malicious or libelous motive, and films dealing with questions of fact which relate to criminal cases pending in the courts."[77] Evelyn Nesbit Thaw's subsequent film stardom is indicative of some of the changes in the positioning of film texts in relation to scandalous material. Although the ten films she made from 1914 to 1922 clearly drew on her notoriety, they did so in a fictional setting.[78] Nesbit performed her own scandalousness but now in a cinema that was more clearly regulated, that was resolutely defined as harmless entertainment (see fig. 3). Even so, the scandalous nature of Nesbit's life would prove hard to defend in the early 1920s, when a number of star scandals reanimated the moral panic about cinema and when film studios began to insert "morality clauses" into contracts with actors. Her career in the movies ended in 1922.

The Unwritten Law, then, stands at the threshold of important decisions about how cinema should function within the social body. The film emerged as a highly visible symbol of the alleged immorality of cinema at a moment when reform and governmental groups were becoming increasingly concerned about the effects of moving pictures on audiences and about the problems of the dangerous spaces of nickelodeons. The subject matter of the film rhymed with some of the concerns that underpinned this regulatory intervention. The film thus functioned as a convenient symbol of the broader immorality of cinema, enabling an intensification of regulation and setting in process a series of decisions and developments that had far-reaching effects on the shaping of cinema: the emergence of regulatory structures, the shaping of textuality and its links to moral discourse, and the definition of cinema principally as harmless entertainment. Such decisions and developments were enmeshed with the broader regulatory space instantiated by the Thaw-White scandal; the filming of that scandal made

Figure 3. Performing scandalousness. Publicity postcard for Evelyn Nesbit during the time she was an actress contracted with William Fox, c. 1918. Nesbit was the first person to capitalize on a scandal to become a film star. Courtesy of the Bill Douglas Centre for the History of Cinema and Popular Culture, University of Exeter.

clear the connections between regulatory projects, illuminating the process by which cinema was regulated and shaped in close conjunction with wider discourses of morality.

NOTES

Thanks to Peter Kramer, Peter Stanfield, Vanessa Martin, and Riley and Lauren Martin-Grieveson for help with the writing of this essay. Thanks to the Bill Douglas Centre for the History of Cinema and Popular Culture, University of Exeter, for permission to reproduce the stills. Thanks are due in particular to Peter Kramer for his characteristically insightful reading of an earlier draft.

1. *New York Times*, June 26, 1906, 1. In truth it was unclear whether Thaw had said "wife" or "life." The policeman had approached Thaw and asked him if he was responsible for the shooting. "'Yes' Thaw replied. Then he added that the man had ruined his life — or wife — I could not distinctly make out." Ibid., 3. The press quickly settled on "wife" and constructed the scandal as a sexual scandal.

2. *New York Evening Journal*, June 29, 1906, 2.

3. Thaw was tried in early 1907, but the jury could not reach a verdict. He was tried again in early 1908 and pronounced insane. John B. Thompson has argued that the press in the nineteenth century transformed the visibility and publicness of scandal, leading to what he terms an arena of "mediated visibility." John B. Thompson, "Scandal and Social Theory," in James Lull and Stephen Hinerman, eds., *Media Scandals: Morality and Desire in the Popular Culture Marketplace* (London: Polity Press, 1997), 60. My interest in the shaping of the scandal by the press has led me to consult the following newspapers: *New York World*, *New York Times*, *Chicago Tribune*, *New York Evening Journal*, *New York Tribune*, and *New York Herald*. For other accounts of the scandal see Evelyn Nesbit Thaw, *The Story of My Life* (London: John Long, 1914); Harry K. Thaw, *The Traitor: Being the Untampered with, Unrevised Account of the Trial and All That Led to It* (Philadelphia: Dorrance, 1924); Evelyn Nesbit Thaw, *The Untold Story* (London: John Long, 1934); Gerald Langford, *The Murder of Stanford White* (London: Victor Gollancz, 1963); Michael Mooney, *Evelyn Nesbit and Stanford White: Love and Death in the Gilded Age* (New York: William Morrow, 1976); and Jay Robert Nash, *Murder among the Mighty: Celebrity Slayings That Shocked America* (New York: Delacorte, 1983). The events are also portrayed in the film *The Girl on the Red Velvet Swing* (Fox, 1955) and in E. L. Doctorow's novel *Ragtime* (London: Random House, 1975) and the film of the same title, directed by Milos Forman in 1981.

4. *New York Times*, quoted in Langford, *Murder of Stanford White*, 62. Thaw's obituary in the *Herald Tribune* in 1947 also suggested the scandal was shaped into melodrama: "In the eleven years between 1906 and 1917 the reading public of America was furnished with a fantastic running melodrama so strange and so varied that even the most imaginative creator of fiction could hardly have conceived the events that unfolded." *Herald Tribune*, February 24, 1947, 14.

5. Peter Brooks, *The Melodramatic Imagination: Balzac, Henry James, Melodrama, and the Mode of Excess* (New Haven: Yale University Press, 1976), 28, 20.

6. See Daniel Horowitz, *The Morality of Spending: Attitudes towards the Consumer Society in America, 1875–1940* (Baltimore: Johns Hopkins University Press, 1985); Roy Rosenzweig, *Eight Hours for What We Will: Workers and Leisure in an*

Industrial City, 1870–1920 (Cambridge: Cambridge University Press, 1983); John D'Emilio and Estelle B. Freedman, *Intimate Matters: A History of Sexuality in America* (New York: Harper and Row, 1988); Kevin White, *The First Sexual Revolution: The Emergence of Male Heterosexuality in Modern America* (New York: New York University Press, 1993); Joanne Meyerowitz, *Women Adrift: Independent Wage Earners in Chicago, 1880–1930* (Chicago: University of Chicago Press, 1988); Gail Bederman, *Manliness and Civilization: A Cultural History of Gender and Race in the United States, 1880–1917* (Chicago: University of Chicago Press, 1995); Paul Boyer, *Urban Masses and Moral Order in America 1820–1920* (Cambridge: Harvard University Press, 1978); Robert Wiebe, *The Search for Order, 1877–1920* (New York: Hill and Wang, 1967); and Morton Keller, *Regulating a New Society: Public Policy and Social Change in America, 1900–1933* (Cambridge: Harvard University Press, 1994).

7. For this stance on the function of scandal see James Lull and Stephen Hinerman, "The Search for Scandal," in Lull and Hinerman, eds., *Media Scandals*; for discussions of the functions of melodrama see Brooks, *Melodramatic Imagination*, and Christine Gledhill, ed., *Home Is Where the Heart Is: Studies in Melodrama and the Woman's Film* (London: British Film Institute, 1987).

8. For details on the play, entitled *The Millionaire's Revenge*, see the file on it held at the Billy Rose Theater Collection, Lincoln Center, New York Public Library. *The Unwritten Law: A Thrilling Drama Based on the Thaw-White Case* was copyrighted on March 4, 1907. Copies of the film exist at the National Film Archive, London, and at the Museum of Modern Art, New York City.

9. Nickelodeons, the first permanent movie theaters, emerged in mid-1905 but began to proliferate rapidly through 1906. Prior to this, moving pictures in the United States had been exhibited principally in the context of vaudeville. "It is not too much to say," Charles Musser asserts, "that modern cinema began with the nickelodeons." Charles Musser, *The Emergence of Cinema: The American Screen to 1907* (Berkeley: University of California Press, 1990), 417.

10. Musser, *The Emergence of Cinema*, 479.

11. *Chicago Tribune*, May 3, 1907, 2. For details on this ordinance see "Police Supervision in Chicago," *Nickelodeon*, January 1909, 11.

12. *Moving Picture World*, May 25, 1907, 179.

13. On the serial and intertextual nature of scandals see Lull and Hinerman, "The Search for Scandal," in Lull and Hinerman, *Media Scandals*, 17; and Jeffrey Weeks, *Sexuality and Its Discontents: Meanings, Myths, and Modern Sexualities* (London: Routledge and Kegan Paul, 1985), 45. A note on my use of *scandal* and *moral panic* here: although scandals can be seen as intertextual and serial, they take the form of a singular event. Moral panics, on the other hand, tend to be ongoing, to be a series of events that challenge prevailing configurations of morality. What I trace out here is the emergence of a moral panic about cinema, a panic that is certainly still ongoing.

14. The phrase "regulatory space" refers to the wider structures and more general aims of particular interventionist systems, in particular to the panoply of regulatory issues subject to public decisions, debates, and often governmental intervention. For further discussion of the phrase, and of the positioning of cinema in relation to other regulatory issues, see my "Fighting Films: Race, Morality, and the Governing of Cinema, 1912–1915," *Cinema Journal* 38 (fall 1998): 42–43.

15. Lewis A. Erenberg, *Steppin' Out: New York Nightlife and the Transformation of American Culture, 1890–1930* (Chicago: University of Chicago Press, 1981), 60–61; Kevin White, *First Sexual Revolution*, 13.

16. Around the turn of the century, movies, amusement parks, dance halls, and department stores created a heterosocial environment that provided young women with access to a wider range of evening pleasures. These leisure sites differed from, for example, saloons, which were traditionally homosocial spaces. For a description and analysis of the emergence of this heterosocial leisure world see Erenberg, *Steppin' Out*, and Kathy Peiss, *Cheap Amusements: Working Women and Leisure in Turn-of-the-Century New York* (Philadelphia: Temple University Press, 1986), esp. 6–33. Miriam Hansen describes the reorganization of the public sphere at the turn of the century in *Babel and Babylon: Spectatorship in American Silent Film* (Cambridge: Harvard University Press, 1991), esp. 90–125.

17. *Harper's Weekly*, July 14, 1906, 978; July 21, 1906, 1015.

18. See, for example, *New York Times*, June 19, 1906, 1–2; July 4, 1906, 1; *New York World*, June 26, 1906, 1; June 27, 1906, 2. *New York World* in particular made much of Nesbit's testimony at the trial that she had swung up and down on the velvet swing and that she had posed for White in exotic clothes (headlines included "Her Confession to Thaw of Swinging in White's Studio" and "Posed for White in Studio Dressed in Japanese Kimono"). *New York World*, February 8, 1907, 3.

19. White, *First Sexual Revolution*, 3; Bederman, *Manliness and Civilization*. Warren Susman quotes Ralph Waldo Emerson's famous definition of character as "moral order through the medium of individual nature" in his description of a transformation of a culture of character into one of personality. Warren Susman, "'Personality' and the Making of Twentieth-Century Culture," in John Higham and Paul K. Conkin, eds., *New Directions in American Intellectual History* (Baltimore: Johns Hopkins University Press, 1979), 214.

20. *Harper's Weekly*, July 21, 1906, 1012. Historians have suggested that the shift from a producer to a consumer culture gathered pace through the years 1880–1920, when the working week declined and people found more time for leisure practices that were increasingly separated from work. For T. J. Jackson Lears, an emerging therapeutic ethos of self-realization involved the substitution of an endlessly deferred desire for traditionally moral and religious kinds of self-control. T. J. Jackson Lears, *No Place of Grace: Antimodernism and the Transformation of American Culture, 1880–1920* (New York: Pantheon Books, 1981).

21. Reverend Samuel C. Deans, quoted in the *New York Times*, July 2, 1906, 3.

22. *The Social Evil in Syracuse*, 1913, quoted in D'Emilio and Freedman, *Intimate Matters*, 189.

23. Social historians such as Mary Ryan and Stuart Blumin have shown how during the nineteenth century the middle class in the United States defined itself through notions of domesticity, gentility, and morality. Mary P. Ryan, *Cradle of the Middle Class: The Family in Oneida County, New York, 1790–1865* (Cambridge: Cambridge University Press, 1981); Stuart Blumin, *The Emergence of the Middle Class: Social Experience in the American City, 1770–1920* (Cambridge: Cambridge University Press, 1981).

24. *New York World*, July 1, 1906, 3.

25. Delphin Delmas, quoted in the *New York Times*, April 9, 1907, 2.

26. Delphin Delmas, quoted in the *New York Times*, April 10, 1907, 1.

27. Ibid.

28. On this tradition see Robert M. Ireland, "The Libertine Must Die: Sexual Dishonor and the Unwritten Law in the Nineteenth-Century United States," *Journal of Social History* 23 (fall 1989): 26–44. Ireland notes that the classic method of de-

fending the killers of "libertines" was to plead temporary insanity, which would allow proof of the sexual aspects of the case and permit defense counsel to argue the unwritten law. From around 1870 though, defenses based on the so-called unwritten law became less successful and as a result less frequent. See also Hendrik Hartog, "Lawyering, Husbands' Rights, and 'the Unwritten Law' in Nineteenth-Century America," *Journal of American History* (June 1997): 66–96. Hartog examines a series of trials where this plea was invoked between 1859 and 1870, arguing that they are useful sources for social, cultural, and political history, visible sites at which the changing understandings of gender, marriage, honor, law, and violence were played out. Such a plea was certainly anomalous by 1907.

29. See the details in Langford, *Murder of Stanford White*, 45.

30. *New York Times*, July 14, 1906, 3.

31. *New York World*, June 27, 1906, 4. Langford, in *The Murder of Stanford White*, has details on Thaw's second trial in 1908. Nesbit would later write about how Thaw whipped her violently after taking cocaine. Nesbit, *Untold Story*, 110.

32. William Travers Jerome, quoted in the *New York Times*, April 8, 1907, 2.

33. *New York World*, June 26, 1906, 2; *New York World*, July 8, 1906, 2. Thaw was the heir to millions his father made from coal mine leases, franchises in railroad feeder lines from mine head to hearth pit, and from the Pennsylvania Railroad.

34. Quoted in the *Chicago Tribune*, April 13, 1907, 3. A consensus gradually emerged that Thaw was suffering from "hereditary insanity." In a strange twist *dementia Americana* — the belief in the sanctity of the domestic sphere — was brought back to the domestic, a dementia of the domestic. This was the grounds on which he was committed to the Matteawan insane asylum in 1908.

35. *New York World*, July 8, 1906, 2.

36. Arnold I. Davidson, "Sex and the Emergence of Sexuality," *Critical Inquiry* 14 (autumn 1987): 41. See Michel Foucault, *The History of Sexuality, Volume 1: An Introduction* (1976), trans. Robert Hurley (London: Penguin, 1990).

37. See, for example, Thomas Elsaesser, "Tales of Sound and Fury: Observations on the Family Melodrama," in Gledhill, *Home Is Where the Heart Is*; and Brooks, *Melodramatic Imagination*.

38. White, *First Sexual Revolution*, 61.

39. *New York Times*, April 9, 1907, 2.

40. Delmas, quoted in the *New York Times*, April 9, 1907, 1.

41. Quoted in the *New York Times*, April 14, 1907, 7.

42. William Travers Jerome, quoted in the *New York Times*, April 11, 1907, 2. My account here centers on the discursive positioning of Nesbit and does not take into account Nesbit's own actions. In her written accounts of her life she presents her story very much as a movement away from a domestic sphere exemplified by her mother. In her first autobiography she notes that after she started working, "I had found a little world outside my own; already I found myself looking back upon the life domestic with the interests and curiosity which the mountaineer reserves for the plains she has quitted." *Story of My Life*, 25. In her second autobiography, after writing of her acceptance of Thaw's marriage proposal, she writes: "Never again the thrill and excitement of an opening night, the hard but congenial work, the smell of grease paints, the sense of freedom and self reliance of the self supported." *Untold Story*, 153. Nesbit has a productivity herself in relation to these debates about women, the domestic sphere, and the heterosocial sphere and exemplifies one way in which a woman negotiated the contradiction of this cultural moment.

43. *Daily Telegraph*, quoted in the *Chicago Tribune*, April 13, 1907, 2.

44. The moral panic over "white slavery" emerged most prominently in the United States in 1907 after the publication of the first of George Kibbe Turner's three influential articles on the topic. Two of these, "The City of Chicago: A Study of the Great Immoralities" and "The Daughters of the Poor," are collected in Arthur and Lila Weinberg, eds., *The Muckrakers* (New York: Capricorn, 1964). For debates about women in the new public spaces of leisure see Peiss, *Cheap Amusements*, and, more generally, Judith R. Walkowitz, *City of Dreadful Delight: Narratives of Sexual Danger in Late-Victorian London* (London: Virago, 1992). On the "new woman" in the 1910s and 1920s see Meyerowitz, *Women Adrift*, and Paula Fass, *The Damned and the Beautiful: American Youth in the 1920s* (Oxford: Oxford University Press, 1977).

45. Joanne Meyerowitz, "Sexual Geography and Gender Economy: The Furnished Room Districts of Chicago, 1890–1930," *Gender and History* 2 (autumn 1990): 288.

46. Advertisement for *The Millionaire's Revenge*, in the file on the play at Lincoln Center, New York Public Library. There are no details as to where this advertisement came from. It also stated: "The most realistic scenes ever enacted on the American stage, without doubt produced on a scale of liberality never before attempted in the world of melodrama."

47. Gerald Langford suggests this in *The Murder of Stanford White*, although without referencing it. Michael Mooney suggests it also in *Love and Death in the Gilded Age*, although his suggestion appears to be based on Langford's. Eileen Bowser has also suggested that Thaw's mother may have had a role in financing the film *The Unwritten Law* a year later. In a memorandum written in 1978, at the time when the Museum of Modern Art (MOMA) acquired a copy of the film, Bowser asked: "could it be that Thaw's mother, a millionairess prepared to spend a fortune to rescue her troublesome son, backed the making of this film to aid in his defense?" See the file on *The Unwritten Law* at MOMA.

48. *New York World*, September 20, 1906, 7.

49. Quoted in Langford, *Murder of Stanford White*, 50.

50. On the topical nature of sensational melodrama see Tom Gunning, "The Horror of Opacity: The Melodrama of Sensation in the Plays of Andre de Lorde," in Jacky Bratton, Jim Cook, and Christine Gledhill, eds., *Melodrama: Stage, Picture, Screen* (London: British Film Institute, 1994); on the structure of sensational melodrama see A. Nicholas Vardac, *Stage to Screen: Theatrical Origins of Early Film: David Garrick to D. W. Griffith* (Cambridge: Harvard University Press, 1949).

51. Christine Gledhill has argued that classical Hollywood cinema is derived from both melodramatic and realist aesthetics, which produces "a cinema in which the melodramatic and the realistic — the metaphoric and the referential, the psychological and the social — mesh." Christine Gledhill, "Between Melodrama and Realism: Antony Asquith's *Underground* and King Vidor's *The Crowd*," in Jane Gaines, ed., *Classical Hollywood Narrative: The Paradigm Wars* (Durham: Duke University Press, 1992), 165. On "sensation" more generally see in particular Ben Singer, "Modernity, Hyperstimulus, and the Rise of Popular Sensationalism," in Leo Charney and Vanessa R. Schwartz, eds., *Cinema and the Invention of Modern Life* (Berkeley: University of California Press, 1995). Tom Gunning observes that "one could argue for the term [*sensation*] being one of the keywords of the twentieth century." Tom Gunning, "Horror of Opacity," 52.

52. *Variety*, March 30, 1906, n.p. (my emphasis).

53. Fred J. Balshofer and Arthur Miller, *One Reel a Week* (Berkeley: University of California Press, 1967), 8. For more general details on Lubin see Linda Kowald, "Siegmund Lubin, the Forgotten Filmmaker," *Pennsylvania Heritage* 12 (winter 1986); and Joseph P. Eckhardt and Linda Kowald, *Peddler of Dreams: Siegmund Lubin and the Creation of the Motion Picture Industry 1890–1916* (National Museum of American Jewish History, 1984).

54. Extant records suggest that only two films were made of the scandal prior to *The Unwritten Law*, and neither of these represented the whole scandal. *The Thaw-White Tragedy* (American Mutoscope and Biograph, 1906) was made quickly after the shooting and was a short reenactment of the actual murder. *In The Tombs* (American Mutoscope and Biograph, 1906) was made in late 1906 and is a brief drama based on Nesbit's visiting Thaw in the prison named The Tombs. The version I saw is at the Library of Congress, and in it Thaw is shown in jail being visited by a woman I take to represent his mother. After she leaves, an actress representing Nesbit enters and Thaw asks a guard to let him out of the cell. The guard refuses but relents when Thaw offers him money, and Thaw and Nesbit kiss, with the guard looking around anxiously.

55. *Chicago Tribune*, April 13, 1907, 3. On the difficulties surrounding the exhibition of the film see below.

56. Quoted in the *New York World*, February 8, 1907, 2.

57. William Travers Jerome, quoted in the *New York World*, February 8, 1907, 3.

58. This concept of allegiance draws on the work of Murray Smith. Smith defines *allegiance* as referring to the spectator's evaluation of certain characters as representing a morally desirable (or at least preferable) set of traits in relation to other characters within the fiction. On the basis of this evaluation, Smith suggests, the spectator adopts an attitude of sympathy (or alternatively antipathy) toward the character and responds emotionally in an apposite way to situations in which the character is placed (or might have been placed). See Smith, *Engaging Characters: Fiction, Emotion, and the Cinema* (Oxford: Oxford University Press, 1995), esp. 186–227.

59. *Moving Picture World*, March 16, 1907, 24.

60. *Moving Picture World*, April 20, 1907, 102. This example suggests that the audience had intended to see this one film, a situation that was unusual at this time, when films were usually less than ten minutes long and were grouped together in short programs. This account also testifies to the interest shown in the film at a moment when Thaw was still on trial.

61. Rosenzweig, *Eight Hours*, 205; *Moving Picture World*, April 27, 1907, 119.

62. There is some confusion over titles here: *Moving Picture World* noted that the exhibitor was fined for showing *The Great Thaw Trial*, a film for which I can find no production details (although it is mentioned by Kevin Brownlow in his *Behind the Mask of Innocence* [London: Jonathan Cape, 1990]). I suspect this was in fact *The Unwritten Law*, which is the only title mentioned in the journal up to that date. Even if *The Great Thaw Trial* was shown, it was not the only one: the judge viewing the films "decided that two of them, the one depicting the drugging of Evelyn Nesbit by White and that portraying what is called the shooting of White on the roof garden, were unfit for children to see." *Moving Picture World*, May 11, 1907, 153. I would hazard a guess that the two films were *The Thaw-White Tragedy* (American Mutoscope and Biograph, 1906), which depicts a brief reenactment of the shooting, and

The Unwritten Law. Janet Staiger also notes the confusion around the existence of films of the case in her *Bad Women: Regulating Sexuality in Early American Cinema* (Minneapolis: University of Minnesota Press, 1995), 197.

63. *Moving Picture World,* May 11, 1907, 153; *Moving Picture World,* May 25, 1907, 179.

64. For a discussion of some of these reports and investigations see Lee Grieveson, "Why the Audience Mattered in Chicago in 1907," in Melvyn Stokes and Richard Maltby, eds., *American Movie Audiences: From the Turn of the Century to the Early Sound Era* (London: British Film Institute, 1999).

65. *Chicago Tribune,* April 10, 1907, 12.

66. *Chicago Tribune,* April 13, 1907, 3. This is an early example of the suggestion that foreign films were immoral, an argument that from 1907 on became increasingly central to debates in the United States about the morality of cinema. The American film industry attempted to construct foreign films, particularly those of the dominant Pathé company, as the cause of the intensified reform concern about cinema. For an account of this development see Richard Abel, "The Perils of Pathé, or the American-ization of the American Cinema," in Charney and Schwartz, *Cinema and the Invention of Modern Life.*

67. *Chicago Tribune,* April 13, 1907, 3.

68. Ibid.

69. For example, George Kneeland observed, "Procurers frequent entrances to factories and department stores, or walk the streets at night striking up acquaintances with girls who are alone and looking for adventure. . . . They attend steamboat excursions, are found at the sea shore and amusement parks, in moving picture shows. . . ." George Kneeland, *Commercialized Prostitution in New York City* (New York: Bureau of Social Hygiene, 1913), 65; *Chicago Tribune,* April 14, 1907, sec.1, 5; Chicago Vice Commission, *The Social Evil in Chicago* (1911), in Gerald Mast, ed., *The Movies in Our Midst: Documents in the Cultural History of Film in America* (Chicago: University of Chicago Press, 1982), 62.

70. Weeks, *Sexuality and Its Discontents,* 45 (my emphasis).

71. See Grieveson, "Why the Audience Mattered," and "Fighting Films."

72. *Moving Picture World,* May 25, 1907, 179.

73. Tom Gunning, *D. W. Griffith and the Origins of American Narrative Film: The Early Years at Biograph* (Urbana: University of Illinois Press, 1991).

74. On the emergence of the National Board of Censorship see Charles Matthew Feldman, *The National Board of Censorship (Review) of Motion Pictures, 1909–1922* (New York: Arno Press, 1977).

75. One finds this criticism more widely in the period. For example, *Moving Picture World* reprinted an article from the *Cleveland Plains-Dealer* on the proliferation of immoral moving picture shows: "Such exhibitions as these should certainly be prohibited. They teach no good lesson, and they do not even furnish amusement." *Cleveland Plains-Dealer,* in *Moving Picture World,* January 11, 1908, 23. In a review of another Lubin film *Moving Picture World* labeled it "a Lubin which seems to be somewhat uncalled for. . . . The photography is good and to a certain extent the picture may interest those who are thoughtless but there is a certain degree of delicacy which should be observed about such matters that is plainly violated here. The picture serves no useful purposes. It is not instructive and cannot be called entertaining." *Moving Picture World,* August 28, 1909, 283.

76. On the emerging distinctions between fiction and nonfiction and their links

to regulatory concerns see Lee Grieveson, "Policing the Cinema: *Traffic in Souls* at Ellis Island, 1913," *Screen* 38 (summer 1997): 149–171. On the broader configuration of Hollywood cinema as harmless entertainment see Richard Maltby, *Harmless Entertainment: Hollywood and the Ideology of Consensus* (Metuchen, N.J.: Scarecrow Press, 1983).

77. Frederick C. Howe, "What to Do with the Motion Picture Show: Shall It Be Censored?" *Outlook*, June 20, 1914, 415.

78. Nesbit appeared in ten films: *The Threads of Destiny* (Lubin, 1914), *Redemption* (Triumph, 1917), *Her Mistake* (Triumph, 1918), *The Woman Who Gave* (Fox, 1918), *I Want to Forget* (Fox, 1918), *Thou Shalt Not* (Fox, 1919), *A Fallen Idol* (Fox, 1919), *My Little Sister* (Fox, 1919), *Woman, Woman* (Fox, 1919), and *The Hidden Woman* (Schenck, 1922). Some of these films clearly reflected on Nesbit's experiences. *Woman, Woman* has Nesbit marrying a young engineer who falls ill, and she earns the money to try to cure him by becoming the mistress of a millionaire (this seems to have some resemblance to the later *Blonde Venus* [1932]). *My Little Sister* has Nesbit playing one of two country girls trapped in a brothel patronized by the wealthy. For a discussion of the figure of Nesbit, mainly in relation to a later film made of the scandal, *The Girl in the Red Velvet Swing* (Fox, 1955), see Stephanie Savage, "Evelyn Nesbit and the Film(ed) Histories of the Thaw-White Scandal," *Film History* 8 (1996): 159–175.

FATTY ARBUCKLE

AND THE BLACK SOX

THE PARANOID STYLE

OF AMERICAN POPULAR

CULTURE, 1919–1922

SAM STOLOFF

It is common in accounts of the establishment of the Hays Office in January 1922 to acknowledge a precursor model for that institution — the Baseball Commissioner's Office, created in January 1921 with Judge Kenesaw Mountain Landis as its first occupant. Both agencies had been established in the wake of major scandals — the Black Sox World Series scandal for baseball, the Roscoe "Fatty" Arbuckle scandal for Hollywood — and both Landis and Hays were charged with "cleaning house" (in addition to serving important trade association functions). The relationship was remarked upon at the time, and some initially referred to Will Hays as "the Judge Landis of the movies."[1]

But the analogy has never been pursued; histories of baseball and Hollywood mention it but only in passing. It is remarkable, certainly, that two different popular culture industries should have thought it necessary, at roughly the same historical moment, to recruit prominent public officials to be their "czars." Once the matter is put this way, however, a prior question asserts itself: was it just coincidence that both professional baseball and the Hollywood film industry suffered definitive scandals within a couple of years of each other after World War I? What made those years — not yet the "roaring twenties" but their shaky preamble — so rich in scandal?[2] The Black Sox and Arbuckle scandals in particular changed the landscape of popular culture for a generation: in the gravity of the charges, in the volume of public response, and in the magnitude of institutional adaptation these scandals were unequaled in their fields, then or (possibly) since. But does it make sense to see them as connected?

Granted, on the surface the Black Sox and Fatty Arbuckle scandals don't seem to have had much in common. One was a case of gambling and game fixing in a professional sport, the other an alleged sex crime committed at a Hollywood drinking party. There is apparently not much to link them. But to regard the Black Sox and Arbuckle scandals as entirely distinct is to see them as happenstance — isolated acts without larger determining causes. The acts that precipitate scandal, or the exposure of those acts, may or may not be matters of accident, but their reception in scandalous terms is not.[3] Not everything that might scandalize becomes a scandal; the event must become the object of a public dispute, usually with different social groups and institutions competing to define the terms according to which the scandalous acts will be understood. In many cases scandals give a symbolic power and focus to ongoing social and economic conflict.[4]

In other words, far from being accidental, the Black Sox and Arbuckle scandals were strongly overdetermined, caught up in the violent political currents of the postwar period, if in somewhat different ways. And as it will be my purpose in this essay to demonstrate, the two episodes resemble one another in certain striking respects and not merely in the way they were subsequently handled.

Of course, it was not just scandal that linked baseball and Hollywood. Both were part of a shared world of commercial entertainment in which given producers, performers, characters, and fictions circulated widely among different cultural forms. A "sporting crowd" of actors, athletes, musicians, and writers all mingled at the ballparks, the vaudeville theaters, the bars and the gambling rooms, along with politicians, gamblers, and entertainment entrepreneurs, and there was considerable overlap in the cultural goods they produced. The different fields competed against one another for audiences; they were similarly reviled as vulgar "urban amusements" and responded by making similarly broad-based class appeals. Professional baseball, therefore, should be seen not merely as an "adjacent industry," in the sense meant by David Bordwell, Janet Staiger, and Kristin Thompson in *The Classical Hollywood Cinema*, with important influences on Hollywood industrial history. Instead, both can be seen as elements of a hybrid field of commercial amusements with continuous overlaps.[5]

More important, both were inscribed within and marked by the same horizon of social, political, and economic history. That horizon drew very near in the postwar period, with its lowering clouds of war inflation and industrial depression, anti-Bolshevik panic, and 100 percent Americanism. The sharp social reaction that came on the heels of armistice — the race riots, nativism, violently suppressed strikes, vigilantism — affected all areas of social discourse, and baseball and Hollywood were certainly not immune.

In what follows I read the scandals in two principal ways. In the first place both scandals were in some measure a function of ideological conflicts concerning nationalism, ethnicity, gender, and social class, and both were interpreted within this framework of interrelated anxieties, anxieties that had been exacerbated by the war. Although not fully amalgamated, the conservative and reactionary coalition of superpatriots, nativists, prohibitionists, and moral reformers that dominated public discourse during these years united in seeing Arbuckle and the Black Sox as potent symbols of social and moral decay and in using the scandals to promote agendas of social control. In the second place, at a time of general corporate consolidation, and during a period of renewed campaign against organized labor, both scandals were sites of power struggle within their industries: struggle for control among rival firms and franchises and struggle between owners and players over salaries and conditions of production.

In the convergence of these forces—in the compound of social crisis and industrial conflict—the scandals were not only like each other but strongly analogous to the Red Scare of 1919–1920. Like the great strikes that precipitated the anti-Bolshevik panic, the scandals were understood by some social groups as the work of alien "subversives," and the prevalent rhetoric of Americanism was consequently deployed against perceived alien influence working behind the scenes. Like those strikes, too, both scandals had a strong underlying element of labor conflict. The Red Scare was significantly fueled by employers attempting to discredit labor organization and to secure managerial control over industrial production; similarly, Hollywood producers and baseball team owners seized on scandal as an opportunity to gain more effective control over their employees. They did so by appointing the "czars" to rule over their industries.

Because they led to the creation of the Landis and Hays agencies, the scandals were thus important for establishing the political-economic basis for oligopolistic control in the 1920s and beyond. Although other historical factors were also involved, such as the Harding administration's support for anticompetitive practices, the scandals provided motive and opportunity. Under the aegis of the Baseball Commissioner's Office and the Hays Office, the major leagues and the major studios, more unified than they would otherwise have been, were able to maintain a nearly unchallenged dominance in their industries for a generation. That dominance, which produced the "golden age" in both baseball and Hollywood, was in part the legacy of the Black Sox and Arbuckle scandals.

SCANDALOUS ACTS

To begin, let me briefly outline the events of the two scandals.

In 1919, shortly before the World Series between the Chicago White Sox and the Cincinnati Reds, meetings took place between several gamblers and a number of White Sox players, whose team was heavily favored to win the championship.[6] The 1919 White Sox (who because of the shabby state of their uniforms

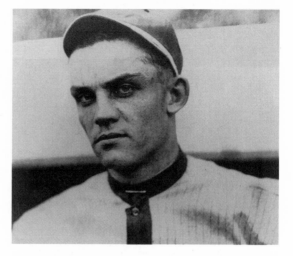

Figure 1. Arnold "Chick" Gandil, first baseman for the Chicago White Sox, and "master of ceremonies" in the 1919 World Series Fix. Courtesy of the Baseball Hall of Fame Library, Cooperstown, New York.

were jokingly called the Black Sox even before the scandal that made the nickname permanent) were one of the best teams in the history of baseball. The team won the American League pennant in 1917 and again in 1919 and boasted some of the game's greatest players, including Eddie Collins, Buck Weaver, and Joe Jackson. For a promised sum of one hundred thousand dollars the conspiring players agreed to lose the Series, which they proceeded to do, apparently deliberately, in eight games.[7] The fix was poorly planned and haphazardly conducted; perhaps four of the eight players whose names subsequently surfaced did the actual work of losing—pitchers Eddie Cicotte and Claude "Lefty" Williams, first baseman Arnold "Chick" Gandil (fig. 1), and second baseman Charles "Swede" Risberg. The others ignored their promise to participate or had only grudgingly agreed to "go along" in the first place, having been told that the fix was on with or without them.

The fix was widely rumored at the time, not least because the odds dramatically shifted in favor of the underdog Reds as the Series got underway. But it was nearly a year before the rumors were confirmed and then only because a grand jury was convened in Chicago to consider other allegations of baseball gambling. White Sox owner Charles Comiskey had made considerable efforts to hush the matter up, but American League president Ban Johnson worked to expose it, mostly out of hostility to Comiskey. Three players testified before the grand jury, confessing their involvement—Cicotte, Williams, and Joe Jackson.[8] The eight players were indicted, along with a number of gamblers—although not New York gambler Arnold Rothstein, whose name was tied to the proceedings and who is widely considered to have been the principal financier of the fix.

After a trial in the summer of 1921, the players were acquitted of all charges. The trial was in a number of ways a fiasco: the players' defense was funded by White Sox owner Comiskey, who had a vested interest in their acquittal, despite the fact that they had conspired against him; among the defense lawyers were former members of the prosecutor's office who had defected; and evidence mysteriously disappeared from the district attorney's files, including, most important, the signed confessions of the players, the theft of which had reportedly been arranged and paid for by Rothstein.

In the meantime hostilities among various owners and officials had led to the collapse of the governing structure of professional baseball. In a panic over the World Series crisis the owners established a new governance system and, after a good deal of wrangling, in January 1921 chose the irascible Chicago federal judge Kenesaw Mountain Landis to be sole Commissioner of Baseball, with absolute power to decide disputes between the major leagues and to rule on player eligibility and ownership. Among Landis's first actions, after his appointment was ratified in January 1921, was to ban the eight accused White Sox players from organized baseball for life.

None of the players ever played in the major leagues again, although several spent a few seasons in "outlaw" and semipro leagues.

•   •   •

In 1921 Roscoe "Fatty" Arbuckle was at the pinnacle of his career (see fig. 2). He was the first comedian to have made the transition from Keystone slapstick to feature films and was apparently the highest paid actor in Hollywood, having signed a deal with Adolph Zukor's Famous Players–Paramount that reportedly paid him $1 million per year in salary plus a percentage of the net profits from his films.[9]

In September 1921 (just one month following the acquittal of the White Sox players), after a party in his suite at the St. Francis Hotel in San Francisco, Arbuckle was implicated in the death of a sometime model and actress named Virginia Rappe. She had been at his party, had become ill, and had died several days later, apparently of peritonitis resulting from a ruptured bladder. The newspapers learned that Arbuckle was a suspect in the case the day after Rappe's death and ran huge banner headlines like "S. F. Booze Party Kills Young Actress," and "Get Roscoe Is Deathbed Plea."[10] The rumors that he had crushed Rappe beneath his weight and/or raped her with a bottle, causing severe internal injuries, began to circulate.[11] Arbuckle was thunderously denounced — in editorial columns, pulpits, meetings of women's and civic organizations, and on the floor of Congress — almost immediately. As the originally reported "evidence" crumbled, the prevailing attitude was that, even if innocent of the actual charge, he was certainly guilty of lewd and immoral conduct.

Arbuckle was tried three times on a charge of manslaughter. In spite of manipulations on the part of the San Francisco district attorney, including witness tampering and destruction of evidence, Arbuckle was finally acquitted, resoundingly,

Figure 2. Roscoe "Fatty" Arbuckle, in a publicity shot from the feature film *Leap Year*. The "black widow" motif would soon be reversed, with Arbuckle portrayed as a spider luring unsuspecting starlets into his web. Courtesy of the Museum of Modern Art, New York.

by the third jury in April 1922. (The first two juries had been unable to reach decisions, the first apparently because a member of the anti-Arbuckle forces refused to vote with the other eleven members, the second because the defense was overconfident and careless in its conduct of the second trial.) All of the serious biographies of Arbuckle conclude that the entire affair was a disastrous mistake: that Rappe had had a long history of medical problems, including frequent abdominal pain, and may have died from complications resulting from an illegal abortion or venereal disease; that she might very well have lived had she received proper medical attention during the days following the party; that the original, mostly uncorroborated, charges had been leveled by a woman who turned out to have a history of blackmail and who was hustled off by the prosecution before the case came to trial and was not allowed to testify; and that the politically ambitious San Francisco district attorney, William Brady, had tried the case, on practically no evidence, as an anti–Southern California vice crusade.

What precisely happened at the St. Francis party will never be known for certain. The participants were mostly drunk; Arbuckle and Rappe were alone in his room for a short period, although there was no evidence of a sexual encounter; the incident was quickly buried under a mountain of speculation, innuendo, accusations, and self-justification. There is a temptation to think that, given the fuss, *something* must have happened. But as evidence from the trial demonstrated, the charges appear to have been wholly manufactured and Rappe's death seems to have been unrelated to anything Arbuckle may have done.

Arbuckle, however, was ruined. His films were yanked from screens and then from general distribution immediately after the scandal hit the press. Meanwhile, under pressure on a number of fronts, especially faced with a renewed censorship campaign in many states and localities, the principal Hollywood studio owners agreed to form a new trade association, the Motion Picture Producers and Distributors of America (MPPDA), and appointed as its head Will Hays, who was then Harding's postmaster general and who had been the chairman of the Republican National Committee during the Harding campaign the year before. This move was modeled on the baseball owners' response to their own crisis less than a year earlier, although Hays was not granted the dictatorial control that Landis had been given.[12] (As I have noted, the parallel was immediately clear.)

After Arbuckle's acquittal in April 1922, Hays, apparently in collaboration with Adolph Zukor and Jesse Lasky, who were the producers and distributors of Arbuckle's films, formally withdrew them from circulation, which amounted to a blacklisting; and although Hays rescinded the formal ban at the end of the year (to renewed public fury), an informal ban continued in effect, and in any event Arbuckle's ruin was already complete. Arbuckle's friends in Hollywood organized a company to hire Arbuckle as a director of short comedy films, which he made under a pseudonym, and he made a brief screen comeback in the early 1930s, just before his death. But these were a shabby, rather shamefaced coda to his once illustrious career. Arbuckle's films now only exist in a few film archives or on hard-to-find videotapes of Hollywood arcana, although the scandal is periodically recycled.

•   •   •

How, then, to explain the proximity of these two scandals? In the first place, as I have suggested, the scandals are best understood as postwar phenomena. When the brief but intense period of total mobilization was abruptly terminated by the war's early conclusion (early for Americans, at least) with the Armistice of November 1918, that sudden halt, and the messy geographic politics and revolutionary skirmishes that made up the war's ragged end, contributed to a feeling of restlessness that overtook the country—both a manic sense of unfulfilled martial enthusiasm and an ominous sense that seditious forces were encroaching. Wars always generate heightened feelings, but the emotions that persisted following the conclusion of the First World War seem to have been particularly intense.

To some extent the wave of postwar reaction can be understood in terms proposed by Richard Hofstadter's classic "The Paranoid Style in American Politics." In that essay Hofstadter describes a tendency, always present among some groups but which becomes most active in U.S. political discourse during periods of crisis or social stress, to see the world in Manichean terms of good and evil and to see the presence of a vast invisible conspiracy that threatens the total destruction of the established order.[13] Such a paranoid worldview, according to which America was vulnerable to a host of foreign evils infiltrating the national body, seized the imagination of many Americans with startling ferocity during the years following the Great War.[14]

But the war seems less to have produced than to have crystallized a wide variety of already existing anxieties. The "fundamental fears and hatreds" that were the war's political residue were only superficially concerned with the conflict in Europe; they were plainly much more concerned with what can be summarily termed modernity: the growth of the cities, continued waves of immigration and the migration of African Americans to northern urban centers, the loss of control in the workplace to mechanization and managerial hierarchies, and women's political gains, among other developments.[15] Movements against these social and cultural shifts had ebbed somewhat since the turn of the century; prosperity for many had undermined the apocalyptic claims that frequently sustained such movements. What the war (and the revolutionary movements that eddied from it) provided was the sense of crisis that made the paranoid discourse of invasion suddenly more persuasive to many. The war mobilized forces of reaction, which focused on social differences, and sought a sense of restoration in matters of race, ethnicity, gender, and class. The period of general panic in the fall and winter of 1919–1920 was fairly brief (if intense), but there were localized manifestations for a number of years thereafter. These included the rise of the Ku Klux Klan, hostility to further immigration, a wave of lynchings, and so on—as well as a decade of conservative Republican rule—and provided a good part of the emotions that fueled the scandals.[16] The scandals, in other words, were considerably exaggerated by the paranoid disposition of the era to see enemies lurking everywhere and to interpret the scandals in terms of much larger conspiracies.

One problem with Hofstadter's analysis is that it fails to adequately specify what social groups have historically been prone to the paranoid view and thus exactly whose "ultimate schemes of values" are threatened during paranoid episodes. But analyses of the Black Sox and Arbuckle scandals suggest that, loosely speaking, the paranoid view was a function of middle-class interests and ideologies.[17]

The class-specific response to the scandals took a number of forms, but perhaps the most direct came in the frequent connection made between Arbuckle's presumed crime and his suddenly acquired wealth as a movie star. Since about 1915 there had been a good deal of fascination with, and anxiety about, escalating star salaries, which had become the subject of detailed commentary in fan magazines.[18] Money was perhaps the most salient factor in the growth of fantasies about the dangers of Hollywood. Richard deCordova has demonstrated that there was a perceptual shift beginning around 1920, when adulation of the stars turned

into suspicion, as "references to divorce, adultery, and moral transgression became a regular feature of star discourse, a part of the formula for writing about
stars."[19] Publicity about the stars' salaries inevitably contributed to the shift toward an attitude of suspicion.

Thus, when the Arbuckle scandal hit the papers, it confirmed what many
people had already come to suspect about Hollywood. The corrupting power of
money was a theme sounded repeatedly in the editorial columns. "For three or
four years the smart set in the movies has been traveling at a furious pace," wrote
the *Los Angeles Times*. "They have taken supreme delight in flinging their money
from the windows."[20] On the same day the *Atlanta Constitution* opined, in an
editorial titled "Ruined by Wealth," that "Arbuckle, made suddenly famous because his grotesque figure and comical antics before the camera was [*sic*] amus-
ing to the 'moviegoing' world, accumulated money so rapidly that his most
difficult problem was to spend it as fast as it came in."[21] The next year, when the
Arbuckle affair was back in the papers with the Hays "Christmas pardon," the
New York Tribune wrote, "Meanwhile a city, peopled with newly enriched actors
who had never had to learn the business of acting, grew up in California. Lacking
the balance that can be supplied only by hard work, their chief aim was to strut
before the public while they spent their vast salaries in the only way that would
occur to people of their sort."[22] The *New York Times* was even more vociferous:

> [The root of the problem] is the sudden acquisition of wealth by persons who
> have neither the mental outlook nor moral fibre necessary to withstand its se-
> ductions. Thrusting large sums of money into their hands inevitably suggests to
> them a plunge into luxury and license. . . . An untrained mind and an undis-
> ciplined character simply cannot, as a rule, bear up against the sudden inrush
> of affluence. . . . The movies have made some people rich who do not know
> what money is for, except that it is to be spent in gratification of barbarian and
> brutal tastes.[23]

In most of these judgments assumptions about social class played a crucial
role. The power of money was seen as corrupting but only (or especially) for those
who did not have sufficiently developed internal restraints ("the balance that can
be supplied only by hard work"). In these accounts Arbuckle fell because he had
been "raised from the position of cuspidor-cleaner in a bar-room to a pedestal of
fame where he may make an income of $5000 a week simply because he is fat
and can make faces."[24] On the floor of Congress Senator Henry Lee Myers of
Montana, arguing in favor of film censorship, denounced Arbuckle and "many
others of like character": "At Hollywood, Calif., is a colony of these people,
where debauchery, riotous living, drunkenness, ribaldry, dissipation, free love,
seem to be conspicuous. Many of these 'stars,' it is reported, were formerly bar-
tenders, butcher boys, sopers, swampers, variety actors and actresses, who may

have earned $10 or $20 a week, and some of whom are now paid, it is said, salaries of something like $5,000 a month or more."[25] In other words, Arbuckle's presumed class status was in itself taken as evidence of his probable guilt.

This preoccupation with star salaries was related to a more general sense that stable measures of value were being undermined during the postwar period. If money could accrue simply because a man "is fat and can make faces," and if it could be flung "from the windows" as if it were confetti, then what was it worth? Such perceptions resonated with people's anxieties about the steep inflation that had sharply eroded the dollar's value during the war years and after: according to Daniel Horowitz, in the years between 1914 and 1921 inflation had cut the dollar's worth in half, and inflation and "profiteering" remained a hot issue after the war.[26]

The same kinds of feelings played a role in the baseball scandal, with players taking the "easy money" offered by gamblers rather than struggling to achieve the athlete's laurels. Part of what made the Arbuckle and Black Sox cases scandalous was that, from a middle-class perspective, ignorant, uneducated men were growing rich without labor, and without the restraining power of "culture," and consequently were debasing values such as diligence and thrift, which served to keep people in "their place."

But calling such reactions "middle-class ideologies" does not do justice to their complexities. Other ideological schemata were closely bound up with these economic anxieties, particularly postwar nationalism, nativism, and anti-Semitism but also anxieties about gender and masculinity. Not all of these ideological terms were coherently related; but as a number of studies have shown, it is often not possible to disentangle these different threads, and for many people (presumably although not necessarily white Protestant men) the terms of social class, Americanness, whiteness, Protestantism, and manliness seemed interchangeable.[27] In a letter to Will Hays, for example, Samuel Abbott, an editor of the *New York Tribune*, wrote of his satisfaction with Hays's decision to ban Arbuckle from the screen: "As the cross symbolizes our religion, the wedding ring our faith in human love and the home; so the flag is our one supreme image of our national unity. We need a stressing of the allied significance of the three, now, to-day. I read with gratitude, this morning, the reports of your wise stand in the Arbuckle matter, for it is in line with the convictions of the men and women who *are* the United States."[28] In this example the intertwined ideologies of nationalism and a Christianized middle-class domesticity were caught up in thinking about the Arbuckle scandal, which thus served as a point of condensation for multiform anxieties about social decay.

Part of the difficulty, therefore, in analyzing paranoid episodes is that it may not be possible to determine ultimate causes. The emotional extremes that define paranoid outbursts are by their very nature multifaceted. But the idea of national subversion during the postwar years covered a multitude of enemies. Hofstadter's anatomy of the paranoid view pointed to the fear of conspiracy as one of its basic features: the agencies of evil operate in secret, quietly infiltrating the institutions of social and political life, which seem to outward appearances to be "normal" but are in fact being contaminated. The fear of conspiracy is one of the clear links between the two scandals and the Red Scare, and charges of Bolshevism were made in the scandals as in the anti-Communist panic, if not as liberally. For example, when the World Series conspiracy was exposed, the *Los Angeles Times*, with its long history of hostility to labor organization, blamed it all on the baseball players' union (which had collapsed several years earlier): "the turbulent element among the players spread a kind of professional Bolshevism among the rest. It is significant that practically every player whose name has been mentioned in connection with the scandals of the last two years was a member of the decadent union." [29] In the Arbuckle case the district attorney and his assistants made repeated accusations and insinuations (never substantiated) that Hollywood operatives backed by wealthy moguls were making secret attempts to corrupt witnesses, bribe jurors, and manufacture evidence, insinuations that created an image of a sinister power at work to undermine the normal processes of law and justice. Assistant District Attorney Leo Friedman, in his closing argument in the third trial, accused the defense of "pulling and tearing down everything, a Bolshevik effort to throw a monkey wrench into the case of the People, in the hope that the real question to be decided by this jury might be covered by the débris." [30]

The Red Scare and the scandals all presented situations in which shocking events seemed to cast a new light on entire cultures and institutions that had until then seemed "normal." Industrial strikes that were not in themselves unfamiliar were suddenly seen, in the glare from the anarchist bombings of May and June 1919, as part of a larger subversive campaign to undermine the state. Headlines about fixed baseball games meant *any* baseball game could be fixed, unbeknownst to spectators: outcomes that they had understood to be based on the chance of skilled competition could suddenly be perceived as products of conspiratorial design. And in the case of the movies the Arbuckle scandal retroactively altered the meanings of all of his films: comedies that had seemed merely playful now seemed vicious and perhaps coded with Hollywood perversion. The disposition to view the world in paranoid terms produced a retroactive "rereading" in which normal surfaces were suddenly perceived to conceal sinister depths.

A good part of this rereading was colored by the postwar hostility toward Jews, which was another strand in the paranoid fabric linking the two scandals. The hatred of the Jew was the major American nativism of the 1920s, as wartime anti-German feeling flowed into postwar anti-Bolshevism, both flowing in turn rather sloppily into anti-Jewish feeling. [31] Just as the mine and steel strikes were thought to be the work of Jewish, Bolshevik agitators, both baseball and the movies were seen as subject to Jewish influence and corruption. For the movies this Jewish element was at the very top: the producers themselves, and much of the hierarchy of the industry. Consider, for example, the assertions made by one Mrs. Rufus Gibbs, of the Citizens League of Maryland for Better Motion Pictures, in a letter to Rev. Charles McMahon, of the National Catholic Welfare Council, some time later: "Motion Pictures are already controlled by a little group of men who are without moral standards; for the most part composed of agnostic Jews, who as a class are becoming a great moral menace to this country and who have no sense of obligation to the youth of the Nation."[32] The movies had always been suspect as an institution, so their workings could easily be seen as Jewish in essence. Baseball, on the other hand, seemed part of the Christian, republican national culture, so the Jewish element was external to the major league structure but encroaching: the "dirty gamblers" who whispered in the ears of gullible ballplayers, and who formed a kind of shadow-world parallel to the sunlit world of sport. Usually the accusations were oblique, as when former Chicago Cubs owner John Murphy wrote in *Baseball Magazine* that many of the gamblers to be found in ballparks were "members of our most industrious commercial race [who] seem to be unable to enjoy a game unless they have a little bet on one side or the other." (The implication here, perhaps, was that Jews could have no loyalty to a team, but only to the wager "on one side or the other," which is similar in a sense to the charge of agnosticism leveled by Mrs. Gibbs.) Or when the *Sporting News* editorialized: "If the newspaper boys want to do the game a real service, let them go after that bunch [the gamblers] — the magnates don't have to tell anybody connected with baseball who they are. Their names and their faces — who could not pick out those faces — are known everywhere followers of baseball congregate."[33] In this case an essentially pure cultural institution was being infiltrated from without, by Jews who conformed to the classic stereotype of the parasite.

The serious anti-Semites, such as Henry Ford's virulent *Dearborn Independent*, drew on what must be considered an Orientalist discourse to describe the Jewish "character." Jews were not in general seen to pose a violent threat; instead, they were seducers, sapping the economic strength of Americans by selling them useless baubles, fashions, and entertainments. The Jewish contamination was a moral one because Jews had no respect for Christian virtue or for properly Anglo-Saxon institutions like sportsmanship. They were licentious and sensual but also cunning. They were loyal to their tribe, not to the nation. The discourse was Orientalist because it implicitly opposed the "Eastern" character of the Jew to the "Western" (or European) character of the ("white") American.[34]

This Orientalist aspect to anti-Semitism crucially ties it to another of the ideological strands in the paranoid fabric, the anxiety about American manliness. One of the qualities of the Jew according to the Orientalist conception is a sort of effeminacy: Jewish sensuality and materiality were opposed to more masculine qualities such as loyalty, valor, or patriotism. By stimulating demand for luxury, fashion, and frivolity, and by appealing to its weak and effeminate tendencies, Jews were softening and "de-moralizing" the "Gentile public."[35]

Of course, the discourse of male anxiety had its own long, independent history as part of the evolution of psychic responses to modernity, for example to the advent of the large corporation and the attendant shift in occupational roles and categories. But World War I served as a point of particular crisis. Wars, which have glittering martial openings, have muddied, disillusioning conclusions; and the men who suddenly had a chance to redeem their whittled masculinity just as suddenly lost it, going back to their homes, their jobs, and an ordinary feminized domestic space that contrasted sharply with the camaraderie of wartime's extraordinary masculine arena. In these terms it makes sense to see the postwar emphasis on a "return to normalcy" as a kind of "male hysteria" in which masculinist anxieties about order, control, and hierarchy, which had grown since the late nineteenth century, coalesced with other antimodern anxieties to create a social explosion.[36]

The anxiety about masculinity was undoubtedly a factor in the paranoid reactions to the scandals, although it played out differently in the two cases. For one thing, the community that responded to the Black Sox scandal was specifically male; much of the audience and all of the sportswriters and editorialists who pronounced on the episode, as well as the great part of their presumed audience, were men. The antimovie crusaders, however, whose voices were raised loudest in the Arbuckle scandal, were women's organizations and other progressive and church-based groups whose constituencies were decidedly female.

The outrage against the Black Sox, and the palpable disappointment their actions caused, stemmed in large measure from an apprehension that their actions were "unmanly." The editorial rhetoric leveled against the players was fraught with gendered language that suggested that they had been seduced, that they had been, in effect, feminized. The involved players were considered a species of monster, having committed the unbelievable act of failing to try to win their sport's highest honor, for the sake of "a few dollars" — that is, they had become prostitutes. This was most evident in the case of Cicotte, whose crying on the stand was widely noted, as was his plea that he had done it to pay off a farm mortgage "for the wife and kids." The *Los Angeles Times* envisioned the players figurally as oak and steel, made soft by "a ring" of gamblers: "To the average fan it still seems unbelievable that those stalwart athletes, with hearts of oak and muscles of steel, could have been debauched by a ring of crooked gamblers." Such contrasts, between "straight" and "crooked," "stalwart" and "debauched," "standing up" and "lying down," the hard and the soft, the linear and the curved, were all figural oppositions between presumed masculine and feminine traits. This could be more explicit, too, as when the *Boston Globe* called the players "weak sisters" (and the term *debauched* suggested a sexual seduction).[37]

Arbuckle, too, represented a failure of manhood. Behind the screen image of masculine heroes the Arbuckle scandal seemed to reveal a yawning sink of depravity. According to the paranoid view, the Hollywood moguls, by paying lavish salaries to actors who were ill-equipped to cope with sudden wealth, had created an atmosphere of vice, of "kept men," "male vamps," dope fiends, and other hothouse species — as the more vivid anti-Hollywood pamphlets described.[38] The Orientalist aspect of this paranoid view was suggested at trial by assistant prosecutor Milton U'Ren in his description of Arbuckle's party in the St. Francis Hotel: "A Babylonian feast was in progress there. The defendant had sumptuous quarters with his friends. . . . Food was spread, wine and liquor were served, and this modern Belshazzar sat upon his throne, surrounded by his lords and their ladies; there was music, feasting, singing and dancing."[39]

However, for a number of reasons, Arbuckle's relationship to masculinity was considerably more complicated than that of the Black Sox. Although the scandal transformed Arbuckle's image in ways that could not have been imagined beforehand, there had always been complex ambiguities in Arbuckle's star persona.[40] Many of these were related to Arbuckle's size and the sexual ambiguities of the fat body. The fat body, for example, was understood to be in some sense childish, especially in the context of slapstick; "Fatty" is a nickname bestowed by children's taunts (and, not surprisingly, it was a name that Arbuckle disliked, although he surrendered to it as a *nom de cinéma*). Arbuckle looked like a giant baby and sometimes played one.[41] This quality of childishness carried with it a kind of implied asexuality. However, with his shift into feature films in 1920 Arbuckle had been marketed as a mock-romantic, sexualized figure, although this sexuality was refracted through a comic lens. The implication was always that considering him as a romantic or sexual figure would inevitably be incongruous. "Still, there's romance in the game," he says in a 1921 article published under his name. "I'm not a Douglas Fairbanks, but girls have loved me. My rotundity seems to fascinate them. Proposals have reached me by the score."[42] And in a 1921 *Photoplay* piece, "Love Confessions of a Fat Man" (on the stands the month of the scandal), he is quoted as saying, "I am convinced that the fat man as a lover is going to be the best seller on the market for the next few years. He is coming into his kingdom at last. He may never ring as high prices or display as fancy goods as these he-vamps and cavemen and Don Juans, but as a good, reliable, all the year around line of goods, he's going to have it on them all."[43] Certainly, these articles were poking fun at the very figure of a "matinee idol" such as Fairbanks. The real joke, however, was that anyone would regard Arbuckle as a sexual object; yet the joke still frames Arbuckle in sexual terms, constructing a sexualized persona even as that possibility is ironically denied.[44]

Arbuckle's very features, his roundness and cherubic qualities, his baby face, suggested a kind of gender ambiguity. Thus, it was not simply his weight, his childishness, or his mock sexualization that made Arbuckle potentially monstrous but the further implication of a body without functioning gender. Arbuckle's penchant for playing roles in drag may have contributed to suspicions concerning his gender. Although the practice was common, Arbuckle was notably fond of female costume, which he had learned to good effect while touring in small-time vaudeville before his film career began.[45]

For these various reasons his body could not be a masculine body. Masculinity is, among other things, an expression of bodily control, whereas the fat body is by definition seen as out of control. Arbuckle's weight became prima facie evidence of his perverted, non-masculine desire — and this was true even though in his athletic slapstick performances Arbuckle could demonstrate exquisite control of his body. In this context the bottle rumor is particularly significant — it apparently suggested a drunken impotence, and it may have gathered force precisely because of the ambiguous persona Arbuckle presented in his films. The implication of the rumor was that Arbuckle exacted revenge on Rappe for his own failed masculinity, making him a sort of vindictive eunuch.

Of course, as a slapstick comic Arbuckle would not have been expected to adhere to some abstract ideal of masculinity in his work; instead, he played with such norms, and his body was an element of that burlesque. Recent works on Hollywood representations of masculinity have pointed out how the representation of masculinity is always complex and contradictory, but comic stars should be seen as proposing another kind of response to masculinity, one that permits transgression of masculine norms without irrevocably breaking them, perhaps as a way of enabling an audience to negotiate the contradictions of gender expectations.[46] A generic consideration enters here; "crazy comedy," and other cinematic forms that emphasize spectacle at the expense of narrative, or that otherwise disrupt the story, also disrupt the star as a locus for identification, thereby permitting a comic modality of light-hearted transgressiveness.[47]

But the scandal changed all that: it denied Arbuckle that lighter touch. In all these various ways the very qualities that made Arbuckle effective as a comic figure — the mayhem and ribaldry of slapstick, the contradiction of the active fat body, and its gender and sexual ambiguities — turned on him. In their comic form they had been available for the management of social anxieties, but in their garish transformation they overstepped the safe boundaries of fantasy and suddenly seemed to represent an actual threat. Anxieties about loss of bodily control in an economy dominated by corporations, about consumption and the excesses that consumerism enabled and provoked, and about maintaining a proper distinction between the sexes in the new age of women's suffrage and bobbed hair all found an object in the reprehensible figure of the condemned Arbuckle.

SCANDAL AND INDUSTRIAL CONFLICT

If the Black Sox and Arbuckle scandals were therefore symptomatic of cultural crisis, they were also a logical outcome of industrial practices that had developed in the amusements business during the first decades of the twentieth century.

The scandals, in other words, were partly a form of economic conflict; and two factors in particular, internal to the culture industries, made that conflict a probability. On the one hand, the rise of a star system in the early part of the century dramatically increased the power of the players in their relations with studio and team owners (although in baseball that power remained mostly latent and unexercised). At the same time, the owners were consolidating their position as oligopolistic producers and by this means were strengthening their position as employers (despite their being frequently at each others' throats). Both the Black Sox and the Arbuckle scandals were strongly determined by this struggle between players and owners, and they should therefore be seen as central skirmishes in long and ongoing labor conflicts.

Actors and athletes perform a unique type of labor: their work cannot be reduced to an abstract labor power precisely because their value as "stars" depends on qualities that they uniquely possess. They are simultaneously workers and branded products: their labor is worth what their brand image will sell. Given a competitive labor market, therefore, star players should be able to earn a large part of what they produce in revenue for their employers (marginal revenue product, in economic terms) — perhaps more, given that stars are often the brand image for the entire output of a given producer.[48] Star power gives players unusual leverage, but this leverage conflicts with the need of producers to have control over production and distribution — a need that was increasing in the teens and twenties as the scale of production was growing, with vertical integration in Hollywood and with the construction of giant concrete-and-steel baseball stadiums.[49]

Until the 1970s, when the outlawing of the "reserve clause" in baseball created a more competitive labor market, baseball players were prevented from fully exercising their star power; professional baseball was organized as a tightly controlled monopoly, leaving players with very little leverage. The reserve clause, which was included in all player contracts, provided that once a player signed with a given team, he had effectively signed away the rights to his services for the duration of his career; he could be sold or traded, or "optioned out" to the minor leagues, without his consent. Because he had no contractual options, he had very little power when it came to salary negotiations; he could not threaten to move to another team because all franchises abided by the "National Agreement" and would not attempt to hire another team's players. A rival major league, the Federal League, had briefly flourished in the mid-teens, giving the players some negotiating power, and salaries had risen accordingly. A union was also formed, the Base Ball Players' Fraternity, and, given the Federal League threat, it was able to force the owners to grant some concessions. With the demise of that league in 1916, however, the union also collapsed, and salaries were slashed; they remained depressed, even when it became clear during the 1919 season that postwar attendance was soaring.[50]

The players, therefore, were held by their teams under a species of peonage. Naturally they resented it. The situation was the same throughout professional baseball. Although Charles Comiskey, the owner of the White Sox, was notorious for paying especially low salaries, and the White Sox players were especially angry, in fact the problem was systemic.[51]

Gamblers, however, were an ever-present source of money if a player was willing to take it. And by all accounts, since baseball's beginnings there had been a certain number of players who were willing. Gambling had always made up a significant part of professional baseball's culture.[52] And it was a central part of the general male social culture; as Luc Sante writes, "gambling permeated every masculine gathering in every station of the social and economic range" in the late nineteenth and early twentieth centuries.[53]

Of course, betting was one thing, but deliberately altering one's play for money (or to win bets) was quite another. Undoubtedly there were far fewer players willing to take this step, but there were some, and the documented cases suggest that there were more whose activities did not become public.[54] Further, nearly everyone in baseball must have known to some extent that gambling was a factor in the game. Given the reluctance of the owners and the baseball hierarchy to bring charges or impose penalties, players who engaged in gambling activities did so mostly with impunity.

The 1919 World Series fix was unusual because it meant agreeing to forfeit the game's highest honors rather than just a single game among the 154 played during a season (or the reduced number played in 1918 and 1919). It is possible to imagine, however, that the resentment among some players on the White Sox had grown to such proportions that they did not care whether they won or lost. Certainly the players knew that they could demand more for losing the Series than for other games, both because of what it would cost them professionally and because of what it would be worth to the gamblers, given the large scale of betting activity the Series inspired.

Then, too, there is the curious incident that occurred during the conspiracy trial of the eight indicted White Sox players in the summer of 1921. At the outset of the trial, during jury selection, several members of the team who were not accused of taking part in the plot, including manager Kid Gleason, pitchers Dickie Kerr and Red Faber, and captain Eddie Collins, came into the courtroom and exchanged pleasantries and expressions of comradeship with the eight indicted players. The press reported critically on this display, and hasty denials were subsequently issued, but the fact remained: some members of the team against whom the indicted players had apparently conspired seemed to bear them no ill will.[55] This suggests that even players who were never suspected of corruption were in fact ambivalent about the issue, whether or not they ever actually contemplated taking bribes. Indeed, allegations surfaced, and were later investigated, that members of the "Clean Sox," who had not participated in the World Series fix, had nonetheless been involved in other incidents of bribery and game fixing in 1917. The entire team, for example, had apparently collected a pool of money (forty-five dollars each, for a total of about eleven hundred dollars) to pay off Detroit (which was not in the running for the pennant) to lose four games to the White Sox (who were in the running) in September of that year. The manager, and owner Comiskey, had also known of the payoff. On inspection, then, the line dividing the "clean" from the "dirty" players comes to seem rather muddy.[56]

It is also true that many, perhaps even a majority of players, knew of gambling activity but considered "squealing" an unacceptable violation of a code of silence. Wrote journalist Hugh Fullerton after the scandal had broken: "The honest ball players, or the majority of them, stand before the public as mildly guilty of being accessories after the fact, in that all save a few knew or suspected that crookedness was going forward and failed to protect their own reputations, their business and the sport from the ones who were guilty. . . . They [dishonest players and gamblers] proved that the game can be and has been successfully manipulated, provided the honest players on the teams do not 'squeal.'" The players' code of silence suggests that they felt they were in league against the owners and the baseball establishment and that they owed more to each other, even in dishonesty, than they did to the magnates. They felt, in other words, a kind of labor solidarity, even if there was more glumness than glory in it.[57]

The World Series sellout, then, was ultimately rather like a strike, a work slowdown, or perhaps like industrial sabotage. To some this will seem an outrageous description, given that the players operated secretly, for financial consideration. But there is no doubt that at heart the World Series fix was a labor rebellion, and most accounts have at least glancingly acknowledged this. (The players had in fact threatened to strike earlier the same season but had been dissuaded by manager Gleason.) The players were refusing to labor at their jobs for the amount of money offered them and without other honest options (short of abandoning their profession) secretly sold that labor to higher bidders — the two groups of gamblers. They felt that their right to be paid what they gauged they were worth overrode their obligations as sportsmen. The fact that the players were willing to engage in such a conspiracy suggests that they saw themselves more as entertainers (saw themselves, that is, from the business perspective) than as sportsmen, and in that case winning and losing came to seem of secondary importance, except as it affected their economic prospects.[58] (This description may only apply, however, to the players who were most bitter about their situations and most active in planning the loss — Gandil, Cicotte, and Risberg. The rest of the participants were rather more reluctant, and their half-heartedness showed in their inattention to where the money in fact went. As I've noted, Gandil apparently took a large part.)[59] The "moral" decay of baseball, in other words, was in fact an economic challenge to a large extent.

Sportswriter Grantland Rice made the connection between the ballplayers and labor militancy at the moment when things began to look suspicious in the Series; describing a key misplay by Cicotte during the first game, he invoked the work stoppage in the steel mills: "Eddie, instead of jumping swiftly for the ball, took his time with all the leisure of a steel striker," wrote Rice. "He made no attempt to hurry this ball along to Risberg for a sure double play." Rumors of the fix had only just begun to circulate, so Rice probably meant nothing particular in the analogy. And the week-old steel strike, representing a peak of postwar labor conflict, was on everyone's mind. Nonetheless, there was some substance (and much prescience) in the remark, which offered a transformative vision of a bad baseball play as a slowdown on a shop floor.[60]

In the film industry, on the other hand, the situation for the players was dramatically different. Because the free-for-all that followed the demise of the Edison Patents Trust in the early teens had created a genuinely competitive field, a number of top performers (such as Arbuckle) had managed to achieve very large salaries and a certain amount of production autonomy by the end of the decade (a movement capped by the 1919 establishment of United Artists). Competition among studios in the race for vertical integration pushed the salaries of proven stars higher and higher. A star's main source of power was the potential of a better offer from a rival studio; in a genuinely competitive situation owners find it impossible not to bid against one another for players, as each seeks a marketing advantage by signing one of the few proven stars and seeks to take those stars out of the hands of other producers. In this way star players are much better able to achieve an equitable share of marginal revenue product. Even when the owners agree in principle not to compete for stars, it has proven extraordinarily difficult for them not to engage in such competition because they tend not to trust each other to abide by informal agreements, and, generally speaking, U.S. law and policy have prevented them from making such agreements formal (and therefore legally enforceable). By the late teens, however, there was a strong feeling among the producers that star salaries were spiraling out of control. Producers were apparently uncomfortable with the publicity given high salaries, and they worried that such publicity gave the stars themselves too strong a bargaining position. But the popular fascination with stars was apparently fixed in part on lavish star lives, and million-dollar salaries contributed to this fantasy of star excess.

Until the Arbuckle scandal shifted the focus, then, producers clearly felt that they gained a marketing advantage from publicizing outlandish star earnings. Magnates and moguls alike were committed to stardom as a way of marketing their cultural products, but they had not yet developed strategies to prevent stars from demanding larger percentages of product revenues, as estimates of their "worth" were raised. The problem was increasingly put in the corporate language of "cost containment" and "stabilization." One source of pressure for control of costs came from the banks, which were taking an increasing role in film financing. As bankers became more involved in the corporate management of film producers, by lending money, floating stock issues, and joining corporate boards, they stressed the need for strict budgeting and for regularization of production. This meant, above all, controlling the star system — not abandoning it, given that its marketing power had become apparent, but limiting the competitive situation that gave stars a relative advantage in their negotiations with producers.[61]

Richard Dyer argues that Hollywood scandals have in some ways been the only "genuine" star publicity, because scandals are inadvertent, whereas in practice all other forms have been controlled by the studios.[62] But scandals may have their deliberate aspects, in the sense that the producers can use them as a means of discipline, even if they do not deliberately cause them. There is reason to believe that, although he undoubtedly would have preferred other means given the damage that the scandal caused to Paramount and to the industry, Zukor wanted to make an example of Arbuckle: he was unhappy with the contract that Joseph Schenck had negotiated in 1919, making Arbuckle the highest-paid actor in the business. Furthermore, Zukor was angry that Arbuckle had refused to make personal appearances for the "Paramount Week" promotion on the very Labor Day when the San Francisco party took place. When Will Hays blacklisted Arbuckle immediately following his acquittal, his action seems to have been taken at the behest of Zukor. Certainly there was great public pressure to take that step, and Famous Players–Paramount had a tremendous amount of money invested in Arbuckle's previously produced films. But Zukor could rationalize those expenses as the price of labor discipline. Even if he was not particularly the object of Zukor's antagonism, Arbuckle's well-publicized paycheck made him an obvious target in the campaign against high salaries.[63]

The Black Sox and Arbuckle scandals, then, represented different but related forms of crisis. In both cases, whether in the underlying causes of scandal or in the ultimate response of owners and producers, what had emerged was a struggle over the control and remuneration of star power. And in both cases scandal presented an opportunity for the owners to establish more effective disciplinary means to ensure that they would win the struggle. For the baseball owners the scandal permitted a consolidation of existing but fraying controls over players, and for the Hollywood studios scandal permitted the establishment of an entirely new system of controls.

But in both cases those controls came through the establishment of internal regulatory agencies: the Commissioner's Office for baseball, and the Hays Office for Hollywood. Both professional baseball and Hollywood had already been moving toward the creation of some kind of trade or regulatory associations, but the specific form those bodies took was largely determined by the scandals: highly public agencies, headed by men drawn from government, whose role was understood to be in some sense custodial. In other words, the advertised function of Landis and Hays was to represent "the public" and on their behalf to "clean up the mess" that the players (and owners) had made, and it was precisely their prestige as public servants that would enable them to impose moral respectability (that is, labor discipline). In this respect the scandals again invite comparison to the Red Scare. Rather like the "Palmer raids," or like General Leonard Wood's marching with federal troops into Gary, Indiana, to round up radicals and suppress the 1919 steel strike (which happened, not entirely coincidentally, while the World Series was being played), the commercial amusement industries installed authoritarian figures to govern their own internal regulatory agencies.[64]

Although the "culture czars" have not ordinarily been seen this way, their main function was to foster collusive behavior among the owners, especially to reduce the competition for the services of players so that star salaries would not be bid up. The position of the players was so weakened by scandalous revelations of gambling, corruption, and debauchery (often but not necessarily spurious) that the owners could openly flaunt their dictatorial, monopolistic control of labor markets under the guise of "cleaning house" and "purging" the corrupt element. They were thus able to turn the discourse of moral outrage engendered by scandal to economic advantage.

CONCLUSION

Ultimately paranoia is about division, and it seeks resolution in the erasure of that division. The paranoid discourses of the postwar period sought a unified national body—unified on particular terms—as well as unified individual bodies: "100 percent Americans" rather than "hyphenated Americans" whose very names bore the marks of social division. Baseball—precisely because it had promoted itself as the "national pastime," and because athletics could be easily aligned with the classical aesthetic of the controlled, contained body—had offered itself as a unifying cultural force, for example claiming particular virtues in campaigns for Americanization. For that reason it was especially vulnerable when the Black Sox scandal revealed divisions in that body. The movies, on the other hand, as "cheap amusements," had always posed the threat of the uncontainable and carnivalesque, although they were increasingly making claims of cultural value.[65]

The resolution of the scandals was an attempt to cleanse sport and film of various taints. What this required was the expulsion of foreign contaminants: the banishment of offending players like Arbuckle or the Black Sox, like the mass deportations of aliens during the Red Scare. This purgation, it was hoped, would restore the national body to health and wholeness—would fashion "one nation, indivisible," and submerge in a "republic of mass culture" the tangible social schisms that had been revealed.[66] Landis was a promiscuous blacklister during the early years of his tenure, and Hays too has been charged with a quieter blacklisting campaign.[67]

The producers and owners, meanwhile, were quite ambivalent about the

forces of the classical body in the guise of middle-class reformers, religious organizations, women's groups, and patriotic societies. They were glad to use them
against their players, and they were eager to appeal to a single mass market; but
they were also aware that these forces were just as likely to be turned against
themselves, for example in reformist campaigns for film censorship or for the
"Blue laws," which prohibited commercial baseball on Sundays. Popular culture,
after all, was itself in some measure a repository of the carnivalesque and could
only be partly allied to the culture of the classical body.

In retrospect, we can see that these years, from 1918 through 1922, marked a
peak of antimodern reaction and in some sense its conclusion as a mass movement. The passage of Prohibition was the conclusion to the greatest of the coercive moral campaigns, and the enactment of stringent immigration restrictions
was the conclusion to the nativist surge that had accompanied the war. For a
variety of reasons, by the mid-1920s the dominance of the cities, of corporations,
of commercial entertainment had come to seem like established facts — less nov-
elties to be feared than signs of progress to be welcomed. As Paul Boyer notes,
"In the 1920s the dregs of the coercive moral-control impulse were left to isolated
fanatics," such as extremist evangelicals, increasingly marginal social organizations, and the Ku Klux Klan, which waned after mid-decade.[68]

The moment of Red Scare and scandal should thus be seen as transitional.
The war produced a social convulsion as a variety of anxieties about lax morals,
unassimilable immigrants, vulgar and corrupting amusements, Bolshevik bomb
throwers, and corporate profiteering briefly coalesced, ignited, and then burned
out. It marked, not a triumph of reaction but its decisive (if incomplete) passing.
Henceforth, the extremes of antimodern reaction would be merely the ragged
end of an increasingly residual cultural formation.

Nevertheless, it would be a mistake to discount the real and lasting effects of
the postwar extremism. In the case of the popular culture industries, the extremist
reaction to scandal ultimately strengthened corporate power and thus contributed to the ascendancy of the "competitive managerial capitalism" that has since
been dominant in those fields.

Notes

1. "One of the alert proposals is the selection of a nationally important man out-
side the picture business to head the body in much the same manner that Judge
Kenesaw Mountain Landis presides over the destinies of baseball." "Again the One
Big Problem," *Moving Picture World*, December 24, 1921, 907. See also Terry Ram-
saye, *A Million and One Nights* (New York: Simon and Schuster, 1926), 815–816.
Harold Seymour notes that Hays was initially known as the "Judge Landis of the
movies." Harold Seymour, *Baseball: The Golden Age* (New York: Oxford University
Press, 1971), 323. As an example of this see the editorial in the *Denver Times*, "'The
Landis of the Movies,'" January 19, 1922. Hays himself disputed the analogy; for

example, in a letter to George Ade of March 28, 1922 he wrote: "Of course, I am in no sense a referee, nor in any sense as has been suggested 'The Judge Landis of the Movies.'" *The Will Hays Papers*, ed. Douglas Gomery (Frederick, Md.: University Publications of America), microfilm edition, reel 4, frame 564.

2. The film industry was shaken, in quick succession, by the Pickford divorce, the William Desmond Taylor murder, and the Wallace Reid narcotics exposé, among other incidents. Kenneth Anger, *Hollywood Babylon* (New York: Straight Arrow, 1975) is the catalogue raisonné of the period's scandals; it is thorough if not reliable. Baseball suffered a variety of game-fixing scandals, including the notorious Hal Chase affair, which is described in some detail below. Seymour, *Golden Age*, 288–293.

3. On this point see John B. Thompson, "Scandal and Social Theory," in James Lull and Stephen Hinerman, eds., *Media Scandals: Morality and Desire in the Popular Culture Marketplace* (New York: Columbia University Press, 1997), 34–64. The Arbuckle affair was more of an accident than the Black Sox sellout given that he had apparently done nothing like what he was accused of, and the scandal depended on a death that, in retrospect, could probably have been prevented if the "victim," Virginia Rappe, had received proper medical attention. But the forces that turned an incident into a scandal, such as newspaper competition, the rivalry between Los Angeles and San Francisco, or hostility to Hollywood during the period, were in no sense accidental.

4. For another examination of the Arbuckle case using these terms see Gary Alan Fine, "Scandal, Social Conditions, and the Creation of Public Attention: Fatty Arbuckle and the 'Problem of Hollywood,'" *Social Problems* 44.3 (1997): 297–334.

5. David Bordwell, Janet Staiger, and Kristin Thompson, *The Classical Hollywood Cinema: Film Style and Mode of Production to 1960* (New York: Columbia University Press, 1985), 88. This is not, of course, to deny the validity of institutional history, merely to point out its necessary limitations.

6. The basic sources for the Black Sox scandal are still Eliot Asinof, *Eight Men Out: The Black Sox and the 1919 World Series* (New York: Holt, 1963); and Seymour, *Golden Age*, 294–339.

7. A second group of gamblers later offered eighty thousand dollars. Neither group paid the promised amounts to the players, who apparently received a total of eighty thousand dollars from the two groups; and Gandil, the main organizer, took the lion's share. That year the Series went to the first team to win five games.

8. Joe Jackson's guilt is still hotly debated. The case for his innocence is convincingly made in Donald Gropman, *Say It Ain't So, Joe: The True Story of Shoeless Joe Jackson*, rev. ed. (New York: Carol Publishing, 1995). Jackson accepted money but appears not to have had an active part in the fix.

9. There are four sober Arbuckle biographies: Andy Edmonds, *Frame-Up!: The Untold Story of Roscoe "Fatty" Arbuckle* (New York: William Morrow, 1991); Stuart Oderman, *Roscoe "Fatty" Arbuckle: A Biography of the Silent Film Comedian, 1887–1933* (Jefferson, N.C.: McFarland, 1994); David Yallop, *The Day the Laughter Stopped: The True Story of Fatty Arbuckle* (New York: St. Martin's, 1976); Robert Young Jr., *Roscoe "Fatty" Arbuckle: A Bio-Bibliography* (Westport, Conn.: Greenwood, 1994). Edmonds states that Arbuckle's 1919 contract with Adolph Zukor was supposed to pay him $1 million per year, although it isn't clear he was ever in fact paid that amount. Edmonds, *Frame-Up!*, 81, 104–106. In an article published shortly after Arbuckle signed the deal with Zukor, his agent Lou Anger is quoted as follows: "I don't mind saying for Mr. Arbuckle, who is a painfully modest man, that the new

contract is the largest one ever signed by Mr. Zukor for an individual artist. It covers a period of three years and involves over three million dollars." *Moving Picture World,* March 8, 1919.

10. "S. F. Booze Party," *San Francisco Examiner,* September 10, 1921. "Get Roscoe," *San Francisco Bulletin,* September 10, 1921.

11. The bottle rumor is the most intractable element of the entire Arbuckle legend. It had no apparent factual basis; certainly it was never mentioned in any of the inquests, hearings, or trials. Instead it was a fantasy condensation, incorporating a number of details from the newspaper accounts of Arbuckle's party. These included the tremendous amount of attention paid to the role of "bootleg liquor" and drinking in the incident (with Prohibition still pretty much a novelty); composite newspaper photographs that superimposed images of Arbuckle, Rappe, and liquor bottles; the fact that Rappe had suffered a ruptured bladder, which seemed to suggest violence; and an incident in which Arbuckle reportedly touched ice to the ailing Rappe, possibly to her genitals. This act, which may have been intended as a joke, with a number of people gathered around, was widely reported in the newspapers as "torture." The bottle story may have been retailed by people whose purposes it served to exaggerate the Arbuckle debaucheries or by people who took pleasure in shocking. But the quickness and ease with which the bottle rumor spread suggests that it satisfied the requirements of myth. It is regarded as the truth of the case to this day. In fact, Yallop argues, it would have been almost impossible for rape with an object such as a bottle to cause the injury suffered by Rappe. Yallop, *Day the Laughter Stopped,* 158, 195. See also Edmonds, *Frame-Up!,* 210–211.

12. This difference was largely a function of baseball and Hollywood's different logics of cultural production and consequently different industrial structures. Baseball was conducted much more as a single entity, with all constituent units—the individual franchises, or teams—subject to a binding regulatory agreement. Following the Supreme Court's 1922 decision in the Baltimore Federal League suit, exempting baseball from antitrust regulation, this monopolistic structure was legally protected. The film industry after 1922 conducted itself much more as a coalition, and ongoing antitrust investigation and prosecution ensured that it would remain that way.

13. Richard Hofstadter, "The Paranoid Style in American Politics," in *The Paranoid Style in American Politics, and Other Essays* (Chicago: University of Chicago Press, 1979). There is considerable overlap between Hofstadter's sociohistorical approach and the more psychosocial implications of the term *hysteria,* which has gained literary-critical currency even as it has become psychoanalytically suspect. Elaine Showalter's usage, for example, in her book *Hystories,* is very similar to Hofstadter's use of the category of paranoia: "Redefining hysteria as a universal human response to emotional conflict is a better course than evading, denying, or projecting its realities." The emphasis, in Hofstadter, on "ultimate schemes of values" points to external challenges, whereas the emphasis in Showalter on "emotional conflict" points to internal states of stress. Both, however, seek to understand historical phenomena in psychologically rooted terms. Elaine Showalter, *Hystories: Hysterical Epidemics and Modern Culture* (New York: Columbia University Press, 1997), 17.

14. This view tapped a long tradition of American thought representing Europe as the decadent Other, a view exacerbated by the unsettlingly intimate contact between this decadent Europe and a virtuous America. With the vastly increased traffic brought by war, the prophylaxis of the Atlantic was breached, and many Americans

were left feeling open to European contagions — from venereal disease (supposedly acquired by troops abroad), to the great "Spanish" influenza (actually indigenous to the United States) that leveled hundreds of thousands, to the infectious ideologies of "international" Jews (about which I say more below). On the flu epidemic see Alfred W. Crosby, *America's Forgotten Pandemic: The Influenza of 1918* (Cambridge: Cambridge University Press, 1989).

15. The phrase "fundamental fears and hatreds" is Hofstadter's: "the fact that movements employing the paranoid style are not constant but come in successive episodic waves suggests that the paranoid disposition is mobilized into action chiefly by social conflicts that involve ultimate schemes of values and that bring fundamental fears and hatreds, rather than negotiable interests, into political action." Hofstadter, "Paranoid Style," 39.

16. Some general, as well as some more specialized, histories of the period, both classic and more recent, that I have relied on include Frederick Lewis Allen, *Only Yesterday: An Informal History of the 1920s* (New York: Harper and Bros., 1931); Lynn Dumenil, *Modern Temper: American Culture and Society in the 1920s* (New York: Hill and Wang, 1995); William E. Leuchtenburg, *The Perils of Prosperity, 1914–1932* (Chicago: University of Chicago, 1958); David Montgomery, *The Fall of the House of Labor: The Workplace, the State, and American Labor Activism, 1865–1925* (Cambridge: Cambridge University Press, 1987); Michael E. Parrish, *Anxious Decades: America in Prosperity and Depression, 1920–1941* (New York: Norton, 1992); and Robert Wiebe, *The Search for Order, 1877–1920* (New York: Hill and Wang, 1967). For more specific information on the cultural crisis in this period see Stanley Coben, "A Study in Nativism: The American Red Scare of 1919–1920," *Political Science Quarterly* 79 (March 1964): 52–75; John Higham, *Strangers in the Land: Patterns of American Nativism, 1860–1925* (New Brunswick, N.J.: Rutgers University Press, 1955); Lawrence W. Levine, "Progress and Nostalgia: The Self Image of the Nineteen Twenties," in *The Unpredictable Past: Explorations in American Cultural History* (New York: Oxford University Press, 1993), 189–205; Robert K. Murray, *Red Scare: A Study in National Hysteria, 1919–1920* (New York: McGraw-Hill, 1964).

17. This conclusion must remain hypothetical in the absence of more substantive information concerning audiences: the baseball fans, moviegoers, and newspaper readers whose responses to scandal went largely unrecorded. The people whose responses *were* recorded, besides the owners, were members of organized interest groups, such as the San Francisco "Women's Vigilant Committee" (which held anti-Arbuckle meetings and courthouse vigils during his trial); other civic and reform organizations, such as the General Federation of Women's Clubs or the YMCA; clergy members; newspaper writers, editorialists, and cartoonists; and judges, lawyers, and politicians (some directly involved in the Arbuckle and Black Sox court cases, some not). Available evidence suggests that the views of the professional moralizers were considerably more hostile than those of the "average" fan. Hofstadter is disinclined to define the paranoid disposition in terms of social class, arguing that in the American context, ethnic and religious conflicts have been primary. But this ignores the ways that ethnicity, race, and religion are intertwined with perceptions of class.

18. See, as just one example, Alfred A. Cohn, "What They Really Get — Now!" *Photoplay*, March 1916, 27–30. Given that baseball players' salaries were tightly controlled, they were not ordinarily subject to the same sorts of commentary. However, there were exceptional cases, such as that of Babe Ruth, whose salary demands when he was sold to the Yankees in 1920 were widely publicized.

19. Richard deCordova, *Picture Personalities: The Emergence of the Star System in America* (Urbana: University of Illinois Press, 1990), 119–120.

20. "The Arbuckle Incident," *Los Angeles Times*, September 13, 1921, 4.

21. "Ruined by Wealth," *Atlanta Constitution*, September 13, 1921, 6.

22. "Not Yet Too Late," *New York Tribune*, December 23, 1922, 8.

23. Editorial, *New York Times*, October 6, 1921, 16.

24. Myra Nye, "The Tin Gods," *Los Angeles Times*, September 16, 1921, pt. 2, p. 4. In one of the few published defenses of Arbuckle at the time of the trials, Gouverneur Morris particularly objected to this kind of argument:

> Even a Mayor [of Los Angeles], in a frenzy of righteousness agreed that it is deplorable to raise people from the "lower orders" and make millionaires of them. What does the Mayor of an American city mean by the "lower orders?" And what is America for if it is not to furnish equal opportunities to all men? And men are not raised. They raise themselves. And God knows it is finer to rise upon the love and laughter of children, as Arbuckle rose, than upon the back of any mercenary campaign—even if one rises all the way up from the "lower orders" whatever they are. Gouverneur Morris, "The Arbuckle Case: An Open Letter to the Editor of *Screenland*," *Screenland*, November 1921, unpaginated; reprinted in Anthony Slide, *They Also Wrote for the Fan Magazines: Film Articles by Literary Giants from e. e. cummings to Eleanor Roosevelt, 1920–1939* (Jefferson, N.C.: McFarland, 1992), 110–113.

25. *Congressional Record*, 67th Cong., 2d sess., June 14–29, 1922, 9657.

26. Daniel Horowitz, *The Morality of Spending: Attitudes Toward the Consumer Society in America 1875–1940* (Baltimore: Johns Hopkins University Press, 1985), 109. According to Horowitz, there were fierce debates about whether thrift or increased consumption was a more appropriate response to the war's end, when the relaxation of patriotic injunctions to economize released a huge pent-up demand for consumer goods. In some respects the arguments fielded by moralists who urged the continuation of thrift directly echoed the editorial condemnations of Arbuckle; consider, for instance, the statement of Christine Frederick, published three months before the Arbuckle scandal began, as quoted in Horowitz: "We have all been participants in a wild, bacchanalian orgy wherein we cast aside our usual sense and caution and flung our money insanely to the winds, gorging ourselves on every delicacy and indulging our desire of licentious spending until we finally achieved an economic debauch." As applied to the postwar consumption habits of the average family this must have seemed rather hyperbolic, but its application to Hollywood stars may have been understood much more literally. Christine Frederick, "The Economic Strike of the American Housewife," *Current Opinion* 70 (June 1921): 751; quoted in Horowitz, 114.

27. For an example see Gail Bederman, *Manliness and Civilization: A Cultural History of Gender and Race in the United States, 1880–1917* (Chicago: University of Chicago Press, 1995).

28. *Will Hays Papers*, letter dated April 19, 1922, reel 4, frame 980.

29. *Los Angeles Times*, September 26, 1920, pt. 2, p. 4. The *Los Angeles Times* had long been an especially vociferous supporter of the open shop and an antagonist to organized labor; see, for example, Kevin Starr, *Material Dreams: Southern California through the 1920s* (New York: Oxford University Press, 1991), 93–94. The Base

Ball Players' Fraternity had claimed a membership of over twelve hundred; not only a fringe "turbulent element" but a very large proportion of active players, including many baseball stars, were at least nominally members of the union. This meant, among other things, that members of the "Clean Sox," White Sox players who had not participated in the fix, had belonged to the union, as well as those who threw the Series. The experience of unionization, and its rather miserable collapse in early 1917, undoubtedly lingered in the minds of the players and disposed them to resent the owners' refusal to bargain. In a general sense, then, rather than a particular one, the *Los Angeles Times* may have been right that unionism was connected to the gambling scandals, although I would argue that it was the frustration of unionism that caused the insurrection, not unionism itself. Some information about Fraternity membership is available in a file containing Base Ball Players' Fraternity documents, which is part of the August Herrmann papers held at the National Baseball Library in Cooperstown.

30. From the transcript of closing arguments, reproduced in "The Trial of Roscoe Arbuckle," in Alvin V. Sellers, *Classics of the Bar: Stories of the World's Great Legal Trials and a Compilation of Forensic Masterpieces* (Baxley, Ga.: Classic Publishing, 1924), 8:106.

31. Higham, *Strangers in the Land*, 277–286.

32. *Will Hays Papers*, letter dated December 29, 1924, reel 19, frame 844. Such sentiments were widely held, if not always publicly expressed, in the early 1920s. A number of other letters and internal memoranda in the Hays files discuss the prevalence of anti-Jewish feeling at the time. A memo concerning nontheatrical film exhibition argued that "a great many of the ministers and members" of Christian churches "are convinced that the motion picture industry is dominated by Jews who have no regard for the Christian religion, if indeed they are not actively hostile to it" (reel 6, frame 438). A letter to Hays from one of his political scouts in St. Louis described his lobbying efforts against a state censorship bill in the Missouri legislature: "this may be plain language but two of the big ones on the Floor and they ought to be broadminded to know better said to me personally this morning when I led up to this legislation as a feeler 'Oh the Movies are owned by damned Jews and let them take their medicine.'" Tilghman Bryant to Hays, January 29, 1923 (reel 8, frame 842). See also Garth Jowett, *Film: The Democratic Art* (Boston: Little, Brown, 1976), 87–88; and Neal Gabler, *An Empire of Their Own* (New York: Anchor, 1988), 2.

33. *Baseball Magazine*, March 1920, 599; *Sporting News*, March 4, 1920, 4.

34. Excerpts from two pamphlets based on articles from the *Dearborn Independent* can be found in David Brion Davis, ed., *The Fear of Conspiracy: Images of Un-American Subversion from the Revolution to the Present* (Ithaca: Cornell University Press, 1971): "The International Jew: The World's Foremost Problem" (1920), and "Jewish Activity in the United States" (1921), 228–240. For some other examples of anti-Semitism as a specifically Orientalist discourse see Leonard Dinnerstein, *Anti-Semitism in America* (New York: Oxford University Press, 1994), 69, 94–95.

35. One of the key terms in the Orientalist discourse is *luxury*: "What power exists whose long experience and deliberate intent enable it to frivolize the people's minds and tastes and compel them to pay most of their money for it too? Why this spasm of luxury and extravagance through which we have just passed?" "The International Jew: The World's Foremost Problem" (1920), in Davis, *Fear of Conspiracy*, 237. This pamphlet is largely a reading of the "Protocols of the Elders of Zion," a document first published in the United States in 1920, which purported to be the plan for Jewish conquest of the world.

36. On the question of reaction and male hysteria see Michael Kimmel, *Manhood in America: A Cultural History* (New York: Free Press, 1996), especially Part Two, "The Unmaking of the Self-Made Man at the Turn of the Century," 79–188.

37. *Los Angeles Times*, September 30, 1920, 4. "The Game Will Go On," *Boston Globe*, September 30, 1920, 14.

38. One of these, "The Sins of Hollywood" (1922), is reprinted in Gerald Mast, ed., *The Movies in Our Midst: Documents in the Cultural History of Film in America* (Chicago: University of Chicago Press, 1982), 176–183. Although some attention has recently been paid to Orientalist representations within Hollywood film, to my knowledge no one has considered the relationship of this filmic discourse to representations *of* Hollywood — e.g., "Hollywood Babylon" — in Orientalist terms that may have been covertly anti-Semitic.

39. Sellers, *Classics of the Bar*, 14. Already, by 1921, Griffith's pseudo-Babylonian "court of Belshazzar" sequence in *Intolerance* had become a kind of shorthand for Hollywood decadence. (Arbuckle's "wild party," had it not been followed by a death, would undoubtedly have seemed rather small and nondescript.)

40. The seminal work in the field of star theory is Richard Dyer, *Stars* (London: British Film Institute, 1979); also important are many of the essays collected in Christine Gledhill, ed., *Stardom: Industry of Desire* (London: Routledge, 1991).

41. For example, in *Brewster's Millions*, Famous Players–Paramount, dir. Joseph Henabery, r. January 1921. In J. Hoberman's words: "Fatty resembles a monstrous toddler. His Humpty Dumpty face is framed by hair as silky as a baby's and there's a correspondingly amoral quality to his glee." J. Hoberman, "Livin' Large," *Village Voice*, September 13, 1994, 59.

42. "The True Story of My Life: Funny Confessions of the Fool of the Films, Specially Written by 'Fatty' Arbuckle," clipping from unidentified publication, February 5, 1921, 445, contained in the Arbuckle file, Museum of Modern Art Film Study Center.

43. "Love Confessions of a Fat Man," *Photoplay*, September 1921, 22–23. For an interesting discussion of *Photoplay's* (non)response to the Arbuckle scandal see deCordova, *Picture Personalities*, 127–128.

44. For a more extended analysis of Arbuckle as a star text see my article "Normalizing Stars: Roscoe 'Fatty' Arbuckle and Hollywood Consolidation," in *A Slightly Different Light: Exploring Marginalized Issues and Forces in American Silent Film* (Carbondale: Southern Illinois University Press, forthcoming).

45. He appeared in female costume at least as early as his sixth Keystone, *Peeping Pete* (1913), in which he played a frumpish, hand-wringing housewife in long dress and apron. In *Miss Fatty's Seaside Lovers* (1915) Arbuckle appeared as a coy, flirtatious heiress with an absurdly tiny parasol and an unexpectedly powerful right cross. In *The Butcher Boy*, the first film he produced for his new Comique company in April 1917, he donned a big flowered dress with a massive bow in back and a curly wig in order to play a schoolgirl at a genteel academy. *Peeping Pete*, Mutual-Keystone, dir. Mack Sennett, r. June 23, 1913; *Miss Fatty's Seaside Lovers*, Mutual-Keystone, dir. Arbuckle, r. May 15, 1915; *The Butcher Boy*, Comique-Paramount, dir. Arbuckle, r. April 23, 1917.

46. Recent works on masculinities in cinema and culture that have been useful in this formulation include Dennis Bingham, *Acting Male: Masculinities in the Films of James Stewart, Jack Nicholson, and Clint Eastwood* (New Brunswick, N.J.: Rutgers University Press, 1994); Steven Cohan and Ina Rae Hark, eds., *Screening the Male: Exploring Masculinities in Hollywood Cinema* (New York: Routledge, 1992); R. W.

Connell, *Masculinities* (Berkeley: University of California Press, 1995); Miriam Hansen, *Babel and Babylon: Spectatorship in American Silent Film* (Cambridge: Harvard University Press, 1991); Peter Lehman, *Running Scared: Masculinity and the Representation of the Male Body* (Philadelphia: Temple University Press, 1993); Constance Penley and Sharon Willis, eds., *Male Trouble* (Minneapolis: University of Minnesota Press, 1993); and Kaja Silverman, *Male Subjectivity at the Margins* (New York: Routledge, 1992).

47. On the relations between spectacle and narrative in comedy, and the form of "crazy comedy," see for example Kristine Brunovska and Henry Jenkins, "Funny Stories," in Kristine Brunovska and Henry Jenkins, eds., *Classical Hollywood Comedy* (New York: Routledge, 1995), 63–86.

48. I take the phrase "marginal revenue product" from Clark Nardinelli, "Judge Kenesaw Mountain Landis and the Art of Cartel Enforcement," *Baseball History: An Annual of Original Baseball Research*, ed. Peter Levine (Westport, Conn.: Meckler, 1989), 104. Although Nardinelli is writing about the labor economics of professional baseball, the same definition applies equally well to other labor markets, including Hollywood's. Nardinelli defines the marginal revenue product of a baseball player as "the increase in his team's revenue attributable to that player."

49. On stadium construction in the early twentieth century see G. Edward White, *Creating the National Pastime: Baseball Transforms Itself, 1903–1953* (Princeton, N.J.: Princeton University Press, 1996), 10–46.

50. The best source for all of these matters is Seymour, *Baseball: The Golden Age.* See also Robert F. Burk, *Never Just a Game: Players, Owners, and American Baseball to 1920* (Chapel Hill: University of North Carolina Press, 1994), 210–240, and appendices.

51. Asinof, *Eight Men Out*, 15–17.

52. See in particular Harold Seymour, *Baseball: The Early Years* (New York: Oxford University Press, 1960), 52–54, 87–88, 295–296, on early gambling (known as "hippodroming"); in a famous case described by Seymour four players on the National League Louisville team were blacklisted for throwing games in 1877.

53. Luc Sante, *Low Life: Lures and Snares of Old New York* (New York: Farrar Strauss Giroux, 1991), 152–153.

54. Hal Chase was the most notorious. A gifted first baseman, Chase, who came up with the New York Americans (later Yankees) in 1905, quickly gained a reputation as a troublemaker: he was constantly tangling with his managers and was suspected of fixing games. Because of his skill, however, he was able to keep playing, moving from New York to the Chicago White Sox in 1913 and then, after a stint with the Federal League, to Cincinnati in 1916. There he became "a full-fledged gambler and fixer," throwing games, bribing players, and collecting commissions on bets he took. When accusations were finally made public, the baseball tribunal that convened to try him in 1919 claimed there was insufficient evidence and dismissed the charges, preferring to sweep the matter under the rug. Reinstated, Chase went back to New York, where he played with John McGraw's Giants until September 1919, when he was finally, and permanently, removed. Seymour, *Golden Age*, 288–293.

55. Asinof, *Eight Men Out*, 242–243. The incident is particularly startling given reports of the players' general hostility toward one another earlier.

56. Seymour, *Golden Age*, 384–385. These charges were made at different times by Oscar "Happy" Felsch and Swede Risberg; in a letter in the "Black Sox Papers," a collection of documents recently released by the Baseball Commissioner's Office to

the National Baseball Library in Cooperstown, the lawyer for Eddie Cicotte is said to have threatened that the indicted players would testify about the Detroit payoff at their trial. However, at hearings conducted by Landis in 1927, when the accusations surfaced again, the majority of the players claimed that the money had been a "reward" to the Detroit pitchers for *winning* several games against the Red Sox rather than a payoff for *losing* the four games to the White Sox. This was also the story told by Eddie Collins in a statement given to Landis's secretary, Leslie M. O'Connor, in February 1921 and by two of the Detroit pitchers, George Dauss and Bill James, in statements made to Landis the same month. (Transcripts of these statements are also in the "Black Sox Papers.") Landis, perhaps in the interests of expediency, dismissed the charges, but Seymour concludes that the "reward" story was concocted, and that in fact Detroit had deliberately lost the four White Sox games. "The Black Sox Papers," vol. 1, no. 145, 155–157. Seymour, *Golden Age*, 384–385. Suggestive also, if not in any way conclusive, is Asinof's comment in his preface that in his research for *Eight Men Out* he found reticence among all the players: a reluctance to talk "was generally true not only of the Black Sox, but also of their innocent teammates. Their recollections of the series were guarded, as if the shame of the scandal was to be shared by them all." Asinof, *Eight Men Out*, xiii.

57. Hugh Fullerton, "Baseball on Trial," *New Republic*, October 20, 1920, 184. See also Asinof, *Eight Men Out*, 167, where he quotes Buck Weaver as saying he is not a squealer; and Seymour, *Golden Age*, 304–305, which discusses a celebratory dinner held by the "Clean Sox" after the scandal came to light, at which they claimed they had suspected all along that their teammates were deliberately losing but had felt bound to a code of silence.

58. On the other hand, Seymour reports that when the Base Ball Players' Fraternity explored affiliation with the American Federation of Labor, the players resisted because of the likelihood that they would have come under the jurisdiction of the "White Rats," the vaudeville union. This suggests that, if they saw themselves as entertainers, that perception did not mean that they considered their work "theatrical." Seymour, *Golden Age*, 241.

59. Asinof, *Eight Men Out*, 188–193.

60. Grantland Rice, *New York Tribune*, October 2, 1919, quoted in Charles Fountain, *Sportswriter: The Life and Times of Grantland Rice* (New York: Oxford University Press, 1993), 174.

61. Janet Wasko, *Movies and Money: Financing the American Film Industry* (Norwood, N.J.: Ablex, 1982), 1–45.

62. Dyer, *Stars*, 69.

63. Edmonds, *Frame-Up!*, 106–107, 120–121, 178–179, 181, 184–185, 221–223. According to Edmonds, Zukor angrily told Arbuckle producer Joseph Schenck that Arbuckle needed "knocking down a few pegs." See also Yallop, *Day the Laughter Stopped*, 259–261.

64. On the events in Gary see Murray, *Red Scare*, 147–148.

65. One need not fully accept the Bakhtinian account of the carnivalesque mode in all its utopian dimensions to recognize its applicability to various modern cultural forms, such as slapstick film comedy or spectator sport. Whether or not the coarse, exuberant, physical, and festive entertainments of modern amusement constituted the cosmic challenge posited by Bakhtin, they were certainly taken to be threatening by cultural conservatives. On reformist hostility to slapstick see, for example, Eileen Bowser, *The Transformation of Cinema, 1907–1915*, vol. 2 of *History of the American*

Cinema (New York: Scribner's, 1993), 179–184. The key text on the carnivalesque aesthetic is Mikhail Bakhtin, *Rabelais and His World* (Bloomington: Indiana University Press, 1984); also valuable is Peter Stallybrass and Allon White, *The Politics and Poetics of Transgression* (Ithaca: Cornell University Press, 1986).

66. I take this phrase from the title of James L. Baughman's *The Republic of Mass Culture: Journalism, Filmmaking, and Broadcasting in America since 1941,* 2d ed. (Baltimore: Johns Hopkins University Press, 1997).

67. On Landis as a blacklister see Seymour, *Golden Age,* 367–399; on Hays see Yallop, *Day the Laughter Stopped,* 261.

68. Paul Boyer, *Urban Masses and Moral Order in America, 1820–1920* (Cambridge: Harvard University Press, 1978), 218.

Shooting Star

Understanding
Wallace Reid
and His Public

Mark Lynn Anderson

*J*ust after the First World War, the word *junkie* entered into American parlance to describe a population of heroin addicts in and around New York City. These addicts were a visible and growing population of male derelicts who supported their drug habit by scouring that city's junkyards in search of scrap metal, which they then sold to junk dealers. As medical historian David Courtwright has noted, the emergence of the term *junkie* at the beginning of the 1920s marked the historical transition in the general demographics of narcotic addiction in the United States. No longer was the typical addict a white, middle-aged, middle- or upper-class rural housewife whose addiction had begun when her physician administered therapeutic doses of morphine to relieve pain. The new addict was more likely to be a young, white male who belonged decidedly to the urban underclass and whose addiction was more likely to have started when he began sniffing heroin with his friends at cheap dance halls.[1] Yet the term *junkie* also describes rather neatly the transformation, in both popular and medical understandings of narcotic addiction, from a notion that morphinism was an organic disorder of the individual that resulted from medical treatment to the view that narcotic addiction was a type of social disease, an unfortunate by-product of a modern industrial society and thus a pressing public health issue.

It was within the context of such a transformation that the popular film star Wallace Reid died in January 1923 at the age of thirty-one from complications resulting from an attempted withdrawal from narcotic addiction. Reid's death is

Figure 1. Wallace Reid in a
Henry Clive portrait from the
early 1920s that was featured
on tin candy boxes.

generally considered one of the three most significant scandals of early Hollywood, along with the three criminal trials of the film comedian Roscoe "Fatty"
Arbuckle in 1921 and 1922 and the sensationalized murder of director William Desmond Taylor in February 1922. Reid was remarkably handsome and had
been a very successful matinee idol from the mid-1910s until his death (fig. 1).
Like a few other popular male stars of the period, such as Douglas Fairbanks and
Thomas Meighan, Reid typified a rugged, "all-American" virility that was a compelling version of psychological and physical health for young white men. Often
reported to stand 6' 3" and to weigh approximately 190 pounds, Reid was usually
portrayed in the fan magazines as a sort of happy and playful giant. He was also
represented as somewhat of a dilettante with scattered interests in music, painting, chemistry, automobile racing, book collecting, golf, and a host of other pas-
times. A young man of many accomplishments, Reid was presumably so full of
wonder at the world that he couldn't be bothered to devote a great amount of
time or attention to any single activity.

Although younger than Fairbanks by almost a decade, Reid was part of the
same generation of film stars who, like Fairbanks, emerged in the mid-1910s to
become public representatives of the newly formed "movie colony" in southern
California. Unlike the newcomer Fairbanks, however, Reid had been working
steadily in the film industry since 1910, making over a hundred films as a featured
player for the Vitagraph, Universal, and Majestic film companies. When Jesse
Lasky signed Reid with his company in June 1915, Reid was already a well-known
and established performer, although his popularity rose rapidly after Lasky paired
him with Metropolitan Opera star Geraldine Farrar in a couple of prestige pic-

tures directed by Cecil B. DeMille. Reid's masculinity also differed from the "vim, vip, and vigor" of Fairbanks, by departing from the latter's insistence on rational self-discipline. Whereas Fairbanks's healthy manliness resulted from the adoption of a youthful mental attitude that valued carefully planned and regimented physical activities, Reid's boyish charm rested more on a naturally robust physique and a much more spontaneous athleticism. Although his many film performances and even the scandal with which his name is linked are largely forgotten today,[2] in the early 1920s, when it appeared as if the film industry itself was in danger of imminent collapse, Reid's drug addiction was a significant moment in the history of the star system and in the consolidation of Hollywood as a mass cultural institution. Reid's death afforded the film industry its first opportunity to explain how good stars can go wrong. The industry succeeded not only in containing the scandal of Reid's drug use but in reinterpreting his death as both a private tragedy and a great public sacrifice.

Although the formation of the Motion Picture Producers and Directors of America (MPPDA) has been repeatedly linked with Hollywood's need to contain the damage caused by the star scandals of the early 1920s, film historians are quick to add that the agency's other, less publicized functions—staving off federal antitrust interventions, maintaining the prevailing relations of production within the industry, arbitrating costly litigious conflicts between distributors and exhibitors, expanding and securing overseas markets, and controlling public information about Hollywood business practices—were far more defining for the institutional mission of the MPPDA and for the film industry's development as a modern international business. The industry's disciplinary responses to the star scandals are, then, often considered publicity diversions behind which the more important exercise of managerial power was concealed.[3]

Nevertheless, part of the MPPDA's implicit public charter was to guarantee the moral quality of the industry's products and its personnel, particularly its stars and leading players. Because of the number of public scandals involving film personalities in the years 1920–1922, Will Hays and Hollywood faced a relatively new type of demand for film censorship. Most movie reform efforts of the late 1910s had targeted film content as in need of improvement and had sought some way of censoring the so-called sex picture, as well as films depicting illegal acts or criminal behavior. In the early 1920s the demand for "cleaner pictures" was soon joined by the demand for "cleaner stars." The identity of the motion picture performer had become a site for possible regulation, and, at least for a year and a half following the arrest of Arbuckle in September 1921, the identity of the performer was one of the principal concerns of censorship efforts outside the film industry. Arbuckle and other scandalous stars posed a relatively new set of complications for the smooth functioning of the star system, and it took Hays and film industry executives quite some time to develop effective strategies for controlling and avoiding particular problems that had suddenly arisen in their marketing of personalities. However, by the time Reid's drug addiction was publicly revealed at the end of 1922, the industry's ability to manage scandals had improved considerably.

Despite the difficulties that the circumstances of Reid's death posed for an industry already attempting to circumvent growing demands for outside censorship, his use of narcotics was made consistent with his earlier star image through a set of industry-directed discourses that purportedly sought to extend the public's knowledge about the social basis of drug addiction. In newspapers, trade journals, and fan magazines the coverage of the scandal drew on specific psychological and sociological images of drug addiction and drug trafficking in order to represent Reid as a tragic, but heroic, figure who sacrificed his life to an adoring public. By examining some of the specific strategies of this coverage and its stages of development during and in the aftermath of the scandal, we can draw some conclusions about the ways his contemporary film audiences were encouraged to understand Reid's stardom and their own relation to his death.

•   •   •

The major interpreter of Reid's identity, once his addiction became widely known, was his wife of nine years, actress Dorothy Davenport. Putting an end to over two years of rumors, she went public about her husband's addiction on December 17, 1922, shortly after committing him to a Los Angeles sanitarium for treatment and approximately one month before his death. Davenport was, at this time, almost always referred to in the press as "Mrs. Wallace Reid." Whether pressured by the film industry or seeking on her own to put an end to mounting press speculations about her husband's condition, Mrs. Reid gave an extensive interview to the Hearst newspapers, detailing her husband's life in order to explain just how he had become addicted to drugs.

A primary aim of the interview was clearly to counter the damaging image of Hollywood as a "den of iniquity," an image that had been so recently promulgated by the tabloids and by many of the would-be reformers of the industry. Mrs. Reid explained her motives:

> I am being criticized severely by some of our acquaintances for having talked so much, but I feel that if the public knows the truth it will not condemn Wally any more than I have condemned him. His is not an individual case symptomatic of a community. The battle Wally is making is the battle that thousands — I might say a million — of men and women are making. . . . If then through telling the truth I can do my part to arouse public sentiment against this nefarious traffic I am willing to suffer criticism.[4]

The idea that an open discussion of Reid's addiction would serve the public good, by fostering a greater public familiarity with an important social problem, allowed the industry to use the "scandal" to its own advantage. A commitment to honest disclosure and frankness in the service of social hygiene was a self-congratulating component of the media coverage of Reid's stardom that would continue in the fan magazines throughout the 1920s, long after his death.

To sever further any connections between her husband's drug use and Hollywood, Mrs. Reid reiterated several times that she was absolutely certain that Reid's drug addiction had begun in New York when he traveled there in the summer of 1921 to work on the film *Forever*, a lavish adaptation of the novel *Peter Ibbetson*. Reid fell ill and began to worry that his "illness was delaying production and adding to the expense." He then asked a local physician for morphine in order to "nerve him for his daily and arduous task." [5] Of course, the place, date, and nature of the commencement of the addiction were continually disputed, and later disclosures and explanations attributed to Mrs. Reid often contradicted one another wildly, sometimes even within the same interview or article.

While making New York the site of Reid's affliction, Mrs. Reid also felt it necessary to mention several accidents earlier suffered by her husband while performing motion picture work. She also indicated that her husband had had enormous demands placed on him by an intense production schedule. The one incident most remarked on later and mentioned by Mrs. Reid in her first interview occurred early in 1919 when the actor was involved in a train accident while making *The Valley of the Giants*, an adventure picture about lumbering in northern California. Various accounts of this particular incident exist, but what is certain is that several members of the film's crew sustained injuries when a caboose carrying them jumped from the tracks and tumbled off an embankment or from a small bridge. Reid mentioned this train wreck in a newspaper interview in July 1919 on the occasion of his signing a new five-year contract with Famous Players–Lasky, a most unusual length of service obligation. Calling *Valley of the Giants* "a tough picture to make," Reid remembered how "in one scene, we were all 'messed up' in a train wreck, and then we had to travel seventy-five miles away from the hotel during the photographing of certain scenes." [6] At the time of the accident Reid was apparently given morphine to ease the pain he experienced from a head injury; but according to later statements by Mrs. Reid, the treatment did not lead to an addiction, and Reid continued to work after the train accident despite suffering lingering pain.

This incident is extremely important because it quickly became the single biographical moment that was most often mentioned in explanations of Reid's death, and even today it is often cited as the event most likely to have been responsible for his morphine addiction. [7] Whether it actually was so is beside the point. The incident accomplished several things that made it a compelling explanation of Reid's fate, both in terms of his established star persona and in terms of popular sociological ideas about drug risks. First, this story somewhat depathologized Reid by characterizing his addiction as the result of a beneficent medical treatment, thereby making it recognizable as an older and more genteel form of morphine dependency. On the other hand, the staging of Reid's first exposure to morphine at the scene of a train accident pushes his addiction closer to an emerging set of representations that linked drug addiction to industrial waste, such as the etymology of the word *junkie.*

The idea that Reid would be susceptible to morphine addiction because of physical exhaustion and injury brought about by arduous working conditions would have been problematic for the film industry, of course, since it suggests that the studio contributed significantly to Reid's illness and impending death. Indeed, only two weeks after her first interviews, we find Mrs. Reid writing a new account of the illness in the *San Francisco Examiner.* Here she begins by stating emphatically that her husband's misfortune was a "personal tragedy" and an "isolated case," and that it had nothing whatsoever to do with motion pictures or with Hollywood. Nevertheless, she retells the story of the 1919 train wreck; however, now the accident no longer takes place during the filming of a scene but occurs as the film's personnel travels to a chosen outdoor location. Reid is also given a more heroic role in this new version of the event, selflessly attending to the other passengers and neglecting his own injuries for several hours. Besides changing these important details, Mrs. Reid also attributes a somewhat nebulous significance to the injuries suffered by her husband in the train wreck: "Against the advice of physicians he went to work [the] next day and the picture was made on schedule. But from that hour Wallace Reid was never the same. I do not know why; it is an intangible thing. I will try to explain as we go along."[8] Together with the very nature of these revisions, the fact that Mrs. Reid was allegedly even writing so many different narratives of her husband's addiction, presumably during a time of great personal stress for her, suggests that she was working at the behest of the industry. Because Reid's illness and impending death constituted a major Hollywood scandal, it is more than probable that both Famous Players–Lasky, the studio to whom Reid was still under contract, and the MPPDA had a hand in determining the changes of the particulars and in the overall direction of Mrs. Reid's accounts. As Danae Clark has demonstrated with respect to the industry's regulation of film labor in the 1930s, the MPPDA often sought to control public representations of the labor of motion picture actors as well as the representations of the conditions of that labor. At times this function would even take priority over the organization's need to protect actors from harmful publicity.[9] The news coverage of Reid's morphine addiction indicates that the MPPDA had made the concealment of film labor a priority from the very beginning of its existence.

Within two weeks, then, the "explanation" of Reid's addiction had shifted from being about an injury sustained at work to being vaguely related to an accident that occurred *on the way to work.* Whereas in Mrs. Reid's first accounts the film star felt compelled to work while experiencing intense physical pain because of the possibility of costly delays in production, he now returns to work "against the advice of physicians." The picture of Wallace Reid the actor, presumably drawn by the person who knew him best, had quickly changed from one of a worker who was also the victim of an industrial accident to one of a hard-working but ultimately self-destructive individual who often placed himself at risk in his desire to serve others. In other words, through these stories Reid had become an addictive personality; Reid was being posed in the media as a compelling individual to whom the public was "addicted" and as an identity whose compulsions were available for multiple interpretations and diagnoses. An attention to Reid's personality was an important intermediate stage in refiguring the scene of his addiction. The further question remains, though, as to why the image of the train wreck continued to play such a central role in Mrs. Reid's and others' accounts if the aim of many of these explanations was to dissociate Reid's illness from the industrial conditions under which he labored.

Several possibilities for the recurrence of the train wreck suggest themselves. First, there is evidence that the story of this injury was already in circulation as a part of the rumors surrounding the star, and it was important to incorporate as much of what people already knew or believed about Reid into the news stories about him. Second, it is also quite possible that even while choosing to protect what she believed were the interests of the industry and of the community to which she belonged, Mrs. Reid understood her husband's addiction to have resulted from the exploitive film work that he was required to perform and thus felt obliged to telegraph to the public the demanding nature of her and her husband's occupation. Third, once Mrs. Reid had incorporated the train wreck into her account, any dramatic shift in the scene of addiction would have called attention to the very constructedness of her disclosures. Finally, as Lynne Kirby has so amply demonstrated in her essay "Male Hysteria and Early Cinema," the fantasy of the train wreck was an important way of organizing the experiences of the perceptual dislocations that were entailed by modernity in general and by the cinema in particular.[10] Mrs. Reid's apparent compulsion to repeat the story of the train wreck thus suggested to the public that the nexus of trauma described by Kirby was an appropriate context for understanding the film star's addiction to drugs. In 1922 such a reception would have still been available to the public and recognized as related to a previous historical mode of film spectatorship. In this way the scene of the accident and the resulting trauma provided a model for dealing with the disruptions caused by news of the addiction, and the train wreck helped link Reid's present condition to the preclassical era of cinema in which he began his film career.

Although all of these considerations probably played some part in the sustained attention given to the injury in the press coverage of the scandal, the train wreck was also highly compatible with Reid's star identity. Reid's insatiable love of automobile racing had become one of the most often remarked-upon interests of the star after he began performing in a popular series of racing pictures for Famous Players–Lasky in 1919 that included *The Roaring Road* (1919), *Double Speed* (1920), *Excuse My Dust* (1920), *Too Much Speed* (1921), and *Across the*

Continent (1922). Aimed at young male audiences and usually based on the popular racing stories of Byron Morgan, these films had heroes with names such as "Speed Carr" (*Double Speed*), "Jimmy Dent" (*Across the Continent*), and "Dusty Rhoades" (*Too Much Speed*). In many ways, of all the films that Reid made during his eleven-year career, the race-car pictures were represented as the most autobiographical. Reid was himself an adept auto mechanic, and he had acquired an amateur racing license. Reportedly, he even had aspirations to compete in the annual race at the Indianapolis Motor Speedway.[11] The type of character played by Reid in these films was usually possessed by a compulsion to compete, either as a successful racer or as an automobile designer with a seemingly insatiable desire to set speed and time records with his inventions. Although Reid's character is never entirely reckless, his great love of auto racing often gets him into trouble, and he is sometimes placed in great physical danger by an unscrupulous competitor or by other, less competent drivers. Yet in the end it is this same love of the sport, together with a consummate mastery over the machines, that pulls him through.

During the same period that Reid was making these racing pictures, he also completed at least twenty-three other feature films before collapsing on the set of *Thirty Days* in September or October 1922.[12] At this time Reid suffered a temporary loss of vision and was reported to be suffering from a severe case of "Klieg eyes," a common industrial hazard for film performers. Named after the powerful arc lamps that had become standard studio equipment in the mid-1910s, Klieg eyes resulted from prolonged exposure to the ultraviolet radiation of the lamps, which produced corneal lesions on the eyes. *Thirty Days* had to be completed with an assistant on hand to provide Reid with a constant verbal description of the film's sets so that the actor could convincingly portray a fully sighted person.[13] At the very height of his stardom Reid was appearing in twice as many pictures as other stars of his caliber, and he was performing in practically every variety of the studio's product, from cheap action and adventure pictures, to romantic social comedies, to specials and prestige costume dramas.

In *The Love Special*, a railroad romance made in 1921, the themes of strenuous labor and physical exhaustion are central to defining Reid's character, Jim Glover. Glover is a construction engineer who designs large architectural structures for a large railroad firm, Great Western. The film begins with Glover not behind a drafting table but at a flood site where a rising river threatens to destroy the total expanse of an important bridge. We learn that he has been awake for over ninety-six hours, stubbornly refusing to rest as he directs rotating crews of workers in a valiant attempt to divert the rising waters away from the bridge. Of course, all his suffering and sacrifice is eventually rewarded when the bridge is saved from ruin. When word of Glover's accomplishments reaches the nearby company offices, Morris Blood (Clarence Burton), a division superintendent, joyously exclaims how invaluable Glover is as an employee and asks, "Who wouldn't give his right hand saving a man like that?" The question refers to Blood's right hand, which appears to be a black rubber prosthesis, but the loss of the original is never fully explained or pursued. With no immediate narrative motivation for this particular disability, the missing hand functions as an index of the danger involved in railroad work, although it is somewhat odd that a regional manager should have to suffer such an injury. Blood is preparing for a visit to the flood site by Great Western's owner and president, Rufus Gage (Theodore Roberts), and in an effort to make a good impression on the boss he asks the now exhausted Glover to be the chief executive's guide. Gage admires Glover for his heroic efforts and sheer physical stamina, but equally taken with the young man's abilities is Gage's daughter, Laura (Agnes Ayers), who is accompanying her father on the tour. When Laura learns of Glover's remarkable feats, she quickly decides to pursue a romance with the dashing young engineer. The missing hand does, then, work at a symbolic level to signify the rail company's need for the aptly named Glover, a sort of "right-hand man" to whom president Gage must eventually forfeit the oedipal battle. In the end it is Glover who wins Laura's hand from the rail magnate by bravely commandeering a locomotive and driving it full-steam through a dangerous mountain pass during a snow storm, arriving just in time to save Gage from a devastating betrayal by an unscrupulous business partner.

When Mrs. Reid first revealed her husband's addiction, the nation's newspapers sought to represent his illness as a heroic life-and-death struggle by a "strenuous actor" against "the drug menace" and as "a human interest story as gripping as many depicted on the motion picture screen."[14] Both in fan magazines and in his film roles Reid had demonstrated an adventurous enthusiasm for the speed of automobiles and trains, and, at least in his film roles, he often placed his life under the threat of mechanical disaster. So despite the fact that the train wreck ran the risk of making the industry responsible for his drug use, it did stage an important moment in Reid's life in a melodramatic way that was consistent with his star image. After all, Reid was still alive when these accounts were first given to the newspapers, and it was important that his illness be integrated into a coherent popular identity that could continue to be profitably exploited.

The relation of Reid's addiction to the excesses of modern industry also had to be negotiated in terms of class identity. When not using generic terms such as dope or narcotics, Mrs. Reid and the nation's newspapers almost always discussed Reid's addiction in terms of morphine. Yet two years earlier, when Variety reported that a "dope-peddler" who claimed to be delivering heroin to a well-known star had been arrested on a studio lot, many people in the industry were certain that the star in question was Wallace Reid. In fact, it is likely that Reid was a user of heroin at the time of his breakdown and throughout much of his addiction.[15] Heroin, a semisynthetic derivative of morphine and generally considered more pharmacologically potent and more addictive, had appeared in the

1890s as a treatment for certain respiratory conditions. Unlike morphine, heroin had a much shorter therapeutic history and was medically prescribed for a fairly limited range of illnesses. Addiction to heroin, therefore, was not so easily associated with legitimate medical treatment as was morphine. From the mid-1910s on, heroin usage was popularly identified with crime and with the so-called criminal classes, those unemployed and unskilled laborers who lived in America's largest cities and who spent much of their time on the streets as members of informal gangs.[16] This transformation of the social identity of the drug addict was also shaping the medical understanding of drug addiction, and available information and statistical data suggest that the urban poor were disproportionately affected by heroin addiction in the 1910s and 1920s.[17] Although it was important for the film industry to present Reid's drug addiction as determined, in part, by the arduous conditions and demands of modern life, it was also important to disassociate thoroughly his plight from the experiences of an urban working class. This was not simply a strategy to make Reid's illness appear more respectable. The insistence that Reid suffered from *morphine* addiction (as opposed to heroin addiction) helped to cover over important relations between economic class and narcotic addiction, thereby making Reid's illness compatible with the ideology of contemporary liberal reform that sought to represent drug addiction as an affliction that could "happen to anyone."[18]

What occurred after Reid's death was more or less a continuation of the changes that were already well under way in the representation of his drug use. Because modern medical discourses and public-health practices were addressing drug addiction as an environmentally determined condition, it remained important for the media to establish a social milieu for Reid's addiction. However, in subsequent accounts given by Mrs. Reid and by others, the industrial world of film production as the scene of Reid's drug use was rapidly being replaced by the private world of domestic consumption. Not only did Reid's posthumous publicity quickly turn to images of a family bereft of a husband, a son, and a father, but the preferred explanation of his addiction now became Reid's private encounters with the "wrong element" during his leisure hours away from the studio and at his home during parties. Drawing on popular fears and fantasies about wild Hollywood parties, the newspapers now told of how Reid's indiscriminate hospitality and the fabulous amenities of his luxurious Beverly Hills home "had drawn to him a mob of hand-shakers which he could not be persuaded were not his real friends."[19] Furthermore, Reid's addiction had become public knowledge in the midst of a moral panic about illicit drug use in the United States, a panic that was in no small way aided by the sensational stories then appearing in the Hearst newspapers about criminal "dope rings" and fraudulent clinics purporting to cure wealthy addicts by providing them with illegal narcotics.[20] This propaganda campaign ultimately sought to strengthen the powers of the police, to create public support for new federal antinarcotic legislation increasing the penalties for those convicted of trafficking, and to establish international agreements halting the production of stimulants and narcotics overseas. Although Reid was only sometimes portrayed as a habitué of wild Hollywood parties, he was increasingly represented as the innocent prey of a criminal traffic in narcotics. Both the Hearst newspapers and the film industry quickly latched on to this image of the dead star and used the publicity generated by Reid's death in their efforts to militarize drug addiction as a public health issue and to win the "war on dope."

Nowhere is this transformation in the understanding of Reid's addiction more evident than in the film *Human Wreckage* (1923), a Thomas Ince production about drug addiction, directed by John Griffith Wray and made with the support of Mrs. Reid and with the cooperation of various public health officials and law enforcement agencies, including the Los Angeles Anti-Narcotic League and the Los Angeles Police Force.[21] Released nationally only six months after Reid's death, *Human Wreckage* tells the story of Ethel MacFarland (Mrs. Reid) and her slow and devastating realization that her husband, Alan (James Kirkwood), is a drug addict. Alan MacFarland is a prominent lawyer who spends many of his evenings at home working on pressing legal cases. To help sustain the attorney's flagging attention to an important murder defense in which an innocent man may be sentenced to die, an incautious physician gives Alan an injection of morphine. This physician is later revealed to be a "dope doctor" connected with the illegal trade in narcotics. As Alan's work continues to place demands on his strength, he comes to rely more and more on the drug, and he is eventually blackmailed by a drug syndicate for whom he must perform legal services in order to procure more narcotics for himself. Even when Alan seeks a cure by going into the seclusion of a countryside cottage with Ethel, a drug dealer is sent to follow Alan and to keep him addicted. Sick and demoralized, Alan fails in his every attempt to break with the drug habit, until Ethel finally pretends that she, too, has become addicted to morphine. Alan, in moral revulsion at what he believes he has done to his wife, finally finds the willpower to conquer his addiction.

The main story of *Human Wreckage* is told against a pair of subplots about two young working-class youths who are not as lucky as Alan MacFarland: both are social welfare cases of Ethel MacFarland, both come from homes without fathers, and both end up dying because of the illegal traffic in narcotics. One of these youths, Mary Finnegan (Bessie Love), is a single mother who has become addicted while mourning the loss of her late husband. When Ethel discovers that Mary has been giving morphine to her infant, she takes the child from Mary and places Mary in a clinic for treatment. Unfortunately, the young mother is too frail for complete withdrawal, and Mary dies "a broken flower" in her own mother's arms, an event the script suggests be treated as "a fairy-book scene." Mary's death prompts the intertitle, "THE BEAST is driven back." The other working-class youth is Jimmy Brown (George Hackatorne), a young man arrested for theft while under the influence of drugs and sent away for a cure. Unlike Mary, Jimmy is hardy enough to withstand the cure, and he returns home to his mother, finding employment as a taxi driver. Unfortunately, because the city's drug dealers know he is an addict and continually tempt him with narcotics, Jimmy eventually suffers a relapse. Deciding that he cannot face the tortures of another withdrawal, he suddenly determines to kill himself and his current fare at that moment, Steve Stone (Harry Northrup), a notorious drug dealer who has been blackmailing MacFarland. Jimmy accomplishes this spectacular murder-suicide by driving his taxi full-speed into a stationary streetcar. The script describes the taxi in the aftermath of the collision as "practically in splinters" and indicates that "lying in the wreckage, and partially covered by it are Jimmy and Stone; they are both dead and the scene should be so shot that there is no doubt of this." Here, the train wreck is no longer the privileged scene of drug addiction or relevant to its explanation. Instead, *Human Wreckage* has made the mechanical disaster a part of the cure.

Human Wreckage worked to unify the differing and potentially disruptive positions of social worker, film actress, and widow that Dorothy Davenport Reid occupied and from which she spoke. The film was promoted and popularly received as based on the particulars of Wallace Reid's drug addiction but not only because Mrs. Reid plays the wife of a drug addict.[22] She also appears at the beginning and at the end of the film as herself, Mrs. Wallace Reid. In a direct address to the camera and with her two children at her side, Mrs. Reid explains: "The picture I have made deals with this great danger and every incident depicted has its parallel in fact." Although the script for *Human Wreckage* was officially credited to C. Gardner Sullivan, the film was widely represented as authored by Mrs. Reid, such as when *Photoplay* published a photograph of Mrs. Reid pensively writing at her desk in mourning attire. The accompanying caption identified her as "at work on her propaganda film to fight the narcotic evil."[23] Preparations for a novelization of the film entitled *Powdered Death* credited Mrs. Reid, first, and Sullivan, second, as the book's coauthors.[24] When the picture was released in June, Mrs. Reid's name appeared above the film's title both on cinema marquees and in newspaper advertisements (fig. 2). She also made several public appearances with the film, lecturing on drug addiction as a medical disease and calling for an end to the unsympathetic representations of drug addicts as moral degenerates and criminals. Asking her audiences to dispense with the common phrase "dope fiend," she stressed the need for greater drug education and for the establishment of clinics devoted to the care of those suffering from narcotic addiction.[25] Yet even as Mrs. Reid publicly supported the greater medicalization of the addict, others were using her and her husband's death to criminalize drug addiction further. U.S. District Attorney John T. Williams, for instance, had blamed Reid's death on "a growing disregard of the law within our own country."[26] The contradictions between law enforcement and the clinical treatment of narcotic addiction had been greatly exacerbated in 1919 when the

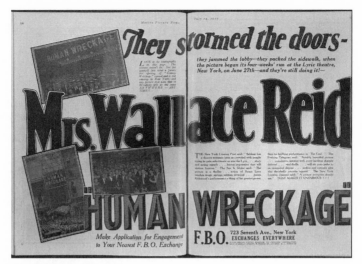

Figure 2. The name above the title. *Human Wreckage* (Thomas H. Ince Corp., 1923) was widely promoted as Mrs. Wallace Reid's personal statement on narcotic addiction, as in this advertisement from *Motion Picture News* (July 14, 1923). Courtesy of George Eastman House.

United States Supreme Court interpreted the Harrison Act of 1914 as proscribing all medical treatment of narcotic addiction through drug maintenance. Because of this decision, scores of treatment centers across the country were forced to close their doors out of fear of prosecution.[27]

Ironically, even *Human Wreckage*, a motion picture promoted as Mrs. Reid's effort to create greater public sympathy for the drug addict, actually supported the further criminalization of narcotic addiction by emphasizing the criminal gang in the addiction process and by portraying maintenance-free withdrawal as the sole possibility for effective treatment, a therapy that was, undoubtedly, the single most significant contributor to Reid's death given his state of physical exhaustion at the end of 1922. The fact that Mrs. Reid could be presented as the author of *Human Wreckage*, a film that in many ways ran counter to, and eventually undermined, her own efforts to obtain better and more humane medical treatment for drug addicts, demonstrates both her importance as a national spokesperson on the issue of narcotic addiction and the power of the industry to determine what she was capable of saying about addiction.[28] Her own reasons for participating in such a project are unclear, although she, like many others, likely believed that the prevailing law enforcement discourse on the criminal traffic in drugs was ultimately compatible with the remedicalization of the addict.[29]

What is certain is that *Human Wreckage* was an important final step in containing the scandal that Reid's addiction posed for the film industry, despite claims that the film required a "special dispensation" from Will Hays in order to be made and released.[30] With Mrs. Reid's guarantee that everything in the film "has its parallel in fact," *Human Wreckage* helped to refigure her husband's drug addiction as the unfortunate result of his personal ambition and his desire to serve the public and to please his friends. Through the story of the MacFarlands, *Human Wreckage* neatly combined both the demands of modern work and the influence of the criminal gang as contributing to narcotic addiction, but it firmly privileged personal contacts with other addicts and with dope peddlers as the most typical, determining, and dangerous cause of habitual narcotic use. Drug addiction is spread in the society only by an alien and contagious criminal element. The film urges sympathy for the drug addict because addiction is shown to cut across class lines, but gone is any sense that addiction is a disease tied to the excesses of mass industrial society. The only remnant of such an idea in the film would appear to be its title, *Human Wreckage*, a title that effectively telescoped the scene of the industrial disaster onto the individual in much the same way that the word *junkie* — a term that once so forcefully called on an active understanding of modern urban life — soon gave way to the absolute identity of the narcotic addict as the American public knows this figure today. As Theodor Adorno observed in his dedication of *Minima Moralia: Reflections from Damaged Life*, "in an individualistic society, the general not only realizes itself through the interplay of particulars, but society is essentially the substance of the individual."[31]

If, however, a substance cannot be controlled, its meanings can. The scandal of Reid's addiction had the real potential of affirming for a mass audience something about the deformation of life under the conditions of twentieth-century capitalism. Clearly, there were many who had not previously concerned themselves with Wallace Reid or his films but had turned their attention to his life and to the terms of his illness in order to learn something.[32] What that something was could not, of course, be abstracted from the very apparatus that made Reid a compelling figure in the first place: the star system. Reid's death helped to pose the star system as a unique source of knowledge not only about the star himself but about cinema as a social institution. Could the star system be used to think about the degradation of modern work or the totality of social relations under monopoly capitalism? The "proper" use of the star system was the ultimate stake the film industry had in controlling the public's understanding of Reid's use of narcotics.

Reid's narcotic addiction aided a reception of his identity as susceptible to a set of conditions entailed by the nature of mass communications, by the supply of and demand for media personalities. Just how those conditions of supply and demand were finally represented and understood through the repeated biographical inscriptions of Reid's life and death points to the importance of film stars in constructing, addressing, and maintaining a mass audience. Reid's personal desire to please others, whether his friends or his vast public, was a pivot on which the institutional representation of his drug use turned. Although images of wreckage, waste, and ruined efficiency continued to dominate the media's coverage of Reid's addiction, these negative qualities of his stardom were effectively detached from the demands of industrial film production and transferred to t.ie excesses of private life and consumption. It is usually assumed that rumors of wild Hollywood parties were essentially harmful to the interests of the film industry, but *Human Wreckage* demonstrated how the image of the lavish "dope party" could be used to portray narcotic addiction as an expression of excessive domestic consumption (fig. 3). Increasingly, the larger institutional context of Reid's addiction became the box office through which the public expressed its adoration for him.

The posthumous coverage of Reid in fan publications usually took the form of either short elegiac pieces written by friends or, more commonly, published letters from loyal fans remembering the great film star. Much of this material emphasized Reid's courage and determination in his fight against addiction and represented his death as a victory against a major social evil and, therefore, a great contribution to the world. In fact, one letter from "a lady" living in New York City claimed that, even in death, Reid was still hard at work: "And I have a conviction unshaken, that his spirit will be at work, MORE EFFECTIVELY for what has happened than it could had he been left here. He is on LOCATION working on a much bigger picture." [33]

In 1924 his friend Buddy Post explained Reid's addiction this way to *Motion*

Figure 3. Images of wild parties helped the film industry to keep star drug scandals at home. Production still from *Human Wreckage*. Courtesy of the Library of Congress.

Picture Magazine: "I shall not attempt to tell when and why Wally started on that fatal journey. A number of circumstances brought about this trouble. To sum up in a philosophical way I might say that Wally did not kill others with kindness but killed himself with kindness to others."[34] Reid's very selflessness and his popularity were now seen as major contributing factors in the etiology of his disease. And if the studio had been initially portrayed as exploiting Reid's popularity with grueling work schedules, his death was now represented as a consequence of an excessive demand placed on the star by a desiring public for whom Reid sacrificed himself and the happiness of his family. The desire of millions replaced the demands of the studio as the source of the damage to which Reid was so susceptible. In 1929 Gladys Hall wrote of the difficulty Dorothy Davenport Reid faced in explaining to her son, Billy Reid, who his father really was: "Difficult to give the boy his father as a human being broken on the wheel of his most endearing qualities. Difficult to explain that dreams are not always best, that the love of millions can break a man as well as make him, that idealism and flattery can lead to degradation, that prowess of body is not always pride of spirit."[35] Yet the public's adoration of and addiction to Wallace Reid was by no means faulted or condemned in such representations. Instead, Reid's death functioned in the posthumous publicity as an uncritical demonstration of the simultaneous emotional proximity of the motion picture star to her/his public and the alienated nature of mass communication. The adoring public was very much welcomed by the media as a part of Reid's addiction.

In 1927 a young college student named Ray Harris organized an international effort to erect a large bay to the memory of Wallace Reid in the Cathedral of St. John the Divine in New York City. Harris had no difficulty convincing several prominent personalities to endorse publicly the construction of the bay and to serve on the executive committee for the memorial project. Members of this committee included film stars, such as Richard Barthelmess, Richard Dix, Douglas Fairbanks, Wanda Hawley, Conrad Nagel, and Mary Pickford; film executives, such as Cecil B. DeMille, Thomas Edison, and Carl Laemmle, as well as Reid's old production supervisor, Jesse L. Lasky; and politicians, such as James Rolph Jr., the mayor of San Francisco, and John W. Smith, the mayor of Detroit. Many of these individuals were quoted in the publicity materials for the fund drive, and several of them testified to the "cleanliness" of Reid's character. Still others employed a language of transcendence to suggest that Reid had been purified in death and that he was exalted in his family's loving remembrance (fig. 4). DeMille told potential fund subscribers how the late star's "mind and soul and spirit was [sic] untouched and always clean, clear and fine," and the national president of the Daughters of the American Revolution, Mrs. Alfred Brosseau, gave her personal endorsement to the memorial campaign by stating how she was "in sympathy with the aims of the wife and mother of Wallace Reid."[36] Fund-raising was complicated by advertising restrictions that the Episcopal Diocese of New

Figure 4. The cost of remembrance. After Reid's death, his narcotic addiction was thoroughly privatized by numerous images of his family in mourning. Here Dorothy Davenport Reid holds a picture of a proposed memorial to her late husband—a bay to be built in the Cathedral of St. John the Divine—while son Billy writes his own check to the memorial's fund. The bay was never built. Courtesy of George Eastman House.

York placed on Harris's organization and later by the onset of the Depression in the early 1930s. After ten years in existence the Wallace Reid Memorial Association was able to raise only $792.79, less than 1 percent of the money required to build the cathedral bay.[37] With the exception of Thomas Edison, who contributed twenty dollars, no major studio executive pledged any money to the fund.

• • •

Social historian Frederick Lewis Allen saw the celebrity scandals of the early 1920s as a kind of misdirection, a distraction for the masses that necessarily kept them from pursuing their real political interests. Discussing the rise in circulation of the tabloids in the period, Allen maintained that it was not simply a "coincidence . . . that as they rose, radicalism fell." Allen portrayed the scandals of the early 1920s as devoid of any real relevance for the lives of working people, and he assumed that the only mode of reception possible for these media events was an uncritical prurience: "Workmen forgot to be class conscious as they gloated over pictures of Miss Scranton on the Boardwalk and followed the Stillman case and the Arbuckle case and studied the racing dope about Morvich."[38] However, it is clear that the scandals spoke to the public's real needs and experiences in some way and that they were not simply the mindless diversions that Allen and, not incidentally, the tabloids, the news media, and the film industry would have us believe. Lecturing to the students of the Harvard Graduate School of Business Administration in 1927, the popular film actor Milton Sills explained the importance of maintaining the illusion of the film star as a harmless diversion for the masses who, he candidly admitted, must work at "routine jobs [that] represent so much inevitable drudgery, and for the most part in the drabbest surroundings." Citing this situation as the reason for "the menace of revolt against our economic system," Sills stressed how the film star "performs an important public service, ameliorating the dreary lives of countless millions, bringing them charm, romance, laughter, grace, and high adventure." [39]

As we have seen, the film industry had to struggle with the media representations of Reid's drug habit in order to make the star's addiction practically incoherent within the terms of industrial production and labor. Instead, the damaged life was finally made into the life that had to be lived and lost at home, where only the grief of a friend, a fan, or a family remained to explain how it all had come about. With the privatization of Reid's addiction complete, newspaper and tabloid attention to him actually ceased after his death, leaving his posthumous celebrity to the fan magazines. In fact, less than one week after Reid's funeral an editorial in the obituary section of *Variety* angrily noted Reid's disappearance from the nation's headlines. Attacking two groups perceived to be serious threats to the film industry during this period, the anonymous writer of this editorial blamed tabloid journalists for exploiting the scandal only to deliver women readers over to the department stores that advertised in their papers, and the writer similarly blamed social reformers for discussing drugs and drug trafficking only in order to "attract morbid crowds of attentive listeners." The important lesson to be learned from Reid's death is given in the editorial's very first sentence: "Wallace Reid died in a fight against the drug habit at 31, more than thirty years before his time and his potential earning capacity of half a million dollars a year." [40] With an astonishing lack of irony, even for a trade journal, the writer expresses the tragedy of Reid's death in terms of loss of an already calculated future income. The appeal is for readers to understand and to remember Reid's death as a lesson about the threat that drugs and drug use pose to the efficiency of rational planning and the realization of future revenue. Throughout the 1920s the major newspapers did remember Reid in the manner advocated here. During this period his name usually came up only in the recurrent news stories about the enormous salaries paid to film stars. His final salary of twenty-five hundred dollars a week was often used as a sort of benchmark against which to measure other stars' earnings. [41] The callous honesty with which the *Variety* writer could invoke Reid only a week after his death had already been made entirely unremarkable by the previous manner in which the publicity around the star had succeeded in evacuating the site of production as a meaningful place from which to understand Reid's addiction. Furthermore, it was Reid's very death, the dead certainty that he would work no more, that allowed the anonymous *Variety* writer to remember Reid as already forgotten, as someone about whom the newspapers would have nothing left to say.

NOTES

An earlier version of this paper was presented on the panel "Regulatory Practices and Historical Methods: The United States Film Industry, 1910–1960," at the 1998 Society for Cinema Studies Conference in San Diego. I wish to thank Lynn Arner, Lisa Cartwright, Kalliope Nikolopoulou, and Eric Smoodin for their insightful comments and helpful suggestions. My gratitude also goes to Rosemary Hanes and Madeline Matz at the Library of Congress and to Becky Simmons at George Eastman House for the invaluable assistance they provided me in researching this project.

1. David T. Courtwright, *Dark Paradise: Opiate Addiction in America before 1940* (Cambridge: Harvard University Press, 1982).

2. Of the three major scandals only the Arbuckle trials and the murder of William Desmond Taylor continue to receive significant popular and scholarly attention. Two full-length books have been written about the Arbuckle case, and, as part of their coverage of the O. J. Simpson murder trial in 1995, news commentators and journalists made continual reference to this earlier celebrity scandal. There have also been numerous treatments of the Taylor murder as an "unsolved mystery," and there is even a monthly newsletter dedicated to the Taylor murder published on-line since April 1993. See David Y. Yallop, *The Day the Laughter Stopped: The True Story of Fatty Arbuckle* (New York: St. Martin's, 1976); Andy Edmonds, *Frame-Up!: The Untold Story of Roscoe "Fatty" Arbuckle* (New York: William Morrow, 1991); see also Sam Stoloff's essay on Arbuckle in this volume. For book-length treatments of the Taylor affair as an entertaining Hollywood murder mystery see Sidney D. Kirkpatrick, *A Cast of Killers* (New York: E. P. Dutton, 1986); and Robert Giroux, *A Deed of Death* (New York: Knopf, 1990). The factual bases of these works are critiqued in Bruce Long, *William Desmond Taylor: A Dossier* (New York: Scarecrow, 1991). The monthly newsletter *Taylorology* can be found on the World Wide Web at <http://www.angelfire.com/az/Taylorology/>. Issues 38 (February 1996) and 39 (March 1996) of *Taylorology* reproduce newspaper and magazine clippings relevant to the Reid scandal. Besides a short chapter in Kenneth Anger's *Hollywood Babylon* and a sixteen-page article published in the 1960s, no substantial attention has been paid to Reid's biography or the scandal of his addiction since the 1928 serial publication in *Liberty* of Adela Rogers St. Johns's idealized portrait of the film actor. Reid's mother wrote and published a sentimental remembrance of her son shortly after his death in 1923. Kenneth Anger, *Hollywood Babylon* (San Francisco: Straight Arrow Books, 1975); Dewitt Bodeen, "Wallace Reid Was an Idol in the Age of Innocence with Feet of Clay," *Films in Review* 17 (April 1966): 205–220; Adela Rogers St. Johns, "The Life Story of Wallace Reid: The Tragedy of an American Idol," *Liberty*, June 23, 1928, 11–15; June 30, 1928, 36–38, 40, 42, 44; July 7, 1928, 59–60, 62, 64–66; July 14, 1928, 50–54; and Bertha Westbrook Reid, *Wallace Reid: His Life Story* (New York: Sorg Publishing, 1923). Bodeen's essay includes an extensive filmography for the actor and is reprinted in Dewitt Bodeen, *From Hollywood: The Careers of Fifteen Great American Stars* (South Brunswick, N.J.: A. S. Barnes, 1976), 91–115. Anthony Slide's entry for Wallace Reid was dropped from the third revised edition of the *International Dictionary of Films and Filmmakers* (Detroit: St. James Press) when it was published in 1997.

3. See for example Robert Sklar, *Movie-Made America: A Cultural History of the Movies* (New York: Viking Books, 1975), 82–85; Lary May, *Screening Out the Past: The Birth of Mass Culture and the Motion Picture Industry* (Chicago: University of Chicago Press, 1983), 179; Ruth Vasey, *The World According to Hollywood, 1918–1939* (Madison: University of Wisconsin Press, 1997); and Stoloff, "Fatty Arbuckle and the Black Sox," this volume.

4. Mrs. Wallace Reid quoted in William Parker, "Mrs. Reid Denies Claim That Husband Is Member of National 'Dope' Ring," *Los Angeles Evening Herald*, December 20, 1922, A14.

5. Mrs. Reid quoted in William Parker, "Reid Got 'Dope' Habit in N.Y., Says Wife," *Los Angeles Evening Herald*, December 19, 1922, A1, A14.

6. Thomas W. Bailey, "Wallace Reid Details Plans of Lasky Firm," *San Francisco Chronicle*, July 27, 1919, 4E.

7. Richard Koszarski, *An Evening's Entertainment: The Age of the Silent Feature Picture, 1915–1928* (Berkeley: University of California Press, 1994), 276–278. Kevin Brownlow refers to this accident as an "explanation [that] was so straightforward one wonders why it did not circulate at the time of his death." Actually, it did circulate widely and was a very important component of the public representation of Reid's addiction, although the explanatory work performed by the story of the train wreck was anything but "straightforward." *Behind the Mask of Innocence: The Social Problem Films of the Silent Era* (New York: Alfred A. Knopf, 1990), 107.

8. Dorothy Davenport Reid, "Wife Pens Dramatic Story of Wallace Reid's Drug Ruin: Dope Curse Traced to Car Injury in 1919," *San Francisco Examiner*, December 31, 1922, 6.

9. Danae Clark, *Negotiating Hollywood: The Cultural Politics of Actor's Labor* (Minneapolis: University of Minnesota Press, 1995).

10. Lynne Kirby, "Male Hysteria and Early Cinema," *Camera Obscura* 17 (May 1988): 113–131. See also Lynne Kirby, *Parallel Tracks: The Railroad and Silent Cinema* (Durham, N.C.: Duke University Press, 1997).

11. Bertha Westbrook Reid, *Wallace Reid*, 74.

12. "Reid Recovering," *Variety*, October 27, 1922, 47.

13. Dorothy Davenport Reid, "Overpowering Mastery of Dope Demon Described," *San Francisco Examiner*, January 4, 1923, 10.

14. "Wally Reid in His Best Stunt Conquers 'Dope'," *Rochester (N.Y.) Herald*, December 17, 1922, 1.

15. The man taken into custody was Claude Tynar (or Tyner) Waltman, a young writer identified in *Variety* as "Thomas H. Tyner, alias Claude Walton, alias, Bennie Walton." Mrs. Reid does not name Waltman but mentions this arrest in her revelations to the Hearst newspapers saying that "the boy's" claims were untrue or misinterpreted. "Had Dope for Star," *Variety*, November 19, 1920, 39. Waltman apparently committed suicide a couple of weeks after Reid's death, leaving a note reading "going to join my pal." *Variety*, February 8, 1923, 47. Waltman's arrest on heroin possession in 1920 is at odds with the general view that during this period heroin use was primarily an East Coast phenomenon, centered mainly in New York City and Philadelphia. Ironically, Mrs. Reid's insistence that her husband became addicted to drugs in New York City in 1921 suggests that heroin played a role in his drug habit because heroin had almost entirely eclipsed morphine in that city as the narcotic of addiction. Mrs. Reid also claimed that on several occasions her husband had received packages of drugs in the mail from New York City. See Dorothy Davenport Reid, "Wally Reid's

Confirmed Use of Drugs Revealed," *San Francisco Examiner*, January 3, 1923, 10. Mrs. Reid also lamented late-night parties at her husband's apartment in New York City, and when Adele Whitely and Gladys Hall interviewed the star there one morning in the summer of 1921, they noted "several festive evidences" and mentioned that "Wally is weary." *Motion Picture Magazine* 22 (September 1921): 22–23. On the prevalence of heroin use in New York and other East Coast cities see Courtwright, *Dark Paradise*, 101–112. On the relation between crime and heroin addiction see "Saving Youth from Heroin and Crime," *Literary Digest* 81 (May 24, 1924): 32–33; and Lawrence Kolb, "Drug Addiction in Its Relation to Crime," *Mental Hygiene* 9 (1925): 74–89.

16. Courtwright, *Dark Paradise*, 87–101.

17. Ibid., 113–147. A psychopathic model of narcotic addiction emerged in the 1920s. As more and more addicts came from the ranks of the lower classes, drug addiction simultaneously came to be understood in terms of abnormal mental or emotional development. The foremost proponent of this theory was Lawrence Kolb, who studied and treated addicts for the U.S. Public Health Service; see "Types and Characteristics of Drug Addicts," *Mental Hygiene* 9 (1925): 303–313. See also Eugene T. Lies, "Constructive Play as a Preventative of Narcotic Addiction," in H. S. Middlemiss, ed., *Narcotic Education: Edited Report of the Proceedings of the First World Conference on Narcotic Education, Philadelphia, Pennsylvania, July 5, 6, 7, 8, and 9, 1926* (Washington, D.C.: H. S. Middlemiss, 1926), 130–136. For a brief comparison of the different public policy approaches taken to narcotic addiction in Great Britain and the United States during the 1920s, see Terry M. Parssinen, *Secret Passions, Secret Remedies: Narcotics Drugs in British Society 1820–1930* (Philadelphia: Institute for the Study of Human Issues, 1983), 201–221.

18. Samuel Hopkins Adams, "The Cruel Tragedy of 'Dope,'" *Collier's*, February 23, 1924, 7–8, 32.

19. Louis Weadock, "Screen Idol Succumbs to Drug Curse," *San Francisco Examiner*, January 19, 1923, 1, 3.

20. At this time Hearst was also busy exploiting Juanita Hansen, a film actress arrested for possession of narcotics in January 1923. Hansen had been a popular serial queen, although her stardom waned considerably after 1920. Although she was acquitted of the drug charge, she publicly confessed to having been a heroin addict in the past. Hearst arranged a speaking tour for the troubled actress and announced plans for an antinarcotics film featuring Hansen. See "Juanita Hansen's Offers," *Variety*, February 8, 1923, 47. Even before Hansen's arrest, though, the Hearst newspapers reported that her name was among those found on a patient list confiscated from a clinic in Oakland, California, whose doors had been shut for providing addicts with illegal narcotics ("Police Seize Records of Dope Hospital," *San Francisco Examiner*, January 3, 1923, 3). Reportedly, Reid had also been a patient at the clinic ("'Sociologist' Arrested as Drug Seller," *San Francisco Examiner*, January 2, 1923, 1). Hansen's addiction was far less disruptive for the industry than Reid's because her film career was effectively over at the time of the scandal.

21. *Human Wreckage* is a lost film. In 1983 Martin Sopocy included *Human Wreckage* in a filmography of extant works by Thomas H. Ince and erroneously reported that a print of the film existed at the Library of Congress; see Jean Mitry, "Thomas H. Ince: His Esthetic, His Films, His Legacy," trans. Martin Sopocy and Paul Attallah, *Cinema Journal* 22 (winter 1983): 2–25. Although there was a film entitled *Human Wreckage* at the Library of Congress, by 1975 that film had been

correctly identified as *Sex Madness* (Cinema Service Corp., 1938), an exploitation feature about venereal disease copyrighted under the title *Human Wreckage*. Citing the scholarship of George Pratt, Sopocy also questioned Ince's actual involvement with the production of *Human Wreckage*, claiming that "the extent of the connection is unclear" and that the film's "relation to the Ince canon remains one of the ambiguities of Ince studies." This "ambiguity" appears to be solely based on the relative lack of prominence given to Ince in the film's publicity. Yet Ince was mentioned in the press coverage as the producer of *Human Wreckage* less than three weeks after Reid's death, from the very moment that the proposed film was announced. See "Watchdogs of Law Aid Dope Film," *Los Angeles Daily Times*, February 7, 1923, sec. 2, p. 7; and "Among 'Dope' Films, Which Will Be First?" *Variety*, February 8, 1923, 46. Additionally, the Thomas H. Ince Corporation is listed as the producer on the copyright registration records for *Human Wreckage*. On the application for license from the Motion Picture Commission of New York State the film's title is given as "'HUMAN WRECKAGE' (A Thomas Ince Production)." Ince was undoubtedly the film's primary producer, and he was probably credited as such in the American release prints of *Human Wreckage*. The relative absence of Ince's name from trade advertising is better understood as evidence of his reticence about the overseas reception of *Human Wreckage*. For example, Ince's distribution agreement for Argentina required that his name be removed from all promotions of the film in that country. Agreement between Argentine American Film Corporation and R-C Pictures, December 23, 1924, Thomas Ince Collection, Carton 46, Manuscripts Division, Library of Congress, Washington, D.C.

22. The reviewer of *Human Wreckage* for *Motion Picture World* was quite taken with the film's "evident sincerity which is naturally greatly enhanced by the presence of Mrs. Wallace Reid, which brings to mind her own tragic experience with this evil." *Motion Picture World*, July 14, 1923, 154.

23. *Photoplay*, May 1923, 84. Sullivan had been the scenarist on many of Ince's most important productions, including *Civilization* (Triangle, 1916). For the script of *Human Wreckage* Sullivan likely "borrowed" material from other writers. For example, in Ince's file for the film there is a seven-page treatment written by Will Lambert for a film about a district attorney who becomes addicted to narcotics while prosecuting a difficult drug case. This untitled story bears more than a few similarities to the Sullivan scripts for *Human Wreckage*. Thomas H. Ince Collection, Carton 31, Manuscripts Division, Library of Congress, Washington, D.C. In 1917 Ince had also supervised the production of *Love or Justice* (New York Motion Picture Corp.), a film based on a Lambert Hillyer script about a lawyer who becomes a drug addict. Kevin Brownlow also reports that Albert Rogell complained of Ince's stealing important material for *Human Wreckage* from Rogell's own antinarcotics film, *The Greatest Menace* (J. G. Mayer, 1923). See Brownlow, *Behind the Mask*, 117–118. Another possible, if somewhat macabre, source for *Human Wreckage* may have been a manuscript authored by "Claud[e] Tyner Waltman" (see note 15). Before committing suicide Waltman gave Mrs. Reid a manuscript on "narcotics evil," a work for which he had been unable to find a publisher. Mrs. Reid claimed to have retained the manuscript in her possession after Waltman's death ("Youth Slays Self to Join Star in Death," *Los Angeles Examiner*, February 4, 1923, 1, 4).

24. Manuscript, Thomas Ince Collection, Carton 31, Manuscripts Division, Library of Congress, Washington D.C.

25. See "Wallace Reid's Widow at the Century," *San Francisco Chronicle*, May 26,

1923, 8; and "Mrs. Reid Makes Anti-Dope Appeal," *San Francisco Examiner*, June 9, 1923, 1.

26. "Reid's Death Warning to Public," *San Francisco Examiner*, January 20, 1923, 3.

27. *Webb et al. v. United States* (1919). See Courtwright, *Dark Paradise*, 106–107.

28. The original script of *Human Wreckage* had proposed that a federal hospital for drug addicts be built on San Clemente Island, but, as Kevin Brownlow has pointed out, the proposed site soon became a practice range for the United States Marine Corps. Brownlow, *Behind the Mask*, 115–116.

29. Indeed, as several statements made by Mrs. Reid attest, she very much supported the efforts of law enforcement to halt the illicit traffic in narcotics, and federal and state law enforcement agencies had lent their support to *Human Wreckage* from the very beginning of its production. However, Mrs. Reid denied early reports that she planned to avenge her husband's illness by exposing the "traffic in narcotics in both Los Angeles and the East." *Rochester (N.Y.) Times-Union*, December 18, 1922, 25. Years later she claimed that her husband had no contact whatsoever with the illegal drug trade because he was capable of "charm[ing] any doctor into giving him the tablets he wanted" (Dewitt Bodeen, "Wallace Reid Was an Idol," 216). Of course, any physician who was so fooled into supplying Reid with nondiminishing doses of narcotics for any length of time would have faced federal prosecution under the Harrison Act if found out.

30. Brownlow, *Behind the Mask*, 109.

31. Theodor Adorno, *Minima Moralia: Reflections from Damaged Life*, trans. E. F. N. Jephcott (London: Verso, 1993), 17.

32. A striking example of this sort of reception is a Wallace Reid scrapbook begun by an unknown person(s) at the moment of the star's death. The first several pages contain newspaper clippings about Reid's illness and death. Moving backward in time, subsequent pages are devoted to fan magazine material from earlier moments in Reid's stardom, such as a rotogravure of Reid with Cecil B. DeMille taken from the June 1921 issue of *Motion Picture Magazine*. Although the scrapbook clearly functions as a memorial, it also poses Reid's career as a type of case study, as a life whose defining moments are narcotic addiction and death. Scrapbook in the care of the author.

33. Bertha Westbrook Reid, *Wallace Reid*, 103 (capitals in the original).

34. Charles A. "Buddy" Post, "Wally Reid, My Friend," *Motion Picture Magazine* 26 (January 1924): 84.

35. Gladys Hall, "Will Wallace Reid's Son Succeed Him?" *Motion Picture Magazine* 36 (January 1929): 50.

36. Wallace Reid Memorial subscription, Wallace Reid file, Paper Collections, George Eastman House, Rochester, N.Y.

37. Memorandum from A. L. Ferguson, September 26, 1939, Wallace Reid Memorial Fund file, Box C-66, Diocese of New York of the Episcopal Church, New York. I am grateful to diocesan archivist Wayne Kempton for information about the institutional history of this memorial fund.

38. Frederick Lewis Allen, *Only Yesterday: An Informal History of the Nineteen Twenties* (New York: Harper and Row, 1931), 81. "Miss Scranton on the Boardwalk" refers to the annual Inter-City Beauty Contest held in Atlantic City, New Jersey, at which the first Miss America was crowned in September of 1921. The press delighted in reporting that Samuel Gompers, president of the American Federation of Labor,

was an enthusiastic member of the audience for the pageant in 1922. In the Stillman divorce, newspaper readers were treated to all the titillating details of the romantic and adulterous adventures of a prominent Wall Street banker and his wife. Morvich was a famous thoroughbred racehorse that achieved an impressive record of eleven wins in eleven consecutive races before winning the Kentucky Derby in 1922, his final victorious start.

39. Milton Sills, "The Actor's Part," in Joseph P. Kennedy, ed., *The Story of the Films* (Chicago: A. W. Shaw Company, 1927), 189–192. I wish to thank Steven J. Ross for reminding me of the existence and importance of these lectures.

40. "The Lesson of Reid's Death." *Variety*, January 25, 1923, 10.

41. See, for example, "Present Production Costs Contrasted with Low Figures of the Past," *New York Times*, December 19, 1926, sec. 7, p. 9; and "A New Phase Opens in the Film Industry," *New York Times*, July 3, 1927, sec. 8, p. 3. The public remembrance of Reid as a structuring absence useful for calculating "reasonable" star salaries is consistent with later popular representations of drug use in Hollywood. When film star Barbara La Marr died from an overdose in 1926, her drug use was generally understood as symptomatic of an excessive Hollywood lifestyle made possible by the inflated salaries of Hollywood stars, many of whom were thought to be inexperienced in handling large sums of money. By the time actress Alma Ruben's drug addiction became public knowledge in 1929, narcotic use had already become a cliché of the film-diva mystique. For example, see the descriptions of morphine addiction in Edward Stilgebauer's pulp-fiction novel *The Star of Hollywood*, trans. E. E. Wilson (Cleveland, Ohio: International Fiction Library, 1929). By the end of the studio era celebrity drug use could even enhance a film star's image. Robert Mitchum's arrest and conviction for marijuana possession in 1948 only contributed to his popular bad-boy appeal. More recently, Drew Barrymore's substance abuse as a teenager ultimately only confirmed the young actress's Hollywood pedigree and her Barrymore lineage (even as it raised some questions about the exploitation of child actors). Drug rehabilitation programs have almost become de rigueur for any celebrity who seeks to cultivate an air of worldliness or who wishes to create the impression of a secret vulnerability. Fancy and expensive detoxification treatments glamorize celebrity drug addiction and help distinguish it from the drug abuse of America's urban poor, who typically make their media appearances as criminals on television's various real-life law enforcement series. Today addicted Hollywood stars only become truly pathetic when, as in the case of Robert Downey Jr., their relapses call forth a repressive response from the state: repeated incarceration. For the sake of stardom death seems preferable to abject criminality.

THE SCANDAL OF RACE

AUTHENTICITY, THE

SILENT ENEMY, AND THE

PROBLEM OF LONG LANCE

NANCY COOK

*I*n 1928 Chief Buffalo Child Long Lance (1890–1932) was hired to star in *The Silent Enemy*, a dramatic documentary about the Ojibwa tribe in Canada. Filmed on location in northern Ontario, *The Silent Enemy* was promoted by its producers, W. Douglas Burden and William C. Chanler, as both an "all-Indian" film that documented what they considered to be a rapidly disappearing way of life and an action picture that would, they hoped, be popular with a general audience. With the publication and popularity of his autobiography and several magazine articles, his achievements in school and in the military during World War I, and finally adoption by and membership in New York's Jazz Age social set, Long Lance himself had already achieved what white culture at that time considered to be the greatest potential of Indians.[1] A paragon of Indian manhood as imagined by whites, Long Lance indeed seemed to be an "ideal" Indian in early-twentieth-century terms.

Promoted by Paramount, which released *The Silent Enemy* in the United States in 1930, as a film with "Real Dangers! Real Indians! Real Romance!," the film has failed nevertheless to receive much attention either from film historians or from scholars interested in realigning literary and film canons by reclaiming the work of minority writers, filmmakers, and actors. In part, the scandal surrounding Long Lance is to blame, for the man the producers believed to be "a chief of a branch tribe of the Blackfoot" was denounced as a fraud during the production of *The Silent Enemy*: rather than being a "full-blooded" Indian, Long Lance was labeled a black man caught in the act of trying to "pass."[2]

Long Lance was born Sylvester Long in 1890, in Winston-Salem, North Carolina. By various accounts, he was of triracial ("White," "Black," and "Indian") or
biracial ("White" and "Indian") heritage but was classified legally as "colored" in
turn-of-the-century Winston-Salem.[3] In his teens Long decided to reject enforced
affiliation with one persecuted minority for a more public affiliation with another, dropped a few years from his age, and applied to Carlisle Indian School as
an eastern Cherokee. Long Lance continued to shed years, realign himself with
increasingly western Native American tribes, and fabricate a more glorious personal past. At times he claimed to have graduated from West Point, to have played
football with Jim Thorpe, and to have won the Croix de Guerre; he also published his autobiography as a hereditary chief of the Blood Indians.

Yet the Long Lance applauded so frequently as an "ideal" Indian in the popular press had been shunned as a "nigger" rather than celebrated at Carlisle; he
had served honorably in World War I but never won the Croix de Guerre; and
his autobiography was fictional. Scandal dogged Long Lance through much of
his career. There were questions about his school and military record, incidents
with married white women, his "unmasking" during the filming of *The Silent
Enemy*, and finally, at the age of forty-one, his death in the home of heiress Anita
Baldwin, under cloudy circumstances, officially the victim of a self-inflicted gunshot to the head.

But as I hope to show here, Long Lance was indeed an "ideal" Indian, although not considered by many of his contemporaries to be a "real" one. Long
Lance, like his autobiography and the "authentic documentary" in which he
starred, performed authenticity; that is, Long Lance imagined and enacted himself in a way that was read by Jazz Age white culture as authentically Indian.
Although labeled a "fraud" during the production of *The Silent Enemy*, Long
Lance nevertheless continued to be used to sell the film's authenticity. Despite
the producers' hesitancy about touting Long Lance in the film's promotional material, neither Paramount nor the film's reviewers could turn away from him. By
providing a successfully "authentic" performance of Indian identity in *The Silent
Enemy*, the "fraudulent" Long Lance became the quintessential Indian at the
same time that he was forced to abandon the role where the scandal was known.
As *Variety* put it in its review of the film, "Chief Long Lance is an ideal picture
Indian, because he is a full-blooded one . . . an author of note in Indian lore, and
now an actor in fact."[4] Perhaps Long Lance's greatest sin was in proclaiming
himself a "full-blooded" Indian, for although that claim helped him attain fame,
it also fed into a biologically determined conception of racial identity that dogs
his reputation to the present day. By investigating the production and exhibition
history of *The Silent Enemy*, I will demonstrate how its producers, director, marketing staff, and critics imagined and represented the "authentic" Indian and
how the effects of their rendering can be seen in the scandals that followed.

This essay explores the nature of more than one scandal involving Long Lance and *The Silent Enemy*. Here I use the term *scandal* in two ways. The first, and more common use, describes the way that supposedly incriminating information about Long Lance was discovered, negotiated, and then suppressed by the producers of *The Silent Enemy*. Combining his own observations with information obtained from the Bureau of Indian Affairs, one of the film's Native American costars told the producers that Long Lance was a fraud. No chief of the Bloods, Long Lance was a black man, the accusation went. Seeking to avoid a national scandal over the racial identity of their star, producers Burden and Chanler responded to the rumors with a private investigation, confronted Long Lance with their evidence against him, then worked both to suppress the rumors and to set a lower profile for their star. Because Burden and Chanler had based much of the film's promotion on its "authentic" cast of "full-blooded" Indians, as well as on its accurate re-creation of Indian life, their fears of exposure seem justified. In spite of the producers' attempts at damage control, the scandal cost Long Lance a great deal, for the rumor had circulated among both New York's Native American community and Long Lance's white social set.[5] Shunned by many former intimates and counseled to "disappear," Long Lance left New York for California, where he died in 1932.

I also use *scandal* in a more general sense, which I take from Herman Gray's work on scandal and racialized discourse. Gray traces a historical trajectory from *The Birth of a Nation* (1915) to the Rodney King "scandal" (1992 and forward). Throughout the twentieth century, he argues, "blackness and difference continue to function as the markers of 'scandalous' threats to the moral and social boundaries":

> I recognize, of course, that the notion of scandal is usually applied to personal, often moral acts of transgression and behavioral lapses of the normative boundaries of the collective. I, however, want to extend and broaden this understanding of scandal by proposing that we consider it as a political and cultural construct which hides and glosses as much as it reveals about the terms of the American moral and social order. Consequently, I apply the notion of scandal to a discursive regime that has invested in representing social, cultural, and political struggles over power in racial terms, framing such struggles to the racial and economic order in moral terms. I want to suggest, moreover, that such racialized discourse works, by naming and rendering as "scandalous" transgressions and oppositions to the dominant order of things.[6]

Following Gray's logic, the scandals involving Long Lance position him as a transgressive figure, and, as such, he is named as "black." The forgotten scandal of Long Lance and *The Silent Enemy* is no less than the scandal of racial identification and affiliation in 1920s America.

But Gray's argument for a reconfiguration of the definition of scandal has further implications here, for I claim that the use of a biologically determined notion of race can be exposed as *scandalous* as it both affects the life and achievements of Long Lance and as it infects the way biographers and critics have represented him. Understanding the nature of the scandals associated with Long Lance throughout his career provides an opening for an examination of racial discourses and authenticity in *The Silent Enemy* and the way in which racial discourse itself continues to be used scandalously in both popular and academic cultures within the United States.

• • •

W. Douglas Burden, a wealthy young naturalist, explorer, and adventurer, developed plans for filming *The Silent Enemy* after seeing Merian C. Cooper's 1927 documentary *Chang*.[7] In later years Burden recalled: "To be sure, we did not have elephants or water buffalo or leopards and tigers and gibbon, but we did have wolves and bear and mountain lion and foaming rapids, and the hardness of deep frost and long, tough winters. In addition, it was all too obvious that the Indians were dying off so rapidly from the white man's diseases that if the story of their endless struggle for survival against starvation — their Silent Enemy — was ever to be captured on film, we had no time to lose."[8]

The filmmakers chose to represent the life of the Ojibwa not as it existed in 1928 but as they imagined it existed before contact with European cultures. Here Burden participates in common assumptions and practices among anthropologists and ethnographic filmmakers of his day. First, he follows an implicit evolutionist narrative popular at the time that saw Native Americans as a "vanishing race," one doomed to die out because of its presumed lower status. The implications of such an argument are consequential, for according to Michael Riley, "in being cast as the last practitioners of a dying way of life, the vanquished Indians . . . are rendered as emblematic of the past, rather than as viable participants in the world of the present."[9] Consequently, and problematically, in this scenario the "natives" are represented as being rescued by the young millionaire-adventurer Burden.

But, as Fatimah Tobing Rony explains, "[w]hile the West implicitly is portrayed as a civilization that can learn from other peoples, indigenous peoples implicitly are seen as threatened with imminent extinction. . . . The ethnographic filmmaker . . . is thus the agent of redemption, but he or she can only really save the West."[10] Citing anthropologist Franz Boas's stated interest in capturing the "'picturesque' ways of 'primitive peoples' — those scenes of rituals, dance, . . . and so on, all that is replete with 'authentic' detail and without the influence of European culture," Rony argues that "the picturesque is a shielding gesture: relations of dominance are preserved in ideologies of death (the 'vanishing races'), in the entertainment of relentless binarisms ('we do this, they do that'), and in the use of text or intertitles to wrest a narrative out of potentially disturbing images."[11] No matter how well intentioned Burden's production of *The Silent Enemy* manufactures, as we will see, its own authenticity, while denying the Ojibwa and other Native American participants their identity in their own historical moment. Robert Berkhofer, among other historians, argues that such practices persist into the present, noting that "most Whites still conceive of the 'real' Indian as the aborigine he once was, or as they imagine he once was, rather than as he is now . . . and far too many anthropologists still present this image by describing aboriginal cultures in what they call the 'ethnographic present,' or as if tribes live today as they once did." [12] Such an ideology required that the Native Americans onscreen perform roles representative of an idealized past. Ironically, to find actors capable of authentically representing the Ojibwa of the past, the producers looked beyond the confines of Ojibwa territory.

According to Burden and Chanler, because there wasn't "much of a chance of getting precisely the kind of character that we wanted just from the Ojibwa, [w]e had to allow ourselves a broader scope." [13] They therefore extended their search to New York, where they cast their leading players. For the female lead they found a Penobscot Indian, Spotted Elk, more often known as Molly Nelson in the city, where she "danced every night . . . at Texas Guinan's Night Club, a well-known speakeasy." [14] They found Chauncey Yellow Robe, the old chief in the movie, in that bastion of authenticity, the Museum of Natural History. Burden remembers: "Here was this striking-looking man, wandering through the halls, looking at the exhibits. He could have been taken right off the buffalo coin. We just started talking to him, and he turned out to be the hereditary chief of the Sioux Indians, a nephew of Sitting Bull. . . . When we told him what we wanted to do, he fell in love with the idea." [15] After seeing a photograph of Long Lance in his autobiography, they cast him to play Baluk, the mighty hunter. As the script notes, he was to be "the epitome of manly development." [16] The producers, then, at least to some degree, viewed Plains Indians as representative of "Indian." Indeed, by the 1920s the combined influences of various Wild West shows and the Hollywood film industry had thoroughly established the image of the Plains Indians as the quintessential Indian. Of the four leading actors in *The Silent Enemy*, both Molly Nelson and Long Lance had performed in Wild West shows as Plains Indians, although only Yellow Robe was of a Plains tribe. Burden's interest in Yellow Robe's illustrious uncle reflects white culture's fascination with Indian royalty, as it were. "Chief" Yellow Robe, "Princess" Spotted Elk, and "Chief" Long Lance represented the height of genetic and cultural achievement in the world of Indians as whites imagined them. As "royalty," each was assumed to be a "full-blood," if not a true "blue blood."

Once they arrived on location in northern Canada, the producers were determined to document "authentic" Indian life, a life, in their estimation, already disappearing. By attempting to hire "'pure blood families' who still lived, at least seasonally, in the bush," Burden hoped to find Indians still living according to the "old ways." It is as though Burden fully subscribed to the ideology of "the ethnographic present." He had difficulty finding full-blooded Ojibwa Indians, and as he soon discovered, few Native Americans (even "full-bloods") still practiced "the old ways" or used old tools or wore animal-skin clothing.[17] For props "some of the Indians brought with them their family heirlooms, while a large assortment of original clothing and other objects were loaned . . . by courtesy of the American Museum of Natural History." Once the props were collected, Burden noted, "we had to teach the Indians their use. Old games, old customs, old methods of making fire and cooking, and many other customs forgotten by disuse were revived. To accomplish this, we consulted authorities on Indian lore and sought the advice of specialists on the subject."[18]

Ironically, the authenticity of these documentary props and details made some fear for its box office failure. "To say that this admirable production is 'educational' is to condemn it to be shown in empty theatres," Robert Sherwood of the *New York Post* lamented in a widely reprinted review. "There is no more demand for education among movie fans than there is among college students. So I shall carefully avoid all use of this ugly word in writing of *The Silent Enemy*, and I urge all other reviewers to do likewise."[19] Sherwood's comments suggest the film offers plenty to viewers besides an authentic rendering of the past, but more on this subject later. What I want to suggest here is that the producers' claims to authenticity, through the use of historically accurate props, help set up an ideological structure wherein the scandal can take hold.

For all of the plaudits for its authenticity, *The Silent Enemy* represents and creates its own particular notions of the "authentic." Although obsessed with authenticity, the filmmakers hired actors from outside the tribe and shot from a dramatic script. Thus, all of the Native Americans in *The Silent Enemy* were actors, "impostors" to some degree. Although such practices are common in Hollywood history, the producers of *The Silent Enemy* had already gone to some lengths to situate their film in the company of documentaries such as *Nanook of the North* (1922) and the aforementioned *Chang* (1927), both of which worked to efface the role of native people as "actors."

Indian, in this context, represents a racial category, a homogenous group that tends to erase regional and tribal difference. Under the rubric "Indian," Chauncey Yellow Robe, a Sioux and hereditary enemy of the Ojibwa, can erase old animosities, play an Ojibwa chief, and claim in the film's prologue that "This is the story of my people."[20] *Indian*, in this construction, becomes a static term that leaves Indians unchanged over time. Yellow Robe vouches for the representation offered:

> Now you will know us as we really are. . . . [E]verything is as it always has been; our buckskin clothes, our birch-bark canoes, our wigwams, and our bows and arrows; all were made by my people just as they always have done. When you see my young men hunting, that is how their fathers hunted; when you see us

cold and starving; when, after the great hunt you see us feasting and singing; that is how we always have lived; those are the songs our forefathers taught us.[21]

As may be apparent from this quotation, sometimes one construction collides with another. Yellow Robe, his authenticity unchallenged both as Indian and Sioux, as corroborated by the producers' frequent mention of his illustrious uncle, Sitting Bull, in all likelihood was no expert with a birch-bark canoe, coming from eastern Montana as he did. Born in 1870 on the Plains, he would not have been familiar with the precontact weaponry of the Ojibwa, nor would he have been familiar with caribou hunting.

According to Molly Spotted Elk, as Indians, Yellow Robe, a Sioux; Nelson, or Spotted Elk, a Penobscot; and Long Lance, ostensibly a Blood, were consulted as experts for this film on Ojibwa cultural practices from a period several centuries earlier. But as Bunny McBride points out, some of the more notable inaccuracies in the representation of Ojibwa culture include "the cliché of an 'evil' medicine man; the bizarre presentation of forty or more Ojibwa tramping about en masse during the winter (the actual strategy against hunger was to divide into small hunting groups); a funeral pyre scene unfounded among the Canadian Ojibwa"; and Yellow Robe appears in Plains Indian attire during his death scene as Chief Chetoga.[22]

As the representative Indian, Yellow Robe himself erases all tribal distinctions in the prologue, which the filmmakers claim Yellow Robe wrote without aid from the producers. Ironically, it will be Long Lance's failure to act according to Yellow Robe's sense of tribal distinctions that precipitates the scandal. In other words, when Long Lance acts Indian, rather than Blood, Yellow Robe becomes suspicious.

Furthermore, in the prologue Yellow Robe links the Indians of *The Silent Enemy* with their ancestors, claiming an unbroken and unchanging set of native practices. As a man dying of tuberculosis Yellow Robe embodies the plight of his race. As a spokesman he represents the past (Sitting Bull), the present (impotence of the Indians as threat), and the future (extinction). Yellow Robe articulates a version of the "ethnographic present," lending another marker of authenticity to the film. Yet the producers, in order to create a compelling need for their film, have claimed that the Indians have broken with tradition, have lost their handcrafts and folkways, and have had to relearn their past from the white man.

In this dizzying confusion where conflicting claims to authenticity vie for authority, authenticity seems to inhere sometimes in the props and sometimes in the activities, and sometimes it seems embodied within the actors themselves. Moreover, with the producer defining, and sometimes manufacturing, the "authentic," authenticity becomes implicated in the power relations between whites and Native Americans. With so much at stake, it is not surprising that the Native Americans on location negotiated or sometimes wielded "authenticity" for and against each other. These contentious strategies become masked through a series of assumptions that help create a coherent, even unitary, notion of "Indian." For both the white production team and the Indian actors, "Indian" signified a set of images and behavior articulated in statements made on location and afterward, in the film text, and in the exhibition materials.

•   •   •

During the shooting other assumptions helped construct the film's notion of Indian.[23] Indians, constructed by the film as "primitive," were thought to have "strong constitutions." In the course of filming, the producers found that despite tuberculosis and other ailments, the actors could perform nearly naked in temperatures as low as forty degrees below zero. Why they were asked to do so remains unclear, although the sight of Long Lance, attired only in a loin cloth, elicited responses from visitors to the location, the publicists, and reviewers. While visiting the winter camp on location in northern Canada, Sheila Lawrence, Burden's sister, had this to say: "Long Lance, stripped to the waist, with his full feather headdress streaming behind him, did a superb Indian dance to the beat of [a production-crew member's] tom-tom. With sweat gleaming on his powerful torso, Long Lance was a thrilling sight."[24] In the finished film all the leading men have their turn appearing clad in only a loin cloth. Long Lance's body, however, is displayed most frequently, alluding, perhaps, to the working title for the film, *Red Gods*.

Stereotypically assumed to be "naturally stoic and reserved," Indians were

Long Lance in a publicity still for *The Silent Enemy*. Courtesy of the Academy of Motion Picture Arts and Sciences.

expected to endure the harsh winter shooting conditions without complaint. Indians, apparently, were only "playing themselves, acting naturally," so they performed all of their own stunts. Although ostensibly from the Plains, Long Lance was expected to perform expertly and comfortably in a birch-bark canoe. He was also badly slashed and scarred during a scene in which he wrestles with and captures two bear cubs. Yet when the censor for the Production Code Administration screened the film, he remarked on images that suggested the abuse of animals, not humans. Listed as possibly objectionable, the censor noted, were "[v]iews of two arrows, which have been shot, actually penetrating the body of bear and of bear, with arrows stuck in it, lying on its side quivering. Views of Indian throwing bear cubs brutally into sack." [25] So although Long Lance is actually injured during the filming of this scene, the censor can't imagine any viewer reacting squeamishly on behalf of the Indian. The animals seem to belong to the "real," whereas the Indian is "mythic." The producers, however, all too aware of the dangers involved, decided to shoot a scene with Long Lance and a bull moose last, for it was so dangerous they feared he might be seriously injured. Stunts, such as one in which Long Lance chases wolves away from the angry moose then spears it as it charges him, were performed with very little coaching, for it was assumed that, as an Indian, he was a "natural outdoors man." Again, for this scene the censor comments not on the danger to the actor, or his near trampling by the moose, but on the image of the "Indian sticking spear into side of moose as it lies prostrate on ground and of moose quivering." [26] One Ojibwa man, an extra, was killed during the production when he slipped through the ice, and both Spotted Elk and Yellow Robe suffered from tuberculosis during the winter shoot, even as they were required to spend time in subzero temperature scantily clad. The dangers to Long Lance and others were absolutely real, the producers claimed repeatedly to the press and in the promotional materials as evidence of the film's authenticity, but the censor was concerned only with the all-too-realistic dangers to the wildlife.

Even though the producers had difficulty finding enough "full-blooded" Ojibwa for the film, they searched diligently and later advertised the fact that theirs was an all-Indian cast. At the time, the dominant assumption was that "real" Indians are "full-blooded." The idea of "mixed blood" had unsettling miscegenational connotations in 1920s America and was best avoided. Further, "full-blooded" Indians are assumed to be unassimilated Indians, who consequently maintain "tradition" and reject the "white man's ways." Producer Burden's emphasis on the "full-blooded" status of his Indian players, both principals and extras, was pervasive on location. In this climate those Indians with any European or other non-Indian ancestry, no matter how traditional their cultural practices, were vulnerable to the derisive term *half-breed*. The term was used by whites and Native Americans alike. Although never challenged or derided as a "mixed blood," Molly Nelson had a French maternal grandfather.[27] Yet Nelson never considered herself a "breed," for she referred derisively to the schoolteacher on location as a "half-breed." [28] Nelson and Yellow Robe were both considered "full bloods" (by themselves as well as by the others) and thus actively, and paradoxically, participated in the reigning (and white) ideology of racial purity that was reinforced nearly everywhere. This, coupled with the producers' assumptions about the social practices of their Ojibwa extras, fostered a social hierarchy wherein the more "primitive" Ojibwa were kept at some distance from both the white film and support crew and the Indian stars.

At the winter camp on location, as Bunny McBride describes it,

> [t]he spatial setup of the living quarters in this wilderness community reflected society's pattern of segregation. The Ojibwa lived four-to-eight family members per tent. Their shelters were set in a cluster about eighty feet away from the two-person staff tents that housed the film's executives and production crew, plus Molly, Long Lance, and Yellow Robe. . . . In the cookery, Hennessey's men [the support staff] ate at one of two long wooden tables, while the film staff dined at a smaller table. The Ojibwa cooked and ate in their tents, with foodstuffs supplied by Hennessey's team. [29]

Although the producers worked assiduously to recruit those whom they considered "unassimilated" Ojibwa Indians for the film, they sought to limit their contact with them when not actually shooting. Long Lance, Nelson, and Yellow Robe presumably were assimilated enough to share in the day-to-day living arrangements of the white film production team. In the problematic logic of racism expressed on location, "full-bloods," as unassimilated, seemed too primitive to socialize with; but "full-bloods," as Indian royalty or "blue bloods," although assimilated (recall their New York addresses), were worthy of association with the white production team.

With the emphasis on "unassimilated" Indians onscreen, it may seem odd that two of the film's stars represented the assimilationist's dream. Both Chauncey Yellow Robe and Long Lance were graduates of the model assimilationist institution, Carlisle. Neither had "gone back to the blanket." Even with much in common, however, Yellow Robe and Long Lance were not allies, and were wary of one another. Rather than assuming that Long Lance's Carlisle training had succeeded in "killing the Indian and saving the man," Yellow Robe suggested to the producers that Long Lance was not who he claimed to be.

What made Yellow Robe suspicious? In Yellow Robe's eyes Long Lance did not act like an Indian. Long Lance danced well, but strangely for a Blackfeet; he was too punctual, too jolly; and he talked too much. Yellow Robe, too, subscribed to many stereotypes of the time, believing that, above all, the Indian is "silent." Long Lance told stories to keep up morale during the long winter shooting, and he laughed readily. Although these traits might have marked his portrayal of an

Ojibwa as authentic, they didn't ring true to the Sioux Yellow Robe. The Indian languages Long Lance drew from most frequently, Yellow Robe would claim, were Cherokee and Sioux. His use of sign language did not correspond with what Yellow Robe knew. So Yellow Robe suggested to the producers that they might investigate the background of their younger star. Long Lance might have picked up this amalgamated set of cultural practices and languages at Carlisle (as Yellow Robe must have picked up a little of the Cherokee language there in order to recognize it in Long Lance's speech) or during his appearances with other Indians at Wild West shows. On location, where all of the Native Americans were performing roles as Ojibwa of the past, nevertheless, Long Lance's performance as a Blood playing an Ojibwa was called into question. Despite the creation of an amalgamated, encompassing, if incoherent, notion of "Indian" by both the production team of *The Silent Enemy* and by the culture at large, Long Lance, apparently, was not a "real" Indian. He concealed his supposed Blood-Blackfeet heritage too well.

William Chanler, an attorney and coproducer of *The Silent Enemy*, took Yellow Robe's charges seriously and began to investigate. He enlisted Ilia Tolstoy, grandson of the novelist and one of *The Silent Enemy*'s production team, to help him. Tolstoy had become friends with Long Lance during the long location shoot and happened to be vacationing in the South when Chanler asked him to travel to Winston-Salem and investigate Long Lance's heritage. In a letter to Tolstoy Chanler lays out what he has learned about his star:

> Yellow Robe called me about three months ago and told me that he had just discovered that Long Lance was not a Blackfoot and that he understood that he was really a negro. He said that the Indians around here [New York] were very stirred up about it and that there would undoubtably [sic] be a formal protest if we featured him. I think the suggestion was somewhat prompted by jealousy: Long Lance was making a tremendous "social success" in New York, being invited by all the swell society hostesses in the City who made a great fuss over him; also he apparently kept aloof from other Indians in the City, which angered them.
>
> However, I wrote to the Indian Department [Bureau of Indian Affairs], and they told me their records showed that he was apparently part Croatan and that he was definitely not a Blood or a Blackfoot. Croatan . . . is a name recently given to a group of people living in North Carolina, previously classed as "free negros," but who claim to be Indians. . . . The Bureau of Ethnology states that they are not of pure blood, although Indian characteristics predominate; that there are very few traces of negro characteristics although it is said that they are part negro. . . .
>
> I gather he is considerable of a fraud. What I want to find out is how much of a one and what can be proved about him. . . . [W]e must try and establish that the Longs themselves are Indians and not negros. . . . Apparently, there

is still some mystery about his mother. Joe Long [Long Lance's father] is reported to have merely said that he thought his mother was a Croatan. Doesn't he know ? . . .

If the evidence against him is really bad, then I shall advise him to simply disappear for a year or two and let it blow over. Otherwise, we will be prepared to defend him.[30]

Chanler's response to the budding scandal of Long Lance's racial identity seems measured, even sympathetic, considering the potential costs of such a scandal for him and Burden and for the film's successful promotion. Long Lance had lied repeatedly to Chanler, fabricating increasingly elaborate stories to cover the incongruities in his official biography. It is ironic that a doctored biography might hurt a film's success given that by 1930 fictional "official" studio biographies were commonplace in Hollywood. But in this case the film's status as authentic documentary is at stake.

Yet Chanler also recognizes that Yellow Robe's own prejudices have played a role in the accusations and works assiduously to recuperate Long Lance as an Indian — of whatever sort. In his letter to Tolstoy the issue of blood quantum comes up, as do various physiological characteristics commonly believed to mark racial heritage. For example, elsewhere in the letter Chanler surmises that if Long Lance's "father had a mustache, he could not have been a full blood," according to Chanler's received ideas about racial characteristics.[31] At that time such markers as body hair, skin tone, and many features simply labeled "Negroid" commonly were used by both anthropologist and lay person to racially identify those not considered wholly white. In the late nineteenth and early twentieth centuries these physiological characteristics were deployed as markers of exclusion. A moustache might disqualify one man as fully an Indian if his heritage were questioned but not another whose racial standing was not under scrutiny.[32] Chanler's question, "Doesn't he know?," posed in regard to Joe Long's heritage, presumes a great deal about the genealogies of oppressed people. Joe Long had been separated from his mother early in life. His mother was a slave, and Joe spent his early life as the property of the Reverend Miles Long, from whom he took his name. Joe Long had been told by his mother that she was Cherokee, but slaves often had neither birth certificates nor complete genealogies. Joe believed himself to be Cherokee and white but could supply no proofs.

Many Native Americans in the South, and particularly in North Carolina, faced similar problems documenting and proving their Indian heritage. A group of such Native Americans, established in the region for well over a century, received partial federal recognition in 1885, when they were officially named Croatan. This name was replaced by Lumbee in the latter part of the twentieth century. When Chanler refers to the Bureau of Ethnology definition of Croatan, he really has no alternative. The Bureau used Frederick Webb Hodge's *Handbook of American Indians North of Mexico* (1907) as its reference, as, indeed, scholars continue to do. But, as Karen Blu points out, Hodge's text was created at a particular historical moment, one during which the status of the Croatan was at a low point. The group of Native Americans, probably of mixed ancestry (perhaps a mixture of various tribal peoples, whites, and blacks, but no definitive description exists), had at various times been classified as "Indian," "free persons of color," "free Negroes," or "free Whites." Until 1835 many such Indians had rights of citizenship, including the right to vote. After 1835 these Indians were more frequently classified with "free Negroes" and consequently denied rights they had previously enjoyed.[33] In fact, some Lumbee trace their own antipathy to African Americans to the legal changes of the early nineteenth century. Blu cites one such conversation: "'When the Whites classified us with the Negroes in 1835, it set back our relations with the Negroes a hundred and fifty years,'" because, Blu adds, "Indians had to fight so hard not to be classified with Blacks"[34] and lose what few privileges their status as "Indians" had afforded.

Moreover, in Hodge's *Handbook* such changes in status are not disclosed; and in the spirit of the "ethnographic present," as described earlier, the history of a people, in the *Handbook* labeled Croatan, is erased and replaced by the recapitulation of the prevailing perception of them in the "Jim Crow" North Carolina of the early twentieth century. In the entry for the tribe the author repeatedly undermines their status as Indians:

> For many years they were classed with free negroes, but steadily refused to accept such classification or to attend the negro schools or churches, claiming to be the descendants of the early native tribes and of white settlers who had intermarried with them. . . . [T]he name itself [Croatan] serves as a convenient label for a people who combine in themselves the blood of the wasted native tribes, the early colonists or forest rovers, the runaway slaves or other negroes, and probably of stray seamen of the Latin races.[35]

Thus, with no definitive evidence that the Croatan are not Indians, but with the official description of Croatan filled with innuendo, the Long family and Long Lance become claimants to Indian status, "coloreds," in the parlance of their place, trying to "pass." There is no place in the economy of racial identification, as played out here, for legitimating the Longs' claims to Native American ancestry. Ironically, although Long Lance and Hodge were both members of the prestigious Explorer's Club in New York and were friends, it was Hodge's book that helped exclude Long Lance from the Club.

Tolstoy went to Winston-Salem, interviewed the Long family and some of their longtime acquaintances in the white community, and established that locally the Longs were considered Indians of mixed white and Indian ancestry. Tolstoy obtained affidavits from some pillars of the white community and notified

Chanler that Long Lance, although not a full-blooded chief of the Blood tribe of western Canada, was nevertheless considered part Indian and not a Negro. But for Long Lance irreparable damage had been done by the rumors about his dubious racial heritage. He was shunned by many acquaintances and friends in New York's "smart set" who had once been drawn to the authenticity with which he embodied the exotic. Always known as a "ladies' man," Long Lance's "new" exoticism wasn't quite exotic enough. Harlem was full of such exotics. He now embodied their fears of miscegenation.

Once the investigation was completed and the producers discovered that Chief Buffalo Child Long Lance had been born Sylvester Long, some promotional plans were changed. Yet both on location and on the screen Chief Long Lance's performance remained powerful. The press releases, as well as the souvenir program for the premiere of *The Silent Enemy*, discuss one scene as particularly compelling. As Baluk, the great hunter, Long Lance has failed to lead his people to caribou, and so at the urging of the wicked medicine man he agrees to sacrifice himself. He will burn on a pyre. He faces death with dignity, but as the flames rise, the lookouts announce the arrival of . . . caribou. Under "Facts about *The Silent Enemy*" in the program we discover that "Cheeka actually believed Baluk was going to be burned to death. Under these circumstances his usual stoicism broke down with the results that are to be seen in the picture." Cheeka, the young boy in the film (played by Ojibwa George McDougall but referred to in all the cast lists only as his character, "Cheeka") cries. The program notes assert that at least one of the "actors" is not, in fact, "acting." What the film audience has seen, then, *is* real, according to the texts.

The program text further explains that "the Indians in *The Silent Enemy*, who were gathered by Mr. Burden, never learned the art of make-believe. They never even knew the meaning of the term. To them it was not acting, but living over again the lives of their remote ancestors." Moreover, "some of the very finest scenes in the picture came without warning, in instant flashes, by a sort of spontaneous, psychic combustion, bringing suddenly to the surface those deeply buried racial qualities which made the actors not merely act but actually live their parts." For the funeral pyre scene the producers knew that "authenticity demanded the singing by the Great Hunter of his Death Chant," but they also knew that it would constitute a serious breach of etiquette were they to ask him to sing it. Long Lance, as Baluk, ascended the pyre, stripped to the waist in the frigid winter air. "Suddenly," the program tells us, "those present heard something — it was night mind you, in the great Temagami Forest — that almost made their blood freeze. There stood Long Lance, surrounded by flames, beating the tom-tom as only the Indians of old knew, now slow, now regular, then increasing in tempo, until it seemed as though forty devils were contriving to make one mad . . . and in the midst of it all a weird, unearthly chant that made icicles come creeping up and down one's back." It was, they later learned, Long Lance's own death chant, for he had been so carried away by the scene that he had found himself singing, much to his own surprise.[36] The filmic strategies are conventional, but the program notes structure and assert them as authentic. The audience is asked to read the scene as other than conventional because the actors are not really actors. Rather, as the text works assiduously to demonstrate, some races are bound to perform their ancestral roles. In some sense they only come into being when they embody these roles. George McDougall cannot perform his own Ojibwa identity, but as "Cheeka" he can. Long Lance does not "act" the part of Baluk but becomes Baluk as he sings his own death chant.

Although Long Lance was not a "real" Indian to his detractors, because he was not a "full-blooded" one, his performance apparently pierced the layers of artifice, carried him away, captured the actors and crew, and presumably the motion picture audience as well. It is, thus, the most "authentic" performance in the film. Yet the scandal and investigation surely influenced some aspects of the film's promotion. Despite his prominence in the film, and although singled out by the critics, Long Lance gets comparatively little coverage in the twenty-page program.

If the producers were hesitant to promote their fraudulent star, the Paramount promotion people seemed compelled to focus on Long Lance. If Long Lance could ruin the film's claim to authenticity with the museum, naturalist, and educator set, he could nevertheless make the film successful as entertainment. With the scandal known in New York, the producers had decided to send Yellow Robe, not Long Lance, to Hollywood for promotional photos and appearances in March 1930. But Yellow Robe was seriously ill (he died in early April), so with some reluctance the producers sent Long Lance. Perhaps in part because of this successful visit, and the photos taken of him there, Long Lance figures prominently in the display advertising for *The Silent Enemy*. In fact, with proclamations of "Real Dangers! Real Indians! Real Romance!" and "Wild Country! Wild Animals! Wild People!" or "Wild Love! Wild Life!," the ads titillate us with the promise of the primitive, and Long Lance is the emblem for it. The marketing staff, too, figures that "Indian" means Plains Indians, for horses appear in the ads but not in the film. And although wild love may have occurred on location, for there were rumors of pregnancies, no sexy scenes appear in the film. By the time the film was released nationally, in the summer of 1930, the Depression had hit hard in most of the United States. With breadlines forming in many cities, nowhere in the ads is it noted that within the narrative the silent enemy is hunger.

Most important, the promotional materials declare, at least visually, that Long Lance himself is the silent enemy. In one sense the promotional materials reveal what the producers sought to cover over: the dangerous sexuality implicit in the well-muscled body of Long Lance, so nearly exposed to the public at large as "Negro." Foregrounded in the ads, he remains unassimilated, both attractive and threatening. One promotional item, a three-by-nine-inch folded "Herald" card, features head shots of Long Lance and Molly Spotted Elk with a menacing mountain lion perched above them, as if on Long Lance's head. Above the images the copy declares: "with NAKED hands they fought for life — that they might live for love!"[37] A newspaper ad mock-up shows drawings of a seated Neewa (Molly Nelson) holding Baluk (Long Lance) by the knee as he spears a caribou. The copy proclaims: "DARINGLY DIFFERENT/AMAZINGLY REAL! Two years of fighting courage beyond civilization created this primal romance!"[38] Under the heading "Catchy Copy," the sexual innuendos continue with "These men know love — they fight terrific dangers to win it! Condemned to burn alive — because he loves too well!"

These bits of "catchy copy" reveal both the attraction and the dangers of racially charged sexual attraction in a historical moment dominated by cultural forces that censured the slightest hint of miscegenation and punished anyone implicated. In these rather menacing images, ones either found nowhere in the film itself or lifted out of context, the *scandal* of racial identification reappears, for it will not be suppressed. As in contemporary media attention that scandal receives, here the focus is on the body — sensual and transgressive, if we are to believe the promotional material prepared for *The Silent Enemy*. And, not surprisingly, it is the darker body of the "primitive" that becomes scandalous in such images. Long Lance, as read by the Paramount promotion department, projects those impulses that cannot be openly acknowledged in public media but that nevertheless fascinate the public. Thus, following the claims made by Herman Gray quoted earlier, Paramount's representation of Long Lance is *scandalous*, for the promotional material invests "in representing social, cultural, and political struggles over power in racial terms, framing such struggles to the racial and economic order in moral terms." The Paramount promotional material erases hunger as "the silent enemy" within the film, even as the film already had rendered it a concern of the deep indigenous past. At a historical moment when many Americans, across racial categories, went hungry, the promotional material shifts attention from "social, cultural, and political struggles over power," to bodily struggles in the realm of the moral: "Wild People!," "Wild Love!," and "primal romance!"

• • •

Beginning in the 1960s, nearly every contemporary treatment of Sylvester Long, or Long Lance, has been somewhat sympathetic to what they have perceived to be his masquerade, as well as the reasons behind it. In his biography of Long Lance, Donald Smith has written sensitively of the challenges Long Lance faced growing up under the shadow of Jim Crow, a system of racial persecution that did not allow for the racial distinctions claimed by his family. Smith also makes clear that regardless of racial background, identification, or misconstrual, Long Lance was an extraordinarily talented man. Yet in every retelling of Long

Lance's heritage and story that I have encountered (at least seven), those who have discovered his place of origin have written of him as "black." For Long Lance geography serves as a linchpin that allows such critics to read race as biologically determined.

In spite of volumes of work across a range of fields, from anthropology to social theory, that proclaim race is *socially*, not biologically, constructed, each account of Long Lance's background relies on retrograde biologically based definitions of race, and thus each concludes that Long Lance is "black." The "blood quantum" discourse so common in early-twentieth-century U.S. culture persists in present-day discussions. For Long Lance the debate shifts from the language of "full-blood" or "half-breed" to the language of slavery: "mulatto," "quadroon," or "octoroon." In the early twenty-first century such reliance on the assumptions, if not the parlance, of the era of Jim Crow is, in Gray's terms, *scandalous*. As James Clifton points out:

> [T]he uncritical use of Indian, White, and Black, and the associated ethnocentric assumptions about ancient differences in behavior and potentialities, history, and culture effectively block analytic thinking. These historically derived, culturally patterned, institutionally reinforced convictions include such persistent ideas as . . . Indianness is fixed by blood. A related assumption is that the labels White and Indian [and Black] mark sharply defined biological, social, and cultural boundaries. . . . A further assumption is that these differences are primordial, inevitable, original, durable, and natural.[39]

As historians, literary scholars, anthropologists, and social theorists grapple with racialist discourse, the sophisticated arguments regarding the historical construction of racism are often undermined by the biological assumptions that remain unexamined within. For example, in her sensitive and sympathetic biography of Molly Spotted Elk, or Molly Nelson, Bunny McBride summarizes Long Lance's "true" background by noting that he was born into a "tri-racial household," that "his father, Joe Long was raised a slave, never knew his real parents," and was of "mixed" ancestry, "part-Indian (perhaps Catawba or Cherokee) and probably European and African as well." McBride describes Long Lance's mother, Sallie, as "part white and part Lumbee (mixed Indian, English, and African)."[40] McBride cites Donald Smith's biography of Long Lance as one of her sources, yet she makes her own assumptions (with some guidance by Smith) about the Longs' family genealogy, reading "black" for "slave." In fact most writers have read "black" for "slave," although we know that many Indians were enslaved along with Africans. McBride claims that Joe Long "never knew his real parents," another commonplace of slavery. Smith recounts that Long spent years trying to trace his mother, that he was eventually successful, and that she told him of his Indian heritage.

Following most sources on the Lumbee, McBride includes African ancestry for Long Lance, even though many Lumbee assert that they are not the descendants of Africans, as Blu's book points out. Yet apparently trapped by the unexamined assumptions of biologically based theories of race, McBride both asserts and denies Long Lance's supposed African ancestry: "With his coppery skin and straight black hair," she writes, "he was able to pass and perform as an Indian — and began to think of himself as one."[41] In her biography of Molly Spotted Elk McBride mentions Spotted Elk's white grandparent but never treats her subject as anything other than fully "Indian." Here, although "coppery skin" and "straight black hair" mark what conventionally might be considered as "authentically" Indian, for McBride such visual signs of race apparently mask Long Lance's "true" identity. In her view Long Lance is really "black." Yet no scholar, Smith among them, has found a documented black antecedent in the Long family. The historically southern-ascribed belief that one drop of black blood makes one black remains *scandalously* omnipresent in McBride's contemporary critical biography. Her conclusion reveals the persistence of the assumptions, if not the social, political, and legal practices, associated with that belief. So Sylvester Long, who knew his Indian-identified maternal grandmother, and who grew up in a family considered by many to be Indian, is reconstructed in recent criticism as one who merely "passes" as an Indian, "performs" as an Indian, and eventually comes to think of himself as Indian. The assumptions found in Hodge's 1907 *Handbook of American Indians* still seem to predominate as perpetually "official," although challenged by many scholars, Karen Blu among them. McBride's assignment of "black" blood is based on assumptions about geography, the institution of slavery, and the authority of historically situated but still powerful "official" texts such as the 1907 *Handbook*. McBride is by no means alone in making these assumptions, for ones like them appear in even the most "theoretical" critical studies of ethnography in the 1990s.

Among the most thorough treatments of Long Lance, and one of few to offer a reading of *The Silent Enemy*, Fatimah Tobing Rony provides a sophisticated analysis of the film in the context of turn-of-the-century ethnography. Still, I am deeply troubled by her reading of Long Lance, as given here:

> The ideology of how *The Silent Enemy* reflects the Western pastime of picturing Native Americans as Noble Savages struggling to survive in the wild is belied by the biographies of the main actors of the film. . . . The handsome star Long Lance was also a Carlyle [sic] graduate, but had embellished a whole Indian biography for himself. Although he claimed he was a chief and a war hero, historians have discovered that he was listed as a "colored" soldier in World War I rosters. Both he and Yellow Robe were part of the New York social life: they could eat at the Explorer's Club, a wealthy elite men's club in New York, a privilege which, as an African American man, Long Lance would never have been granted.[42]

Rony names privileges enjoyed by Indians that recall the ones named by Karen Blu, for which the Lumbee were willing to "fight so hard not to be classified with Blacks." In order to establish the distance between Indians pictured as "Noble Savages" and Indians as active participants in elite forms of white culture (eating at the Explorer's Club), Rony uses Long Lance, figured as "African American," to help gauge the distance. With Long Lance figured as black for comparative purposes, other assumptions associated with blackness are given free play.

Rony asserts that an "Indian" biography, rather than a *Blood* Indian biography, is an embellishment. Again, the "biological" one drop of "black" blood asserts itself. In Rony's passage not only does it make Indian identity an embellishment, but also it keeps Long Lance from occupying the category of "war hero," as if "war hero" and "'colored' soldier" are mutually exclusive categories. And finally, when inside the Explorer's Club, where Long Lance hobnobbed with the very ethnographers who were best able to expose his ruse (among them Hodge, the *Handbook of American Indians* editor), Long Lance loses any possible remnant of his Indian heritage as Rony names him "an African American man." Once again Long Lance has been figured as one who "passed," not as a Blood Indian chief but as an Indian. Rony becomes complicit in the same biological racism she critiques so ably elsewhere in the book. For all her elaborate critique of the way that white imperialist culture imagined and then realized socially a racialized, and inferior, "Other," Rony can't refuse all of the biologically racist assumptions white imperialist culture has created.

These writers and others tolerate, justify, or even celebrate Long Lance's transgressions: his almost Franklinian self-invention and self-improvement, his attractive sexuality, his masquerade as a Blood Indian chief, his place among a white social elite, and the way in which, through his published writing and film performance, he flaunted his "imposter" status. Although some of these writers critique the system that encourages performances such as Long Lance's, each identifies *blackness* as the signifier, par excellence, of transgression. And thus we return to Herman Gray's claims in his work on scandal and race:

> Race continues to quietly organize the discursive terms through which the boundaries of the American social, cultural, and moral order are made visible and maintained. . . . [R]ace as a signifier helps to make such boundaries and those who transgress them visible and representable; thus black social visibility, in contrast to white social locations and discursive positions, and the racist cultural discourse through which blackness is assigned negative value, also helps to subject such transgression to intense policing, mythical representation, and, where necessary, brutal enforcement.[43]

The narrative of transgression constructed around the life of Sylvester Long/ Long Lance demands that he be figured as "black." After all, what story would we tell of an Indian trying to "pass" as an Indian?

Although compulsively represented as "black," Long Lance also remains the "ideal" Indian, an almost mythic figure around whom fantasies of racial identification have been constructed. As the silent enemy, he threatens to expose the social construction of racial identity and calls into question persistent ideas about a biological basis; as emblematic, he threatens both white America's image of the Indian and Native Americans' image of themselves. In this role Long Lance indeed proves paradoxically both mythic and problematically real, revealing that to be represented as or to represent oneself as Indian is to play a role. Moreover, Long Lance reminds us that we are all enacting our own narratives of "passing."

NOTES

Many thanks to Kelly Dennis for her helpful insight and guidance in the revision of this essay, to Donald Smith for his dedication to Long Lance and his thorough scholarship, and to Barbara Hall of the Margaret Herrick Library of the Academy of Motion Picture Arts and Sciences for assistance in my research.

1. Throughout this essay I will use *Indian* to signify the conceptualization and representation of Native Americans as they were imagined during the historical periods discussed. I will use *Native American* to suggest a contemporary, and distinct, notion of identity for the tribal people of North America.

2. Kevin Brownlow, *The War, the West, and the Wilderness* (New York: Alfred A. Knopf, 1979), 551. I preserve Burden's spelling of "Blackfoot," a spelling more common in Canada. The preferred spelling for tribal members in the United States is "Blackfeet." Producer Douglas Burden recounted Long Lance's résumé for film historian Kevin Brownlow, but he left out any information that would suggest the scandal involving Long Lance's identity. Either Burden's memory had faded significantly when he spoke with Brownlow (Burden had been involved in the investigation into Long Lance's identity and knew he was not a chief of the Blood band of the Blackfeet) or his desire to preserve the illusion of authenticity in *The Silent Enemy* prevented him from recalling for Brownlow the circumstances of Long's unmasking during the film's production.

3. The city of Winston-Salem is important here, for had Long been born and raised in another part of North Carolina, particularly the southern region, he and his family might have been legally recognized as Indians.

4. "The Silent Enemy," *Variety*, May 21, 1930.

5. Author Irvin S. Cobb, Long Lance's one-time friend, was among those who shunned him. On hearing the rumor, Cobb allegedly said, "To think we had him here in the house. We're so ashamed! We entertained a nigger" (anecdote told to Donald B. Smith by Earl Parker Hanson, quoted in Donald B. Smith, *Long Lance: The True Story of an Imposter* [Lincoln: University of Nebraska Press, 1982], 196).

6. Herman Gray, "Anxiety, Desire, and Conflict in the American Racial Imagination," in James Lull and Stephen Hinerman, eds., *Media Scandals: Morality and Desire in the Popular Culture Marketplace* (New York: Columbia University Press, 1997), 86, 89.

7. Cooper, like Burden, fashioned himself an explorer-adventurer, and *Chang* (1927) remains a quintessential example of a film in the tradition of "ethnographic

romanticism." For a good treatment of this tradition, and of *Chang*, see Fatimah Tob-ing Rony, *The Third Eye: Race, Cinema, and Ethnographic Spectacle* (Durham, N.C.: Duke University Press, 1996), 129–137.

8. Brownlow, *The War*, 550.

9. Michael J. Riley, "Trapped in the History of Film: Racial Conflict and Allure in *The Vanishing American*," in Peter Rollins and John E. O'Connor, eds., *Holly-wood's Indian: The Portrayal of the Native American in Film* (Lexington: University Press of Kentucky, 1998), 62, 67.

10. Rony, *Third Eye*, 138.

11. Ibid., 78, 80.

12. Robert Berkhofer, *The White Man's Indian: Images of the American Indian from Columbus to the Present* (New York: Vintage Books, 1979), 29. I preserve Berk-hofer's use of the masculine pronoun here because the assumptions Berkhofer articu-lates are gendered and because the masculine ideal for Native Americans is important in the construction, as well as defamation, of Long Lance.

13. Brownlow, *The War*, 551.

14. Smith, *Long Lance*, 168.

15. Brownlow, *The War*, 551.

16. Smith, *Long Lance*, 167.

17. W. Douglas Burden, quoted in Bunny McBride, *Molly Spotted Elk: A Penob-scot in Paris* (Norman: University of Oklahoma Press, 1995), 105.

18. Brownlow, *The War*, 554.

19. Robert E. Sherwood, "Motion Picture Album," *New York Post*, May 17, 1930.

20. Smith, *Long Lance*, 175.

21. *The Silent Enemy* (Paramount, 1930; reissued in 1991 by Video Yesteryear [Sandy Hook, Conn.]).

22. McBride, *Molly Spotted Elk*, 113.

23. The following series of naive assumptions and stereotypes of Native Ameri-cans have a long and complex history. Assumptions such as the ones I enumerate can be found in "classics" of American literature such as Cooper's Leatherstocking books and the works of Francis Parkman. That they persisted into the twentieth century is evidenced by the program and press book for *The Silent Enemy*, which will be dis-cussed in this essay. For overviews of stereotypical and racist assumptions about Native Americans see Berkhofer, *White Man's Indian*; and Scott B. Vickers, *Native American Identities: From Stereotype to Archetype in Art and Literature* (Albuquerque: Univer-sity of New Mexico Press, 1998), two among dozens of treatments of this subject. For clarity I have placed such assumptions within quotation marks.

24. Quoted in McBride, *Molly Spotted Elk*, 117.

25. Sheet 3, PCA file "Red Gods," *The Silent Enemy* files, Paramount Collection, Special Collections, Margaret Herrick Library, Academy of Motion Picture Arts and Sciences, Beverly Hills, Calif.

26. Ibid.

27. McBride, *Molly Spotted Elk*, 19.

28. Ibid., 118.

29. Ibid., 110.

30. Letter from William Chanler to Ilia Tolstoy, March 26, 1930, from the Long Lance papers deposited at the Glenbow Museum, Calgary, Alberta.

31. Ibid.

32. Fatimah Tobing Rony describes how such markers could be both literally and

symbolically erased when it suited ethnographic needs for authenticity: in Edward S. Curtis's 1914 film, *In the Land of the Headhunters*, which was promoted as an authentic representation of Kwakiutl tribal life at the time, the native actors "wore cedar bark costumes and wigs and were made to shave off moustaches." Rony, *Third Eye*, 93.

33. For a thorough treatment of the Native American peoples now called "Lumbee" see Karen I. Blu, *The Lumbee Problem: The Making of an American Indian People* (Cambridge: Cambridge University Press, 1980). My discussion of the politics of racial identification, the Croatan, and the Lumbee owes much to her work.

34. Blu, *Lumbee Problem*, 32.

35. Quoted in Blu, *Lumbee Problem*, 77–78.

36. Souvenir program, *How "The Silent Enemy" Was Made*, 5, 7.

37. From Paramount *Press Sheets*, August 1, 1930–July 31, 1931 (release date August 2, 1930), 7. Paramount Collection, Margaret Herrick Library, Academy of Motion Picture Arts and Sciences, Beverly Hills, Calif.

38. Ibid., 3.

39. James A. Clifton, "Alternate Identities and Cultural Frontiers," in James A. Clifton, ed., *Being and Becoming Indian: Biographical Studies of North American Frontiers* (Chicago: Dorsey Press, 1989), 23.

40. McBride, *Molly Spotted Elk*, 104.

41. Ibid.

42. Rony, *Third Eye*, 143.

43. Gray, "Anxiety," 86–87.

Ecstasy

Female Sexual, Social, and Cinematic Scandal

Lucy Fischer

'Ecstasy Girl"

> Mass newspapers use stars for their own ends: they can be the occasion
> of scandals. . . . Stars [also] provide newspapers with the vehicle for dis-
> cussion of sexuality, of the domain of the personal and the familial.
>
> John Ellis[1]

In its long and checkered history Hollywood has survived a variety of scandals. Some, like those surrounding Fatty Arbuckle or Charles Chaplin, have involved a performer's supposed sexual "misconduct" and troubles with the law. Others, like those circulating around Dalton Trumbo and the members of the "Hollywood Ten," have entailed an individual's political beliefs and activities. In certain cases, like those concerning John Belushi or Robert Downey Jr., a star's alleged drug use has taken center stage. Other instances have attached more to the filmic object than to any human being. In 1997, for example, a controversy swirled around the release of a new version of *Lolita* — considered too prurient for American tastes. Thus, if Hollywood has been our quintessential Dream Factory, it has also been our premier School for Scandal.

If this is true, one of its star pupils was Hedy Lamarr (or "Hedy Glamarr," as *Photoplay* once deemed her).[2] For in 1933 she assumed a leading part in a Tinseltown scandal that engaged both her person and persona and revolved around her role in the film *Ecstasy*. It was this screen incarnation that, *Photoplay*'s Sara

Hamilton observed, "upset . . . the motion picture apple cart" and "brought back to the screen at a time when motion pictures needed it most—sex and glamour" (74). It also led to Lamarr's perennial fame as The Ecstasy Girl.

Originally entitled *Extase*, the film was made by Gustave Machaty in Czechoslovakia in 1933. It concerns a young bride, Eva (played by Hedy "Kiesler," later to become "Lamarr"),[3] whose elderly husband, Emile (Jaromir Rogoz), is sexually impotent. Leaving him, she returns to her father's country estate where she meets Adam (Aribert Mog), a young engineer with whom she has a passionate affair. When her husband realizes this, he kills himself, an act that dampens the lovers' illicit ardor. In most versions the film ends with the couple setting out together on a train voyage, but at the last moment (while Adam naps on a railroad platform bench) Eva steals away.[4]

Predictably, it was the lovers' sexual liaison that caused an international uproar (that "stirred up" a "hornet's nest," as a *Variety* critic put it).[5] *Ecstasy* was denounced by Pope Pius XII in Rome,[6] banned in Nazi Germany, and cut for its Paris release at the Pigalle Theater. In London, although screened by small film societies, it was not released from an L.C.C. ban until 1938.[7] In New York the film was attacked by Al Smith, active in the Legion of Decency.[8] When an attempt was made to exhibit it in 1935, the U.S. Customs Department labeled the film obscene—a decision supported by the Customs Court and the New York Department of Education.[9] When the distributor (J. A. Koerpel of Eureka Productions) later challenged these pronouncements, the case was taken to the United States Supreme Court, which, in 1937, upheld the lower court's decision. *Ecstasy* did not have an American commercial run until 1941. But if, as one reporter claimed, the "picture . . . startled censors wherever shown," we might still inquire: What was so "startling" about it?[10]

Had *Ecstasy* passed the Board of Censors it still would have been denied wide exhibition in America because it failed to meet the standards of the Hollywood "Production Code." In fact, Joseph Breen (the Code's administrator) called *Ecstasy* "dangerously indecent."[11] Various aspects of the film contravened the Code's moral assumptions. Primary was Eva's extramarital interlude, a lapse that countered the Code's commitment to "correct standards of life."[12] The Code quite explicitly privileged the "sanctity of the institution of marriage" and forbade the direct or empathetic treatment of adultery (242). In one reedited, postcensorship version of *Ecstasy* (dating from the 1930s), a passage was inserted in which Eva files for divorce, an action meant to mitigate her marital trespass. And a writer for *Variety* noted that in a version prepared for the film's 1940s New York City release the distributor, Sam Cummins, "ingeniously introduced into the film a diary and—shortly before the much-billed 'ecstatic' moment—written in the book are the words '[We] were secretly married today.' Also, just to make sure the official snippers get the idea, the moment before le moment ecstatique, a voice, supposed to be Hedy's declares in very measured and clear English: . . . 'I must—tell—father—WE—ARE—MARRIED.'" [13] The columnist notes further that although the marital plot of this "whitewashed" version made the couple's relationship "legal," it also made it "dull" (24). The title of his column says it all: "Cummins gives *Ecstasy* the Switch (And How!)."

Although the suicide of Eva's husband, Emile (and the resultant "pall" it throws on Eva's romance), constitutes a certain "punishment" for her sexual malfeasance, the film remains sympathetic to her plight, another affront to the Production Code's rules for moral identification. Emile's sexual dysfunction might also have violated the Code, which warned against the portrayal of "perversion." [14]

One of the most outrageous aspects of the film was the sequence in which Eva runs nude through a field then takes a swim in the buff—the occasion for her meeting Adam. The camera voyeuristically tracks through the trees to discover her at a distance, in full figure, undressed. In other closer shots her bare torso emerges from the water as she comes up for air. The Code specifically bars "complete nudity" (even in "silhouette") or any "lecherous or licentious notice thereof" (243). Evidently, in Cummins's 1941 version of the film, a minute of this sequence was cut. As a *Variety* critic reveals, however, "it was *the* minute."

Hedy Lamarr in the nude scene from *Ecstasy.* Courtesy the Museum of Modern Art Film Stills Archive.

He complains that, now, "even the most imaginative adolescent will have to stretch some to get a flicker" of wantonness.[15]

A WOMAN'S FACE

My face has been my misfortune. It has attracted six unsuccessful marriage partners. It has attracted all the wrong people into my boudoir and brought me tragedy and heartache for five decades. My face is a mask I cannot remove: I must always live with it. I curse it.

HEDY LAMARR[16]

But it is the manner in which Machaty filmed Eva and Adam's first sexual encounter that was most scandalous in its evasion of the Code's prohibition of "scenes of passion."[17] Specifically, the Code shunned "lustful embraces" and "suggestive postures and gestures" that might "stimulate the [audience's] lower and baser elements."

Viewed from today's perspective, the sequence is amazingly chaste. Both characters are fully clothed as they make love on a bed, and often Adam seems to be sitting beside Eva rather than embracing her. What we do see is a montage of synechdocal close-ups that evoke the sinful event: Eva's hand dropping, skimming the shag rug; her necklace of pearls breaking and falling to the ground; her chest heaving in erotic hyperventilation; and finally, her face in a grimace of ecstasy. It was this final iconic image for which the film became notorious. As the actress recalls, "The primary objection was *not* the nude swimming scene, which you have no doubt heard so much about, or the sequence of my fanny twinkling through the woods, but the close-up of my *face*, in that cabin sequence where the camera records the reactions of a love-starved bride in the act of sexual intercourse."[18] It will be our project to inquire why this woman's visage was so provocative and whom it provoked. What proved so shocking about A Woman's Face?

According to Teresa de Lauretis, in the traditional tale female characters are passive, whereas males are the prime movers of the drama. Women are "inscribed in hero narratives, in someone else's story, not their own; so they are figures or markers of positions . . . through which the hero and his story move to their destination and accomplish their meaning."[19] For a film of 1933 *Ecstasy* radically opposes this pattern, especially around the locus of sexuality. It is Eva's desire (an improper one at that) that propels the story forward, that makes her *act*. On Eva's wedding night (like a traditional Sleeping Beauty) she awaits her groom, only to find that he avoids sex by obsessively folding his clothes, arranging his slippers, straightening the fringe on a rug, and fussing with his toilette. Finally, she acts — by confiscating his toothbrush and attempting a seduction. When this aborts, she languishes on the bed and looks out the window, despondently eyeing an amorous pair. On another occasion, as she and Emile sit at a lakeside cafe, she furtively regards romantic couples dancing, jealous of their intimacy. She soon leaves Emile, returning to her father's baronial estate. If Eva represents Eros, Emile signifies Thanatos; if she acts sexually, he fails to "perform."

After meeting Adam, Eva pursues the relationship, brazenly invading his cabin one night (making *him* the Sleeping Beauty). It is here that they engage in their infamous erotic encounter. Hence, she is the actor within the drama on both a physical and scopophilic level. If woman is usually that "obscure *object* of desire," here she is the desiring *subject*. This reading is foregrounded by Eva's longing gazes that affix to the lovers she watches. But it is also figured in Machaty's visual representation of her passion. Depressed and frustrated on her wedding night, she lies alone on her bed, positioned upside down on the covers (as though to signal transgression). As she throws her head backward, the camera cranes down her body in a highly sensual fashion. Later it scans her torso, revealing the conjugal void beside her.

Clearly, these shots operate on a variety of levels. The cinematography is beautiful and offers a lush cinematic surface. The actress is gorgeous and can be appropriated by the male heterosexual look. But something more than this happens. The sequence communicates to us *her* desire, her wish to act in a sexual way. Hence, it also addresses the female heterosexual spectator who does not desire Eva but desires to be *like her*. In certain respects the film's tendency toward "muteness" augments its eroticism, for, as Roland Barthes notes, "Bliss is unspeakable, inter-dicted."[20] Although *Ecstasy* is technically a sound film, it has only moments of dialogue, and proceeds more like a silent movie with musical score.

Part of its sensuous effect resides in its temporality; for Machaty expends enormous footage documenting Eva's longing, eschewing the tyranny of plot and event. At the time of the film's failed American release, a *Newsweek* critic commented on this (with a degree of irony), tying the film's pacing to its eroticism: "One sequence shows Hedy's face in close-up while in the arms of her lover. Last week Representative Culkin (Republican) introduced a measure to outlaw pictures 'which unnecessarily prolong expressions or demonstrations of passionate love.' The representative suggested no time limit."[21]

The same languishing pace marks the segment preceding Eva's sexual tryst with Adam. One night she sits in her father's house alone, dressed in a lounging gown. As though to quell her corporeal heat, she stirs and imbibes an iced drink. She sits by a window and smokes a cigarette (as though to mark herself a modern woman). Intercut are images of her father's statuary — all evocative of the erotic: muscular horses, a Pan figure with pipes. The curtains blow in from the mounting wind, as though nature mirrors her physical turmoil. It is then that she walks to Adam's cabin. As she kisses him a superimposed image of her body separates from its "original" — as though to connote her rebirth through sexuality. Again, what we have here is a sense of Eva as the female agent of the narrative. It is her desire that is blatantly represented, that moves the drama toward frenzy. If, as Mary Ann Doane tells us, the forties cinema imagined a woman who could only desire *to* desire, Eva was well ahead of her time.

The Pleasure of the Text

> The geography of feminine pleasure is not worth listening to. Women are not worth listening to, especially when they try to speak of their pleasure.
> LUCE IRIGARAY[22]

But what of the sequence that follows, the film's most torrid—the segment that one critic ironically deemed "le moment ecstatique"?[23] Clearly, in the breaking of Eva's necklace we have an intimation of her loss of virginity—a state originally intended for her wedding night. On that evening, however, when she asked her husband to undo her necklace, he managed only to scratch his finger on its clasp. Thus, strangely, *he* bleeds for their nuptials rather than she. But it is Eva's face (photographed from above, on the bed) to which we must return—as to the repressed.

What seems scandalous about this iconic image (one registered abstractly in the Czechoslovakian film poster used to sell the movie) is its simple *acknowledgment* of female sexual pleasure—a fact that, Irigaray tells us, must be denied. As we apprehend Eva's face there can be no doubt that she experiences promised ecstasy. Gloria Steinem, in fact, deems it "the first female orgasm on screen."[24] It has been a commonplace of contemporary feminist criticism to remark how man is uncomfortable with female sexuality as it connotes for him a phallic "lack" and an absence of something to *see*. As Irigaray remarks, woman constitutes "a defect in [the masculine] systematics of representation and desire. A 'hole' in its scoptophilic lens."[25] (Perhaps this is why Machaty continually shows Emile fussing with his spectacles—a sign of his discomfort with vision.) In *Hard Core* Linda Williams argues that pornography's relentless focus on the ejaculating penis bespeaks its inability to figure *female* sexual response. As she notes, "The history of hard-core film could . . . be summarized in part as the history of the various strategies devised to overcome this problem of invisibility."[26] The shots of Eva are one such solution—one that no longer shocks or convinces us.

After their initial kiss, Adam disappears below the frame line, embracing Eva as he sinks down. What is intimated here is that he is kissing her lower body parts and, perhaps, engaging in oral sex. Thus, her pleasure may not be purely vaginal—a fact that subverts woman's "proper" Freudian sexual maturation.[27] Thus, *Ecstasy* allows for female *jouissance* and a "sex which is not one." It also represents female desire as a driving force within the natural schema: hence the film intercuts Eva's affair with shots of horses mating, bees pollinating, and flowers dripping dew (images worthy of Georgia O'Keeffe). Hence, woman acts not only on a diegetic level (as agent of the narrative) but in the erotic realm (in the delta of Venus).[28]

On one level the story told in *Ecstasy* has an archetypal aura. With the hero and heroine named Adam and Eve, it invokes the biblical story of Genesis. One senses that Machaty proposes that we begin the world anew, with a healthier, more earthy, attitude toward sexuality. And for some viewers he succeeded: one critic claims that the "portrayal of passion" in the film is "sometimes primitive . . . but never crude."[29]

But the film can also be placed within a particular social/historical context — that of the 1920s and early 1930s. Frederick Lewis Allen speaks of the twenties (in both Europe and the United States) as involving a "revolt of the younger generation";[30] similarly, Walter Lippmann notes a "revolution in . . . sexual morals."[31] Various causes are cited for this social upheaval, some attaching to World War I. Allen speaks of the hedonistic "eat-drink-and-be-merry, for-tomorrow-we-die spirit,"[32] and Samuel D. Schmalhausen talks of soldiers' sexual experimentation.[33] But commentators also realized that the upheaval was tied to the status of *women*. V. F. Calverton writes: "One feature of this revolt that is seldom recognized is that its predominant emphasis is feminine."[34]

Numerous changes configured a New Woman. Allen speaks of her cosmetics, short skirts, cigarette smoking, liberation from housework, and job outside the home.[35] But central was the revolution in sexuality. Calverton cites the advances in contraception that "could remove [woman's] fear, and shift the emphasis in sex life from the procreational to the recreational."[36] The effect of this was twofold. It loosened the constraints linking sex to marriage. As Calverton writes: "The sexual element in life can be satisfied outside of marriage and without many of the impediments which the marital life enforces upon the . . . woman" (122). This led to an increased divorce rate,[37] with a rise in the number of women leaving men.[38]

Contemporary morals also allowed that women might seek erotic satisfaction in and of itself. Calverton states, "The 'sowing of wild oats' is no longer the particular prerogative of the man."[39] Other commentators bemoaned how the cult of premarital purity made women sexually dysfunctional. As Floyd Dell notes, "[I]t was not easy for angels to become suddenly human. Sex did not cease to be 'disgusting' when it was permitted in marriage. . . . The most thoroughgoing successes of the teaching of youthful 'purity' thus resulted in sexually frigid wives."[40]

The turmoil of the twenties also revealed a certain "theatricality" in the established moral universe. Allen calls the "wholesome," "old-fashioned lady" a "sham";[41] Lippmann questions whether society is seeing "more promiscuity or less hypocrisy";[42] Schmalhausen talks of how the "*props*" of "civilized etiquette" are disintegrating;[43] Calverton calls modern marriage a "fiction"[44] and uses the same term to describe its Victorian fantasy of a virginal wife: "certain women have had to prostitute themselves in order that other women might remain respectable and that monogamous marriage continue as a flexible *fiction*" (169, my italics). Hence, the twenties liberated women from a certain degree of social posturing.

Unfortunately, with the stock market crash of 1929 and the onset of the Depression, many gains were lost. Lois Banner suggests that the "'lady-like look' once again became the cynosure of the American woman,"[45] and Robert L. Daniel notes that, with the Depression, there came a reactionary trend. Thus, "[w]omen's magazines . . . repeatedly reaffirmed traditional views of woman's role as wife and mother."[46]

Clearly, the traces of social uproar are evident in *Ecstasy*. Eva is a New Woman who feels a right to sexual fulfillment. With divorce no longer an insurmountable obstacle, she can leave her husband. With fears of pregnancy abated, she can experiment with extra-marital intercourse because sex no longer "induce[s] ruin."[47] (Interestingly, one of the images that scandalized censors in the film was a box of condoms on the groom's nightstand—a prop that, ironically, goes unused.) Even the famous ecstatic shots of Eva's face invoke a new order. As Schmalhausen notes, "The happy slogan of the newer generation of feminists, honoring love as radiant passion, is: orgasms for women."[48] Finally, Eva's identification with Nature (with horses, flowers, and bees) marks her resistance to the rigid gender masquerade of the human world.

Although most of *Ecstasy* attests to the rise of female freedom in the 1920s, its highly ambiguous (and contested) ending may represent its foreclosure in the 1930s. In the prints of the film that currently circulate in the United States, after Eva leaves Adam at the train station, the narrative implies a temporal ellipsis. We next find Adam at one of his work sites, supervising laborers in the construction of some public work. A Soviet-influenced montage transpires of men wielding pickaxes, drills, and shovels. As Adam oversees the project, he looks around and notices several of the workers' wives tending to their babies. As he contemplates this scene, we see a shot of Eva with a baby, a shot we interpret as imagined from Adam's point of view. In the next shot we see the silhouettes of a man and a woman (ostensibly Adam and Eva) meeting and embracing in the woods.

The status of this denouement is highly questionable as most descriptions of the original film imply that it ends at the railroad platform.[49] At what point this additional material was added is not clear, but it seems to be one of many responses to the censorship battles. Its effect is to radically tame the scandalous aspects of the narrative. It marks a shift of erotic energy into the more "productive" social field of masculine manual labor. It also charts the move of Eva's sexual work to her maternal labor in its postpartum figuration of her. Hence female sexuality is once more harnessed to maternity in true Freudian fashion. Even the language in which social commentators described the sexual revolution of the time revealed the connection of eroticism and motherhood. As Schmalhausen remarks, "The newer freedom must go through its *birth pangs* that are anything but beautiful and delay while in disgusting *swaddling clothes* . . . until freedom in sex and love *creates an individuality* of its own."[50]

Interestingly, after Lamarr had spent several years in Hollywood, press coverage of her worked to inoculate the public against her scandalous aura by highlighting her new maternal role. A 1940 interview with Louella Parsons (melodramatically entitled "My Fight for Jimmy") catalogs Lamarr's travails in maintaining custody of her adopted child once her second marriage (to Gene Markey) had collapsed. We are told that, eventually, "[t]he Children's Society . . . saw the tears on Hedy's cheeks — and wisely decided that the screen's greatest beauty is also one of the finest mothers in the world."[51]

HER LIFE AS A WOMAN

Hedy's is one life story I should love to film, but wouldn't dare. Audiences wouldn't believe it.

A HOLLYWOOD PRODUCER[52]

When *Ecstasy* was released, Kiesler was only twenty years old. As a teenager, she had been enamored of the theater and had gone to study with Max Reinhardt in Berlin.[53] She recalls: "By 1919, I was spending my pocket money 'escaping' into the world of make-believe offered by the movie magazines. I began to think about becoming an actress."[54] Returning to Vienna, she was cast in a series of movies: *Geld Auf Der Strasse* (1930) and *Sturm Im Wasserglas* (1931), both directed by George Jacoby; *Wir Brauchen Kein Geld* (1931), directed by Karl Boese; and *Die Koffer Des Herrn O. F.* (1932), directed by Alexis Granowsky.

In her much-contested 1966 autobiography, *Ecstasy and Me: My Life as a Woman*, Lamarr describes the circumstances of the making of her most famous film. She claims that, initially, she was not told there would be a nude scene. When she hesitated to film it, Machaty intimidated her. As Lamarr recalls, "The director shouted: 'If you do not do this scene, the picture will be ruined, and we will collect our losses from you!' . . . To emphasize his masterfulness, he picked up a small block of wood, and threw it in my general direction." To add insult to injury, he fired a gun on the set, to signal the moment she should undress.[55]

According to Lamarr, a similar sadism informed his filming of the infamous intercourse scene. Machaty told her to lie down with her hands above her head. As Aribert Mog caressed her, she closed her eyes. Machaty ordered her to stop, dissatisfied with her simulation of sexual climax. As she recollects, "He mumbled about the stupidity of youth. He looked around and found a safety pin on a table. He picked it up, bent it almost straight, and approached. 'You will lie here,' he said. 'I will be underneath, out of camera range. When I prick you a little on your backside, you will bring your elbows together and you will *react!*'" (29). According to Lamarr, that is how the sequence was filmed. She reminisces further:

"Some of those pinpricks shot pain through my body until it was vibrating in every nerve. I remember one shot when the close-up camera caught my face in a distortion of real agony . . . and the director yelled happily, 'Ya, goot!'" (30).

We cannot attest to the veracity of Lamarr's story, although it sounds so bizarre (and unselfserving) that it would be hard to comprehend why she would concoct it. What her narrative, at least, imagines is that the iconic pose of female ecstasy was not only acted (as would be any movie sequence) but performed as a transposition of *pain* —her face masking her agony. Hence the sequence that shocked the world for its claims to female sexual *jouissance* may have been derived from familiar patterns of patriarchal subjugation — "prick" and all. Curiously, her feigned cinematic pleasure mimics that which she would later face in her troubled first marriage to munitions magnate Fritz Mandl (a man who, like Emile, was much her senior): "He would demand a night of fervent love-making and I was afraid to complain. . . . I had learned to play that role well, and I appreciated the drama of it" (33).

Lamarr eventually left Mandl in a scene rife with intrigue. *Photoplay's* Hamilton relates Hedy's dramatic "escape": "Having no money of her own, except a small sum saved from household expenses, she packed her luxurious clothes. . . . And then quietly one night during her husband's absence, with the aid of a faithful maid she crept to the depot and caught the train." (Shades of Eva fleeing the unsuspecting Adam.) For Hamilton Lamarr played "in her own life story . . . a part so thrilling that anything that [could] now happen to her on the screen [was] just so much aftermath."[56]

After leaving Mandl Lamarr was soon approached by Louis B. Mayer, and, in 1937, she signed a contract with MGM. (Mayer's choice of name for Kiesler — "Lamarr" — linked her to another scandalous star, Barbara La Marr, the "woman who was too beautiful," who died of a drug overdose in 1926.) Drawing on the fame of *Ecstasy*, MGM sold Lamarr as a "pulse-quickening" *femme fatale* for her American premiere in *Algiers* (1938).[57] This is how *Collier's* Kyle Crichton represented her to the public:

> Not only have I called on Hedy Lamarr . . . but I have come forth unscathed. My eyebrows are unsinged and anyone who says that he can smell the odor of burnt flesh about me is merely kicking the truth around. . . . It is also untrue that the asphalt in the street before Miss Lamarr's house has buckled up and is lying in a steaming cauldron. . . . Nothing so hot as Hedy Lamarr has appeared in America since Theda Bara . . . and it may be comforting to have my report that it is possible to approach within hailing distance of the lady without suffering the fate of the damned.[58]

If Lamarr failed to experience *jouissance* on the set of *Ecstasy*, she claims to have done so in countless moments of her private existence. As she tells us in her book: "In my life, as in the lives of most women, sex has been an important factor."[59] She recounts an evening at a shady nightclub, when a man mistook her for a prostitute and she went along with the ruse (22). She catalogs her lesbian attractions and the woman who "introduced [her] into . . . mysterious girl-girl relationships." (Part of that mystery, she confides, is that whenever she engaged in homosexual relations, she immediately "wanted a man" [202].) She also advises women on the joys of sexual release: "Have you ever heard a girl say she was so happy she could burst? That's what sex does at a joyous time. It really helps you 'burst'" (67). And she claims that men valued her exceptional erotic endurance: "I know this is terribly personal but [my husband] loved me because I had frequent orgasms. . . . What he didn't know was that during love affairs with all men, I had frequent orgasms" (157). At moments, she wonders if she suffers from "a kind of nymphomania" (220).

Hence, the woman who scandalized the world in the 1930s as the "Ecstasy Girl" ends her career with another scandal. For, *My Life as a Woman* extends her screen reputation to the personal realm — merging the historical and pictorial senses of the term *biograph*. While Fritz Mandl once paid huge sums of money in an attempt to acquire and suppress all extant prints of *Ecstasy*, Lamarr's autobiography exploits her notoriety some thirty years later.

But, ironically, beyond its racy content there was another scandal associated with Lamarr's literary exposé. According to David Shipman, she attempted, unsuccessfully, to suppress the production of the book, then sued her collaborators for "misrepresentation."[60] In Lamarr's *New York Times* obituary (of January 20, 2000) she is quoted as claiming that the volume was "deliberately written as an obscene, shocking, scandalous, naughty, wanton, fleshy, sensual, lecherous, lustful and scarlet version" of her life.[61] Despite such extreme charges, her lawsuit failed.

One of the odd features of Lamarr's autobiography is its prefatory and introductory testimonials, written by a physician and a psychologist. J. Lewis Bruce, M.D., attests to the miracle of Lamarr's success in a high-pressured industry: "An actress such as Miss Lamarr . . . can be thankful she survived the rough and treacherous grind at all."[62] Dr. Philip Lambert presents Lamarr as a sexual pioneer and role model: "Miss Lamarr's manifold sexual experiences, male and female, led her to the delightfully ingenuous self-prognosis that she is 'oversexed.' Her admitted talent for quick and joyful orgasm indicates an uncomplicated natural sex response. Her curious search for new love-play settings and her candid delight in unexpected sexual episodes place her in a position of psychological unassailability."[63] He recommends Lamarr's books to the "guilt-ridden reader for whom this gutsy confessional may offer resultful therapy, if not instant emancipation."

Thus, capitalizing on the moral freedom of the 1960s (and endorsements by the "male medical gaze"), it offers up an erotic scandal of the 1930s in a revised and modern form — that of sexual liberation and therapy. Hedy Lamarr meets Dr. Kinsey or, perhaps, Dr. Ruth.

Notes

1. John Ellis, "Stars as a Cinematic Phenomenon," in Gerald Mast, Marshall Cohen, and Leo Braudy, eds., *Film Theory and Criticism*, 4th ed. (New York: Oxford University Press, 1992), 617.

2. Hamilton, "Hedy Wine," *Photoplay*, October 1938, 23.

3. When Hedy Kiesler came to America in 1937, MGM renamed her Hedy Lamarr. According to Christopher Young (*The Films of Hedy Lamarr* [Secaucus, N.J.: Citadel Press, 1978]), her birth name was Hedwig Eva Maria Kiesler.

4. Given the censorship constraints around *Ecstasy*, numerous versions of the film have existed over time. Even a 1933 review in *Close Up* (signed by T. W.) refers to an "original" version that the reviewer apparently did not see (196).

5. Anonymous, "*Extase*," *Variety*, April 11, 1933, 20.

6. Jay Robert Nash and Stanley Ralph Ross, *The Motion Picture Guide, E–G, 1927–1983* (Chicago: Cinebooks, 1986), 744.

7. Peter Galway, "The Movies," *New Statesman and Nation*, February 19, 1938, 287–288.

8. Anonymous, "Entertainment/Screen: Beautiful Girl Tripping through Wood Too Much for Censors," *Newsweek*, January 19, 1935, 26.

9. Tim Kennedy, "*Ecstasy*," in Frank Magill, ed., *Magill's Cinema Survey: Foreign Language Films* (Englewood Cliffs, N.J.: Salem Press, 1985), 922–923.

10. Anonymous, "Entertainment," 26.

11. Gerald Gardner, *The Censorship Papers: Movie Censorship Letters from the Hays Office, 1934–1968* (New York: Dodd and Mead, 1987), 74.

12. Raymond Moley, *The Hays Office* (New York: Bobbs-Merrill, 1945), 241.

13. Walt., "Cummins Gives *Ecstasy* the Switch (And How!); Now It's Up to Lawyers," *Variety*, January 8, 1941, 24.

14. Moley, *Hays Office*, 242.

15. Walt., "Cummins Gives *Ecstasy*," 24.

16. Hedy Lamarr, *Ecstasy and Me: My Life as a Woman* (USA: Bartholomew House, 1966), 273. (No city of publication listed.) As regards this citation, it is important to note that, in David Shipman's *The Great Movie Stars: The Golden Years* (New York: Crown, 1970), Shipman states: "In 1966 she unsuccessfully sought an injunction against the publication of the book [*Ecstasy and Me*], and three years later, she sued her collaborators for $21 million damages for misrepresentation" (321). Similarly, in a newspaper piece ("Life after the Casbah," *Pittsburgh Post-Gazette*, August 8, 1999, G1, G4), Kate Connolly claims that Lamarr's autobiography was "written by a ghost writer" and concurs with Shipman that the actress "successfully sued the publisher for misrepresentation" (G4).

17. Moley, *Hays Office*, 242.

18. Lamarr, *Ecstasy and Me*, 18.

19. Teresa de Lauretis, *Alice Doesn't: Feminism, Semiotics, Cinema* (Bloomington: Indiana University Press, 1984), 109.

20. Roland Barthes, *The Pleasure of the Text*, trans. Richard Miller (New York: Hill and Wang, 1975), 21.

21. Anonymous, "Entertainment," 26.

22. Luce Irigaray, *This Sex Which Is Not One*, trans. Catherine Porter (Ithaca, N.Y.: Cornell University Press, 1985), 90.

23. Walt., "Cummins Gives *Ecstasy*," 24.

24. Gloria Steinem, "Women in the Dark: Of Sex Goddesses, Abuse, and Dreams," *Ms.*, January-February 1991, 37.

25. Irigaray, *This Sex*, 26.

26. Linda Williams, *Hard Core: Power, Pleasure, and the Frenzy of the Visible* (Berkeley: University of California Press, 1989), 49.

27. In her article "On Sara Kofman's *L'enigme de la femme*" (*DisCourse* 4 [winter 1981–1982]: 34), Evlyn Gould summarizes the Freudian position as follows: "In order for a young girl to become a woman, the ambivalence of the female child towards her mother must be transformed into hatred and the clitoral erogenous zone given up for the vagina. Freud explains that this transfer of erogenous zones predisposes women to hysteria since it requires the repression of the virile, phallic pleasure of clitoral masturbation. In fact, hysteria . . . is almost inevitable in female sexuality because of the double erogenous zones: one masculine, one feminine."

28. I am referring to the erotic writings of Anais Nin in *Delta of Venus: Erotica* (New York: Harcourt Brace Jovanovich, 1977). Although, for its time, *Ecstasy* went a long way toward representing female desire, I would not want to downplay its more conventional aspects. Clearly, Eva is, selectively, figured for the male gaze; there are no nude shots of Adam nor any in which he is equally privileged as an object of beauty. Nonetheless, within the context of the narrative, Eva's imaging also allows for a more progressive reading—one that foregrounds her desire rather than the spectator's.

29. Anonymous, "*Extase*," 39.

30. Frederick Lewis Allen, *Only Yesterday: An Informal History of the Nineteen-Twenties* (New York: Harper, 1931), 94.

31. Walter Lippman, *A Preface to Morals* (New York: Macmillan, 1929), 288.

32. Allen, *Only Yesterday*, 94.

33. Samuel D. Schmalhausen, "The Sexual Revolution," in V. F. Calverton and S. D. Schmalhausen, eds., *Sex in Civilization* (New York: Macaulay, 1929), 373.

34. V. F. Calverton, *The Bankruptcy of Marriage* (New York: Macaulay, 1928), 22.

35. Allen, *Only Yesterday*, 89–97.

36. Calverton, *Bankruptcy*, 121.

37. Allen, *Only Yesterday*, 115.

38. Calverton, *Bankruptcy*, 75.

39. Ibid., 91.

40. Floyd Dell, *Love in the Machine Age* (New York: Farrar and Rinehart, 1930), 62.

41. Allen, *Only Yesterday*, 112.

42. Lippman, *Preface*, 186.

43. Schmalhausen, *Sexual Revolution*, 367 (my italics).

44. Calverton, *Bankruptcy*, 169.

45. Lois Banner, *Women in Modern America: A Brief History* (New York: Harcourt Brace Jovanovich, 1974), 197.

46. Robert Daniel, *American Women in the Twentieth Century: The Festival of Life* (New York: Harcourt Brace Jovanovich, 1987), 87.

47. Calverton, *Bankruptcy*, 142.

48. Schmalhausen, *Sexual Revolution*, 380.

49. Young, *Films of Hedy Lamarr*, 96.

50. Schmalhausen, *Sexual Revolution*, 402.

51. Louella Parsons, "My Fight for Jimmy: An Exclusive Interview with Hedy Lamarr," *Photoplay*, October 1940, 82.

52. Quoted in Hamilton, "Hedy Wine," 74.

53. Young, *Films of Hedy Lamarr*, 13.

54. Lamarr, *Ecstasy*, 17–18.

55. Ibid., 27–28. See note 16 for the reasons I refer to Lamarr's autobiography as "much-contested."

56. Hamilton, "Hedy Wine," 74.

57. Richard Griffith, ed., *The Talkies: Articles and Illustrations from "Photoplay Magazine," 1928–1940* (New York: Dover, 1971), 198.

58. Kyle Crichton, "Escape to Hollywood," *Collier's*, November 5, 1938, 14.

59. Lamarr, *Ecstasy*, 11.

60. Shipman, *Great Movie Stars*, 321.

61. Hedy Lamarr quoted in Richard Severo, "Hedy Lamarr, Sultry Star Who Reigned in Hollywood of 30's and 40's, Dies at 86," *New York Times*, January 20, 2000, B15.

62. J. Lewis Bruce, introduction to Lamarr, *Ecstasy* (no page numbers listed).

63. Phillip Lambert, "Preface" to Lamarr, *Ecstasy* (no pages listed).

As Red as a Burlesque Queen's Garters

Cold War Politics and the Actors' Lab in Hollywood

Cynthia Baron

In February 1948 a small but remarkably significant skirmish in the series of encounters between Hollywood craftspeople and the anticommunist movement came to a head. The confrontation took place during what might seem a hiatus in the divisive investigations that sought to expose un-American activity in the film industry. The events in 1948 did not eventually lead to the imprisonment of the individuals who declined to answer the question, "Are you now, or have you ever been, a member of the Communist Party?" Nor did the events prompt an outpouring of highly visible support as had been the case a few months earlier in October 1947, when Hollywood luminaries traveled to Washington to express their objections to the proceedings of the U.S. House Un-American Activities Committee (HUAC). The confrontation in early 1948 did, however, result in the blacklisting of numerous craftspeople, among them actors Roman Bohnen, J. Edward Bromberg, Rose Hobart, and Will Lee, who were called to appear before the California State Fact-Finding Committee on Un-American Activities, known as the "little Dies Committee," or the Tenney Committee for its chairman and driving force, Jack B. Tenney. The confrontation would also lead directly to the closing of the Actors' Laboratory, a respected Hollywood theater company and one of the nation's most important centers for actor training, and precipitate the deaths of Lab members Roman Bohnen and J. Edward Bromberg.

The showdown between the Tenney Committee and the Actors' Lab was one of many occasions in which Americans of opposing perspectives performed their respective positions in large gesture. It dramatized the political, economic, and social tensions that defined American society in the Truman years and underscored the dynamics of an important scandal of the period, communist influence in Hollywood. Fears about communist influence in Hollywood were tied to beliefs that the Communist Party had gained control of craft organizations in the industry and that its influence would jeopardize the capital investment and profit system already in place. Studio executives were not alone in their concerns about communist influence. A Gallup Poll conducted in April 1947 reported that 61 percent of the American public supported outlawing the Communist Party. In February 1948 another Gallup Poll revealed that 35 percent of the public believed the Communist Party "was getting stronger and was already in control of important elements in the economy [and that] ten percent of the public thought that the Communist Party was reaching the point where it could dominate the nation."[1]

Growing union membership (from three million in 1932 to nine million in 1940) represented the most important social change of the decade. Moreover, as George Lipsitz points out, with labor unrest fueled by 25 percent of war workers out of jobs by the winter of 1945–1946, "more strikes took place in the twelve months after V-J Day [August 14, 1945] than in any other comparable period in American history."[2] In Hollywood, as elsewhere, critics of the labor unrest sweeping America consistently stressed the idea that communists were instigating strikes as part of a larger plan to overthrow the country. In such a climate demands by Hollywood craftspeople for wage increases, employment benefits, and policies that reflected fair labor practices were seen by some segments of the film industry as threats to "American ideals." Based on the rationale that Hollywood workers would have been satisfied with their wages and working conditions were it not for Communist Party agitators, industry professionals—who, like 35 percent of the American public, believed that the Communist Party had "control of important elements in the economy" — interpreted the strikes as indications of communist influence. For those who identified the Communist Party as the source of labor unrest, symbolic gestures such as picketing and the production of "political" plays represented threatening signs of communist influence that had the potential to sway public opinion and encourage Hollywood craftspeople to press their demands for improved wages and working conditions.

The scandal surrounding the Actors' Lab is best understood in this context. Although some scandals might involve behavior marked by sexual outrageousness that thumbs its nose at the status quo; might be related to actions that are shocking, spectacular, and perhaps secretly exciting; or might begin with behavior that is offensive to moribund propriety or conventional morality, the "scandalous" behavior by members of the Actors' Lab cannot in any useful way be considered in such terms. Instead, the case of the Actors' Lab reveals that scandalous behavior can simply be behavior that is open to attack by members of an opposing ideological position. As John B. Thompson points out in his essay "Scandal and Social Theory," because "values and norms are contested features of social life . . . scandals are often rather messy affairs, involving the *alleged* transgression of values and norms which are themselves subject to contestation."[3]

The methods used by the opponents of the Actors' Lab indicate that scandal can sometimes have less to do with the actions of what Thompson calls the "participants" than with the reactions of the "non-participants" who work to generate public disapproval of the participants' actions, damage the participants' reputations, and discredit the participants' beliefs while validating their own. Moralizing and establishing guilt by association were strategies pioneered by U.S. Representative Martin Dies in his tenure as chairman of HUAC from 1938 to 1945. Jack Tenney effectively employed these tactics as well. Far from using hearings and reports to bring new facts to light, Tenney orchestrated public appearances to disgrace his opponents and martial support for his rebuke and condemnation of their actions.

The Tenney Committee's methods illustrate the logic, processes, and consequences of public figures using slander and malicious gossip to silence potentially powerful adversaries. Tenney and other anticommunists circulated false and misleading accusations to shape public opinion, and they masked their tacit agenda to maintain privilege by using inflammatory statements about the impending threat of international gangsters set on destroying civilization. Moreover, the confrontation between Tenney and the Lab shows how "republican" ideals of privatism and individualism could be brought to bear in a political, economic, and social struggle for power with individuals who sought to assert the country's opposing "democratic" priorities of an egalitarian and collective society. Tenney and other anticommunists used the communist scandal in Hollywood to further the interests of established representatives of the film industry and the American electorate, over and against those of liberal-minded craftspeople who were not only "undesirable" but expendable as well. As Robert Vaughn notes in his study of the blacklist period, "people who had the most to lose by being blacklisted managed . . . to avoid the problem" of having their careers disrupted, but when, as was often the case, lesser known figures were caught up by investigations, their "careers and incomes in virtually every case" were diminished to almost nothing.[4]

Long interested in communist activity in Hollywood and an expert in actions marked by grand gesture, Jack Tenney issued subpoenas to four members of the Actors' Lab on Friday, February 13, 1948, the opening night of *Declaration*, a play scripted by soon-to-be-blacklisted writers Janet and Philip Stevenson. The Lab's mounting of the play, directed by Daniel Mann and produced with a cast of fifty that included Lloyd Gough as "Thomas Jefferson," represented an equally dramatic gesture: just months before, the film industry had adopted an official policy of blacklisting anyone suspected of being a communist, and *Declaration* compared the contentious hearings held by HUAC in 1947 to the highly un-popular legislation passed by the Federalist Party in 1798 known collectively as the Alien and Sedition Acts.

Declaration "consisted of eighteen scenes drawn together by a narrator who commented on the proceedings and at other times read from Jefferson's writings" and established parallels between the events in Jefferson's time and the contem-porary period through staging and the use of modern dress.[5] In giving a voice to the (more progressive) Republican Party led by Thomas Jefferson, the 1948 play claimed the moral high ground for contemporary "unfriendly witnesses" who openly challenged the right of political committees and political parties to use domestic security concerns as a ruse to discredit political opponents and impose restrictions on freedom of speech and the press. The Lab's production, staged on weekends from February 13 to March 7 and then nightly from April 13 to the end of that month, received favorable reviews. Virginia Wright of the *Los Angeles Daily News* told readers that the play "will make you see our times in greater clarity."[6] Noting that the play "steps hard on important toes," *Variety* called *Dec-laration* a "hard-hitting portrayal of government conflict and the repression of individual thinking." The trade review told readers that *Declaration* was "a well-written play that adds up to sock entertainment" and that it was "ripe for Broad-way, a definite asset to any theatre season."[7]

The Lab members' decision to mount the production of *Declaration* becomes especially significant in light of the events that precipitated their showdown with the Tenney Committee. One of the most highly publicized confrontations of the period began on October 20, 1947, when HUAC opened its hearings on alleged communist influence in Hollywood. A month later these hearings would lead to contempt charges against "unfriendly witnesses" John Howard Lawson, Dalton Trumbo, Albert Maltz, Alvah Bessie, Samuel Ornitz, Herbert Biberman, Edward Dmytryk, Adrian Scott, Ring Lardner Jr., and Lester Cole (listed here in order of their appearance before HUAC). Although these members of what came to be known as the Hollywood Ten would not be fined and imprisoned until June 1950, their collective decision not to answer questions about their political affili-ations had one immediate consequence. As of November 24, 1947, they could not be employed by the film industry under the policy outlined in the "Waldorf Statement."

The statement, which announced that executives of the film industry would not "knowingly employ a Communist or a member of any party or group which advocates the overthrow of the Government of the United States by force, or by any illegal or unconstitutional method," did not exactly represent a capitulation to external pressure. Instead, the announced policy can best be understood as the culmination of intensive effort by the industry's own anticommunist organiza-tion, the Motion Picture Alliance for the Preservation of American Ideals, estab-lished in February 1944 and led by industry figures such as Sam Wood, Cecil B.

DeMille, Walt Disney, Lela Rogers, Hedda Hopper, Borden Chase, Rupert Hughes, Morrie Ryskind, and Roy Brewer (an anticommunist expert and the West Coast head of the International Alliance of Theatrical Stage Employees [IATSE]). As early as March 1944, the Motion Picture Alliance (MPA) had sought government assistance to combat labor unrest in the industry. In the months that followed, this influential anticommunist network had used the Conference of Studio Unions strikes, which profoundly disrupted Hollywood production even before the war ended in 1945, as evidence that government intervention was vital to preserving the existing system.[8] Labor unrest represented a tangible threat to the economic structure underlying the MPA's vision of American society. Individuals who allegedly incited Hollywood's craftspeople to press for financial concessions became central targets in the MPA's initiative to preserve a system that reflected their "ideals." As Greg Mitchell explains, "[T]he crusade against the Hollywood Ten was rooted in the long-simmering labor wars within the movie industry [where] union activists had been accused of pro-Communist leanings since the early 1930s [and where these attacks] had only intensified following World War II."[9]

The blacklisting policy adopted by the Hollywood film industry contributed to efforts by Republicans and conservative Democrats to reverse legislation passed during the Roosevelt administrations that was seen as aiding the rising demands of workers and craftspeople. By enacting their blacklisting policy industry executives not only vindicated the assumptions, objectives, and methods of HUAC, and validated Truman's foreign and domestic anticommunist policies; they also ensured a long life for a coalition whose members shared a commitment to "countersubversive" action against "agitation" caused by unions, communists, Jews, blacks, Hispanics, and other "aliens." As Ellen Schrecker explains in her study of McCarthyism, the hearings in October 1947 came to represent a crucial turning point because "by precipitating the blacklist, the hearing established the pattern of economic sanctions that was so central to the committee's success and that of the rest of the anticommunist crusade."[10]

The Waldorf Statement, which connected economic policies to political policies as shared expressions of anticommunism, succinctly articulated the ideological framework through which many Americans viewed the communist threat and the period's increasing bond between corporate America and American government. Strengthened by New Deal policies, this bond, characterized by scholars such as Michael Rogin and George Lipsitz as the corporate-liberal position, was cemented by a package of policies that included the Truman Doctrine for Greece and Turkey, announced March 12, 1947, which claimed America's right to intervene abroad (militarily, politically, and economically) in defense of "American definitions of freedom and stability"; Executive Order 9835, announced March 21, 1947, which instituted a loyalty oath and stipulated that federal employees would be dismissed if investigators found them disloyal to their government; the Marshall Plan, first proposed by Secretary of State George Marshall on June 5, 1947, which established the policy of using massive government loans abroad to create a "favorable economic and political climate for American business"; and the Taft-Hartley Act, passed into law on June 23, 1947, which virtually overturned the Wagner Act of 1935 to provide substantial protection for employers and insure that union leaders were not members of the Communist Party.[11]

The American public's support of these measures reveals that in the postwar years even disparate segments of the American public were prepared and persuaded to believe that substantially expanding American control in foreign markets represented the only credible line of action for the country's national security, that the growth of American corporate power depended on establishing and maintaining political and economic stability abroad and at home, and that governmentally sanctioned anticommunist policies were a legitimate component of securing that stability. Flying in the face of principles at the heart of laissez-faire capitalism, the "communist issue" provided a basis for fiscal conservatives to support significantly increased levels of government involvement in American business. Establishing a state of emergency that allowed for the suspension of constitutional protections, the postwar "red scare" provided a basis for securing consent from social liberals who would otherwise have balked at the federal government's underwriting corporate activity in foreign markets rather than social programs at home.

Given this political environment, the Lab's production of *Declaration* could be seen on the one hand as foolhardy and on the other as heroic. Did Lab members understand that by mounting the production they were inviting attack by substantially better-armed forces? Probably. Did they honestly believe their showcase production would by its own integrity change the course of events? Probably not. Did they so believe in a "democratic" ideal that they felt compelled to voice their opposition to the suspension of civil liberties? It seems so. Does the Lab's decision to produce the play reflect long-standing principles? Yes. The group's decision to produce *Declaration* arose out of priorities the Actors' Lab Executive Board had agreed on in September 1945. The priorities included working with returning veterans, building a new theater, and supporting people opposed to "native forms of fascism." This last point would set them on a collision course with Tenney and the MPA. But the priorities outlined in 1945 were not new for the Lab. From its inception in 1941 the Lab's philosophy had been shaped by its members' concerns about the rise of fascism and the outbreak of war in Europe. The Lab's "Statement of Policy" explains that its mission was to develop actors' understanding of and participation in society, especially when "the preservation of democracy and democratic culture [is] a matter of life or death."[12] Lab members rejected the notion that actors were disreputable outcasts, as well as the idea that they were colorful, romantic figures "inhabiting an ivory tower above the petty affairs of daily life." The organization's pragmatic approach to acting and citizenship found expression in its Constitution, which defined the Actors' Lab as a place where craftsmen could work together for artistic self-improvement, the elevation of the craft of acting, and the good of the community.

Established in 1941 and housed in two ramshackle buildings behind Schwab's Drugstore in Hollywood from 1943 to 1949, the Actors' Laboratory was an acting school, a theater company of actors who worked as supporting players in Hollywood films, and one of the principal sites of exchange between film and theater professionals. As blacklisted actor Jeff Corey points out, the Lab was "a very important theater at the time [and] the in place [to be]. It was really the hub of theater activity and everyone used to come to see the Lab plays — Freddie March, Danny Kaye, the whole Hollywood community."[13] Based on interviews with a collection of Lab members, Delia Nora Salvi explains that for its members the Lab was "more than just a workshop or theater; it was also their social life and refuge [and] the Lab people not only clung together out of a shared artistic belief, but also out of a need for spiritual and human fulfillment." Salvi notes that "the 'alley' became the symbol of this creative-social aspect of the Lab [for] when the Lab moved to [its permanent location on] Laurel Avenue in 1943, the narrow alley which ran alongside its buildings [behind the drugstore] became the favorite 'hanging-out' place for members, students, and Lab friends."[14]

Lab members took their civic duty seriously. Several actors including Will Lee volunteered for active duty during the war, and a founding member of the Lab, Richard Fiske, was killed in action. Between 1942 and 1946 the Lab put together fourteen productions for the U.S.O. in the States and overseas, formed two of the first Hospital Units to tour the country, and provided special training for enlisted personnel who would be producing shows for the armed forces. After the war the Actors' Lab produced a radio series for the Veterans Service Center and provided acting classes for returning GIs. Between 1945 and 1948 the Actors' Lab received more than three thousand applications from veterans wanting to enroll in courses there, and the Veterans Administration supported veterans' work at the Lab because it believed acting would help veterans adjust to postwar existence. By the mid-1940s Lab stage productions began getting attention as well. In 1945 Jonson's Elizabethan comedy *Volpone* became the Lab's first big theatrical success. *Variety* told the industry that the Actors' Laboratory seemed "bound for Broadway at last."[15] That same year *Life* magazine announced that "some of the most skillful acting in the United States today is being done in Hollywood by some part-time refugees from the movies."[16]

The Lab's origins provided its opponents with material that would later be used to discredit the theater company and its members. Founders of the Actors' Lab had been members of the Group Theatre and the Hollywood Theatre Alliance (HTA). The Lab's connection to the HTA seemed especially significant to concerned anticommunists, for the HTA had evolved from the Los Angeles—

based company of the Federal Theatre Project, a successful but highly controversial national program dissolved in 1939 following an investigation by the Dies Committee. Yet because Lab members were skilled actors, effective teachers, had served in the armed forces, and supported the war effort with U.S.O. and hospital tours, in its first several years the Lab seems to have been viewed by industry executives as no worse than many "artistic" groups. That perception changed, however, following an incident in October 1945. A few Lab members had been sent to observe the ongoing conflict that had developed outside the Warner Bros. lot in the wake of the Conference of Studio Unions strike against the studio. Setting aside the board's decision to take no public stand, some of the observers decided to join the picket line. Prior to that moment the Lab had enjoyed an especially good relationship with Warner Bros. The studio's drama coach, Sophie Rosenstein, had lectured at the Lab; on several occasions Warner Bros. press releases proudly announced that Lab members were in the cast of its films; the studio had even loaned the sets and props the Lab was using for its current production of *A Bell for Adano*. Yet after Lab members were seen joining the picket line, studio head Jack Warner had his property picked up and, like other industry figures committed to preserving "American ideals," began to see Lab members as communist agitators.

Efforts to nail down that perception for the public began in earnest less than a month later when the "Rambling Reporter" column of the *Hollywood Reporter* warned the studios and the Veterans Administration about sending students to the Actors' Lab and told the film community that "people of repute" were stating quite openly that the Lab was dominated by people who were "as red as a burlesque queen's garters." [17] The column asserted that the reports were of "public concern" and threatened that "a denial of the communistic affiliations of members of the faculty is due and vital to the Lab itself." Joining the picket line was the participants' first obvious confrontational action, and the non-participants moved quickly to define the significance of that action for the American public. Through their warnings, threats, and assertions the non-participants sketched a compelling argument: taxpayer money was paying for classes taken by veterans at the Actors' Lab; Lab members had shown support for craftspeople locked in a labor dispute with a studio; labor unrest in the film industry was (or could be) the consequence of communist agitation; joining the picket line revealed that Lab members were sympathetic to communist agitation (or at least showed they were unconcerned about raising that suspicion); "public concern" was warranted because taxpayer money was going to individuals who supported (or seemed to support) the work of international gangsters set on destroying the American way of life. Effectively stifling questions about evidence, for example, proof that the strike against Warner Bros. had been caused by communist agitators (and that joining the picket line signified support of communist agitation), the non-participants essentially dared the American public to contradict views expressed by "people of repute." Effectively silencing objections that walking a picket line did not represent support of the Communist Party but instead the expression of a legal right exercised by thousands of Americans, especially in the years following World War II, the non-participants carefully failed to discuss Lab members' actions (including those that had led to their sound reputations as actors and acting teachers) and instead insinuated that Lab members were by their very nature markedly different from "people of repute."

Drawing attention away from Lab members' actual behavior, and counting on the public to make a series of inferences, the *Hollywood Reporter* column blotted out the individual identities Lab members had acquired as a result of their craftsmanship and replaced them with a conglomerate, hyperbolic identity embodied in the image of the skirt-lifting, red-gartered burlesque dancer who, like the international communist agitator, would always in the end show herself to be the lowest kind of professional, someone engaged in immoral actions to calculated effect. Thus, with their opponents' and their own character traits and motivations already outlined in November 1945, long before the Lab began rehearsals of *Declaration*, the anticommunists' lead players began preparing for the Tenney Committee's performance at the public hearings on the Actors' Lab in 1948.

•   •   •

With shouting matches and fights sometimes breaking out, with people attending the hearings often physically removed for what Tenney deemed heckling, with long stretches of time filled by investigator and counsel Richard Combs reading material into the record, with no occasion for the attorneys of unfriendly witnesses to test the strength of the testimony given by friendly witnesses, the hearings held by the committee throughout the 1940s must have been curious public performances. The Tenney Committee staged its performance using members of the Actors' Lab in the Assembly Chambers of the State Building in Los Angeles, and from beginning to end it was Tenney's show. The committee never asked questions about the actual operations of the Lab, refused to hear statements prepared by the individuals who had been subpoenaed, and strategically withheld its most powerful and libelous "evidence" until the findings could be submitted without interference: the day following the Lab members' appearances, with the chambers emptied of their attorneys and supporters, Richard Combs gave official sanction to the *Hollywood Reporter*'s insinuations, that communists at the Lab were using tax dollars to subvert the government, by explicitly pointing out that the Lab's certification by the Department of Public Education meant that "any veteran attending the institution could demand that he be given GI money and the government would have no alternative under the law except to give it to him."[18]

Cast once again in supporting roles, Lab members served to forward the narrative designed by the anticommunist network. The first Lab member called before the committee, World War II veteran Will Lee, appeared on February 18, 1948. The Tenney Committee's report for 1948 states that Lee explained he was "an actor, employed as a teacher at the Actors Laboratory Theatre [and that] like all of the other Communists who had appeared before the committee . . . Will Lee [had] refused to answer whether or not he had been, or was, a member of the Communist Party" (106). The next day the three other members of the Lab were called. Again the committee asked only the most basic questions: how and where the "witnesses" were employed; were they, or had they ever been, members of the Communist Party? Rose Hobart was called first and "refused to say whether or not she was a member, or had been a member, of the Communist Party"; Roman Bohnen was called next, and, as the 1948 Tenney Report insinuates, Bohnen "followed the same pattern set by Rose Hobart"; J. Edward Bromberg was called last and like the others, refused to state his political party affiliation (105).

Given that the Tenney Committee's questions to the Lab members yielded only information that was already a matter of public record, namely that they were actors and members of the Actors' Lab, the hearings seem to have been designed primarily to assert the rightness of the non-participants' position. In his exhaustive study of the Tenney Committee Edward Barrett points out that "on the whole, it appears that the hearings of the Tenney committee were not conducted in a manner calculated to permit rational finding of fact [and] that prosecution rather than investigation was the theme."[19] Barrett explains that "the hearings appear to have been planned for the purpose of publicizing conclusions already reached [and that] when previous investigation had convinced the committee chairman . . . that certain organizations were communist fronts . . . hearings were arranged to publicize . . . these conclusions" (45). Barrett also notes that "much of the testimony before the committee was not tested for reliability [and thus failed to provide a basis] for any rational finding of facts" (46).[20]

For Tenney's committee, providing an occasion for the "witnesses" from the Actors' Lab to decline answering the question about political party affiliation appears to have been a central purpose of the hearings, for as its 1948 report explains, the testimony of the Lab witnesses followed "the usual, evasive and argumentative pattern set by Communists who [had] been brought before the committee."[21] Given that the hearing served at most to confirm the assumptions of the committee, it does seem that the entire exercise was designed to punish and discredit the witnesses, to provide material for the committee's reports, and, from there, to provide material for the public pronouncements of other interested non-participants. A strong supporter of the Tenney Committee in the first several years of its existence, Hearst columnist Lee Mortimer explained: "the beauty of Tenney's publications is that the citations may be repeated or republished without fear of civil or criminal action because they are the official reports of a legislative body, issued under the imprint of the State, and thus are privileged."[22]

An integral link in a nationwide anticommunist network, the Tenney Committee worked with substantial resources, including $153,000 in appropriations from the California legislature between June 1941 and June 1949. For information on communist activity it depended on "evidence" derived from its own investigations, from material contained in HUAC's seven-volume publication *Appendix IX*, and from FBI files given directly to the committee or channeled to it through the offices of Attorney General Earl Warren and later those of Governor Earl Warren. As California's attorney general from 1939 to 1943, Warren played a pivotal role in the operations of the state's first committee to investigate communist activity, the Relief Investigating Committee established in 1940, as well as that group's successor, the Fact-Finding Committee on Un-American Activities established in 1941. For example, working behind the scenes, in 1941 Warren orchestrated the Fact-Finding Committee's investigations of University of California Boalt Law School professor Max Radin to effectively scuttle his appointment to the California Supreme Court.[23]

Although Warren is remembered as a liberal Supreme Court justice, he was also a nativist concerned about "alien" influences in California. An active anticommunist even as the governor of California from 1943 to 1953, Warren had what Sigmund Diamond describes as a "particularly close and cooperative relationship" with FBI director J. Edgar Hoover "that began when Warren was a 'law and order' district attorney in Alameda County, California" from 1925 to 1938.[24] Diamond explains that "no state governor was more diligent in using the FBI than Earl Warren" and that "to judge from the FBI files, no state governor received more FBI information than Earl Warren."[25] When he moved to national politics, Warren's anticommunist efforts had a public component as well, for as Thomas Dewey's vice presidential running mate in the 1948 election against Democrat Harry Truman, Warren took the public position that Truman "coddled Communists." Although the Republican defeat in 1948 reinvigorated and sustained that political party's anticommunist agenda, after Warren became chief justice in 1953 the evolution of his personal views led him, in cases such as *Emspack v. the United States* (May 23, 1955), to issue opinions that began to dismantle the legal and economic superstructures of the anticommunist movement.

Yet before Warren's decisions as chief justice would help erode blacklisting policies, the California Tenney Committee, a committee Warren himself had first empowered, would play a central role in the federal investigations of Hollywood craftspeople. As Edward Barrett explains, in 1945 the Tenney Committee "held no public hearings, but assisted the House Committee in its investigation of communism in Hollywood."[26] The HUAC investigation of Hollywood was announced by Congressman John Rankin on July 1, 1945, in the *San Francisco Chronicle*, which quoted him as saying that "one of the most dangerous plots ever instigated for the overthrow of the government" was headquartered in Hollywood (30).[27] Congressman Karl E. Mundt confirmed the need for a House investigation by stating that the Tenney Committee's existence proved that the situation in the Hollywood film industry "must warrant investigation" (30).[28] Contributing to these statements, Tenney announced that his committee was providing House members with "volumes of information from our investigations which have shown widespread Marxism in the film colony, [and that the Tenney Committee's] official reports for 1943 and 1945 contain summaries of the programs of individuals and organizations in Hollywood for the destruction of the Constitution and the American way of life" (30).[29] As a final embellishment, Tenney noted that "Congressman Rankin is guilty of understatement in his announcement that Hollywood is full of Reds" (30).[30]

Building on HUAC's interest, Tenney stepped up his investigations of Hollywood. Beginning in 1945, he worked to expose communist infiltration of the Conference of Studio Unions led by Herb Sorrell, and in July 1946 Tenney was invited to speak at the national IATSE convention to describe his battles against Sorrell and other alleged communists in Hollywood. In October 1946 Tenney held hearings to question Paul Robeson and to assert his findings on alleged "communist fronts" such as the Screen Writers Guild, the Hollywood Community Radio Group, and the Hollywood Independent Citizens Committee of the Arts, Sciences, and Professions. Tenney's unrelenting efforts to expose communists were rewarded, for in March 1947 he was invited to appear before HUAC as an expert witness, and he "testified at length regarding communist infiltration in California."[31]

Tenney's public hearings a few months later on the Actors' Lab were staged when he was perhaps at the height of his career. On February 15, 1948, the Sunday before the hearings opened, Tenney presided over the first meeting of his Citizens Advisory Committee, which was so well attended the meeting was held in the auditorium of the State Building in Los Angeles. A formidable network of non-participants, the Advisory Committee included the state's most powerful and proactive anticommunist organizations, among them the American Legion, the Associated Farmers, the IATSE (represented by Roy Brewer), and the MPA (represented by Borden Chase). Tenney's affiliation with these "selected patriotic organizations" strengthened the support he had enjoyed from the press since 1941. Yet during this period Tenney first began to lose widespread public approval, and in late 1947 criticism of his committee began to appear sporadically in newspapers. By April 1948, following the publication of its report in March, which listed over 175 groups as communist front organizations, what Edward Barrett describes as "a mounting tide of criticism of the committee" started to make itself heard (35). In June 1948 two leading church groups announced condemnation of the Tenney Committee, and by the middle of the year Tenney's public opponents included the State Bar of California, the League of Women Voters, and the California National C.I.O.-P.A.C. Then, with little warning, on June 20, 1949, Republican senator Tenney was required to withdraw from his committee. His 1949 report, published on June 8, had listed fourteen high-ranking elected Democratic officials as having communist affiliations and thus provided a way for critics to openly oppose him now that "the issue had been shifted from communism to party politics" (323).

Edward Barrett explains that Tenney's removal could be expected because from the beginning "the weakest point in the committee's reporting had been its failure to present any detailed analysis of the organizations that it termed communist fronts" (78). He observes that "a basic reason why so many people were [by 1949] so bitterly opposed to the committee, why it was widely denounced as a 'smear' agency, was its failure to convince the public of the communist character of most of the organizations denounced by it" (350–351). Barrett points out that the committee's circular reasoning proved entirely unreliable. People were called communist sympathizers because they belonged to organizations deemed communist fronts, and organizations became communist fronts because of their membership. This led to an ever-increasing number of people and organizations under suspicion, and as Barrett notes, "by 1949 the group of people involved was so large as to make patently ridiculous many of the committee's findings" (350). Although Tenney was reelected in 1950, he was no longer a central figure in the anticommunist movement. He tried to reestablish himself by campaigning as Gerald L. K. Smith's running mate during Smith's presidential bid in 1952, but Tenney's public life ended when, in a national wave of anti-McCarthy sentiment, he was voted out of office in 1954.

• • •

Charges published against the Actors' Lab suggest that Tenney subpoenaed the four people he did because Rose Hobart had lectured on the history of guilds and unions; J. Edward Bromberg had spoken at the People's Education Center, which Tenney believed was a communist front; Roman Bohnen had performed a monologue at the Soto-Michigan Jewish Center, which the committee believed was a communist front because it rented films from the People's Education Center; and someone named William Lee (no relation to Lab member Will Lee) had authored an article in *People's Daily World*, a newspaper affiliated with the Communist Party. Beyond these individual instances the committee's report in March 1948 presented a host of allegations to prove that the Lab's primary function was "to draw ambitious young actors and actresses into the orbit of Communist front organizations" and that it "donated funds and talent to help put across pro-Communist demonstrations," meaning perhaps picket lines like the one Lab members joined outside the Warner Bros. studio in 1945.[32]

In the 1948 report important "evidence" against the Lab was its "affiliation with" Hollywood Ten figures Alvah Bessie, Samuel Ornitz, John Howard Lawson, Albert Maltz, and Edward Dmytryk. Bessie and Ornitz had attended Lab productions; Lawson had once lectured at the Lab; Maltz had been among thirty people who endorsed the Lab in an ad published in *Variety* in 1944; and, like other people connected with the Lab, Dmytryk had been an instructor at the People's Education Center. Other "evidence" was that the Actors' Lab was on a mailing list used by Hollywood Writers' Mobilization, a suspected communist front, and that Roman Bohnen had been part of a radio workshop at the League of American Writers' School in Hollywood, another suspected front. As evidence of communist affiliation, the 1948 report noted that Lab members had signed a letter of protest against HUAC published by the *Hollywood Reporter* on November 3, 1947, and, as the most salient "proof" of communist activity, the 1949 report listed Lab members among the hundreds of the Tenney Committee's "more notorious critics."[33]

With Tenney's charges against the Lab part of public record by mid-1948, an open display of "subversive" behavior by Lab members in September, namely their holding a fund-raising event on Labor Day, quickly drew public attack from anticommunist figures such as Jim Henagan of the *Hollywood Reporter* and syndicated columnist Hedda Hopper. Writing in the *Los Angeles Times*, Hopper did not openly attack the Lab for holding its fund-raiser on Labor Day but instead focused attention elsewhere by heatedly censuring the Lab for holding a racially integrated event. Claiming that the group's behavior would lead to race riots, Hopper announced that the great balance of the community "was shocked at this public display on the part of the Actors' Lab."[34] Other non-participants moved into action, and an article entitled "Justice Department Labels Actors' Lab Theatre a Communist Front," published on September 8, 1948, by the *Los Angeles Examiner*, reviewed the evidence that "proved" the Actors' Lab was a communist front: the four Lab members had refused to answer questions about their political party affiliations; Lab member Jacobina Caro had been married to Sidney Davidson, an instructor at the People's Education Center; and the Lab had staged Sean O'Casey's *Pound on Demand*, Irwin Shaw's *The Shy and the Lonely*, and Anton Chekhov's *The Bear* and *On The Evils of Tobacco* —which actor Gene Kelly, who often attended Lab performances, later characterized as "innocuous and hilarious short comedies."[35]

A few months after the Labor Day exchange, and following a year of struggling as a blacklisted actor, "Bud" Bohnen died suddenly on February 24, 1949, at the age of fifty-four. Bohnen had been a member of the Group Theatre (1931–1941) and was recognized as an actor whose work could, as Jeff Corey puts it, be "absolutely poetic."[36] Bohnen, who appeared in some forty Hollywood films and is best remembered for his work in *Of Mice and Men* (1939), *The Song of Bernadette* (1943), and *The Best Years of Our Lives* (1946), had since the Lab's inception been its most invaluable member. In her interviews with Lab members Delia Salvi was told that Bud "had been the one to whom everyone looked for guidance, inspiration, and mediation of whatever controversy arose."[37]

While appearing in a Lab production of *Distant Isle*, Bohnen suffered a heart attack at the climax of the second act; he collapsed and died on stage; the curtain was closed, and the audience was asked to leave. Amid the shock and chaos that followed Bohnen's collapse, fellow actor Ed Bromberg took the task of calling Lab members who were out of town to tell them the news. On December 6,

1951, Bromberg would himself suffer a heart attack and die at the age of forty-seven while in rehearsals for a West End production of *The Biggest Thief in Town* by blacklisted screenwriter Dalton Trumbo. Bromberg, another member of the Group Theatre, was a round-faced character actor who had appeared in over fifty films, among them *Rebecca of Sunnybrook Farm* (1938), *Hollywood Cavalcade* (1939), *Lady of Burlesque* (1943), and *A Song Is Born* (1948). In the months before his death Bromberg's heart condition, which had developed after his appearance before the Tenney Committee and worsened as he attempted to make ends meet as a blacklisted actor, had become even more serious after he had been required to appear before HUAC on June 26, 1951.

The crucial assertion made by the non-participants in the case of the Actors' Lab, first voiced just after Lab members joined the picket line outside Warner Bros., was that the Lab had been using studio and taxpayer money to subvert students with un-American teachings. This false and inflammatory accusation would eventually pay off when, just a little over a year after the subpoenas were issued, the Veterans Administration chose not to renew its contract with the Actors' Lab, deciding suddenly that the facilities were inadequate. In the same period the Internal Revenue Service revoked the Actors' Lab's nonprofit, tax-exempt status. With its members blacklisted, its productions playing to semiempty theaters, and its classes failing to enroll sufficient students, in the fall of 1949 the Lab paid its debts to the individuals it owed, closed its school, and declared bankruptcy. On February 8, 1950, a few remaining Lab members opened a production of *The Banker's Daughter*. After its final performance May 6, 1950, many in the cast simply left town, for, as Delia Salvi puts it, "the majority of the prominent members of the Lab found it impractical to remain in Hollywood."[38]

Long after the Lab had closed its doors as a theater company and drama school, its status as a front organization was used by anticommunists to prove communist affiliation. In the extensive HUAC hearings chaired by John S. Wood in 1951, several individuals were questioned about their relationship to the Lab, including friendly witnesses Larry Parks and Marc Lawrence and unfriendly witnesses Howard da Silva, Anne Revere, Helen Slote, and Waldo Salt, who refused to answer questions about the Lab because, as Salt pointed out, "California State Senator Jack Tenney had already investigated the organization and labeled it subversive."[39] Other Lab members were subpoenaed by HUAC throughout the 1950s, among them Morris Carnovsky, Lloyd Gough, Jeff Corey, Howland Chamberlain, Mary Virginia Farmer, and Hy Kraft, and even as late as 1958, Joe Papirofsky, also known as Joseph Papp, was called before the committee.

For more than two decades the non-participants' definition of the Lab as a communist front organization profoundly affected the lives of everyone found to have been associated with the Lab. That definition has also had important lasting consequences in the realm of scholarship. In studies of film and theater the middle years of the 1940s have rarely been seen as a remarkably productive period when the Actors' Lab built on the aesthetic innovations of the Federal and Group Theatres; instead, those years have been viewed as "dead time" between the Group Theatre and the Actors Studio in New York, which opened its doors in October 1947.

• • •

Extant Lab records suggest that the organization subscribed to principles that could be described as humanistic, progressive, and often exhaustively democratic. It would be these principles that set them on a collision course with anticommunists, for although *Declaration* was perhaps the Lab's most overtly political production, Lab members consistently worked from assumptions that led them to explore avenues for participatory citizenship. Their fateful skirmish with Tenney represents a moment when anticommunists effectively asserted the validity of a "republican" vision of America in which individualism, privatism, and rights emerging from the possession of private property were the central values — over and against a "democratic" vision of the American way of life that valued egalitarian and collective ideals and that in the Roosevelt years had become more pervasive in the industry and the country because of working-class and craft activism or "agitation."

The non-participants never presented the actions of Lab members as signs of a "democratic" vision of America but instead consistently asserted that Lab actions represented a well-orchestrated communist threat. That anticommunism was the driving force behind American political scandals throughout the twentieth century is surprising, considering that in comparison with other nations, America has been the least threatened by communism. Because Americans have been, as Joel Kovel puts it, so "floridly anticommunist," the energy devoted to exposing and punishing communists seems to reflect not simply Americans' efforts to "save civilization and preserve freedom" but also the public's tacit desire to preserve and strengthen the power of the republic's representatives whose interests have, over time, become identified with those of the country as a whole.[40]

To entertain that possibility is to take seriously Marxist analyses of ideology's role in contemporary societies and to recognize that policies that further the interests of an elite group can in fact shape the views of people who are not even members of that class. To consider the possibility that the American public gives over decision making to those deemed suitable for the task can also mean recognizing that in conception and practice the dominant vision of the American way of life has been a "republican" vision where political, economic, and social power is exercised by representatives of those entitled to vote and — as indicated by the comparatively recent passage of the Nineteenth Amendment, which extends voting privileges to women, and the Twenty-fourth Amendment, designed to secure voting rights long withheld from African Americans — where suffrage is extended only to defuse "agitation" by the politically disenfranchised.

That America is a republic where elected and appointed representatives belong to a political, economic, and social vanguard is underscored by the assumptions, objectives, and methods of anticommunists active in the postwar years. During this period these guardians worked to protect the interests of the republic's "suitable" representatives who would be deposed and dispossessed if, as the Tenney Committee's 1948 report explained, the Communist Party were to obtain its final objective of "a world dictatorship of the proletariat."[41] Issuing from the sense of crisis that led to various countersubversive measures when war broke out in Europe, the first report published in 1940 by the California committee investigating un-American activity explained that "we must not permit ourselves to be fooled by the Communist Party, into thinking that it is anything else than a part of a lying, scheming, pernicious army of international gangsters, determined to destroy and desecrate human dignity and civilization."[42] This assumption would lead to the anticommunists' central objective — to expose and punish communists and fellow travelers, as well as the methods used to fight the "army of international gangsters."

In an environment where political leaders were calling for Americans to respond to a crisis situation, many people were prepared to cede power to a political vanguard led by anticommunist experts such as Edward Gibbons, who, in writing the 1949 report of the Tenney Committee, explained that the committee would continue its work in the face of communist threats and *"the apathy, complacency, ignorance and gullibility of many individuals who stand to lose everything they hold dear."*[43] Discussing the role played by the guardians of the republic, Ellen Schrecker explains that the postwar anticommunist movement was "an elite phenomenon, the product of complex interaction between the Truman administration's need to enlist support for its foreign policy and the Republican Party's search for a popular domestic issue" after twenty years of Democratic rule.[44] Yet the scandals generated by Tenney and others would have failed to disarm their opponents had they not struck a chord with the American public. The public supported the elite movement because it tapped into people's "republican" view of the American way of life, where political, economic, and social power was bestowed on a select, deserving few whose positions were to be respected by the populace at large. By calling on the public's "republican" vision of America, legal actions that supported the demands of craftspeople could be presented as scandalous behavior that threatened "American ideals." By appealing to a well-established "republican" vision of the American way, leaders could safely secure support for the capital expended to discredit the opposing "democratic" vision of America that threatened to unseat the republic's economic and political representatives.

In the confrontation between the Actors' Lab and the Tenney Committee, the actions of individual Lab members were seen as symptomatic of a larger political crisis, and the Lab came under investigation because, as an alleged communist front, it held a special place in the contest for political, economic, and social power. Was the Lab a political organization designed to bring down the American government? No. Was it a "subversive" organization? Perhaps. Lab members supported the organization of craftspeople, were interested in ending racism, were in favor of child care, and openly advocated a "democratic" vision of the American way of life. Rose Hobart, who was blacklisted long into the 1960s, gives us an indication of Lab beliefs in the statement she prepared for the Tenney Committee. Had she been allowed to read it, she would have argued that "American ideals" were not ends to be achieved by any means necessary but instead were constituted by the actions of every American and existed only insofar as they were practiced; as she explains, the "freedom the Constitution gives the theatre, and our citizens and this Committee must [with humility and graciousness] vouchsafe [freedom to all Americans] if our ideal of a democratic society . . . is to survive."[45] Will Lee echoed her views in his statement for the committee, and summing up the source of the scandal perhaps better than anyone, the veteran surmised that Jack Tenney had called him before the committee because "Mr. Tenney and I hold divergent views as to what is good for the American people."[46]

The confrontation between the Actors' Lab and the Tenney Committee underscores the fact that scandal necessarily involves two distinct categories of performers, what John B. Thompson calls "participants" and "non-participants," and it illustrates how "non-participants" can sometimes play the pivotal role in a scandal. The Tenney Committee, with active support from influential newspapers, state and federal agencies, and private anticommunist organizations such as the Motion Picture Alliance for the Preservation of American Ideals, had the authority to investigate and subpoena members of the Actors' Lab, read material about them into the official records of their hearings, make public announcements about their hearings, and publish assertions about Lab members that could be repeated and republished by individuals, the press, and film industry organizations without fear of civil or criminal action being taken in response. Secure in their complementary positions of power in public and private institutions, the Tenney Committee and other "non-participants" were the ones who shaped public perception of the Actors' Lab and its members' moral character, for they brought the Lab scandal into being by calling attention to behavior preemptively defined as shameful and made certain their condemnation had lasting consequences by playing to long-standing concerns that "democratic" behavior might be dangerous as well.

NOTES

1. Thomas C. Reeves, *The Life and Times of Joe McCarthy* (New York: Madison Books, 1997), 209.

2. George Lipsitz, *Rainbow at Midnight: Labor and Culture in the 1940s* (Urbana: University of Illinois Press, 1994), 99.

3. John B. Thompson, "Scandal and Social Theory," in James Lull and Stephen Hinerman, eds., *Media Scandals: Morality and Desire in the Popular Culture Marketplace* (New York: Columbia University Press, 1997), 41 (my italics).

4. Robert Vaughn, *Only Victims: A Study of Show Business Blacklisting* (New York: Putnam, 1972; reprint, New York: Limelight Editions, 1996), 172 (page citations are to the reprint edition).

5. Delia Nora Salvi, "The History of the Actors' Laboratory, Inc., 1941–1950" (Ph.D. diss., University of California, Los Angeles, 1969), 190.

6. Salvi, "History," 192. *Los Angeles Daily News*, February 14, 1948.

7. Salvi, "History," 192; *Variety*, February 18, 1948.

8. See Larry Ceplair and Steven Englund, *The Hollywood Inquisition in Hollywood: Politics in the Film Community, 1930–1960* (New York: Doubleday, 1980; reprint, Berkeley: University of California Press, 1983), 209–225. See also Edward Dmytryk, *Odd Man Out: A Memoir of the Hollywood Ten* (Carbondale: Southern Illinois University Press, 1996), 34.

9. Greg Mitchell, *Tricky Dick and the Pink Lady: Richard Nixon vs. Helen Gahagan Douglas — Sexual Politics and the Red Scare, 1950* (New York: Random House, 1998), 60.

10. Ellen Schrecker, *Many Are the Crimes: McCarthyism in America* (Boston: Little, Brown, 1998), 319.

11. See Lipsitz, *Rainbow at Midnight*, 157–204, esp. 178–191.

12. See Actors' Laboratory Collection, Special Collections Department, University of California, Los Angeles, Boxes 1–19 (hereafter cited as Actors' Laboratory Collection).

13. Patrick McGilligan and Paul Buhle, eds., *Tender Comrades: A Backstory of the Hollywood Blacklist* (New York: St. Martin's, 1997), 185.

14. Salvi, "History," 36.

15. Actors' Laboratory Collection.

16. Ibid.

17. *Hollywood Reporter*, November 9, 1945.

18. Jack B. Tenney, Chairman of the Senate Fact-Finding Committee on Un-American Activities, *Fourth Report of the Senate Fact-Finding Committee on Un-American Activities, 1948: Communist Front Organizations* (Sacramento: California Legislature, March 25, 1948), 347.

19. Edward L. Barrett Jr., *The Tenney Committee: Legislative Investigation of Subversive Activities in California* (New York: Cornell University Press, 1951), 44.

20. See also ibid., 330–354.

21. Tenney, *Fourth Report*, 105.

22. Stefan Kanfer, *A Journal of the Plague Years* (New York: Atheneum, 1973), 94.

23. See G. Edward White, *Earl Warren: A Public Life* (New York: Oxford University Press, 1982), 34–67. Throughout his career Warren seems to have been guided by carefully reasoned arguments colored by strongly felt personal grudges and allegiances. As California's attorney general, Warren had felt slighted and left out of important decisions by Governor Olson. Once again working behind the scenes, Warren directed the Tenney Committee to investigate the King-Ramsay-Conner case and guided the committee to its decision that Governor Olson's release of the three men, whose case had been ardently prosecuted by then District Attorney Earl Warren, resulted from communist influence. Some fifteen years later, forces shaping Warren's

position would lead to a decision at the opposite end of the political spectrum. When *Emspack v. the United States* was first argued in January 1954, Chief Justice Warren found that individuals could not appeal to the First or Fifth Amendment when asked questions about Communist Party membership. His opinion changed completely, however, when the case was reargued in April 1955, a little more than a year after the first Army-McCarthy hearings. Claiming that the investigation was being stonewalled, on May 20, 1955, Senator Joseph McCarthy accused President Dwight Eisenhower, who had appointed Warren to the Supreme Court, of taking the Fifth Amendment. On May 23, 1955, Warren handed down the landmark decision in the case of *Emspack v. the United States*.

24. Sigmund Diamond, *Compromised Campus: The Collaboration of Universities with the Intelligence Community, 1945–1955* (New York: Oxford University Press, 1992), 345.

25. Ibid., 259.

26. Barrett, *Tenney Committee*, 30.

27. *San Francisco Chronicle*, July 1, 1945 (quoted in ibid.). All quotes from the *San Francisco Chronicle* are reprinted here from Barrett, *Tenney Committee*; parenthetical pagination in the text refers to Barrett.

28. Ibid.

29. *San Francisco Chronicle*, July 21, 1945.

30. Ibid.

31. Barrett, *Tenney Committee*, 31.

32. Tenney, *Fourth Report*, 104, 105.

33. Jack B. Tenney, Chairman of the Senate Fact-Finding Committee on Un-American Activities, *Fifth Report of the Senate Fact-Finding Committee on Un-American Activities, 1949* (Sacramento: California Legislature, June 8, 1949), 688. See also Tenney, *Fourth Report*, "Actors' Laboratory Theatre," 95–106, "Communist Front Organizations: Arts and Culture," 50–52, and references throughout, including 129, 159, 259, 276.

34. See Salvi, "History," 200; Actors' Laboratory Collection contains reprint of article in the *California Eagle*, September 16, 1948.

35. Barrett, *Tenney Committee*, 365.

36. McGilligan and Buhle, *Tender Comrades*, 182.

37. Salvi, "History," 10.

38. Ibid., 225.

39. Vaughn, *Only Victims*, 125.

40. Joel Kovel, *Red Hunting in the Promised Land: Anticommunism and the Making of America* (New York: HarperCollins, 1994), x, xi.

41. Tenney, *Fourth Report*, 45; Part 1 of the report, "Analysis of Communist Front Organizations," 23–89, was written by Edward Gibbons, publisher of *Alert*.

42. Tenney, *Fifth Report*, 701.

43. Ibid., 687 (italics in original).

44. Ellen Schrecker, "McCarthyism and the Decline of American Communism, 1945–1960," in Michael E. Brown, Randy Martin, Frank Rosengarten, George Snedeker, eds., *New Studies in the Politics and Culture of U.S. Communism* (New York: Monthly Review Press, 1993), 125.

45. Salvi, "History," 291.

46. Ibid., 289.

THE CINDERELLA PRINCESS AND THE INSTRUMENT OF EVIL

REVISITING TWO POSTWAR HOLLYWOOD STAR SCANDALS

ADRIENNE L. MCLEAN

*T*he scandalous affairs of Rita Hayworth and Ingrid Bergman with, respectively, Aly Khan and Roberto Rossellini are often linked in Hollywood lore because they occurred nearly simultaneously (from the end of 1949 through 1950) and featured similar narrative details: both involved married women who consorted publicly with married men who were not their husbands and by whom they became pregnant. According to conventional wisdom, Bergman's Hollywood career was badly damaged as a result, but Hayworth's was enhanced — an outcome frequently invoked as evidence that scandal affects a star's career in direct proportion to the compatibility of the transgressive activity with the star's textual and extratextual image as promulgated in popular discourse.[1] The following, transcribed from a cable-television "documentary," is a standard rendering of this point of view: "Ingrid's career was ruined in America, and she was even denounced on the Floor of Congress as an 'instrument of evil,' because she wasn't behaving as the public expected; she was supposed to be like Joan of Arc, which she had just played on the screen. But Rita Hayworth's career only grew bigger; she was the movies' Gilda after all; she was *supposed* to be a vamp."[2]

Yet, as we will see, even the clearly marked differences between the two stars do not provide an explanation in which cause (behavior, matched or mismatched with star image) generates effect (career damaged or enhanced). First, Richard Dyer's description of the star as a "reconciler of contradictions," one who combines ordinarily irresolvable attributes in the same body, and John Ellis's definition of the star as a "paradox" who is both ordinary and extraordinary, indicate that tension is inherent in star images.[3] Although Bergman and Hayworth were hardly identical, their images shared many more features than the standard account would suggest—particularly off the screen, where each was given core values like integrity and honesty and kindness by fan magazine writers and publicists. Thus, we need to do more than assert that it was acceptable for Hayworth to be a vamp in real life because she played vamps on the screen. It was more unusual, in fact, for Bergman's prescandal image to be so seamlessly pure, so tension free. I will address these issues by examining in detail how Hayworth and Bergman were constructed and described in popular discourse.

Second, the two scandals were also qualitatively distinct as *events*. Not only did Hayworth's affair take place during years in which she was off the screen entirely, but her postscandal career scarcely "got bigger." Instead, it slowly but steadily declined. Conversely, what *Variety* liked to call the "war whoop of the bluenoses" represents only one part, albeit a prominent part, of the response to Bergman's actions. There is considerable evidence that Bergman retained significant fan and industry support throughout her ordeal, and she seems to have remained an audience favorite despite her "banishment" from American films. Indeed, it remains to be seen whether Bergman was ever banished at all.

The material presented here is meant, then, to open up and complicate certain widespread assumptions about a series of specific events in Hollywood's history. Thus, it is partly a detailed recounting of the way the scandals were narrativized for the public and partly an attempt to understand some of the choices and actions undertaken "behind the scenes." A primary problem with any work of this kind is, of course, the absence of the very public one is talking about; to study material produced by Hollywood or the popular press does not give us much access to how that material was received, circulated, discussed, or on what terms. I can claim only that the surviving textual material indicates that some members of the public responded to both scandals in a variety of ways; that Hollywood itself tried to fit the scandals to what it believed were the public's desires; and that the standard account has, for whatever reason, dimmed this complexity of address and response. The Bergman scandal, particularly, was never simply the result of "'real-life' events" overwhelming "even the manipulative efforts of the studios' public-relations departments,"[4] the point of view taken by James Damico in his 1975 essay "Ingrid from Lorraine to Stromboli."[5] Nor were the scandals only the predictable result of what happens when, in James Lull and Stephen Hinerman's words, a "public persona enters the public arena under circumstances that are outside the star's control."[6] Neither scandal, within limits, was foreordained as such from the beginning merely by the unfortunate revelation that certain inappropriate "real-life" events had occurred.

Rather than focusing on the scandals only as examples of star-image mismatch, or as what happens when women violate societal "norms," I want to examine the scandals through the terms by which, and why, they were defined as such. The fame of the two stars allowed many others—the most notorious being Senator Edwin Johnson of Colorado, who denounced the women in Congress—to use the scandals to further their own careers. Senator Johnson did not simply condemn actions that had already occurred, however; his exploitation of Bergman and Hayworth, whom he called "apostles of degradation," helped in large measure to "scandalize" their images and their subsequent film careers (with consequences that will be discussed below). But, in his turn, Johnson would learn, no less than the stars he lambasted, that the effects of scandal can be unpredictable.[7] To condemn the actions of others in the name of conventional morality is also, always, to risk altering the very constitution of those terms and the ideology they support.

To begin, I present background material on Bergman's and Hayworth's star images up to the time of the scandals.

THE NORDIC NATURAL AND THE SHY SIREN

Ingrid Bergman was already married (to a Swedish doctor, Peter Lindstrom) and had a young daughter when she was "found," already well trained as a stage and film actress, and brought to America to make films by producer David Selznick in 1939. It is part of the Bergman star image that, because of her resistance to being made over physically in the usual Hollywood way—having her eyebrows plucked, her hair dyed, her lips redefined, etc.—Selznick made a conscious decision to exploit her as a healthy and uncomplicated "Nordic natural."[8] (As Damico notes, this required editing out of Bergman's persona certain features thought to be more characteristic of a femme fatale—for example, her earthiness, stubbornness, and selfishness.) But although the publicity about Bergman emphasized her unspoiled wholesomeness and domesticity, her professionalism and devotion to her work, and her quiet family life (fig. 1), this image was often contradicted by Bergman's film roles.

Bergman played a nun in *The Bells of St. Mary's* (1944) and the title role in the film *Joan of Arc* (1948), but she also played prostitutes or promiscuous women in several films, including two (*Notorious* [1946] and *Arch of Triumph* [1948]) released immediately before the scandal. Damico claims that these textually discordant Bergmans were subsumed into the "wholesome" paradigm under the rubric of her devotion to her "art" (acting). He concludes that the extratextual discourse about Bergman's "purity" overwhelmed or suppressed her promiscuous film roles, with audiences and critics "simply accepting the validity of [Bergman's] acting while denying the character it portrayed" (249). The question is why this should have been true for Bergman and not for Hayworth. That is, given Bergman's extraordinary popularity, combined with the contradictory textual evidence, why were there not attempts to incorporate the Rossellini affair into her star image (such attempts had after all worked before, for example with Mary

Figure 1. A prescandal photomontage from *Movie Stars Parade* (December 1948) showing Ingrid Bergman visiting "a special Joan of Arc exhibit" in France. The photo on the bottom left is one of the few in which Bergman and Rita Hayworth appear together. Copyright 1948 by Ideal Publishing Corp.

Astor in the thirties)?[9] Such attempts *were* made; the problem is that Bergman herself refused to participate in ameliorating her public image. This alone represents a critical distinction between the Bergman and Hayworth affairs.

Rita Hayworth, on the other hand, *was* a "made-over" star. From the beginning of her career two primary components of her star image were her Latin heritage (she was half Spanish) and the fact that her good looks were the result of much manipulation. The transformation of Margarita Carmen Cansino (her real name) to Rita Cansino, and finally to Rita Hayworth in the late 1930s, involved extensive manipulation of her body and face: her eyebrows *were* plucked, her hairline was raised through electrolysis, she "reduced," her hair color was changed from brown to red. But these routines only made her different, not necessarily less admirable or even less "authentic" in the public's eye, than Bergman.[10] Hayworth did play vamps in some of her forties star vehicles (*Gilda* [1946], *The Lady from Shanghai* [1948], *The Loves of Carmen* [1948]), but she always retained elements of her equally popular musical persona (for example, that of *You Were Never Lovelier* [1942], *Cover Girl* [1944], or *Tonight and Every Night* [1945]) in the vamp roles—the single exception being *The Lady from Shanghai*, which was also a notable box office failure.

Most important, while there is a disparity in what might be taken as the physical natures of Bergman and Hayworth—Bergman's beauty was "natural," Hay-

worth's manufactured—as well as in their types of performing talents, there are many similarities in the representations of their private lives prior to the scandals (see fig. 2). Like Ingrid Bergman, Hayworth was rendered often as a maternal figure (her daughter, Rebecca Welles, was born in 1944) whose romantic escapades and forays into Hollywood nightlife were only the result of her search for a husband and home life that would give her child the security that Hayworth herself—as a professional performer since the age of twelve—had never had.[11] Even Hayworth's divorces, both from men not well liked in Hollywood generally (Edward Judson, more than twice her age, and Orson Welles, the father of her child), are described in positive terms: Hayworth, so sweet but insecure, so humble and so "nice," deserved to be happy, and neither of these husbands were seen as suitable mates.[12]

   In both Bergman's and Hayworth's images, therefore, an effort to maintain, on the one hand, or to find, on the other, a happy home life for their daughters is clearly marked and, in turn, marks both stars as "decent." Why, then, have we so often assumed that the public's "positive" response to the Hayworth–Aly Khan scandal can be traced to Hayworth's vamp film roles? Or that Bergman's image could not accommodate any contradictory elements? Hayworth *was* invoked in much of the discourse about Bergman and Rossellini, but so were other stars such as Lana Turner, who at that point in her career had not been involved in any

Figure 2. A characteristic depiction of Rita Hayworth, this one a spread from *Photoplay* (July 1947), in which she is represented as at once sweet, erotic, and maternal. Copyright 1947 by Macfadden Publications.

Photoplay's headline reporter breaks the silence that could be heard from Hollywood to New York when Rita Hayworth left Orson Welles

scandal.[13] Upon close reading, the action that Hayworth and Turner, but not Bergman, could easily get away with turns out to be divorce itself, not merely the glamorous public carousing that went on afterward. Both Hayworth and Turner had already been through several divorces; Bergman, on the other hand, was supposed to have had a stable home life and a happy marriage.

The primacy of the discourse about marriage and family in both scandals suggests that some of their "meaning" can be linked to uncertainties and anxieties about how married women generally were supposed to act, what roles they would play in the postwar world. (Films such as *Mildred Pierce* [1945], as well as the cycle of film noir, of which *Gilda* and *The Lady from Shanghai* are a part, also seem to exemplify this concern.)[14] Neither Hayworth nor Bergman "were" only mothers; they were also working women, forced by the times to valorize in public what Bergman apparently had and Hayworth as yet could only "yearn" for—a stable and happy nuclear family. But the tension between what appears on the surface to be consensus about the primacy of their symbolic roles and their actual professional existence as actors with hidden offscreen lives has parallels with revisionary views of the 1950s themselves. According to Elaine Tyler May, Joanne Meyerowitz, Todd Gitlin, and others, the apparent complacency and consensus of the fifties shielded, and was also a shield from, an extraordinary amount of inconsistency, confusion, doubt, and change.[15] Hayworth's initial plight was not

Rita Hayworth flying high in "Down to Earth"

that she was a vamp but that she was a married woman, with a child, consorting with someone else's husband. Bergman's behavior was shocking because she apparently willfully destroyed what every American woman, including Hayworth, was supposed to covet: a perfect family. The controversy, rather than the consensus, with which the women's transgressions were met indicates their relevance to wider debates about the role of women and freedom, public and private sexuality, and the nuclear family at a crucial time in American social history.

In order to explore what the Bergman and Hayworth scandals consisted of as actions, as well as metaphors, I will discuss them at some length chronologically, drawing on letters, studio histories and archival documents, and trade journals, as well as more widely circulated popular sources. I begin with the "facts" as we can know them at this point of the Hayworth–Aly Khan affair.

"THE ALY, THE AGA, AND THE RITA"

Separated, but not divorced, from Orson Welles, Rita Hayworth was introduced to Prince Aly Khan at a party given on the French Riviera by the "international hostess" Elsa Maxwell in July 1948.[16] Hayworth was riding the wave of *Gilda's* popularity both in America and in Europe. Aly, who was separated but not divorced from his wife, Joan Guinness (the mother of his two young sons), pursued Hayworth with all the considerable resources at his disposal. Known as one of the world's "great lovers," Aly Khan was also purportedly one of the richest men in the world, as well as heir to the throne of the Aga Khan, ruler of the "world's Ishmaili Muslims." When Hayworth returned to Hollywood in September 1948, Aly (and the press, which had been trailing the pair throughout France and Spain) followed. Hayworth suddenly refused to report to Columbia for work, citing an unsuitable script, and was put on suspension (occasioning the famous *Hollywood Reporter* headline "From Cohn to Cannes to Khan to Canned"). She then fled to Mexico, with Aly close behind.

To quell the adverse publicity that was beginning to appear in the papers, Aly and Hayworth held a press conference in Mexico City, denying jointly that they were having an affair. Perversely, they attempted to support their denial by pointing out the fact that they were both still married and therefore were *not free* to be romantically involved. (Not surprisingly, this explanation did nothing to stop the press attacks.) But in November 1948 Hayworth's divorce from Orson Welles became final; she left for Europe again in December. By January 1949 the affair had been in the headlines for several months, and there were calls by religious groups and women's clubs to boycott Hayworth's films.[17] Aly Khan issued a joint statement from Cannes that as soon as his divorce became final, he would marry Hayworth, although a date could of course not yet be set. By April, thanks to the cooperative Joan Guinness (who providentially did not name Hayworth as co-respondent in her divorce suit), Hayworth and Khan announced that the wedding would take place on May 27, 1949, which it did, to great fanfare in the press.[18] Shortly after Christmas, some seven months after the wedding ceremony, their daughter, the princess Yasmin Aga Khan, was born. (Yasmin's noticeably "premature" birth was remarked upon in some quarters.)

There is not much, of course, that would mark any of this as particularly scandalous today. Everything had fallen into place for Hayworth and Aly Khan: no party acted acrimoniously, divorce decrees were granted without delay, there were no real hitches in the wedding plans, and suddenly the impending nuptials became "the most talked about trivia of the year"[19] (see fig. 3). In fact, as Aly's biographer puts it, "with the announcement that they would wed, Rita's and Aly's romance took on a whole new fairy-tale aspect; forgotten were the harsh words of yesterday, replaced by allusions to Prince Charming and Cinderella."[20] The Hearst press set the cap on this aspect of the affair by commissioning from Louella Parsons a fourteen-part life story of "Cinderella Princess" Hayworth, which ran immediately after the wedding in newspapers across America.[21]

It is important to remember, however, what might have been, had events not conspired so nicely: had spurned spouses been recalcitrant and uncooperative, and divorces not come through on time; had Aly Khan not been a wealthy prince; and had the announcement of *a* wedding, at least, not taken place eleven months before the birth, thus preventing gossips from speculating that the marriage *had*

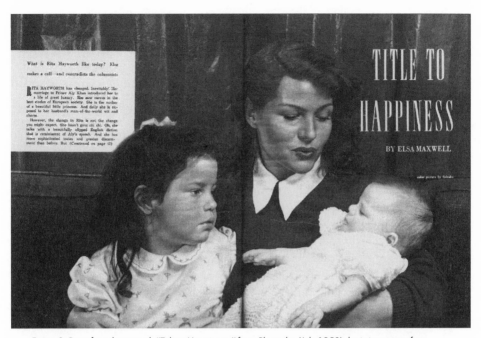

Figure 3. Part of a color spread, "Title to Happiness," from *Photoplay* (July 1950) depicting scenes from Hayworth's new "fairy-tale" life. Despite being the wife of a prince and the mother of a "beautiful princess," Hayworth has "not gone chi-chi," Elsa Maxwell assures us, and remains the same shy, down-to-earth woman she has always been. Copyright 1950 by Macfadden Publications, Inc.

to take place. Had these or any number of other circumstances been different, might not Hayworth have ended up, like Bergman, purportedly "banned" from the movie screens of America?

Perhaps. Perhaps not. Vamp image or no, had the timing of Hayworth's affair not worked out so neatly — had she actually given birth to an illegitimate child — she, and any other female star, would clearly have been in the same boat as Bergman in terms of facing the reactions of public watchdogs and moral interest groups.[22] But at the same time it is not clear whether public censure of Bergman was really based simply on the fact of the affair or, instead, on the way it was apparently conducted. Contrary to popular belief, Hollywood itself actively attempted to exploit the transgressive sexual behavior of Bergman, as well as that of Hayworth, and how it did so matters much more than previous accounts have acknowledged.

"IF YOU NEED A SWEDISH ACTRESS . . ."

Ingrid Bergman wrote a letter to Roberto Rossellini on April 29, 1948, expressing her admiration for his neorealist films *Open City* and *Paisà* and offering her services as "a Swedish actress who speaks English very well, who has not forgotten her German, who is not very understandable in French, and who in Italian knows only 'ti amo.'"[23] Accounts differ as to when and why Rossellini replied, but in the summer of 1948, while Bergman was making *Under Capricorn* for Alfred Hitchcock in Paris, Rossellini and Bergman met to discuss making a film together. Early in 1949 Rossellini went to Hollywood to finalize the film deal with Bergman and RKO; because he had no money, he stayed with Bergman and her husband and child in their Beverly Hills house. In February 1949 Rossellini returned to Rome, and Bergman followed in March. In April, shooting began on the film *Stromboli*, named for the volcanic island on which it was shot (the volcano itself figured in the film's plot). Within weeks rumors were circulating in America that Bergman and Rossellini were having an affair. When *Life* magazine published a picture of the two holding hands in May, clouds began to gather.[24]

Joseph Breen, director of the Production Code Administration, wrote to Bergman, demanding that, for the good of Hollywood's reputation, she publicly denounce the rumors that she and Rossellini were romantically involved.[25] This Bergman did not do, and although her 1980 autobiography is full of recollections about how surprised she was by all the furor, there is more than a little evidence that she tried to play both ends against the middle. But she was also plagued by Peter Lindstrom's intransigence in granting a divorce when she requested it. This situation became particularly critical when she announced in August 1949 that she would quit making films altogether; it was rumored, and the rumors subsequently proved true, that she was pregnant, and that Rossellini was the father.

What was coming to be known as the *Stromboli* scandal was not, however, even at this point irrecuperable. To account for later developments, four things need to be taken into account: how Bergman's recent films had fared at the box office; how *Stromboli* was to be financed; how Bergman, Rossellini, and to a certain extent Peter Lindstrom tried to influence public opinion; and finally, who actually ended up with control over *Stromboli* in America, and what that meant to the reception of the film.

In terms of Bergman's recent films, the three that she had chosen to make since leaving Selznick—*Arch of Triumph*, *Joan of Arc*, and *Under Capricorn* (1949)—were box office disappointments.[26] But it is hard to determine to what extent her reputation as a box office favorite was tarnished by this fact, irrespective of the scandal. That is, if Bergman's marquee value had measurably diminished already by 1948, attempts to manage the effects of the scandal may have been confused by an uncertainty about *why* her audience was rejecting her and thus how to translate *Stromboli*'s notoriety into box office success. As to the financing of the film, the profit-sharing deal Bergman and Rossellini made was with RKO; and it is critical to subsequent machinations that megalomaniac Howard Hughes then owned the studio (surprisingly, Damico does not mention this) and was apparently infatuated with Bergman (as he was with many female stars). Bergman received $175,000 for the film and also 40 percent of the profits;

Rossellini got a salary and would receive 20 percent of the profits. In addition, Bergman received a $50,000 subsidy from the Italian government for making a film on Italian soil.[27] If *Stromboli* were a success, Bergman and Rossellini stood to make a substantial amount of money.

Next, when Bergman discovered she was pregnant, she knew that unless *Stromboli* could be quickly released (before her pregnancy became certifiable public knowledge) or unless she could marry Rossellini within a reasonable amount of time before the birth, the film might be banned in America by local censorship boards, and, if that happened, there would be no profits to share. At this point, the story becomes very confused, but several events stand out as turning points. For example, Bergman seems to have tried to stop the rumors of her pregnancy from spreading by publicly denying it to Hollywood columnist Hedda Hopper in Rome in August 1949. Thinking she had Bergman's word of honor, Hopper announced in the press that the rumors of pregnancy were false; Hopper had seen Bergman with her own eyes, had heard the denial from her own mouth. When the story was contradicted in a December scoop by Hopper's arch rival Louella Parsons, Hopper's enmity knew no bounds. It is astonishing that Bergman would think deceiving Hopper was a smooth ploy; Bergman later wrote how she had often watched Hopper, a fierce moralist, threaten other actresses for far less monumental slights or offenses.[28]

What might have happened had Lindstrom granted Bergman a divorce at an earlier date? Around the time that Bergman was trying to deny her pregnancy and saying that she would retire from the screen because of the furor over the affair alone, public sympathy was beginning to turn toward her and away from her husband. By September American columnists, as well as Bergman's lawyer in Los Angeles, were criticizing Peter Lindstrom for essentially forcing Bergman to act like a loose woman by not acceding to her plea for a divorce, for squabbling over money, and for using their eleven-year-old daughter, Pia, as a bargaining chip. Lindstrom's self-aggrandizing and holier-than-thou attitude gave the public a different view of Bergman's "perfect" marriage and happy home life[29] (see fig. 4). Lindstrom's refusal to give Bergman a divorce, coupled with the fact that Rossellini's annulment of his first marriage did not come through until January 1950 (a month before the baby's birth), is one of the several points of potential similarity at which the Rita Hayworth–Aly Khan affair and the Bergman-Rossellini affair significantly diverged.

Finally, sometime between August and November 1949 Howard Hughes offered Bergman and Rossellini $600,000 for their shares of the American and European rights to *Stromboli*, and they refused it.[30] They apparently believed they stood to make more from *Stromboli* at the box office. In December Joe Steele, Bergman's devoted publicist, learned from Bergman that the rumors about her pregnancy were true.[31] Horrified by the implications for the success of the film, Steele decided to confide in Hughes, to convince him to release *Stromboli* immediately in as many as five hundred theaters across America. If *Stromboli* were

Figure 4. Part of a long article, featuring color photos, about Ingrid Bergman's "new life" with Roberto Rossellini from the 1949 Christmas issue of *Photoplay* (note thumbnail of smiling "cover girl" Bergman, with reindeer and candles in the background). A typical example of immediate efforts to redefine Bergman's image and that of her "happy marriage" to Peter Lindstrom, the article dates, of course, from before the announcement of the pregnancy. Copyright 1949 by Macfadden Publications, Inc.

released with public knowledge that Bergman was going to have an illegitimate child, pressure on exhibitors would likely force bans in some conservative neighborhoods. Although Steele believed that Hughes was agreeable to the scheme—which would, he thought, financially benefit not only Bergman and Rossellini but RKO as well—his relief was short-lived. The next morning, December 12, 1949, the syndicated headline of the *Los Angeles Herald Examiner* (byline, Louella O. Parsons) read "INGRID BERGMAN BABY DUE IN THREE MONTHS AT ROME."[32] Yet even at this point, recuperation was obviously still thought possible, for Parsons specifically attempts to define Bergman's plight in terms of romance: "Few women in history, or men either, have made the sacrifice the Swedish star has made for love," Parsons writes. She goes on to compare Bergman to Mary Queen of Scots, Lady Hamilton, and Wallis Simpson.[33]

"THIS IS IT!"

We know now that Howard Hughes himself leaked word about the pregnancy to Louella Parsons, although many gaps remain in our knowledge about why he might have done so.[34] For example, did Hughes believe that ratcheting up the notoriety level would increase the box office take on *Stromboli*?[35] This seems likely. Or was his release of the final "Bergman bombshell" an egocentric and irrational response to Bergman's and Rossellini's refusal of Hughes's earlier offer for their rights to the film? Was there any relationship between Hughes's infatuation with Bergman herself and the subsequent "butchering" of Rossellini's film at the hands of RKO editors? These questions cannot be answered unequivocally; but they are the kinds of specific questions we need to ask if we are to understand more clearly the substance of Hollywood scandal in general terms and the American fate of *Stromboli* and Bergman in particular.

Bergman's and Rossellini's baby was born in Rome on February 2, 1950. By the following week a version of *Stromboli* "disowned" by Rossellini because of RKO's reediting was set to be booked into theaters across the United States. (On February 9 Bergman received a Mexican divorce. Peter Lindstrom, giving in at last to the inevitable, filed a countersuit in California, which was decided in May. Immediately after Lindstrom's California divorce was granted, Bergman and Rossellini were wed by proxy in Juarez, Mexico.)

Although we can only speculate at this point, Hughes did have a history of outrageous advertising campaigns (his fights with local censors and the Motion Picture Association over publicity for *The Outlaw* in 1943 and 1946 are famous).[36] This, as well as the possibility that Hughes may have believed that *Stromboli* was already irretrievably notorious, would help to explain the overtly sensational nature of the film's advertising campaign. "RAGING ISLAND . . . RAGING PASSIONS!" the ads read. "This is IT! The Place: STROMBOLI/ The Star: BERGMAN/Under the Inspired Direction of ROSSELLINI." RKO also decided to time the release of the film with the birth of the child. Frantic memos abound in the Production Code Administration files about the ad campaign, detailing how offensive and "unfortunate" the Breen Office found it but also how difficult it was for them to prevail, at that time, over the "unrelenting pressure" of the will of Howard Hughes.[37] The phrase "This is IT!" was thought particularly unfortunate because of what *it* implied in relation to the baby's birth, and the Breen Office was dismayed to find that, despite its protestations, "this is the very thing that Mr. Hughes picked for heavy use, and the other ads were thrown out."[38] And to make things "just about as bad as they could be, of course, the ads broke just at the time the news broke about the birth of the baby."[39]

What exactly was the public's response to the baby's birth? Damico writes that ministerial groups, women's organizations, and private citizens "bombarded Hollywood with resolutions and letters" and that legislatures "the country over spent hours discussing the scandal" (243). He describes editorials written by newspapers "of all sizes and persuasions, most condemning Bergman but some championing the artist's right to individual freedom" (243). Adding the fact of Edwin Johnson's denunciation of Bergman on the floor of the U.S. Senate, Damico states that the extent of the furor aroused by the Bergman-Rossellini affair is "evident" (244). Because other sensationalized indiscretions—for example, Robert Mitchum's arrest for possession of marijuana in 1948—which Damico calls "transgression of an even stronger societal taboo" — raised nothing like the "storm of disapproval" that Bergman's actions did, Damico decides that the *Stromboli* affair can be explained only, or at least "essentially," by the "peculiarities of the Bergman image" (244).

Although it is true that the *Stromboli* affair aroused more public denunciation than Mitchum's arrest, it is arguable whether having a child in wedlock by a man who was not your husband represented *less* of a "societal taboo" than possession of a drug that had only relatively recently become illegal.[40] Indeed, it was not only Mitchum's rebel image but his "real-life" devotion to his family that was used to "rehabilitate" him.[41] The point is that some ministerial groups and women's organizations could more or less be counted on to denounce even the mildest sorts of "immoral" public behavior. It was their potential ability to turn denunciation into actual boycotts, of films or stars, that had always worried Hollywood, leading it to try continually to placate such groups through tight self-regulation. This self-regulation is missing from the handling of *Stromboli*.

DEFERRING THE INGRID VERDICT

It is by no means clear that any exhibitors were set on banning *Stromboli* before its release; what mattered to most of them was whether the film did business or not. As *Variety* put it in one headline, "Many Exhibs Defer Verdict on Ingrid Until They See 'Stromboli' B.O. Returns."[42] The article continues:

> Film industryites who've been through similar campaigns before are entirely cynical on how many theatres can be expected to join the currently mounting boycott on "Stromboli." They declare that the number of exhibs deciding to nix the [film] will hinge entirely on what success the pic achieves at the b.o. in early engagements.
>
> If RKO's Italian-made film gives promise of providing heavy profits for exhibs, it's said, there will be very few who will find it advisable to skip the film. On the other hand, should it fail to do business, hundreds of theatremen may be expected to decide that "moral considerations are too great" to play "Stromboli," according to observers in New York.
>
> Reports of bans and boycotts were gradually building up throughout the country yesterday (Tuesday). Nevertheless, the total number of theatres and censoring bodies that had stamped "No" on the much-publicized film remained comparatively unimpressive in light of the size of recent headlines. (1)

On Wednesday, February 15, *Variety* ran another front-page article headed "BEEFS NO BAR TO 'STROMBOLI' BOOKINGS," which reported that despite the "multiplicity of squawks" against the film, RKO had booked "every one of the available 300 prints" into a theatre. Again, although several theaters *did* ban the film, it is unclear that opposition to the film per se did anything other than "[whet] public curiosity, rather than [dampen] b.o. chances" (1). In *Variety's* and the *Motion Picture Herald's* trade reports through the weeks that followed, one finds not only that business varied wildly from city to city but that in certain cities *Stromboli* did, in fact, do better business because rather than in spite of the ban. For example, *Stromboli* was banned in Memphis, Tennessee; so Memphis fans trooped across the Mississippi River to West Memphis, Arkansas, where it was not. Indeed, because of the influx of *Stromboli* "biz" from Memphis, *Variety* reported, "matinees are being held daily for the first time in the history of the Crittenden [the West Memphis theater]."[43]

Yet in the same issue in which *Variety* reported on the Memphis situation, it also called *Stromboli* a "One-Day B.O. Wonder." Three weeks after *Stromboli's* initial release, RKO was having a hard time getting bookings. But what we cannot tell is whether "moral considerations [had become] too great" to exhibit the film (a response to censure) or whether the quality of the film itself caused the public's lack of interest. Almost without exception reviews of *Stromboli* were unenthusiastic, but it was not judged salacious (no bans were requested based on the picture's content). Critics thought it both hard to understand (literally, since the dubbing was poor) and to follow, with little interesting action other than a tuna harvest and a volcanic eruption. Several reviewers did acknowledge that some faults were possibly the result of RKO's tampering with the film. Whatever the reason, *Stromboli's* box office fade-out after "tremendous" openings was rapid. Nevertheless, there are indications that the film still made considerably more than its $800,000 cost.[44] Although discussion of *Stromboli's* nonclassical narrative structure and its neorealist ethic would be out of place here, it should be noted that the fervor, naturalism, and emotional strength of Bergman's performance were favorably singled out by some, if not all, American critics.[45]

Had *Stromboli* been less difficult to "read" by American audiences—if it had become a popular film—it might still have made money, even with fewer bookings. Because the film faded so quickly, however, the question now becomes why Senator Johnson would have felt compelled to denounce the film and Bergman (much less Hayworth, who had not made a film since 1948, and who had apparently retired from the screen) so strongly on March 14, 1950.

The answer to this is complex. It derives from the exploitation by RKO of the film itself but also from Johnson's own exploitation (1950 was an election year) of the "headline heat"[46] generated by the HUAC investigations of the communist "infiltration" of Hollywood and its films. As Victor Navasky points out, the HUAC investigations were themselves an attempt to turn the nation's focus away from the very recent communist spy scandals in Washington.[47] If Johnson's paranoid blasts against Hollywood are impossible to take seriously now, it is clear that the climate in which they occurred had less to do with Hayworth's and Bergman's indiscretions than with the cold war and the "success," thus far, of the HUAC investigations in finding Hollywood to be a place "literally reeking with Communism."[48]

Certainly Johnson's own campaign to "get his name in the papers" à la Joe "Tailgunner" McCarthy was aided by RKO's (and presumably Hughes's) decision to capitalize on *Stromboli's* notoriety by defining Bergman through passion rather than romance in its publicity campaign.[49] The ads for *Stromboli* are luridly drawn but cheaply printed in black and white. Bergman is portrayed in profile, embracing an unidentifiable dark-haired man, the orgasmic expression on her face visually tied to the erupting volcano beneath them. Along with "This is IT!," the slogan "raging passions," placed against both "raging island" and the "inspired direction of Roberto Rossellini," seems to have been particularly offensive both to reviewers and to Senator Johnson. Again, the film itself was mild; it had no trouble getting a seal of approval from the Breen Office. *Stromboli* could not be banned because of its content. It was being banned precisely because of what RKO trumpeted so baldly was its appeal: the transgressive but *extratextual* sexual misconduct of its star and its director. RKO, as well as Bergman and Rossellini (that they would be the primary beneficiaries of the film's success had been widely reported in the popular press), appeared to be trying to profit from, rather than pay for, their sins — and at American expense.[50]

The few letters and petitions contained in the Production Code files (there are four denouncing Bergman and her films, as well as one supporting her from the National Council of Freedom from Censorship) are interesting in this regard; none of the letters condemning Bergman date from before the baby's birth. They seem, in fact, to have been incited by it, and most mention Bergman's unrepentance (the fact that there is no "expressed shame or regret") and the way she appeared to "capitalize subtly, though flagrantly, upon this immoral and illicit romance" as the primary reason for their denunciation. The petitions are from small churches, a Parent-Teacher Association, and two Missouri Baptists.[51]

Bergman's lack of penitence, combined with RKO's heavy-handed response to attempted local bans against the film, was all Johnson needed to go to the floor. For when the exhibitors of some small theaters in small towns bowed to local pressure and agreed not to show the film, RKO sought injunctions against them in court, claiming that a film *could not be censored* for reasons that were not contained in the film itself.[52] Because *Stromboli* was patently not offensive as a film, exhibitors had no legal right to ban it. Whether RKO had the law on its side or not, it looked as if RKO was trying to force small-town exhibitors to show the film. Even if poor box office prospects rather than deeply held moral convictions were the main reason for the exhibitors' resistance, RKO's strong-arm tactics only fanned the flames, and infuriated Senator Johnson.

Johnson's proposition was to license movie stars in order to keep them in the future from being able to profit financially from illicit or immoral behavior.[53] It was the profitability of *Stromboli* that he made the issue—the fact that RKO, Bergman, and Rossellini (whom Johnson later called a communist *and* an "infamous Nazi collaborator," a "ruthless, blood-sucking, black market operator of the greediest variety," an "associate of dope smugglers," and a "bedroom prowler," as well as a "partner of RKO" [4118]) would get some of the "ten to twenty-five million dollars [*sic*]" the film was going to make (3281). Indeed, the scandal itself, Johnson believed, was engineered to "bolster the box-office take" of a film that "[lacked] appeal of its own" (3282). RKO "watched this sickening scandal develop and unfold," and "smacked their greedy lips and laid deep plans to convert its morbid appeal into cash" (3282). Johnson continues:

> [RKO's] disgusting publicity campaign for it permitted no revolting bedroom scene to escape, and stressed passion in its worst sense. RKO had word that the anticipated birth should take place about February 15, so that was the day RKO selected to run the film in their theatres. The nauseating commercial opportunism displayed by this corporation and their partner, the vile and unspeakable Rossellini, sets an all-time low in shameless exploitation and disregard for good public morals. When they deliberately exhibited the moral turpitude of the leading lady to pack their theatres, how can they contend that since the weak, pointless, and ugly film was not definitely immoral, no question of morality was involved? (3282)

The RKO publicity "stressed passion and brazenly termed Rossellini inspired. If this swine is inspired," Johnson blasts, "he is inspired by the devil" (3287).[54]

The terms Johnson uses to describe the attitudes and behavior of Bergman and Rossellini, Rita Hayworth, and Hollywood itself— "sneering," "haughty," "high-handed," "disrespectful" — crown his assertion that the movie industry had a "people be damned" attitude and had "forced [*Stromboli*] down their throats." Bergman is censured because she "took the money," and "neither she nor anyone else can have her cake and eat it too" (3284). Bergman, Rossellini, and RKO have "*invited restraints by law* and I shall do my best to see that they get what they have *asked for*" (3284; my italics).[55] Hollywood, Johnson says, "thinks more of the quick dollar than it does of its own good name" (3288). Bergman, Rossellini, RKO, Robert Mitchum, Rita Hayworth ("who got herself involved in a triangle and ended up with a new baby and the title of princess" [3288]), and others are described as part of a Hollywood phenomenon—moral degradation—that he contrasts with professional sports. In the sports world, Johnson claims, "perpetrators" are not allowed to get away with even "lesser offenses" without "drastic punishment" (3288). Johnson ends his tirade with a statement that supports the notion that he was making Bergman into a scapegoat for the combined sins of Hollywood generally: "If out of the degradation associated with Stromboli, decency and common sense can be established in Hollywood, Ingrid Bergman will not have destroyed her career for naught. Out of her ashes may come a better Hollywood" (3288).

Despite Johnson's attack (which ended up bringing Johnson himself a lot of unwanted publicity about his own fondness for "headline-hunting" activities) [56] and some inconclusive newspaper items, Bergman was probably never actually banned from American soil. [57] According to a March 1950 "Letter from Rome" published in the *New Yorker*, Bergman's American base of support remained strong. [58] Eight out of ten of the some thirty- to forty thousand letters Bergman received during her ordeal, for example, were favorable, declaring her "wonderful" or "courageous." Many of the letters contained criticisms of the press: there were references to "'filthy scandal sheets in our land,'" "'the disgust and outrage I feel for the press,'" and "'contempt for a press which thinks we have to know it all.'" Even Louella Parsons heard "a thing or two about her nasty tongue." Magazines ran a number of articles that either supported Bergman outright or reported that audience affection for her still ran high. [59] According to one, her fan mail was still running to at least thirty letters a week, all favorable, one year later — *except* for one "recurring exception," the mail from one "vigilant lawmaker" (Senator Johnson) who has "chosen not to let his constituents forget what they did." [60]

Certainly David Selznick remained positive about Bergman's appeal in America; within three months of the baby's birth he was trying to sign her to a contract, and he faced competition from other producers. [61] Several of Bergman's subsequent films with Rossellini were released in America, if not as widely as *Stromboli*. And if one looks at the discourse about *Anastasia* (1956), Bergman's next American film and one for which she won an Academy Award, there is remarkable similarity between its pro-Bergman tone and that of the pre-*Stromboli* years. She was starting all over again, "fresh," on a new cultural terrain whose contours she, and Rita Hayworth, had helped in some measure to reshape. [62]

• • •

James Damico does demonstrate convincingly how reviewers, gossip columnists, and journalists continually reified Bergman's image as spiritual rather than sexual even in the face of mounting evidence to the contrary, but his conclusion that Bergman was a "totem figure" that had "despoiled itself" and therefore was pulled from its pedestal by a "wrathful public" (252) is too pat. Although there was overt public outcry against the conduct of Bergman and Rossellini, the narrow focus of Damico and other commentators makes both the affair and the outcry more remarkable than they were. Damico points with amazement to the "extensive and spontaneous national reaction" that accompanied "one film star's adultery" (242) and remarks that the breadth of the attack on Bergman was "totally unexpected" (243). But Hayworth's affair not only preceded Bergman's in the news; it too was accompanied at the outset by equally indignant attacks and tirades, from the same quarters.[63] And, as we have seen, there was no single "spontaneous national reaction" to the events nor any single cause for them.

Thus, although star image did play a role in fostering expectations about how Bergman and Hayworth "normally" behaved, neither scandal was destined to be such simply because of unanticipated revelations in public about unseemly activities that had occurred in private. It was not only their images but the actions and choices that the stars and others made offscreen that helped to determine the way Bergman's and Hayworth's transgressions were represented and perceived both publicly and privately. Bergman and Rossellini could have diffused public criticism through apology or repentance, for example, but chose not to. RKO could have played down the scandal rather than "forcing it down the public's throat." Conversely, had the timing of Hayworth's and Aly Khan's affair been "off" and Princess Yasmin's birth occurred out of wedlock, Hayworth too would have been an "instrument of evil" rather than a "Cinderella girl."

We can also ponder what the outcomes might have been for the two "apostles of degradation" if Rossellini had been rich and a prince rather than (in Senator Johnson's words) a "vile and unspeakable" Italian; if Aly Khan had been a poor Moslem commoner rather than the most eligible bachelor in the world; if Bergman had been an American; or, perhaps most important, if America had not been in the throes of anticommunist witch-hunts, spy scandals, and crises of containment. Senator Johnson's grotesque exhibition and self-aggrandizing sensationalism — his own star performance, as it were — played an enormous role in constituting the stars' behavior as scandalous, and we need to connect his exploitative actions, as well as the wider HUAC investigations of Hollywood, with Washington's desire to divert attention from its own corruption and the notoriety resulting from it.

At issue is, precisely, who speaks for "the public," and who constitutes it in, and for, the popular imagination. Even during the height of the scandal Bergman had supporters who decried her persecution by both the "bluenose" public and the press. But her continued allegiance to family life with Rossellini, despite some problems with her relations to daughter Pia, helps also to account for this.[64] Conversely, Hayworth's first film after her return to Hollywood was a success financially ("She's back!" screamed the ads for *Affair in Trinidad* in 1952), but her affair did not, in the long run, help her career as much as Bergman's eventually did hers. After her divorce from Aly Khan — barely three years after the "fairytale" wedding — Hayworth made some of her most interesting films (for example, *Miss Sadie Thompson* [1954] and *Fire Down Below* [1957]); but by the mid-fifties and her short, brutal marriage to Dick Haymes, her career and even her life were seen as being in decline.[65] (Aly Khan, who never married again, died in a car crash in 1960.)

In the end the effects of the scandals on Hayworth's and Bergman's images mirror each other. The "courageous" and sexually transgressive Bergman was able to reify herself as respectable through apparent devotion to domesticity, and scandal injected interesting contradictions into her impossibly "saintly" and tension-free image both on- and offscreen. Bergman's career was hardly ruined; it was given a new lease on life, and she ended up rejuvenated as an actress and a star. Conversely, scandal dimmed the complexity of Hayworth's star persona, reducing its earlier unique combination of sweetness, domesticity, optimism, and eroticism to the sum of the failed romantic liaisons and darkening events of her personal life.[66] It was not so much that "'real-life' events" overwhelmed even the manipulative efforts of Hollywood but that the manipulative efforts took on a life of their own. What this discussion of the Hayworth and Bergman affairs suggests, then, is that scandal, perhaps inevitably, produces paradoxes: attempts either to deny its magnitude or to exploit its transgressive pleasures often end up revealing the incongruities and inconsistencies of the very ideological assumptions on which transgression, as an act, depends.

NOTES

1. See, e.g., Molly Haskell, *From Reverence to Rape: The Treatment of Women in the Movies* (New York: Penguin, 1974), 10, 254, 306; Ethan Mordden, *Movie Star: A Look at the Women Who Made Hollywood* (New York: St. Martin's, 1983), 264–265. Marshall McLuhan's *The Mechanical Bride: Folklore of Industrial Man* (New York: Vanguard Press, 1951) seems to have been particularly influential as well. McLuhan could have had no point of view on the outcome of the scandals, but his assessment has become standard: "Recently, the furor over [Bergman's] Rossellini affair was an interesting example of what happens when two dreams get crossed up. She wantonly stepped out of her Hollywood stereotype, endangering a large investment. Rita Hayworth's stereotype, on the other hand, was not shattered by her affair" (120). Marsha McCreadie relies on McLuhan's assessment in *The American Movie Goddess* (New York: John Wiley and Sons, 1973), 37.

2. From a special about Hollywood scandal, narrated by Robert Osborne, broadcast on cable television's Movie Channel several times in the early 1990s.

3. Richard Dyer, *Stars* (London: BFI, 1979/1998); John Ellis, "Stars as a Cinematic Phenomenon," *Visible Fictions: Cinema, Television, Video* (London: Routledge, 1982), 91–108.

4. Jeremy G. Butler, ed., *Star Texts: Image and Performance in Film and Television* (Detroit: Wayne State University Press, 1991), 240.

5. James Damico, "Ingrid from Lorraine to Stromboli: Analyzing the Public's Perception of a Film Star" (1975), in Butler, *Star Texts*, 240–253. All subsequent references will be cited in the text.

6. James Lull and Stephen Hinerman, eds., *Media Scandals: Morality and Desire in the Popular Culture Marketplace* (New York: Columbia University Press, 1997), 21.

7. See John B. Thompson, "Scandal and Social Theory," in Lull and Hinerman, *Media Scandals*, 34–64; and the introductory discussion in William A. Cohen, *Sex Scandal: The Private Parts of Victorian Fiction* (Durham, N.C.: Duke University Press, 1996).

8. See Kirtley Baskette, "Nordic Natural," *Photoplay*, October 1941, reprinted in Barbara Gelman, ed., *Photoplay Treasury* (New York: Crown, 1972), 336; and the first three of the eight volumes of the Ingrid Bergman scrapbooks (hereafter referred to as IBS) in the Constance McCormick Collection, University of Southern California Cinema-Television Library, Los Angeles. Another frequently applied appellation was "Divine Swede."

9. At least four separate polls in 1947 alone—by *Box-Office Journal, Woman's Home Companion, Country Journal*, and Gallup's Audience Research Institute—named Bergman the "lead" female performer in America.

10. For details on the fabrication of Rita Hayworth and how it was represented publicly, see Adrienne L. McLean, "'I'm a Cansino': Transformation, Ethnicity, and Authenticity in the Construction of Rita Hayworth, American Love Goddess," *Journal of Film and Video* (fall 1992/winter 1993): 8–26.

11. Conclusions drawn from the seven volumes of the Rita Hayworth scrapbooks (hereafter referred to as RHS), as well as clipping files and other scrapbooks, in the Constance McCormick Collection, University of Southern California Cinema-Television Library, Los Angeles; and in the Margaret Herrick Library, Academy of Motion Picture Arts and Sciences, Beverly Hills, Calif. (hereafter Margaret Herrick Library).

12. RHS, vols. 1–5; see also Hedda Hopper, "Rita Hayworth Found to Be Two Individuals," *Los Angeles Times*, November 1948; Hedda Hopper, "Rita's Sweeter Than Ever," July 18, 1948, in the Hedda Hopper Collection ("Sunday Stories"), Margaret Herrick Library.

13. IBS, vols. 1–4. See also Louella O. Parsons, "The Bergman Bombshell," *Photoplay*, July 1949, reprinted in Gelman, *Photoplay Treasury*, 359.

14. There are many discussions of women's roles in films of the forties; see, for example, Michael Renov, *Hollywood's Wartime Woman: Representation and Ideology* (Ann Arbor: UMI Research Press, 1988).

15. See Elaine Tyler May, *Homeward Bound: American Families in the Cold War Era* (New York: Basic Books, 1988); Brett Harvey, *The Fifties: A Woman's Oral History* (New York: HarperCollins, 1993); Joanne Meyerowitz, ed., *Not June Cleaver: Women and Gender in Postwar America, 1945–1960* (Philadelphia: Temple University Press, 1994); Todd Gitlin, *The Sixties: Years of Hope, Days of Rage* (New York: Bantam, 1987). For an ethnographic analysis of the active, multiple, and changing meanings of women's engagement with wartime and postwar star images, see Jackie Stacey, *Star Gazing: Hollywood Cinema and Female Spectatorship* (London: Routledge, 1994).

16. Information in this and subsequent paragraphs about the Hayworth–Aly Khan affair is gathered from the Hayworth scrapbooks and clipping files cited above and from biographies of Hayworth and Aly Khan, including John Kobal, *Rita Hayworth: The Time, the Place, and the Woman* (New York: Norton, 1977), chaps. 6 and 7; Barbara Leaming, *If This Was Happiness: A Biography of Rita Hayworth* (New York: Viking, 1989), chaps. 13–20; Leonard Slater, *Aly: A Biography* (New York: Random House, 1965), chaps. 18–22. See also chap. 6 in Louella Parsons, *Tell It to Louella* (New York: G. P. Putnam's Sons, 1961).

17. See, for example, "Hayworth Ban Asked," *Hollywood Reporter*, January 14, 1949; "Clubwoman Asks Boycott of Rita's Films," *Los Angeles Times*, January 14, 1949; "Club Women Plan Boycott of Hayworth Pix," *Variety*, January 14, 1949; and the British "This Affair Is an Insult to All Decent Women," *The People*, January 9, 1949: "the extravagant expeditions of this coloured Indian prince and his 'friend' have

become an insult to decent-minded women the world over." American journalists seem never to have referred to Aly as "colored" but did call him the "Moslem prince," the "Mohammedan prince," the "Indian prince," and the "brown-skinned prince." Hayworth's ethnic background, on the other hand, is never discussed in connection with Aly Khan's except in the terms already mentioned (e.g., "the former Margarita Cansino" or "her European background").

18. RHS, vol. 4; clipping file (Rita Hayworth), Margaret Herrick Library. See also Robert Coughlan, "The Aga, the Aly, and the Rita," *Life*, May 16, 1949, 125–142: "The details of what a London editorialist ungenerously called [Aly's] 'squalid love affair' with Miss Hayworth must be known to all who can read: their meeting on the Riviera a year ago, Aly's visit to Hollywood, the trips to Mexico and Cuba, the bizarre flight to Ireland and the Continent and at last back to the Riviera, with reporters and photographers yammering in hot pursuit" (139). A riotous compilation of Louella Parsons's reporting on the wedding can be found in A. J. Liebling, "The Wayward Press (Right Up Louella's Ali)," *New Yorker*, June 11, 1949, 76–81.

19. Slater, *Aly*, 163.

20. Ibid.

21. Louella Parsons, "Cinderella Princess: Colorful Career of Cinderella Girl Told by Film Writer," 6 chaps., *Los Angeles Examiner*, May–June 1949 (RHS, vol. 4). The series was originally to have comprised fourteen chapters, but Hearst stopped running them when Aly "beat up" three reporters, an incident that, according to Parsons, Hearst took personally as an assault on the dignity of the press.

22. As it was, the differences in Hayworth's and Aly's social backgrounds, and the implications of those differences for the viability of the marriage, were remarked upon. See, e.g., "Rita and Aly: The Most Dangerous Marriage of the Year," *Hollywood Yearbook* 1 (1950): 8–9.

23. Information in this and subsequent paragraphs about the Bergman-Rossellini affair is gathered from the Bergman scrapbooks cited above; Damico, "Ingrid"; Ingrid Bergman (with Alan Burgess), *Ingrid Bergman: My Story* (New York: Delacorte Press, 1980), chaps. 12–18; Laurence Leamer, *As Time Goes By: The Life of Ingrid Bergman* (New York: Harper and Row, 1986), chaps. 12–15; Donald Spoto, *Notorious: The Life of Ingrid Bergman* (New York: HarperCollins, 1997); Lawrence J. Quirk, *The Films of Ingrid Bergman* (New York: Citadel Press, 1970); Rudy Behlmer, ed., *Memo from David O. Selznick* (New York: Viking, 1972), 126–137, 357, 393, 406–408; Parsons, *Tell It to Louella*, chap. 4.

24. "Strombolian Idyl," *Life*, May 2, 1949, 48; IBS, vol. 3.

25. Breen's letter, dated April 22, 1949, is in Bergman, *My Story*, 235–236. See also Leamer, *As Time Goes By*, 178.

26. Leamer says they were "humiliating failures" (161), and in Bergman's auto-biography Alan Burgess notes that Bergman was "setting a record for the number of [film] companies she helped put out of business" by 1950 (283).

27. Leamer, *As Time Goes By*, 164.

28. As at a party where Hopper excoriated Gene Tierney and promised to do the same to her forthcoming film, merely because Tierney had not told Hopper that she was pregnant — and Tierney was safely married at the time (Bergman, *My Story*, 139–140; Leamer, *As Time Goes By*, 190). See also Hedda Hopper and James Brough, *The Whole Truth and Nothing But* (New York: Doubleday, 1963), 77–78.

29. See Arthur L. Charles, "The Secrets Behind the Bergman Tragedy," *Modern Screen* 39 (November 1949): 56–57, 72–75 (which also describes Bergman's saintly

image as always having been a myth); Joseph Steele, "The Ingrid Bergman *Love Story*" [italics in original], *Photoplay* (cover story), December 1949, 36–39, 94–95; "Ingrid in Stromboli," *Screen Guide*, December 1949, 50–51; "Ingrid and Roberto: A Tight Halo Got Some Adjusting," *Hollywood Yearbook* 1 (1950): 26–27; Parsons, *Tell It to Louella*, 73–74; Leamer, *As Time Goes By*, 193–196.

30. Leamer, *As Time Goes By*, 196.

31. In a letter to Steele dated November 26, 1949, Bergman advised him that "if again somebody prints that I'm pregnant, don't sue them, because you will be sure to lose your case." Leamer, *As Time Goes By*, 198.

32. On Tuesday, December 14, 1949, another *Los Angeles Examiner* headline proclaimed, "BERGMAN BABY DUE FEBRUARY; SECRET TO RELATIVES / Ingrid True Story Known to Only 3" (one of them apparently Louella Parsons). Parsons, *Tell It to Louella*, 75.

33. For other articles linking both the pre- and postpregnancy affair to "true love" and romance, see Steele, "The Ingrid Bergman *Love* Story"; "Ingrid in Stromboli"; and IBS, vol. 3, particularly Adela Rogers St. Johns, "Love, Laughter and Tears," *American Weekly*, c. 1951; Crawford Dixon, "Ingrid Bergman: Saint or Sinner?" *Modern Screen*, c. 1949–1950, which claims that "the whole truth about Ingrid Bergman is this: she is neither a saint nor a sinner, neither devil nor deity. She is a fine, forward, uprighteous [sic], honest, talented, and incomparably lovely young woman"; "Ingrid Bergman's Love Story," a two-part *Look* cover story by Howard Taubman that ran in January and February 1952; David Chandler, "Bergman Today," *Modern Screen*, c. 1951–1952.

34. See Spoto, *Notorious*, 284–285; Parsons, *Tell It to Louella* ("I was given a message from a man of great importance not only in Hollywood, but throughout the United States. He was close to Ingrid and had been close to her for a long time. He had connections in many parts of the world — including Italy — whose sources of information could not be questioned"), 74; see also Donald L. Barlett and James B. Steele, *Empire: The Life, Legend, and Madness of Howard Hughes* (New York: Norton, 1979), 169.

35. See, for example, "Bergman-Rossellini Idyll Seen as B.O. Boost for 'Stromboli,'" *Variety*, August 10, 1949, 3.

36. *The Outlaw* was made in 1943, released in 1946 by United Artists and, significantly, rereleased in an expurgated version in 1950 by RKO. See Murray Schumach, *The Face on the Cutting Room Floor: The Story of Movie and Television Censorship* (New York: William Morrow, 1964), 51–62; Tony Thomas, *Howard Hughes in Hollywood* (Secaucus, N.J.: Citadel Press, 1985), chap. 6; Betty Lasky, *RKO: The Biggest Little Major of Them All* (Englewood Cliffs, N.J.: Prentice-Hall, 1984), pts. 8 and 9; Leonard J. Leff and Jerold L. Simmons, *The Dame in the Kimono: Hollywood, Censorship, and the Production Code from the 1920s to the 1960s* (New York: Doubleday, 1990), 109–125. Surprisingly, Schumach mentions neither the names of Rossellini and Bergman nor *Stromboli*, not even in connection with the *Miracle* decision of 1952, in which movies were declared in a unanimous opinion by the Supreme Court to be entitled to guaranties of free speech. *The Miracle* was a 1948 Rossellini film that had been deemed sacrilegious by local censorship boards on its American release in 1950, and it seems reasonable to assign a connection to their resistance to the film and the concurrent furor over *Stromboli*. See also Garth Jowett, "'A Significant Medium for the Communication of Ideas': The *Miracle* Decision and the Decline of Motion Picture Censorship, 1952–1968," in Francis G. Couvares, ed., *Movie Censor-*

ship and American Culture (Washington: Smithsonian Institution Press, 1996), which also does not mention Bergman or *Stromboli*.

37. Memo to Mr. [Eric] Johnston, February 27, 1950, from Gordon S. White (?) in the Production Code Administration Files (*Stromboli*), Motion Picture Association of America, Margaret Herrick Library.

38. Ibid.

39. Gordon S. White to Joseph I. Breen, February 6, 1950 (memo), Production Code Administration Files (*Stromboli*).

40. Even *Photoplay* produced evidence to this effect in its defense of Mitchum; see Florabel Muir, "The Truth about Dope in Hollywood," *Photoplay*, December 1948, 32–33, 72. Muir notes that "federal narcotics agents have not been greatly concerned with the arrest of tea smokers" because marijuana is smoked "for fun" and is not "addictive," unlike the evil "poppy drugs." See also David F. Musto, *The American Disease: Origins of Narcotic Control* (New Haven: Yale University Press, 1973), chap. 9.

41. For example, Adele Whitely Fletcher, "The Strange Case of Robert Mitchum," *Photoplay*, November 1948, 52–53, 90. Within a few years fan magazines often did not so much as mention Mitchum's "case," even in articles about him with titles like "Don't Push Me!" *Motion Picture*, December 1953, 25, 66.

42. *Variety*, February 8, 1950, 1.

43. *Variety*, February 22, 1950, 1, 20; see also *Motion Picture Herald*, February 25, 1950, 28.

44. For example, according to "Movie Notes" in *Newsweek* (March 6, 1950), "Whatever happens to 'Stromboli' now, RKO executives aren't greatly worried. They estimate that the picture grossed $2,000,000 in its first week against an investment of $800,000, plus some frozen funds in Italy" (12). Some of the revenue was the result of saturation booking. According to *Variety*, RKO broke a record set in 1946 with Selznick's *Duel in the Sun* by booking a February 15 "day and date opening" for 102 theaters in the greater New York area (*Duel in the Sun* had "day-and-dated" in 54 theaters). Saturation booking indicates uncertainty about a film's box office staying power, but it is hard to tell whether an actual ban or simply bad word of mouth about *Stromboli* as a film was feared. *Variety* only says that RKO was "[a]nxious to get the film into release while the front pages are still hot with the Bergman-Rossellini situation," and that Loew's was "miffed" when RKO withdrew its tentative booking with that theater chain because the earliest play date it had available was March 15. See *Variety*, February 8, 1950, 19.

45. See Red Kann's review in the *Motion Picture Herald*, February 18, 1950: "It would be difficult to imagine Miss Bergman delivering a bad performance. Nor does she here. . . . Those who play [*Stromboli*] will get an attraction of passing interest and established star value morally unobjectionable for adults" (21). For a discussion of the reaction of American censors to Italian neorealism see Leff and Simmons, *Dame*, 141–161. For a close analysis of *Stromboli* see Peter Brunette, *Roberto Rossellini* (New York: Oxford University Press, 1987), 109–127; Peter Bondanella, *The Films of Roberto Rossellini* (Cambridge: Cambridge University Press, 1993), 17–20.

46. Terry Ramsaye, "It's Clouding Up!" *Motion Picture Herald*, April 15, 1950, 7. Ramsaye discusses Johnson's "sensation-seeking investigation" as an attempt to get his own "name in the papers" and also refers to the

possible demand, this tortured election year, for a big load of what someone has so aptly called "red herring." When there are such matters around as the fragrant references to homosexuality in some certain, and some very uncertain government offices . . . and innumerable other less aromatic but equally compromising embarrassments such as what might be called the "red spy situation continued" such convenient material [as the *Stromboli* affair] to take some of the headline heat off Washington and put it on Hollywood may be handy to have around. There are plans to have it around.

47. Victor S. Navasky, *Naming Names* (New York: Viking, 1980).

48. See Navasky, *Naming Names*; see also "Johnson Has More Steam; Rankin Helps," *Motion Picture Herald*, April 1, 1950: "Senator Edwin C. Johnson of Colorado and Representative John Rankin of Mississippi teamed up this week in vicious blasts against the motion picture industry in general" (34).

49. See Mary Beth Haralovich's "Advertising Heterosexuality," *Screen* 23 (July-August 1982): 50–60, for a historical overview of why what Haralovich calls "sensational heterosexuality" became more and more common in motion picture advertising in the forties. *Stromboli*'s campaign was obviously still excessive, however. See also Janet Staiger, "Announcing Wares, Winning Patrons, Voicing Ideals: Thinking about the History and Theory of Film Advertising," *Cinema Journal* 29 (spring 1990): 3–31.

50. In a lengthy confidential document dated February 27, 1950, George Gallup's Audience Research Institute assured RKO executives — and how widely this information was subsequently circulated I do not know — that according to its research (polls conducted on February 4, 5, and 6) the scandal had "added greatly to the picture's potential" and, most important, had had "no apparent net negative effect on the picture's want-to-see." No one involved in the polling had, of course, *seen* the film at that time. *Gallup Looks at the Movies: Audience Research Reports 1940–1950*, American Institute of Public Opinion (Wilmington, Dela.: Scholarly Resources, 1979), Reel 4.

51. They are also remarkably self-aggrandizing, most urging that "this petition" or "this letter" be published and circulated "widely."

52. See *Variety*, February 22, March 1, 1950.

53. All of the Johnson testimony is taken from the *Congressional Record*, 81st Cong., 2d sess., March 14, 1950, 3281–3288, and March 27, 1950, 4118. Specific page references are cited in the text.

54. Johnson said elsewhere that Rossellini was "inspired by cocaine" (4118).

55. Bergman seems actually to have been granted some leeway in the conduct of her personal affairs because she was foreign; as one senator put it, "these people . . . are not Americans but foreigners, so why not leave the thing alone" (*Congressional Record*, 81st Cong., 2d sess., February 15, 1950, 1820). But because her career was "made in America," her transgression could also be seen as a betrayal.

56. For a rundown of Johnson's involvement with other "controversial stories" see George Spires, "Hollywood under the Lens — or Stalked by a Headline Hunter," *Motion Picture Herald*, April 22, 1950. See also "Senator Calls Off the Dogs but Holds Fast to Leash," *Motion Picture Herald*, May 6, 1950, 28.

57. Bergman canceled her contract with her agent, MCA, in 1950 because she had "no *intention* of visiting or working in America in the near future" (Bergman, 283–284; my italics). On Friday, February 3, 1950, a *Los Angeles Herald Express* piece indicated that "U.S. May Bar Ingrid's Return / . . . Ingrid Bergman may be barred from returning to the United States as a result of the birth of her son, it was disclosed today" (IBS, vol. 4), but the fact is that Bergman never *tried* to return to America. See "A Visit with Ingrid," *Look*, May 20, 1952: "After the baby [her second by Rossellini, who turned out to be twin daughters, Isabella and Ingrid], a visit to

America, maybe" (IBS, vol. 4). Because references to Bergman's having been banned occur mainly in the literature surrounding her return to the screen in 1956, it is interesting to speculate whether the banishment was actually only a rhetorical reaction to Bergman's *refusal* between 1952 and 1956 to return to the States.

58. Genêt, "Letter from Rome" (March 27), *New Yorker*, April 8, 1950, 88–100.

59. IBS, vol. 4, particularly David Chandler, "Bergman Today," *Modern Screen*, c. 1951–1952: "[The] rush of Christmas mail also proved something else to Ingrid. . . . / The Italian post office had to put on special men to handle the mountain of cards and letters she received from people in America who sent encouraging and reassuring messages." See also "Dear Ingrid Bergman—," *Look* (?) (c. February 1951): "All in all, one can conclude from the letters received by Miss Bergman that: / 1. A majority of American fan-letter writers can't spell. / 2. Several writers who claim to have strong religious feelings know a remarkable number of profane words. / 3. Seventy-five per cent of the letters were kind and encouraging. Of the 25 per cent that were unkind, only five per cent were signed. / 4. Seventy per cent of the letters urged Miss Bergman to resume her career."

60. "Dear Ingrid Bergman—." In 1952 Elsa Maxwell and *Photoplay* provided ballots on which audiences could indicate whether or not they "want[ed] Ingrid Bergman back" (*Photoplay*, August 1952, 39, 91). Of the 10,293 ballots *Photoplay* received, "four out of every five were in favor of the actress's return." "Your Verdict on Ingrid Bergman," *Photoplay*, December 1952, 56–57).

61. In a letter dated June 13, 1950, Selznick writes: "I think there has been, and increasingly will be, a strong sentiment that [Bergman] has been persecuted to a ridiculous and untenable extent, and perhaps to a growing conscience that if Lindstrom had granted her a divorce, when she wanted it, the whole situation would not have existed as a scandal. / In any event, I should be happy to welcome Ingrid back to the fold and actually . . . I'd like very much to have Ingrid under contract again." Behlmer, *Memo*, 406–408. The other producers interested in Bergman were Sam Spiegel, Walter Wanger, and (again) Howard Hughes; the problem for all is that Bergman is "under Roberto Rossellini's thumb." See also Chandler, "Bergman Today": "No American producer of any consequence who passes through Rome fails to make a proposal that Ingrid do a picture for him."

62. See "Ingrid's New Role," *Collier's*, September 18, 1953, 30–31; Geoffrey Bocca, "Love Against Odds: A New Look at the Bergman Scandal," *American Weekly*, January 29, 1956; Robert J. Levin, "The Ordeal of Ingrid Bergman," *Redbook*, August 1956, 36–39, 82–86; "Ingrid: A Fresh Start at Forty," *Look*, September 18, 1956, 100–102, 104–107; Ingrid Bergman, with Bill Davidson, "I am not doing penance for anything," *Collier's*, October 26, 1956, 35–41. On April 19, 1972, Congress officially "apologized" to Ingrid Bergman for Senator Johnson's "bitter attack" twenty-two years before.

63. Johnson enters as evidence for his testimony a newspaper item from Providence, Rhode Island, dated February 13, 1950: "Newspapers should not have printed the Ingrid Bergman–Rossellini or the Ali [*sic*] Khan–Rita Hayworth stories, according to Gov. John O. Pastore" (3287). See also "Rita and Aly: The Most Dangerous Marriage": "Half the world sighed enviously, the other half wanted to sic the Johnston office on the lovers" (9).

64. According to some accounts, public opinion turned completely toward Bergman when Rossellini began to "dally" with the star of one of his films. I believe it is more likely that the dalliance provided a means for fully justifying publicly what

had already occurred to a substantial extent among Bergman fans. For a discussion of Sweden's reaction to Bergman after the scandal see Erik Hedling's essay in this volume.

65. As *Life* (October 5, 1953) wrote of the Hayworth/Haymes wedding in Nevada, "For Rita, the girl who four years ago had starred in a diamond-studded matrimonial production staged by Prince Aly Khan, this was a skid into the rhinestones" (35).

66. See Liza Wilson, "Should Rita Change?" *Photoplay*, December 1951, 46–47, 93–94; "What Price Will Rita Pay?" *Modern Screen*, c. 1952; Alyce Canfield, "Is Rita Still Acting the Princess?" *Motion Picture*, March 1952, 46–47, 64; Peter Sherwood, "The Shadow in Rita Hayworth's Life," *Screenland*, September 1952, 26–27, 58–60; Jane Corwin, "The Not-So-Private Life of Rita Hayworth," *Photoplay*, October 1952, 50–51, 105–107; "Rita, Goddess of Love," *Movieland*, April 1955, 34–35, 66–67; "The Life and Loves of Rita Hayworth," *Inside Story*, December 1957, 44–51. See also Thelma McGill, "Rita's Forgotten Child," *Modern Screen*, November 1953, 56–57, 92–93; and Ruth Seymour, "Love's Lonely Fugitive," *Movie Secrets*, August 1956, 26–29, 68–72, in which Hayworth is castigated for not providing a stable home for daughters Rebecca and Yasmin.

EUROPEAN ECHOES OF
HOLLYWOOD SCANDAL
THE RECEPTION OF
INGRID BERGMAN
IN 1950S SWEDEN

ERIK HEDLING

*I*n 1949 the Swedish actress Ingrid Bergman caused a scandal in Hollywood when she left her Swedish husband, Aron Petter Lindström, and their young daughter, Pia, for the Italian film director Roberto Rossellini, with whom she had a child out of wedlock in 1950. The effects of this scandal on Bergman's career in America have received considerable attention from journalists and gossip columnists, as well as from historians and film scholars.[1] No work at all, however, has been done on her fate in Sweden or on how the scandal affected Swedish culture and sexual politics. But Bergman received very rough treatment at the hands of the Swedish quality press; in the newspaper *Svenska Dagbladet*, for example, a bastion of Swedish conservatism, she was even accused of having tainted the Swedish flag.[2]

This essay explores how Bergman, Rossellini, and the scandal itself were represented in the Swedish daily and weekly press in 1955, when Bergman returned to Sweden for the first time since the scandal to perform in the Artur Honegger–Paul Claudel oratorio *Joan of Arc at the Stake*, a production staged and directed by Rossellini that opened at the Royal Opera in Stockholm on February 17. This occasion became the opportunity for a contentious class struggle, played out in the press, between "high art" (masculine, modernist, classical, "legitimate") and "low art" (feminine, popular, sentimental, commercial). The terms of this encounter, examined here with new translations from the Swedish, provide information not only about Swedish class and gender politics in the 1950s but about how a well-known scandal, whose substance in America derived apparently from issues of morality and sexual impropriety, was recast and reframed in a different cultural context.[3]

Below I establish some normative frames of reference[4] for film criticism and appreciation in Sweden at this time (the only exhaustive study of Swedish journalistic arts criticism is aimed exclusively at literature).[5] Then I describe in detail the reception of *Joan of Arc at the Stake* in order to discuss why the spectacle of a popular Swedish Hollywood star performing in an opera directed by an Italian film director provoked such a passionate and sustained set of responses.

First, in Sweden in the 1950s the "establishment" — the quality daily press, institutions of higher education, the government, and so on — was led by a predominantly male literary culture that strongly emphasized the importance and superiority of high art. Film was not given much social or aesthetic status in 1950s Sweden, in contrast to other European countries such as France and Italy. For example, a Swedish film later canonized as a masterpiece by international critics and film historians, Ingmar Bergman's *Smiles of a Summer Night* (1955), was disposed of in the Swedish press by the leading literary critic of the postwar period as "the miserable imaginings of a spotty youth, the insolent dreams of an immature heart."[6] In their recent history of Scandinavian film, Tytti Soila, Astrid Söderbergh Widding, and Gunnar Iversen even trace the lack of a coherent film history of Scandinavia to the fact that film "still has low status generally in these countries."[7]

Second, and ironically, film was immensely popular in Sweden, and movie stars — both domestic and foreign — enjoyed a huge following. No one at the time was more popular than Ingrid Bergman, who had become a Swedish star at the age of nineteen in 1934, before her "discovery" by Hollywood. Film historian Rune Waldekranz, formerly a film producer, writes about the discovery of Bergman by director Gustaf Molander that "she would become a movie star as shining as Greta Gustafsson Garbo, but her star would shine considerably longer than Garbo's — for her entire lifetime."[8] In her study of female identity in Swedish film melodramas of the 1930s, Tytti Soila claims that Bergman's star image in Sweden was contradictory from an ideological point of view.[9] In *Valborgsmässoafton* [*Walpurgis Night*] (1935), for example, Bergman played a woman subdued by patriarchal demands for procreation, whereas her final and most popular starring roles before her move to Hollywood — for example, *Intermezzo* (1936) and *En kvinnas ansikte* (1938) — would strongly challenge that demand, thus allowing for the development of a more diverse female subject positioning.[10]

This contradictory aspect of Bergman's early star image in Sweden helped account for her huge popularity among both men and women and was perhaps linked to repressed fears and desires circulating around the strongly demarcated class and gender lines of prewar Swedish culture. In Hollywood Bergman's image became much more harmonious and "pure" offscreen, even while onscreen her

Ingrid Bergman as Joan of Arc at the Royal Opera, Stockholm, Sweden, in 1955. Copyright Enar Merkel Rydberg.

stereotyped Madonna/whore roles—as the nun in *The Bells of St. Mary's* (1944), for example, and the promiscuous Alicia in *Notorious* (1946)—conformed to the limited diversity of the repertoire available to Hollywood's leading women. James Damico and Adrienne McLean have described how Bergman's Hollywood persona remained separate from any discordant roles she "acted"; in spite of playing a brassy barmaid in *Dr. Jekyll and Mr. Hyde* (1941) and a saint in *Joan of Arc* (1948), she was in the American public's eye the exemplary and uncomplicated Nordic housewife, sold as "natural" and "unaffected" and, above all, "wholesome." In Sweden, however, her star image seems to have remained more contradictory even throughout her American career; like her characters in her Swedish films, Bergman was potentially a perfect family wife, but at the same time she was strong and self-dependent.

The Lindström-Rossellini scandal did undoubtedly alter Bergman's reputation in Sweden, although it is difficult to say to what extent. In some quarters, namely in the "quality" daily press, Bergman became characterized as a threat because she was the immensely successful star of an intellectually scorned popular medium. The arrival, therefore, of Bergman back in Stockholm in 1955—the fallen movie star trying to appear in a literary and musical high-art context—provided an excellent opportunity for this press firmly to reassert the old aesthetic hierarchies.

These hierarchies ultimately engaged the question of money and financial success, by tradition a somewhat problematic topic in Sweden, where various media scandals over the years have been generated simply by people receiving too much pay in the public eye. The amount of money paid to Ingrid Bergman came in for particular attention. John Russell Taylor actually states about the *Joan of Arc at the Stake* debacle that "she had to face the most concentrated hostility and outright malice in her whole career": "Any Swede will tell you that it is deeply ingrained in the national character: whereas in France, say, any success a French performer has abroad only intensifies popularity at home . . . in Sweden any success a Swede may have outside the country is fiercely resented and dis-missed — the very fact of leaving Sweden, if only temporarily, is regarded as some sort of betrayal." [11] Although this generalized argument cannot be sustained on all levels (as in, say, the case of former United Nations general secretary Dag Hammarskjöld), it certainly was true for director Ingmar Bergman, for tennis champion Björn Borg, for sex symbol Anita Ekberg, and especially for Ingrid Bergman. Yet, arguably because of the very tensions in Swedish culture her 1955 return revealed, Ingrid Bergman would, at least, later receive both respect and support from her homeland.

THE PRESS RECEPTION OF *JOAN OF ARC AT THE STAKE*

The theatrical production of *Joan of Arc at the Stake* had originally premiered on December 5, 1953, as *Giovanna al rogo*, in Naples, Italy. Tag Gallagher de-scribes in some detail Rossellini's directorial strategy for this production:

> His production would resemble medieval paintings or passion plays. . . . To change scene from landscape to church, he would use rear-projectors and lan-tern slides, fake flames and colored spots, stars, mist, and passing clouds. His curtain would open with a small girl tied to the stake stage-rear, flames would rise up, and Ingrid would ascend out of the darkness on an elevator, in black, with only her face showing, which would represent her mind looking at her past. The moral would be that freedom means commitment, accepting chains, and going to the stake, like in *Paisà* [Rossellini's neorealist film of 1946].[12]

The performance in Naples received excellent press, and Rossellini was hailed as a reviver of opera; reviews of Ingrid Bergman as Joan were, in Gallagher's words, "ecstatic." [13] In 1954 the production was taken to the Paris Opéra, where composer and author, Honegger and Claudel themselves, gave it their blessing. It was an astounding success in Paris. In London, however, reviews were much more critical (perhaps because the British establishment was also historically deeply ambivalent about the cultural status of popular films), although the pro-duction fared well in Barcelona, where additional performances were given in French.

The February 1955 performances in Stockholm were heavily advertised and highly anticipated, particularly because it was Bergman's first visit to her home country with her new family; her last visit had been with Aron Petter Lindström in 1948. The press saluted her, and the weeklies greeted the Rossellini family by running big interviews; journalist Anita Thomasson provided two, one each for the "highbrow" *Vecko-Journalen* and the "lowbrow" *Veckorevyn*.[14] The tickets for the five performances were released on February 2, and the newspaper *Stockholms-Tidningen* reported that tickets were already being offered on the black market at exorbitant prices half an hour after the box office had opened.[15] In commercial terms, in fact, the production was a huge success. Performances were given in Swedish, after a translation of Claudel's libretto by Swedish writer Nils-Olof Franzén.[16]

The Stockholm quality press, however, had a field day, spurning both Bergman's performance and Rossellini's staging. *Morgon-Tidningen*, a social-democratic daily paper, printed two separate reviews under the same heading, one on Honegger's music by a musical scholar, Folke Törnblom, and one on Claudel's libretto by the arts editor of the paper, Erwin Leiser.[17] Both were tough in their judgments. Törnblom was indirectly critical, lamenting the fact that the real star of the evening, Honegger, had been totally forgotten in the aggressive marketing of the piece (he was referring, of course, to the publicity about the Rossellinis). Leiser was more openly aggressive, claiming that the Rossellini presentation of Claudel's and Honegger's work of art was "shocking." Leiser also directly attacked the "cinematic" aspects of the production: "Rossellini is a film director and thus alien to the demands of the stage. He presents the piece in CinemaScope and bright colors. And he lets Ingrid Bergman act as if she were in front of a camera."[18] He also explicitly mocked the cost of hiring the Rossellinis: "The honoraria paid to the Rossellinis seem to have made it impossible for the Opera to invest properly in stage props," and there was apparently not enough money left "to dress the choir, who were hidden among the orchestra instead of being on stage where they should be in this mystery play." Finally, Ingrid Bergman was criticized for the limitations of her acting ability.

The attack on Bergman's acting was repeated by the newspaper *Aftonbladet* in a review by drama critic Teddy Nyblom, who had quarreled with Rossellini personally at a press conference before the premiere: "The eye beats the ear to death in this cinematic, commonplace version. One thought one had seen a short movie in color and CinemaScope."[19] Nyblom also complained about Rossellini's not having directed Ingrid Bergman properly, even though she was "no great actress."

Ebbe Linde, a poet, scholar, and drama critic for the daily *Dagens Nyheter*, was less vicious.[20] However, he also marginalized Rossellini's artistic abilities: "Rossellini has created a prologue to the music and he himself has described how it happened: he listened to the records and experienced a vision, without in the least knowing about Claudel." He also gave Bergman her share of criticism: "Just Like Rossellini, Ingrid Bergman has enjoyed greatness completely within realist

filmmaking. On the stage, she is too rigid and her voice has a too-limited register." Linde also claimed that the strongest impression on him, paradoxically, was
when Bergman performed a simple song, and here he went on to allude, explicitly—the only critic to do so—to the Lindström-Bergman-Rossellini ménage à
trois and the five-year-old scandal: "She still has that clear, relentlessly Nordic
appearance which in its time enchanted America, before moral bigotry lit a fire."
Linde finished his review by adding that Swedish theater and opera directors
like Alf Sjöberg or Göran Gentele (later, ironically, the director of New York's
Metropolitan Opera) would have done much better. As it were, he continued,
Honegger was the real star of the evening, and the Swedish musicians also performed well. Only the third rank, Linde concluded, could be given to the famous
guests.

Musical critic Yngve Flycht of the daily *Expressen* was, with Linde, somewhat
lenient toward Ingrid Bergman personally.[21] Still, he claimed that Rossellini's direction demanded an actress with a richness of voice that Bergman just did not
possess. Also, the Rossellini device of placing the choir among the orchestra was
nothing less than "a disaster." Rossellini's direction removed everything that was
"monumental" about the piece, and in what was left he "loses himself in a close-
up technique that has nothing to do here." Yet Flycht added a few kind words
about Ingrid Bergman: "This world-famous Swede, whom we adore so much for
her freshness, happiness, courage, and firmness, allowed us to hear her most formidable Swedish. . . . But, in such a demanding auditorium, her voice lacks the
necessary musical quality." And, he added, he was sorry "to have to welcome
Ingrid Bergman home to her old country with so few words of warm sympathy."

The only female critic in the daily review sample, drama critic Kajsa Rootzén,
writing for the *Svenska Dagbladet*, was also very critical of Rossellini's direction
and claimed that the English critics had been absolutely right: Rossellini's direction clearly falsified Claudel's intentions, and the staging worked against the dramatic text.[22] Ingrid Bergman did not have the stature to carry her role properly,
being too "vague" and "cool." Bergman did, however, contribute something
through her considerable vocal resources, shown off by the musical presentation.
The staging, on the other hand, was destroyed by Rossellini's idiosyncratic direction. In the end, by far the most affirmative review came from composer Kurt
Atterberg, reviewing *Joan of Arc at the Stake* for the liberal paper *Stockholms-
Tidningen*.[23] Even so, Atterberg's review contained a few sneers aimed at Rossellini, whose "illustrated edition" of Claudel's difficult and complex oratorio "is
intended to make it easier or at least to speed up the grasping of the text."

READING THE CRITICS OUT

Some common traits are obvious in these reviews, and they all relate to the
hierarchy of discourses described earlier: the predominantly male establishment

press that valorized high art over popular culture, the relative lack of aesthetic status of film at the time, the foregrounding of fame and money as contemptible aspects of the star persona. The importance of the oratorio as an event is obvious from the fact that the Stockholm papers sent their most prestigious critics to the performance, and their reviews in some cases were the size of critical essays. Yet the purpose of these essays was to establish an aesthetic hierarchy in which Roberto Rossellini and Ingrid Bergman were firmly placed at the very bottom. Nevertheless, although Bergman acted "vague" (Rootzén) and "like she was in front of a camera" (Leiser), was "no great actress" (Nyblom), and had a voice of "limited register" (Linde) that lacked "musical quality" (Flycht), her appearance was praised and her suffering at the hands of the American press (when it was mentioned) was denounced as "unfair." Despite general condemnation of the amount of money earned by the Rossellinis—which Leiser cunningly blamed for the bad quality of the entire production—the fact remains that the enormously popular Bergman was not attacked as much as Roberto Rossellini and the medium of film itself.

Of the six reviews mentioned so far, the majority were quite explicit in belittling Rossellini's background as a filmmaker. Because he was a film director he was inherently "alien" to the "demands of the stage," and all was in CinemaScope and bright colors (Leiser) or "like a short movie in color and CinemaScope" (Nyblom). Likewise, the direction was "cinematic" and "commonplace"—that is, commonplace *because* cinematic (Nyblom). Rossellini's "close-up technique" (Flycht) was a ludicrous but derogatory reference to a cinematic convention, obviously used metonymically as a *pars pro toto* for bad art, namely the cinema. Even Atterberg's reference to Rossellini's production as an "illustrated edition" of Claudel's literary masterpiece conforms to anticinema rhetoric, which at the time referred to cheap and considerably bowdlerized versions of literary works in the shape of popular editions and comics, both of which were implicitly tied to the cinema and its "readers." Rossellini's "shocking" direction was also couched in hierarchical terms—his insolence in transforming art into entertainment, his "not knowing the least about Claudel" and his inferiority to Swedish directors (Linde), his "falsifying" of Claudel's intentions (Rootzén), the fact that he did not "understand" (the implication being that Rossellini was uneducated) that *Joan of Arc at the Stake* was an oratorio and not an opera, and so on. The reader, of course, was supposed to agree with these assessments and certainly to apprehend all of the cinematic attributes as vulgar. Not one of the critics mentioned that Rossellini enjoyed world fame outside of Sweden precisely as an exemplar of a cinematic movement, Italian neorealism, that challenged such norms of Hollywood-style cinema.

Taken together, the highbrow critics conformed to some or all of the three frames of reference I established earlier. As highbrow critics they were most predictable in their contempt for the popular appeal of the Rossellinis' visit to Stockholm and their getting "mixed up" with high art at the Royal Opera. The few references to the earlier scandal make it difficult to assess to what extent it contributed to the critics' scorn. But the outright aggression against and the blatant disrespect for Rossellini's person — shared by all of the male critics, with Kajsa Rootzén being noticeably more subdued — indicate that there was both a gender and a class bias at work. Ingrid Bergman, the Swedish beauty, had married an Italian film director who was certainly not to be accepted by the male Swedish highbrow establishment.

TO BE EXHIBITED FOR MONEY

These prejudices of class and gender became more obvious a week after the oratorio's first performances in Stockholm, when longer articles began to appear in the highbrow weeklies like *Vecko-Journalen*. If the reviews in the daily papers had been harsh, they had been relatively respectful, especially toward Bergman herself. Now, in *Vecko-Journalen*, Ingrid Bergman and Roberto Rossellini were lambasted in terms far more biased and scornful than the dailies had employed.

Vecko-Journalen had covered Ingrid Bergman in negative terms before. When Bergman visited Stockholm in 1948, before she left Hollywood and Lindström for Rossellini, Lars Ulvenstam, who at the time was a young doctoral student in comparative literature (and later a highbrow media personality), produced an article that was highly critical of the actress.[24] The article indulged in elitist clichés and openly mocked the purity of Bergman's Hollywood image, her lack of educated values, and her financial greed. It also expressed various anti-American sentiments common in Swedish highbrow culture at the time (and another normative frame of reference for the reception of Ingrid Bergman, a Hollywood star). Birgit Tengroth, a former actress with literary ambitions, also wrote an article on Bergman in 1952. Tengroth related how she and Bergman had been in acting school together and how Bergman became the unchallenged star of the class. Tengroth willingly admitted her jealousy of Bergman but added, with malicious pleasure, that Ingrid Bergman had finally gotten her comeuppance: "To me she was like a sunflower. The sunflower that looks so strong and luxuriant until one day a storm comes and robs it of its crown."[25]

For the *Joan of Arc at the Stake* production, *Vecko-Journalen* came to wage war again on Ingrid Bergman. They assigned Erik Lindegren to write the review. Lindegren was at the time one of Sweden's most esteemed modernist poets, an author of famous librettos, and also sporadically the opera critic for *Vecko-Journalen*.[26] His very first opera review, in fact, and his first review for the magazine, was on Ingrid Bergman in *Joan of Arc at the Stake*. He was scathing, to say the least:

> Ingrid Bergman and Rossellini hosted the masked ball of the year, on both sides
> of the proscenium, and contributed ambitiously to the entertainment with the
> divertimento *Joan of Arc at the Stake*, otherwise known as a masterpiece by

Claudel and Honegger. . . . The way [Rossellini] solves staging problems seems to be founded on a film director's nightmare of a work in which song, speech, music, and movement must add up to such an impossibly unified entity that the main role least of all seems to be written for Ingrid Bergman. . . .

It is just natural that the message . . . that Claudel had died would cast even more shadow on Rossellini's sophistically hackneyed and confused version. On the other hand, in the light of [Claudel's death] the production became too insignificant even to be called a disaster. . . .

Rossellini thus cuts the pulse out of the strong dramatic content of the work, and undermines the roles of the choir and the music respectively. On the other hand he gives us Ingrid Bergman *au naturelle*, where in reality the work demands a genial and musically talented actress — along with a few kitsch cinema effects, project closeups, intertitles, smoke screens, and false spaces, which make the available and confusingly arranged stage even poorer. . . .

Those of us who left the premiere disappointed could reflect ourselves on the cool reception in the morning papers in reviews surrounded by advertisements for Ingrid Bergman blouses and Rossellini's used car tires. . . . But Claudel's and Honegger's work still is great and should be presented soon in purified shape.[27]

Here the same old discourses are echoed. Rossellini and Bergman are ridiculed in much the same terms employed by the dailies. The only ones who come in for praise are several of the Swedish participants in the performance, such as the male actors and the musical director. The review does not, then, wholly support Lindegren's own assertion that the version was "too insignificant even to be called a disaster." It is in fact a mixture of diplomatic praise for the resident Swedes and personal attack against the Rossellinis.

That in *Vecko-Journalen*'s handling of the matter there was something personal, and yet also profoundly ideological, is made clear in by far the worst attack on the Rossellinis, launched by Stig Ahlgren, a regular chronicler well known in Sweden for his wit and his extremely nasty way of reviewing. His background was academic, highbrow, and literary; many of his pieces of criticism have become minor classics. "To Be Exhibited for Money," his attack on Bergman and Rossellini, is certainly one of his most famous.[28]

According to some sources, the biographical background to Ahlgren's vicious attack on Bergman was actually his wife — Birgit Tengroth, the actress-novelist mentioned earlier, who had been in school with Bergman — and her personal hatred and jealousy of the star. "Ahlgren," she is reputed to have said as he left for the opening of *Joan of Arc at the Stake*, "don't you dare write any nice words about Ingrid."[29] More interesting from my point of view is the fact that the highbrow *Vecko-Journalen* sent not only Erik Lindegren but also its senior writer, Ahlgren, to the event — and that Ahlgren had never before written, and never would again, any review of a theatrical production.

I quote Ahlgren's review below at some length because it has heretofore been excerpted only in tiny bits in English: [30]

Criticism, both here and abroad, has contained some acid about Ingrid Bergman. Her artistic range is too narrow, her voice is trivial, she does not know what passion means, and so on.

What she has earned from playing Joan of Arc at the stake is, as is well known, not just nickels and dimes; but she hardly deserves even this. Ingrid Bergman is not really an actress in the established sense. Her career has taken place at an entirely different level. To compare her, as has frequently been done, to professional actresses is both nasty and unfair.

She travels around and is exhibited for money. The exhibitor is Roberto Rossellini, with whom she has three children and one Rolls Royce. This travelling troupe has very little or nothing to do with art. . . .

Ingrid Bergman is not an actress but a clever businesswoman. In cold blood she has calculated her chances of earning money on her particular attractiveness for the masses. "If you got something people wants [*sic*], sell it!" This golden rule she has made her own. In the eyes of Hollywood, for many years she incarnated the myth of the sound woman, the unproblematic comrade wife. When the myth cracked up, she could not be exhibited for money any more in America.

Back in Europe, she was condemned to play her life's role number two: the courageous woman who takes her fate into her own hands. She is still no actress. She is and can only be herself, exhibiting phases from her private life. The Joan of Arc that she is set to play is the hurt martyr of free love against whom a stupid and clumsy process has been opened by puritan bigotry. Two things that she has said in American interviews bear witness to her complete insensitivity towards what Joan of Arc is about. One of them was "Only affected people like classical music." That one was for Honegger! The other one was "I do not believe in the supernatural." That one was for Claudel! With sympathetic openness she replies to the question why she, a somewhat lukewarm and uncomplicated Swedish "country girl," has chosen to play Joan of Arc, a great tragic role: "It just happened that way."

It just happened that way that when Rossellini and Ingrid Bergman had created flawed films one after the other, there was nothing left for them to do but travel from city to city, from country to country, and exhibit Ingrid for money. . . .

One has to keep things separate. That an oratorio was performed at the same time that Ingrid was on stage at the opera, exhibiting herself for money, has created many unnecessary misunderstandings, mostly by critics, since the audience never doubted for a moment what it paid to see: Ingrid, our Ingrid, playing the role of a friendly and well-brought-up Swedish girl . . . , the role she performed in the weeks before the premiere while the press kindly carried wood for the publicity fire. . . .

The best review — still another proof of her sound and natural spirit — came from Ingrid Bergman herself after the performance: "I thought it went rather well." A different view can only be held by someone who still tried to judge Ingrid Bergman as if she were an actress. Why do we love her, if not for her happiness; yes, precisely happiness, since she lacks precisely that which is the inner core of being an artist: self-criticism, and the humility it takes to represent life which is not one's own. Theatre is performance. Theatre is according to Ingrid Bergman herself "affected" and "supernatural," something entirely alien to her own uncomplicated self.

Ingrid Bergman exhibits herself for money. That is nothing to be ashamed of.[31]

Once again, the terms are familiar: utter disrespect for Rossellini and his art, and contempt for the amount of money paid to the international stars (it should be noted that Ahlgren, a Marxist in the 1930s, was extremely well paid himself).[32] But his tone is harsher and more cruel; to write that Rossellini was the leader, the "exhibitor" of a "travelling troupe" was highly insulting.[33] The outrage against Bergman personally, as an object to be "exhibited" (not in a museum, of course, but in a circus, or a zoo) for money, is nastier than that of any other critic to that point.

What is most puzzling, however, is that Ahlgren — one of the great literary stylists of twentieth-century Sweden — draws so heavily on the article about Bergman written by Lars Ulvenstam seven years earlier, without attribution of any kind. Only Ahlgren's expression "country girl" was put within quotation marks, being obviously taken from Ulvenstam. The attacks on Bergman for what she had said about classical music and the supernatural were also taken from Ulvenstam's text. Most striking of all, the grammatically incorrect English sentence — "If you got something people wants, sell it!" — was directly plagiarized. A possible explanation is that Ahlgren in 1948 had been the editor-in-chief of *Vecko-Journalen*, for which Ulvenstam's article was written; thus, he knew the earlier article and used the very same words in order to hurt Ingrid Bergman even worse and to remind her of the former attack.

The day after the publication of Ahlgren's article, Ingrid Bergman defended herself publicly at a charity event in Stockholm.[34] And from that moment things began to take a different turn. Ahlgren's attack provoked a backlash, and a fierce debate began in *Vecko-Journalen*. Gustaf von Platen, Ahlgren's biographer and also editor-in-chief of *Vecko-Journalen* at the time, claims that the article created "a storm, worse than any storm a Swedish review ever before had created."[35] And for three weeks *Vecko-Journalen* published many letters to the editor, of which an overwhelming majority attacked Ahlgren: "Dr. Ahlgren's words about Ingrid Bergman are more than harsh. . . . Ingrid Bergman's private life, now once again the issue, is really exemplary. We should neither be conventional nor formal. She has had the courage to stand up to the world and follow her own conscience."[36] "It is a pleasure to see somebody fight Mr. Ahlgren back — for too long it has looked like nobody dared to fight this fencer with a poisoned blade."[37] But some letters could also take Ahlgren's side: "I want to thank you. . . . To let 'Circus Rossellini' loose on our Opera is to say the least irresponsible."[38] One could also find support for Ahlgren in the sneering remarks made about Bergman's marriage: "Public opinion would not have concerned itself with Ingrid Bergman's private life, had she divorced and remarried under normal conditions. . . . Some moral values should also be expected from Ingrid Bergman."[39] But most of the letters raged at Ahlgren.[40]

One of the harshest letters was quoted by Ahlgren himself in his personal response to one that read, "Baldhead! Go to hell, you fucking swine, dungheap," and was signed "Educated reader of *Vecko-Journalen*."[41] Ahlgren replied that he meant that Ingrid Bergman was a "sacred cow" who just could not understand, nor accept, that she was a mediocre actress. She also could not realize that she owed her popularity to Hollywood, where she "was backed by American housewives (who later let her down when she did not conform to the myth of the jaunty, faithful, and erotic ideal spouse)" (305–306). Ahlgren also quoted an article by Ivar Harrie, editor-in-chief of *Expressen* (and yet another respected highbrow personality of the literary establishment), who claimed that Ingrid Bergman was "an idol, protected by everything stuck-up and pharisaic in this country" (304).

In his later version of the background of the entire Bergman affair, von Platen writes:

> She had been worshipped in Sweden during her Hollywood years, but then came the divorce from her Swedish husband and the passionate affair with Roberto Rossellini. It was hard for the Swedish people to forgive her. It was not the fact that she had let down her husband and child that most bothered the Swedes. Instead, it was that she had proved her image—young, beautiful, chaste, sinful Hollywood's Virgin of Orléans—false. Ingrid Bergman, the Nordic vestal, was indeed like the rest of us. (296–297)

Yet neither Ahlgren's justification nor von Platen's contextualization accounts for the contentiousness the events elicited. In 1955 the conflict did not concern itself much with Bergman's marital infidelity or the falseness of the "Nordic vestal"; when these were referred to, it was to criticize American "moral bigotry." Rather, the conflict in Sweden depended much more on the class- and gender-based opposition between "high" and "low." Von Platen's description mainly replicates later Hollywood lore that links the downfall of the actress to her perfect image; in Sweden, however, Bergman's image had been quite different.

The reception of Ingrid Bergman, Roberto Rossellini, and *Joan of Arc at the Stake* represented a cultural battle over the arts in which the dominant, male literary culture attempted to use Ingrid Bergman, both as a woman and as a representative of commercial film culture, to consolidate and increase the power of an existing aesthetic hierarchy. They were not, it seems, completely successful.

Several women's weeklies, for example, later defended Bergman more vociferously, both on the protofeminist ground of her rights as a human being and a woman's "right to love."[42] In fact, Bergman was never again the subject of press attack in Sweden. She continued to be a heroine of the women's weeklies until her death, with her life story reiterated again and again.

• • •

Regarded more than forty years later, the storm over *Joan of Arc at the Stake* is interesting primarily because it brought out into the open the polarization in Swedish cultural politics between "low" and "high," and the "low" for once responded to the attacks from the "high." If Ingrid Bergman was, in Ahlgren's terms, a "sacred cow," the conflict showed that the Swedish literary culture of which he was a part was an even bigger one, its highbrow and establishment "priests" more in need of humility and self-criticism than Bergman and Rossellini. Another dimension is the difference between America and Sweden regarding cultural and sexual politics. In America Bergman had, like her heroine Joan of Arc, been "burnt at the stake" for her alleged moral inadequacies. In Sweden, which was much more liberal in sexual terms than America, this was clearly not as much of an issue. But the scandal Bergman had created in the past could be used ideologically in Sweden for another purpose, which was much more important to internal power relations: that is, to oppress the popular culture mostly connected with women by fabricating yet another "scandal" in the name of art.

NOTES

I am greatly indebted to Adrienne McLean for her most helpful editing.

1. Standard works are Ingrid Bergman (with Alan Burgess), *My Story* (New York: Delacorte Press, 1980), simultaneously published in Sweden as *Mitt Liv* (Stockholm: Norstedts, 1980); Laurence Leamer, *As Time Goes By: The Life of Ingrid Bergman* (New York: Harper and Row, 1986), simultaneously published in Sweden as *As Time Goes By: Den sanna bilden av Ingrid Bergman*, Swedish trans. Riina Larsson (Stockholm: Forum, 1986); and Donald Spoto, *Notorious: The Life of Ingrid Bergman* (New York: HarperCollins, 1997). Other biographical accounts are Joseph Henry Steele, *Ingrid Bergman: An Intimate Portrait* (New York: David McKay, 1959); John Russell Taylor, *Ingrid Bergman* (London: Elm Tree Books, 1983); and John Kobal, ed., *Legends: Ingrid Bergman*, with an introduction by Sheridan Morley (London: Pavilion, 1985). A recent biography of Rossellini, Tag Gallagher's *The Adventures of Roberto Rossellini: His Life and Films* (New York: Da Capo Press, 1998), contains useful information. Academic studies of Bergman include James Damico, "Ingrid from Lorraine to Stromboli: Analyzing the Public's Perception of a Film Star" (1975), in Jeremy G. Butler, ed., *Star Texts: Image and Performance in Film and Television* (Detroit: Wayne State University Press, 1991), 240–253; and Adrienne L. McLean, "The Cinderella Princess and the Instrument of Evil: Surveying the Limits of Female Transgression in Two Postwar Hollywood Scandals," *Cinema Journal* 34 (1995): 36–

56, and expanded version in this volume. Bergman continues to be the subject of new "documentaries" for biography series that run regularly on television cable channels in America.

2. Spoto, *Notorious*, 291.

3. Although the conflict I explore was largely carried out in the media, it was not a media scandal of the sort James Lull and Stephen Hinerman describe in "The Search for Scandal" in their anthology *Media Scandals: Morality and Desire in the Popular Marketplace* (New York: Columbia University Press, 1997). Rather, Bergman's star scandal, her affair with Rossellini, was used as an opportunity to discuss Bergman's personal and professional shortcomings in a language and a context and for reasons that have since become shocking on their own and that might, now, from a different vantage point, be thought scandalous as well. See also the introduction to this volume.

4. The phrase "normative frame of reference" is derived from Janet Staiger, *Interpreting Films: Studies in the Historical Reception of American Cinema* (Princeton: Princeton University Press, 1991), 79–97. Staiger argues that critics make their points in a context that includes their own social positions and their understanding of a presumed audience for whom they write. Although notions of value are not in this sense "universal," they can be used as "political weapons."

5. Per Rydén, *Domedagar: Svensk litteraturkritik efter 1880* (*Days of judgment: Swedish literary criticism after 1880*), Press & Litteratur 14 (Lund: Litteraturvetenskapliga institutionen, 1987).

6. By Olof Lagercrantz, literary scholar, critic, arts editor, and editor-in-chief of *Dagens Nyheter*, October 3, 1956. Quoted in Ingmar Bergman, *The Magic Lantern* (London: Penguin, 1988), 155.

7. Tytti Soila, Astrid Söderbergh Widding, and Gunnar Iversen, in Tytti Soila, Astrid Söderbergh Widding, and Gunnar Iversen, eds., *Nordic National Cinemas* (New York: Routledge, 1998), 5.

8. Rune Waldekranz, *Filmens historia* (Stockholm: Norstedts, 1986), 2:851.

9. Tytti Soila, "Kvinnors ansikte: Stereotyper och kvinnlig identitet i trettiotalets svenska filmmelodram" (Ph.D. diss., Stockholm: Institutionen för Teater-och Filmvetenskap, 1991).

10. Ibid., 179. Both *Intermezzo* and *En kvinnas ansikte* were remade in Hollywood, the first as *Intermezzo: A Love Story* (1939) and the latter as *A Woman's Face* (1941). Soila, however, claims that in both these films the "fissures" widened in the Swedish versions are "mended." That is, the patriarchal discourse is "stronger in the American films" (179). It should be noted that Soila's analysis of *En kvinnas ansikte* has been challenged in other Scandinavian feminist readings. Anne Jerslev claims that the Bergman character instead expresses melancholy over an essential loss. Anne Jerslev, "*En kvinnas ansikte*: En melankolisk berättelse om kvinnligheten," in Erik Hedling, ed., *Blågult flimmer: Svenska filmanalyser* (Lund: Studentlitteratur, 1998), 107–125.

11. Taylor, *Ingrid Bergman*, 87–98.

12. Gallagher, *Adventures of Roberto Rossellini*, 424.

13. Ibid.

14. Anita Thomasson, "Pappa är barnvakt" (Daddy's babysitting), *Vecko-Journalen*, February 5–12, 1955, 9, 17–18; and "Pappa, mamma, barn" (Daddy, mummy, and the children), *Veckorevyn*, February 12–19, 1955, 18–20.

15. Unsigned, "800 i Jeanne d'Arc-kön, alla kunde köpa biljetter," *Stockholms-Tidningen*, February 3, 1955.

16. Gallagher claims that Franzén was one of "Sweden's most famous writers" (*Adventures*, 445). In reality Franzén wrote mostly children's fiction.

17. Folke H. Törnblom och Erwin Leiser, "Herrskapet Rossellini på bål" (Mr. and Mrs. Rossellini at the stake), *Morgon-Tidningen*, February 18, 1955. All translations from the Swedish in this and other quotations are my own.

18. That Leiser ridicules the cinema is a bit ironic given that he would later become famous as a documentary filmmaker and film historian in Sweden.

19. Teddy Nyblom, "En stjärna går upp i rök" (A star goes up in smoke), *Aftonbladet*, February 18, 1955.

20. Ebbe Linde, "Talaktrisen på Operascenen bäst när hon sjöng enkel visa" (Speech artist on the opera stage best when singing a simple song), *Dagens Nyheter*, February 18, 1955.

21. Yngve Flycht, "Jeanne d'Arc efter bålet" (Joan of Arc after the stake), *Expressen*, February 18, 1955.

22. Kajsa Rootzén, "Jeanne d'Arc på Operan" (Joan of Arc at the opera), *Svenska Dagbladet*, February 18, 1955.

23. Kurt Atterberg, "Känslolös Ingrid på bålet: Jeanne d'Arc på Operan framgång för Rossellini" (Insensitive Ingrid at the stake: Joan of Arc at the opera success for Rossellini), *Stockholms-Tidningen*, February 18, 1955.

24. Lars Ulvenstam, "Ingrid Bergman osminkad" (Ingrid Bergman without makeup), *Vecko-Journalen*, no. 42, 1948, 20, 27.

25. Birgit Tengroth, "Ingrid den granna" (Ingrid the beautiful), *Vecko-Journalen*, no. 11, 1952, 20–21. Tengroth became known as a novelist in the early 1950s; Ingmar Bergman's *Three Strange Loves* (*Thirst*, 1949) was based on her collection of short stories.

26. See Erik Lindegren, *Operakritik* (Opera critique), ed. with an introduction by John Stenström (Lund: Ellerströms, 1994), 8.

27. Erik Lindegren, "Rossellinis ringlinje," *Vecko-Journalen*, March 5–12, 1955, 9–11. The article is reprinted in Erik Lindegren, *Operakritik*, 17–21.

28. Stig Ahlgren, "Visa sig för pengar," *Vecko-Journalen*, February 26–March 5, 1955, 15.

29. Ahlgren's other claim to international fame is that he was the real-life model for the mean engineer Alman (played with a striking physical likeness by actor Gunnar Sjöberg) in Ingmar Bergman's *Wild Strawberries* (1957). The engineer's wife, played by Gunnel Broström, was in turn based on Ahlgren's wife, Birgit Tengroth. Ahlgren and Tengroth's marriage was, apparently, very unhappy. See Gustaf von Platen, *Min vän Stig Ahlgren: Kvickhetens konung* (My friend Stig Ahlgren: The wizard of wit) (Stockholm: Fischer and Company, 1997), 31–40, 299. In *Images: My Life* (New York: Arcade, 1994) Ingmar Bergman claims, "Over the years I have not intentionally created a multitude of malicious portraits of people I know. The quarreling marital couple, Stig Ahlgren and Birgit Tengroth in *Wild Strawberries*, is a sad exception, one which I regret" (164).

30. In Gallagher, *Adventures*, 445; Leamer, *Ingrid Bergman*, 234; Bergman, *Mitt liv*, 385.

31. The article is reprinted in Gustaf von Platen, *Min vän Stig Ahlgren*, 301–304.

32. Ibid., 42.

33. "Exhibitor" and "travelling troupe" refer to low-status traveling theater companies or circuses. Even if Ahlgren was not a racist—he would elsewhere, for instance, publicly denounce prejudice against Gypsies—the phrase "travelling troupe"

could also connote "tattare," or "travelers," an ethnically undefined group with no-madic living patterns in Sweden. The "travelers" enjoyed very low social status and were often depicted as swarthy, promiscuous, and violent in Swedish popular cul-ture, especially in the cinema. Rossellini, as an Italian, conformed in his appearance, at least a little bit, to this stereotype. Åke Grönberg, who plays the circus director Albert in Ingmar Bergman's *The Naked Night* (aka *Sawdust and Tinsel,* 1953), wears makeup in the film that easily connects him to the "travelers." In the 1950s, ethnically stereotyped films about "travelers" were common in Sweden. See Rochelle Wright, *The Visible Wall: Jews and Other Ethnic Outsiders in Swedish Cinema* (Carbondale: Southern Illinois University Press, 1999), 95–147.

34. Ingrid Bergman's speech is quoted in extenso in Spoto, *Notorious,* 318.

35. Gustaf von Platen, *Min vän Stig Ahlgren,* 298.

36. Carl-Gustaf Lundberg, letter to the editor, "I angeläget ärende" (Of immedi-ate concern), *Vecko-Journalen,* March 12–19, 1955, 6.

37. Eric Ahlström, letter to the editor, "I angeläget ärende," *Vecko-Journalen,* March 12–19, 1955, 7. The writer also mentions approvingly articles defending Berg-man written by personal friends, journalists Barbro Alving and Mollie Faustman; see Ingrid Bergman, *Mitt liv,* 354–356.

38. Runa Wendler, letter to the editor, "Extra angeläget ärende," *Vecko-Journalen,* March 19–26, 1955, 22.

39. Holger Dahlberg, letter to the editor, "I angeläget ärende," *Vecko-Journalen,* March 26–31, 1955, 16.

40. I have actually spoken to one letter writer to *Vecko-Journalen,* a medical stu-dent at the time. He claimed that his family admired Ingrid Bergman greatly for her strong personality and that they were outraged by Ahlgren's attack. The writer of the letter had never held any opinions about the Lindström-Rossellini-Bergman scandal.

41. In Gustaf von Platen, *Min vän Stig Ahlgren,* 307.

42. The extremely popular *Hänt i veckan* provides a good example. In 1966 this women's weekly published a special edition devoted entirely to Bergman's life. Most of the issue covers the story of her three divorces, her relation to her children, and her brave struggles to pursue her career (*Hänt i veckan,* March 4, 1966).

Systematizing Scandal

Confidential Magazine, Stardom, and the State of California

Mary Desjardins

*I*n his groundbreaking history of the development of the Hollywood star system, Richard deCordova argues that the star scandals of the 1920s were an actualization of "something that had previously had an existence as a more virtual set of pressures, contradictions, and fantasy scenarios."[1] DeCordova's description of scandal in the 1920s is also useful for thinking about star scandal from the studio era of the 1930s and 1940s to the poststudio, postmodern media period of today. Star scandals—everything from Rock Hudson's death from AIDS in 1985 to the Woody Allen/Mia Farrow/Soon Yi Previn triangle of the early 1990s—do still seem to "erupt" into actualization, promising "a full and satisfying disclosure of the star's identity."[2] Yet the "ante" for what signifies the "promise of a full and satisfying disclosure" of a star's identity has been upped considerably, and this is not only because of changing sexual mores in the social sphere. The deregulated, globalized, multichannel, multimedia environment of postmodern culture allows for competing star discourses of morality and scandal to circulate simultaneously (both at the level of the individual star and on a more general register of stardom), and some contemporary stars' personas are based to a considerable extent on scandal itself.[3]

To state the obvious, we are in a culture of scandal, a culture in which scandal—both the alleged event and the response to it—can be, and often is, compatible with systematic, mass-produced forms of public media discourse. Scandal may still be experienced by any number of players (the readers/spectators, the media producers, and even sometimes the transgressors) as an eruption, but it now breaks as news in carefully preconstructed narrative and imagistic frameworks to a public that at some level expects that that behavior is possible, inevitably documented by technologies and witnesses, and made accessible for interpretation through multiple media sites. The fantasy scenario deCordova described as the location of the preactualized star scandal of the 1920s has not just moved from the public's unconscious to its preconscious but could be said to reside most of the time in the zone of consciousness.

This essay, however, will not be concerned with the current positionings of stars vis-à-vis scandal. Instead, by focusing on a pivotal period and phenomenon between the studio era and now—the 1950s and the rise of the scandal magazines—I will examine the changes in social, industrial, and legal regulations of public discourse about stars that helped create this contemporary environment. Specifically, I will discuss the way scandal magazines of the 1950s attempted to construct star scandal with a kind of "systematicity" that would give them an unlimited supply of copy, ensure an ongoing difference from Hollywood-produced discourse, and protect them from legal action. This will entail a discussion of their personnel (private investigators, writers, tipster call girls), research methods and evidence gathering (wiretapping, spy photography, historical research into past press coverage), and their aesthetic (the creation of the "composite" photo and the "composite fact" story, repackaging of past narratives about stars).

I will also examine the ways the Hollywood film industry and the state of California responded to these magazines. Any attempt to understand the origin, context, and ultimate impact of these magazines must examine these responses because the magazines' own forms of systematicity—their operating procedures and the aesthetics of their product—were shaped out of a canny anticipation of the possible reprisals from the film industry and the state, two other institutions that had a stake in the production of knowledge about personal and social identity in terms of a public/private, surface/depth logic. Because it was *Confidential* magazine that the state of California brought to trial in 1957 for criminal libel and obscenity, I will use articles from that publication as my specific examples of scandal magazine stories.

• • •

Publisher Robert Harrison claimed that the excitement caused by the 1951 televised hearings of Senator Estes Kefauver's committee on organized crime was the inspiration for creating *Confidential* magazine in 1952. In other words, Harrison learned that the spectacle of secrets being revealed about powerful people had public appeal that could be commercially exploited. Although the hearings may have been the most immediate inspiration for his launching of a scandal publication venture, Harrison was already poised for entry into scandal magazines by the start of the decade. He had vast experience in tabloid newspapers and film-industry trade publications since the 1920s, and by the 1940s he was producing "girlie" magazines like *Whisper* (which he later successfully revamped into a scandal magazine after *Confidential's* popularity was proven). "Girlie" or "cheesecake" magazines did well in the 1940s, helping to create and sustain the American GI's interest in pinup art. These and other tabloid publications flooded the market as wartime paper rationing was lifted in 1950. Although many of the titles failed, the theme of female sexual transgression was an already established frame, and *Confidential's* success in featuring scandal stories about stars and other famous people, as well as exposing racketeering, consumer scams, and political peccadilloes, resulted in dozens of copycat magazines and hundreds of "one-shots" (onetime publications focused on one star or theme) in the 1950s.[4] Those magazines, like *Confidential*, that enjoyed sustained prosperity throughout much of the decade did not owe all their success to the availability of cheap paper and exploitation of name figures. At least three other dynamically related factors secured their popularity with the public and (at least temporary) protection from actions taken by Hollywood and the state: 1) the general legal climate in the 1950s surrounding issues of libel, privacy, and obscenity; 2) the magazines' uses of sources (many who willingly signed affidavits), state-of-the-art surveillance research methods, and what we may call today a "tabloid" or "trash" aesthetic for narratives and graphic design; and 3) the ability to sustain plausible fictions about stars at a time when it was no longer clear that the official voices of Hollywood could do so — that is, the magazines realized that the studios' power was declining and that stars, as the symbols of that system, were left vulnerable to attack.

Cultural commentary and legal cases concerning alleged scandalous behavior or the reporting of it tend to conceptualize libel, privacy, and obscenity as mutually imbricated notions even though each has a separate legal definition and each can be the cause of a distinct legal action. Various historians have pointed to how legal and social institutions have understood — even if only tacitly — all three concepts as concerned with the boundaries and regulation of civility, of what should remain private and what should be public.[5] It is beyond the scope of this essay to explore all the complex issues surrounding the mutual imbrication of libel, privacy, and obscenity as legal and social concepts throughout history or even in the 1950s, but I will return to their intertwining when I discuss the state's response to *Confidential* in the 1957 trial. First, I will briefly sketch out the status of each concept as it might apply to scandal magazine activity in the 1950s.

Although the status of defamation laws in the 1950s still made libel "the celebrity's most desirable remedy against scandal magazines,"[6] the outcome of civil libel cases was uncertain at this time, at least in the California courts. Not only did testimony at defamation trials require the further recycling of the scandalous stories alleged to be libelous, but if the celebrity had not suffered pecuniary loss, the libelous material had to be defamatory on its face. In other words, it must be defamatory without the need of innuendo or inducement. Under a special civil code in California law, which exemplified the degree to which the first amendment concept was held sacred, if the judge or jury believed that the article was susceptible to an innocent as well as a defamatory interpretation, it was highly likely that the ruling would be in favor of the defendant.[7] As I discuss below, because the scandal magazines anticipated the legal implications of civil libel cases, they followed a number of "research" procedures and made stylistic choices to elude "defamation on its face" interpretations of the law.

Celebrities could bring action against the scandal magazines for invasion of privacy, but as one federal judge put it in 1956, the state of the privacy law was like "a haystack in a hurricane."[8] Originally devised out of the famous argument by Samuel Warren and Louis Brandeis in 1890, civil privacy cases concerned the more nebulous area of private feelings, protecting the individual from emotional distress. Warren and Brandeis had argued for privacy law as "a remedy for the threats to personality and feelings posed by 'recent inventions and business methods,' such as sensationalist journalism, advertising practices, and . . . newly invented Kodak, and similar cameras."[9] Warren and Brandeis had thought the technological and media developments of the 1890s made legal protection of privacy especially pressing, so it is not surprising that an increasing number of cases concerning privacy came to state or federal supreme courts in the 1950s as new media, like television and scandal magazines, and new technologies, like sophisticated, often miniature, surveillance devices (sound recorders, wiretaps, and cameras), proliferated in use throughout the decade. As with libel cases, bringing action against the scandal magazines for invasion of privacy was tricky — celebrities had to prove not only that the magazines inflicted emotional distress (not too difficult) but that they were devoid of any educational or entertainment value (much harder). Yet the law could favor the privacy of the star over the press's constitutional privileges if the material published was considered to be of such an intimate nature that its disclosure violated the community's notions of decency.[10]

However, at this time definitions of obscenity — that vague concept having to do with what was considered outside the bounds of decency — were in a shift mode, expanding legal, commercial, and social ideas about that issue. Social historians John D'Emilio and Estelle Freedman suggest that the 1946 Supreme Court decision that overturned the Post Office's denial of mailing privileges to *Esquire* magazine resulted in an increased accessibility of erotically explicit material.[11] This ruling paved the way for the appearance of *Playboy* magazine in 1953, which would never be denied mailing privileges, although it did not escape negative commentary. At the same time, publishers of cheaply produced paperback books that were easy for newsstand owners to accommodate in crowded stalls, started using sexy graphics on book covers to much public controversy but ultimately little successful legal regulation. The famous Roth Supreme Court case of 1957 (which came down the month before the *Confidential* trial started in California), although upholding local censorship efforts, established that sex and obscenity were not synonymous, making it clear that obscenity was intended to arouse prurient interests. Within the film industry, expansion of what were considered morally appropriate representations of sexuality became possible after the 1952 *Miracle* case, which extended freedom of speech to motion pictures, denied them since the *Mutual v. Ohio* ruling in 1915. Although this ruling did not result in immediate changes to the Production Code, it weakened local censorship efforts. In the mid 1950s successful challenges to the Code by Hollywood insiders, such as director-producer Otto Preminger, preceded Code expansions of admissible representation by the late 1950s.

The scandal magazines exploited this changing climate around obscenity, as well as the complexities of current libel and privacy laws, in their efficient mass production of salacious stories about stars. To ensure a constant flow of scandal narratives for bimonthly publication, they evolved a particular philosophy toward hiring and directing personnel and used surveillance research methods and writing techniques that recycled old stories or created "composite" facts as the basis for new ones. Although the magazines usually retained a small permanent writing and editing staff, they employed many writers who were already experienced in news, either with "legitimate," mainstream papers and magazines or with tabloids. For example, Edythe Farrell, who eventually edited the successful scandal magazine *Suppressed*, had once been a writer and editor for earlier Harrison tabloid publications, and she had also edited the *Police Gazette*, a notorious precursor to scandal publications in its taste for combining sex, crime, and a fascination with the techniques of uncovering secrets to titillate a largely male readership. Harrison's smartest move in relation to personnel was the bankrolling of the organization Hollywood Research Incorporated, run by his niece Marjorie Meade and her husband. This Los Angeles–based business existed as a separate corporate entity from *Confidential* (a shrewd legal protection for Harrison and the magazine in New York), and its main purpose was to recruit writers and hire/pay tipsters and private investigators. Tipsters ranged from call girls and ex-spouses of stars to disgruntled film-industry or press employees. Harrison claimed sometimes a star's press agent, or even an important producer, such as Mike Todd, might serve as a story source.[12]

Tipsters provided initial kernels of gossip or leads for information, as well as confirmations of rumors. Sometimes the work of tipster call girls dovetailed with that of private detectives, such as when they allowed their phones to be tapped or wore wristwatches equipped with tiny recorders in hope of getting taped confirmation of what was rumored to be true about a star. Next to call girls, private investigators were among *Confidential's* most infamous research personnel, mostly confirming facts for stories already in process. These detectives used state-of-the-art surveillance equipment for both audio and visual "proof" of scandalous behavior. The concern for electronically recorded or photographed evidence, like the practice of having some tipsters sign affidavits about their stories, was part of *Confidential's* careful anticipation of legal reprisal.

The magazine's writing methodology and aesthetic included practices of re-cycling, combining, and recombining of story material. Some articles, often grouped around a particular scandal theme, basically just recycled various scan-dal stories from earlier press accounts, drawing on oft-told narratives about Mary Astor's diary and divorce in the 1930s, Errol Flynn's trial for statutory rape in the 1940s, and Fatty Arbuckle's trial for murder in the 1920s. The "composite" fact principle permeated almost every scandal story, old or new. The core facts of such a story might have occurred or had been reported elsewhere as occurring, but the narrative contained important omissions, combined several events that had no necessary causal relationship, and added embellishments, such as salacious titling, colorful graphics, alliteration, and constant reminders that the story was the result of "on the scene" reporting. Most articles that did not have photos taken at the scene were accompanied by one or more "composite" photos — photos that were taken at another scene, usually when the celebrity was caught off-guard, or that were doctored so that material from one photo would be com-bined with another (a trick of tabloid newspapers for many years). Together these composite forms imputed that the celebrity had engaged in immoral or indecent conduct.

The *Confidential* article "It Was the Hottest Show in Town When Maureen O'Hara Cuddled in Row 35" was one such composite-fact story (fig. 1).[13] In it a theater usher alleges that he caught O'Hara having sex with an unnamed Latin

Figure 1. What *Confidential* alleged about Maureen O'Hara. Copyright 1957 by Confidential, Inc.

American "lothario" in the back row of Grauman's Chinese Theatre. *Confidential* attorney Daniel G. Ross claimed at the trial that the magazine had an affidavit from the former usher that the story was true, but he also admitted he and editor Harrison were influenced by a number of legitimate newspaper headlines about O'Hara when they were considering publication of the story.[14] These headlines, such as "Ex-Husband Says Star Lives in Sin," concerned allegations made by ex-husband Will Price in 1955 that O'Hara was openly "consorting" with married Mexican businessman Enrique Parra "at all hours of the day and night" in both her Los Angeles home and his in Mexico.[15] Price was attempting to get custody of their eleven-year-old daughter, Bronwyn, and the matter was eventually settled out of court with Price withdrawing the allegations, the lawyers renegotiating the terms of Price's visitation with his daughter, and O'Hara agreeing to stay silent about the agreement.

The scandal magazine *On the QT* had already used the newspaper reports as composite facts in its 1956 story "The Strange Case of Maureen O'Hara."[16] The magazine rehashed the custody battle but also took the opportunity to construct rumors of a conspiracy—why had Price withdrawn his allegations so quickly, the article asked; was it industry pressure? Although *Confidential* would often claim that the film industry was behind many a hush-up of scandal, its story about O'Hara drops all aspects of the star's involvement with Parra that were linked to the child custody battle, as well as suggestions about industry attempts to silence Price. It reimagines what "consorting" with a Latin American boyfriend "at all hours of the day and night" might include. The article describes the behavior of O'Hara and her escort as "torrid," as so uncontrollable that the usher has to ask them three times to break up their "petting." The unnamed Parra supposedly sits with his coat off, "his collar hanging limply at half mast," while O'Hara's white silk blouse is apparently no longer "neatly buttoned." To add to the story's spice, the magazine illustrates the article with a photo of O'Hara taken elsewhere in which she seems to be adjusting the top button of her dress or blouse. The caption of the photo states, "Redheaded Maureen's blouse needed plenty of fixing after bouncing and bundling with that Latin lad in Grauman's Chinese Theatre."[17]

The use of composite-fact stories had considerable power, as they seemed to offer plausible chronologies for events that had a ring of truth about them because readers had probably encountered some aspect of them before in newspaper gossip columns, traditional fan magazines, other scandal magazines and tabloids, and even sometimes in feature stories of the mainstream press. They also had power in the legal realm because they provided libel juries or judges with interpretive challenges as to their defamatory or intrusive status—after all, some aspects were true, or had been reported before, hadn't they? The magazines' use of surveillance techniques and insider-tipsters, in turn, gave them tremendous power in their relations with the film studios. For example, if the scandalousness of an act is based partly on the secrecy of its commission, certainly for the 1950s homosexuality or homosexual acts would be among the most scandalous.[18] *Confidential* did "out" Marlene Dietrich and Liberace, but the most significant "outing" the magazine had at its disposal was Rock Hudson's. At least one participant in an all-male party at the home of Henry Willson (the agent of Hudson, Tab Hunter, Rory Calhoun, Robert Wagner, Natalie Wood, and Guy Madison) had apparently signed an affidavit stating that he saw Hudson engage in group sex with men. In 1955 *Confidential* traded that information about Hudson to Universal Studios for a story about Rory Calhoun (another Universal contract star) as teenage felon (he had been incarcerated for stealing cars).[19] As David Ehrenstein observes, this hardly seems an "even" trade.[20] Surely the Hudson story was the better scandal; but if the "trade" is conceptualized in terms of the magazine's systematizing of scandal, it was better for the future workings of their mass production system — it forever gave *Confidential* leverage over the studio (and over a major star and his agent) for future stories, as well as exhibited the publication's own mastery over the mass production of star discourse. The Calhoun story also was less likely to create the kind of complaints that often got *Confidential* in legal hot water. In fact, because the story included Calhoun's conversion by a prison chaplain, it also gave the magazine an opportunity to claim the moral and legal high ground if challenged in court — how could Calhoun claim that such a story hurt him, when it sympathetically chronicled the transformation of a criminal teen into a spiritual and material success? Wasn't this the kind of story so often published by the fan magazines?[21]

From the point of view of the historian or theorist of scandal, the scandal magazines' research and writing methodologies also demonstrate the publications' own understanding of scandal's definition. In his study of Victorian era scandals, William A. Cohen does not define scandal as an offensive act *or* the reaction to an offensive act, as dictionaries typically do. He suggests that the event cannot be disarticulated from the public recapitulation of it — they are two moments in the temporal dimension or continuum of scandal.[22] The scandal magazines refused the same disarticulation, as they devised ways, such as surveillance, that made sure the alleged event could move to the stage of recapitulation. Legally conceptualized, such surveillance strategies look *forward* to the probability of a crime or scandal (rather than backward to a committed criminal act, as search-and-seizure tactics do).[23] From a business standpoint the attitude that scandalous behavior is (and has been) always available to be "caught" by surveillance technologies constructs and protects the magazines' systematicity, ensuring the continual flow of copy for a regularly scheduled, mass-produced publication. It also links the magazine to a number of alluring practices — espionage, forensic science, etc. — some of which could be seen as "legitimate" or "objective." Although mock "paste-up" graphics and blaring headlines imparted an air of immediacy to the stories, in some cases the magazines made surveillance strategies and the on-the-scene reporting of the event somewhat irrelevant to the telling, as they rewrote old stories or fabricated new events (such as the O'Hara–Grauman's Chinese narrative).

The recyclings and rewritings of old scandal stories were also important to the power of the magazines to construct a plausible fiction about their motivations. They editorialized constantly about how they would tell readers the *truth*, rather than the packaged, formulaic "domestic bliss and patriotic service" narratives created by studios and press agents of the stars, which were fed to legitimate newspapers, general interest magazines, and film fan magazines alike. The scandal magazines, they argued, would uncover what had been hidden about the stars all these years. Using mottos for their magazines like "the stories behind the headlines" (*Whisper*), "stories the newspapers won't print" (*On the QT*), and "uncensored and off the record" and "tells the facts and names the names" (*Confidential*), the magazines claimed that they would uncover what had been hidden about stars all these years (fig. 2). They attempted to gain their own moral weight in describing their work as historical investigation and heroic journalism.

Figure 2. *Confidential* defends its tactics. Copyright 1957 by Confidential, Inc.

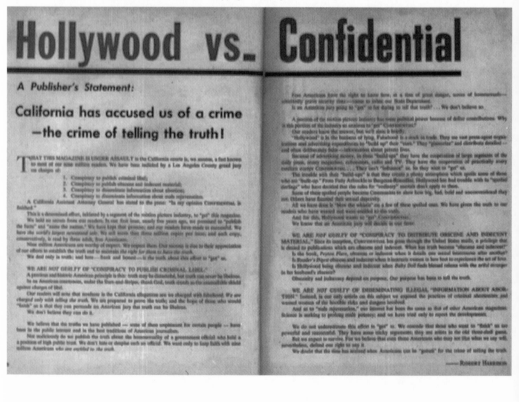

Allusions to past scandals or repetition of those stories, as well as unearthing new ones, were important proofs that *Confidential* was *not* the one lying:

> "Hollywood" is in the business of lying. Falsehood is a stock in trade. They use vast press-agent organizations and advertising expenditures to "build up" their "stars." They "glamorize" and distribute detailed — and often deliberately false — information about private lives. . . . The trouble with their "build ups" is that they create a phoney atmosphere which spoils some of those who are "built up." From Fatty Arbuckle to Bergman-Rossellini, Hollywood has had trouble with its "spoiled darlings." . . . All we have done is "blow the whistle" on a few of these spoiled ones. We have given the truth to our readers . . . who . . . were entitled to the truth.[24]

The scandal magazines' fiction about their strategies was relatively sustainable in the late 1950s because Hollywood's own ability to sustain a fiction about stars at this time was waning. Since the studio breakup following the Paramount divestment decree of 1948, many stars were no longer under long-term contract. Some stars had independent production companies, and others were only under contract to studios on a per-picture basis (however, Rock Hudson, Rory Calhoun, and Tab Hunter — all stars who had articles about them published or threatened by *Confidential* — were under long-term contracts to studios). Beyond promotion and publicity for single films, which the studios still managed, much of the star-oriented publicity was coming from other sources — from the press agents stars could hire on their own in the wake of the studio breakup and from the stars themselves, such as in their television appearances. Although all could be said to work on behalf of the industry's benefit, the difficulties of sustaining the power of studio-contract morality clauses, the coherencies of star personas, or a unified discourse about Hollywood, for that matter, were becoming more apparent as the decade wore on.

The traditional fan magazines exemplify these difficulties. Since the Ingrid Bergman-Roberto Rossellini adultery and pregnancy scandal and the Robert Mitchum marijuana bust in the late 1940s, the fan magazines went into overdrive to protect readers' beliefs in Hollywood morality. Yet their response to scandal under the cloak of moral uplift was contradictory. In some articles published between the Bergman and Mitchum scandals in the late 1940s and the *Confidential* trial in 1957, the fan magazines rather paradoxically supported traditional morals through a marked investment in specific details of stars' possibly indecent behavior. In other instances they assumed a strategic silence that discretely "spoke" about scandal through a self-conscious avoidance of its name.

In the late 1940s and early 1950s — before the scandal magazines' arrival — some stories were surprisingly explicit in particularizing the Bergman and Mitchum situations. For example, *Photoplay*'s 1948 article "The Truth about Dope" not only gives details of the actual drug bust involving Mitchum but speculates that Mitchum might have smoked marijuana in order to feel more confident. The article's attempt to clarify the "truth about dope" and not completely condemn Mitchum before his trial puts it into the interesting — and by current standards, sensible — position of suggesting that what Mitchum did wasn't too bad because marijuana is not as harmful and addictive as heroin.[25] In February 1949 *Modern Screen's* "An Open Letter to Robert Mitchum: The Case for the People" also explicitly states why Mitchum is in trouble with the law, but it takes the scandal as an occasion to flatter its readers by extolling their sense of fair play toward the unconvicted and their charity toward those who, found guilty, pay their debt to society.[26] *Photoplay's* April 1949 "What Now for Mitchum?" praises the actor for pleading guilty and sparing Hollywood and the nation — especially the young teenagers who idolize him — the scandal of a long trial and the subsequent sensational press coverage.[27]

Generally sympathetic to Mitchum in this specific scandal — in fact, they served as one important venue for his public rehabilitation, as they did for Bergman[28] — the fan magazines at this time also published many articles that replaced understanding with condescension for stars whose lives included rebellious, unhappy, or generally scandalous behavior in the past. In *Photoplay's* June 1950 article "I Call It Scandalous!," what is scandalous, according to author Elsa Maxwell, is that Bergman thought Hollywood was wrong for her and left for Italy, Robert Mitchum was not properly schooled by his studio in his responsibilities as a star, and Shirley Temple was not taught that testifying negatively against husband John Agar at their divorce trial would have been more seemly if done in another state.[29] In *Modern Screen's* June 1952 "Hollywood's Most Tragic People," author Louella Parsons argues that most stars who have been involved in scandals, from Wallace Reid and Mabel Normand in the 1920s to Judy Garland, Robert Walker, Franchot Tone, and Carole Landis in the late 1940s and early 1950s, are to be pitied rather than condemned. One of the photo captions even describes these figures as pathetic.[30]

Another fan magazine response was to publish articles that dealt with issues of star morality while avoiding a rehashing of previous scandals. These provided more general, simultaneously obscure and heavy-handed, responses to charges that Hollywood was an environment for scandalous behavior. Some of these, such as *Modern Screen's* February 1950 "Hollywood's Ten Best Citizens" and *Photoplay's* August 1950 "The Other Side of the Hollywood Story," are inspired to report stars' charitable activities from a desire to rectify what is vaguely described as misplaced emphasis in newspapers and magazines on the less positive contributions of Hollywood citizens. Both pieces pompously exaggerate their mission, with *Modern Screen* declaring its article as one of the most important it has ever published.[31] *Photoplay* offers, with "editorial pride," a chart that "took months of concentrated effort" to put together. The chart exhaustively details statistics for about 150 stars that apparently prove their worthiness as model citizens: statistics of their marital, parental, and home-ownership status, as well as of community service and honors.[32] These were "objective" measures to counter other kinds of surveillance, such as that employed by *Confidential*. *Modern Screen's* September 1950 issue includes a "special report" on Hollywood morals, grouping together under this rubric articles on Mitchum, Judy Garland (who had recently attempted suicide), and Hedda Hopper's efforts to keep stars out of trouble (if only they had taken her advice, claims Hopper!). Although this report dares to actually speak the terminology of scandal ("How Sinful Are Movie Stars?" asks the title of one article), like the stories in *Modern Screen* and *Photoplay* earlier that year, it works to prove its argument that contemporary Hollywood is very moral indeed through statistics. A chart accompanying the report proclaims that in the Hollywood of the previous fifteen years only ten of fifteen thousand actors were in major scandals; there were only two murders and six prostitution cases; and there were eighty-four times more sex offenses in New York City! (Should any historian of Los Angeles, or even a casual reader of Raymond Chandler or James Ellroy, question those statistics about murder and prostitution cases in Hollywood during this period, the text accompanying the chart clarifies that those figures are really for Beverly Hills, an upscale, largely residential town where many stars at the time lived.)[33]

After the scandal magazines started to make an impact, signaled by the national attention that articles in *Time* and *Newsweek* and a series of civil libel suits gave them in the mid-fifties, the fan magazines became even more reticent to name specific scandalous allegations made about stars.[34] Because the Bergman and Mitchum scandals had made headline news in legitimate national newspapers and magazines, the fan magazines could be explicit in their referencing of details. As noted in the case of Mitchum, they could even turn these into recuperative copy. But the scandal magazines were considered illegitimate and were read by a smaller audience than the legitimate press (although the circulation figures claimed for *Confidential* ranged from 250,000 to 4,000,000, which put them in good competition with fan magazines). It was believed that repeating information from them could provide further means for circulation and amplification of alleged scandalous behavior.

Instead, the fan magazines resorted to a strategic silence about specific details of the scandals broken by *Confidential* and its imitators. This resulted in titillation and incoherencies. For example, an editorial entitled "Scandal in Hollywood" in the July 1955 issue of *Photoplay* claims that stars have been recently subjected to vicious attacks, but the article never describes the specifics. It states that the "scandal-mongering" had not only implied marital infidelity but "the worst in human behavior." The reader is left to wonder which kind of scandal applies to which of the stars listed in the editorial (Rory Calhoun, June Allyson and Dick Powell, Alan Ladd and Sue Carol, Burt Lancaster, Van Johnson, Lana

Turner) and what exactly constitutes the "worst" in human behavior.[35] *Photo-play*'s February 1956 story "Kim Novak: Stabbed by Scandal"[36] never mentions the article but was written in response to *Confidential*'s January 1956 "What They 'Forgot' to Say about Kim Novak."[37] *Confidential*'s story claimed that Novak was "kept" by a New York businessman. *Photoplay* argues that Novak had been scandalously depicted as "ambition-driven" and discovered by an agent while she was riding her bicycle in town. With these vague and seemingly inoffensive details, the reader might ponder why stories about her discovery on a bike or her ambition would be so upsetting or scandalous and imagine the same, or a worse, emplotment of Novak's "ambition" that *Confidential* had.

The fan magazines' strategic silence about scandal was characteristic of their balancing of secrecy and revelation since the 1920s, a tension that fascinated readers even as it allowed the publications to maintain the boundaries of social propriety. Gaylyn Studlar argues that the fan magazines of the 1920s resorted to "a strategy of indirection that relied heavily upon the reader's preexistent knowledge of events gleaned from other sources, not the magazines themselves."[38] Although this method was a voluntary response to the social pressures and economic risks stemming from a series of Hollywood scandals in the early 1920s (those involving Fatty Arbuckle, Wallace Reid, and William Desmond Taylor), its manifestation in fan magazines of the 1950s might have been puzzling to readers who remembered the publications' obvious investment in other scandals (such as the Mitchum and Bergman scandals) just a few years earlier. Although their cooperation with the film industry in the 1920s was more or less voluntary, by the 1930s the fan magazines had more or less capitulated to the demands of the studios to publish positive articles written by studio-approved writers; now in the 1950s, because of the studio breakup, competition with the scandal magazines for readers, and changing societal beliefs about obscenity, fan magazines seemed uncertain about what the readers wanted, what they might already know, and what the implications of too explicitly acknowledging reader desires and knowledges might be.[39]

Although its control over the coherency of publicity and promotional discourses was clearly weakened in the 1950s, the film industry still had the production of motion pictures as a potential weapon against the scandal magazines. MGM produced *Slander* in 1956. Starring Van Johnson as Scott Martin, Ann Blyth as his wife, Anne, and Steve Cochran as H. R. Manly, *Slander* tells the story of how fictional scandal magazine *Real Truth* ruined the life of newly popular television puppeteer Martin when it runs an article about his arrest for robbery as a teen. Magazine publisher-editor H. R. Manly really wants to run a story on Mary Sawyer (never seen in the film but described in such a manner as to suggest an Ingrid Bergman–like star who has played Joan of Arc and other saintly characters). His "researchers" have found that Sawyer knew Martin's mother. The film implies Mrs. Martin once arranged for Sawyer to get an abortion or give up an illegitimate child for adoption.[40] Manly attempts to use the story about Martin's juvenile-delinquent past to blackmail him for details and verification of the information about this more important star. When Martin refuses to turn a scandal magazine "tipster," his wife leaves him, the story about him is published, he temporarily loses his job, and his son is killed (he runs in front of a car to escape the children taunting him about his "jailbird" father). Manly is then shot and killed by his mother (Marjorie Rambeau), who hates the way her son's magazine has ruined lives.

Anticipating the kind of interest the state would take in the scandal magazines' operating strategies, the film focuses on the way the magazine orders researchers to find damaging dirt about famous people, uses blackmail to pressure tipsters, engages in trade-offs of stories, and revels in its cynical attitude (Manly declares that "there's something dirty in everyone's past . . . [and that] the cleaner they are on the surface, the dirtier they are underneath"). The tipster system of research and fact validation is seen as almost as dangerous as the publication of scandal. Martin's wife leaves him because he doesn't choose that option in the face of his own sordid past's being revealed. Even though his son is killed as a result, Martin gains self-respect and confidence (and eventually wins back his job) through the way he stands up to the magazine. Clearly drawing on *Confidential*'s story on Rory Calhoun (of course the trade behind that story could hardly be revealed in 1956), *Slander* reiterates a typical fan magazine discourse about the digging up of old scandals about stars. That is, no story from the past reflects what the star has become in the present—which is hard-working, home-owning, and family-loving. Hollywood was willing to concede that times had changed to the extent that the public was beginning to expect some scandal in a star's past, but it was still hoping to shape public discourse into accepting that whatever their pasts, stars were now ideal citizens of 1950s America.

The film industry probably wished that the scandal magazines could be as easily dispatched as the fictional H. R. Manly was by his mother's gunshot. Certainly, reports of how studio bosses pressured California politicians into quashing the scandal magazines are not uncommon in histories of the *Confidential* trial.[41] However, evidence suggests a much more complicated picture of the film industry's relationship to the political and law enforcement activities directed at *Confidential* in 1957. In February of that year two hearings by California state senate committees—the Interim Committee on Collection Agencies, Private Detectives, and Debt Liquidators, and the Judiciary Committee investigating the use of surveillance equipment in the state—had used in their evidence the "research tactics" of the scandal magazines as examples of abusive intrusions of privacy. The former committee had even subpoenaed famed baseball hero Joe DiMaggio and media star Frank Sinatra to testify about the role of private investigators in the famed "wrong door raid," in which DiMaggio, Sinatra, and others had allegedly broken down the door of an apartment expecting to find DiMaggio's ex-wife

Marilyn Monroe in flagrante delicto. *Confidential* had reported this incident, using the files of one of the private investigators hired by DiMaggio to follow Monroe. Sinatra's very reluctant testimony and its aftermath (the state considered filing perjury charges against Sinatra because his story differed from the private investigator's), as well as private investigator Fred Otash's testimony on how he spied on Hollywood figures to confirm stories for *Confidential*, resulted in high-profile coverage of the committee's work in national media.[42]

Given the news media's almost exclusive, and rather embarrassing, focus on only one aspect of the hearings' evidence gathering—the Hollywood–private eye–scandal magazine connection—the film industry probably would have supported the legislation to curb the scandal magazines' operations that both senate committee chairman Fred Kraft and California governor Knight proposed to the media as the hearings finished up in March.[43] The legislation did not materialize, but state attorney general Pat Brown worked with the Los Angeles district attorney to bring charges against *Confidential* of criminal conspiracy to commit criminal libel and to publish obscenity. Because of failure to extradite Harrison from New York, however, the only individuals they could bring to trial were the Meades, who ran Hollywood Research, Inc., as a front for the magazine. Conspiracy to commit criminal libel meant that the magazines had malicious intent in publishing the scandalous stories. Yoking the charge to conspiracy to publish obscene material worked as a contaminating factor in two ways. It put the case into a social arena in which the magazine might be judged as a moral contaminant in society (as moral crusade discourses usually described obscenity), and it "contaminated" the libel charge, potentially predisposing jurors to find the magazine's whole operation sleazy and therefore to find its stories malicious in intent and its reporting of private acts outrageous and of no social value.[44]

Film-industry support of legislation was one thing—it meant the "dirty work" of fighting the scandal magazine would be in the hands of legislators in Sacramento—but support of a criminal trial to take place in Los Angeles was surely another. Stars would be subpoenaed for testimony, and the scandal stories would be read aloud in court, become part of the public record, and be reported on by national media. Also, the verdict outcome would be unpredictable. Reports early on in the July-October 1957 trial indicated stars would like to settle out of court (and sure enough, once subpoenas were prepared, many managed to be out of town).[45] When the Motion Picture Industry Council made statements to the media through its president, actor (and future senator) George Murphy, it focused on the way the trial provoked "disgust and anger" in Hollywood and how it was trying to make sure that such a trial would never again take place.[46] Although Murphy ostensibly meant that the council wanted to attack the magazine's libelous activities, an underlying meaning was that the council wished there had not been a trial to reveal so many negative stories. A *New York Times* article appearing the same day Murphy's remarks were made public quoted an unnamed source as saying that the industry had considered doing something to stop the magazines but dropped the project "when the studio heads became apprehensive of becoming involved with the magazines and feared a boomerang."[47]

Famed Hollywood attorney Jerry Giesler (he represented Mitchum and Lizabeth Scott in their civil libel cases against *Confidential* and had been Mitchum's attorney in the 1948 trial) did not just impute that the industry was apprehensive but also cowardly when he publicly stated on numerous occasions at the time of the hearings and trial that Hollywood "never gives help on the battlefield, but is always glad to provide a pat on the back after the fight is over. . . . It's strange how all their organizations run to cover."[48] Kenneth Anger claims that the film industry sent a public relations man to Pat Brown, threatening withdrawal of campaign funds to the Republican Party in the next election if his office filed criminal charges that would involve a trial. This seems dubious because Brown was a Democrat (the withdrawal of campaign funds to the Republicans would only help Brown in his political rise if he were to accept such a bribe), but the general picture Anger paints of the industry as reluctant to have the case go to trial seems to be compatible with evidence found elsewhere.[49]

News reports indicate Hollywood was nervously anticipating the recirculation and amplification the trial would give the scandal stories. Contemporary accounts don't point out how the film industry might have been justifiably apprehensive about other revelations the trial might provoke, such as how Hollywood's systematizing of star discourse also involved fabrication, invasion of privacy, and intimations of sexual misbehavior (even if in the service of recuperating that sin with stories of reconciliation and domestic reunion). The state was interested in raising issues about the magazine's surveillance tactics to demonstrate how it was not just reporting old scandals but actively (maliciously) creating situations to construct scandals, that it was "a smut factory."[50]

However, neither the state nor the industry might have anticipated that *Confidential*'s attorneys (their libel attorneys used in consultation, not the defense attorneys for Hollywood Research, Inc.) would justify these activities in testimony as being a response to Hollywood's successful mass production of star discourse and the breakdown in its once systematized regulatory functions. For example, *Confidential* attorney Daniel G. Ross claimed that press agents and fan magazines were the ones lying about the stars, and their success had resulted in the stars' being worshiped as "false idols" by the public. *Confidential*, said Ross, was providing a public service in telling "the truth about these personalities."[51] At another point defense witnesses changed strategies and claimed that some "true" material about sexual behavior had come from Hollywood itself, from press agents, studio employees, and even from fan magazines. *Confidential* legal advisor Albert DeStefano stated that the magazine had taken material from a fan magazine in writing "How Long Can Dick Powell Take It?," an article describing trouble in the Dick Powell–June Allyson marriage because of Allyson's relationship with star Alan Ladd.[52] Fred Meade, one of the principal defendants in the case, argued that it was the film industry's refusal or inability to act on one of its main regulatory procedures, the exercise of morality clauses in star contracts, that was responsible for the success of magazines like *Confidential*.[53]

Meade's defense, blaming breakdown on Hollywood's own systematicity in regulating morality, like Ross's claim that *Confidential* performed a public service by revealing the sins of "false idols," was not only a defense against libel (and invasion of privacy, which the magazine was not "officially" on trial for) but also against obscenity charges. These claims took the moral high ground in justifying the publication of sexual material as educational, but the defense witnesses also had to argue that the articles were not obscene because they did not arouse "a sexually itchy reaction, an uncontrolled desire to commit depraved acts."[54] In fact, said DeStefano, many of the articles were humorous, and a story "cannot be obscene if it makes the reader chuckle."[55] Furthermore, went the argument, if obscenity is determined by the standards of the community, then *Confidential*'s repetition of material accepted previously by the public — that is, already in the public record — such as the accusations about O'Hara's relationship with Parra first mentioned at the O'Hara-Price custody dispute, could hardly be obscene.[56]

The sensational trial involved high drama and humor — the assistant district attorney, an avowed churchgoer, reading racy *Confidential* magazine articles aloud to the court; *Confidential* attorneys pulling out novels like *Peyton Place* to suggest the magazine was no more obscene than many best-selling books; Maureen O'Hara angrily declaring that she could prove that she was out of the country at the time *Confidential* alleged she was having sex with Parra in Grauman's Chinese; and Dorothy Dandridge, calmly testifying that she could and would never have had sex in the Lake Tahoe woods with a white musician, as *Confidential* claimed. She would not have even taken a walk with a white man because "Lake Tahoe . . . was very prejudiced. Negroes were not permitted that freedom."[57] Despite the powerful and convincing testimony provided by O'Hara and Dandridge, the jury deadlocked over the verdict in early October 1957. When the state declared a willingness to start with a new trial, *Confidential* agreed to cooperate and to change its policies in order to avoid mounting another expensive defense.

The strategies Hollywood and *Confidential* devised in 1957 to defend their own systematization of star discourse in the face of a public trial seem understandable, but the state's motivations in attacking *Confidential* and in not bowing to the film industry's wish to avoid a trial is not entirely explainable, or at least not verifiable. One significant possibility is to be found in relation to the state senate committee hearings several months before the trial. Both hearings examined the role of non–law enforcement institutions (collection agencies, debt liquidators) or individuals (private investigators, criminals) using tactics that invaded citizen privacy and sometimes challenged constitutional rights concerning protection from search and seizure (Fourth Amendment) and self-incrimination (Fifth Amendment). Examples from scandal magazine surveillance practices were used by both committees in their hearings and garnered them much publicity during the actual proceedings. However, the reports published at the hearings' ends, which were certainly not read by very many in the public, suggest that these examples were only a small part of the committees' concerns.[58] Did the highlighting of the scandal magazines by the committees and the press during the hearings function as a public display of the state's concern for protecting citizen rights to privacy?

Why would this be necessary? Possibly because the state—both the state of California and the federal government—were massively undercutting those very rights in the 1950s and had been doing so since at least the beginning of the cold war at the end of the 1940s. Loyalty oaths and surveillance through FBI wiretapping and U.S. Post Office monitoring of publications had been used in both Washington and California as means to expel communist or other "subversives" (such as homosexuals) from civil service and other forms of public life.[59] The House Un-American Activities Committee had targeted the film industry in two large "show trial" hearings in less than a decade, and the University of California had much-publicized firings of professors suspected of leftist sympathies. Both California senate committee reports demonstrate concern with the way non–law enforcement uses of surveillance were increasing at this time. Recent Supreme Court restrictions on law enforcement surveillance tactics and rapid developments in sophisticated surveillance devices are discussed as providing new opportunities for law enforcement abilities to be outstripped by individuals and institutions that are shown to be ruthlessly and criminally intrusive.[60]

These reports suggest that the state could be constructing an "other" to take the blame for its own perceived diminishing surveillance powers or what the historian might perceive as its abuse of surveillance power. The trial could be seen as an extension of the state's "othering" of the scandal magazines to mask its own power. However, libel laws and their enforcement also raise broader issues about community that are central to another important facet of this case. Robert C. Post argues that defamation laws, when understood as protection of reputation as dignity, are concerned not only with the individual's interest in dignity, but with "the enforcement of society's interest in its rules of civility, which is to say its interest in defining and maintaining the contours of its own social constitution."[61] This notion of defamation entails an understanding of how societies exercise power to designate who is a member of society (who deserves respect) and who is not (who is a deviant because of unacceptable behavior). Protection of dignity is a "confirmation of membership" in a community. Defamation threatens this confirmation, and libel trials are "an arena in which the parties [the defamed and the defaming] are free to present 'competing interpretations of behavior.'"[62] The *Confidential* trial was not just about the state's proving its power over scandal magazines but was also a ready forum to raise, and perhaps settle, "competing interpretations" of a number of behaviors, most involving sexuality, that troubled and fascinated 1950s society.

For most of the twentieth century, stars had been constituted by the very terms—the private self behind the public image—that suggest the "processes through which our society constitutes sexuality as an object of knowledge and fascination."[63] Knowledge of the stars is a knowledge of sexuality is a knowledge of the self. Knowledge of the stars was regulated by Hollywood to create desire *and* maintain certain boundaries of sexuality—monogamous heterosexuality practiced by people of the same race—which, presumably, were internalized by the public through acts of self-policing. The *Confidential* trial raises questions about the sustainability of stars as the vehicles and models for sexual self-policing. If *Confidential* could be convicted of libel and obscenity, it could be seen as the deviant member of society, and the stars could be reembraced by the community.

The state has an investment in seeing that people police themselves so that its work is all the more effective. But the way the state became invested in particular *Confidential* stories through the willingness of those star subjects to participate in the state's case is instructive in this regard. An examination of the state's use of Dorothy Dandridge, Liberace, and Maureen O'Hara as grand jury witnesses undercuts simple assumptions about the meaning of the trial: 1) that it was merely a mask for the state's totalitarian tendencies, 2) that the state did not have complicated or ambivalent notions about who should be included in the membership of society, or 3) that the public understood the state's motivations in the way the state hoped it would.

For instance, Pat Brown claimed many years after the trial that his office filed criminal charges against *Confidential* not because of industry pressure but because he believed it maliciously defamed Dorothy Dandridge.[64] In his version of the state's motivation, Brown, a devout liberal who wanted his legacy to include defending civil rights for black Americans, remembers it in terms of Dandridge's dignity and right to full membership in American society. Fabricating, hinting at, or documenting instances of interracial sex was a prime tactic of the FBI and right-wing groups to smear civil rights activists at this time. *Confidential* had a similar smear ethic, especially regarding female African American entertainers. Not only did this kind of defamation attempt to exclude such African American entertainers from membership in society by appealing to racial bigotry that abhorred miscegenation, but it usually described African American women as animalistic, always primed for sex. *Confidential*'s story portrayed Dandridge in this way, so Brown's use of the article as generator of the charges was an attack on this system of defaming African Americans and on negative stereotypes of black femininity.[65] However, from another perspective, no matter what Brown's motivation, the state's defense of Dandridge might have confirmed intolerance for interracial sexual relationships because it considered the plaintiff's assertion that black-white sex took place as a smear, as well as confirmed that the only African American woman whose privacy was worth protecting was the "proper" — that is, asexual — lady.

Liberace's willingness to give testimony at the grand jury that preceded the trial was a major part of the publicity surrounding the state's case (although to my knowledge, he never testified at the trial). The *Confidential* story "Why Liberace's Theme Song Should Be 'Mad about the Boy!'" suggested Liberace aggressively demanded kisses and other attention from a male press agent.[66] A star's homosexual identity at this time was a more explosive secret than interracial heterosexual romance, but Liberace's case is complicated by the degree to which his sexuality might be considered an "open secret" to at least portions of the American public (in a way that Hudson's was not, although it was an open secret in Hollywood). It is beyond the scope of this article to fully explore the possibility of Liberace's sexuality as an open secret. However, his willingness to bring libel charges against *Confidential* and to participate in an attempt to indict them for criminal libel by the grand jury suggests what is at stake in the 1950s for homosexuality to be considered in terms of libel as an assault on reputation as dignity. By accusing the magazine of libel, Liberace is suggesting their story has threatened his membership in the community. In asking the court to consider this story alleging his homosexual behavior as libel, Liberace is in essence asking the court to affirm that the community's identity excludes homosexuals. By doing so Liberace assents to a homophobic idea of community, and the court also shows its assent and rewards him by taking his accusations seriously enough to serve as testimony in indicting *Confidential*. However, if we do momentarily agree that some people "knew" or wondered about his sexuality, even if only the writer and several million readers of the *Confidential* article,[67] the homophobic community who allows him to sustain his homosexuality as an open secret in this way knows, at some level, that the story is not entirely libelous. This meant that defamation law as a tool for some part of the community to maintain its power might be seen by some or participated in by some as itself an "open secret." In other words, in supporting Liberace the state not only maintains a homophobic community but risks exposing the (libel) law as adjudicating not truth but who shall have power to stay a member of the community and under what conditions.

The *Confidential* story about Maureen O'Hara plays with the growing fascination in the 1950s with the sexually experimenting woman, eagerly read about in the Kinsey Report and *Playboy* but usually counterposed to the wife and mother ideal prevalent in so many other representations in this period. O'Hara defended her accusation of *Confidential* as libelous by appealing to how it hurt her as a professional, and it concerned her as a mother that such material would be available to children.[68] The latter defense allied her stance with both the maternal ideal of the 1950s and the moral crusades of the era that decried a number

of popular culture representations and media (like comic books) as bad influences on children. Her concern for her standing as a professional was both a plea
for recognition that one's believability or attractiveness as a public figure can
depend on the dignity accorded by the community and for recognition that she
was a worker and image with a value in the market. Unlike many of the witnesses,
O'Hara displayed obvious anger on the stand. Although this was "allowed" her
because of stereotypes about the Irish temper, it was not a trait encouraged by the
feminine mystique of the time. The state (through the trial) provided certain
contexts for O'Hara performances that represented nontraditional feminine images, even as it was attempting to silence *Confidential's* nontraditional feminine
portrait of the actress.[69]

• • •

The jury's inability to come to a decision about the charges against *Confidential*
might have been because the complexity of the legal issues and/or of star personas
as they were revealed by the *Confidential* case involved too many contradictions
that were salient but not solvable, fully understood, or perhaps speakable at the
time.[70] For that reason either convicting or clearing *Confidential* for libel would
send a message about the stars as members of the community that was impossibly definitive. *Confidential* and the other scandal magazines became tamer in
the years immediately following the trial (Harrison sold off *Confidential* a few
months later) and would eventually be replaced by the tabloid papers popular
today. Many of their aggressive methods find a legacy in the surveillance strategies of today's paparazzi. However, to fully understand what legacy the scandal
magazines left in relation to the public's attitudes about stars, privacy, libel, and
obscenity, it is important to remember those figures and concepts could be linked
together in the 1950s only when the state, the film industry, and the magazines
interacted briefly in social and legal contexts that exposed a power struggle over
community membership.

NOTES

1. Richard deCordova, *Picture Personalities: The Emergence of the Star System in America* (Urbana: University of Illinois Press, 1990), 139.

2. Ibid., 141.

3. For a discussion of scandal and media globalization see John Tomlinson,
"'And Besides, the Wench is Dead': Media Scandals and the Globalization of Communication," in James Lull and Stephen Hinerman, eds., *Media Scandals: Morality and Desire in the Popular Culture Marketplace* (New York: Columbia University
Press, 1997), 65–84.

4. The histories of many of these magazines can be found in Alan Betrock,
Unseen America: The Greatest Cult Exploitation Magazines 1950–1966 (New York:
Shake Books, 1990), 3–9.

5. See, for instance, Rochelle Gurstein, *The Repeal of Reticence: America's Cultural and Legal Struggles over Free Speech, Obscenity, Sexual Liberation, and Modern Art* (New York: Hill and Wang, 1996), and Robert C. Post, "The Social Foundations of Defamation Law: Reputation and the Constitution," *California Law Review* 74 (May 1986). For a discussion of how legal theories about privacy became foundational for laws and theories concerning rights to publicity see Jane Gaines, *Contested Culture: The Image, the Voice, and the Law* (Chapel Hill: University of North Carolina Press, 1991).

6. Irwin O. Spiegel, "Public Celebrity v. Scandal Magazine: The Celebrity's Right to Privacy," *Southern California Law Review* 30 (1957): 287.

7. Ibid., 285–287.

8. C. J. Biggs, quoted in Edward J. Bloustein, "Privacy as an Aspect of Human Dignity: An Answer to Dean Prosser," *New York University Law Review* 39 (December 1964): 962.

9. Robert E. Mensel, "'Kodakers Lying in Wait': Amateur Photography and the Right of Privacy in New York, 1885–1915," *American Quarterly* 43 (March 1991): 27.

10. Spiegel, "Public Celebrity v. Scandal Magazine," 307–311.

11. John D'Emilio and Estelle Freedman, *Intimate Matters: A History of Sexuality in America* (New York: Harper and Row, 1991), 280.

12. Thomas K. Wolfe, "Public Lives: *Confidential* Magazine; Reflections in Tranquility by the Former Owner, Robert Harrison, Who Managed to Get Away with It," *Esquire*, April 1964, 87–90, 152–157.

13. R. E. McDonald, "It Was the Hottest Show in Town When Maureen O'Hara Cuddled in Row 35," *Confidential*, March 1957, 10–11, 46. I discuss this article in more detail in my *Recycled Stars: Hollywood Film Stardom in the Age of Television and Video* (Durham, N.C.: Duke University Press, forthcoming).

14. Jack Jones, "Witness Tells of Wild Pool Party," *Los Angeles Times*, August 21, 1957, 18.

15. This headline appeared in the *Los Angeles Mirror News* (June 21, 1955) and possibly in New York papers. Other Los Angeles headlines included "Ex-Mate Accuses Maureen O'Hara, Demands Custody of Daughter, 11," *Los Angeles Times*, June 21, 1955; and "Maureen O'Hara Lashes Back in Custody Fight," *Los Angeles Times*, June 24, 1955. On the witness stand Ross also mentions the headline "Accuses Star of Consorting with Wealthy Latin" from an unnamed paper.

16. Robert Durant, "The Strange Case of Maureen O'Hara," *On the QT*, March 1956, 10–11.

17. McDonald, "Hottest Show," 46.

18. This definition is provided by William A. Cohen, *Sex Scandal: The Private Parts of Victorian Fiction* (Durham, N.C.: Duke University Press, 1996), 1–96.

19. There are many versions of how and why the Hudson story was suppressed by *Confidential*, and many of them are intertwined with stories that Hudson was pressured into marrying Phyllis Gates in 1955 by his agent and/or studio to disprove the scandal stories should *Confidential* or another magazine publish reports of his homosexual activity. It is beyond the scope of this essay to go into the latter issue. Stories about the former range from narratives about monetary payoffs to the magazine; to agent Henry Willson's hiring of a gangster to "rough up" the article's author, the editor, or those who signed affidavits (it isn't clear from accounts which); to Universal Studios and agent Willson offering up the story of another of their mutual clients/ employees, Rory Calhoun. See Fred Otash, *Investigation Hollywood!* (Chicago:

Henry Regnery, 1976), 31–38 (Otash doesn't use Hudson's name, but it is very easy to figure out whom he is talking about); Rock Hudson and Sara Davidson, *Rock Hudson: His Story* (New York: Avon Books, 1987), 95–97; Phyllis Gates and Bob Thomas, *My Husband, Rock Hudson* (New York: Jove Books, 1989), 207–208. The account concerning Calhoun is supported by Ezra Goodman, *The Fifty-Year Decline of Hollywood* (New York: Simon and Schuster, 1961), 52–53 (like Otash, Goodman doesn't use Hudson's name, but it is clear from context that Hudson is the figure in question); by an interview with writer Maurice Zolotow in the 1988 British television documentary *Hollywood Confidential*, in which Zolotow claims that Calhoun told him that the story about him had been offered up to kill the story about Hudson; and rather unenthusiastically by David Ehrenstein, *Open Secret: Gay Hollywood 1928–1998* (New York: William Morrow and Company, 1998), 99–100. Not only did the trade for the Calhoun story make sense in terms of *Confidential's* mass production of scandal, but Calhoun was, like Hudson, contracted to Universal and a client of Henry Willson (who, from every account I have ever read of him, used his clients like pawns, even blackmailing them about the affairs they had with *him*), and the story came out in 1955, about the time the story about Hudson was supposedly "killed." For an interesting account of Willson's relationships with his clients by a former client see John Gilmore, *Laid Bare* (Los Angeles: Amok Books, 1997). The story about Calhoun was Howard Rushmore, "Rory Calhoun: But for the Grace of God, Still a Convict," *Confidential*, May 1955, 23–25, 51–52. An unsigned editorial in the magazine's September 1955 issue followed up the story with quotes of praise for *Confidential's* treatment of Calhoun's story from the priest who had helped the star.

20. Ehrenstein, *Open Secret*, 99–100.

21. In fact, when Calhoun was informed that the story was going to be published by *Confidential*, he worked with gossip columnist Hedda Hopper to have his past crimes first revealed by her, a Hollywood insider with a syndicated column in the "legitimate" press. In the next few months and years numerous general interest magazines and fan magazines published stories about Calhoun's past, using an "uplift" narrative similar to *Confidential's*. See, for example, Rory Calhoun, "My Dark Past," *American Weekly*, August 21, August 28, 1955; and Rory Calhoun, "Look, Kid, How Stupid Can You Be?" *Photoplay*, February 1957.

22. Cohen, *Sex Scandal*, 8.

23. Telford Taylor, *Two Studies in Constitutional Interpretation: Search, Seizure, and Surveillance and Fair Trial and Free Press* (Columbus: Ohio State University Press, 1969), 80–81.

24. Robert Harrison, "*Confidential* vs. Hollywood," *Confidential*, September 1957, 22–23.

25. Florabel Muir, "The Truth about Dope," *Photoplay*, December 1948, 32–33, 72.

26. Wade Nichols, "An Open Letter to Robert Mitchum: The Case for the People," *Modern Screen*, February 1949, 27.

27. Florabel Muir, "What Now for Mitchum?" *Photoplay*, April 1949, 31, 98–99.

28. For discussions of discourses that rehabilitated Bergman and Mitchum see Adrienne L. McLean, "The Cinderella Princess and the Instrument of Evil: Surveying the Limits of Female Transgression in Two Postwar Hollywood Scandals," *Cinema Journal* 34 (spring 1995): 36–56; and McLean's essay in this volume.

29. Elsa Maxwell, "I Call It Scandalous!" *Photoplay*, June 1950, 100–102.

30. Louella Parsons, "Hollywood's Most Tragic People," *Modern Screen*, June 1952, 30–31, 95–96.

31. "Hollywood's Ten Best Citizens," *Modern Screen*, February 1950, 46–47, 73–74.

32. Fred Sammis, "The Other Side of the Hollywood Story," *Photoplay*, August 1950, 31–35.

33. "*Modern Screen* Special Report: Morals in Hollywood," *Modern Screen*, September 1950, 25, 54–60.

34. In 1955 stars Robert Mitchum and Lizabeth Scott and heiress Doris Duke filed libel suits against *Confidential*, and star James Mason filed a libel suit against *Rave*. The magazines received attention in "The Press in the Sewer," *Time*, July 11, 1955, 90; and "The Curious Craze for 'Confidential' Magazines," *Newsweek*, July 11, 1955, 50–52.

35. Ann Higginbotham, "Scandal in Hollywood," *Photoplay*, July 1955, 29.

36. Ted Maddox, "Kim Novak: Stabbed by Scandal," *Photoplay*, February 1956, 54–55, 86–87.

37. Robin Sharry, "What They Forgot to Say about Kim Novak," *Confidential*, January 1956, 31–34. The scandal magazines were mostly bimonthly publications and often came out almost two months before the dates listed on covers (for example, the July 1957 *Confidential* issue with a story about Liberace was already on newsstands when he testified before the Los Angeles grand jury in May 1957). Also, advance copies of the magazine were usually available (and often sent) to the celebrities (or the celebrity's studio) about whom a story was written. Although this was often a ploy to pressure stars into trading a story for the one to be published, it could also give the fan magazines (via press agents and studios) time to quickly write articles in reply. Thus, *Photoplay* was able to quickly respond to the story about Novak in its February issue.

38. Gaylyn Studlar, "The Perils of Pleasure? Fan Magazine Discourse as Women's Commodified Culture in the 1920s," *Wide Angle* 13 (January 1991): 11. DeCordova, *Picture Personalities*, also discusses how the fan magazines both silenced and spoke about scandal.

39. For information on studio–fan magazine relations in the 1930s, which were characterized by the studios' clamping down on control over what the magazines published through "blacklisting" and "whitelisting" certain writers and story themes, see "Publicity Heads Unite to Curb Fan Mags," *Hollywood Reporter*, August 10, 1934; "Fan Mags Promise to Be Good," *Hollywood Reporter*, August 16, 1934; and Goodman, *The Fifty-Year Decline and Fall of Hollywood*, 77.

40. The film is vague as to what Sawyer's trouble is; Martin says only that his mother helped her out of a "jam." According to notes by screenwriter Jerome Weidman, Sawyer was raped by an older man when she was a teen and gave birth to his child (Martin's mother helped her in childbirth); when the child died and its father was murdered, Sawyer went into a mental institution. Weidman expresses displeasure in this back story, and makes notes to make Sawyer less victimized so that Manly can appeal to Martin on the basis of Sawyer's complicity in her own past "sins." However, none of these details are in the film or even in later drafts of the screenplay. See MGM production file on *Slander* (July 23, 1956), University of Southern California Archive of Performing Arts; and Production Code Administration file on *Slander*, Margaret Herrick Library, Academy of Motion Picture Arts and Sciences, Beverly Hills, Calif.

41. Bob Thomas, *Liberace: The True Story* (New York: St. Martin's, 1987), 129. Thomas also makes this assertion in the 1988 British television documentary *Hollywood Confidential*, as do two other Hollywood columnists from the period. In the same documentary Pat Brown, who was California's attorney general in 1957, claims that Hollywood did not pressure him into bringing charges against *Confidential*.

42. Just a few of the articles covering the committee hearings are "Scandal Magazine Curb Looms after Raid Probe," *Los Angeles Herald-Examiner*, February 18, 1957; James Denver, "Girl Reveals Tips to Scandal Mag," *Los Angeles Mirror News*, February 19, 1957; "Giesler May Be Called in Scandal Hearings," *Los Angeles Times*, February 21, 1957; Gladwin Hill, "Sinatra Version of Raid Disputed," *New York Times*, February 28, 1957; "Film Star Blackmail, File Thefts Charged," *Los Angeles Mirror News*, February 28, 1957; Gladwin Hill, "Detective Tells Inquiry He 'Checked Out' 150 'Scandal' Articles for *Confidential*," *New York Times*, March 1, 1957; Gladwin Hill, "Scandal Inquiry Finds No Answer," *New York Times*, March 2, 1957.

43. "Scandal Magazine Quiz by U.S. Urged," *Los Angeles Times*, March 5, 1957.

44. See D'Emilio and Freedman, *Intimate Matters*; Rochelle Gurstein, *Repeal of Reticence*; and Walter Kendrick, *The Secret Museum: Pornography in Modern Culture* (Berkeley: University of California Press, 1996), for discussions of moral crusades against obscenity.

45. "Film Stars Move to Quash Scandal," *Hollywood Citizen News*, July 29, 1957, 1.

46. "Maureen O'Hara Denies She 'Cuddled in Row 35,'" *Los Angeles Herald-Examiner*, August 18, 1957, 1, 15.

47. Gladwyn Hill, "Film Colony Fidgets in Confidential Case," *New York Times*, August 18, 1957, sec. 4, p. 7.

48. "Film Biz Giving Only 'Lip Service' in Fight Against Smear Mags — Giesler," *Daily Variety*, April 19, 1957.

49. Kenneth Anger, *Hollywood Babylon* (San Francisco: Straight Arrow Books, 1975), 265. Typically, Anger gives no citations for his information. See Matthew Tinkcom, "Scandalous! Kenneth Anger and the Prohibitions of Hollywood History," in Ellis Hanson, ed., *Out Takes: Essays on Queer Theory and Film* (Durham, N.C.: Duke University Press, 1999), 271–287, for an interesting discussion of Anger's fascination with *Confidential*.

50. "Hearing on Publisher," *New York Times*, July 24, 1957. Assistant Attorney General of California Clarence A. Linn made these remarks in the context of an argument made to the state of New York to extradite *Confidential* editor-publisher Robert Harrison to California.

51. Jones, "Wild Pool Party," 18.

52. This claim is attributed to DeStefano in "The *Confidential* Story," *Inside*, December 1957. *Inside* was a pseudoscandal magazine published for a short time in the late 1950s that tried to capitalize on the scandal caused by the scandal magazines. The fan magazine articles in question were probably Louella Parsons, "How the Ladds Reconciled," and William Barbour, "How Long Can It Last?," in *Modern Screen*, May 1955. The *Confidential* article even plays with the title of the latter story, turning "it" into "Dick."

53. "Laxity of Studios Charged in Trial," *New York Times*, August 26, 1957.

54. Jones, "Wild Pool Party," 18.

55. "Atty Calls *Confidential* Tales Funny," *Los Angeles Mirror News*, August 30, 1957. See also "*Confidential* Trial to Move Over to Grauman's Theater," *Los Angeles Times*, August 31, 1957, sec. 3, pp. 1, 8, for testimony about the humorousness of the magazine's articles.

56. Jones, "Wild Pool Party," 18.

57. Jack Jones, "Maureen O'Hara Angrily Denies Magazine Story; Dorothy Dandridge Also Charges Article about Her in *Confidential* Was Falsehood," *Los Angeles Times*, August 4, 1957.

58. California Senate Judiciary Committee, *The Interception of Messages by the Use of Electronic and Other Devices* (Sacramento: Senate of the State of California, 1957); and Fred H. Kraft, *Report of the Senate Interim Committee on Collection Agencies, Private Detectives, and Debt Liquidators* (Sacramento: Senate of the State of California, 1957).

59. The literature on this topic is too voluminous to cite individually, but especially helpful to me were Alexander Charms, *Cloak and Gavel: FBI Wiretaps, Bugs, Informers, and the Supreme Court* (Urbana: University of Illinois Press, 1992); John D'Emilio, *Sexual Politics, Sexual Communities: The Making of a Homosexual Minority in the United States, 1940–1970*, 2d ed. (Chicago: University of Chicago Press, 1998); Richard F. Hixson, *Privacy in a Public Society: Human Rights in Conflict* (New York: Oxford University Press, 1987); Carey McWilliams, *Witch Hunt: The Revival of Heresy* (Boston: Little, Brown, 1950); and Alan Theoharis, *Spying on Americans: Political Surveillance from Hoover to the Huston Plan* (Philadelphia: Temple University Press, 1978).

60. Kraft, *Report*, 5–8; California Senate Judiciary Committee, *Interception of Messages*, 12–16.

61. Robert C. Post, "Social Foundations of Defamation Law," 711.

62. Ibid., 712.

63. DeCordova, *Picture Personalities*, 143.

64. Brown's on-camera interview is used in *Hollywood Confidential.* Although the documentary was produced in 1988, judging by the film stock quality, décor, and dress styles in the Brown interview, it appears that it was filmed in the 1970s.

65. James L. Boyd, "Only the Birds and the Bees Saw What Dorothy Dandridge Did in the Woods," *Confidential*, May 1957. According to Donald Bogle, *Dorothy Dandridge* (New York: Amistad, 1997), 375, Dandridge had a copy of the issue by March 1957.

66. Horton Streete, "Why Liberace's Theme Song Should Be 'Mad about the Boy!'" *Confidential*, July 1957, 16–21, 59–60. See Bob Thomas, *Liberace*, for discussion of a famous 1959 libel trial in which Liberace defended his reputation against charges of homosexuality from a British columnist pen-named "Cassandra."

67. We might also consider what the British public believed about Liberace's sexuality after the 1956 publication of the "Cassandra"-authored column in the British *Daily Mirror.* This column used language to "out" Liberace that was so vicious that *Confidential's* article seems pro-gay in comparison. See Bob Thomas, *Liberace*, 121–124.

68. "Maureen O'Hara, Liberace Hit 'Lies,'" *Los Angeles Times*, May 15, 1957.

69. Desjardins, *Recycled Stars.*

70. Gurstein, *Repeal of Reticence*, might see the jury's indecision as representative of a society and its legal system that link privacy and obscenity too closely to individual rights and property. Because the state didn't prove that the stars written about by *Confidential* were hurt by the libelous obscenities in terms of property, the jury was indecisive about the magazine's harmfulness. Gurstein argues that protection of the privacy of individuals—including things about them that might be considered "indecent"—is good for the whole society, protecting basic human dignity.

BARBARELLA GOES

RADICAL

HANOI JANE AND

THE AMERICAN

POPULAR PRESS

SUSAN MCLELAND

*J*ane Fonda's July 1972 trip to Hanoi, during which she broadcast addresses to U.S. bombers asking them to stop their raids on North Vietnam, marked a change from earlier star scandals, which usually revolved around a star's private behavior — drug use or choice of sexual partners, for example. Even the "scandal" of the Red Scare of the 1950s focused on (mostly male, and usually "intellectual") stars' prior (and often recanted) political activities rather than a female sex symbol's current beliefs. Fonda's trip and her desire to speak out against U.S. involvement in Vietnam raised the issues of the appropriateness of stars' involvement in national affairs (despite Ronald Reagan's election to governor of California), and the role of women in Left political circles. It also led to a reinterpretation of Fonda's previously established star persona in the popular press, focusing on her disloyalty toward American values through a variety of radical, unfeminine behaviors. This effort to contain her actions by equating the larger betrayal of Americanness with a betrayal of her established body image of all-American sexuality and liberation would mark a turning point in Fonda's image in newspapers and magazines in the United States. By examining the changes in her persona at a critical time in its continuing construction, this essay will explore some of the ways Jane Fonda illuminates crises in the juncture of women's roles, politics, Hollywood, and American society.

This essay will most closely consider public discourse in the United States from 1968 to 1974, beginning in the last days of Fonda's marriage to French film director Roger Vadim, shortly before the birth of her first child, Vanessa Vadim, and ending after her marriage to American activist Tom Hayden and the birth of their son, Troy Donovan Garity. In this period representations of Jane Fonda went through four distinct but intimately connected stages: in 1968 and 1969, while she was still married to Vadim and not yet politically awakened, Fonda was portrayed as "the sex kitten next door"; beginning in 1969 and continuing through 1971 or early 1972, she was a "political dilettante"; in 1972 and 1973 Fonda and new husband Tom Hayden were represented as "dangerous radicals"; by 1974 Fonda and Hayden had mellowed and become almost "respectable moderates"—a timing that will suggest the possibility of marriage and motherhood containing her radical tendencies.

BARBARELLA, FUTURISTIC SEXPOT (1968–1969)

In "The Politics of 'Jane Fonda'" Tessa Perkins makes an interesting point concerning Fonda's screen persona: "of the sixteen films Fonda made before 1968 *Barbarella* is overwhelmingly the one that is referred to—and almost comes to stand in for all the others. This is important in so far as it becomes part of the 'knowledge' about Fonda which is constantly referred to and has to be 'dealt with.'"[1] Many of those films, in fact, were light "sex comedies" in the same sense as *Barbarella*, although not as sexually explicit.[2] In 1968 *Barbarella* was Fonda's most recent screen performance and the one most freshly inscribed on public consciousness; as such, it was the film that most completely worked with extra-textual discourses to define Fonda in terms of a mutely compliant body. Based on a popular French comic strip chronicling the exploits of a forty-first-century outer space adventuress (in both senses of the word), *Barbarella* features the nearly nude Fonda exploring strange new worlds and battling evil galactic forces.

Fonda as *Barbarella* was both symbol and product of a "revolution" that capitalized on free love and sexual pleasure as shocking and therefore resistant. Manifested in the late twentieth century as the "*Playboy* discourse," for Fonda it took the form of both performance and lifestyle in the late 1960s. *Playboy*'s pseudo-Freudian discourse distinguished it from other discourses that viewed sex as merely "normal"—as an important, but not defining, force in human existence. Instead, *Playboy* situated sexual experience as a natural expression of "healthy" (male) bodily desires, investing sexual expression with a quasi-medicalized urgency. At the same time, women's display of their bodies (for men) also was legitimated through a nationalist discourse that celebrated the *Playboy* pinup as "all-American," in contrast to the artificial eroticizing of European-style "art photography." By re-creating the nude pinup as the all-American woman (in part by picturing her elsewhere in the magazine as secretary, cheerleader, or some other icon of familiarity and desirability), *Playboy* played off of a stereotypical dichotomy that divides white women into Americans (whose sexuality is characterized by frankness, naturalness, and a bit of naiveté) and Europeans (whose sexuality is steeped in mystique and artifice).[3]

For *Life* magazine's 1968 profile "Fonda's Little Girl Jane," Jane Fonda appears on the cover in a form-fitting futuristic Barbarella costume, staring defiantly — but seductively — at the camera while she clutches an enormous rifle; inside she peers out frankly from a tangle of windswept hair — and nothing else — on what is identified as "an Italian beach." Both photographs are updated versions of classic pinups, challenging the viewer to possess Fonda and constructing Fonda's body as the repository of a healthy, liberated, utopian sexuality that promises a host of once-forbidden pleasures. Yet although Fonda's exhibitionism is constructed in "utopian" and "natural" terms in the two photographs, their effect is not indifference to the objectifying gaze but open provocation of it. Fonda's acknowledging expression constructs her as accepting — even inviting — the woman's place in patriarchy: "to-be-looked-at-ness." We now know Fonda (thanks to the pictures) through her body; it is as a body that we come to recognize her as a grown woman. Her "history," which is inscribed on her body through its depiction in extrafilmic discourse, also carries the imprint of her Father — and the danger that his wrath implies. The text by Thomas Thompson that accompanies these photographs underscores both the contrived naturalness and patriarchal threat surrounding the display of Fonda's body: "It wasn't so much her right-out-in-the-open nudity that smarted but the fact that this was, after all, *Henry's* daughter."[4]

Although he never appears in person in this particular article, Henry Fonda haunts Thompson's description of Jane Fonda and her lifestyle. A film star since the 1930s, Henry Fonda had built his career around a series of portrayals of stoic, honest, heroic American icons, including Abraham Lincoln in *Young Mr. Lincoln* (1939), Tom Joad in *The Grapes of Wrath* (1940), Wyatt Earp in *My Darling Clementine* (1946), and the honorable Lieutenant Douglas Roberts in *Mister Roberts* (1955). Henry Fonda was positioned as a prototypical American patriarch, and the fact that his daughter had embraced the sexual revolution boded ill for less heroic American fathers who desired to keep their daughters chaste. Thompson's allusion uses Henry Fonda's screen persona as iconic American male to erase the actual Henry Fonda's rocky marital history — by this time he was divorced from the fourth of his five wives, the Italian countess Afdera Franchetti Fonda.[5] Such accounts that portrayed Henry Fonda as all-American also would rewrite the historical Henry Fonda's troubled relationship with his children (best illustrated, perhaps, by son Peter's possibly accidental suicide attempt while Henry Fonda was away on his third honeymoon).

Jane Fonda's material, bodily presence — especially her place as a sexy body — defines how she is portrayed both onscreen and off. Thompson reports that as Barbarella, Fonda "plays a French comic-strip character who never lets clothes cramp her style — when she gets around to wearing any."[6] He draws parallels between her onscreen performance and offscreen lifestyle with the swinging French director of the film, Roger Vadim, whose "reputation has him more knowledgeable in matters sexual than Kinsey, Freud and Krafft-Ebing, due partly to his many and spectacular wives and lovers and partly to the films that he makes." Vadim was well known worldwide in the late 1960s as the director of (among other films) . . . *And God Created Woman* (1956) and the discoverer and mate of a series of 1950s and 1960s sex symbols—Bridget Bardot, Annette Stroyberg, and Catherine Deneuve. His alliance with Jane Fonda marked a powerful melding of the French reputation for libertine behavior with the *Playboy* discourse's insistence on sex as "natural."

Fonda's reluctance to marry Vadim, preferring instead to cohabitate for two years first, further solidified her reputation as the representative of an era of sexual freedom while ignoring her experience as the child of a much-broken home. But still she retained her status as the "girl next door" through occasional prudishness, as when she refused to allow her husband to film her in a nude scene that she believed was not dramatically motivated. The sexually liberated Fonda of the *Barbarella* era, although temptingly exotic, remained safe for American admiration—a mixture of "apple pie and soufflé, or Montgomery Ward and Dior."[7]

Fonda's next major film role, as the doomed Depression-era marathon dancer Gloria in *They Shoot Horses, Don't They* (1969), marks a sharp departure from the "sex kitten" Jane toward a more serious—and less sexy—political awareness. *Look*'s Henry Ehrlich focuses on the spectacle Fonda's body has become by painting an ugly picture of her: "she . . . cut back her voluptuous yellow hair to a marcelled 1930-ish dark-blonde bob and dieted away her curves."[8] That Fonda actually cut her hair, rather than wearing a wig for this role, suggests her willingness to bid her sexy image good-bye. The action divorced Fonda from the long blonde hair that signified femininity and sexiness in the late 1960s, especially in terms of the sex symbols Vadim had nurtured. Thus Fonda's action can be read as an attempt to break with her playful, sexy past and her sexually progressive husband with a sweep of the shears.

Fonda herself concentrates on her sexy body image as the key to her star persona: "After they see how I look in this picture," she remarks to Ehrlich, "nobody will ever hire me again." Her onscreen dowdiness ties in with a new offscreen "maturity" through her other new physical role—motherhood, which features prominently in both the *Look* article and a fashion feature in the *New York Times* entitled "Jane Fonda, on Clothes and No Clothes."[9] Although the *New York Times* article links Fonda to maternity only in terms of her own fourteen-month-old daughter, Vanessa Vadim, *Look* traces her maternal instincts to her childhood. Much had been written about Fonda's experience as daughter to an American icon or wife of a French Svengali, but Ehrlich is one of the first to explore her roles as older sister to Peter and mother to Vanessa as well. In the article Peter Fonda asserts that Henry Fonda hardly knew his children. "He had an image of us as nice clean kids, just like in the stupid photographs," Peter growls. The two children learned to depend on each other rather than on their father or stepmothers. As adults they took separate paths to find out, as Peter describes it, "What did we two innocent kids do to get so screwed up? . . . It took me two weeks [to understand] with LSD; Jane spent a lot of years at a shrink." [10]

Ehrlich reports that Jane is determined that her relationship with her own daughter will be different. Still, she sacrificed precious time with Vanessa to make *They Shoot Horses, Don't They* — including giving up their physical bond. "I had to stop nursing Vanessa," she explains. "They took away what belonged naturally to her" (75). Here Fonda brings together attitudes toward her breasts from a number of discourses: *Playboy*, which regards them as "natural," as well as a relatively new (in the 1960s) maternal appreciation of the nurturing abilities of the female body, primarily focused on the inherent value of breast- rather than bottle-feeding infants. Thus, although "Jane has been identified with healthy on-screen nudity, not motherhood" (70), the contrasting roles can be reconciled in her unfolding persona via their common focus on the female body as the site of plenitude for others.

SLOB: THE POLITICAL ANIMAL (1969–1972)

By 1970 Fonda was embarking on a period of personal and political exploration that was interpreted in the press as her "political dilettante" phase. For Fonda and a number of other actors of her generation, charged by the variety of heterodox movements that peaked in the 1960s and early 1970s, the rewards of stardom — fame and wealth — paled in comparison with the satisfaction one could achieve through political involvement. Fonda is widely quoted in her pronouncement that "Being a movie star is not a purpose." [11] Fonda's growing involvement with radical causes — and her increasing "mouthiness" — was represented in the popular press at this time by two stereotypes: the "Republican Mother" and the "lib" subset of the "disorderly woman." Both stereotypes, which use femininity as a position from which to critique dominant patriarchal culture, have ample precedent. The Republican Mother has been a common trope of American rhetoric since the Revolutionary War, and the disorderly woman has been documented in Western discourse since early modern Europe. [12] Beginning with her pronouncement in Ehrlich's profile that she was now reading the news "as a mother," Fonda called on a tradition of maternal concern for the future of her children as she embarked on a career in the public sphere of war and politics.

In general, the disorderly woman's image is a comic one, "poking fun" at culture rather than straightforwardly criticizing it. This laughter — and its lack — are significant for both the unruly woman and her audience, a significance that the "newly liberated" Fonda grasped along with other women striving for "liberation" in the late 1960s and early 1970s. At this time the movement had gone beyond ingratiating itself to men to request equality and into a phase of criticizing and antagonizing them to demand it. Although feminists retained a sense of humor, humor took a backseat to (or served as an open expression of) serious — even angry — analysis of inequalities in opportunity, in pay, in legal protection, and in the social and sexual division of labor.[13]

Descriptions of Fonda during the early 1970s match the "humorless" designation designed to denigrate "libbers" in the popular press. A *Life* article entitled "Nag, Nag, Nag!" notes that Vadim was publicly calling her "Jane d'Arc" but that she "wasn't smiling" about it; the Hollywood Women's Press Club had given her the "Sour Apple Award" for giving the industry "a sour image," and she was castigated for "walk[ing] around with a solemn Red Guard face." William F. Buckley Jr. repeats the "Red Guard" line, appealing to American stereotypes of life under Stalinism — apparently the ultimate end of any change from the status quo. Fonda is "Miss Grim . . . her solemn, Red Guard face never smiling, never laughing, never, obviously, looking into the mirror."[14]

Fonda's new "seriousness" is signaled in the roles she chose to portray during this period, as well as in her offscreen work. In fact, between *Barbarella* in 1968 and *Fun with Dick and Jane* in 1977, Fonda played primarily "straight" characters in serious dramas.[15] Although Fonda's gravity at first pleased critics and audiences (she was awarded the New York Film Critics' Best Actress award for *They Shoot Horses, Don't They* and *Klute*, nominated for an Academy Award for *They Shoot Horses*, and won her first Oscar for *Klute*), it reinforced her image as a woman who "can't take a joke," thereby linking her with the radical feminists who could be written off as extremists in an occasionally successful attempt to contain their revolutionary messages.

The contrast between Fonda's image and her voice provides another deviation from the unruly woman stereotype. Although Fonda-as-disorderly-woman had the *potential* to serve as a revolutionary model in this period, her representation within the popular press — especially as she was split between the naturally beautiful body (which patriarchy interpreted as compliant) and the unruly voice — undermined her ability to convey any sort of coherent message about potentially radical causes. As a result, representations of Fonda continuously critically scrutinized her physical appearance even when they claimed to concern her political activities. This tactic, which focused attention on Fonda-as-body at the same time that she was working to be heard as a potentially revolutionary voice, typified early 1970s responses to feminism by both the establishment and most of the leftist political movements, which also were firmly entrenched in patriarchy. The woman's place in the political revolution was prone, providing support and pleasure for the men who did the "real work" — just as it had been in the sexual revolution trumpeted by Hugh Hefner and Vadim. As the women's liberation movement gained attention and notoriety, it was able to take many of the Left's leaders to task for their sexism, including Fonda's husband-to-be, Tom

Hayden. The attention to Fonda's body at this stage of her political career, then, was not particularly unusual; what was unique was the way that Fonda's experience as a previously exemplary model and actress enabled her to draw attention to both the construction of her femininity and its intentional deconstruction. Thus Fonda's assertion that her new "look" served as a sign of her new political awareness brought her body renewed public attention. Where she once had dared the public to accept the beauty of her "natural," unclothed body, now she challenged people to view the ugliness of her "natural," unadorned self.

By 1970 it was widely reported that Fonda had left Vadim and his lifestyle to become, as *Newsweek* labeled her, "The Cause Celeb." [16] Reports now focused on the laundry list of "causes" to which she had donated her bodily presence and/or her money. William F. Buckley Jr. characterized her involvement in 1972 as "Citizen Jane": "She has been greatly fired up about Women's Liberation, Indians, Cesar Chavez, grapes, lettuce, the Dutch elm disease and poison ivy." [17] She also became more "newsworthy," crossing over from entertainment and fashion sections to infiltrate the (male, public) domain of hard news. Dozens of *New York Times* reports for 1970 catalog her activities for the Black Panthers, Native Americans, and the antiwar movement, as well as controversial stances on a number of other issues—as opposed to the paper's four film-related articles on her in 1969.

Although *Newsweek* still considered her "sexy" in 1970, her apparent disregard for fashion and her appearance was portrayed as an equally important issue. *Newsweek* quoted her: "I'm a renegade actress, a slob who doesn't fit into the Hollywood mold." [18] Rex Reed, in a controversial *New York Times* interview during which Fonda doctored a cigarette with marijuana, further investigated her repudiation of the sexy image. "It was the critics who gave me the sex symbol image in the first place," Fonda tells Reed. "In this country, if you do a Dostoevski film and take your bra off, you're a sex symbol." Instead, after another haircut (this time, the cropped *Klute* look) she was fulfilling "a deep-rooted psychological need to be a boy." Reed notes, in fact, that with the new haircut she looks just like her father, only prettier. "Masculinizing" Fonda's appearance cannot recreate her as a radical because her physical resemblance to Henry Fonda is a constant reminder of her link to patriarchy and Americana. Although Reed's profile is generally positive, the Hirschfeld caricature that accompanies it grotesquely emphasizes a prominent chin, bulging eyes, the infamous cigarette, and a mop of straight, dark hair as she converses with her unseen interviewer. [19] This marks a striking contrast to the traditional glamour shots that accompanied her *Barbarella*-era profiles, in which it is apparent that Fonda neither talks, nor offends.

Because a "masculine" young Fonda could not help but be confused with her brother Peter, it is not surprising that the two found their personas conflated when Jane Fonda was arrested for drug possession in Cleveland in November of 1970. Jane and Peter Fonda had embodied the twin hedonistic fantasies of the 1960s, sex and drugs (respectively), and whereas Jane upped the rebellious ante with her political activities in the 1970s, Peter remained identified with chemical self-liberation. That both *Newsweek* and the *New York Times* highlighted her political work in feature articles reporting on the drug possession arrest suggests that these mainstream reports found all of the obsessions of the youth culture — drugs, sex, and political involvement — equivalent. And the fact that the charges, when dropped, received scant attention underscores her identification with a set of phenomena that could not be differentiated in the mainstream press and for which rebellion in one sphere signified treason in all.[20]

After a year away from Vadim, Fonda had apparently shed her sensual femininity in favor of a new, unacceptably dour, more "masculine" identity — and a greater emphasis on the presence of her voice. Although Mel Gussow's *New York Times* review of her performance in the antiwar cabaret *FTA Show* (either "Free The Army" or "Fuck The Army," depending on your source) celebrated her "fetching" fatigues, the *Saturday Review*'s Goodman Ace found her new political awareness less attractive. Before she spoke on a television talk show, Ace noted that "she looked divinely feminine in her smartly tailored, form-fitting pants suit." Even after she began discussing Vietnam, Ace still felt the animal urge to state, "Me fellow, you Jane." But as the interview wore on, "what began as an extraordinarily pretty butterfly seemed to me now . . . a caterpillar." Ace finally was prompted to say, "You fellow, me fellow," to this political — and therefore masculine — caterpillar who had once been a beautiful, silent *Barbarella* butterfly.[21]

The barbs concerning her personal appearance and the growing attention given to her voice continued throughout 1972. William F. Buckley Jr. reports that she is now "young middle-age." Even more appalling, she "goes tirelessly about the college circuit and grunts out her views on international policies."[22] The *FTA Show*'s tour of Japan, as reported in *Time*, occasioned further criticism of Fonda's sexiness, especially in comparison with Bob Hope's troupe's concurrent tour. "[FTA's] performers determinedly hide their physical charms . . . under jeans and baggy sweaters," *Time* notes. Fonda herself is identified in boldface print as "No Barbarella."[23] And a disappointed fan, presumably one of the American servicemen Fonda had traveled to entertain, complained that "she looks too undistinguished and sounds too shrill."[24] That her voice becomes "shrill" or produces unattractive "grunts" at this time suggests a turning point in its perceived effectiveness: Kathleen Rowe Karlyn notes that "voices in any culture that are not meant to be heard are perceived as loud when they do speak, regardless of their decibel level ('shrill' feminists, for example)."[25] Although the content of Fonda's "voice" takes a backseat to its form in these articles, and the presence of her body continues to overwhelm its message, that message was beginning to be noticed, as her tenacity provided Fonda with a grudging accumulation of what Pierre Bourdieu calls symbolic capital — hence authority — in her public representations.[26]

Jane Fonda's most popular and widely acclaimed film role in this period — as part-time call girl Bree Daniel in *Klute* — mirrors popular press depictions of this body/voice dichotomy. This character marks a sharp contrast to the purring, fetishized, and unified *Barbarella* voice and body. Disembodied voices are a significant motif in the film, from the murderer who audiotapes his victims' last tricks, to Daniel's verbal seduction of a blind John, to her voiced-over therapy sessions. Yet throughout *Klute* actions performed by Fonda's body contradict the messages conveyed by her words — from her encouragement of a murderous client while she fights off his brutal attack to the closing voice-over in which she denies the possibility of a future in suburbia while we see her pack up her New York apartment to leave with the small-town detective.

In addition to the beautiful body/shrill voice split that informs Fonda's persona in the post-*Barbarella*, prebroadcast years, the popular press sought to contain her politics within another discourse that traditionally had defused the unruly woman's explosive potential: a corresponding split between low and high, the emotional woman and the intellectual man. Nathalie Zemon Davis describes this as one strategy that was used both to liberate and to contain the unruly woman's social commentary. Because the unruly woman was a captive of her lower material and bodily functions (unlike men, who were ruled by higher intellectual laws), "she was not accountable for what she did. Given over to the sway of her lower passions, she was not responsible."[27] As a creature of emotion, passion, and materiality, she was indulged by public tolerance for — and even expectation of — her transgressions; thus, her message also could be ignored easily because the messenger could be considered so clearly inadequate.

Popular press depictions of Fonda's political involvement from late 1969 to early 1972 bear out her place on the bottom half of this split. Her interest is continually described as "emotional" rather than "intellectual." *Newsweek* calls her "passionate" and "fervent"; Goodman Ace determines that she is "investing her emotion in defending and embracing Hanoi." Margaret Ronan's "Whatever Happened to Baby Jane" casts her activism as a part of Fonda's "education" — a process babies and children undergo to develop control over their emotions and bodily functions. And *Life* comments, "She is a sincere advocate, though her command of facts and complexities is unconvincing. . . . In her mind, all causes fit together into one complaint about our society."[28] Although a variety of respected Left activists found links between the individuated causes of Native American genocide, civil rights, the Vietnam War, sexism, and capitalist consumer culture, Fonda's efforts to connect them were considered an intellectual failing. *As a body* — "a star doing it" — she could share her symbolic capital with her chosen causes, but her status as an unmistakably *female* body paradoxically limited the general public's ability to listen to her voice as an expression of a "higher" intellectual analysis of those causes.

The general representational restriction of Fonda to the lower, emotional, corporeal, and sexual sphere parallels the tendency in contemporary accounts to overlook the repercussions of her six years' residence in France, which included a social life peopled by radical intellectuals. Since her return to the United States, Fonda's All-American persona appeared to sweep away the traces of her life in France in the 1960s for the popular press. The few articles that acknowledge her past dismiss it with the "low" rhetoric of *Barbarella* and Vadim's sex comedies. Yet a closer look at the context of France in the late 1960s—which influenced even hedonists like Vadim—shows a historical moment ripe with radical activity that culminated in the political events of May 1968. Fonda and Vadim maintained close ties to political French filmmakers like Jean-Luc Godard, as evidenced by Fonda's starring role in Godard's *Tout va bien* in 1972. Vadim, as well, was directly involved in the May 1968 rebellion; as president of the filmmakers' union he represented his more radical friends in negotiations that would eventually be breached by de Gaulle's government.[29] Perhaps even more significant, in light of the next phase of Fonda's political activism, was the cynicism permeating French intellectual culture as a result of their own failed imperialist mission in Vietnam. Ignoring Fonda's experience with French politics enabled Americans to continue to see the Vietnam conflict as an American effort in the international struggle against communism rather than as an indigenous people's fight for self-determination against a series of colonizers. This reinforced popular American depictions of Vietnam as a conflict without context or past before U.S. involvement. Keeping Fonda All-American helped portray Vietnam as an All-American war.[30]

DISEMBODIED VOICE (1972–1973)

Unlike the unruly women in early modern Europe, Jane Fonda had the technological means to escape the confines of her body—at least temporarily—through radio broadcasts. And it was through this medium that Fonda's "nagging" voice was finally understood for the radical, and potentially dangerous, instrument that it had become. In July of 1972 Fonda began her tour of North Vietnam, where she made the infamous broadcasts. The *New York Times* first reported her trip on July 8 with a short paragraph on page 15, a day before the *Chicago Tribune* noted it on page 8. News of her first broadcast appeared in the July 15 editions of the *New York Times*, *Los Angeles Times*, and *Chicago Tribune*. The *Chicago Tribune*'s quotation from her broadcast suggests that Fonda tried to humanize the North Vietnamese for American soldiers. "These are peasants. They grow rice, and they rear pigs. They are similar to the farmers in the Midwest many years ago in the U.S." Both the *Tribune* and the *New York Times* reported that after visiting a bombed-out North Vietnamese village, she appealed to American bomber pilots to "reconsider their participation in the Vietnam war": "I implore you, I beg you to consider what you are doing. In the area where I went it was easy to see that there are no military targets, there is no important highway, there is no communication network." State Department officials attacked the source of the broadcasts: "It is always distressing to find American citizens who benefit from the protection and assistance of this Government *lending their voice* in any way to governments such as the Democratic Republic of Vietnam" (my emphasis).[31]

Yet Fonda had been expressing the same sentiments in the *FTA Show* for almost two years. The State and Defense departments had been able to keep Fonda and her troupe physically off American military bases — even though the *FTA Show* always had been able to find nearby theaters willing to house them. In fact, the *FTA Show* had recently completed a tour of "far eastern" bases that may have included performances in South Vietnam — which indicates that her bodily presence combined with her voice had not been considered dangerous even when it was on or near the front lines of battle. Yet the radio broadcasts allowed the *disembodied Fonda voice* access to places where the physical woman's presence could be banned — or where the message inscribed on the Fonda body would overwhelm or undermine the message carried by her voice.[32]

Public reaction to Fonda's broadcasts — more violent and negative than that surrounding her previous political activities — signals that Fonda's voice had finally managed to be heard. This allowed her vocal opposition to the war to threaten the status quo in a way that the *Fonda body* uttering the same words never had. Whereas the protesting Fonda voice within the Fonda body had inspired indulgence (at best) or contempt (at worst), her disembodied voice was labeled a traitor worthy of censorship and censure. Her earlier attempts to "masculinize" her body could not make it less an object, but her moments as a disembodied voice, which transformed her into a political being, managed to temporarily re-create her body as a desexualized object that was not the gendered object of the male gaze. Even when a photograph documenting her (bodily) appearance in North Vietnam appeared later in the month of July 1972, its content (featuring Fonda in military gear) only confirmed the radical message of her voice, contributing to the growing hostility against her.

The *New York Times* chronicles a litany of charges against Fonda: Representative Fletcher Thompson of Georgia called for a treason investigation; the Veterans of Foreign Wars named her a "traitorous meddler in official Government security" who should be subjected to the "legal machinery of the Federal Government"; First Lady Pat Nixon scolded her for her remarks; the House Internal Security Committee voted to ask the Justice Department to investigate her trip and the broadcasts; Representative Richard Ichord of Missouri suggested that similar trips, *especially those involving radio broadcasts*, be subject to criminal penalties, then introduced a bill to restrict travel by American citizens in the area; her speeches were canceled around the United States; and she was pelted with red paint during an antiwar demonstration in Stockholm.[33]

The "Voice of the People" in the *Chicago Tribune* carried a lively debate over her words and their repercussions. Scott Wilde of Illinois suggests that "the verbose Miss Fonda doesn't realize how very much she sounds like Axis Sally and Tokyo Rose." Illinois resident Aileen Widerquist was "sickened and grieved" by a photo of Fonda but angered by her words. "Miss Fonda doesn't mention all the cities Hanoi has destroyed. . . . Does Miss Fonda really think or believe her statements . . . ?" "Disgusted Citizen" of Chicago similarly attacks her powerful words and silences. "Another [Fonda defender] writes that *she tells it like it is.* We haven't heard one word from her about the butchery the North Vietnamese carry on in South Viet Nam. . . . Why doesn't she broadcast from Saigon, urging the regime in Hanoi to stop this murder?" And Kenneth Platt of Michigan defines *war* and *treason* to refute charges by Fonda and another letter writer who accused President Richard Nixon of treason: "A state of war is caused by an act, *not by spoken words.* . . . [Nixon] has not violated our Constitution by carrying the war to an enemy nation." Yet Fonda also has supporters, including Louis Kale of Chicago, who, paradoxically, valorizes her words as actions: "I think [Jane Fonda] is truly a great American. A lot of us say we would like to do something about the war if we could. Well, she can, and she is."[34]

The *Los Angeles Times*, however, felt compelled to take an official stance on Fonda's words and actions, in an effort to recontain her as an embodied woman. In its lead editorial for August 7, 1972, the *Times* complained that

> the measured and documented reporting of [U.S. journalist Joseph] Kraft and a few other professionals has been almost lost because of reports bordering on the hysterical from some of the other visitors. Their emotionalism has not served the purposes they intended, for their excesses and exaggerations have been seized as ammunition by those who seek to discourage all criticism of American action in Vietnam. One can appreciate the horror felt by Miss Jane Fonda, the actress, upon seeing the damage and casualties she is convinced were caused by Americans allegedly against civilian targets.[35]

Fonda is tarred with all the epithets previously established by her embodiment as an uncredentialed woman protesting the war: she is an "actress," not a "professional", (although one wonders what type of professional the *Times* would trust), who "felt horror" (rather than experiencing an intellectual exercise); her report, which "borders on the hysterical," is marked by "emotionalism," "excesses," and "exaggeration," which have rendered it useless for determining "the truth." Yet the *Times's* call for a more reasoned response to Fonda's words based on the source from which they emanated, the famed Fonda body, could not stem the tide of controversy she had raised.

But what did people hear when Fonda's voice became audible? What was so controversial about the content of her speeches? The ambivalence of popular representations of the Vietnam War in 1972 provides some sense of the volatility of the subject as a site of contesting interpretations. Mainstream newspapers and newsmagazines of the day continued to report in every issue on combat and peace negotiations using the wartime terminology honed in previous clashes in Korea and World War II, even equating the terms "North Vietnamese" and "the enemy." With their tight deadlines and a readership concerned about the fate of specific individuals, units, and battles, these news sources tended to be bogged down in the details to the detriment of providing a larger understanding of the war. Yet more than five years of outspoken antiwar rhetoric among civilians, politicians, and returning veterans had made a dent in both domestic reporting on home-front morale and occasional attempts at in-depth reporting on policy analysis. Combined with nightly television reports that showed the squalor, grit, and confusion of fighting in Vietnam, these everyday sources of information provided a regular dose of daily horror and everyday heroism, bodies shattered by mines, falsely optimistic politicians, business-as-usual generals, angry student radicals, and homesick soldiers. Given these options, is it any wonder that the tone of the mainstream newspapers and magazines overwhelmingly valorized the soldiers?

In 1972, higher-brow monthlies, with the luxury of extended publication deadlines, as well as a readership less immediately invested in the war, were willing to openly equate the words *Vietnam* and *mistake*. The *Atlantic Monthly*, for example, regularly reported on policy missteps in Vietnam and featured on its July 1972 cover an interview with a retired American general who had served in Vietnam, second-guessing American diplomatic and combat positions from the beginning of the nation's involvement. The *New Republic* questioned the president's psychological motivations and constitutional prerogatives, and the *Nation* described Vietnam as "The Greedy War" on its cover and analyzed the American leaders' failure to comprehend the petty thievery that the war encouraged under the guise of the victory of American capitalism. *Psychology Today* even suggested in a 1972 ad that, had the magazine existed in the early 1960s, its popularization of psychological concepts such as "groupthink," which accounts for the lack of constructive dissent in organizations committed to unanimity, could have prevented American involvement in the region.[36] In these publications blame for the war, when it was assigned, was placed on diplomatic and defense strategies, not on the everyday soldiers whose presence was barely acknowledged in their pages. Privileged by distance from the actual events, just as upper-class families were able to debate the war dispassionately while they provided their sons with educational deferments and National Guard commissions, in 1972 these magazines presented a sanitized view of Vietnam as a historical error that we might have prevented, had opportunities to escape, but continued to perpetuate.

What, then should anyone do about Vietnam? And how were Jane Fonda's "solutions" framed as "treasonous" given the lack of consensus about the war's meaning or its ability to be represented? A letter from Gary Scott Goodman of Santa Monica to the *Los Angeles Times* offers a clue: "As a conscientious objector I am crucially aware that one who believes in an antiwar philosophy must be against all wars, and those nations that engage in them. Ms. Fonda finds it sensationally appropriate to openly support the North Vietnamese, and their acts of human destruction, while posing to be 'antiwar' at the same time. The two guises are mutually exclusive."[37] Because Fonda's broadcasts focused on the North Vietnamese and their pain rather than on the generalized horrors of war perpetuated on both sides, it was possible to interpret her position as "For North Vietnam" rather than "For Peace." As a result, Fonda could be isolated not only from those who supported the war effort but from the pacifists who refused to support any war whatsoever. Rejected by both the establishment that labeled her treasonous and the antiwar movement that dismissed her as pro-North Vietnam, Fonda was subject to derision from both sides of the Vietnam debate.

Similarly, Fonda's broadcast descriptions of the damage American aggression caused against civilians in North Vietnam could be interpreted as direct criticism of American soldiers rather than attacks on war in general. Personalizing the war by asking soldiers how they reconciled their consciences to the deaths of innocent women and children came dangerously close to calling them "baby killers." Even though Congress later dismissed charges of treason based on transcripts of Fonda's addresses, the impression that she had verbally attacked the soldiers in her pleas for their cooperation in ending the war persists, causing continuing conflicts between Fonda and Vietnam veterans' groups. Reaction to Fonda's broadcasts establishes a continuum of possibilities for attitudes toward Vietnam and the Vietnam conflict. On the one hand, the "traitorous" Fonda and the "average American" postulated by the newsmagazines both support and oppose fairly concrete beings, whereas those who take the "antiwar" stance deal in abstractions. Such abstractions as "the War Machine" and a generalized peace, however, lack the potency of embodied experiences to generate action on a widespread scale and therefore remain safe options for dissenters. On the other hand, the tendency to personalize conflicts as Fonda did has roots in the narrative conventions of the well-made play and the classical film.[38]

Fonda's very real efforts to embody "the enemy" for her countrymen — even going so far as to compare them to their Midwest pioneer forefathers — suggests her effort to rework the narrative of the average soldiers' war experience from one of heroism to one of treachery and to reinterpret their actions from "following orders" or "fighting Commies" to "betraying fellow human beings." Her later efforts to turn the "treasonous" label, with which these interpretations of her broadcasts had branded her, back on President Richard Nixon represents her further attempt to personalize the enemy of the people. The popular misunderstanding of her mission, however, led to her own personification as that enemy.

MRS. TOM HAYDEN, RECUPERATED RADICAL (1974–PRESENT)

For the rest of 1972 and most of 1973 Fonda's voice retained its power, serving as the focal point for her popular press persona. Shrillness in particular became an important motif depicting the disembodied Fonda. *Time*'s Jesse Birnbaum, in a discussion of Fonda's role in the filming of Henrik Ibsen's *A Doll's House*, focuses on Fonda's vocal opposition. She "declared" her objections to the script, "announced" new cues that she had written, and "demanded" seventy pages of rewrites. Fonda's own use of her body as an actress — to develop the friendship between her character, Nora, and Kristine, played by Delphine Seyrig — was denounced by director Joseph Losey as "the unwarranted intrusion of lesbianism into the story." Yet Losey assured Birnbaum that "he can cut out Jane's verbosity in the editing wherever it gets in the way." [39]

Other limited efforts to contain Fonda in 1973 focus on her continuing pronouncements but suggest action against her bodily presence. The *New York Times* reported that Colorado state legislator Michael Strang, describing her as "a foul-mouthed offensive little Vassar dropout," proposed a resolution banning Fonda from the state. The chief Fonda controversy during the year was over a statement she made that spring regarding the veracity of returning POWs' charges that the North Vietnamese had tortured them. The *New York Times* reported on her clarification of this statement at a "much-heckled talk" to University of Southern California students: "I never blanketly said that all prisoners of war are lying. I said the primary lie comes from the U.S. Government, and that is the one we have to concern ourselves with." Some students then hanged her in effigy. [40]

By the end of 1973, however, Fonda had entered a stage that was more easily contained by patriarchal hegemony. Her marriage to radical leader Tom Hayden early in 1973 helped to redefine her as a woman who possesses — and is ruled by — a body, emotions, and a man. But the new Fonda lacks the sensuality and sexual charge of the *Barbarella* (and even the "slob") years — thanks to the return of her repressed maternity. A profile in the *New York Times Magazine* compares life with her new husband to the luxury of her years with Vadim, noting that the Haydens' "connubial mattress rests on the bare bedroom floor" of their "pinched and unfashionable," "colorless" duplex. In contrast author Martin Kasindorf describes again the "sexy" glass-walled Vadim bedroom/bath and their "showplace 130-year-old farmhouse west of Paris." [41] He also reports throughout the interview on her physical responses to questions and interruptions. She "lovingly nurses" son Troy, flashes "a dazzling smile," lugs groceries into the apartment and grouses with a plumber. Although Kasindorf implies she has gained substance during her years in the limelight, he also suggests that her new domestication has destroyed the magic that made her a dangerous woman.

But the crowning blow in the war of containment against Fonda came in her reconciliation with Henry Fonda — a settlement that could be considered to bridge the previous decade's generational conflict. In an interview that was quoted in James Clarity's *New York Times* column, Henry Fonda issued a public pardon for his daughter's offensive actions. "I've not said much about Jane before and I resent people who expect me to denounce her," her patriarch the American icon stated. "Hers is not my way of life, and hers is not too often my exact way of thinking. But I love her, I respect her right to say what she says and she and her husband are obviously deeply in love."[42] A series of alliances created and repaired — with her husband, her son, and finally her father — combine to restore Jane Fonda's ability to accumulate and invest symbolic capital in both the entertainment and political fields.

Henry Fonda's continuing approval of his daughter — signaled by a benefit performance of his Broadway show *Clarence Darrow* for Jane Fonda's Indo-China Peace Campaign — prompted reporter John Corry to refocus on her appearance rather than her pronouncements. "Miss Fonda is the La Pasionaria of the antiwar movement, but up close she is indistinguishable from the girl next door," he comments. Corry, in fact, reinterprets her commitment — not in the "traitorous" terms of the last two years but under the harmless epithet "radical chic."[43] Her father's benefit performance helped to realign her with the moneyed (and therefore respectable) interests of mainstream liberalism. She was containable once again. In fact, Fonda's return trip to Hanoi late in 1974, accompanied by the all-male team of cinematographer-director Haskell Wexler; husband, Tom Hayden; and infant son, Troy, was not even considered "hard news" — it rated only a few mentions in the "Notes on People" column. Now, Fonda's activities were closely linked to her body through onscreen appearances in the documentary she and Wexler were producing, as well as through her physical connection with Hayden and Garity. In these reports her once-strident voice is oddly silenced.[44]

To some extent Fonda's temporary recontainment represents her effort to address mainstream America and to put her radical past behind — not merely for economic reasons but to widen the audience for her message, she indicates. "I'm still committed but not reckless anymore," she tells Geraldo Rivera on a late-night talk show.[45] In fact, Fonda and Hayden seem more chastened than triumphant, in light of the "victory" of their well-publicized opinions, with the withdrawal of American troops from Vietnam and impending impeachment proceedings against President Nixon. The "Huck Finn"-look-alike Hayden, once leader of the radical Students for a Democratic Society and member of the Chicago Seven, for example, is particularly restrained in light of the turn of events. Hayden, now considering a run at mainstream electoral politics, tells the *New York Times*, "You can become a prisoner of the image you were. . . . [We're] learning to talk to the middle now. I don't think we ever really won anything in the sixties."[46]

Fonda outlines her plan for producing "message films, but in subtle, commercially viable ways," to Kasindorf. "I don't want to play liberated women, roles where people say, 'Oh, that's Jane Fonda, that's the way she perceives herself.'" Instead, she wants to play "the antithesis of what I feel—a prowar or apolitical kind of woman existing in a situation most average people live in" so she can help "to clarify the situation for other women."[47] This statement provides a blueprint for most of the roles she would produce and play in coming years: in *Coming Home* (1978) she plays a military wife awakened to the injustice of the Vietnam War; in *The China Syndrome* (1980) she portrays a features reporter awakened to the dangers of capitalist-controlled nuclear energy; in *Nine to Five* (1981) she plays a displaced homemaker awakened to the inequality of sexist corporate America; in *The Dollmaker* (1984, for television) she portrays a simple mountain woman awakened to the subjugation of unskilled urban workers; in *Stanley and Iris* (1990) she plays a repressed factory worker awakened to the problem of illiteracy in the working classes; and in *Old Gringo* (1989) she portrays a spinster awakened to the oppression of colonialism in Mexico *and* the cruelty of revolutionary justice. In most of these films Fonda's character's awakening is accompanied by a transformative sexual experience, which works to tie her intellectual enlightenment with a sensuously embodied arousal. Thus, her film roles have enabled Fonda to have it both ways—as a mind and a body—in a manner that her image as a public figure in the popular press cannot. For throughout the last twenty years, representations of Fonda's body and voice have continued to battle for legitimacy in the construction of her political image.

Jane Fonda never will be a completely "safe" actress as far as pockets of the public are concerned. From the 1970s until today her name has continued to surface in letters to the editor as a synonym for "traitor." A bumper sticker distributed at a small-town Texas gun shop states that "Vietnam veterans will forgive Jane Fonda when the Jews forgive Hitler," equating her embrace of the North Vietnamese during the war with the planning and execution of the Holocaust. And the Republican joke that circulated during the 1992 presidential election—"What's the difference between Bill Clinton and Jane Fonda? Jane went to Vietnam."—indicates that although mainstream conservatives can laugh at her now, she still serves as a potent signifier for un-Americanness.

Another incident suggests that the popular press has continued to try to contain her radical past. During the 1991 baseball playoffs, when her then-fiancé Ted Turner's Atlanta Braves played in the World Series, Fonda was held up to public scrutiny for cheering the team on with "the Tomahawk Chop," a gesture that Native American groups had identified as demeaning to their heritage. As in the 1970s, when her (apparently true) history as a sex kitten was used to undermine her (false) revolutionary message, her (apparently true) insensitive actions today are used to discredit her (still false) radical past, calling both message and messenger into question. The one moment in Fonda's history in which she transcended her representation as merely a female body to express a potentially radical thesis, when framed in the context of her present, becomes aberrant. Although still a signifier of treason for the Radical Right, Fonda degenerated through popular representations of her traditional marriage to iconoclastic but conservative Turner into a disorderly woman recuperated by the power of (the right sort of) heterosexual coupling—a "shrew" who was tamed by a real man, at last. And the continuing volatility of the union, despite Fonda's and Turner's joint statement in January 2000 that they "continue to be committed to the long-term success of our marriage,"[48] further discounts her effectiveness as a mainstream political activist, especially because she abandoned her own power bases in film and fitness early in the 1990s to be simply an internationally famous, fabulously wealthy, gorgeous, adoring, and sympathetic spouse.

NOTES

1. Tessa Perkins, "The Politics of 'Jane Fonda,'" in Christine Gledhill, ed., *Stardom: Industry of Desire* (London: Routledge, 1991), 244.

2. *Tall Story* (her 1960 debut), *La Ronde* (1964), and *Barefoot in the Park* (1967) all can be considered "sex comedies" in the sense that they focus on heterosexual male-female attraction. Other films, including *Walk on the Wild Side* (1961), *The Chapman Report* (1962), *Cat Ballou* (1965), *The Chase* (1966), *The Game Is Over* (1966), and *Histoires Extraordinaires* (1967), deal more frankly with sexual themes or feature Fonda in roles characterized by their sexuality.

3. See Richard Dyer, *Heavenly Bodies: Film Stars and Society* (New York: St. Martin's, 1986), chap. 2, and Barbara Ehrenreich, *The Hearts of Men: American Dreams and the Flight from Commitment* (New York: Anchor Books, 1983), chap. 4, for discussions of *Playboy*, pinups, and the American male.

4. T. Thompson, "Fonda's Little Girl Jane," *Life*, November 29, 1968, 68.

5. Three of Henry Fonda's marriages ended in divorce. His second, to Jane and Peter's mother, terminated when Frances Seymour Brokaw Fonda's suicide prevented Henry Fonda from divorcing her to marry third wife Susan Blanchard, who was only a few years older than Jane. Henry Fonda would marry once again; his fifth wife, Shirley, nursed him through his fatal bout with cancer.

6. Thompson, "Fonda's Little Girl Jane," 66.

7. Ibid., 70.

8. Henry Ehrlich, "Jane Fonda: Shining in Two New Roles," *Look*, May 13, 1959, 70.

9. Joan Cook, "Jane Fonda, on Clothes and No Clothes," *New York Times*, December 5, 1969, 38.

10. Ehrlich, "Shining," 75.

11. See, for example, Leslie Halliwell, *Halliwell's Filmgoer's Companion*, 8th ed. (New York: Scribners, 1983); and Matt Martin, *Did She or Didn't She: Behind the Bedroom Doors of 201 Famous Women* (New York: Citadel Press, 1996), both of which use this quotation as their defining comment on Fonda and her careers in the two fields of entertainment and politics.

12. See, for example, E. Ann Kaplan, *Motherhood and Representation: The Mother in Popular Culture and Melodrama* (London: Routledge, 1992), for discussion of the Republican Mother; see Nathalie Zemon Davis, "Women on Top:

Symbolic Sexual Inversion and Political Disorder in Early Modern Europe," in Barbara Babcock, ed., *The Reversible World* (Ithaca: Cornell University Press, 1978), 147–190, for discussion of the disorderly woman's precedents and uses. The disorderly woman has been celebrated by Bakhtinian scholars as a significant site of struggle against hegemony; see, for example, Kathleen Rowe [Karlyn], "Roseanne: Unruly Woman as Domestic Goddess," *Screen* 31 (winter 1990): 408–419, for a particularly elegant analysis along these lines.

13. See Robin Morgan, ed., *Sisterhood Is Powerful: An Anthology of Writings from the Women's Liberation Movement* (New York: Vintage, 1970), for documentation of these shifts in the movement.

14. John Frook, "Jane Fonda, Nonstop Activist: Nag, Nag, Nag," *Life*, April 23, 1971, 52C; William F. Buckley Jr., "Secretary Fonda," *National Review*, August 18, 1972, 919.

15. *FTA*, the filmed version of her sketch comedy road show for military personnel, and *Steelyard Blues*, in which she reprises her role as a hooker, mark her only "comic" performances during this time, and neither was particularly well received at the box office or by critics. Both, in fact, were comedies with a political message that could still be considered "serious."

16. "Cause Celeb," *Newsweek*, November 16, 1970, 65.

17. Buckley, "Secretary Fonda," 918.

18. "Cause Celeb," 65.

19. Rex Reed, "Jane: 'Everyone Expected Me to Fall on My Face,'" *New York Times*, January 25, 1970, sec. 2, pp. 15, 22.

20. Articles reporting on Fonda's arrest include "Jane Fonda Accused of Smuggling," *New York Times*, November 4, 1970, 52; and "Cause Celeb," 65; announcement of the charges' dismissal appeared in "Personalities," *New York Times*, May 29, 1971, 9. It is interesting to note, as well, that the cover of *Life's* "Nag, Nag, Nag" issue identifies Fonda as "a Pusher of Causes," incorporating drug lingo to discuss her political activism.

21. Mel Gussow, "Anti-Army 'F.T.A.' Show,'" *New York Times*, November 23, 1971; Goodman Ace, "You Jane, Me Fellow," *Saturday Review*, June 5, 1971, 5.

22. Buckley, "Secretary Fonda," 918–919.

23. Histories of the *FTA Show* note that Fonda's burgeoning feminist consciousness was the main force behind the desexualization of the revue. According to George Haddad-Garcia, *The Films of Jane Fonda* (Secaucus, N.J.: Citadel Press, 1981), this was a source of tension between male and female members of the troupe. Still, Fonda's fame and politically useful alliances allowed her vision of the show to win out. "We're not going to do that kind of chauvinist show with topless dancers and a lot of breasts," she was reported to announce, in a dig at Bob Hope's government-sanctioned tours. Yet Fonda was widely rumored to have shared her sexual favors with a variety of sympathetic GIs, as well as a number of the Black Panthers.

24. "Typhoon Jane," *Time*, January 3, 1972, 71.

25. Rowe [Karlyn], "Roseanne," 413.

26. See Pierre Bourdieu, *Language and Symbolic Power*, trans. Gino Raymond and Matthew Adamson (Cambridge: Harvard University Press, 1991), esp. chaps. 3 and 9, for a full discussion of the ways a variety of types of capital contribute to our ability to speak in society. Bourdieu distinguishes between monetary capital, relational capital (connections), cultural capital (education), and symbolic capital (general fame — the ability to catch the public's attention), all of which provide their owners with enhanced opportunities to address the public and its leaders.

27. Davis, "Woman on Top," 176.

28. "Cause Celeb," 65; Ace, "You Jane," 5; Margaret Ronan, "Whatever Happened to Baby Jane," *Senior Scholastic* (November 1971): 36; Frook, "Nag, Nag, Nag," 51. Ronan also quotes part-Indian singer Buffy St. Marie on Fonda's work with Native American rights: "she has unintentionally blown a couple of our most important issues by not really understanding our problems" ("Whatever Happened," 36).

29. See Roger Vadim, *Bardot, Deneuve, Fonda: My Life with the Three Most Beautiful Women in the World,* trans. Melinda Camber Porter (New York: Simon and Schuster, 1986), chap. 30, for Vadim's version of the events of May 1968 and his (and Fonda's) relation to them.

30. This effort to overlook the failed French regime has not been confined to the 1960s and 1970s. Even the more recent American Vietnam stories erase the French history in the region. Consider Oliver Stone's celebrated Vietnam trilogy, which would seem to suggest that the conflict began with the Kennedy (or perhaps Eisenhower) administration. Eleanor Coppola noted in her documentary *Hearts of Darkness* that her husband had originally shot a segment meant to symbolize the French occupation of Vietnam, but it was deleted from the final cut of *Apocalypse Now* because it interfered with the narrative flow of the American characters' journey. Television's *China Beach* offered one of the few popular American depictions of the war that featured occasional French characters.

31. "Jane Fonda in Hanoi," *New York Times*, July 8, 1972, 15; "Jane Fonda Arrives in Hanoi for Visit," *Chicago Tribune*, July 9, 1972, sec. 1, p. 8; "Jane Fonda Appeal Reported by Hanoi," *New York Times*, July 15, 1972, 9; "Hanoi Broadcast by Jane Fonda Reported," *Los Angeles Times*, July 15, 1972, sec. 1, p. 11; "Jane Fonda Plea in Bombing Told," *Chicago Tribune*, July 15, 1972, sec. 1, p. 2.

32. See, for example, Kaja Silverman, *The Acoustic Mirror* (Bloomington: University of Indiana Press, 1988), for a discussion of the silencing of women's voices in the classical Hollywood cinema. Silverman argues that cinema (and perhaps other representational forms) almost always binds the female voice to a visually represented body, thereby reinforcing the woman's place in patriarchy as "to-be-looked-at-ness."

33. James Clarity, "Notes on People," *New York Times*, July 19, 1972, 43; "VFW Urges Prosecution of Clark and Miss Fonda," *New York Times*, August 24, 1972, 9; "Mrs. Nixon Asserts Jane Fonda Should Have Bid Hanoi End War," *New York Times*, August 9, 1972, 12; "House Committee Refuses to Subpoena Jane Fonda," *New York Times*, August 11, 1972, 59; "Rep. Ichord Requests Laws Covering Jane Fonda Trip," *New York Times*, August 15, 1972, 20; James Clarity, "Notes on People," *New York Times*, September 21, 1972, 25; "Jane Fonda Denied a Hall," *New York Times*, October 5, 1972, 36; James Clarity, "Notes on People," *New York Times*, December 27, 1972, 52.

34. Scott Wilde, "Letter to the Editor," *Chicago Tribune*, August 2, 1972, sec. 1, p. 20; Aileen Widerquist, "Letter to the Editor," *Chicago Tribune*, August 2, 1972, sec. 1, p. 20; "Disgusted Citizen," "Letter to the Editor (Jane and the War)," *Chicago Tribune*, September 8, 1972, sec. 1, p. 10; Kenneth Platt, "Letter to the Editor (Treasonous Conduct)," *Chicago Tribune*, September 6, 1972, sec. 1, p. 24; Louis Kale, "Letter to the Editor (Jane Fonda and Peace)," *Chicago Tribune*, September 2, 1972, sec. 1, p. 6.

35. "Search for Truth in North Vietnam," *Los Angeles Times*, August 7, 1972, sec. 2, p. 6.

36. "Could Psychology Today Have Prevented the Vietnam War?" (advertisement), *Harper's*, July 1972, 27. The ad states in part, "What if [Yale University

psychologist and "groupthink" discoverer Irving L.] Janis's conclusions had been developed ten years earlier? And what if there had already been a magazine called *Psychology Today* to communicate world-changing ideas like these to a wide general audience of thoughtful readers? Might it have prevented the tragic American military intervention in Vietnam?"

37. Gary Scott Goodman, "Letter to the Editor (Jane Fonda's Visit to North Vietnam)," *Los Angeles Times*, August 2, 1972, sec. 2, p. 6.

38. See, for example, Linda Seger, *Making a Good Script Great*, 2d ed. (Hollywood: Samuel French, 1995), 174.

39. Jesse Birnbaum, "Oh, You Militant Doll," *Time*, March 12, 1973, 67.

40. James Clarity, "Notes on People," *New York Times*, April 6, 1973, 37; April 14, 1973, 21.

41. Martin Kasindorf, "Fonda: A Person of Many Parts," *New York Times Magazine*, February 3, 1974, 16.

42. James Clarity, "Notes on People," *New York Times*, August 21, 1973, 25.

43. John Corry, "About New York: Theater Party for a Cause," *New York Times*, March 27, 1974, 35.

44. James Clarity, "Notes on People," *New York Times*, April 2, 1974, 35; April 12, 1974, 27; April 26, 1974, 31.

45. As reported in John O'Connor, "TV: Rivera Tries Hand as a Late-Hour Celebrity," *New York Times*, June 6, 1974, 74.

46. Corry, "About New York," 35.

47. Kasindorf, "Many Parts," 19.

48. "Alone on the Range: After Eight High-Profile Years, Jane Fonda and Ted Turner Announce a Trial Separation," *People*, January 17, 2000, 115.

WHAT BUSINESS DOES A CRITIC HAVE ASKING IF BLAKE EDWARDS IS GAY?

RUMOR, SCANDAL, BIOGRAPHY, AND TEXTUAL ANALYSIS

PETER LEHMAN AND WILLIAM LUHR

When Max Bercutt, former head of publicity for Warner Bros., arrived for an interview concerning his work with Blake Edwards in the 1960s, he casually remarked during the preinterview discussion that he presumed we knew Edwards was gay. This comment did not surprise us because it has long been rumored that Edwards is gay. Since his marriage to Julie Andrews, those rumors have been compounded with rumors that she is a lesbian and that they have a "marriage of convenience."

In recognition of and in response to these rumors, both Edwards and Andrews have vehemently denied them in published interviews in such places as *Playboy* and the *Advocate*, as well as in private interviews with us. Speaking in the *Advocate* about rumors of her lesbianism and Edwards's homosexuality, Andrews has said, "'The rumors I was aware of were the ones that concerned the two of us.' She admits, 'You know, it's the easiest thing in this town for people to say, "Oh, my God, he's gay" and trash somebody. That's the way it used to be. Blake and I were definitely spoken of as being gay.' The rumors, she adds, were printed: 'The gutter press usually prints something silly, and it gets picked up at the hairdresser's by a whole bunch of ladies or gentlemen, and before you know it, the gossip becomes fact.'" [1]

Edwards has a long history of embracing public controversy and has told us that, were he gay, he would freely admit it: "I've been 'gay' since I really started in the business. There has been that rumor that I'm gay, and there is nothing further from the truth. I don't say that proudly, or anything else. In fact, I say to people who bring it up, . . . 'If I was gay, . . . I'd be out of the closet and say, "I'm gay."'"[2] Similarly, responding to questions about the appeal of his films to gay fans at the 1998 Hamptons International Film Festival, he said that he believed he had a gay guardian angel who guided him but added, "And if I was gay myself, I'd be the most 'out' gay man there ever was."[3] Indeed, Edwards claims to be unable to comprehend bisexuality and says that he has never known a bisexual: "I don't understand them. I don't know any bisexuals. I mean, I probably do, but I don't know that I do, you know? And bisexuality, I, in my lifestyle, have never really considered, never really felt it."[4] Furthermore, Edwards acknowledges that he is aware that the rumors about him have extended to his close colleagues such as Tony Adams, a producer of his films from the mid-1970s to the mid-1990s: "But there is a heavy rumor, you know, that Tony and I are supposed to be lovers. I mean, it goes from one person to another that I'm associated with."[5]

Edwards presumes that the rumors about his and his wife's sexuality originated with people insecure in their own: "If people are sniping about our sexuality, it's the very proof of what I say: They're so fearful of their own sexuality that they have to snipe at others'." He, however, openly acknowledges anxieties about his sexuality: "Many years ago, when I began analysis, the first thing I contended with was my own *great* fear of being a homosexual. That sort of thing is operative in everybody. . . . I thought, Oh, my God, I'm a fag. And little by little, I found out that I was a very normal human being who might have had some homosexual fantasies. . . . Anyway, within a couple of months' time, I realized quite honestly—and with great relief—that I was not a homosexual. Not because I couldn't have dealt with it but because I preferred not to be a homosexual in this country, particularly then, when they were so discriminated against and when they were *all* in the closet."[6]

In this essay we examine the issue of Edwards's rumored homosexuality with relation to a biography on which we are currently working, as well as to our past and ongoing critical analyses of his work. We begin by placing the question of whether or not biographers should explore the sex lives of their subjects, including rumors and scandals about them, within the historical context of biographical traditions. This leads us to the related issue of what such biographical data may contribute to an understanding of an artist's work. We then turn to a brief overview of our past reading of Edwards's films based on the assumption that they adopt a white male heterosexual mode of address. In conclusion, we indicate how our past analyses of Edwards's oeuvre would be affected were documentation to emerge that he, in fact, is gay or bisexual. Our goal is to map the touchy terrain between rumor, scandal, and scholarly analysis.

The distinguished biographer Frederick R. Karl, writing recently about the focus on sexual and cultural issues in Gloria Erlich's *The Sexual Education of Edith Wharton* (1992), commented, "This is biography of one type, and a type that seems to be more and more credible. We see it in John Maynard's 'sexual life' of Charlotte Brontë, [and] in part in Ian Watt's first volume of his Joseph Conrad 'biography.'"[7] The credibility given the biographical exploration of sexual issues that Karl acknowledges was not always the case. When the practice of modern biography began in the eighteenth century, it was generally perceived as the recording of the public lives of public men. The private affairs of people such as Samuel Johnson were not considered significant, and published biographies, by and large, ignored them. Similarly, nineteenth-century biographers also presumed that the secrets of their subjects should be withheld and their privacy protected.

But as Ira Nadel has observed:

> This attitude toward the hidden changed in the post-Freudian twentieth century as the exposure of secrets became expected. Victorian fiction may have indirectly prepared the way with its constant exposure of secrets as a plot device. . . . Our age of self-exposure is one of self-justification: to reveal one's self completely is almost a requirement. Psychoanalysis has sanctioned the Romantic desire to confess which Rousseau had initiated for the modern reader. We all possess secrets, but it is now acceptable to uncover them—and a biographer's task to record them. . . . Freud, and the discipline he initiated, made the release of secrets acceptable, . . . which in turn intensified the public's wish to know more of them.[8]

Although some contemporary biographies focus on aspects of their subjects' lives outside the realm of sexuality, few of substance, if any, use the notion of a split between a subject's public and private life to justify a claim that the private is irrelevant. In fact, the late nineteenth century produced a dramatic example of the explosive eruption of the private into the public life with the case of Oscar Wilde, subject of countless twentieth-century biographies, that provides a signpost to the dangers of presuming the two can be separated.

Furthermore, much of twentieth-century biography has explored a subject's private life to critique, either implicitly or explicitly, the often hagiographic practices of nineteenth-century biographical writing. Lytton Strachey's *Eminent Victorians* (1918) provides a signal example; part of the modernist backlash against Victorian culture, the book's very title is profoundly ironic. It gives biographical sketches of four figures, greatly esteemed during the Victorian Age as models of British righteousness, and underlines their self-righteous and at times hypocritical motives or behavior. The book is significant not only for its revisionist presentation of its subjects but also for its rejection of the Victorian trend toward "heroic" biography; its interrogation of its subjects' private lives is central to both of these aspects.

Notions of what constitutes a private life have shifted with cultural norms. The institution of marriage is a public act that serves to produce a socially sanctioned private life, and even nineteenth-century biographers celebrated the marriages of artists, such as that of Robert and Elizabeth Barrett Browning. Twentieth-century biographers have also examined dysfunctional marriages, such as those of F. Scott and Zelda Fitzgerald or Sylvia Plath and Ted Hughes. Such biographies commonly imply a relationship between the artist's sexual life and art.

Things get more difficult with relationships that exist outside of traditional social sanctions, whether heterosexual affairs such as that of Dickens and Ellen Ternan or, even more socially forbidden and scandalous, homosexual relationships like that of Gertrude Stein and Alice B. Toklas. The revelation of such relationships may have real social consequences for living figures who wish to conceal their sexuality or even for the legacy of long-dead ones, as with the rumored relationships of Thomas Jefferson with Sally Hemings or George Washington with Venus. Most historians accept the relationships of Dickens and Stein as part of the factual record of their lives, whereas the rumors that Jefferson produced illegitimate children with his slave Sally Hemings and that Washington sired an illegitimate son with his brother's slave Venus remain controversial (although recent DNA tests have given greater credibility to the Jefferson rumor). Although these examples hold a different biographical status — the scandalous relationships of Dickens and Stein are presumed to have been historically verified, whereas those of Jefferson and Washington are not — much of contemporary biographical practice would consider all as holding a legitimate place within the historical record.

Notions of what validly constitutes the historical/biographical record have changed radically in the past twenty-five years. The widespread disclosures, both in the mainstream press and in biographical writings, of information about scandals in the sexual lives of national political figures like Gary Hart and Bill Clinton (in Clinton's case, a dominant aspect of the first impeachment trial in over a century) would have been unthinkable as recently as the 1960s. Comparable scandalous information about John F. Kennedy or Franklin Delano Roosevelt was available to informed researchers during the lives of those men but was not published then. One might say that things have come full circle from the eighteenth-century notion of public lives of public men, in which the private was ignored, to the recent fascination with the private lives of public men and women, in which the private, particularly the scandalous, often obscures the public.

The pressures of deviating in a scandalous manner from the dominant sexual model are extraordinary and can give a central tension to the story of a life. If a subject is a closeted homosexual, the simple fact of living a masquerade under the terror of exposure (as discussed and implicitly compared with the pressures of living as a spy in Sam Tanenhaus's 1997 *Whittaker Chambers: A Biography*) cannot help but constitute a central aspect of the life.[9] As Edwards and Andrews have testified, even if a subject is heterosexual (or at least claims to be) but subject to rumors of homosexuality, the strain of living in a homophobic culture can be intense.

But what does sexual orientation have to do with an artist's work? According to much contemporary cultural discourse, a great deal. The cultural, racial, sexual, ethnic identities of any group, marginalized or mainstream, can provide individual artists with unique perspectives on experience that may inform the work the artist produces and may speak in a special way to others with similar experiences.

•   •   •

Raising the question of an artist's sexual orientation is more complex than at first may seem the case. It sounds like a simple enterprise that invites an easy judgment. On the one hand, those opposed might claim that one shouldn't raise the question because an artist's sexual orientation is a private matter and that the artist's work should stand on its own merits. From this point of view sexual orientation simply doesn't matter. On the other hand, those who consider it relevant may argue that *only* a gay artist can accurately portray gay experience. But both positions are woefully inadequate. Most obviously, the distinctions involved in either of the above examples are dubious. What does it mean to say a work should stand on its own? Why privilege an idealized, hermetic notion of art that, somehow, fully contains its meanings and aesthetic accomplishments? Similarly, why should one presume that, just because one is gay, one has special insight into gay experience? Or that such experience can somehow itself be "accurately" represented?

In place of simple and, inevitably, inadequate declarations about the relationship of an artist's sex life to his or her work, it is necessary to identify the function that raising the question fulfills. Understanding who is posing the question to whom and for what purpose is critical in evaluating and understanding it. The question "Is Blake Edwards gay?" is not really one question, nor is the rumored affirmative answer simply one rumor. Rumors, gossip, revelations, and confessions about private sexual matters, scandals, and sexual orientation are part of varying discourses that give different meanings to what seems like the same thing. One cannot understand or really answer the question "Is Blake Edwards gay?" without asking, "Who wants to know and why?" In this regard discourses of sexual rumor may be compared to comic discourse. As Jerry Palmer has argued in *The Logic of the Absurd*, the exact same joke may be racist in one context but not in another. It depends on who is telling the joke to whom, when, and where.[10]

In order to illustrate this we will discuss four instances in which we have encountered the rumor that Blake Edwards is gay from different people in very different contexts: one from within the industry, one from within academia, one at a public forum, and one from students. We caution at the outset that we are not claiming that these individuals represent any groups or anything essential about the groups with which we have identified them. They are, rather, concrete instances of the diversity of specific contexts in which we have encountered rumors of Edwards's homosexuality.

We referred to the first instance, from within the film industry, in our introduction. Max Bercutt, former head of publicity at Warner Bros., considered the issue so important that he introduced it before even beginning a formal interview with one of us. During the interview he spoke about Edwards's sexuality as a man secure in his "knowledge" of the factuality of the subject, as well as of its significance. "When he divorced his wife and left his children, he became a different man," Bercutt claimed, thus pinpointing a pivotal moment in Edwards's life when the alleged homosexuality began. "I think that, because of his bisexuality, I think that's why he left his wife and his kids. And I think that's why he married Julie; they were two bisexuals who walked hand in hand into the sunset." Here Bercutt claims similar knowledge about Edwards's marriage to Andrews, asserting Edwards's "bisexuality" as his motive for leaving one wife and marrying another. Furthermore, Bercutt claims that Edwards has been perceived as gay or bisexual throughout his career. "They [studio executives] knew about it [Edwards's bisexuality] . . . by *Days of Wine and Roses*. When he was doing his TV, they knew it." Bercutt claimed that his job as a publicist was to keep the public from learning about Edwards's homosexuality, something he described as comparatively easy in Edwards's case: "We [publicity and the studio] weren't worried about bisexuals, we were just worried about out and out homosexuals." Bisexuals, Bercutt observed, "had kids, were married, and you weren't worried about them." [11] Presumably, a bisexual lifestyle would not imperil the dominant image of heterosexuality then considered important for mainstream audience acceptance.

We in no way want to imply that Bercutt was homophobic or prejudiced against gays or bisexuals. Indeed, he mentions in the interview that he "liked" Edwards and even intervened on his behalf with angry studio executives. We have quoted extensively from our interview with him to document an instance of Edwards's rumored homosexuality within the industry, a rumor that dates back to 1962 and confirms Edwards's own claims, quoted above, that he has always been perceived as gay within the industry. However ironic it may be (a point to which we shall return), it is, of course, possible that Edwards's image as gay within the industry is simply based on groundless rumor and that publicity departments were involved in covering up a nonexistent "problem" or, perhaps more accurately stated, a problem that they brought into existence. In what sounds like an ironic twist from Edwards's film *The Tamarind Seed* (1974), which deals with international espionage and whose characters engage in elaborate duplicity in both their public and private lives, the studios may have been creating a heterosexual veneer of wife and kids for a heterosexual with a wife and kids!

The second instance of the "you know Edwards is gay" assertion was made to us, in a manner strikingly similar to Bercutt's, within academia. At a professional lunch, a self-identified gay academic seated next to one of us virtually repeated the "you know Edwards is gay" line and once again at the outset of the conversation. Whereas Bercutt spoke with "insider" industry "knowledge," the professor also spoke with "insider knowledge"—he said that Edwards's homosexuality was widely known within the Los Angeles gay community. This time the topic arose within the context of pedagogy and research; the professor complimented us on our books on Edwards's films, saying he used material from them in a lecture on Edwards in a film class. As with Bercutt, however, the segue to the rumors of Edwards's sexuality was immediate, implying some "essential" and privileged knowledge about Edwards that should be quickly shared. And much as Bercutt seemed secure in his knowledge about Edwards's sexuality on the grounds that it was widely accepted in the industry, the academic seemed equally secure in his on the grounds that it was widely circulated in the gay community.

As with Bercutt, there was nothing malicious in the manner in which the academic conveyed the rumor. He liked Edwards and identified himself as a fan. In both instances it seemed like the speakers wanted to help us as scholars by passing on their privileged "information," which they thought we might not know because we were not, in the one instance, a member of their professional community and, in the other, a member of their subculture. Neither speaker presumed himself to be spreading rumors. On the contrary, each offered what he perceived as factual information. This widespread presumption of knowledge poses a significant issue for biographers because they no longer have the option of choosing not to investigate their subjects' private sexual lives; it is already part of the discourse about the subjects and, in a sense, is thus not really private, as our next example illustrates.

The third instance occurred in December of 1984, when one of us conducted a question-and-answer session following a Manhattan screening of Edwards's *The Man Who Loved Women* (1983), hosted by the Media Educators Association. A woman from the audience stood up and announced, "Of course, everybody knows Edwards is gay." When she was told that we had heard rumors to that effect but had no direct knowledge and couldn't really speak to the subject, the topic was dropped. Again, what is striking is the "you know" attitude (although the context here is more ambiguous than those recounted above). Why did this woman feel it was relevant to a postscreening discussion of a film about a womanizer to assert the common "knowledge" that Edwards was gay? Most likely, she felt that it somehow explained some aspect of the film, something that has also occurred in our experiences with students.

The fourth instance occurred in a large, multisection, lower-division course on American film genres that one of us taught over a number of years. It included a unit on Edwards's comedies, with screenings and lectures on a couple of the Pink Panther films, "10," and *Victor/Victoria*. The lectures dealt in part with Edwards's representation of failed normative, heterosexual masculinity. Every year students raised questions about Edwards's sexuality. Students asked the teaching assistants if Edwards was gay, and, because the assistants regularly responded by saying Edwards is married to Julie Andrews, the students then asked if the professor was gay — presumably feeling that the very introduction of such issues was "suspect." Indeed, during one discussion section led by the professor, a woman bluntly asked, "Is Blake Edwards gay?"

Most of these students were not passing on rumors they had heard about Edwards's sexual orientation before taking the class but may have been responding to material in the class that challenged cherished and unquestioned norms. In effect, such students were looking for a gay person to whom to attribute these challenges. Why would any "normal" man want to do that? Wouldn't a "normal" man celebrate cultural norms of heterosexual masculinity? Some students found in homosexuality an explanation for the presence of the strange ideas in the films and even the lectures. The woman who interrupted the discussion section to inquire whether Edwards was gay recognized, by the end of the semester, the homophobia implicit in her question. Homosexuality perceived as an evil perversion could explain away troubling ideas with which, otherwise, the student would have to grapple as a legitimate and integral part of his or her culture. Such students could avoid the discomfort of engaging such ideas by adopting the posture that, if Edwards was being critical of conventional masculinity, it was not because of any problems with conventional masculinity but, rather, because of something sick within Edwards.

The above four examples stemming directly from our own experience illustrate a potentially varied range of contexts and meanings for the question "Is Edwards gay?" or for the assertion, "Of course, he is gay." The student's question in our last example may share something with the woman's declaration at the public forum in that both the question and the assertion seem to provide explanations for the presence of certain themes, plots, or characters in Edwards's films. The last two examples also contrast with the first two in that neither the industry professional nor the academic presumed that knowledge of Edwards's homosexuality explained anything in his films, whereas the second two presumed some sort of relationship between the two.

Even when the comments and questions are not openly homophobic, one could argue that the obsessiveness with which such rumors spread is, itself, frequently a sign of homophobia. If so many people in our culture weren't afraid of homosexuality, would there be so many rumors about its presence? But, as the second example shows, such rumors are also present in the gay community. The gay man's interest in Edwards's sexual orientation obviously provides an entirely different context from that of the female heterosexual student upset by the situations within the films. The student's response might resemble the industry professional's in one regard: it is certainly possible that some industry insiders perceive Edwards's films as being unusual in a manner that feeds the rumors that he is gay. He has, for example, long been interested in plots that concoct cross-dressing scenarios (for example, *What Did You Do in the War, Daddy?* [1966], *Gunn* [1967], *The Revenge of the Pink Panther* [1978]); films with unusual, intense male bondings (the Clouseau/Cato relationship, *Wild Rovers* [1971]); and films with homosexual and lesbian characters (*Gunn*, "*10*" [1979], *Victor/Victoria* [1982], *Sunset* [1988], *Switch* [1991]).

This complexity of response to allegations of gayness, whether verified or rumored, was nicely summed up by Manohla Dargis in an article about George Cukor, a now acknowledged gay director of the classical Hollywood cinema. Dargis commented that Cukor "was about as 'out' as was possible for a gay man to be during those days. None of this might matter except for the fact that Cukor's sexuality was used both as an argument for his work and as an argument against it." [12] Cukor was famous as a director of "women's movies," and some made connections between his sexuality and the content and style of his films. Joan Crawford, whom he directed, said, "George was a better woman's director because he was more feminine by nature." [13] Just as people have frequently drawn on a person's life to make inferences about that person's creative work, they can just as readily use aspects of the work as the basis for assumptions about the creator's life.

Victor/Victoria supplies an interesting illustration of this point because it was a rare combination for Edwards of critical acclaim and box office success and because, years after its release, he adapted it as a high-profile Broadway musical marking Julie Andrews's return to the Broadway stage after a prolonged absence. Both the film and the play have a high public visibility within Edwards's career. In the film James Garner plays King Marchand, a Chicago gangster who falls in love with Victoria (Julie Andrews) only to learn that "she" is a female impersonator. Determined to prove his heterosexual manhood, he spends much of the film trying to discover Victoria's "true" sex and, once he succeeds, trying to romance her.

The film's central cross-dressing premise has a woman pretending to be a man pretending to be a woman. If the public associates drag and cross-dressing with the gay community in general, this film's convoluted plot adds a layer to the masquerade. Another obvious "gay" element of the film is the character of Toddy (Robert Preston), Victoria's agent, and the gay subculture to which he belongs. The film, in fact, begins not with its heterosexual characters but with a scene devoted to Toddy and one of his lovers. Homosexuality is thus posited as an integral part of the film's representation of "gay Paree" in 1934.

But these aspects of the film would not necessarily lead those inclined to do so to conclude that Edwards is gay. Films that deal with cross-dressing or gay subculture don't necessarily cause speculation about or bring attention to their director's sexual orientation. To the best of our knowledge, when Sydney Pollack made *Tootsie* (1982), there were no rumors that he was gay openly circulating within the industry, the gay community, or among the general public. One significant way that *Victor/Victoria* differs from that film is in how Edwards critiques the film's central heterosexual character and simultaneously celebrates its central gay character. King Marchand is a scared, insecure man whose heterosexual identity is presented as a masquerade. King travels with Norma, a blonde "bombshell," but he fails in nearly every effort to control her behavior or to satisfy her sexually. In one scene he flees her rage by seeking shelter in his bodyguard's bedroom as Norma hurls objects at him. Similarly, he travels with golf clubs in December. Both the athletic equipment and the blonde are little more than accoutrements for his (not very effective) performance of heterosexual masculinity.

The film critiques the notion of sports as a "natural" expression and sign of heterosexual masculinity. King is shocked to learn that Squash, his bodyguard, is gay because Squash had been an award-winning football player (and the character is played by Alex Karras, an actor recently retired from a highly successful professional football career). Furthermore, King discusses this with Squash when he is about to fight a boxing match with a man who, unbeknownst to him, is both a world-class professional boxing champion and a homosexual. For Edwards, then, such signifiers of conventional masculinity as beautiful "molls," golf clubs, and boxing matches mean nothing because they, like cross-dressing, can be little more than a masquerade.

The heterosexual world is, thus, not as far removed from the cross-dressing, gay subculture as may at first seem the case.[14] Far from being natural, the heterosexual masculine norm appears to be just one more masquerade. Certainly this view of heterosexual masculinity might distress some heterosexuals who consider their sexuality "natural," as opposed to gay sexuality, which they consider perverse. For such people it might be literally unimaginable that any man could address such issues without being gay himself.

The situation is intensified with the character of Toddy. In contrast to King he is entirely comfortable with his sexuality. He never anguishes over being gay, and he doesn't need to prove anything about his sexuality to himself or to others. Nor, until the final scene, does Edwards use his sexuality or lifestyle as the source of humor. On the contrary, for most of the film King's predicament of first needing to discover the "truth" about Victoria, and of then having to deal with the perception of others that he is gay and living with a man, provides most of the comedy. Only when Toddy replaces Victoria onstage in drag at the end of the film does he become a comic spectacle. But even this scene can easily be read as a celebration of Toddy and drag queens as a vital, energetic force that upsets the staid world of heterosexual order.

Like Toddy, Squash is an attractive character. He is a sweet, caring man and the end of the film celebrates his union with Toddy when Toddy throws a rose from the stage to Squash in the audience.

In short, *Victor/Victoria* critiques the world of normative heterosexual masculinity and simultaneously celebrates the world of cross-dressing homosexuality. The Broadway musical version intensifies these elements by making "King's Dilemma" (the title of one of the songs) even more explicit and by having Squash, in the play's final scene, burst into song by addressing the audience with the question, "Why can't we just love one another?" Indeed, this line may very well sum up the point of this brief example: Edwards's embrace of the world of homosexuality may, in the words of the film, seem to some "scared heterosexuals" proof that he is really a homosexual. They may consider him too fascinated with the world of homosexuality to be a heterosexual.

The films, the play, and other works of Edwards could conceivably have fueled the rumor that he is gay. But the important question remains: what importance, if any, is there in either laying the rumor to rest or in verifying it? What difference does it make to a critical assessment of his films given that, either way, they are the same films? As we shall demonstrate, the answer to this question is more complex than at first may seem the case. It is helpful to begin by placing this issue within a larger perspective.

The most publicized recent instance of speculation about an artist's sexual orientation in the United States occurred not about a movie director but, rather, about Ellen DeGeneres, a television star. Ever since the premiere of her successful show, *Ellen*, the media indulged in a great deal of speculation about whether the star was a lesbian. The speculation included interpreting various episodes of the show in ways consonant with a gay reading: few episodes dealt with heterosexual dates, and others dealt with close interactions between Ellen and another woman. Finally, in a highly publicized episode that scored high Nielsen ratings, the character came out as lesbian.

The attention given to Ellen DeGeneres foregrounds some of the possible benefits of inquiring about an artist's sexual orientation. The obsession with sexual rumor need not be a simple invasion of privacy, nor is it necessarily prurient or reactionary (although it clearly can and frequently is all of those things). Such inquiry may have benefits. Gay men and lesbians exist in an often marginalized subculture, and their awareness that an artist also belongs to that subculture may not only serve as a source of identification and pride but also may cue them to look for certain meanings and messages in the work that speak to them in a significant manner.[15] The "outing" of gay and lesbian artists also helps destroy the popular perception that they are extremely isolated exceptions. Indeed, some feared that after the character of Ellen came out as a lesbian, she would stand alone as a token lesbian character. If so, her appearance might even set back the proliferation of lesbian characters on television if the broadcast industry should believe it could point to her and her alone to ward off potentially troublesome allegations of homophobia.

Kobena Mercer's work on Robert Mapplethorpe serves as an example of what the stakes may be in publicizing an artist's sexual orientation.[16] Mercer, a black homosexual, originally condemned Mapplethorpe's work as racist: he felt that it exploited black men and perpetuated stereotypes of them as oversexed with large penises. Mercer later returned to Mapplethorpe's work with the knowledge that Mapplethorpe was a gay artist personally involved with his subjects, some of whom were his lovers when he photographed them. For Mercer this perspective gave Mapplethorpe's work new and positive meanings. He now saw Mapplethorpe not as a mainstream photographer who had exploited and eroticized a marginalized community but rather as part of that community—as someone who photographed a community he knew and loved. Mercer now saw the photos as revealing desire for the black male bodies depicted rather than simply fascination with their exoticness. By bringing certain kinds of images normally reserved for the world of gay porn into the world of high art, Mapplethorpe created a radical displacement of the nude white female body that normally lies at the center of that artistic tradition. As such, he challenged many patrons of high art to see beauty in the black male body.

Although the photographs had not changed, Mercer's two readings of them profoundly illustrate the complexities of considering an artist's sexual orientation when interpreting that artist's work. One perspective finds evidence in the photographs to condemn Mapplethorpe as an exploitative racist; another perspective finds evidence in the same photographs to categorize him as an innovative artist boldly challenging centuries of artistic traditions. This goes beyond the simple issue of the first being "wrong" and the second "right" due to new evidence, as would be the case, for example, were new evidence to emerge about the first person to discover the circulatory system or to walk on the moon. An art critic would not necessarily be "wrong" to find material in Mapplethorpe's photographs to support a categorization of racism and exploitation or of cultural innovation. Indeed, many informed critics still make such racist charges, and clearly a white gay man with a black lover can be a racist. Furthermore, there is a long-standing tradition of heterosexual artists exploiting their models/lovers. Cultural criticism of this sort is complex and multifaceted.

We turn now to a reading and rereading of Blake Edwards's films. First we will sketch a reading of them that presumes his public persona of a heterosexual filmmaker. We will refer to our previous work on Edwards's films because that presumption was crucial to those readings and was stated explicitly in them. We will then indicate how that reading would shift were Edwards gay. In doing so, we do not presume that Edwards is a major or even important filmmaker. Although we have tried to make the case in our books for the importance of his films, the artistic status of the films is irrelevant here; even if Edwards is a mediocre or bad filmmaker and we have overrated him, the same issues are at stake.

•   •   •

In our two books devoted to critical analyses of Edwards's oeuvre we examine Edwards's films as made from the perspective of a frightened, white, male heterosexual positioned within a historical period—the post–World War II era—that increasingly challenged white, heterosexual, male privilege.[17] Our critical position admires the way Edwards's films question the centrality and normality of white, heterosexual masculinity, presenting us with heroes who are neurotic, insecure, incompetent, and unable to live up to their culture's norms. Rather than condemning the apparent failures of these heroes, however, the films call the very norms into question and critique rather than emulate them. The true failures in these films have seemed to us to be not the central male characters but rather the cultural notions of heterosexual masculinity by which those characters are defined and judged. From this critical perspective, the films appear painfully honest, particularly because Edwards has often drawn attention to similarities between these characters and himself, even to the extent of calling some of the films semiautobiographical.

Edwards has frequently declared that he has drawn the central characters in films like "10," S.O.B., and That's Life! (1986) from his own life. Furthermore, he has placed markers of his life in the films themselves, each of which is about a successful and creative heterosexual man hysterically undergoing a crisis. Edwards cast his own wife, Julie Andrews, as the poorly treated sexual partner of these characters in each of the films; her character in S.O.B. is even a parody of her "Mary Poppins" public persona. That's Life! was shot literally in their own home, cast with their family and friends, and coauthored by Milton Wexler, Edwards's psychologist. In fact, in a press release for the film Edwards explicitly linked two of the films: "'That's Life!' could almost be considered a sequel to "10," in that it's the same mid-life crisis, but almost 20 years down the line." [18]

In addition to being heterosexual, the Edwards surrogates in these films are striking for the unsympathetic manner in which they are portrayed. They are grotesquely self-centered, desperate, and ugly in much of their behavior, often profoundly and destructively indifferent to the concerns of their mates and others around them. In this they resemble central characters in other Edwards films, such as The Man Who Loved Women, Skin Deep (1989), and Switch. One might say that, in relationship to biographies that have been dubbed "pathographies," Edwards has made a collection of pathographies about himself. This relentless exploration of his own worst qualities has struck us as a painfully honest and admirable aspect of Edwards's films. We have associated such brutal self-investigation with his long interest in psychoanalysis, as well as with what we have perceived as his uncompromising honesty in interviews with us.

We have argued that Edwards's critical self-examination of heterosexual masculinity distinguishes his work. To extend that argument to a film made after the publication of our second book, the central character in Switch so smugly seduces women that some of his lovers murder him. Instead of being able to revel in the thought of having "conquered" them, he only learns that they genuinely hate him at the moment that they kill him. The plot contrives to have his soul return in a woman's body; his redemption depends on the nearly impossible task of finding just one woman to vouch for him. Consequently, he not only experiences life in a woman's body but also learns how contemptible his behavior as a privileged heterosexual male had been. But the film's central mode of address, even when within a woman's body, is aligned with the very heterosexual male whom the film critiques.

The destructiveness of traditional heterosexual masculinity also appears in such films as "10," *The Man Who Loved Women*, and *Skin Deep*, where the womanizing central male characters literally cannot control their actions. The Inspector Clouseau films also relate to this problem in several ways. Much of their humor comes from Clouseau's inability to control his mind or his body in the manner culturally prescribed for men. As if this were not enough, he repeatedly asserts his superiority over women and people of color, while consistently making a fool of himself. In *Revenge of the Pink Panther* (1978), for example, as he runs in terror from a leather-clad, whip-wielding dominatrix, he rants, "I am opposed to the women's libs" and "Man is the master." He also makes disparaging comments about his Asian manservant Cato's "little yellow skin," entirely oblivious to his own moronic behavior.

Edwards has never made a film centering on a gay male or on a heterosexual male tormented with anxieties that he might be gay. We have argued elsewhere that a major strength of his work lies precisely in his refusal to presume a "liberal" understanding of alternative subject positions and in his ability to focus repeatedly on the inadequacies, complexities, and limitations of the dominant subject position in his films, that of a heterosexual, white male. For example, in 1989, we claimed:

> One of Edwards's greatest strengths derives from his nonliberal approach to women and homosexuals. He in no way pretends to understand them or speak for them as, for example, a film like *Tootsie* does. Many of Edwards's films engage areas important to feminism and the gay movement, but his films are ultimately about his concerns of male heterosexuality. They gain their ideological complexity not from claiming to understand women or gays but, rather, from a piercing investigation beneath the surface of the normative male sexuality that structures the Hollywood cinema. His films lack both the conservative and at times reactionary appeal of the new Hollywood films that nostalgically yearn for the old images of men and women, and they lack the liberal appeal of the films that attempt to make their audiences feel fashionably sympathetic with the plights of women and gays. In a profound sense, Edwards understands the limitations and potentials of being a heterosexual male filmmaker at this moment in history.[19]

Many of Edwards's films have centered on heterosexual males in privileged positions who suffer indignities to their presumed position of power, at times leading to hysterical terror and mental breakdown. Most are comedies that derive their humor from the constant embarrassment of these men as they fail to live up to their culture's notion of heterosexual masculinity. This can be seen even early in his career when Edwards made a number of comedies about men in the military, such as *The Perfect Furlough* (1959) or *Operation Petticoat* (1959), in which he used the military image of brave and resourceful manhood under pressure as a backdrop against which to highlight the inadequacies of his central characters. These films, made in the 1950s and 1960s, spoke to Edwards's generation, whose main image of the U.S. military was its role in World War II, at a time when it was perceived as having triumphed over fascist dictators and establishing the United States as the dominant world power. Instead of reinforcing this image of triumphant masculinity, however, Edwards in his comedies pointed to its absurdities.

In 1981 we observed that *Operation Petticoat*, which deals with World War II submarine warfare, has a rich sexual subtext in which the phallic shape of the submarine plays a prominent role. Yet this submarine and the men on it are subjected to all kinds of indignities by the standards of conventional masculinity. By the time the film is over women have invaded the male space, and the submarine has been painted pink and saved from destruction by women's undergarments!

The irony implicit in the title of *Operation Petticoat* is also implicit in *What Did You Do in the War, Daddy?* The title of this World War II film implies that the answer will reveal the kind of masculine heroics glorified in *Saving Private Ryan* (Steven Spielberg, 1998), but these conquering soldiers are involved in sham battles, drunken revelry, and transvestism and are often driven insane. Instead of depicting righteous, purposeful masculine action, this film makes men in war appear ludicrous.

In *Gunn* the central character is ostensibly a tough, competent private detective, another postwar icon of strong masculinity; but middle-aged, middle-class Peter Gunn is repeatedly disoriented by a world in which his fundamental presumptions and securities no longer function. Like Inspector Clouseau the detective is a heterosexual male and represents the traditionally male-encoded power of the law and of deductive reasoning. But like *A Shot in the Dark* (1964), *Gunn* shows that power to be eroding. Clouseau fails in his many efforts at seduction and survives only because he is so incompetent in that world of declining masculine power, and Gunn stands by helplessly at the film's climax as he watches a woman kill a transvestite. All he can do is ask, "Why?"

In *Wild Rovers* (1971) Edwards engages another culturally and generic potent image of masculinity, that of the ruggedly individualistic cowboy of the Old West. This film deals with two cowhands who, feeling that a bold, decisive move will make their fortune, rob a bank. They do not, however, ride into the sunset and a new life; instead, all ends in failure, and they die sadly. Julie Andrews has told us that she feels that the two cowboys represent different sides of Edwards's character, and the film is intriguing in that neither of those characters reinforces traditional images of Western masculinity.[20] They fail at virtually everything they think strong men should do, partially because of the inadequacies of those images of masculinity, and the film shows the characters "caught up in processes that they don't understand and about which they can do nothing."[21]

One of the major processes that these cowboys and other Edwards male protagonists don't understand is masculinity. But this masculinity is always explored and critiqued from the perspective of white, heterosexual males rendered desperate by a world in which they can barely cope and in which their privilege is no longer presumed, whether the hysterical middle-aged men of *"10," S.O.B., Victor/Victoria, The Man Who Loved Women, Micki and Maude* (1984), *Skin Deep, Switch,* or others. Our work has categorized Edwards as virtually a spokesman for their plight and not for the perspective of any of the kinds of people who menace these men, such as women, gays and lesbians, or people of color. For us this has both limited his work and given it a special integrity.

But what if Edwards *is* gay? Such a disclosure would obviously influence biographies of him, but it would also have a complex effect on analyses of his work. His apparent mode of heterosexual address would indicate not ruthless self-examination and critique but, rather, a duplicitous mask. Instead of using his work to reveal and explore, he could be seen as using that work to hide. Such a shift would neither imply that the value of the films had diminished nor that previous criticism of them was irrelevant; it would, however, necessitate a reexamination of a central aspect of Edwards's work. The mode of address of his films would shift from that of a brutally honest heterosexual acknowledging failures, fears, and doubts to that of a closet homosexual or bisexual hiding both within the films and his public persona the reality of his sexuality. Rather than seeming aligned with, for example, Peter Gunn, a very heterosexual character confused by the world of homosexual transvestism in which he finds himself, Edwards would, in fact, be a very part of that world of both masquerade and homosexuality; rather than being aligned with King Marchand in *Victor/Victoria,* who is also very heterosexual and confused by the world of homosexuality, Edwards would actually be more at home in the world of Victoria's masquerade and Toddy's homosexuality; and rather than being aligned with the frightened heterosexual hero of *"10"* (Dudley Moore), he would be more at home with that character's gay songwriting partner.

Within such a context Edwards's insistence that were he gay he would be out of the closet, and the related claim that he cannot even understand bisexuality and has never known any bisexuals, would switch from being candid admissions to a carefully constructed ruse designed to cover up his secret life.

•   •   •

Our project therefore resembles Kobena Mercer's in that we are able to return to our earlier published work and demonstrate how our assumption about Edwards's sexual orientation affected our readings of his films. In at least two respects, however, there is a strong difference. First, where Mercer's rereading supplied a more sympathetic account of Mapplethorpe's work, our possible re-reading is likely to do the opposite. Were it to be proven that Edwards is gay, he would emerge not as an honest filmmaker baring his soul, doubts and all, but rather as a dissembler hiding his homosexuality. This would be true not only of the obvious strong denials in interviews quoted above but, also, of the semiauto-biographical films analyzed above as being virtual pathographies.

In this regard Edwards would ironically resemble François Truffaut, whose *The Man Who Loved Women* (1977) he remade. In a public exchange of letters and angry comments in 1973, Jean-Luc Godard accused Truffaut of creating a false image of himself in *Day for Night* (1973), Truffaut's highly personal, fictional account of filmmaking. In the film Truffaut plays a film director who, unlike others around him, is removed from any sexual intrigue or adventure. Instead, he appears wise and preoccupied with important matters. However, it was widely known in the French film industry that Truffaut regularly had affairs with his leading ladies during production. In Godard's words, "one wonders why the director is the only one who isn't screwing around in 'Day for Night.'"[22] Richard Brody notes of this situation, "Although Truffaut would eventually mine his romantic entanglements for their comic potential in 'The Man Who Loved Women,' the exchange of insults over 'Day for Night' highlighted the fact that the ostensibly autobiographical elements in Truffaut's films were less a matter of self-revelation than of self-reconstruction or self-exploitation."[23]

Brody's analysis of Truffaut's films, like Mercer's analysis of Mapplethorpe's photographs, reveals how consideration of an artist's private sex life may play a significant critical function. Here criticism and biography become interrelated. Biographers need to establish the reliable historical record of their subjects' lives, and critics exploring the relationship between an artist's work and life must be able to rely on the biographical information rather than, perhaps unknowingly, only working with and passing on scandalous rumors. In this regard it is important to verify whether Truffaut actually had affairs with his leading ladies or if the rumors were simply unsubstantiated gossip. Proof of either alternative would substantially affect the positions of Godard, Brody, and, of course, Truffaut in the exchange.

Brody's distinction in Truffaut's work between "self-revelation" and "self-reconstruction" is also applicable to Edwards's oeuvre. If, as we presumed when we wrote our critical studies of Edwards's films, he is a heterosexual, then his semiautobiographical films are self-revelations; if he is a homosexual, however, then they are "self-reconstructions." Brody summarizes the latter notion when he notes, "Truffaut seems to re-project, for his own psychological benefit, a coherent alternative vision of himself—one that is, above all, distinguished by its merciful detachment from the chronic pain of his mutilated childhood" (87). From this perspective even "self-reconstructions" shouldn't simply be dismissed as false—

they may serve complex functions such as, in Brody's view of Truffaut, a way of coping with childhood trauma; they may also reveal important aspects of the subject's psychic imperatives.

It is important to conclude by emphasizing a final distinction between Mercer's rereading of Mapplethorpe and our potential one of Edwards. Mercer's reading is based on substantiated knowledge about Mapplethorpe's homosexuality. Our potential reading is entirely hypothetical, predicated on the speculation of verification of what is now purely rumor. In fact, we have no reason to believe the rumor to be true. For the record we have no direct knowledge of anyone claiming to have been a homosexual lover of Edwards's. Nothing in our interactions with Edwards and Andrews suggests that theirs is a marriage of "convenience": to the contrary, they appear to have a close, meaningful relationship. Edwards has appeared candid with us in interviews, and we have never seen evidence of any dissembling about his sexual orientation or anything else. Indeed, he is remarkably open when touchy topics of any kind come up — he listens carefully, considers, and tries to answer as best he can.

Nevertheless, scandalous rumors of the kind circulating around Edwards and Andrews pose a very real danger, as Madonna inadvertently makes clear in an interview with the *Advocate:* "Certainly everybody in the Hollywood community knows who the gay people are and who aren't [*sic*]."[24] Many would undoubtedly agree with such a glib generalization, but there is simply no evidence that rumors are always right. Certainly the Hollywood community has known about the hidden private homosexual lives of many of its members while the general public has remained in the dark, Rock Hudson being one highly publicized example. But that does not mean that everyone rumored to be a homosexual is one. Indeed, Martin Duberman, author of a highly regarded biography on Paul Robeson, claims that while he was researching his book, despite widespread rumors that Robeson was bisexual and a claim in the *Advocate* that he was gay, "I had found absolutely no evidence of Robeson's erotic interest in men."[25] Duberman was astonished by the fact that even the publication of his biography did nothing to lay these rumors to rest.

We would like to close by returning to the central question posed by this essay: "What business does a critic or biographer have asking if an artist or performer is gay?" At times, a fine line may separate rumor, scandal, criticism, and biography. If the purpose of raising these questions is simply to revel in the shocking/titillating notion of the creator of the Pink Panther films as gay or of "Mary Poppins" as a lesbian, then we may have little more than gossip, although even such gossip should not necessarily be pejoratively dismissed. Although in this essay our focus is on the relationship of rumor, scandal, and gossip to biography and critical analysis, we do not wish to imply that that is the only legitimate enterprise or even a privileged one. As we have indicated, for example, knowledge about the sexual orientation of artists may serve valuable nontextual functions for fans, and gossip may be important within that context. If, however, posing the question of sexual orientation leads to a significant reevaluation of a body of work, including its meaning and accomplishments, it may also be a complex and meaningful critical enterprise.

NOTES

1. Michael Szymanski, "Our Fair Lady: Julie Andrews Discusses Gay Fans, AIDS, and Her TV Movie Debut," *Advocate*, May 21, 1991, 72.

2. Blake Edwards, interview by the authors, Los Angeles, August 8, 1989.

3. Quoted in "Ear's News of Hampton's Flickfest," *New York Post*, October 22, 1998, 10.

4. Edwards, interview.

5. Edwards, Interview.

6. Lawrence Linderman, "Playboy Interview: Julie Andrews and Blake Edwards," *Playboy*, December 1982, 85–86.

7. Frederick R. Karl, "Some American Biography: An Article-Review," in Frederick R. Karl, ed., *Biography and Source Studies* (New York: AMS Press, 1998), 4:103.

8. Ira Nadel, "Authorized Secrets Or Lives of the Living," in Karl, *Biography and Source Studies*, 4:89–91.

9. See Sam Tanenhaus, *Whittaker Chambers: A Biography* (New York: Random House, 1997).

10. Jerry Palmer, *The Logic of the Absurd: On Film and Television Comedy* (London: BFI Publishing, 1987).

11. Max Bercutt, interview by Peter Lehman, Tucson, Ariz., May 5, 1989. We wish to thank Susan Hunt for arranging the interview.

12. Manohla Dargis, "All He Did Was Create a Parade of Classics," *New York Times: Arts and Leisure*, July 25, 1999, sec. 2, p. 27.

13. Ibid.

14. In a related manner, the studio head in *S.O.B.* (1981) is a cross-dressing heterosexual man whom we see in a dress and heels as he makes love to a woman.

15. For a sophisticated discussion of these issues and for an examination of the distinction between a textual notion of lesbianism and one focused on a persona see Judith Mayne, *Directed by Dorothy Arzner* (Bloomington: Indiana University Press, 1994).

16. Kobena Mercer, "Skin Head Sex Thing: Racial Difference and the Homoerotic Imaginary," in *How Do I Look: Queer Film and Video*, ed. Bad Object-Choices (Seattle: Bay Press, 1991), 169–210.

17. See Peter Lehman and William Luhr, *Blake Edwards* (Athens: Ohio University Press, 1981), and William Luhr and Peter Lehman, *Returning to the Scene: Blake Edwards, Volume 2* (Athens: Ohio University Press, 1989).

18. Unpublished publicity release for *That's Life!*, quoted in Luhr and Lehman, *Returning to the Scene*, 222.

19. Luhr and Lehman, *Returning to the Scene*, 10.

20. Julie Andrews, interview by the authors, London, 1992.

21. Lehman and Luhr, *Blake Edwards*, 193.

22. Quoted in Richard Brody, "Drowning in the New Wave," *New Yorker*, May 24, 1999, 87.

23. Ibid.

24. Don Shewey, "The Saint, the Slut, the Sensation: Madonna," *Advocate*, May 7, 1991, 50.

25. Martin Duberman, "Writing Robeson," *Nation*, December 28, 1998 (accessed on January 9, 2000), <http://www.thenation.com/issue/981228/1228duberman.shtml>.

HOLLYWOOD GOES

TO WASHINGTON

SCANDAL, POLITICS,

AND CONTEMPORARY

MEDIA CULTURE

JAMES CASTONGUAY

*W*hile still in theaters, Barry Levinson's *Wag the Dog* (1997) received an astonishing amount of media attention for anticipating scandalous events in the Clinton White House. In the film a fictional U.S. president hires a spin doctor and a Hollywood producer to create a fake war to divert attention away from a presidential sex scandal shortly before a national election. The connections made by the media between the fictional film and political reality became so ubiquitous[1] that, according to *USA Today*, the *Encarta World English Dictionary* "consider[ed] adding the term 'wag the dog' to its next edition after real-life events mimicking the 1997 film caused the phrase . . . to 'instantly become part of our political language.'"[2]

In February 1998 *Dateline NBC* produced a segment devoted to the many coincidences between *Wag the Dog* and the actual scandal, reporting that the uncanny similarities boosted the film's box office receipts by tens of millions of dollars.[3] Shortly after the "Clinterngate" (or Zippergate, Sexgate, Monicagate, etc.) story broke on January 17, 1998, President Clinton increased the pressure on Saddam Hussein to give UN inspectors full access to potential weapons sites. As Clinton continued to warn Hussein not to "defy the will of the world" and embarked on an inexorable march toward "Desert Storm II," references to *Wag the Dog* were routinely used by television and print media to discuss the ongoing "scenario" or "saga."

During Monica Lewinsky's testimony before the federal grand jury in August 1998, President Clinton ordered attacks against suspected "terrorist installations" in Sudan and Afghanistan. The timing of these raids — just three days after the president admitted to having "inappropriate relations" with Lewinsky in the White House — prompted the *New York Times* to track down Larry Beinhart, the author of the novel on which *Wag the Dog* was based, and report that Beinhart "was having an I-told-you-so kind of day."[4] Following yet another series of air strikes against Iraq's weapons programs on the eve of the impeachment vote in December 1998, several politicians (in addition to the media) invoked *Wag the Dog* to criticize President Clinton. Journalists went so far as to ask White House officials during press briefings if various presidential decisions were "*Wag the Dog* scenarios," and Kenneth Starr was encouraged by reporters to share his thoughts about the film (which he had seen).[5]

Wag the Dog's intertextual ubiquity points to its privileged position within the hierarchy of media culture and among representations of scandal (as the inclusion of "wag the dog" in *Encarta* suggests). This essay explores the ways in which *Wag the Dog* — and the phrase it popularized — became the remarkably mobile signifiers[6] described above, deployed for a wide range of political and commercial purposes. Following the multicontextual approach exemplified by star studies, I ground *Wag the Dog* within the context of "the Bill Clinton text" and the political economy of Hollywood in the late 1990s, while also engaging with several salient theoretical problematics raised by contemporary theory and cultural studies.

POLITICAL CELEBRITY, SCANDAL, AND THE CULTURE WARS

Because media scandals are inordinately intertextual, hierarchical, and polysemic,[7] their meanings cannot be adequately understood apart from broader discursive networks and social formations. Indeed, like other cultural productions, media scandals are interpreted differently depending on the historical, cultural, and geographical contexts of reception, in addition to various categories of cultural difference (for example, race, ethnicity, gender, class, sexual orientation, age, religion, education, and political affiliation). Below, I explore the ways in which President Clinton was a scandalous cultural production long before *Wag the Dog* or his affair with Monica Lewinsky. Rather than focusing on the various scandals themselves, I examine the ways that President Clinton became a site of cultural negotiation and contestation, hyperscandalized or valorized, depending on the interpretive community. As I will show, these contexts of reception are central to the meanings of Clinton's media scandals and the responses to (and appropriations of) *Wag the Dog* in popular and political culture.

Patricia Mellencamp has argued that gossip, like media scandal in general, "is a genre with its own conventions . . . [that] traverse . . . media and formats . . . which are rigidly hierarchized and stylized according to education and profession — whether tabloid, mainstream, or upscale press, or TV, whether syndicated or nightly news." In addition, Mellencamp stresses that gossip and media scandals are symptomatic "of the shifting border between private and public domains and issues."[8] Media scandals thus exemplify what popular pundits and academic critics often diagnose — and lament — as the putative blurring of various boundaries in an increasingly mass-mediated world. To offer just one recent example, in a 1998 *USA Today Magazine* article, Professor David Zarefsky claims that television's conflation of "publicness with celebrity . . . [has caused Americans to] react to political figures as they might to movie stars, concerned to know the details of their personal lives and to pass judgement on their life choices, whether or not they are relevant to governance."[9]

President Clinton complicates this star-politician conflation because from the beginning of his administration, Clinton's connection with Hollywood has been a recurring topic in the popular press. For instance, following *Murphy Brown's* response to Dan Quayle's attack on the series' lead character for having a child "out of wedlock," the vice president observed that "[the episode] was a good campaign contribution to Bill Clinton, but he gets a lot of campaign contributions from Hollywood."[10] Quayle is referring to the long list of celebrity "FOBs" (Friends of Bill), including *Wag the Dog* stars/producers Dustin Hoffman and Robert DeNiro, as well as dozens of other entertainment celebrities (for example, Jane Fonda, Steven Spielberg, Barbra Streisand, Richard Dreyfus, Sharon Stone, Richard Gere, and Cindy Crawford) who either visited the White House or stayed in the Lincoln bedroom.[11]

On the campaign trail Clinton shunned the legitimate press and upscale genre of television news in favor of the lower, more populist (and popular) media forms like MTV and talk shows (for example, *Donahue, The Arsenio Hall Show, Larry King Live*, and *The Tonight Show*). Stories and interviews in popular magazines like *TV Guide* and *People* about the first family's domestic politics and television viewing habits further positioned the president as a willing and eager participant in, and fan of, popular culture.[12] After the president was elected, the *Washington Post* proclaimed that "Clinton's inauguration [was] shaping up as an exercise in pluralism and popular culture,"[13] and the *Chicago Sun-Times* criticized "the wretched excess" and "orgy of self-indulgence" during what it dubbed "Hollywood Inauguration Week."[14] "It's no secret that Bill Clinton is star struck," *Newsweek* claimed in April 1993, reporting that the president's "image meisters worry that 1600 Pennsylvania Avenue is starting to look more like the Dorothy Chandler Pavilion on Oscar night than the Executive Mansion."[15]

Although during the early days of his administration Clinton continued to be described by the media as "star-struck," less than a year later journalists would refer to Bill Clinton not only as an adoring fan but "a celebrity" in his own right, "whose presence brings . . . star-struck crowds and jogging groupies . . . rushing forward to touch his hand."[16] Referring to the height of Clinton's public celebrity during his campaign, one commentator went so far as to claim that "[President Clinton] is not only John Wayne, Marlon Brando and James Dean, but also Franklin Delano Roosevelt, Huey Long and John F. Kennedy. *He is bigger than life.*"[17]

Soon after President Clinton took office, however, ABC's *Nightline* dedicated an entire program to pondering "the big fuss about Hollywood and Washington" after Clinton experienced a backlash of public opinion driven in part by vengeful members of the White House press corps out to prove that they could not be ignored by a putatively populist president. In addition to jilted journalists intent on showing that they could not be usurped by television's "lower" genres, in the wake of Clinton's rumored two-hundred-dollar haircut aboard Air Force One, Republican leaders attempted to transform Clinton's pop-cultural populism into a star-struck complicity with "Hollywood's cultural elite." Later bewildered by the American public's continued support for the president during the impeachment process and the ongoing Kenneth Starr investigation, frustrated critics conceived of Clinton supporters and the American electorate like they do the film and television audience: as passive consumers who uncritically accept ideological messages and are hopelessly duped by the media-savvy politician Bill Clinton (or "slick Willie").

To be sure, every U.S. president's image has been mediated; yet the cultural production of "Bill Clinton" differs in important ways from the formation of Ronald Reagan through his Hollywood roles,[18] or the televisual construction of John F. Kennedy (to name two obvious mass-mediated examples). Unlike the conservative Reagan, who was an actual television celebrity and movie star before entering politics, or the aristocratic Kennedy, Bill Clinton was a poor southerner raised in a widely publicized untraditional and dysfunctional family and — like most post–World War II baby boomers — was the first president to have been immersed in television culture. As the *New York Times* speculated during the 1992 presidential campaign, "during his time at Hot Springs High School in Arkansas, . . . the young Mr. Clinton was no doubt affected by popular culture . . . [including] 'The Donna Reed Show,' reported to be [Clinton's] favorite television show."[19] It was also widely reported that Clinton was a fan of TV and the movies, worshiped Elvis Presley (an Elvis impersonator was in the inaugural parade and Clinton performed "Heartbreak Hotel" on *The Arsenio Hall Show*), and was managed by the first couple's good friends Harry Thomason and Linda Bloodworth-Thomason (the creative team responsible for the situation comedies *Designing Women* and *Evening Shade,* Clinton's inaugural ceremonies, and the influential fourteen-minute campaign biopic "The Man from Hope").[20]

All of this suggests that class politics and concomitant questions of "taste" are central to understanding the cultural presence of Bill Clinton and his many media scandals. As communication professor Marita Sturken puts it, "there is no denying that Clinton is the president for whom class has always been an issue":

> Criticisms of Clinton throughout his political career have consistently deployed class stereotypes of the white cracker or a bubba, someone who can't control his appetite, who eats junk food, who hugs other politicians with little reserve. The Washington Beltway crowd has never forgiven Clinton for being too Arkansan. And nowhere is this more obvious than in his choice of extramarital women. . . . Roseanne used to joke that she was America's worst nightmare: white trash with money. But Lewinsky is worse, the perverse offspring of the circus of American politics and media: white trash with a sense of entitlement.[21]

When Hollywood entertainers continued to support the president after he admitted to having an "improper relationship" with Monica Lewinsky, Geoffrey Wheatcroft argued that there was "a certain logic in the affection which the rich white trash from Hollywood show for the poor white trash from Arkansas."[22] Finally, economics professor Thomas Hazlett asked rhetorically: "Is it mere coincidence that, in the era of Bill Clinton, Jerry Springer has surpassed Oprah in the daytime talk ratings war?"[23] Hazlett's explicit association of Clinton with "trash TV" recapitulates classist attacks against daytime talk television more generally. Like the racially specific phrase "white trash" employed by Wheatcroft, the implication is that these genres—and the people who watch and appear on them—are economic waste or social excrement, evacuated of any positive cultural attributes ("cultural rot" as William Bennett baldly put it). We could thus paraphrase Laura Grindstaff's discussion of daytime talk shows to argue that Bill Clinton has been "especially maligned" because he violates "conventional middle-class standards of moral conduct and 'good taste.'"[24]

I would argue that "the texts of Bill Clinton" lend themselves to what cultural historians and feminist critics have theorized as the metaphoric construction of "mass-culture-as-feminine."[25] Indeed, as I noted earlier, whereas Reagan was associated with the *production* of Hollywood images, history, and mythologies, Clinton has been positioned primarily as a *consumer* of mass culture, thus associating him with a symbolically "subordinate" cultural position. We could further extend the argument made by television scholars that the medium has been gendered "feminine,"[26] to include Clinton's association with this "lower" medium and the further devalued entertainment genres such as talk TV (as opposed to "masculine" news journalism). Seen in this light, the repeated attempts to scandalize Clinton's personal and political life—and his own hypermilitaristic policy toward Iraq—could be viewed as hypermasculine responses to these cultural anxieties.

The fact that news of the Clinton-Lewinsky sex scandal—and *Newsweek's* suppression of the story—was first published on the Internet by gossip journalist Matt Drudge (described by the *Boston Globe* as "the *Drudge Report's* scandalous scoop") is also significant because it further intensifies the crisis in journalism's institutions.[27] As University of Texas professor Gary Chapman wrote in response to Matt Drudge's article on the scandal, "A communications medium some of us hoped would be the means to a new age of democratic discourse among genuine and engaged citizens has apparently been swamped by the sewage of sleaze, gossip, celebrity worship and competitive consumerism."[28]

Although Bill Clinton and Monica Lewinsky may offend the aesthetic sensibilities of Washington's political culture and liberal and conservative critics, Clinton's lower-class origins from Hope, Arkansas, also construct an *ethos* of ordinariness that accounts for much of his strong appeal outside of the normative white middle- to upper class. For instance, in order to explain to its readers "Why America Still Loves Bill!," the *National Enquirer* quoted a professor to remind its readers that "[Clinton] is not some elitist with a vast fortune":

> He's known hard times. Like many of us, he's struggled with a weight problem, enjoys fast food, wears a baseball cap, and plays a saxophone poorly enough that he keeps his day job. He has a disobedient dog, a wide variety of friends—not just politicians—and is clumsy enough to fall and damage his knee. We like to see him succeed because it's as if we're watching ourselves succeed. We're cheering for him because we see him as one of us.[29]

Similarly, in a *New Yorker* piece that uncannily anticipates issues raised by Warren Beatty's *Bulworth* (1998),[30] Toni Morrison argued that many African American men supported Bill Clinton during the impeachment process because, "white skin notwithstanding, [Clinton] is our first black president. . . . [He] displays almost every trope of blackness: single parent household, born poor, working-class, saxophone-playing, McDonald's-and-junk-food-loving boys from Arkansas."[31] Alvin Poussaint would later claim, according to the *New York Times*, that many African Americans were circulating rumors that Clinton "must have had black ancestry," thus providing biological proof for Morrison's social construction of Clinton's blackness.[32]

Following Morrison's (and Gloria Steinem's earlier remarks that Clinton is the first woman president because he was elected "without the proper 'masculine' behavior, . . . his origins were lower class unlike most men's, he married a woman who was at least his equal, he refused to go to war; and he actually listens"), the *Christian Science Monitor* published a piece about "The Clinton Presidency's Feminine Mystique": "It's not just because Bill Clinton stands for 'women's issues'—as he has stood for African-American issues—that he's being credited with feminizing the presidency. It's also a matter of style—a listening, empathetic, some would say 'touchy-feely' approach that appeals to many women voters. . . .

'He's one of us,' whether he behaves like a 'black president' or a 'woman president,' says [Professor] Barber."[33] The problematic appeal to gender and racial stereotypes notwithstanding, these arguments are symptomatic of the transgendered and multiethnic construction of "President Clinton," demonstrating that "Bill Clinton" is a highly contested site of cultural negotiation and identification. A polysemic hybrid of racialized, classed, and gendered meanings, Bill Clinton's lower-class economic background and "white trash" aesthetic at once allies him with other nonnormative and nonprivileged groups and also explains the polemical responses to his behavior by many members of the middle and upper classes, especially conservative white male politicians.

As with the O. J. Simpson trial and the Anita Hill–Clarence Thomas hearings, then, gender and race — in addition to social class — are crucial to understanding the mediation, meanings, and politics of the Lewinsky-Clinton sex scandal. I would argue that the inability of "anti-Clintonites" to understand the popular support for the president is a result of their social position, which blinds them to the different social realities through which many Americans experience and view institutions like the judicial system, law enforcement, and the presidency. In the end the shifting borders of race, gender, and class provoked by Bill Clinton, combined with his alignment with "lower" popular forms, genres, pleasures, and people, pose a serious threat to the political order of things and the rigid hierarchies of media culture.

As if responding to the anxieties generated by the threats to a traditional model of patriarchal presidential masculinity, a *USA Today* article (accompanied by a photograph of Bill Clinton and Chelsea "enjoying *American Gladiators*") wrote, "Rest assured when Bill Clinton moves into the White House he'll be in control. When it comes to the TV remote control, Clinton tells *TV Guide* he zaps past the commercials, 'political ads included. Hillary doesn't do that.' So Bill, not Hillary Clinton, operates the remote? 'Well,' smiles the president-elect, 'it can often be a struggle.'"[34] A *Time* cover story in June 1993 featuring a minuscule President Clinton dwarfed by the issue's already emasculating title "The Incredible Shrinking President" literalized the cultural anxieties caused by having a "soft" (or flaccid) "draft-dodging democrat" in the White House. Facing "dismal approval ratings" as a result of his lack of demonstrated leadership in international politics, especially on the Bosnia question, Clinton discovered a political aphrodisiac when, less than three weeks after the special *Time* issue, he ordered the bombing of Iraq's intelligence headquarters, dramatically increasing his approval ratings overnight.[35] The *New Statesman & Society* argued the following in the wake of the bombing:

> Clinton is also well aware of the "wimp factor." His problems with the military, over his draft evasion during the Vietnam war and his support for gays in the armed forces, has laid him open to charges that he is weak on military matters.

In fact, he is far weaker in standing up to his military advisors (who were as responsible for his backdown over intervention in Bosnia as the differences with European allies). The Baghdad bombing, then, is a measure of his weakness, not his strength. "The wimp that roared" . . . has done so to no real purpose — and at the expense of yet more innocent lives in the Iraqi capital.[36]

Thus long before the Lewinsky affair, Clinton's "feminine mystique" had at times been translated into a damaged masculinity in need of repair. Ella Shohat and Robert Stam's comments about the Gulf War are instructive in this context. For them Operation Desert Storm "reiterated the [imperial] trope of 'regeneration through violence'[,] the process whereby the fictive 'we' of national unity is reforged through salutary massacres."[37] As I have argued elsewhere concerning the Gulf War and its mediation,[38] Clinton's continued acts of violence and the continued killing of Iraqi civilians can be viewed as a response to historical anxieties that resulted from gender, racial, and class politics in the 1990s — a regeneration of the president's image through hypermasculine militarism, violence, and death. Although several critics voiced their opposition to the president's actions, his intention and the motivation for this obvious attempt to improve (and remasculinize) his image through violence were not scrutinized in any significant way by the pre-Lewinsky press or anywhere else in pre–*Wag the Dog* popular culture.

WAG THE DOG AND POSTMODERN MEDIA CULTURE

My use of the phrase "media culture" in this chapter refers in part to what Douglas Kellner describes as the "images, sounds, and spectacles [that] help produce the fabric of everyday life, dominating leisure time, shaping political views and social behavior, and providing the materials out of which [people] forge their very identities."[39] Driven by giant entertainment conglomerates, media culture is a transnational, commercial, and high-tech culture that includes — among other media — film, television, video, the Internet, print, and music. Although it is tempting to suggest that Clinton is the first true TV president or that his administration is the first "postmodern presidency," I use the term *postmodern* somewhat reluctantly because ambiguities, misrepresentations, and theoretical clichés continue to inform academic and popular discussions of postmodernism and postmodernity. As Kellner points out, within contemporary theory and cultural studies postmodernism remains largely undertheorized, at times synonymous with "contemporary society" or defined by a set of arbitrary characteristics covering "a bewildering diversity of cultural artifacts, social phenomena, and theoretical discourses."[40] Having said that, I do feel that it is necessary to describe 1990s media culture and the Clinton-Lewinsky media scandal as "postmodern" due to the sheer scale and intensity of their mediation, which amount to a difference in kind. Instead of focusing, however, on whether the texts of Wag the Dog exhibit characteristics of postmodern style (that is, are "postmodern"), in what follows I explore the implications of what I see as the film's blending of Frankfurt School pessimism toward popular culture with Jean Baudrillard's brand of media postmodernism.

My discussion of "Bill Clinton" addressed issues of class as they intersect with gender and race within the hierarchy of media and political culture. Wag the Dog is particularly instructive in this regard because it exploited the cultural capital of its actors/producers (Hoffman and DeNiro), writers (David Mamet), and director (Levinson) to position itself as a work of high culture satirizing the lower medium of television. Like several other recent Hollywood films (The Truman Show [Weir, 1998], Pleasantville [Ross, 1998], and EdTV [Howard, 1999]), Wag the Dog is very much about television, and the film's mise-en-scène offers a steady televisual flow within the public and private spheres, from the bedroom to the "war room," airports, jets, limousines, warehouses, and restaurants. Like Levinson's "quality" television series Homicide, Wag the Dog employs the conventions of documentary realism with an expressionistic style to separate itself from the usual Hollywood and television fare.

In short, according to Wag the Dog, television is largely to blame for the decline of American culture and politics. As the dominant medium of the 1990s, television is presented as being responsible for manipulating an unthinking American public and media audience through whatever images and rhetoric political spin doctors and Hollywood decide to produce. Wag the Dog is thus reminiscent of the critical approach to mass media exemplified by the Frankfurt School theorists' conception of mass culture as the "deadening antagonist of individual creativity"[41] that forces ideology and commodities on passive consumers of popular culture. (Winifred Ames [Ann Heche], a top presidential aide in the film, makes this argument explicitly when she smashes a small television for "destroying the electoral process.") Of course, Wag the Dog's arguments about the relationship among "the media," scandal, and politics could be viewed as radical for a film produced by a major Hollywood studio. Indeed, its relentlessly cynical satire of the commodification of war and the art of political spin-doctoring and media manipulation separates it in important ways from most other Hollywood films. In this sense film critic Stanley Kauffmann is right to praise the film's criticism of the monologic mass media and a system of governance that have evacuated a democratic public sphere from our political reality.[42]

Whereas conservatives attacked President Clinton's personal morality, Wag the Dog focuses much of its criticism on the aesthetic and intellectual banality of commercial media culture. Indeed, central to Wag the Dog's diegetic and larger intertextual project is an attempt to distance the film from the tabloid and mainstream press's concerns with President Clinton's private behavior. For instance, in several interviews and articles in popular magazines Barry Levinson insists that

Wag the Dog is about Hollywood and the media, not President Clinton and sex scandals. This point is reiterated in a short, interview-style video documentary titled "From Hollywood to Washington and Back," which follows *Wag the Dog* in its DVD and VHS releases. As Levinson argues in the concluding segment,

> We only have certain visual images of the Gulf War. It's almost like [we're] a shared . . . collective. That [nose-cone image] was . . . all we got. . . . It was incredibly controlled and you could have faked any one of those pieces very easily, the way they showed the [smart bomb hitting] the building. . . . David Mamet and I [began to] discuss how much you can fake. By the time you find out if it's true it doesn't matter [because] we're on to something else. And the possibility of faking images for whatever purpose is certainly possible. Will it happen? To what extent will it happen? Ya' know, that's the basis of *Wag*.[43]

Earlier in the interview Levinson claims that he doesn't think *Wag the Dog* has "anything to do [with] Clinton," instructing the viewer that the film is "really [about] the presidency, as opposed to a specific president." Furthermore, Levinson argues, *Wag the Dog*

> is more [about] . . . how much [media] manipulation is taking place on a day-to-day basis . . . to the point that we are no longer quite sure where reality is and those things which are fabricated. . . . It's a hard thing when once upon a time some things were real and some things weren't real, and we begin to blur those lines between fact and fiction. Once the lines between fact and fiction blur, then we begin to become much more skeptical and much more cynical.

I quote Levinson at length not to embrace auteurism or directorial intention uncritically but to suggest that the explicit articulation of Levinson's preferred meanings does indeed function to contain the film's polysemy and to establish the boundaries of reception (especially political interpretations).[44] In addition, Levinson's claims are an accurate representation of the film's dominant narrative themes, which, in addition to the film's Frankfurt School pessimism, are unwittingly underpinned by the kind of media postmodernism associated with the French theorist Jean Baudrillard, who in the early 1990s made the infamous claim that "the Gulf War did not take place." Baudrillard (who had insisted in a different context that "*Watergate is not a scandal* . . . [but] a simulation of scandal to regenerative ends")[45] argues, in short, that because television constructed the reality of the Gulf War for most Westerners, and because TV gave us no images of the actual war, the Gulf War was pure simulation.[46] It is instructive in this regard that the VHS version of *Wag the Dog* ends (after the closing credits of the postfilm documentary) with Tom Brokaw insisting that "television *is* reality," thus expressing in literal terms an extreme version of media postmodernism.

It has been argued that Baudrillard's argument represents a major "flaw . . .

[of] all postmodernist thinking," which Paul Patton summarizes as the "confused epistemological argument which begins by denying that we have any means of access to 'what happens' other than what is provided by the media, and ends by concluding on this basis that there is no 'operative difference between truth and falsehood, veridical knowledge and its semblance.'" Patton admits that "understood in this manner, the thesis that the Gulf War did not take place would indeed be ludicrous," yet he defends Baudrillard by arguing that he does in fact "make truth-claims about what happened," including the argument that "the reality of the media Gulf War . . . is a different kind of event from those which occurred in the desert, a simulacrum rather than a distorted or misleading representation."[47]

I would argue, however, that *Wag the Dog's* rhetoric is symptomatic of the clichéd and caricatured position assigned (unfairly or not) to Baudrillard. Indeed, in Larry Beinhart's novel on which *Wag the Dog* was based,[48] President George Bush fabricates *an actual* Persian Gulf War — and his motives for waging it — to deflect attention away from domestic problems (thus giving fictional reasons for starting the actual war). In *Wag the Dog's* adaptation, however, the president hires the Hollywood producer Stanley Motss (Dustin Hoffman) and Conrad "Mr. Fix-it" Brean (Robert DeNiro) to construct a *completely fictional* U.S. war against Albania, thus evacuating the original satire a priori of much of its political punch.

Wag the Dog's and Levinson's fascination with "faking visuals" is epitomized by the sequence in which Motss uses a soundstage and production crew to produce fake news footage of an Albanian peasant girl dodging artillery fire while

Figure 1. Stanley Motss (Dustin Hoffman) directing fake war news footage in *Wag the Dog.*

clutching a kitten under her arm (fig. 1). Shot digitally in front of a blue screen, the actress holds a bag of chips while Motss decides to optically "punch the kitten in later." The faked footage is leaked through a satellite uplink and broadcast as a special television news report just hours later. Brean and Ames watch the report while sipping champagne with Motss in his Hollywood mansion. "They used the same process in the last Swarzenegger movie," Motss explains, "but wait till we get the song. Then you'll have the song, the image, and the merchandizing tie-ins. . . . This is only the beginning." *Wag the Dog*'s fetishization of digital or virtual reality was further exploited by a Web site tie-in for the film, which invited the Internet user to "play political spin doctor" by constructing his or her own virtual war (and victim), thus positioning the user as a director in the control booth (fig. 2). The new medium of the World Wide Web thus allows Internet users to partake in a long tradition of mass-mediated war simulation, dating back at least to J. Stuart Blackton's scale-model reenactments of Spanish-American War naval battles (reminding us that progressive politics do not necessarily inhere in interactivity).[49]

Figure 2. A Web site tie-in for *Wag the Dog* invites Internet users to "Play Political Spin Doctor" by recreating a scene from the film, although the real game is virtual war "live from Albania." (Note the choice of a SCUD missile on the control booth panel.) Original URL: *http://www.mediadome.com/Webisodes/Wag/Game/gameframe.htm*. Copyright Intel Corporation.

Wag the Dog does refer to this longer history of representations of war in the sequence in which Brean and Ames convince Motss to produce their media war. Brean accomplishes this by listing the following phrases: "Tippecanoe and Tyler too," "Fifty-four forty or fight," "Remember the Maine." "We remember the slogans," Brean insists, "[but] we can't even remember the fucking wars. Ya' know why? It's show business." He then offers the following descriptions: "Naked girl covered in napalm, 'V' for victory, five marines raising the flag [at] Mount Surabachi." "You'll remember the picture fifty years from now," he insists," but you'll have forgotten the war." Brean's paradigmatic example, however, is Operation Desert Storm: "The Gulf War, smart bomb falling down the chimney, twenty-five hundred missions a day, a hundred days, one video of one bomb, Mr. Motss. The American people bought that war. War is show business. That's why we're here." When Motss insists that at "some point [the public has] gotta know" that there is no real war, Brean also uses the Gulf War as his definitive counterargument: "They gotta know? Stan? Get with it. . . . You watched the Gulf War. What did you see? Day after day, the one smart bomb falling into a building. The truth? I was in the building when they shot that shot. They shot it in a studio in Falls Church, Virginia [using a] 1/10th scale model of the building." When Motss asks Brean if he is telling the truth, Brean answers, "How the fuck do we know? You take my point?"

As media critics have already argued, the Gulf War was an instantaneous televisual historiography that was forgotten almost as quickly as last year's television series. Yet Wag the Dog takes these arguments and Baudrillard's thesis one step further, suggesting that, unlike the previous wars, in the electronic and digital age the actual Gulf War was a technical fraud that never took place in historical reality.[50] Consequently, I would argue that Wag the Dog is closer to the genre of media conspiracy films like Capricorn One (Hyams, 1978) than to political satires like The Mouse That Roared (Arnold, 1959) and Dr. Strangelove (Kubrick, 1964), critiques of corporate capitalism like Network (Lumet, 1976), or other political films from the 1990s, such as Bulworth, Dave (Reitman, 1993), Absolute Power (Eastwood, 1997), and Primary Colors (Nichols, 1998).

Interestingly, Baudrillard too has insisted that the Gulf War "is not a war any more than 10,000 tons of bombs per day is sufficient to make it a war. Any more than the direct transmission by CNN of real time information is sufficient to authenticate a war. One is reminded of Capricorn One in which the flight of a manned rocket to Mars, which only took place in a desert studio, was relayed live to all the television stations in the world."[51] It is one thing to question whether Operation Desert Storm constituted a war in the traditional sense of the term and quite another to suggest, as Baudrillard and Wag the Dog do, that we cannot make claims to the historical facticity of the Gulf War. I am not arguing, of course, for a naive positivism that suggests history and reality are somehow unmediated but arguing instead for a more nuanced theoretical and critical approach to postmodern media culture that examines gradations of abstraction and degrees of mediation. In *The Ecstasy of Communication* Baudrillard has alluded to his writings as an "attempt to reconstitute the society they describe,"[52] and, like *Wag the Dog*'s arguments, his book on the Gulf War may be true enough on a descriptive level (diagnosing a postmodern cultural condition). It ultimately retreats, however, from politics into ideological complicity with the very process or phenomenon it sets out to critique. Similarly, *Wag the Dog* neglects to engage substantively with the economics of the media systems and structures behind the production of texts generated by, among other things, the process of political "spin" central to the film.[53]

John Frankenheimer's and Tom Brokaw's comments from *Wag the Dog*'s VHS / DVD documentary are relevant in this context. Frankenheimer recalls his days as an assistant director to legendary CBS radio and television news journalist Edward R. Murrow, who, according to Frankenheimer, would "really, really be in an uproar" over the current state of television news because "any semblance of purity and high intentions has vanished." Echoing my earlier discussion of aesthetic objections to popular culture, Frankenheimer concludes, "It's a pity, it's all the *[National] Enquirer*. It's shocking really." After an interview with the film's coproducer Jane Rosenthal, who laments the tabloidification of media culture by the *Jerry Springer Show*, Tom Brokaw offers the following comments from behind the helm of the NBC news desk: "I sometimes feel like I'm living in the world of *Network*. But I'm hanging on for dear life maintaining standards. And what I always say to people is that you have to separate us from all that's going on around us. I think there is a lot of comment about the line of news and entertainment dissolving but the fact of the matter is that it was always a blurred line." Brokaw proceeds to historicize media journalism, referring to publisher William Randolph Hearst as "one of the great showmen of our time" and pointing out that Edward R. Murrow, "one of the founding fathers of television news, appeared on camera . . . with a cigarette dramatically lit . . . off to the side, enveloped in a cloud of smoke. . . . So the line has always been blurred."

In addition to historicizing the distinction between news and entertainment, Brokaw, who argues that "television *is* reality," nonetheless takes issue with the version of television reality offered by *Wag the Dog*. In the film Ames informs Brean that the fake war production is a huge success because "the *New York Times*, the *Washington Post*, *Detroit Register*, and *Sacramento Bee* are all in remission. No mention of the firefly girl. None." Brokaw argues, however, that news professionals "commented at length about the possibility that [Clinton] was ratcheting up the pressure on Iraq as a diversion from the Monica Lewinsky story. . . . The Washington press corps and the rest of us . . . are greatly flawed individuals, but we ain't stupid. And that was asking us to buy something that I just don't think people would buy."

On the one hand, Brokaw's comments separate him from the vast majority of journalists and television commentators who seemed, ironically, to miss *Wag the Dog*'s premise that journalists are the pawns of political handlers. On the other,

Brokaw is also correct to argue that the Lewinsky-Clinton media scandal demonstrated that *Wag the Dog* was wrong to assume that a war would distract journalists from a presidential sex scandal given that, as Brokaw points out, the media habitually speculated about "*Wag the Dog* scenarios." (One could argue, of course, that *Wag the Dog* was responsible for alerting journalists to this possible connection.) What Brokaw fails to realize or acknowledge, however, is that the Lewinksy-Clinton media scandal demonstrated that *Wag the Dog* got it backwards because, in the 1990s, sex scandals function to divert attention away from immoral military actions and unethical foreign policy rather than the other way around. Furthermore, although Brokaw's comments provide an important corrective to ahistorical claims about the uniqueness of postmodern media culture and the end of legitimate journalism, he also relativizes the historical specificity of late-twentieth-century consumer-oriented media and entertainment industries. Brokaw thus diminishes the consequences and realities of what is a scandalously undemocratic American society (exemplified by NBC's parent company, General Electric, producing the weapons that fought the Gulf War, while Tom Brokaw delivers reports of their success). As Todd Gitlin has recently put it, "Today's media conglomerates have a grander scale than the trusts of the late nineteenth century . . . [and] intense and informed discussion of [this matter] is long overdue."[54]

GLOBAL MEDIA SCANDAL

There is no question in my view that *Wag the Dog* is a nicely crafted, well-acted, and intelligently written film, which explains the overwhelmingly positive reviews and critical acclaim it received.[55] In the end I would argue that the film is primarily a satirical jab at Hollywood tastes and personalities (exemplified by Dustin Hoffman's character, who would rather die than not receive the credit for his war production). And in its attempt to document a lack of a democratic media culture, the film aestheticizes the art of political handling and public relations to such a degree that the spectator is positioned by the narrative to be complicit with, and encourage, the process of media manipulation. Although its "hypodermic needle" theory of media manipulation is, like the Frankfurt School approach, highly problematic, even more troubling in light of Gitlin's remark is the lack of any critique of the industrial-military-government-media complex that makes cultural productions like the Gulf War and the "*Wag the Dog* phenomenon" possible. Indeed, as I will show, the production and marketing of *Wag the Dog* were inordinately illustrative of many of the processes that the film supposedly satirizes.

Wag the Dog's fifteen-million-dollar budget and twenty-nine-day shooting schedule (extremely low and short, respectively, for Hollywood) were foregrounded in the film's prepublicity in an attempt to place the film outside of the "wretched excesses" of Hollywood and closer to the spirit of an independent production. From the outset this is misleading because Hoffman, Levinson, and DeNiro all coproduced the film with their own production companies, thus lending their acting (and directing) skills to the film up front. In addition, the major financial backer and distributor of the film, DVD, and VHS, is New Line Cinema, whose parent company, Time-Warner, also owns CNN. Despite studio spokespeople's claims that *Wag the Dog* would not exploit allegations about Clinton's affair with Lewinsky, the *Los Angeles Times* suggested that New Line was trying to capitalize on the troubles at the White House to promote the film with advertisements that "seemed to draw comparisons to the real-life drama unfolding in Washington."[56] There was also an explicit connection between the people involved with *Wag the Dog* and the president because several days before the Monica Lewinsky affair became news, *USA Today* reported that President Clinton attended a fund-raising dinner sponsored by *Wag the Dog*'s coproducer Jane Rosenthal.[57] According to the *Sacramento Bee*, Barry Levinson, who was also in attendance, told the president, "I hope you have a sense of humor." Clinton, who hadn't yet seen the film, reportedly assured Levinson that his sense of humor was "very deep."[58]

Although I would not got so far as to argue, as some media conspiracy theorists have, that *Wag the Dog* producers knew of the Lewinsky scandal *before* Matt Drudge, the conglomerate connection between CNN and New Line Cinema makes this argument seem almost plausible. Regardless, Time-Warner "franchised"[59] *Wag the Dog* through intertextual (or cross-promotional) publicity throughout CNN's media formats and genres. CNN constructed a tie-in for the film on its CNNInteractive Web site in which Internet users could win a free trip to Washington, D.C., and CNN's *ShowBiz Today* broadcast live from the film's premiere. More interesting for my purposes, however, were the banner advertisements for the DVD release of *Wag the Dog* that were strategically placed on the front page of the CNN Web site, directly above stories about the White House scandal. For instance, on August 1, 1998, CNNInteractive featured an article about the Clintons accompanied by a montage of large images of Monica Lewinsky, Ken Starr, and President Clinton layered over dozens of smaller images of other "players" from the media scandal. Even though *Wag the Dog* had been released on DVD a month earlier, the banner advertisement announcing the DVD release reappeared directly above the sex scandal story. (Unfortunately, CNNInteractive denied my request to authorize the use of a screen capture I made of this Web page.) This blatant hypercommodification of scandal for Time-Warner's New Line Cinema by CNN and *Wag the Dog*'s producers is a striking example of the seamless conflation of the fictive and the real, tabloid and legitimate news, as well as news and entertainment during the "crisis in the White House." (See fig. 3.) Indeed, the CNN Web site collapses TV's generic boundaries and programming conventions (for example, the "commercial break") into the *mise-en-scène* of one Web page.

Figure 3. *National Enquirer*, September 8, 1998.

These inter- and intratextual strategies are symptomatic of the news media's ability to create the news while constructing an illusory sense that the network is objectively reporting naturally newsworthy events as they unfold.[60] Although brief disclaimers appear when CNN is reporting on its parent company Time-Warner, such "admissions" are a stamp of integrity for the serious genre of the news division that, in turn, allow the "softer" formats to do their ideological work. For instance, CNN produced a special segment on the popularity of the *Wag the Dog* video in which CNN correspondent Cynthia Tornquist reported that "video stores are scrambling to meet the skyrocketing demand for the 1997 film."[61] The segment's "movie analyst," Martin Grove, informs us that "a lot of people who consider themselves informed want to become more informed and therefore are going to see the movie."

Grove's comments suggest the pedagogical role *Wag the Dog* has adopted, gaining the epistemological status of documentary and thus educating the U.S. public about actual media scandals and real politics. Although Baudrillard may be guilty of propagating apolitical abstractions, the Baudrillardian sensibility in *Wag the Dog* demands even closer scrutiny precisely because the film became such an all-encompassing signifier for understanding not only the scandal but U.S. foreign policy and actual military actions. Unlike the "harder" news reports, we were never informed in this report or elsewhere on CNN that *Wag the Dog* was produced by a sibling company of the network. In addition, the possibilities of "wag the dog scenarios" were endlessly debated across CNN's television programming, and metastories about the coincidences between the film and real events circulated alongside metadiscussions about whether it was appropriate for the news media to be framing the debate in terms of a fictional film in the first place. This seemingly inevitable ethical navel-gazing by media professionals serves to further distance the American public from any discussion of the real scandals of the 1990s, such as the Gulf War; Bosnia; Rwanda; the Savings and Loan theft; the digital spectrum giveaway; institutionalized racism, classism, and sexism; and the scandalous crisis in democracy produced by industrial-military-government-entertainment-media conglomerates.

CONCLUSION

Although I have already discussed many of the ways that Wag the Dog was deployed for different political and commercial purposes, in his discussion of the globalization of communication John Tomlinson reminds us that "media scandals, like all media representations, lose some interest, some 'immediacy,' as they cross cultural distance . . . [because we] . . . only fully engage with scandals insofar as they seem relevant to our ongoing, lived experience."[62] Illustrating this, a January 26, 1998 CBS This Morning segment devoted to "opinions around the world on the latest White House sex scandal," reported that the British were ambivalent, that the French were indifferent, and that Israel was "showing signs of concern." We are also told that "America's enemies are having a field day. In Baghdad the newspapers are talking about the moral corruption at the top in the United States and there's more of the same in Iran."[63]

In addition to these different local receptions of global media scandal was the appearance of Wag the Dog in several of the regions that President Clinton bombed throughout 1998 and 1999. In fact, during the U.S. strikes on Iraq, Sudan, and Yugoslavia, Wag the Dog explicitly surfaced in all of the local contexts of the countries being bombed. On the January 26, 1998, CBS This Morning, Vicki Mabrey reported the following from Baghdad:

> And something that's pretty rare here, on the inside of the paper, they're devoting entire pages to this. There are articles titled: "The International Implications of Clinton's Low Morals" and "Monica Pushes Clinton to the Brink." There's also one that says: "Clinton Between the Tail of the Dog." So I have to tell you that the term "wagging the dog" has gotten into the vocabulary over here. They're wondering if life is going to imitate art and the president will follow the plot of the movie Wag the Dog and decide to bomb Iraq. Or also, they're wondering if this is going to force him to resign or be impeached.

Frank Rich reported in the *New York Times* that Saddam Hussein later "de-light[ed] in the mockery of Bill Clinton's motives and resolve" by the airing of a bootleg copy of *Wag the Dog* on Iraqi state television (followed by edited se-quences from the infamous Columbus town hall meeting in which CNN broad-cast protestors voiced their opposition to Clinton's policy on Iraq).[64]

Mamet and Levinson's decision to make Albania the enemy became yet an-other coincidence — in this case a potentially unfortunate one for the produc-ers — as news that minority Serb nationalists were massacring ethnic Albanians in Kosovo started making headlines in March 1998. The *Cleveland Plain Dealer's* prediction that "the situation in Kosovo could become *Wag the Dog* for real" became a political and historical reality during the "crisis in Kosovo."[65] The *Mil-waukee Journal-Sentinel* later cited wire reports claiming that as NATO pounded the environs of Belgrade, Serbian television aired *Wag The Dog* replete with live news updates of the bombing.[66] In April Yugoslavia's film academy awarded its top prize to *Wag the Dog* and invited the producers and director to travel to Belgrade to accept the award.[67] In the wake of Clinton's strikes in Afghanistan and Sudan, *CNN Headline News* showed images of Sudanese protestors chanting and holding makeshift signs that read "Clinton: Wag the Dog" in English and Arabic (fig. 4). Print and television reports of these appropriations of *Wag the Dog* by the "enemy" (including an ABC segment showing *Wag the Dog* being shown on Serbian TV) may have functioned to mitigate domestic criticism of

Figure 4. Protesters in Sudan hold makeshift "Clinton: Wag the Dog" signs in response to U.S. bombing raids on suspected "terrorist installations." Courtesy of CNN ImageSource. Copyright 1999 Cable News Network, LP, LLP. All rights reserved.

U.S. policy because many Americans, including journalists, would not want to be aligned with a buzz phrase that had been poached for these very different political purposes.

The culmination of this dizzying flow of global images and rhetoric reached its apogee when the *New York Times* took "a detour into the absurd" to report that "Yugoslav official, Goran Matic, claimed . . . that there are no real Kosovar refugees. That the people we see acting like refugees are just . . . actors, 3,000 to 4,000 of them, getting paid $5.50 a day by NATO. The way it was in the film *Wag the Dog*. As if to match him, a NATO spokesman would deny the story only on condition of anonymity."[68] These examples suggest that we must consider local receptions of global media scandal, and they provide further evidence that meaning does not inhere solely in the text itself. Yet as Frank Tomasulo has warned, "[a]lthough a healthy epistemological skepticism . . . is an important corrective to dominant ideology, extreme nihilism . . . can undermine even the most settled of historical facts."[69] *Wag the Dog* unwittingly lends credibility to Matic's claim that the horrors in Kosovo, like the massacre in the Persian Gulf, did not take place (as Baudrillard argues), thus pointing to the problematic ethical and political consequences of media postmodernism and *Wag the Dog*.

NOTES

I am grateful to Larry Beinhart for providing helpful information.

1. The Lexis-Nexis database returned over seven hundred references to *Wag the Dog* in network television news reports about President Clinton's attacks against "terrorist installations" in Afghanistan and Sudan in August 1998.

2. César G. Soriano, "Enshrining the Wag," *USA Today*, December 21, 1998, 1D.

3. *Dateline NBC*, February 6, 1998. Trade journals and "box office analysts" would later claim that the real scandal hurt the film *Primary Colors* financially because "the Bill-and-Monica show" was on television every night for free.

4. James Barron with Jacques Steinberg, "Public Lives: A Waggish Tale In Washington," *New York Times*, January 23, 1998, B2.

5. Jill Lawrence, "Comparisons to 'Wag the Dog' Never Far Behind," *USA Today*, August 21, 1998, 6A.

6. I am glossing on Tony Bennet and Janet Woollacott's analysis of "the texts of Bond" and "James Bond" as a "mobile signifier" in *Bond and Beyond: The Political Career of a Popular Hero* (New York: Methuen, 1987), 42–43.

7. See James Lull and Stephen Hinerman, "The Search for Scandal," in James Lull and Stephen Hinerman, eds., *Media Scandals: Morality and Desire in the Popular Culture Marketplace* (New York: Columbia University Press, 1997), 17–19.

8. Patricia Mellencamp, *High Anxiety: Catastrophe, Scandal, Age, and Comedy* (Bloomington: Indiana University Press, 1992), 155.

9. David Zarefsky, "The Decline of Public Debate," *USA Today Magazine*, March 1998, 56–58. The subtitle of Zarefsky's piece makes another familiar argument about the relationship between media and the audience: "Thanks largely to television," he writes, "people have been transformed into passive consumers of mes-

sages and images, rather than participants in a dialogue." For a critical overview of scholarship that has posited a passive television viewer see Lynne Joyrich's *Re-viewing Reception: Television, Gender, and Postmodern Culture* (Bloomington: Indiana University Press, 1996). See also Kathleen Hall Jamieson and Sean Aday, "When Is Presidential Behavior Public and When Is It Private?" *Presidential Studies Quarterly* 28.4 (fall 1998): 856–860.

10. Alan Bernstein and Mark Smith, "Quayle Takes Aim at Clinton in Visit: Hollywood Is Issue in Speech," *Houston Chronicle*, September 23, 1992, 3. See also Greg Braxton and John M. Broder, "It's Murphy Brown's Turn to Lecture Vice President," *Los Angeles Times*, September 22, 1992, A16.

11. See Jennifer Rowland, "Hollywood Welcomes Clinton," U.P.I., September 17, 1992; Robert W. Welkos, "Hollywood Plays a Starring Role in Financing Politics," *Los Angeles Times*, August 25, 1996, A1+.

12. According to *Variety*, "Aides say Bill Clinton usually has several books going at once. A typical collection includes a mystery, a biography, a book on popular culture and a treatise on world economics." See Jeff Strickler and Lewis Cope, "Hot Topics," *Variety*, December 16, 1992, 1E.

13. Michele L. Norris, "Angling to Catch a View of Clinton," *Washington Post*, November 22, 1992, B1.

14. Richard Roeper, "Clinton's Party Week Is Wretched Excess," *Chicago Sun-Times*, January 20, 1993, 11. The five-day ceremonies were also dubbed "Woodstock '93" by Bob Dart in "Clinton Party Crowd Will Groove to Woodstock of '93," *Atlanta Journal and Constitution*, January 7, 1993, 4.

15. Gregory Cerio and Lucy Howard, "Bel Air on the Potomac," *Newsweek*, April 26, 1993, 7.

16. Victor Gold, "Stay in Touch," *Washingtonian*, March 1993, 1.

17. Elizabeth A. Kaiden, "Colours Emerge amid the Mud and Grey," *The Straits Times*, June 23, 1998, 1 (emphasis in original).

18. See Michael Rogin, *"Ronald Reagan," the Movie: And Other Episodes in Political Demonology* (Berkeley: University of California Press, 1987).

19. Linda Lee, "A Wrinkle in Time: Bill Clinton's Wonder Years," *New York Times*, January 10, 1993, sec. 2, p. 27.

20. Diane Haithman, "Designing Presidential Politics," *Los Angeles Times*, July 25, 1992, calendar sec., p. 1; "Morning Edition," NPR, January 18, 1993; *Showbiz Today*, CNN, February 10, 1993; "The 52nd Presidential Inauguration: Bill Clinton Becomes President," *Times-Picayune*, January 17, 1993, A10; Michael Leahy, "Linda & Harry & Bill & Hillary," *Playboy*, November 1993, 78+.

21. Marita Sturken, "The Beltway Class System Has Never Accepted Bill Clinton," *Los Angeles Times*, December 20, 1998, 5.

22. Geoffrey Wheatcroft, "Profile: Friends of Bill," *Independent*, December 27, 1998, 16.

23. Thomas W. Hazlett, "Review of *The Jerry Springer Show*," *Reason* 29 (April 1998): 74.

24. Laura Grindstaff, "Producing Trash, Class, and the Money Shot: A Behind-the-Scenes Account of Daytime TV Talk Shows," in Lull and Hinerman, *Media Scandals*, 190.

25. See Andreas Huyssen's *After the Great Divide: Modernism, Mass Culture and Postmodernism* (Bloomington: Indiana University Press, 1986); Patrice Petro, "Mass Culture and the Feminine: The 'Place' of Television in Film Studies," *Cinema*

Journal 25.3 (1986): 5–21, and *Joyless Streets: Women and Melodramatic Representation in Weimar Germany* (Princeton: Princeton University Press, 1989).

26. See Lynne Joyrich, *Re-viewing Reception: Television, Gender, and Postmodern Culture* (Bloomington: Indiana University Press, 1996).

27. Mark Jurkowitz, *"The Drudge Report's* Scandalous Scoop," *Boston Globe*, January 22, 1998, E1.

28. Gary Chapman, "Digital Nation: When High Technology Stoops Low," *Los Angeles Times*, February 9, 1998, D6. During the late 1990s the World Wide Web has increasingly begun to be viewed as the TV of the Internet (a conflation literalized by the proliferation of Microsoft's WebTV) at the same time as the emerging technology of the Web also has become more and more synonymous with Internet itself. As WebTV promises to "bring the Information Superhighway right into [American] living room[s] without a personal computer," the Web may already be assuming a position alongside or beneath television in the aesthetic hierarchy of media culture (as Chapman's comments suggest). Consequently, just as film and television studies scholars have turned their attention to intellectually devalued popular forms, so, too, should we expand our purview to include the intertexts of the important medium of the World Wide Web.

29. John Blosser, "Why We Still Love Bill!," *National Enquirer*, October 5, 1999 (accessed on July 8, 1999), <http://www.nationalenquirer.com/archive/stories/1198.html>.

30. In her discussion of the media's "Hortonization of Clinton" after the release of the Starr Report, Anna Everett argues:

> President Clinton as public text is essentially Senator Bulworth in several respects. Both men use sex to ease the mid-life crisis. Both men are "down" with black people. Both men are liberal politicos. Both men engage in scandalous behavior. Both men are viewed as a friend to blacks — they are black people's "niggah," as the Halle Berry character affectionately rechristens Beatty's Bulworth. (Of course it should go without saying that for Lani Guinier, Dr. Jocelyn Elders and the countless numbers of black deinstitutionalized welfare recipients, with a Democratic friend like Bill Clinton, who needs Republican enemies?). *"Bulworth,* Clinton and the Starr Report: Some Eerie Parallels," *Screening Noir Online: A Newsletter of Film and Video Culture* 2 (spring/summer 1999) (accessed July 20, 1999), <http://www.film-studies.ucsb.edu/faculty/everett/news_letter/>.

31. Toni Morrison, "The Talk of the Town," *New Yorker*, October 5, 1998, 32.

32. Kevin Sack, "Blacks Stand by a President Who 'Has Been There for Us,'" *New York Times*, September 19, 1998, A1.

33. Referring to the "boxers-or-briefs question" from Clinton's 1992 campaign appearance on MTV, Barber also points to Clinton's "ordinariness": "You wouldn't ask your dad what kind of shorts he wears, but you would ask your brother. Clinton is willing to answer these kinds of questions." See Francine Kiefer, "The Clinton Presidency's Feminine Mystique," *Christian Science Monitor*, June 7, 1999, 2+.

34. One could also argue that the details of Clinton's "sexual encounters" with Lewinsky contained in the infamous Starr Report and articles in the tabloids constructing Clinton as a borderline sexual predator function to remasculinize the president in a different way.

35. The *New York Times* reported that "President Clinton's decision to attack Iraq has brought him a substantial boost in approval ratings for handling both foreign policy and his overall job as President and has diminished uncertainty over his leadership on the world stage according to the latest New York Times/CBS News Poll." See Richard L. Berke, "Raid on Baghdad," *New York Times*, June 29, 1993, A7+.

36. "The 'Wimp That Roared,'" *New Statesman & Society*, July 2, 1993, 5–10.

37. Ella Shohat and Robert Stam, *Unthinking Eurocentrism: Multiculturalism and the Media* (New York: Routledge, 1994), 130.

38. See James Castonguay, "Masquerades of Massacre: Gender, Genre, and the Gulf War TV Star System," *Velvet Light Trap* 39 (1997): 5–22. Kristin Hoganson has suggested that criticisms of Bill Clinton's inability to lead as "commander-in-chief" of the armed forces were uncannily similar to the gender politics and discourses of masculinity that provoked the Spanish-American and Philippine-American Wars. Clinton's lack of intervention in Bosnia inspired a 1994 letter published in the *Wall Street Journal* demanding that "[t]he prissy-pants lemon-suckers running our State Department . . . be replaced by real men who will speak the naked truth." See Kristin Lee Hoganson, *The "Manly" Ideal of Politics and the Imperialist Impulse: Gender, U.S. Political Culture, and the Spanish-American and the Philippine-American Wars* (Ph.D. diss., Yale University, 1995), 484.

39. Douglas Kellner, *Media Culture: Cultural Studies, Identity, and Politics between the Modern and the Postmodern* (New York: Routledge, 1995), 1.

40. Ibid., 43.

41. Steven Connor, *Postmodernist Culture: An Introduction to Theories of the Contemporary*, 2d ed. (Cambridge: Blackwell Publishers, 1997), 190.

42. Stanley Kauffman, "Vengeance and Vexation," *New Republic*, February 2, 1998, 24–25. On the public sphere see Jurgen Habermas's classic study *The Structural Transformation of the Public Sphere: An Inquiry into a Category of Bourgeois Society*, trans. Thomas Burger and Frederick Lawrence (Cambridge: MIT Press, 1996). Recent work has criticized Habermas for not recognizing social inequities in relation to the public sphere. See the contributions to Bruce Robbins, ed., *The Phantom Public Sphere* (Minneapolis: University of Minnesota Press, 1993).

43. Levinson reiterates this in a print interview: "Take the Gulf War visual of the smart bomb going down the chimney and blowing up the building. You could really fake that quite easily with digital work with today's technology. And so I said, that's sort of fascinating to me, and then wondered how that would play out." See Denis Hamill, "Barry Levinson Looks Back at *Diner* and *Rain Man* and Ahead to the Release of *Wag the Dog*," *Daily News*, December 21, 1997, Sunday Extra Sec., p. 2.

44. This attempt to distance the film from discussions of "life imitating art" functions similarly to the strategy of denial espoused in *Wag the Dog*. In order to divert attention away from the potential sex scandal, Brean tells Winifred Ames to introduce disinformation by initiating a series of denials. For instance, Brean instructs a staff member to leak information to the press that the reason the president extended his trip to China "has nothing to do with the B3 bomber program." "But there is no B3 bomber," an aide replies. "That's right," says Brean, "and we don't know how these rumors get started."

45. Jean Baudrillard, *Simulations* (New York: Semiotext[e], 1983), 26, 30.

46. Jean Baudrillard, *The Gulf War Did Not Take Place* (Bloomington: Indiana University Press, 1995).

47. Paul Patton, introduction to *The Gulf War Did Not Take Place*, 16.

48. See Larry Beinhart, *American Hero* (New York: Ballantine Books, 1993).

49. I am not suggesting that the Internet is inherently undemocratic. I would argue, however, that we should avoid the kind of crude technological determinism that often informs both utopian and dystopian visions of the Internet. Web sites dedicated to the politics of the Clinton-Lewinsky scandal suggest a wider range of discourses than those available through television or in mainstream print media. Not surprisingly, the phrase "Wag the Dog" also informs many criticisms of the president on the Internet and the Web. See, for instance, <http://www.actionworks.org/guides/wag/wagdog.htm>, <http://www.doctorliberty.com/wag the dog.html>, and <http://www.antiwar.com/>.

50. Baudrillard does in fact insist at one point that the Gulf War was truly scandalous: "If this war had not been a war and the images had been real images, there would have been a problem. For in that case the non-war would have appeared for what it is: a scandal. Similarly, if the war had been a real war and the information had not been information, this non-information would have appeared for what it is: a scandal." As I argue, however, Baudrillard does not elaborate a critical account of the scandal of the Gulf War but offers a largely descriptive account of the event's effacement by the media. See Baudrillard, *Gulf War*, 81.

51. Baudrillard, *Gulf War*, 61.

52. Jean Baudrillard, *The Ecstasy of Communication* (New York: Semiotext(e), 1983), 9.

53. See Stuart Ewen, *PR!: A Social History of Spin* (New York: Basic Books, 1996).

54. Todd Gitlin, introduction to Erik Barnouw, ed., *Conglomerates and the Media* (New York: New Press, 1998), 9.

55. Michael Sprinker expresses a similar ambivalence in his review of Levinson's *Tin Men* (1987) when he writes, "Given the obvious superiority of Levinson's film to the bulk of Hollywood's current pulp production, one feels almost churlish in criticizing *Tin Men*. Yet it is precisely Levinson's intelligence which disappoints." See Michael Sprinker, *"Tin Men,"* in Frank N. Magill, ed., *Magill's Cinema Annual 1988: A Survey of the Films of 1987* (Pasadena: Salem Press, 1988), 357.

56. Robert W. Welkos, "Are 'Wag's' Ads Taking Real Life by the Tale?" *Los Angeles Times*, January 29, 1998, Calendar Sec., F47.

57. "'Dog' Has Its Day with the President," *USA Today*, January 8, 1998, 2D.

58. Ed Fishbein, "Clinton in Good Humor at Fund-Raiser," *Sacramento Bee*, January 10, 1998, A2.

59. I am adapting this term from Thomas Schatz's "The New Hollywood Studio System," in *Conglomerates and the Media*.

60. See Daniel C. Hallin, "Commercialism and Professionalism in the American News Media," in James Curran and Michael Gurevitch, eds., *Mass Media and Society*, 2d ed. (London: Arnold, 1996), 243–262; and Michael Gurevitch, "The Globalization of Electronic Journalism," in Curran and Gurevitch, *Mass Media and Society*, 204–224.

61. *CNN Sunday*, August 23, 1998.

62. John Tomlinson, "'And Besides, the Wench is Dead': Media Scandals and the Globalization of Communication," in Lull and Hinerman, *Media Scandals*, 71–72.

63. Tomasz Kitlinski, Pawel Leskowicz, and Joe Lockard have also argued, however, that "[a]rguments in the Arab press for an anti-Clinton conspiracy varied between those who believed the scandal was generated in response to an emergent White House opposition to Israeli expansionism and those who viewed Clinton's

misfortunes as political cash being converted by the Jews." Tomasz Kitlinski, Pawel Leskowicz, and Joe Lockard, "Monica Dreyfus," *Bad Subjects: Political Education for Everyday Life* 44 (May 1999): 23.

64. Frank Rich, "Dying in Columbus," *New York Times*, February 21, 1998, A11.

65. Elizabeth Sullivan, "Kosovo Violence Threatens Neighbors," *Plain Dealer*, March 8, 1998, 7A.

66. "Serbian TV Viewers See *Wag The Dog*," *Milwaukee Journal-Sentinel*, March 27, 1999, 8. The front page of the *Boston Herald* described this as "a novel twist in the propaganda war with America," apparently unaware that Saddam Hussein had used the same tactic. See Andrew Miga, "Escalation: Kosovo Conflict Spills into Bosnia, Albania," *Boston Herald*, March 27, 1999, 1.

67. "Envelope Please: *Wag The Dog* Gets Serb Prize," *Boston Globe*, April 18, 1999, A35.

68. Larry Beinhart, "Book, Movie, War, Reality," *New York Times*, May 18, 1999, A23.

69. Frank P. Tomasulo, "'I'll See It When I Believe It': Rodney King and the Prison-House of Video," in Vivian Sobchack, ed., *The Persistence of History: Cinema, Television, and the Modern Event* (New York: Routledge, 1996), 81.

SCANDAL AND FILM

A SELECT BIBLIOGRAPHY

COMPILED BY ADRIENNE L. MCLEAN

The following bibliography of published English-language books and essays is divided into two sections. The first features a wide range of general or "mass-market" works published by commercial presses about particular people or events; many are the memoirs of or biographies about stars, gossip columnists, press agents, journalists, and other Hollywood "insiders" of various kinds. The list also includes books and articles by mainstream cultural critics that seem to be aimed at a general audience. Not included are individual articles from fan magazines or scandal sheets or works about stars whose lengthy careers were only occasionally notorious. The second section references works, published primarily by university or academic presses, that tend to concentrate on larger theoretical or historical questions raised by celebrity and stardom, scandal, gossip, rumor, innuendo, and popular treatments thereof. Given the pervasiveness of scandal as an aspect of mass-mediated representation, however, this section also includes particularly useful scholarly works whose subjects might more properly be considered social science, politics, literature, film censorship, or star studies. Although no value judgments are meant by characterization of a work as "mass-market" or "academic," it is recognized that such terms are, unfortunately, ideologically loaded and our designations may seem arbitrary. For further references see also the endnotes of individual essays.

POPULAR WORKS

Anger, Kenneth. *Hollywood Babylon.* San Francisco: Straight Arrow Books, 1975.
———. *Hollywood Babylon II.* New York: Dutton, 1984.
Austin, John. *Hollywood's Babylon Women.* New York: S. P. I. Books, 1994.
Bacon, James. *Hollywood Is a Four Letter Town.* Chicago: Henry Regnery, 1976.
Betrock, Alan. *Unseen America: The Greatest Cult Exploitation Magazines, 1950–1966.* New York: Shake Books, 1990.
Bosworth, Patricia. "Hollywood on Trial." *Vanity Fair,* April 1997, 236–259.
———. "That Old Star Magic" [*Photoplay*]. *Vanity Fair,* April 1998, 188–198.
———. "The Gangster and the Goddess" [Lana Turner and Johnny Stompanato]. *Vanity Fair,* April 1999, 244–271.
Collins, Amy Fine. "Idol Gossips" [Hedda Hopper and Louella Parsons]. *Vanity Fair,* April 1997, 358–375.
Collins, Gail. *Scorpion Tongues: Gossip, Celebrity, and American Politics.* New York: William Morrow, 1998.
Davidson, Bill. *The Real and the Unreal.* New York: Harper and Brothers, 1961.

Edmonds, Andy. *Frame-Up! The Shocking Scandal That Destroyed Hollywood's Biggest Comedy Star, Roscoe "Fatty" Arbuckle*. New York: Avon Books, 1991.

Eells, George. *Hedda and Louella*. New York: Putnam, 1972.

Ehrenstein, David. *Open Secret: Gay Hollywood, 1928–1998*. New York: William Morrow and Company, 1998.

Ernst, Morris L., and Pare Lorentz. *Censored: The Private Life of the Movie*. New York: Jonathan Cape and Harrison Smith, 1930.

Forman, Henry James. *Our Movie Made Children*. New York: Macmillan, 1933.

Friedrich, Otto. *City of Nets: A Portrait of Hollywood in the 1940's*. New York: Harper and Row, 1986.

Gabler, Neal. *Winchell: Gossip, Power, and the Culture of Celebrity*. New York: Alfred A. Knopf, 1995.

Giroux, Robert. *A Deed of Death: The Story behind the Unsolved Murder of Hollywood Director William Desmond Taylor*. New York: Alfred A. Knopf, 1990.

Hadleigh, Boze. *Hollywood Babble On: Stars Gossip about Other Stars*. New York: Carol Publishing, 1994.

Hampton, Benjamin B. *A History of the Movies*. 1931. Reprinted as *History of the American Film Industry from Its Beginnings to 1931*. New York: Dover Publications, 1970.

Hopper, Hedda. *From under My Hat*. New York: Doubleday, 1952.

Hopper, Hedda, and James Brough. *The Whole Truth and Nothing But*. New York: Doubleday, 1963.

Kamp, David. "When Liz Met Dick." *Vanity Fair*, April 1998, 366–394.

Kashner, Sam. "The Color of Love" [Sammy Davis Jr. and Kim Novak]. *Vanity Fair*, April 1999, 378–386, 405–409.

Kohn, George C. *Encyclopedia of American Scandal*. New York: Facts on File, 1989.

Lemann, Nicholas. "Scandalizers-in-Chief: Five Presidents and How They Shrank." *New Yorker*, July 5, 1999, 76–81.

Machlin, Milt. *The Gossip Wars: An Exposé of the Scandal Era*. New York: Tower Publications, 1981.

Madsen, Axel. *The Sewing Circle: Hollywood's Greatest Secret, Female Stars Who Loved Other Women*. Secaucus, N.J.: Birch Lane Press, 1995.

Mann, William J. *Wisecracker: The Life and Times of William Haines, Hollywood's First Openly Gay Star*. New York: Viking, 1998.

Muir, Florabel. *Headline Happy*. New York: Henry Holt, 1950.

Nash, Jay Robert. *Murder among the Mighty: Celebrity Slayings That Shocked America*. New York: Delacorte Press, 1983.

Navasky, Victor S. *Naming Names*. New York: Viking, 1980.

Otash, Fred. *Investigation Hollywood!* Chicago: Henry Regnery, 1976.

Palling, Bruce, ed. *The Book of Modern Scandal*. London: Weidenfeld and Nicolson, 1995.

Parsons, Louella. *The Gay Illiterate*. New York: Doubleday, 1944.

——. *Tell It to Louella*. New York: G. P. Putnam's Sons, 1961.

Powdermaker, Hortense. *Hollywood, The Dream Factory: An Anthropologist Looks at the Movie-Makers*. Boston: Little, Brown, 1950, chaps. 3, 12, and 13.

Reid, Bertha Westbrook. *Wallace Reid: His Life Story*. New York: Sorg Publishing, 1923.

Robinson, Jill. "Polanski's Inferno." *Vanity Fair*, April 1997, 150–170.

Rosenstein, Jaik. *Hollywood Leg Man*. Los Angeles: Madison Press, 1950.

Rosten, Leo C. *Hollywood: The Movie Colony, the Movie Makers.* New York: Harcourt, Brace and Company, 1941, chaps. 5 and 8.

Schudson, Michael. *Watergate in American Memory: How We Remember, Forget, and Reconstruct the Past.* New York: Basic Books, 1992.

Shevey, Sandra. *The Marilyn Scandal.* London: Sidgwick and Jackson, 1987.

Skolsky, Sidney. *Don't Get Me Wrong—I Love Hollywood.* New York: Putnam, 1975.

Spacks, Patricia Meyer. *Gossip.* New York: Alfred A. Knopf, 1985.

Stallings, Penny, with Howard Mandelbaum. *Flesh and Fantasy.* New York: Harper and Row, 1978.

Walker, Alexander. *Stardom: The Hollywood Phenomenon.* New York: Stein and Day, 1970, chap. 12.

Yallop, David A. *The Day the Laughter Stopped: The True Story of Fatty Arbuckle.* New York: St Martin's, 1976.

ACADEMIC WORKS

Bernstein, Matthew, ed. *Controlling Hollywood: Censorship and Regulation in the Studio Era.* New Brunswick, N.J.: Rutgers University Press, 1999.

Bird, S. Elizabeth. *For Enquiring Minds: A Cultural Study of Supermarket Tabloids.* Knoxville: University of Tennessee Press, 1992.

Black, Gregory D. *Hollywood Censored: Morality Codes, Catholics, and the Movies.* Cambridge: Cambridge University Press, 1994.

Borden, Diane L., and Kerric Harvey, eds. *The Electronic Grapevine: Rumor, Reputation, and Reporting in the New On-Line Environment.* Mahwah, N.J.: Lawrence Erlbaum Associates, 1998.

Braudy, Leo. *The Frenzy of Renown: Fame and Its History.* New York: Oxford University Press, 1986.

Castor, Laura. "Did She or Didn't She? The Discourse of Scandal in the 1988 U.S. Presidential Campaign." *Genders* 12 (winter 1991): 62–76.

Cohen, William A. *Sex Scandal: The Private Parts of Victorian Fiction.* Durham, N.C.: Duke University Press, 1996.

Couvares, Francis G., ed. *Movie Censorship and American Culture.* Washington: Smithsonian Institution Press, 1996.

Damico, James. "Ingrid from Lorraine to Stromboli: Analyzing the Public's Perception of a Film Star." In Jeremy G. Butler, ed. *Star Texts: Image and Performance in Film and Television,* 240–253. Detroit: Wayne State University Press, 1991.

DeCordova, Richard. *Picture Personalities: The Emergence of the Star System in America.* Urbana: University of Illinois Press, 1990.

Doherty, Thomas Patrick. *Pre-Code Hollywood: Sex, Immorality, and Insurrection in American Cinema, 1930–1934.* New York: Columbia University Press, 1999.

Dyer, Richard. *Heavenly Bodies: Film Stars and Society.* New York: St. Martin's, 1986.

———. *Stars.* London: BFI, 1979/1998.

Fine, Gary Alan. "Scandal, Social Conditions, and the Creation of Public Attention: Fatty Arbuckle and the 'Problem of Hollywood.'" *Social Problems* 44 (August 1997): 297–334.

Goffman, Erving. *Frame Analysis: An Essay on the Organization of Experience.* Cambridge: Harvard University Press, 1974.

———. *Stigma: Notes on the Management of Spoiled Identity.* New York: Jason Aronson, 1974.

Goode, Erich, and Nachman Ben-Yehuda. *Moral Panics: The Social Construction of Deviance.* Oxford: Blackwell, 1994.

Jacobs, Lea. *The Wages of Sin: Censorship and the Fallen Woman Film, 1928–1942.* Berkeley: University of California Press, 1995.

Johnson, Sally. "Theorizing Language and Masculinity: A Feminist Perspective." In Sally Johnson and Ulrike Hanna Meinhof, eds. *Language and Masculinity*, 8–26. Oxford: Blackwell, 1997.

Johnson, Sally, and Frank Finlay. "Do Men Gossip? An Analysis of Football Talk on Television." In Sally Johnson and Ulrike Hanna Meinhof, eds. *Language and Masculinity*, 130–143. Oxford: Blackwell, 1997.

Leff, Leonard J., and Jerold L. Simmons. *The Dame in the Kimono: Hollywood, Censorship, and the Production Code from the 1920s to the 1960s.* New York: Doubleday, 1990.

Lewis, Jerry M., assisted by Linda Powell. "Comedy and Deviance: The Fatty Arbuckle Case." In Clinton R. Sanders, ed. *Marginal Conventions: Popular Culture, Mass Media, and Social Deviance*, 18–28. Bowling Green, Ohio: Bowling Green State University Popular Press, 1990.

Lull, James, and Stephen Hinerman, eds. *Media Scandals: Morality and Desire in the Popular Culture Marketplace.* New York: Columbia University Press, 1997.

Marshall, P. David. *Celebrity and Power: Fame in Contemporary Culture.* Minneapolis: University of Minnesota Press, 1997.

May, Lary. *Screening Out the Past: The Birth of Mass Culture and the Motion Picture Industry.* New York: Oxford University Press, 1980.

McLean, Adrienne L. "The Cinderella Princess and the Instrument of Evil: Surveying the Limits of Female Transgression in Two Postwar Hollywood Scandals." *Cinema Journal* 34 (spring 1995): 36–56.

Mellencamp, Patricia. *High Anxiety: Catastrophe, Scandal, Age and Comedy.* Bloomington: Indiana University Press, 1992.

Morin, Edgar. *The Stars.* Trans. Richard Howard. New York: Grove Press, 1961.

Oderman, Stuart. *Roscoe "Fatty" Arbuckle: A Biography of the Silent Film Comedian, 1887–1933.* Jefferson, N.C.: McFarland, 1994.

Perkins, Tessa. "The Politics of 'Jane Fonda.'" In Christine Gledhill, ed. *Stardom: Industry of Desire*, 237–250. London: Routledge, 1991.

Rosnow, Ralph L., and Gary Alan Fine. *Rumor and Gossip: The Social Psychology of Hearsay.* New York: Elsevier, 1976.

Rubington, Earl, and Martin S. Weinberg, eds. *Deviance: The Interactionist Perspective.* 7th ed. Boston: Allyn and Bacon, 1999.

Sanders, Clinton R. "'A Lot of People Like It': The Relationship between Deviance and Popular Culture." In Clinton R. Sanders, ed. *Marginal Conventions: Popular Culture, Mass Media and Social Deviance*, 3–11. Bowling Green, Ohio: Bowling Green State University Popular Press, 1990.

Savage, Stephanie. "Evelyn Nesbit and the Film(ed) Histories of the Thaw-White Scandal." *Film History* 8 (1996): 159–175.

Thompson, Kenneth. *Moral Panics.* London: Routledge, 1998.

Tinkcom, Matthew. "Scandalous! Kenneth Anger and the Prohibitions of Hollywood History." In Ellis Hanson, ed. *Out Takes: Essays on Queer Theory and Film*, 271–287. Durham, N.C.: Duke University Press, 1999.

Turner, Patricia A. *I Heard It through the Grapevine: Rumor in African-American Culture.* Berkeley: University of California Press, 1993.

About the Contributors

MARK LYNN ANDERSON is currently a visiting assistant professor in the Department of English and Comparative Literature at Hobart and William Smith Colleges. He is working on a book about the early star system and its relation to the development of the human sciences.

CYNTHIA BARON is an assistant professor of film studies at Bowling Green State University in Ohio and has written several articles and book chapters on screen acting.

JAMES CASTONGUAY is chair of the Media Studies Department at Sacred Heart University in Fairfield, Connecticut. He has published several articles on war and the media and is a contributor to *American Quarterly*'s Project for Hypertext Scholarship in American Studies. He is currently the Information Technology Officer for the Society for Cinema Studies.

DAVID A. COOK is a professor of film and director of the Film Studies Program at Emory University. He has published numerous articles in the fields of English literature and film studies, and his most recent books are the third edition of his *A History of Narrative Film* and *Lost Illusions: American Cinema in the Shadow of Watergate and Vietnam, 1970–1979* (volume 9 in Scribner's History of the American Cinema series).

NANCY COOK is an associate professor of English at the University of Rhode Island. She has published a number of articles in the areas of film, American literature, and Western American studies.

MARY DESJARDINS is an assistant professor at Dartmouth College, where she teaches film, television, and women's studies. She has published widely in the areas of film and television and is completing a book called *Recycled Stars: Hollywood Film Stardom in the Age of Television and Video*.

LUCY FISCHER is a professor of film studies and English and director of the Film Studies Program at the University of Pittsburgh. She has published extensively on issues of film history, theory, and criticism, and among the books she has authored or edited are *Jacques Tati, Shot/Countershot: Film Tradition and Women's Cinema, Imitations of Life, Cinematernity: Film, Motherhood, Genre,* and *Sunrise*. She is currently working on a book entitled *Designing Women: Art Deco, Cinema, and the Female Form*.

LEE GRIEVESON is a lecturer in Cinema Studies at the University of Exeter and Assistant Director of the Bill Douglas Centre for the History of Cinema and Popular Culture. He has published several articles on cinema history and film theory and is currently completing a book on the regulation of early American cinema.

ERIK HEDLING is an associate professor of film studies at the Department of Comparative Literature, Lund University, Sweden. He has published a number of journal articles and book chapters in English and Swedish, and among his books in English are *Lindsay Anderson: Maverick Film-Maker* and *Interart Poetics: Essays on the Interrelations of the Arts and Media*.

PETER LEHMAN is a professor of film in the Interdisciplinary Humanities Program and the Hispanic Research Center at Arizona State University. His books on film theory and criticism include *Running Scared: Masculinity and the Representation of the Male Body, Close Viewings*, and *Defining Cinema*. He has coauthored several books with William Luhr, among them two volumes on the films of Blake Edwards and a textbook, *Thinking About Movies*.

WILLIAM LUHR is a professor of English at Saint Peter's College in Jersey City, New Jersey, and Cochair of the Columbia University Seminar on Cinema and Interdisciplinary Interpretation. He has published widely in film journals and written and edited several books, among them *Raymond Chandler and Film, World Cinema since 1945, The Maltese Falcon: John Huston, Director*, and, as mentioned above, he has collaborated with Peter Lehman on several projects.

ADRIENNE L. McLEAN is an assistant professor of film studies in the School of Arts and Humanities at the University of Texas at Dallas. She has published several articles and book chapters on film and television history and theory and is completing a book called *Being Rita Hayworth: Labor, Identity, and Hollywood Stardom*.

SUSAN McLELAND received her Ph.D. from the Department of Radio/Television/Film at the University of Texas, Austin. She has published several journal articles and book chapters and is completing a book about the star image of Elizabeth Taylor.

SAM STOLOFF received his Ph.D. from the Department of English at Cornell University; his essay is drawn from his dissertation on Fatty Arbuckle and the Black Sox and the normalization of commercial culture in the 1920s. He has published several essays in film journals and anthologies.

Index

Page numbers in italics refer to illustrations.

MAGGIE SHAYNE

PRINCE OF TWILIGHT

MIRA

MIRA

Recycling programs
for this product may
not exist in your area.

ISBN-13: 978-0-7783-2906-0

PRINCE OF TWILIGHT

For questions and comments about the quality of this book please contact us at
Customer_eCare@Harlequin.ca.

www.MIRABooks.com

Printed in U.S.A.

Praise for the novels of

MAGGIE SHAYNE

"The latest from bestselling Shayne
is an interesting, inventive tale."
—*Publishers Weekly* on *Demon's Kiss*

"Suspense, mystery, danger and passion—
no one does them better than Maggie Shayne."
—*Romance Reviews Today* on *Darker Than Midnight*

"A tasty, tension-packed read."
—*Publishers Weekly* on *Thicker Than Water*

"Maggie Shayne demonstrates an
absolutely superb touch, blending fantasy and romance
into an outstanding reading experience."
—*RT Book Reviews* on *Embrace the Twilight*

"Maggie Shayne is better than chocolate.
She satisfies every wicked craving."
—*New York Times* bestselling author Suzanne Forster

"Maggie Shayne delivers sheer delight,
and fans new and old of her vampire series can rejoice."
—*RT Book Reviews* on *Twilight Hunger*

"Shayne's haunting tale is intricately woven... A moving mix
of high suspense and romance, this haunting Halloween
thriller will propel readers to bolt their doors at night!"
—*Publishers Weekly* on *The Gingerbread Man*

"Shayne's talent knows no bounds!"
—*Rendezvous*

"Maggie Shayne delivers romance
with sweeping intensity and bewitching passion."
—*New York Times* bestselling author Jayne Ann Krentz

Prince of Twilight

Prologue

Fifteenth Century
Romania

"We have to bury her, my son."

Vlad stood in the small stone chapel beside his beloved new bride. Elisabeta's skin was as cold as the stone bier on which she lay. She wore the pale green wedding gown the servants had found for her on the day their hasty vows had been exchanged. The skirt draped on either side of her, swathing the stone slab in beauty. Her hair, pale as spun silver and endlessly long, spread around her head, as if pillowing her in a cloud.

"My son—" This time the old priest's words were accompanied by his hand, clasping Vlad's shoulder.

Vlad whirled on the man. "No! She is not to be put in the ground. Not yet. I won't allow it."

A little fear joined the pity in the old man's eyes. Not enough, not yet. "I know this is difficult—I do. But she deserves to be laid to rest."

"I said no," Vlad repeated, his tone tired, his heart dead. Then he turned from the priest and focused again where he needed to focus: upon her, upon his bride. Their time together had been too short. One night and then part of a second before he'd been called into battle. It wasn't right.

The priest still hovered.

"Get out, before I draw my blade and send you out in pieces." Vlad's words were barely more than a hoarse whisper, yet filled with enough menace to elicit a clipped gasp from the cleric.

"I'll send in your father. Perhaps he can—"

Vlad turned to send a warning glare over his shoulder. Brief, but powerful enough to reduce most mortals to tears.

"I'm going, my liege." The priest bowed a little as he backed through the chapel doors.

Vlad sighed in relief when the doors closed once again, leaving him alone with his grief. He leaned over Elisabeta's body, lowered his head to her chest, and let his tears soak the gown. "Why, my love? Why did you do this? Was our love not worthy of a single day's grieving? I told you I would come back. Why couldn't you have believed in me?"

A soft creaking sound accompanied by a stiff night breeze and the gentle clearing of an aging throat told him that his respite was over. Vlad forced himself to straighten, to turn and face his father—for truly, the man had become as much a father to him as any had been, since Utnapishtim.

The old king was pale and unsteady. He'd lost a daughter-in-law he'd been close, already, to loving—and for three days he had believed that he had lost his son, as well.

He crossed the small room, his gait uneven and slow, then wrapped his frail arms around Vlad's shoulders and hugged him hard, as hard as his strength would allow. "Alive," he muttered. "By the gods, my son, you're alive after all."

Vlad closed his eyes as he returned his father's embrace. "Alive, father, but none too glad to be, just now." As he said it, he looked back at his bride.

His father did, as well, releasing his hold on Vlad to move closer to the bier. "I cannot tell you how it grieves me to see you in such pain, much less to witness the loss of such a precious young woman as Elisabeta."

"I know."

"Your friend, the foreign woman—she told you what transpired?"

Vlad nodded. "Rhiannon is…an old friend. And a dear one. She said she arrived here for a visit just after I was called to defend our borders."

"So she did. We put her up. Fussy one, she is, and I don't believe she thought highly of your chosen bride. Were the two of you…?"

"As close as any two people can be," Vlad told him. "But we had no claims on each other. She would not have been jealous."

"She called the princess a—now what was the word she used…? Ah yes, a *whiner*," the king said softly. "To her face, no less."

Vlad nodded, not doubting it.

"When word came that you'd been killed on the field of battle, poor Elisabeta took to the tower room and bolted the door. I had men trying to break it down right up until—"

"I know, Father. I know you did all you could."

The king lowered his head, perhaps to hide the rush of tears into his clouded blue eyes. "Tell me what I can do to ease your grief."

Vlad thought about that, thought about it hard. Rhiannon was no ordinary woman but a former priestess of Isis and daughter of Pharoah. She was skilled in the occult arts, and she had told Vlad that he would find Elisabeta again—she had foreseen it—in five hundred years' time, if he could live that long. What she hadn't promised was that Beta would be the same woman he had loved and lost, or that she would remember him and love him again.

"There is something I can do for you," the king said softly. "I can see it in your eyes. Speak it, my son, and it shall be done, whatever it is."

Vlad met his father's eyes and felt love for the man. True love, though the king was not his true father. "I cannot let them bury her. Not yet. I need you to send our finest riders upon our fastest mounts, Father. Send them out into the countryside to gather the most skilled sorcerers, diviners, wizards and witches in the land. I don't care what it takes. I must have them here before my beloved is put into the cold ground."

The king looked worriedly into his eyes. "My son, you must know that even the most skilled magician won't be able to bring her back. Buried or not, she resides among the dead now."

He nodded once, closed his eyes against that probing, caring stare. "I know that, Father. I only need to be sure she's at peace."

"But the priest—"

"His prayers are not enough. I want to be sure. Please, Father, you said you would do anything to ease my pain. This shall ease it, if anything can."

The king nodded firmly. "Then it shall be done."

"And Father—until they come, keep everyone from here. And even then, let them in only by night."

The old man was used to Vlad's nocturnal nature by now. He nodded, and Vlad knew the promise would be kept.

The king left, and Vlad drew his bloodstained sword, then stood between the bier and the chapel door. When the sun rose, he barred the door, drew a tapestry from the wall and wrapped himself in it. When the sun set again, he was forced to lay the fabric over Elisabeta's body or witness it begin to change with the ravages of death. And before the third night was through, the scent of death and decay hung heavy on the air.

But finally, at midnight of the third night, the chapel doors opened again, and several men entered. No women were among them. They entered in a rush of wind, dressed in dull white traveling robes of wool, for the most part, though one wore a finer fabric in rich, russet tones, its edges embroidered with a pattern of twisting green vines.

They all dropped to one knee, bowing low before

him. The one in the brown said, "My prince, we came as rapidly as we could manage. Our hearts are heavy with grief at the loss of the princess."

"Yes," he said. "Rise. I need your help."

The men looked at one another nervously. There were five, he saw now. Locals, mostly, though one appeared to be from the East, and another was Moorish in appearance.

"We are honored if we can be of service," the apparent spokesman said. "But I know not what we can do. Against death, even we are powerless."

He nodded and thought of Gilgamesh, the legendary king of Sumer. His own desperate search for the key of life had resulted in the creation of an entire race—the Undead. Vampires. Like Vlad, and Rhiannon, and so many others. But it had never resulted in the great king's dear friend Enkidu returning from death.

Maybe, Vlad thought, his own quest was just as mad. But he had to try.

"I do not ask you to conquer death. Only to ensure that when I find her again, I will know her—and that she will know me. And remember. And love me again."

The magicians and sorcerers frowned, seeking understanding in each other's faces.

"A powerful seer has told me that the princess will return to me in another lifetime. But it will be in the distant future."

"But, my liege, you would be aged and she but an infant."

"That's not your concern, sorcerer. I want only to ensure that when she does return—and reaches a decent age—she will remember all that came before, that she will be the woman she was in this lifetime. Can you or can you not fulfill this request?"

One man began to whisper to another, and Vlad caught the words "unnatural" and "immoral," but the man in brown held up a hand to silence them. Then he approached Vlad slowly, cautiously, and at last he nodded. "We can and we shall, my liege. Go, get sustenance, rest. She'll be safe in our care, I promise you."

Vlad gazed at the shape beneath the tapestry. No longer his Elisabeta, but a shell that had formerly held her essence. He looked at the men again. "Do not fear to try. It is a lot I ask of you. I give my word, I will not exact punishment should you fail, so long as you do the very best you can. On her memory, I vow it to you."

The men bowed deeply, and he glimpsed relief on their faces. Truly, Vlad was not known for his mercy or understanding. He left them to their work. But he didn't rest, and he didn't feed. He couldn't—not until he knew.

It was four a.m. when a servant boy came to fetch him back to the chapel, and as he hurried there, he saw that the door was open and the priest was coming out, wafting a censer before him. Behind him, men came bearing the corpse, buried in flowers, upon a litter.

And behind *them* came the wizards and sorcerers, who met Vlad's eyes and nodded to tell him that they had been successful. The man in russet came to him, while the others kept the slow pace behind the funeral procession. The priest's servant rang a bell, and the gruff-voiced cleric intoned his prayers loudly, so that others from the castle and the village joined in as they passed, many carrying candles or lamps. No one in the village had slept this night, awaiting the princess's burial, and so the procession grew larger and longer as it wound onward, a writhing serpent dotted with lights.

"My prince," said the man in brown. "We have done it. Take this."

He handed Vlad a scroll, rolled tightly and held by a ruby ring—the ring he'd given to Elisabeta. It had been on her finger. Seeing it caused pain to stab deeply, and he sucked in a breath.

"I don't understand," he said. "You removed her wedding ring. Why?"

"We performed a powerful ritual, commanding a part of her essence to remain earthbound. The ring is the key that holds her and will one day release her. When a future incarnation of Elisabeta returns to you, all you will need to do is put this ring upon her finger and perform the rite contained on this scroll, and she will be restored to the very Elisabeta she was before. She will remember everything. And she will love you again."

"Are you sure?" Vlad asked, afraid to believe, to hope.

"On my life, my prince, I swear to you it is true. There is only one caveat. And this could not be helped, for we risk our very souls by tampering with matters of life and death and the afterlife. The gods must be allowed their say."

"The gods. It was they who saw fit to take her from me this way. To hell with the gods."

"*My prince!*" The sorcerer looked around as if fearing Vlad's blasphemy might have been overheard by the deities themselves.

"Tell me of this caveat, then," Vlad snapped. "But be quick. I must attend to my wife's burial."

The man boldly took hold of Vlad's arm and

began walking beside him, catching them up to the procession, while keeping enough distance for privacy. "If the rite has not been performed by the time the Red Star of Destiny eclipses Venus, then the gods have not willed it, and the magick will expire."

"And what will happen to Elisabeta then?"

"Her soul will be set free. All parts of her soul, the part we've held earthbound, and any other parts that may have been reborn into the physical realm. All will be free."

"And by free, you mean…dead," Vlad whispered. He gripped the man by the front of his russet robes and lifted him off his feet. "You've done nothing!"

"Death is but an illusion, my liege! Life is endless. And you'll have time—vast amounts of time—in which to find her again, I swear."

He narrowed his eyes on the sorcerer, tempted to draw his blade and slide it between the man's ribs. But instead, he lowered him to the ground again. "How much time? When, exactly, does this red star of yours next eclipse Venus?"

"Not for slightly more than five hundred and twenty years, my liege, as nearly as I can calculate."

Vlad swallowed his pain and his raging grief. Rhiannon had predicted he would find his Elisabeta again in five hundred years. His chief concern at the time had been wondering how the hell he could manage to survive so long without her; how he could bear the pain.

Now he had an added worry. When he did find her, would it be in time to enact the spell, perform the rite, and restore her memory and her soul?

By the gods, it had to be. He was determined. He must not fail.

He *would not.*

He was no ordinary man, nor even an ordinary vampire, after all.

He was Dracula.

1

Present day

"Melina Roscova," the slender blond woman said, extending a hand. "You must be Maxine Stuart?"

"It's Maxine Malone, and no, I'm not her." Stormy took the woman's hand. It was cool and her grip very strong. "Stormy Jones," she said. "Max and Lou are busy with another case, and we didn't think it would take all three of us to conduct the initial interview."

"I see." Melina released her grip and dug in her pocket for a business card. "I guess this must be out of date."

Stormy took the card, looked it over. The SIS logo superimposed itself over the words Supernatural Investigations Services. In smaller letters were their names, Maxine Stuart, Lou Malone, Tempest Jones and beneath that, in a fancy script, Experienced, professional, discreet and a toll-free number.

She handed the card back. "Yeah, that's pretty old. Maxie and Lou got hitched sixteen years ago now. Of course, we didn't get new cards made up until we'd used all the old ones. You have to be practical, you know."

"Naturally."

"So why all the mystery?" Stormy asked. "And why did you want to meet here?"

As she spoke, they moved through the entrance and into the vaulted corridors of the Canadian National Museum. Their steps echoed as they walked. Melina paid the entry fee in cash, and led the way deeper into the building.

"No mystery. I want you to handle a sensitive case for me. Discretion—" she tapped the old business card against her knuckle "—is imperative."

"You can trust us on that," Stormy said. "We wouldn't still be in business after all this time if we didn't know how to keep our mouths shut." She looked at a threadbare tapestry on display inside a glass case. Its colors had faded to gray, and it looked as if a stiff breeze would reduce it to a pile of lint. "So why this place?"

"This is where it is," Melina said, eyeing several tarnished silver pieces in another case. Bowls, urns, pendants.

"Where what is?"

"What you need to see. But it won't be here for long. It's part of a traveling exhibit. Artifacts uncovered on a recent archaeological dig in the northern part of Turkey."

Stormy eyed her, waiting for her to say more, but Melina fell silent and moved farther along the hall, among line drawings and diagrams of dig sites, framed like pieces of art. Then she turned to go through two open doors into a large room. There were items lining the walls, all of them safely behind glass barriers. Brass trinkets, steel blades with elaborately carved handles of bone and ivory. Stormy glanced at the items on display, then rubbed her arms, suddenly cold to the bone. "You'd think they'd turn on the heat in here. It's freezing," she muttered. Then, to distract herself from the rush of discomfort, she snatched up a flyer from a stack in a nearby rack and read from it. According to it, the items found didn't match the culture of the area in which they'd been located, and many were thought to be the spoils of war, brought home by soldiers who looted them from faraway lands and conquered enemies. The dig site was believed to have been a monastery of sorts—a place where men went to study magic and the occult.

"Here it is," Melina said.

Stormy dragged her gaze from the flyer to where the other woman stood a few yards away, in front of a small glass cube that sat atop a pedestal. Inside the cube, resting on a clear acrylic base, was a ring. It was big, its wide band more elaborately engraved than the gaudiest high school class ring she'd ever seen. Its gleaming red stone was as big as one of those, too, only she was pretty sure this stone was real.

"It's a ruby," Melina said, confirming Stormy's unspoken suspicion. "It's priceless. Isn't it incredible?"

Stormy didn't reply. She couldn't take her eyes off the ring. For a moment it was as if she were seeing it through a long, dark tunnel. Everything around her went black, her vision riveted to the ring, her eyes unable to see anything else. And then she heard a voice.

"Inelul else al meu!"

The voice—it came from her own throat. Her lips were moving, but she wasn't moving them. The sensation was as if she had become a puppet, or a dummy in some ventriloquist act. Her body was moving all on its own, her hands reaching for the glass case, palms pressing to either side of it, lifting it from its base.

A hand closed hard on her arm and jerked her away. "Ms. Jones, what the hell are you doing?"

Stormy blinked rapidly as her body snapped back on line. She saw Melina holding her upper arm while looking around the room as if waiting for the Canadian version of a SWAT team to swarm in.

Stormy cleared her throat. "Did I set off any alarms?"

"I don't think so," Melina said. "There are sensors on the pedestal. They kick in only if the ring is removed."

Frowning as her head cleared, Stormy stared at her. "Why do you know that?"

"It's my job to know. Are you all right?"

Nodding, Stormy avoided the other woman's eyes. "Yeah. Fine. I…zoned out for a minute, that's all."

But it wasn't all. And she wasn't fine. Far from it. She hadn't had an episode like that in sixteen years, but she knew the sensations that had swamped her just now. Knew them well. She would never forget. Never. She hadn't felt that way in sixteen years, not since the last time she'd been with him. With Dracula. The one and only. And though her memory of the specifics of that time with him was a dark void, her memories of…being possessed remained. And memories of Dracula or not, she'd heard his voice just a moment ago, whispering close to her.

Without the ring and the scroll, I'm afraid there is no hope.

What did it mean? Was he here? Nearby? And why, when she remembered so little about their time together, had that phrase come floating in to her memory now?

No. He wouldn't come back to her when he knew what it did to her mind and body. He'd let her go in order to spare her going through that madness anymore. Or so she liked to believe. She'd awakened in Rhiannon's private jet, on her way back home. And, like all of Vlad's victims before her, her memory of her time with him had been erased.

But not her feelings for him. Inexplicable or not, she had felt a deep sense of loss, and she'd been dying inside a little more with every single day that had passed since.

He wasn't here. He wouldn't put her through that again. Unless…

She looked again at the ring. God, could this be

the ring he'd been talking about? And what had he meant by that cryptic phrase? It was hell not remembering. Sheer hell. She should hate him for playing with her mind the way he had. Over and over she'd struggled and fought to recall the time she'd spent with him, after he'd abducted her in the dead of night so long ago. She'd even tried hypnosis, but it hadn't worked. Nothing had. He'd robbed her of memories she sensed might be some of the best of her life. Damn him for that.

"Ms. Jones? Stormy?"

Turning slowly, she met Melina's far too curious brown eyes. "The ring is the reason you want to hire us?"

"Yes. What's your connection to it?"

Stormy frowned. "I don't know what you mean. I have no connection to it."

"You certainly had a strong reaction to it."

She shook her head. "I had a head injury a long time ago. Occasional blackouts are a side effect."

"Speaking in tongues is a side effect, as well?"

"It's gibberish. It doesn't mean anything. Look, the condition of my skull is really not the issue here. Are you going to tell me what this job entails or not?"

Melina looked at her, pursed her lips and lowered her voice. "I want you to steal it," she whispered.

* * *

Stormy wasn't sure what she had said as she had made a hasty exit from the museum. She thought she had told Melina Roscova to do something anatomically impossible, and then she'd left. She hadn't stopped until she'd pulled up in front of the Royal Arms Hotel, where she handed her car keys and a ten-spot to a valet.

"Be careful with her," she told him. "She's special."

He promised he would be, and she watched him as he drove her shiny black Nissan, with the customized plates that read Bella-Donna into the parking garage across the street. As he moved into the darkness, she heard tires squeal and winced. "One scratch, pal. You bring Belladonna back with one scratch…"

"Madam?"

She turned to see a doorman with a question in his eyes. "You're going inside?" he asked.

"You tell that moron when he gets back that if he scratched my car, I'll take it out of his hide. And it's *mademoiselle*. Not every thirtysomething female is married, you know."

"Of course, *mademoiselle*." He opened the door, his face betraying no hint of emotion. It would have been much more satisfying if he'd been defensive or hostile or even apologetic. But…nothing.

She headed straight for her room and started a bath running, intending to phone Max and fill her in from the tub. She was upset. She was shaken. She was damned scared of what the sight of that ring had done to her.

She'd spoken in Romanian. And she knew exactly what she'd said, even though she didn't speak a word of the language and never had.

The ring belongs to me.

Elisabeta. It had to have been *her* voice.

Sixteen years ago, she'd begun having these symptoms. Blacking out, speaking in a strange language, becoming violent, attacking even her best friends and, usually, remembering nothing. It was as if she were possessed by an alien soul, as if her body were a marionette with some stranger pulling the strings.

Max said her eyes changed color, turned from their normal baby blue to a dark, fathomless ebony, during those episodes.

Through hypnosis, she'd learned the intruder's name. Elisabeta. And she knew, in her gut, that the woman had some connection to Vlad. An intimate one.

Vlad had been under attack, had taken her hostage to aid in his escape. Even then, she'd been drawn to him. His muscled, powerful body. His long, raven's wing hair. His eyes—the intensity in them when he looked at her. She remembered kissing him as if there were no tomorrow. Or maybe that had never happened; maybe that was fantasy. A delicious erotic fantasy that left her with a deep ache in her loins and her soul. She remembered hoping he could help her solve the mystery of who Elisabeta was and why she was haunting Stormy. Trying to take over. And maybe he had. But though, upon her return, Max had told her that she had been Vlad's captive for than a week, Stormy remembered nothing.

She only knew that since her return, she'd felt almost no sign of that intruding soul's presence. And she'd determined that it was Vlad's nearness that stirred the *other* to life. As it would stir any woman.

She was still there, though. Stormy had never doubted it. Hoped she was wrong, but never truly doubted. Elisabeta, whoever she was, still lurked inside her, waiting…for something.

Stormy stopped pacing and held her head in her hands as she stared into the mirror that was mounted on one of the lush hotel room's antique replica dressers. "Dammit to hell, I hoped you were gone," she whispered. "I honest to goodness was beginning to let myself believe you were never coming back. Not a peep out of you in sixteen years. And now you're back? Why? Will I ever be rid of you, Elisabeta?"

A tapping on her door startled her and brought her head around, and she swore under her breath. She had things to work through, and there was a nice hot bath—and maybe a few tiny bottles from the mini-bar—in her immediate future.

"Please, Ms. Jones," Melina Roscova called from the hallway. "Just give me ten minutes to explain. Ten minutes. It's all I need."

Stormy sighed, rolled her eyes and stomped into the bathroom to turn off the faucets. She pulled the plug on the steamy water with a sigh of regret, then went to yank the door open. She didn't wait for Melina to come inside, just turned and paced to the small table at the room's far end, yanked out a chair and nodded toward it.

"We are *investigators*," she told her unwelcome guest, her tone clipped as she bent to the mini-bar and yanked out a can of ginger ale and a tiny bottle of Black Velvet. She popped the tops on both and poured them into a tall glass that sat beside an empty ice bucket. "Not thieves for hire. We don't break the law, Ms. Roscova. Not for any price."

"Call me Melina," the woman said as she sat down. "And all I want you to do is listen to what I have to say. That ring…it has powers."

"Powers." Stormy said it deadpan, dryly, without a hint of inflection. Then she took a big slug of the BV-and-ginger.

"Yes. Powers that could, in the wrong hands, upset the supernatural order—perhaps irrevocably."

"The *super*natural order?"

"Yes. Look, this is very simple. Just…just let me make my pitch, promise me it will remain confidential, and then, if you still refuse, I won't bother you again."

Stormy downed half the drink and sat down. "And my word that this will remain confidential is going to be enough for you?"

"Yes."

"Why?"

Melina blinked, and it seemed to Stormy she chose to answer honestly and directly. "Because my organization has been observing yours for years. We know you never break your word. And we know you've kept far bigger secrets than ours."

Another big sip. The glass was getting low, and she was going to need a refill. Seven Canadian bucks a pop for the BV. And worth it, right about now. "Your…organization?"

"The Sisterhood of Athena has existed for centuries," Melina said. She spoke slowly, carefully, and seemed to be giving each sentence a great deal of thought before uttering it. "We are a group of women devoted to observing and preserving the supernatural order." She licked her lips. "Actually, it's the natural order, but our focus is the part of it that most people refer to as supernatural. Things are supposed to be the way they are supposed to be. Humans tend to want to interfere. We don't, unless it's to prevent that interference."

Stormy lifted her brows. "Humans, huh?" She eyed the woman. "You say that as if there are non-humans running around, as well."

"We both know there are."

They both fell silent, staring at each other as Stormy tried to size Melina up. Could she truly know about the existence of the Undead?

Finally, Stormy cleared her throat. "This is sounding awfully familiar, Melina. And not in a good way. You ever hear of a little government agency known as DPI?"

"We're nothing like the Division of Paranormal Investigations, Stormy. I promise you that. And we're privately funded, not a government agency." She licked her lips. "We protect the supernatural world. We don't seek to destroy it or experiment on it the way the DPI did. We are guardians of the unknown."

Stormy nodded. "And why do you want the ring?"

"Strictly to keep it from falling into the wrong hands and being used for evil."

"And I'm supposed to take your word for this? And then, based on nothing more than that, break into a museum and steal a priceless piece of jewelry?"

"Yes." Melina lowered her head. "I'm sorry I can't tell you more, but the more people who know of this ring's powers, the more dangerous it becomes."

Stormy sighed. "I'm sorry. Look, I just can't do this. And even if I wanted to, Max and Lou would never go along with it."

Melina nodded sadly. "All right. I guess…we'll just have to find another way."

"You do that. Good night, then, Melina. And… good luck. I guess."

"Good night, Stormy." She got up and saw herself out of the hotel room. Stormy followed just long enough to lock the door. Then she restarted the bath and refilled her glass.

* * *

Vlad reread the piece in the *Easton Press* four times before he could believe it wasn't only a figment of his imagination. It was a tiny piece, a two-inch column tossed in to fill space, about a new exhibit of artifacts found in Turkey, currently on display at a museum in Canada. *The most exceptional of the artifacts is a large ruby ring with rearing stallions engraved on either side of the flawless, 20 karat gemstone.*

That was the line that had caught his attention. The one he kept reading, over and over again, until his eyes watered.

"It can't be...." he whispered.

But it could. Surely it could. There was no reason to doubt that this might be the ring he'd placed on his bride's finger centuries ago. And yet, he didn't *want to* believe it. Belief led to hope, and hope led to grief and loss. He wasn't certain he could stand any more of those.

He didn't suppose he'd done a very good job of avoiding them, all these years, though. He'd tried, but dammit, he couldn't let her go. It wasn't in him. She had a hold on him as powerful as any thrall he'd ever cast over a mortal.

Vampires didn't dream; their sleep was like death. But Dracula dreamed. Of *her*. Tempest...or Elisabeta or…hell, the two were so entwined and confused in his mind, he didn't know how to distinguish his feelings for one from his feelings for the other. He didn't know how to distinguish them.

He'd purchased a tiny peninsula on the coast of Maine, used his powers to disguise the place. A passer-by would see only mist and fog and forest. Not a towering mansion built to his specifications. It was twenty miles from Easton, where Tempest, who insisted on calling herself "Stormy," lived with her friends, Maxine and Lou, in a mansion of their own.

He'd kept track of her, all these years. He'd watched her, but from a distance. Never getting too close. Never touching her or letting his presence be known. But he knew. He knew everything she did. He knew about the vampires who shared the mansion with the mortals and helped them in their investigations—Morgan de Silva and Dante, who'd been sired by Sarafina, who'd been sired by Bartrone. The vampiress Morgan was the mortal Maxine's twin sister, and though the two hadn't been raised together, they were close now.

He knew about Tempest's family—her parents, retired now and living in a condominium in Florida. She visited twice a year, no matter what. He knew about her relationships with men—though it killed him to know. She saw men sometimes. Dated. And every time it filled him with a rage that he found nearly impossible to contain.

He was dangerous at those times. And when the anger got beyond his endurance, he would force himself to go away for a time. It was the only way to prevent himself from murdering every bastard who laid his hands on her, and possibly her with them.

Nothing ever came of any of her liaisons. He never sensed her falling in love, feeling the kinds of things he liked to think she had felt with him.

He knew *everything* about her. Everything she did, everything she loved. And he knew her time was short. The deadline was approaching rapidly, the one those magicians had included in their spells. It had been driving him to desperation as it drew ever nearer. The so called Red Star of Destiny was due to eclipse Venus in a mere five days. And when it did, Elisabeta would cross to the other side, along with Tempest. He would lose them both. God, he couldn't bear the thought!

Although, in every practical way, he'd lost them both already. Unless…

Tempest wasn't in residence at the mansion now. She and her partners had taken off on one of their cases, and since he didn't sense any danger to them, he'd remained behind. And now he was glad he had.

He stood, brooding, at the arched windows of his parlor. The fireplace at his back was cold and dark. He didn't need it, didn't need warmth, sought no comfort, because there was nothing, really, that could grant it to him. Outside, a storm raged, the ocean dancing at its commanding touch, shuddering with the furious breaths of the angry wind. Lightning flashed, and the wind howled. He loved nights like this.

Vlad looked again at the newspaper, noting the location of the exhibit. The Canadian National Museum in Edmunston. Less than 200 miles away.

He could be there in four hours by car. Less, if he drove quickly.

But he was Dracula, and had far more efficient ways to travel. He pulled on his coat. It was long and leather, with a caped back, and in keeping with his mood, it was black.

He reached to the windows' center clasp, turned it and pushed the panes outward. Then he whirled, faster and faster. Like a cyclone he spun, as he focused his mind and altered the shape of his body.

When he soared into the night, into the storm,

it was in the form of a giant black raven. He would find out soon enough whether the ring on display in Canada was his ring.

Her ring.

Stormy didn't know what the hell to do. She did know one thing. She was going to have to get her hands on that ring—because if it was *the* ring, she couldn't risk anyone else possessing it. Including Melina and her precious organization. She didn't know anything about this Sisterhood of Athena, and she didn't even consider trusting them. And not Vlad. God, not him.

That ring had some kind of power over her. That ring had brought Elisabeta to the surface, allowed her to take over again. And that ring, she was more certain than ever, must have been the one he had referred to in the tiny bit of memory that had resurfaced in her mind.

If he learned the ring was here, he would come for it. Nothing would stop him, if that was his goal. And God only knew what he would do with it once he had it. Use it, perhaps, to bring his precious Elisabeta back to screaming, bitching life inside her? She couldn't go back to that. Not again. She needed to be rid of the intruder, once and for all.

She needed to destroy the ring. Maybe that would do it. If the damn ring didn't exist, then its power, whatever that power was, couldn't exist, either. So that was the answer. She had to destroy it, melt it down and smash its gemstone to dust.

But first she needed a plan. She decided not to call Max and Lou on this matter. Not just yet. First, because they were involved with another case, one that had taken them out of the country, and second, because Max was far too protective of her. And this wasn't her problem. Stormy needed to deal with this on her own, without feeling the need to justify or explain or defend her decisions to her best friend.

So she filled her glass for the third time, and she soaked in the tub, and she thought and thought about how she might go about getting the ring from the museum, not for Melina, but for herself, and how she could do it without getting caught.

She fell asleep in the tub, her empty glass on the floor beside it, her mind reeling with scenes from the classic old movie *It Takes a Thief* and trying to ignore the other images that plagued her. Images of Vlad.

And then—in her dreams—it came. A memory.

* * *

Vlad had sent her to bed in the tiny cabin of the sailboat he'd used to make his escape after abducting her.
He'd told her that they would reach his place on the Barrier Islands soon.

They must be there by now, she thought as she woke,
and she wondered if she might be in his home already,
because she didn't feel the gentle rocking and swaying of
the sea beneath her. But it was pitch dark in this bedroom—too dark to tell where she was.

She rolled to one side, began to reach out in search
of a lamp or something, but her hand hit a solid wall.
Odd. They must not be in the boat anymore, because
that wall was farther away from the bed than this. She
ran her palm along the smooth wall and frowned. It was
lined in fabric. Something as smooth as satin.

Blinking and puzzled, she moved her hand downward, then upward, only to find another smooth, satin-
lined wall behind her head.

Something clutched in her belly, and she rolled quickly
to the other side, thrusting both hands out, only to hit
another wall. She was closed in tight on three sides, and
a terrifying suspicion was taking root in her mind. Her
breath coming faster now, her heart pounding, she
pressed her palms upward. They moved only inches before hitting a satin lined ceiling.

I'm in a coffin! *she screamed inwardly.* I'm trapped in a tiny box and God only knows what else! I'll suffocate!

Panic twisted through her body like a python on crack, and she clenched her hands into fists and pounded on the ceiling, bent her legs as far as the space would allow and kicked at the bottom and sides. She shouted at the top of her lungs. "Let me out. Open this Goddamn box right now and get me the hell out!"

To her surprise, her pounding resulted in the ceiling above her rising with every strike, and she realized belatedly that, while she might be in a box, she wasn't locked in.

The lid gave when she pushed it, and she'd barely had time to process that fact when it opened all the way, as if on its own.

She could see at last, and what she saw was the man himself standing there, staring down at her. He looked harried, tired. His white shirt's top three buttons were undone, and his hair was loose and long.

Then he was reaching for her.

She slapped his hands away and, gripping the sides of the box, pulled herself up into a sitting position, swung her legs over the side, narrowly missing him on the way, and jumped to the floor. She gave a full body shudder, then snapped her arms around her own body, tucked her chin and closed her eyes.

He touched her shoulders. Her body reacted with heat and hunger, but she fought to ignore those things. "I'm sorry, Tempest. I fully intended to have you out of there by the time you woke, but I—"

She punched him. Hard. Straight to the solar plexus. It gave her a rush of satisfaction to hear his grunt, and when she opened her eyes and saw him stagger backward a few paces, it felt even better.

"Bastard."

"Tempest, if you'd let me explain—"

"How dare you? How dare you stick me in some fucking box like that? And why, for God's sake? What the hell were you thinking?" She drew back a fist and advanced on him, fully intending to deck him again, right between the eyes this time.

He had her by the forearms before she could swing, so she kicked him in the shin. He yelped but didn't release her.

"You know, that's what I like best about you freakin' vamps. You feel pain so much more than humans do."

"Enough!"

He shouted it, using the full power of his voice—or she guessed it was full power, but maybe not, maybe he had a lot more he wasn't tapping into just yet. But either way, the sound was deep and as potent as if her head were inside a giant bell. It rang in her ears, split her head and temporarily deafened her.

She pressed her hands to her ears and closed her eyes until the reverberations stopped bouncing around her brain. Then, slowly, she lowered her hands, opened her eyes, lifted her head. He was still standing there in front of her, staring hard, anger glinting in his jet black eyes.

"I've told you, I'm sorry about the coffin. It was the only way."

She narrowed her eyes on him, about to cut lose with another stream of insults, accusations and possibly profanity, but then she caught a glimpse of the space beyond him, and she was shocked into silence.

Stone walls climbed to towering vaulted ceilings. Inverted domes housed crystal chandeliers. Sconces in the walls looked as if they could hold actual torches. The windows were huge, arched at the top, with thick glass panes so old the night beyond them appeared distorted. Sheet-draped shapes were the only furniture in the place. And a wide curving staircase wound upward and out of sight.

"This is…your place?" She swallowed hard as she took in the dust and cobwebs; then, turning slowly, she started a little at the sight of the two coffins lying side by side, both of them open. "Doesn't look as if anyone's used it in a while."

"It's been a long time since anyone has lived here, yes."

Blinking, she went to the nearest window, passing a double fireplace that took up most of one wall on the way. Wiping the dust from the glass with her palm, she stared outside.

The impression was of sheer height and rugged, barren rock. The moon hung low in the sky, nearly full and milky white. It spilled its light over cliffs, harsh outcroppings of rock and boulders jutting upward from far, far below. Beyond the cliffs, she could see grassy hills and valleys. But around this place, there was none of that. It was dark. It was bereft. Even the few pathetic trees that clung for their lives to the steep cliff-sides were scrawny and dead looking.

Stormy swallowed the dryness in her throat—she could barely do it. She was dehydrated, thirsty, starving and a little bit scared. This didn't look like any island off North Carolina.

"Where the hell are we, Vlad?"

2

Vlad kept his distance from the others who were visiting the museum. Mortals. Tourists. Groups of children being led about by young tour guides. He slipped into the Anatolian exhibit, which was housed in a room all its own, and stared at the ring in its glass case. Memories came flooding into his mind, into his soul, but he drove them back. It wasn't easy. He recalled taking the precious gem from his little finger and slipping it onto Elisabeta's forefinger, the only one it came close to fitting. He remembered how, within an hour, she'd wound it around with twine, to make it fit more snugly, and how seeing it on her made him feel proud and protective. It was large and strong and powerful on her small, delicate hand. It seemed to denote his claim to her. It seemed to mark her as his own.

"Sir? Excuse me, sir?" a woman asked.

Vlad blinked the memories away and turned to face the uniformed woman who had approached him. He hadn't even been aware of her presence, much less of how much time had passed while he'd stood there staring at the ring.

"The museum is closing sir. You'll have to leave now."

"Ahh. Yes, of course."

She left him alone, and he turned again to the ring. It was the one. He'd found it at last. And yes, he would leave the museum—for now. But no power on earth would keep that ring from him.

He closed his eyes, turned and left the museum, but as soon as he stepped out into the fresh air of the night, he sensed something else, something he had not expected.

"Tempest," he whispered. And he turned slowly, scenting the air, feeling for her energy, certain she was close.

And she was. He began to move, barely looking, drawn by the feel of her. Like following the trail left by a comet's tail, he homed in on her warmth, her light, the sparkling energy that was hers alone.

He wouldn't get too close. He couldn't, not without running the risk of her knowing. In all these years, all this time, he hadn't come close to her, despite the temptation he could barely resist. And as long as he'd kept his distance, Elisabeta had slept. She'd been dormant, deep inside Tempest. Somewhere. He knew she hadn't left this plane. She hadn't died or moved on. She was still there. He felt her there. But she hadn't stirred.

As long as he stayed away from Tempest, he thought, she wouldn't. It was easier on Beta that way, or he hoped it was. Let her rest and bide her time. But time—God, time was running out for both of them. And now that he'd found the ring, he almost didn't dare to hope there could be a chance. Yet he couldn't help but hope.

So he followed her trail as her presence hummed in his blood, stroked his senses like a bow over the strings of a violin, until his longing for her vibrated into a pure, demanding tone. It was more powerful now, he realized as he drew closer, than it had been before. Even harder to resist, perhaps because he was allowing himself to move closer to her than he had in sixteen years. It drew him, drove him, until he stood on the sidewalk beside a hotel, staring up at the room where every sense told him she was.

God, it was all he could do not to climb the wall and go to her.

Always before, he'd been prepared to resist his own urges. Always before, he'd had time to steel himself before getting within range of her energy. But this had been entirely unexpected. He hadn't come here for this, for her. He'd come for the ring. His plans beyond that were uncertain. Without the scroll, the ring was useless.

Why was Tempest here? Had she come for the ring, as well? Why? How could she know?

He couldn't let her obtain it, if that was her goal. For her to possess it would be far too dangerous.

As he stood there, staring up at the room, Tempest stepped out onto the balcony, leaned on the railing and gazed out into the night.

He couldn't take his eyes from her. And his preternatural vision didn't fail him. He managed to drink in every detail of her face in a way he hadn't been close enough to do in far, far too long.

The blush of youth had faded from the body of the woman in which his love lay sleeping. In its place were the angles of a female in the prime of her life. Her face was thinner, her eyes harder, than they had been before. Her hair was still blond but not as pale; still short but less severe. Its softness framed her face and moved with every touch of the breeze. She still bore a striking resemblance to Elisabeta, her ancestor. He longed to bury his fingers in those sunlight-and-honey strands, to bury himself inside her; to feel her shiver under the power of his touch.

She wanted him.

God, he could feel her wanting him. Yearning for him. And she knew he was close. She sensed him, perhaps not as powerfully and clearly as he sensed her, but it was there. And consciously or not, she was calling out to him. She wanted him still.

He had to school himself to patience. He had to know why she was here, what she was doing. He'd waited sixteen years to be with her again—more than five hundred before that. Surely he could wait one more night. But not much more than that.

He was hungry. He needed sustenance, blood to satisfy his body and perhaps calm the raging desire in his veins. To keep himself from going to her, for just a little while longer. And then, in the early hours just before dawn, he would go after the ring.

And that was precisely what he did. But when he got to the museum, it was to find the window broken, the alarms shrieking, sirens blaring and the ring...

Gone.

* * *

Stormy woke to the insistent sun beaming through the hotel room's windows and searing through her eyelids. She rolled over in the bed and hid her face in the pillows, but the memory of her dreams woke her more thoroughly than the sun ever could have.

She'd dreamed about Vlad.

But she hadn't dreamed about the two of them making love—which was odd, because she'd dreamed of *that* many times over the past sixteen years, never sure whether it had actually happened, or if it was just part of her senseless yearning for him. Or something more sinister—perhaps the longing of her intruder or one of *her* memories.

No. This dream had been more like a memory. Until the end. Then it had become a vision. He'd been standing there on the shores of Endover, where she had first met him. His castle-like mansion hovered on its secret island behind him, and the sea was raging in between. He'd been just standing there, staring at her.

Wanting her.

Calling to her.

The wind had been whipping through his long dark hair, and she'd remembered—yes, remembered!—the way it felt to run her fingers through it.

His chest had been bare, probably because, in her mind, that was the way she preferred to remember him. His chest. Next to his eyes, and that hair, and his mouth, it was her favorite part of him. She'd touched that chest in her dreams. She'd run her hands over it and over his belly. Had it ever been real?

It felt real. More real than anything else in her life.

She rolled onto her back and pressed her hands to her face. "God," she moaned. "Am I ever going to get over him?"

But she already knew the answer. If she hadn't been able to forget Dracula in sixteen years, it wasn't likely to happen anytime soon. He had a hold on her. Maybe it was deliberate. Maybe it was him messing with her mind, refusing to let her forget him, even while making her forget the details of their time together. Or maybe it was because of that other soul that lurked inside her. Because, though it had been dormant for a long time, Stormy knew that *the other* was still there. And if she'd begun to doubt it, Elisabeta's recent appearance had driven the truth home. She lived still.

But was that why she couldn't forget Vlad? Or was it just because he was the only man who had ever made her feel…desperate for him. Hungry for him. Certain no one else would ever suffice.

And no one else ever had. Or ever would. She couldn't even climax with another man.

He certainly hadn't had the same issues, though, had he? He'd never made contact, not once in sixteen years. And it hurt, far more than it should. Some days she convinced herself it was because he truly *did* care about her. That he was keeping away to protect her from the inner turmoil Elisabeta would cause if he did otherwise. But most of the time she believed the more likely reason. It was, after all, Elisabeta, not Stormy, he loved. And since he couldn't have her, he couldn't be bothered with Stormy at all.

She closed her eyes, and revisited, mentally, the initial parts of her dream—and knew it had been a memory. A snippet of the weeks Vlad had erased from her mind. He'd taken her to Romania, not North Carolina, smuggled her there inside a casket. She'd awakened in his castle, furious with him.

But why? What had happened there? Why had he let her go? God, why had he ever let her go?

Groaning, Stormy dragged herself out of bed, shuffled across the room and kicked the clothes she didn't remember wearing out of her path. She went to the door and hoped, for the hotel staff's sake, that her standing order had been delivered on time.

It had. Outside the door was a rolling service tray, with a silver pot full of piping hot coffee and a plate with several pastries beside it. There were a cup, a pitcher of cream, and a container with sugar and other sweeteners in colorful packets. Beside all of that was a neatly folded—and hot of the presses, by the smell of the ink—issue of the daily newspaper.

Her order had been filled to perfection—assuming the coffee was any good—and delivered on time. She'd specified this be brought to her room every morning of her stay between 7:30 and 8:00 a.m., and that it be left outside her door so that her sleep wouldn't be disturbed.

Yeah, she was a pain in the ass as a hotel guest. But given what they charged for rooms these days, they ought to throw in a little extra service, the way she saw it. Not that they were throwing it in, exactly. She would be billed, she had no doubt. But the agency was thriving, so what the hell?

She wheeled the cart into her room, filled the cup with coffee and snagged a cheese and cherry Danish. It wasn't Dunkin' Donuts, but it was the closest she could get at the moment. Then she sat down to enjoy her breakfast and unfolded the newspaper.

The banner headline hit her between the eyes like a fist.

BOLD BREAK-IN AT NATIONAL MUSEUM—PRICELESS ARTIFACT STOLEN.

"No," she whispered. But she already knew, even before she read the piece, what had been taken. The hole in the pit of her stomach told her in no uncertain terms.

And her stomach was right.

According to the article, the burglary had been a graceless smash-and-grab. Someone had kicked in the window of the room where the ring was on display, so they clearly knew right where it was. They had set off every alarm in the place but were back out the window and gone before the security guards even made it into the room.

It didn't seem a likely M.O. for Melina Roscova. Stormy would have expected more grace, more finesse, from a woman like that. But who else would want the ring?

The answer came before she had time to blink. Vlad. That was who.

She'd dreamed of him last night. Had it been coincidence? Or had it been his real nearness making his image appear in her mind?

Did he have the ring? Just what kind of power did that thing have?

She shivered and knew that whatever it was, it

frightened her. But she shook away the fear and squared her shoulders.

"One way to find out," she muttered. She finished the Danish, slugged down the coffee, and headed for the shower for a record-breaking lather and rinse, head to toe. But halfway through, she stopped. Because…damn, hadn't she fallen asleep in the bath last night? Why the hell didn't she remember getting out of the tub and into bed?

She frowned as she toweled down and yanked on a pair of jeans and a black baby T-shirt with a bad-ass fairy on the front above the words Trust Me.

"I must have been more tired than I thought," she muttered. "It'll come back to me."

Telling herself she believed that, she slapped a handful of mousse into her hair and gave it three passes with the blow dryer. "And that," she told her reflection, "is why I love short hair."

She stuffed her feet into purple ankle socks, and her green and teal Nike Shocks, then grabbed a denim jacket and her bag—a mini-backpack—on the way to the door. There she paused before going back to grab her travel mug off the night stand. She filled it from the coffee pot, snatched two more pastries and the business card Melina had left her the night before, then headed out the door.

She moved through the hotel's revolving doors and turned to tell one of the uniformed men who stood there to go get her car, but Belladonna was already there, waiting. She was parked neatly just beyond the curved strip of pavement in front of the hotel's doors, along the roadside. Had she called down last night and arranged for the car to be there, then forgotten doing it? That didn't seem likely, but between the drinks she'd had last night and the stress of being in the same city with that ring, much less Vlad, she supposed it was possible.

And that was as far as she allowed that train of thought to travel. She would deal with the burglary now. Just focus on that. The intricate and tangled web of her mind and her memory would only distract her. She had to see Melina Roscova. Because she had to find out what had happened to that ring.

My ring, a little voice whispered deep inside her mind.

It wasn't Stormy's voice.

It was a four-hour drive to Athena House, or would have been if she hadn't gotten lost on the way, and stopped for lunch to boot. Stormy inched Belladonna's shiny black nose into the first part of the driveway and stopped at the arched, wrought-iron gate that had the word ATHENA spelled out in its scroll work. The gate was closed, but there was a speaker mounted on one of the columns that flanked her on either side.

She got out of the car and headed for the speaker. The big iron gate hung between two towering columns of rust-colored stone blocks. The entire place was surrounded by a ten-foot wall of those same hand hewn stones, and beyond the gate, Stormy could see that the house was built of them, as well.

Giant stone owls carved of glittering, snow-white granite perched on top of each column, standing like black eyed sentries to guard the place. Those glinting onyx eyes gave Stormy a shiver. Too much like Elisabeta's eyes, she supposed. And the notion of them sparkling from her own face, the way witnesses had said they did, sent a brief wave of nausea washing through her.

A speaker with a button marked Talk was mounted to the front of the left stone column. Stormy poked the button. "Stormy Jones, from SIS, here to see Melina Roscova."

"Welcome," a feminine voice said. "Please, come in."

The gate and swung slowly open. Stormy went back to the car, sat down on her black seat covers with the red Japanese dragons on them, which matched the floor mats and the steering wheel cover, and waited until the gate had opened fully. Then she drove slowly through and followed the driveway, which looped around a big fountain and back on itself again. She stopped near the mansion's front entrance and shut the car off. Then, stiffening her spine and hoping to God that Melina would admit to having stolen the ring herself, she got out and went up the broad stone steps to a pair of massive, darkly stained doors that looked as if they belonged on a castle, right down to the black iron hinge plates and knobs, and the knocker, which was held in the talons of yet another white owl.

The doors opened before she could knock, and Melina stood there smiling at her. "I know we didn't discuss a fee before, but I'll pay whatever you ask. I'm just so glad you changed your mind."

She continued babbling as Stormy's stomach churned, and she led the way through the house's magnificent foyer into a broad and echoing hallway, and along it into a library. As they walked through the place, they passed other women, all busy but curious. All between twenty and fifty, Stormy thought, taking them in with a quick sweep of her well trained eyes. All attractive and fit. *Really* fit.

"You certainly work fast once you make up your mind," Melina said, as she closed the library doors, and waved Stormy toward a leather chair. "Did you bring it?"

Stormy walked to the chair but didn't sit. Instead, she turned to face Melina, her back to the chair, and asked as calmly as she could manage, "Did I bring what?"

Melina's smile showed the first sign of faltering. "The ring, of course."

Disappointment dealt her a crushing blow. So much so that Stormy sat down heavily in the chair behind her and lowered her head. Dammit, she'd been hoping, but she didn't think Melina was acting. She drew a breath. "I don't have the ring, Melina."

"Well, what did you do with it?"

"Nothing." She forced herself to lift her head, to face the woman, who was, even then, sinking into a chair of her own, looking as deflated as Stormy felt. "So it's safe to say *you* didn't break into the museum and steal it last night," Stormy said.

"I didn't." Melina closed her eyes briefly. "I assumed you had. Figured you'd had a change of heart or…something."

"I didn't," Stormy said, echoing Melina's own denial.

"Then that means—"

"It means someone else has the ring," Stormy said.

Melina rose slowly, walked to a cabinet and opened it, then poured herself three fingers worth of vodka. Stolichanya. Good shit. She downed it, then turned and held the bottle up.

"No, thanks. I'm driving."

"Not for a while, I hope."

"No? Why wouldn't I be?"

Melina grabbed another glass and poured, then refilled her own. She capped the bottle and put it away, then walked across the room to hand the clean glass to Stormy. "Because I need your help. Now more than ever, Stormy. You have to agree to take the job."

"The job was to steal the ring," Stormy said. "Someone's already done that."

"Yes. And now the job is to find out who has it and take it from them. Before it's too late."

Stormy was pretty sure she knew who had the ring. And she didn't look forward to going up against him, although it seemed she wasn't going to have a choice about that. Maybe with the money and resources of this Sisterhood behind her, she would have an edge. A shot, at least. God knew she couldn't let Vlad decide what to do with the ring.

She didn't know what sort of power the thing possessed, but she sensed, right to her core, that whatever it was, it might very well destroy her.

Melina sighed. "I have to let my Firsts know what's happened, so we can begin the search."

"Your Firsts?"

"My...lieutenants, for want of a better term. Not to mention my superiors." As she said that, she lowered her head and wiped what might have been a bead of sweat from her forehead. "Stay for dinner. As soon as I have things squared away, I'll tell you everything I know about the ring. Everything, Stormy. Although..."

Stormy lifted her brows, and when Melina didn't finish, she prompted her. "Although?"

Melina shrugged. "I get the feeling you already know as much as I do," she said softly. "Why is that, Stormy?"

Stormy shrugged. "I never set eyes on that ring until yesterday, Melina. I think your imagination is working overtime."

Melina studied her for a long moment, then seemed to accept her words with a nod. "Will you help me?"

"You keep your word and tell me all you know— and I mean everything, Melina—and I'll do my best to find and...*acquire* the ring."

Melina smiled. "Thank you, Stormy. Thank you so much." She clasped Stormy's hands briefly.

Stormy felt a little guilty accepting such senseless gratitude from the woman. After all, she hadn't said anything about giving the ring to her. And she didn't intend to.

When the sun went down, Vlad rose from the crypt where he'd spent the day. The crushing devastation that returned the moment his mind cleared of the day sleep was nearly enough to send him sinking to his knees. But he fought it. All was not lost. It couldn't be.

To be so close—so close to having the ring—and then to lose it that way…

He could only reach one conclusion. Tempest. She must have the ring. She had come for it, just as he had. And she'd beaten him to the theft.

So there was still a chance. He need only find her and—

She's gone.

The knowledge seeped into his mind, as real and as palpable as air seeping into a mortal's lungs. Tempest had left the city.

No matter. There was nowhere on earth the woman could go where he would be unable to follow. To find her. To feel his way to her. She would never escape him.

So he followed the trail she had left. A trail of her essence, woven with her yearning for him. And he found her.

She was behind the walls of a mansion, beyond a stone barrier and an iron gate marked by the word ATHENA.

He recognized the place for what it was—it wasn't the first he'd seen—a base for the Sisterhood of Athena.

They were involved with Tempest? With the ring? By the gods, how? Why? Why would Tempest entangle herself with the likes of them?

Vlad planted himself outside the tall stone wall that surrounded the place, though he could easily have leapt it. He didn't need to. His power over Tempest was strong enough that he could crawl inside her mind, see everything she saw, hear everything she heard. He could *feel* her thoughts.

And damn the repercussions. She'd stolen the ring and…what? Brought it to these meddling mortals? How dare she betray him that way?

No, he would do whatever was necessary to get to the bottom of this, to find the ring and get it back. So he made himself comfortable in the darkness beyond the walls of the mansion, and he slid as carefully as he could into his woman's mind.

3

Dinner was late at Athena House, but well worth the wait: a tender glazed pork loin with baby carrots and new potatoes. Enough side dishes to satisfy anyone, and the promise of dessert later on.

As she ate, Stormy tried to match the names she'd been given to the faces around her, but she determined she would never keep them all straight. There were three she knew for sure. Melina, of course. Then there was Melina's apparent right-hand woman, Brooke, with sleek, shoulder length red hair parted on one side, as straight as if it were wet. She looked as if she'd stepped off the set of a Robert Palmer video and was so thin Stormy wondered if she ever ate anything at all. She wore a tweed skirt that hugged her from hips to knees, with a buttoned-up ivory silk blouse. And third was Lupe, a shapely Latina who reminded Stormy of

Rosie Perez every time she opened her mouth. She was five-two, way shorter than her two cohorts, and curvy as hell. She had full, lush lips and copper-toned skin. Her hair was longer than Brooke's, jet back, and curled as if it had been left out in a windstorm, and her brown eyes were like melted milk chocolate. She wore designer jeans and a chenille sweater that had probably cost more than Stormy's entire wardrobe.

Those three she remembered. And those three were the ones who went with her into the library when the meal had ended. And yes, Stormy thought, Brooke *had* eaten—about enough to feed a baby bird.

A fourth woman brought a china tray with matching coffee pot, cups, cream pitcher and sugar bowl into the room, set it down and left without a word.

"This place is…odd," Stormy said.

"Is it?" Melina poured coffee into four cups, took one and sat down. She took it with cream, no sugar, Stormy noticed. Smooth but strong.

"It feels like a cross between an army barracks and a convent."

"Because that's what it is," Lupe said with a grin and a combination Spanish-Brooklyn accent. She took her own cup, added four spoons full of sugar and sat back. Hot and sweet, but dark, Stormy thought.

She eyed the room. It was large, a towering ceiling and four walls lined with books and bound manuscripts, many of which seemed very old. The scents of old paper and leather permeated the place. At the farthest end of the room there was a table that stood about desk height. It might have *been* a desk, for all Stormy could tell, since it was hidden under a purple satin cloth. Antique pewter candle holders with glowing tapers stood on top, to either side of an aged leather book.

Stormy eyed the book, watching only from the corner of her eye as Brooke took her own cup of coffee, adding nothing to it at all. Dark and bitter.

She took her own with just enough cream to mask the bite, and just enough sugar to lull her into forgetting that caffeine could kick her ass. She smiled a little as she fixed it and thought that you could tell a lot about a person by the way they took their coffee.

Melina said, "We first learned of the ring in 1516, when a member of the Sisterhood acquired the journal of an alleged mage who'd lived a century earlier."

"The Sisterhood of Athena is that old?" Stormy asked.

"Older." Melina watched her staring at the book.

"So this is the one? The old journal?" Stormy asked, stepping toward the book on the table.

"Yes."

She set her coffee cup down and moved closer, then reached for the book, only to pause when Brooke put a surprisingly chilly hand over hers. "It's very delicate. Be careful."

"Like she's planning to rip off the cover?" Lupe asked with a toss of her head. "Give it a rest, Brookie."

There was no question, the nickname was not a term of endearment.

Stormy looked from one woman to the other. They were opposites and maybe equals. There was tension there. But that wasn't her problem. She steadied herself and touched the book with great care, opening its leather cover and staring down at the brittle, yellowed pages within.

Words flowed across the pages in some foreign script, where words were even visible. Many had faded to mere shadows. She wanted to turn the page, but didn't dare, for fear it might disintegrate at her touch.

"It's not in English." After she said it, she realized she had stated the obvious.

"No," Melina said. "Many pages are missing or

only partly there. Many more cannot be read, but we've translated those that can. It's written in a long-forgotten language, so some of the translations are piecemeal or educated guesses. But the journal does speak of 'The Ring of the Impaler.'"

Stormy nodded. She didn't bother trying to feign surprise. She'd never been a good actress. "Meaning *Vlad* the Impaler, aka Dracula."

"That's the conclusion we've reached, yes. The timing would have been right, and since it was found in Turkey, and the Turks were at war with the Romanians during Vlad's reign, it makes sense."

Stormy felt herself shiver. This *was* the ring Vlad had referred to sixteen years ago in the words that had so recently echoed in her head. If there had been any doubt, it was gone now. It was the ring he'd been seeking for more than five centuries. She forced herself to retrieve her coffee, to sip it slowly and not tremble visibly.

"And this journal…it says something about the ring?" she asked.

Melina moved past her to the aged book and opened it to a section marked with a blood red ribbon. "This is the reference," she said. "If you prefer, you can copy it out and take it to your own translator. But I can assure you, you won't find a more accurate interpretation than ours. We use only the best linguists for this sort of thing."

"I believe you," Stormy said. "But if it's all the same to you, I'd prefer to copy it. Or better yet..." She dipped into her backpack, which she'd slung over the back of her chair, and pulled out a state of the art digital camera, tiny and light and packing 8.5 megapixels. "May I?"

Melina nodded, but her face was pinched. Stormy snapped several shots of the book, including close ups of the page to show the text as clearly as possible. Then she put the camera away and turned to Melina. "So are you going to tell me what it says?"

"Of course." The other woman moved behind the large table that held the book, and confirmed Stormy's suspicion that it was actually a desk when she lifted the purple cloth and opened a drawer. She removed a notebook and an eyeglass case. Then she slid the glasses on—gold framed bifocals in their stereotypical rectangular shape. She opened the notebook and began to read.

"'At the prince's bidding, we imbued the ring with his bride's essence and created a powerful rite, which we transcribed upon a scroll. These were given to him, along with our instructions. When he finds the woman, he must place the ring upon her finger and perform the rite we created. At once the essence of the one he lost will return. Her mind, her memories, her soul, will be restored. Certain physical traits—mysteries to us but known to the prince, or so said our divinations—will return, as well. This was perhaps the greatest work of magic I have ever performed. The power of all of us together, the most accomplished mages of our time, was an awe-inspiring experience. And yet my heart remains heavy, for the work we did has a shadow side. The soul of the lost, while a part of the whole, is not the whole. For it to return, it must also displace. It is unnatural, and I fear the repercussions upon the whole, upon the innocent, and upon my own soul for my part in creating what I fear is a dire wrong. We did, however, set a way for the gods to subvert our work. A time limit, in the tried and true method of occultists from time immemorial. When the Red Star of Destiny eclipses Venus, the time of this spell will expire. And all parts of the sleeping soul—both the woman she was and her spiritual descendant— will be set free to begin anew.'"

Melina closed the book and lifted her head. She removed her glasses and folded them with care.

Stormy looked at the other faces in the room and realized this was the first time either of the other women had heard these words aloud. Brooke looked excited and intrigued, while Lupe seemed puzzled and troubled.

"So the ring has the power to bring someone back from the dead?" Lupe asked.

"Not the body," Melina told her. "Only the soul."

"Creating what? A ghost?" Lupe asked.

Stormy set her cup down. "It's a soul-transferal. The dead spirit comes into the body of a living person. It…takes over." She got a chill when she said it. "Correct?"

Melina nodded. "That's my best interpretation, yes."

"And by spiritual descendant…some sort of re-incarnation?" Stormy asked, though she thought she already knew the answer.

"But wouldn't a reincarnation already *be* the dead woman's soul?" Lupe asked.

Stormy shook her head. "Not necessarily. Some theorize that when we die, our soul returns to meld with a greater one. A higher self. All the experiences are shared, and the higher self spins a new soul from its parts. That's the reincarnation. It's part of the whole, but not the same whole that lived before. A new individual."

Lupe nodded, as if that made sense to her. Stormy

wondered how, when it had taken her sixteen years to wrap her mind around the notion. It had been explained to her by the hypnotist she'd seen in Salem, and she hadn't believed it at first. Hadn't wanted to believe that the enemy lurking within her was her spiritual ancestor. A part of her.

Now she had a whole new nightmare to wrap her mind around. Elisabeta was Vlad's bride. His wife. His dead wife, and she was already hiding in Stormy's body, waiting for the chance to take over. And the ring he had in all likelihood stolen last night could bring her back to raging life in Stormy's own body. It could give her full control.

"So the question is," she asked slowly, "what happens to the living person? The rightful owner of that body? Does she just get…booted out when Elisabeta takes over?"

Melina licked her lips. "How did you know her name was Elisabeta?"

Stormy's eyes flicked to hers quickly, then just as quickly away. "Come on. You said you've been observing my company for years. You must know vampires are an area of expertise for me."

Melina nodded but kept looking at Stormy for a beat too long. Then she sighed. "I don't know what would happen to the rightful owner of the body. But the rite spoken of in this journal could very well be a recipe for metaphysical murder."

"Not necessarily, though," Brooke said. "Some people, myself included, believe that two souls could conceivably co-exist within the same body, providing both agreed to it."

"It would be like having a split personality," Stormy said softly. "Constant conflict, fighting for control." She was speaking, of course, from personal experience. "It could never be over until one of them died."

"I disagree," Brooke said. "They could share. Perhaps even…meld, given time. Melina, does the rite say the person the soul resides in has to be a spiritual descendant?"

"No."

"It's obscene," Lupe said softly. "A slap in the face of the supernatural order, no matter how it works."

"Exactly," Melina said. "A lifetime ends when its time is over. That's the way things are supposed to be. You cannot interfere with that and think there won't be serious repercussions. And now…" She closed her eyes. "Someone has the ring."

"But what about the rite?" Stormy asked. "Is the actual rite given in the journal?"

"No," Melina said softly. And as she said it, her eyes met Brooke's very briefly, then slid away again.

"We don't even know if the rite exists anymore. It could easily have disintegrated, as so many pages in this journal have done."

"Could it be recreated?" Stormy asked.

Melina tipped her head to one side, studying Stormy a little too closely again. "Perhaps. A talented witch or sorcerer might be able to create a spell that would work. They could certainly try, with God only knows what sort of results. And no doubt there are some stupid enough or power hungry enough to want to." She shook her head in disgust. "Which is why we must get the ring out of circulation. It has to be secured. As long as it exists, there is the risk that an innocent life will be lost or altered beyond repair."

Stormy agreed. Particularly since the innocent life in question was her own. "What did that last part mean," she asked. "That part about the Red Star of whatever?"

"We don't know. We have no way of knowing what modern astronomers have named whatever star those old ones were referring to. Or if it was a star at all." Melina carried the notebook to the desk and put it into a drawer, then locked it. "That's it," she said. "That's absolutely everything we know. Brooke and Lupe, because they are second in command to me, are the only two here who know all this. And now you know it, as well." She moved across the room to Stormy. "Do you think you can find the ring and take it from whoever stole it?"

Licking her lips nervously, Stormy nodded. "I think I have to."

It had been so long. Far, far too long.

Elisabeta lived still. He sensed her, alive and aware, deep inside Tempest's consciousness. Waiting for him to rescue her.

And maybe the things he'd overheard while eavesdropping from deep within Tempest's consciousness were things that required him to take action. To see her. To speak to her. Or maybe he was only allowing himself to believe they did, because he couldn't be this close and not get a little closer. Close enough to touch.

The one called Melina—the leader of this little coven—suggested Tempest stay there at the mansion for the night, rather than driving all the way back to the city and her hotel. When Tempest agreed, he sagged in relief, because he couldn't wait much longer. He needed to go to her.

But he would have to be careful. As angry as he was that she would betray him by agreeing to help the Sisterhood of Athena steal the ring, he didn't want to traumatize her unnecessarily. He would, no doubt, be forced to do enough of that later. Soon, in fact.

He had no idea how she felt about him now. He didn't how she would react to seeing him again for the first time in sixteen years. But he could not leave without seeing her. So be it.

The bedroom to which she was shown had a minuscule balcony. Vlad stood beneath it, watching her shadow play against the curtains as she moved around the room beyond them. He tried to be patient when her movements stopped, but he didn't succeed. Instead, he leapt from the grassy lawn behind the Athena mansion, clearing the rail and landing softly on the balcony. And then he went still, listening and sensing for her in the room beyond.

The shower was running. The bedroom lights were turned off, but a sliver of illumination came from beneath the closed door of the adjoining bathroom. And so he waited there, aching, silent and bleeding inside.

Eventually the sound of flowing water stopped. He waited, still and alert, watching her as she stepped into the bedroom wearing only a towel. And then she dropped the towel to the floor, and he swore his body caught fire at the sight of her, nude and damp and beautiful still. So beautiful.

She crossed the room, tugged back the covers, settled into the bed and closed her eyes.

She was tired; he felt that in her. And then she sensed something, someone near, might even have known on some deep level that it was him, lurking in the night, hungering. But it didn't trouble her enough to keep her from sleep. And he wondered briefly why she was so exhausted.

He had to know what she was doing. He had to know why she was involved with the Sisterhood of Athena, and what she planned to do with the ring if and when she found it. He'd overheard enough to be fully aware she intended to search for it on behalf of the Sisterhood. Did she honestly intend to hand it over to them? What could have instigated such an idiotic, not to mention disloyal, act?

He waited until he was certain she slept—it didn't take long. Then he slid the glass door open and moved silently into the room, up beside her bed.

For a long moment he stood there, just experiencing her. The scent of her, familiar and arousing, filling him. The sounds of her breath, moving softly, deeply, in and out of her lungs. The sight of her. Her once purely platinum hair had new tones, honey and gold, woven through with paler highlights. It was slightly longer than before, softer. And there were lines, tiny ones, at the corners of her eyes. He wanted to touch her, taste her, and the knowledge that the blankets and sheets were the only things covering her burned in him.

But he wasn't there for those things. He was there for information. And the ring.

He lowered himself into a chair, focused on her mind and crept inside, carefully. He didn't want her aware of his intrusion, nor did he wish to rouse Elisabeta, who still lingered. His eyes fell closed as he felt her exhaustion, and then he sank into her dreams. She was on a sailboat, lying on the deck, bathed by the light of a full moon so big it lit the entire sky and the sea beneath it. It painted her in its milky light. She wore a stretch of sheer white fabric that draped from one shoulder all the way to her feet.

She was smiling up at someone. It was with a little rush of shock and pleasure that he realized it was him. He was in her dream. And he was moving closer to her, reaching out to her, telling her not to be afraid.

"I'm not afraid," she told him. "Not of you." And she tilted her head. "She can't get to me in my dreams. Did you know that?"

The real Vlad was surprised, as he watched her dream image of him react with a knowing nod. "It's the one place you're safe from her. That's why I come to you here."

Was it true? Was it real? It almost seemed as if she had dreamed of him before. Could it be true?

He had to put it to the test. Had to. He stepped out of her consciousness, so that he was looking at her lying there in the bed, rather than looking out through her eyes within her own dream.

"You will not wake. You will stay safe in the haven of your dream," he told her. "Do you understand?"

He felt her agreement, though she didn't speak aloud. He also felt her longing for him, wanting him, craving his touch. It was almost too much to resist, and yet…

"I have questions for you, Tempest."

"Yes."

He was sitting on the edge of his chair now, leaning closer to her. He couldn't stop himself from touching her, just a little. He commanded her not to wake with the power of his mind as he trailed his fingertips over her cheek.

She leaned into his touch, and she shivered a little with a rush of pure desire. So responsive to him still. Maybe even more so than she had been before.

"Tempest, why are you looking for the ring?"

"Have to find it. Said I would." She spoke the

words aloud, startling him. But she remained asleep, lost in the throes of her dream. When he started to move his hand away, her smaller hand closed over it to press it closer to her face. Then, slowly, she moved it downward, over her neck, her collarbone, underneath the blanket to her breast.

He released a shuddering breath as his palm rubbed over warm, soft skin and the stiff peak pressing into its center. Softer than before, not as firm or perky, but warm and full. He told himself to take his hand away. She arched her back, and he couldn't do it. Instead he drew his fingers together on her nipple, pressing and rolling it to give her a taste of the pleasure she so craved.

"Why, Tempest?" he asked. "Tell me why?"

"Make love to me, Vlad."

"Talk to me, first. Answer my questions," he told her.

She twisted in the bed, pushing at the blanket until it slid and bunched up around her waist, leaving her upper body bare and fully exposed.

He shivered at the sight of her. Still so incredibly beautiful, with creamy skin almost begging to be touched. Hips a little wider than before, body a little fuller. It wasn't the body of a twenty-three-year-old now. It was a woman's body, and he burned with desire to bury his own inside it.

"Tell me why you have to find the ring." He cupped her untouched breast with his other hand, and squeezed and lifted it, then pinched the nipple softly, because he loved the way she gasped and shivered every time his fingers closed tighter on the hard little bud.

"If you have it, you'll kill me."

"I would never hurt you, Tempest." Another pinch. Harder this time. She sucked air through her teeth. Gods, he wanted her.

"Use your mouth," she whispered.

"Tell me why you think I'll kill you." He couldn't take his eyes off her breasts. He wanted to taste them. And he didn't have the will to do otherwise. He bent his head, squeezing her breast in his hand, so the nipple thrust upward, and lapped its tip with his tongue.

She gasped. "More."

He loved this part of her, this new part. The girl she'd been would have waited to see what he would do, how he would touch her, then reacted when he did. But the woman she had become told him exactly what she wanted. And it made him all too eager to comply.

"Tell me, Tempest, and I'll give you what you want," he whispered, his breath bathing her sensitive skin as he spoke.

"If you have the ring, you'll put it on me. You'll perform the rite." She arched her back. "Please, Vlad."

He closed his mouth around her nipple, suckled her deep and hard for a long moment. Her hands closed in his hair, and she held him to her. He bit down a little, and she arched against his mouth, silently begging for more.

He stopped. "Keep talking, Tempest. Tell me what I need to know."

Breathless, she whispered, "If you perform the rite, I'll die. My soul will go away. And she'll take my body. Take you." She pressed her breast to his lips, and he took it again, drawing on it, nipping and tugging.

She writhed beneath him, arching and moaning until the blanket fell to the floor at the foot of the bed, leaving her completely naked and exposed to him. Vulnerable to him.

Gods help him.

His hand slid over her body, across her belly, to the soft curls between her legs. She let her thighs fall open wide, arching her hips against his hand.

"What will you do with the ring when you find it?" he asked.

"I can't tell you. You'll stop me."

He slid his fingers between her folds. She was wet. Dripping, and so hot. "Tell me, Tempest," he whispered, and he thrust his fingers inside her.

She shuddered from her head to her toes, and pressed him deeper.

"Will you give the ring to the woman? Melina?"

"I don't know her. Don't trust her," she said. Then, "Harder!"

He drove his fingers into her more deeply, withdrew and did it again. "Tell me what you'll do with the ring."

"I'll...destroy it," she whispered.

He went still. Shocked. Destroy it? By the gods, she couldn't. She *wouldn't*.

Her eyes fluttered.

He saw it, knew she was starting to lose her grip on sleep, and called up the full power of his mind. "Don't you dare wake up, Tempest. Sleep. Dream. Enjoy."

She relaxed a little, and he rewarded her by sliding his fingers into her again. In, and then out. Over and over. "Give yourself to the pleasure, my beautiful Tempest. Give yourself to me."

"You'll hurt me...destroy me."

"If that's my will, there is no point in fighting it.

Surrender to me, Tempest. Let go." He worked her body and her mind, bending to take her breast in his mouth again, in his teeth, using his thumb to torment her clitoris while his fingers drove deeper into her, until he felt her give way. She writhed and moaned as the orgasm gripped her, and he spoke to her mind, commanding her to remain asleep, to remember it all as no more than a pleasant dream. Her body jerked and shuddered with her release, and she whispered his name over and over as she came.

He caressed her until the last shivers finished, until the spasms eased and she calmed slowly back down. He stroked her body and, leaning close her ear, whispered that she was his, that her will belonged to him, and that she would trust him, believe what he told her and do what he bade her, always. He tugged the blankets over her body and tucked her in tightly.

"You've hurt me," she whispered. "You never came back to me, Vlad. You only came now for the ring. And now you have it!"

She was getting agitated. He soothed her, stroking her hair, her cheeks. "I don't have it Tempest. I didn't take it."

"You don't? You didn't? But you want it. And you have to know...have to know... Even Melina knows."

"Knows what?"

Her head twisted from side to side on the pillows, her eyelids beginning to flutter rapidly without quite opening. "You don't care, do you? You want to clear the way for her to come back, even if it means my soul. You want me dead. Nothing can hurt more than that."

"You will trust me, Tempest. Your will is mine. I own your soul. Know that, and stop fighting it. You'll do my bidding, whatever that might entail. But for now, sleep, Tempest. Just sleep."

She relaxed slightly, and as he continued petting her, rubbing her shoulders and neck, she calmed down, bit by bit.

"I love you, Vlad," she whispered. "I never wanted to. But I do."

He didn't know how to respond to such a declaration. It shocked him. He'd hoped, secretly, that she still harbored feelings for him, because it would make doing what he had to do easier if he could do it with her cooperation. But he'd never imagined those feelings could be so intense, especially since he'd erased her memory of the time they had spent together.

She rolled onto her side and relaxed as he gently urged her mind into an even deeper sleep, a dreamless, restful sleep.

He rose then, went into the bathroom, washed his hands of her scent, her essence, with no little rush of regret, and then splashed cold water onto his face.

He hadn't intended what had just happened between them. And yet, he'd learned far more than he'd ever hoped to learn. He knew now that she wasn't working for the Sisterhood of Athena—not really. She didn't know anything about them, didn't trust them any more than he did. He knew that she hadn't stolen the ring. But she intended to find the ring and destroy it, and he knew why. She feared that ring—feared wearing it would be the death of her soul, and would result in her body being surrendered to an intruder.

And so it would.

And he'd learned that she loved him. Tempest loved him, and it hurt her to believe that he didn't love her in return. That he would choose Elisabeta over her. Even if it meant her life.

Above all else, he'd learned something more vital than anything else. Tempest believed herself immune to invasion from Elisabeta in her dreams. But she was wrong. Elisabeta had been there. She'd heard, felt, experienced, all of it. He'd felt her there. Why she hadn't come into full control, he didn't know. It might be that she was too weak after so much time. Or it might be that she was waiting, listening, trying to learn the same things he was. Who had the ring and how to obtain it.

He could visit her as often as he liked. He could make love to them both, Tempest and Elisabeta, if only in dreams.

Was it wrong to visit Tempest's body this way? Probably. But it wasn't against her will—he knew her will, could sense it in her mind. But the will to make love to a vampire in her dreams might not be the same as it would be in her waking state.

Did he give a damn if what he was doing was right or not? Gods knew he'd done worse things in the centuries he'd been alive. And if this was the only way he could have her, so be it.

He knew he would return—night after night if he could manage it. He was like an addict craving a drug, and having found a font of it, endless and undefended, he couldn't do less than take his fill.

Especially being fully aware just how little time remained. Four days. Four short nights until the Red Star of Destiny eclipsed Venus. And then they would both die.

Beyond the physical pleasure he would give, and eventually receive, as well—yes, why the hell not? Beyond those things, he would be able to keep himself fully apprised of Tempest's progress and her interactions with the Athena group.

He returned to the bedroom, leaned over her and whispered in her ear, "Remember me only as a dream, Tempest. Remember and know you will dream of me again. From now on, beautiful Tempest, your nights, and your will, belong to me."

"Don't go," she whispered. "Don't leave me again."

He leaned closer, pressed his mouth to hers, kissed her softly, deeply, and wished for more. And more. He had to leave. He had to find a victim, feed on hot, rich blood, before his will failed him and he took hers instead.

That would make him vulnerable to her. It would strengthen the already powerful bond and create a weakness in him. One that might make him falter in the things he needed to do.

And he could not falter. He had to move forward with his plan or all would be lost.

4

Stormy felt warm all over. She rolled onto her side to hug her pillow to her with a deep contented sigh and felt a smile tug at her lips. And then she came fully awake and the smile died. The sigh died. The warmth turned to a chill that shivered from her toes to her throat, where it caught and lodged.

Vlad had been there.

She sat up in the bed, scanning the darkness of the room around her. The balcony doors were closed, their curtains still, blocking out the night beyond them. She saw no one lurking in the shadows. The luminous red eyes of the digital clock beside the bed read 4:15. There were no other eyes glowing at her from the corners. She reached out, groping for the lamp just to be sure, found the switch after a couple of false starts, and turned it on.

Light flooded the bedroom. She saw no one. But

she *felt* them: eyes on her, watching her. The sensation was so real, she spun around to look behind her, but no one was there. Even so, it felt as if someone was standing right behind her, breathing down her neck.

Shivering, hugging herself, she moved across the room to the French doors of the balcony and tested them. Locked. Swallowing the dryness in her throat, she went to the closet and closed her hand around the cool brass doorknob. She stiffened her spine and jerked it open.

But no one was lurking inside. Sighing in relief, she turned and moved to the bathroom, reaching in first to flip on the light, then scanning the room. She'd left the shower curtain open, but she glanced behind it anyway.

Nothing.

She left the bathroom light on when she retreated to the bedroom, though it was a stupid, childish thing to do. Dropping to her knees beside the bed, she gripped a handful of covers and lifted them so she could peer underneath. But there was nothing there except an expanse of the same carpet that covered the rest of the floor. And then she shook her head at her own foolishness. The very notion of Vlad hiding under a bed… It was ludicrous.

She was alone.

But he'd been there. She was sure of it. It hadn't been just a dream. She ought to know, she thought. She'd been dreaming of him for sixteen years. She'd never felt like *this* upon waking. She felt relaxed; fulfilled. *Sated.*

Swallowing hard, she moved to the French doors again, unlocked and opened them, then stepped out onto the balcony and faced the darkness.

"Vlad? Where are you?"

The only answer was the gentle whisper of the wind moving through nearby trees, and sliding around the eaves and the railing.

"I know you're out there, Vlad. And I know you want that damned ring. Don't you try to put it on me, Vlad. Don't do it. I'm warning you."

There was still no answer. She stood there for a long time as bits of the dream that wasn't a dream came back to her. She remembered the way he'd touched her, the way he'd made her body come alive, made it sing.

Don't be stupid! It was me he was touching, me he wants, not you! Never you!

The voice, familiar and hated, shouted the words inside her mind, and Stormy gasped, gripped her head and closed her eyes. *That* was who she'd felt watching her. Elisabeta! She was getting stronger again. Rising up again.

She closed her eyes, chasing away the shivers of fear racing through her body. She had to focus on what he'd said, not on what he'd done.

He'd said he didn't have the ring.

Had he been telling the truth? Maybe so. Because if he had it, why hadn't he put it on her last night? Why wait?

Perhaps because he still hadn't located the rite that went along with it. Maybe he was just waiting for the one missing piece, biding his time.

From now on, Tempest, your nights, and your will, belong to me.

She heard his passionate whisper, a command, not a request. She lifted her head, staring out at the night. "No part of me belongs to you, Vlad. Understand that. I'm not the young, cow-eyed girl I was before. And I've been working with your kind for long enough to know how to shield myself. My will is too strong to be broken by a vampire. I'm my own woman, and no man owns me. Not even you."

She thought she had told him she loved him last night. But surely he couldn't take that declaration seriously. Not when she'd been asleep, believing it all to be a dream.

"That was wrong, Vlad. What you did last night, making me stay asleep, and trying to convince me it was just a dream? It was wrong. You violated me."

To get to me! And he will again and again and again, and you'll have no say in the matter.

"Shut up, Beta!"

She felt no response from Vlad, swallowed hard and lowered her head. She'd loved every second of it. But that didn't make it all right. He hadn't asked. He'd only taken.

Given, actually. But still... She wondered briefly if she was truly angry that he'd touched her without asking, or was it more that he had denied her seeing him again when she'd longed for nothing else for all this time? He'd kept her asleep, used his power over her to keep her from waking up. She wanted to see him. She wanted to throw her arms around him and weep for joy. She wanted to tell him how much she'd missed him.

"Right. The man has come to murder me. Get over it, Stormy."

Because it was true. He hadn't come for her. He'd come for the ring, and for Elisabeta.

"Don't let it happen again," she whispered. And on some level, she was sure he was out there, somewhere, listening. "Just don't."

She went back inside, locked the French doors and crawled back into the bed, determined to get another hour or two of sleep before it was time to get up and face the day. He wouldn't come back again tonight, she told herself. It was too close to dawn for that.

She only wished she could be as certain about Elisabeta. The sleeping intruder had awoken, strong and ready for a fight. It wasn't one to which Stormy was looking forward.

She rolled over, punched her pillow and closed her eyes. And she did get the sleep she'd been so determined to get. But it was far from restful, and filled with more pieces of her missing memories.

Vlad built a fire in the giant hearth and yanked the dusty sheets from the furniture, making a place for them to be comfortable on the ancient but still sturdy chairs. He located food, canned stew with gravy, certainly not cuisine, but she declared it edible and proved it by devouring every bit. She was starved. The castle's caretakers, he told her, only came in one weekend a month, and though he'd phoned ahead to tell them to prepare a room for her, the supplies they'd left in the pantry were meager at best.

"*I'm not the original Vlad Dracula,*" *he told her at length.*

Stormy looked at him quickly. "*You're not?*"

"No. I am…far older. But that's unimportant right now. I was centuries old, already, when my travels took me to Romania. I cannot help but think it was fate that led me there. To her."

"Elisabeta?"

"Yes."

He was intense, his eyes focused on the dancing fire that painted his face in light and shadow, giving him an even more frightening appearance. And even more beautiful.

"The prince, the real son of the king, had been killed in battle before he was out of his teens, his body left to rot, unidentified and unclaimed. His father never knew what had become of him, and by the time I arrived, he had been mourning his lost son for some years. I knew the young prince's fate. I'd heard it directly from the enemy who'd slain him. That man panicked when he realized he'd killed the prince, knowing the vengeance the king would wreak should he learn of it. So he stripped the prince of his clothes, obliterated his face and dragged his body into a stand of brush, never to be found." He lowered his head. "When I arrived, the king mistook me for his long-lost son. I didn't have the heart to kill the joy in the old man's eyes. I saw no harm in playing the role."

"I see." She didn't, not entirely, but she was eager to hear more of his story. About Elisabeta, the woman who terrified her, seeming to possess her at times.

"I'd been living as Prince Vlad for nearly five years when I met her. We married a day later."

She shot him a quick, searching look. "That's it? You met her and married her a day later? That's all you're going to say about your...courtship?"

Vlad lifted his brows, spearing her with his steady gaze. "What else is there to say?"

"I don't know. How you met her. Where. What made you fall in love with her. It must have been...intense, if you married her so quickly."

"Intense." He turned his eyes toward the fire, stared into the snapping flames. "That describes it as well as anything. The details...the details are unimportant."

"The details are the only thing that's important."

He shrugged as if it didn't matter, and she knew he wasn't going to share his private hell with her. Not now. And maybe not ever. "The outcome is the same, with or without my most intimate memories being spilled at your feet, Tempest. I was called into battle on our wedding night. Enemies had crossed our borders. I led our soldiers to meet them, but we were severely outnumbered. It was ugly. Bloody. Many died. I was struck down, but one of my men dragged me into shelter and left me there, safe from the sun."

She sighed, disappointed that he'd refused to go into

detail about his time with Elisabeta. She sensed that he didn't trust her with that kind of power.

"Was it luck that your soldier put you under cover?" she asked softly. "Or did he know?"

Vlad glanced her way. "No one really knew what I was. But by then my father and my closest comrades were used to my nocturnal leanings. They all knew I detested daylight, took to my rooms whenever the sun was shining. They knew I slept by day and that disturbing my sleep was an offense of the most dire sort." He shrugged. "They may have suspected more. Gods know the villagers did. Rumors about my nature were flying, even then."

"So it was you, not the original prince, who inspired all the stories," she said softly.

"Yes. It was me."

She nodded slowly, then swallowed the lump that came into her throat. "Some of them…are pretty gruesome."

He paused a moment. "I am not proud of the things I have done in the past, but I won't make excuses. I returned to the castle to find my new bride dead. And yes, I wreaked havoc on my enemies after that. I was brutal. Perhaps even insane, at the time. But it's done, and I can't undo it."

She drew a breath and shivered a little. "So you blamed them, your enemies, for her death?"

"It was well deserved."

"Did they kill her? Storm the castle while you were

away and—" She broke off there because he was shaking his head. "*How did Elisabeta die, Vlad?*"

He set his jaw, fixed his eyes on the fire. "*She received word that I had been killed in battle, and in her grief, pitched herself from a tower window.*"

At her tiny gasp, he shifted his gaze toward her again. She held her hand to her lips involuntarily and felt her eyes go damp.

"*I'm so sorry,*" she whispered.

He shrugged and looked away.

"*Why do you do that?*"

"*Do what?*" he asked without looking at her again.

"*Pretend it doesn't matter. That it doesn't hurt anymore.*"

"*It was a long time ago.*"

"*And it's been eating you up inside ever since.*"

"*Don't pretend to understand me, Tempest. You couldn't begin—*"

"*You've spent all these years waiting for her to come back to you, searching for her. Don't try to pretend this obsession of yours isn't based on unbearable pain, Vlad. It won't wash, not with me.*"

"*My pain is not the subject of this conversation. You wanted to know about Elisabeta. I'm telling you about her.*"

"*Not really,*" she said. "*But maybe I can piece it to-*

gether from the scraps you're willing to share. Go on, Vlad. Finish the story. What happened next?"

"Her body lay in the chapel. My dear friend Rhiannon had arrived in my absence. It was she who told me what had led to Beta's death. And she told me more, as well. She told me that Elisabeta would return to me in five centuries."

She nodded slowly. "I know of Rhiannon. She's well versed in the occult arts, or so the stories go. Magick, divination, prophecy."

"She was a priestess of Isis, after all."

"So you believed her."

"Believed her? Yes. But I was not convinced Elisabeta's return would be enough. I wanted to ensure that she would remember me, that she would still be the woman I had loved. That she would love me again."

Tempest rose from the chair and moved to stand in front of him, staring down at him, blocking his view of the flames, so he had little choice but to look at her instead. "How could you do that?"

"I couldn't. But I knew of those who could. Rhiannon took her leave, and I had my father send horsemen into the farthest reaches, to bring back sorcerers, witches, magicians of every sort. I charged them with the task, and they assured me they had accomplished it. They gave me the ring from Elisabeta's finger, along with a scroll, rolled tightly and held within its circle. The told me they had somehow bound her essence to the ring, and that when she returned, I need only replace it on her finger and perform the rite contained in the scroll to restore her completely."

He went quiet and watched her face, her eyes, awaiting her response. She stared at him, her eyes moist. "And you think I'm her. And you think that with this ring and scroll, you can...make me remember the past?"

He nodded slowly. "I am not convinced you are her. Not yet. But if you are, then I think the rite would accomplish it, yes."

Stormy closed her eyes, lowered her head. Vlad rose to his feet and began to pace. "We were attacked after burying her, by the same army we'd been battling in the days prior to her death. Ambushed. Everyone was killed. The king, the villagers, the priests. Everyone. Even me."

She frowned, but then it faded as realization dawned. "But you revived."

"I did, just before sunrise. But my body had been searched, stripped of anything of value. The ring and the scroll were gone."

He moved past her, paced to the fireplace, bracing one hand on the huge stone hearth and staring into the flames. "I thought if I brought you here, to Romania,

*showed you the places she knew, your memory might re-
turn on its own."*

"Not my memories," she said, her throat dry. "Hers.
And so far that's not happening, Vlad."

"No. Nor would it, not in this castle. She never set
foot here, as far as I know. No, it's the places she lived
that I want to show you." He looked toward the window.
"But dawn is coming soon. I must rest. Tonight I'll take
you to the village. To my father's castle. To the places she
knew. Perhaps…perhaps it will stir something to life."

"Oh, I've got no doubt. It'll probably stir her to life.
She'll take over, and I won't have any control over my
own body, my own actions. God, you have no idea what
a horrible feeling that is, Vlad. I don't want to go through
it again."

"If that happens," he said, turning slowly, "I'll take
you away from whatever seems to have instigated it. I'll
care for you until you return to yourself."

She did not for one minute believe his lies. "And will
you also keep me from doing anything I wouldn't do, if
I were myself?"

He stared at her but said nothing, and she closed her
eyes, her face heating as she turned away from him.
"When she takes over, Vlad, you know what happens.
Between us. Are you going to make me say it?"

He still didn't respond. And she was under assault

from within by the memories of the things she'd done during the episodes she'd spoken of. She'd flung herself into his arms. She'd kissed him, fed from his mouth with her tongue while moaning endearments in Romanian. She'd arched into him, pulled his hips hard against her and told him how she wanted him. Only it hadn't been her. It had been Elisabeta. Stormy had been no more than a silent witness. And yet she'd burned with the same desire the other woman felt for him.

"I need your promise, Vlad. Promise you won't make love to me…not unless you're certain it's really me."

He caught her shoulders and turned her to face him, then lifted her chin so that he could watch her face. "And if I am certain it's really you?" he asked. "Do you intend to take me to your bed then, Tempest?"

"I don't know. I don't know if what I feel for you is real, my own desire, or something she's planted in me. I just don't know."

"And you don't wish to engage in sex with me until you do," he said, completing the thought for her.

She swept her lashes downward. "I know you don't have to wait. You can take me any time you want to, either by brute force or by using the power of your mind to bend me to your will. I'm not even going to lie to you and say I would hate you for it. I want it. I crave it. But I'm asking you not to do that. I'm asking you to wait."

He caught a handful of her hair in his fist and tipped her head up, bent his head and took her mouth, but only briefly. It was a hungry kiss, and he swept his tongue into her mouth to taste her. Then he lifted his head away.

She was trembling. "Even if she takes over. Even if she begs you to take her."

"It would be a test of my control. One I cannot promise I will pass." He trailed a finger over her cheek and downward, tracing her jawline and then her neck. "But rest assured, Tempest, if I find out this is a game—if I learn you've been lying to me, trying to convince me you are my Elisabeta as other women have tried to do over the years—I'll take all you have and then some. I'll make you my slave, a mindless drone without a will of your own. You will exist only for my pleasure and only for as long as I will it."

She lifted her eyes to his and whispered, "Is that supposed to be a threat, Vlad? Because it doesn't really sound all that horrifying."

He lifted his brows but said nothing. Still, she saw the fire in his eyes and thought maybe it was for her, for once, and not the woman who possessed her.

She touched his shoulder, her eyes fixed on his. "I want to be whole again. I want to understand this thing, and more than that...I feel something for you, Vlad. Something powerful. And it's killing me that I can't tell whether it's my own emotion or hers. I want to sort this out, and for the first time I feel as if there might be a chance to do just that. So yes. I'll go with you to the places she knew."

He averted his eyes just as something came into them. He hardened his features. "It's not as if you have a choice, you know."

She lowered her head and turned away quickly. "No, I don't suppose it is." She sighed deeply, wondering if she were insane to be feeling so much desire for a man who'd abducted her against her will. Though in truth, it hadn't been against her will. Not really. She wanted to be with him. She wanted to figure all this out. And if she really wanted to get away, she doubted even Dracula himself could stop her. She wasn't exactly helpless.

Slowly, very slowly, she faced him. "What if she does manage to return, to take up residence in my body? Have you wondered about that? What future could you possibly have together, either way? Vlad, you're a vampire. I'm not. I'm not one of The Chosen. This body can't be transformed. Have you considered what that means?"

He lowered his head sharply. "I will not consider the inevitability of finding my love only to lose her again. I cannot."

"Fine. Then consider this. If she comes back, Vlad, what happens to me?"

He glanced toward the windows. "The sun is coming. I feel it."

Stormy felt as if a blade had been sunk into her heart. It didn't matter to him what happened to her, she realized slowly. He didn't care.

Stormy hadn't expected to have a companion with her for the day, but she couldn't find a way to get out of taking Brooke along when she returned to the museum. Frankly, she didn't know why she bothered returning to the scene of the crime at all. She knew damn well who had taken the ring. Vlad. It had to be Vlad, no matter what he had said. Who else would want it? And she knew he was near. She felt him. How big a coincidence would it be that he was in town when that cursed ring was stolen? Too big, that was how big. He must have taken it. He was still determined to evict her from her own body just to bring back his lunatic of a wife.

It shouldn't hurt, but it did.

"That's the room, isn't it?" Brooke asked as they moved through the corridors of the museum. There was no yellow police tape, but the doors were closed.

"Yeah, that's it."

"Doesn't look like we're going to get a look at it from out here."

"Well, you never know."

Stormy glanced up and down the hall, and seeing no one, she gripped the knob and twisted it, then smiled. "Unlocked. What do you know?"

"Do you really think we—"

"It'll only take a minute. Look, why don't you go on a little tour? I won't be long."

"No way. If you're going in there, I'm going with you."

Stormy frowned but quickly ducked inside the room, with Brooke right behind her. She closed the door and took a look around. As she did, she asked the question on her mind. "Melina doesn't trust me, does she?"

Brooke seemed surprised. "Why would you think that?"

"She sent you along. And you act like someone under explicit instructions not to let me out of her sight."

Brooke shook her head. "It's not Melina. It's me. I've...got a real interest in this case."

"Really?"

She nodded. "I find it fascinating. Are you telling me you don't? I mean, you do this shit for a living."

"Sure I do. That's why I'm in this business. But then

again, so are you, in a way. You and this…Sister-hood."

Brooke nodded.

"So why the special interest in this case?"

Brooke shrugged and looked around the room, then pointed. "That must be how they got in, huh?"

Stormy eyed the window. A sheet of blue plastic had been affixed over it, probably just to keep out the elements until a crew arrived to replace the glass. She moved closer, lifting the plastic. The window glass was shattered, the remaining shards leaning inward. "Point of entry. Yes." She looked beyond the glass. "There's a ledge out here. I suppose the intruder could have climbed up there, worked his way along to this window and then come in." *Unless*, her inner voice whispered, *he just jumped up from the ground. It's only the second story. No challenge for a vampire.*

Brooke peered around her, but Stormy let the plastic fall back into place. "So again, I ask you. Why the special interest in this case, Brooke?"

The other woman met Stormy's eyes and maybe realized she wasn't going to evade the question quite as easily as she'd hoped to. She thought for a moment, then said, "It's not often I disagree with Melina on anything. This time I do. And I'm eager to find proof of which theory is the right one."

"It's important to you, being right?" Stormy asked. "Or is it her being wrong?"

Brooke shrugged. "I just want to know, one way or the other."

"Okay." Stormy filed that away and examined the room further. She spotted the surveillance camera mounted high in one corner, and her heart beat a little faster. If only she could get her hands on a copy of that tape. What it *didn't* show would tell her as much as what it did.

Voices in the hall jerked her off that train of thought, and she held up a hand to tell Brooke to be quiet. Brooke's eyes widened and shot toward the door, but she stayed still and silent, and the voices passed, fading away.

"We'd better get out of here. I think we've seen all there is to see."

Brooke nodded, and Stormy moved to the door, pressed her ear to it for a moment, then opened it and, after a quick look up and down the hall, moved through. Brooke followed. No one saw.

"That's it, then? We're heading back?"

"Not just yet," Stormy said. "I want to get a look at the point of entry from outside."

They exited the museum, and walked down the sidewalk and around the corner to the side of the building where the broken window was located. As Stormy took in the street from end to end, not missing a single detail, she tried to make small talk. "So how long have you been with the Sisterhood, Brooke?"

"Eighteen years. How long you been in the supernatural investigation biz?"

"Officially? About sixteen years now. Max and I were teenage sleuths before that. Kind of the Scooby Gang of our town, you know?"

"That's funny." Brooke smiled, relaxing a little.

"You must have been just a kid when you joined this group, then, huh?" Stormy asked. She noticed a trash can that looked out of place. It was painted green and had a maple leaf symbol on it. It stood underneath a tree with a large, low hanging limb, right next to the museum building.

"Seventeen."

"Really? And what about Melina?" A person could have climbed from that trash can to the limb, she thought, and from the limb, they could easily make their way to the ledge.

"What *about* her?" Brooke asked.

"I'm guessing you two are about the same age, aren't you?"

"She's a year older. But she came in about a year before I did."

"Hmm."

Brooke eyed her. "What?"

"Nothing." Stormy had located other trash cans. They were green and bore the same logo. But they were not on the sidewalk. They were across the street, in a small park, spaced at intervals along the walking path.

"Come on, that 'hmm' definitely sounded like something," Brooke said.

Stormy shrugged. "Well, I don't know. I guess I was just wondering how it is that she's the one in charge and not you. Does it go by seniority or...?" Not one green trash can anywhere else on the street or on the sidewalk, Stormy noticed. They were all in the park. So someone had definitely placed that can underneath that tree. Deliberately.

A vampire would not need to move a trash can, climb a tree or inch along a second story ledge to reach that window. For the first time, she honestly wondered if Vlad had been telling the truth. Maybe he *didn't* have the ring.

"The former leader picks the new one. To be honest, Eleonore was grooming both of us to take her place. But she had to choose one or the other."

"And she chose Melina."

"Yes."

"That must have hurt."

Brooke shot her a look, her brows furrowed. "Don't be ridiculous. If I didn't like it, would I still be here?"

"I suppose not."

"So are you getting anything out here? Any clues or whatever it is you Scooby-types look for?"

Stormy thought she was getting a lot. Mainly, a question. If Vlad didn't have the ring, then who the hell did? And why was it she suddenly felt more vulnerable than she already had, when she knew damn well no one was more of a threat to her than he was?

"What do you say we get some lunch, huh? And then maybe we'll pop by the police department and see if we can get them to drop any hints about what they've got on this case so far."

"You think they'll tell us anything?" Brooke asked.

"Not on purpose. Come on."

5

The day was unproductive, for the most part. Stormy knew now that it was possible an ordinary mortal, not Vlad, had stolen the ring. And she knew the police had the tape from the video surveillance camera, but not whether anything was on it.

Maybe the night would provide more answers.

She'd pleaded exhaustion and gone to her room early. But she wasn't tired. She was eager and afraid and excited and terrified. He would come to her tonight. She knew he would. The fear made sense. Not the longing. Never that, she told herself, knowing she was lying.

She opened the windows, one after the other, so the night wind whispered into the bedroom and the curtains sailed like ghosts. And she left them that way while she headed into the bathroom for a long, steamy shower. When she stepped out again, dried herself off and padded, naked, back into the bedroom, he was there. Waiting for her.

He sat in a chair, in the shadowy corner. She wasn't surprised or startled or even embarrassed to be standing naked in front of him. It felt normal, natural and expected.

"Hello, Tempest," he said softly.

She felt herself tense as she reached for a robe. "I knew you would show, now that the ring has surfaced. So tell me, Vlad, was it real, last night?"

He got to his feet and came to her, took the robe from her hands before she had a chance to pull it on. Her heart skipped and her belly tightened. And even then, she felt that foreign presence stirring, deep inside her.

"I like looking at you. Give me that, at least," he said, very softly.

"You know I can't, Vlad. You know what it would do to me." She stared into his eyes, wondering if he even gave a damn about that. "Even now, she's waking up, trying to take over. Just being close to you—"

"I know, Tempest. Believe me, I know."

"Of course you do. It's why you're here."

He seemed surprised but didn't let it throw him. "I've never been far from you," he told her.

That got her. True or bald-faced lie, her heart went for it, and seemed to go soft and squishy in her chest.

"I've missed you so damn much," she whispered, a wrenching confession.

He bent his head and kissed her, wrapped his arms around her waist and pulled her nude body against his clothed one. His tongue delved into her mouth, and she took it, loved it, welcomed it, as she arched against him. But the *other* was coming alive, clawing her way to the surface, demanding possession of Stormy's own body.

She pulled free of Vlad and took a step back.

"I want you." His words were nearly a growl. And, she noted, he didn't say her name. She suspected he was speaking to Elisabeta, not her.

When she spoke, her voice was broken, trembling. "It wouldn't be me. You'd be making love to her. My body, her soul." She met his eyes, held them hard. "Maybe you wouldn't mind that so much. She's the only one you really want."

"Does it matter, Tempest? I don't think you would refuse me. And I know she wouldn't."

"Do it, then," she said.

She saw him frown. "Tempest?"

"Yes, it's still me, dammit. Do it. Take me and see

what happens. But I warn you, Vlad, if you put that ring on my finger—"

"I don't have the ring."

She went silent, staring at him, trying hard to see if he were telling the truth or lying. But, for the life of her, she couldn't tell.

"Please don't lie to me, Vlad. Please—"

"I don't have it, Tempest. I did come here for it. But someone else got there first. Until last night, I had assumed it was you."

She closed her eyes, wanting to believe him.

"I made a discovery last night, Tempest," he said softly. "And you know what it is, don't you? Elisabeta can't invade your dreams. Everything but that. Last night, I came to you in your dreams. And she didn't take over your mind. She couldn't. Your dreams are you own. Safe ground, apparently."

Stormy blinked her eyes open and stared at him. "But it was only my mind you invaded."

"No, Tempest. It was real. I touched you, kissed you. I wanted—" He closed his eyes.

"I didn't know getting a woman's permission was on your list of priorities, Vlad."

He lowered his head. "You still don't. It's only a token effort, really. I heard you, cursing me, just before dawn. I'm still unsure how much of it was sincere. But I think we both know I'm going to take you either way."

She didn't want to think about that, not now. "I don't think I believe you."

He looked her squarely in the eyes. "Refuse me and find out."

She lowered her eyes and didn't answer. Her body was screaming for him. She wanted to tell him yes, to take her in every imaginable way. She wanted to tell him no and enjoy being ravaged by his will rather than her own. She wanted. She just *wanted*.

"I brought you something." He reached over to a night stand and picked up something she hadn't seen there before. A videotape.

"What is this?" she asked as he handed it to her.

"The museum's surveillance footage from the night the ring was stolen. I liberated it from the police department."

Her brows rose. "Is there anything on it?"

"I don't know. I haven't viewed it. I'll leave that to you and ask you to tell me what you find."

She blinked, shocked by the gesture. "You're showing a hell of a lot of trust in me to give me this tape. What makes you think I'll tell you what's on it, though? My goal is to keep you from getting the ring, not to help you find it before me."

"View it. At least then you'll know I don't have the ring. I have neither the time nor the inclination to sit through hours of footage, nor easy access to audio-visual equipment. And if you choose not to tell me what you find, it will be a simple enough matter for me to command you to tell me, or simply invade your mind and read what is there."

"You want me to find it first, don't you?" She scanned him with her eyes narrow, wondering what he was up to.

"I don't care which of us finds it first. If it's you, I can take it from you without so much as exerting any effort."

"You're that sure of yourself. Of your power?"

He met her eyes, smiled slowly, evil lighting his face. "Where you're concerned? Yes, Tempest, I am. You'll do whatever I command."

He glanced at the bed. She did, too, and she knew what he was thinking. She was thinking the same thing. Her pride wanted to refuse him, but she told her pride to go to hell. She wanted him—it was a force she didn't even try to resist. Was he compelling her to feel this way, even now? Was it Elisabeta's desire burning her up inside? Or could it be her own?

It didn't matter. She wanted him so much she was trembling with it. Her breaths came short and hitched, and her heart pounded. She walked to the bed, put the videotape on the night stand and peeled back the covers, then lay down, pulling them over her. She closed her eyes. "I'm going to sleep now, Vlad. And you are more than welcome in my dreams. You…you always have been."

He moved to the bed, sat on its edge. "Open your eyes, Tempest."

She did, and found his locked with them. "Don't blink, and don't look away. Just look into my eyes. Know my will. Feel my will. Do you feel it?"

"Yes," she whispered.

"Good. Close your eyes now. And sleep. Sleep, Tempest, sleep. Be alert, and aware, and remember everything—but sleep. And do not wake until I tell you to wake."

"Yes." She licked her lips as the last vestiges of control melted away from her hands. "Make it good, Vlad," she whispered.

She was asleep. And yet…not. Vlad was pulling the covers away from her, bending over her, touching her body, and she felt everything, all of it, but for the life of her, she couldn't move or respond. It was as if she were a marionette and he was holding her strings. When he wanted her to move, she did, but of her own will, there was nothing in evidence. Nothing.

His hands moved over her breasts, rubbing and squeezing them. And then his lips followed, and he kissed and suckled her. She wanted to clutch his head and hold him closer, but she couldn't do that. Her arms would not move. Not unless he told them to.

His hand slid between her legs. *Open to me,* he whispered inside her mind. And then her legs suddenly had the power to move, but only if they moved the way he'd instructed, to part, and when she thought they were wide enough and would have gone still, his will pushed them farther, wider, and she lay there, more exposed than she had ever been. He touched her then, explored her with his fingers, probed deep inside her, pinched her pulsing nub lightly, then harder.

She heard herself whimper in response to that rough touch, and to his teeth on her nipple, mimicking the motion of his fingers. Pinching, tugging. Hurting so deliciously that it felt good. She wanted to arch her back, to push her breasts up in offering. She wanted to wriggle her hips in time with the motions of his hand. But she was motionless. Paralyzed. Helpless.

And then he was sliding down her body, his mouth moving wet and hungry over her belly, her abdomen, before settling finally over her center.

The sensation was too much, and she would have

tugged her thighs together to slow it down, but they would not budge. If anything, they opened wider— he made them open wider, made her hips tip upward to give his mouth even greater access. His tongue snaked out, lapped over her lips and then between them, and then deeper, plunging inside her. Too much. She wanted to draw back, to slow it down. Instead her body obeyed his will, not her own, and her hips thrust upward, grinding her mound against his mouth. He fed from her, licking her as if in a frenzy of hunger. His teeth scraped her, caught her and bit down just enough. And then his hands were on her, spreading her wider, laying her open to his plundering mouth. He ravaged her, and his puppetmaster mind made her own hands go to her breasts, made her own fingers twist her nipples and pinch them.

It was his will, all his. She was no more than a ragdoll, awash in sensation, with no ability to do or say anything in her own defense. He could do what he wanted, and that was precisely what he did. She would not, could not, resist or refuse. And God help her, she didn't want to.

His mind whispered to hers, *Give yourself to me. Come for me, Tempest. Do it now.*

Her body responded to his command, as he bit and sucked her harder than before, and forced her hands to pinch her nipples harder, until they throbbed and grew hot. She exploded at his command, and he plundered on, taking her while her body convulsed. She wanted to twist away, the sensations were so overpowering, and yet he wouldn't let her, made her lie there, open and utterly helpless to him, until he had taken his fill and reduced her to a shuddering, whimpering mass of sensation.

And then, even before the convulsions had stopped, he was moving up her body and sinking himself deep, deep inside her.

"Again," he whispered as he began moving deeper, withdrawing, moving inward again. "Move with me now."

She did, even though the actions brought too much sensation to bear. And the passion began building before it had even ebbed.

He held her, and drove into her over and over, so deeply he drove the breath from her lungs. And this time, when he neared climax and she did as well, he sank his teeth into her throat, and he drank her essence, her blood.

The power of it nearly made her body shake apart with the release. It was above and beyond any orgasm she'd ever experienced. She felt everything. His body hard and pulsing, invading hers, filling her.

His teeth embedded in the flesh of her throat as his mouth drained the very lifeblood from her body. She was his, utterly and completely his, and her mind and body exploded around him, because he commanded it. And it was powerful.

So powerful, in fact, that she woke from her lucid sleep to find him lying there, still inside her, on top of her, holding her, kissing her neck and licking at the wounds he'd left in her throat, even as he began moving again to rebuild the fire.

Elisabeta came to fierce, fighting life, and Stormy barely had time to whisper "No" before she was gone. Her time with Vlad was over. The invader had driven her out.

When her nails raked his back, Vlad realized she had changed. No longer responding only to his mind's suggestions, Tempest had instead taken control. She was moving frantically beneath him, making demands of her own, unspoken but clear in the movements of her body. He drew back to stare down at her, wondering how she had managed to escape the power of his mind, and he saw that her eyes were wide open and blazing…

…and jet-black.

"Tempest…"

"She's gone. And I won't let her come back. Not this time, Vlad. This body is mine." Elisabeta wrapped her arms around his neck to draw him more deeply inside her.

He drove once, twice, then closed his eyes and gave in to the passion that rose up in him. He was shaking with desire and need. And it didn't matter who owned the body any more than it mattered who owned the blood that he needed to stay alive. He took what he needed from anyone he pleased. He always had. This was no different.

And he took her. He took them. Elisabeta, Tempest, both of them. Neither would have turned him away. He wouldn't have cared if either of them had.

Harder and harder he rode her, until she was panting and gasping beneath him, her nails raking his back until the pain burned along every path she made, but it only enhanced his pleasure. The bed slammed against the wall with the force of his thrusts, and he pushed her still harder. He didn't care if he hurt her.

"Elisabeta!" He growled her name as he spurted into her, holding her hard and mercilessly as he drove to even greater depths and then held there, pulsing, throbbing, into her.

She grunted, perhaps in pain or maybe in pleasure. He couldn't be sure and told himself it didn't matter. Slowly he eased himself out of her, but he didn't lie there on the bed to embrace her. He got up. Got to his feet, began reaching for his clothes.

"I've come back to you, Vlad," Elisabeta whispered. She twisted in the bed like a contented cat, hugging the pillow, clutching the sheet. "And this time, it will be forever."

"Is she dead, then? Have you managed to evict her from the body without my help after all?"

Beta thrust out her lower lip, sitting up in the bed. "Why do you care? I'm the one you love. I'm the one you're meant to be with. Your wife, Vlad. I'm your wife."

"You don't have to remind me of that. I've been trying to find you again since you died, Elisabeta."

"But I didn't die," she told him. "Not completely. Your magicians and your sorcerers wouldn't let me die. They imprisoned my essence in some in-between state—they bound it to the ring. I couldn't have moved on even had I wanted to. But I didn't want to, Vlad. I didn't want to leave you. And I haven't."

She blinked those huge, dark eyes up at him, and he saw them fill with tears. "Vlad, why aren't you happy? Isn't this what you wanted?"

"It's all I've wanted," he told her. He put on his

clothes, but she was still weeping, and he didn't have it in him to turn a cold shoulder to her. Even as unused as he was to showing affection, he couldn't remain cold. Not to her, not to his Elisabeta. He sank onto the bed and pulled her into his arms, holding her gently. "I've never stopped loving you, Beta. Nor stopped wishing you could return. But I have to know—is she dead?"

She stared at him, and he knew, before she even spoke, that she would lie. So he pressed his lips to hers to stop her from speaking at all, and as she melted in his arms and opened to his kiss, he entered her mind as easily as a warm knife through butter, and he read what was there.

But there were no specific thoughts, no answers. Just a sense of vehemence, hatred and fury that shocked him, and he drew away from her kiss as if burned by it. He also felt Tempest still there, alive, but trapped. Like a captive inside her own body.

"My love?" Elisabeta whispered. "Can't you stay with me? Just for a short while longer?"

"No, Beta. I must go. And so must you. Tempest's friends will be coming for her soon. They'll know what you've done unless you…recede. Go back to sleep inside her, and wait until the time is right."

Her lips went tight. "I won't. It's too hard to get

control. If I release it, I might never get it back again."

"You will," he promised. "I'll help you. Don't you trust me?" He cupped her cheek. "Please, Beta. Let her come back to herself. Just for now."

She held his gaze, and for a moment he saw anger glittering in the depths of her eyes. But then she blinked it away, averted her face and nodded once. "All right. I'll do as you ask. For now."

She lay down in the bed, pulled the covers over herself, and closed her eyes. In a few moments her breath came slowly and evenly.

Vlad touched her face, her hair. "Tempest?"

She didn't reply, just kept on sleeping. He tried probing her mind but found it blocked to him. She'd taken refuge, put up the blocks she'd somehow learned to build—most likely by years of working with and for his kind—to keep him out.

Elisabeta. She wasn't the woman he remembered. But whatever she'd become, he knew he bore the blame. Imprisoned, trapped for hundreds of years—how could she not lose herself to fury and anger and…perhaps even madness?

"I'm sorry, Beta. I'm sorry for what I did to you. I promise I'll make it up to you, no matter what I have to do."

Pressing a kiss to her forehead, he rose from the bed and went to the windows and leapt to the ground, but never landed. Instead, he changed forms and flew as a nightbird over the walls of the Athena mansion.

6

He wanted another woman.

Elisabeta's borrowed heart felt as if it were slowly turning to a chunk of cold ice. Her prince, her husband, who had promised her eternal life, still wanted her, yes. But he wanted his precious Tempest, as well.

Well, she'd fooled him. She'd pretended to obey his wishes, to withdraw and allow Tempest to return to control. In truth, she'd only feigned sleep until he left the room.

But no more.

The woman whose body she possessed, Tempest, who called herself Stormy—the enemy—writhed within, struggled to regain control. Elisabeta felt her own grip weakening and knew she had to work fast. She had to do what was necessary and do it quickly. And she wasn't certain she trusted Vlad to do it for her. She had to do this on her own.

"You're not coming back," she told the one she'd displaced. "Not this time."

Stormy dreamed. And more pieces of her past returned. Once again she was in Romania, in Vlad's castle.

Vlad carried an oil lamp from the great room, and led her toward the wide and cold stone staircase. The bannister was wood, solid and coated in dust. Not ornately carved, but beautiful in a rough and rustic way. He didn't take her hand as he led the way. She walked beside him, and when a piece of one of the stone stairs fell away beneath his foot and he had to grip the rail to keep from falling, she clasped his upper arm instinctively.

He looked at her, the lantern glow flickering between them, his eyes intense, as if he, too, felt the power that seemed to surge between them with any physical contact whatsoever. It surged even in something as innocuous as her hand on his biceps.

She had to lower her gaze from the burning intensity in his eyes. She shifted it to the lamp instead. "Maybe I should carry that, given that your kind are nearly as combustible as the lamp oil."

He lifted his brows but didn't object as she took the lamp from his hand. She held it by its slender neck, between the wide glass base and the sphere that held the oil. Its chimney was tall and narrow, sooty near the top. It was warm to the touch, unlike the man who'd been carrying it.

They resumed climbing the stairs and moved along a high-ceilinged corridor past arching doors that each seemed to be cut from a single slab of wood. Black iron hinges and knobs gave the place a gothic feel that was fitting, she thought. Pausing at one of the doors, he pushed it open wide and let her precede him with the light.

Its golden warmth spilled onto a huge canopy bed with sheer white curtains surrounding it. It was stacked high with pillows and covered by a thick comforter. And the room was remarkably dust free. She moved closer to the bed, noting the tall windows in the far wall, the thick red draperies held back with fringed golden ties. Bending, she ran a hand over the comforter and caught the freshly washed scent coming from the bedding.

"It's clean," she said, glancing over her shoulder at him.

He stood near the doorway. "I phoned ahead. Asked the caretakers to come in and make up a room for you. I hope it's comfortable."

"It's fine." It was more than fine. It was darkly beautiful, like something out of a gothic fairy tale. She turned and held up the lamp to look around, noticing the ornate, ancient-looking furnishings, a rocking chair, writing desk and chest of drawers and wardrobe. There was *a fireplace here, too, and she set the lamp on the mantle, and glanced into the hearth to see wood and kindling laid ready for the touch of a match.*

He came closer then, removed the screen and took a long wooden match from a tin holder on the mantle. With a flick of his thumbnail on the matchhead, it flared to life, and he bent to light the kindling.

"You do mess around with fire a lot, for a vampire."

He shrugged. "I'm careful."

She nodded toward the windows. "What about those? Are the drapes thick enough to…?" She let her words die as he turned to look at her, the question in his eyes.

"I hadn't planned to rest here with you, Tempest. Though if you would prefer me to, I—"

"No. No, that's not what I meant." She averted her eyes, shaking her head in denial, though it had been exactly what she had meant. She'd just assumed…. "Actually, I'll be grateful for the privacy. I have a lot of thinking to do. I just—I'm not used to sleeping by day, and the sun streaming in might keep me awake."

"I see." She was afraid he did. All too well.

He moved to the windows, untied the golden cords and tugged the draperies together, blocking out the graying sky beyond. "Better?"

"Much. But I could have done that." She dared to look at his face again and was surprised to see that his *eyelids had become heavy, kept drifting closed.* "Go on, go to bed. I can handle things from here."

He nodded but seemed hesitant to leave, even then.

"I'm not going to run away, Vlad. We made a deal. I always keep my word."

"That's good to know. Good rest, then, Tempest."

"You too. See you at sundown."

He nodded and left her alone in the room.

As the fire licked to life, the room grew brighter. Bright enough to let her explore it more thoroughly. There was a dressing table, and its surface was far from bare. There were a gorgeous silver hairbrush, comb and hand mirror lying on the top, and she wondered if they'd been there before or if he'd had them brought in for her. She wondered if they'd been Elisabeta's, then thought they would surely be tarnished with age if they had. Curious, she opened some of the drawers and found that they were not empty, either. A selection of undergarments—bras and panties, nightgowns and camisoles, and a few pairs of socks—filled them. Frowning, she moved to the wardrobe and opened its doors, wondering if she would find fancy dresses and gowns.

She didn't. Its hangers were filled with jeans and blouses, and a warm coat. Two pairs of shoes sat on a shelf—hiking shoes and running shoes. She picked up a shoe and looked at the number on the bottom. It was her size. The chest of drawers held sweaters and T-shirts. He'd definitely had these things brought in for her. And he knew her sizes, and her style.

Another door revealed a bathroom that was surprisingly modern, at least in comparison to the rest of the castle. Indoor plumbing must have been a more recent addition. The tub was old, claw footed and deep. The sink was a pedestal model, the toilet a huge one that must have been manufactured in the fifties. All the fixtures were brass and shining. Towels and washcloths, all clean smelling, were stacked on a shelf. And a small stand with a mirror behind it and a stool in front held bottles and jars—familiar ones.

Hair care products, moisturizer, soaps and razors, and a supply of makeup. All her brands. All her colors.

My God, how did he know so much about her?

Stormy wasn't sure whether to be touched that he'd gone to so much trouble, taken so much care, to provide for her comfort, or creeped out by the fact that he seemed to have dug into her life—or maybe her mind—so deeply without her knowledge.

Maybe she was a little of both.

She would have loved a shower, but that wasn't an option. No showerhead. Sighing, she put the stopper into the tub and started a bath running. Then she went back into the bedroom to choose a nightgown. The one she pulled out was long and white and flowing. Perfect attire for the heroine in a gothic novel, stranded in a strange castle in a foreign land with a vampire for a host. Why not?

The bath relaxed her; the nightgown felt heavenly against her skin. She hadn't expected to be able to sleep at all, but when she crawled into the bed, she knew she would. The mattress was covered in a downy featherbed, and her body sank into it as if she were sinking into a cloud. So comforting and warm, with the down-filled comforter snuggling her and the pillows cradling her head. She thought it would put the most hopeless insomniac to sleep. She sank into slumber as soon as she'd pulled the covers around her shoulders.

She slept for a long time. Deep, uninterrupted, blissful, restful sleep.

Until the dream came.

In the dream, she wasn't herself. She was someone else. Elisabeta. Oh, it was Stormy's body, her face, but the other woman's eyes lived in it. She was standing on the edge of a cliff, getting ready to jump.

Stormy felt as if she were inside the body of the other woman but not in control. It was as if she was just along for the ride. But she knew everything Elisabeta knew, felt everything she felt, as she stood on that precipice, high above a thundering waterfall. The night *sky above her was dotted with stars, and behind her, grasses and wildflowers spread out as far as she could see. But her gaze was drawn to the woman again. Somehow she could see her, even though she felt trapped inside her.*

Elisabeta wore a simple dress that reached to her feet. There were grief and loneliness, a great yawning emptiness, inside her, filled only with pain beyond human endurance. It hurt so much. Stormy felt it. She ached with it.

I've lost everyone. Everyone I ever loved. I have nothing left.

The Plague, Stormy thought slowly. Elisabeta's family had been taken by the Plague. Her mother. Her father. Her brothers. Her baby sister.

"Alanya." *Stormy whispered the baby's name as it floated into her awareness.* "She was only two." *Her throat went tight, and she felt tears burning in her eyes. Tears…for Elisabeta.*

There was something else wrong with the woman. Woman? No, she wasn't even that. She was barely more than a girl. Her mind was awash with overwhelming emotions, and her body—her body was weak and sick. She'd been growing weaker for a long time now, and she knew, deep down, that whatever was wrong with her would get no better. She saw no need to go on living, suffering from a mysterious malady that would surely kill her anyway, now that her family was gone.

She's one of The Chosen, Stormy realized. One of those mortals with the Belladonna Antigen—the only ones who can become vampires. They always weaken and die young, but God, not that young.

The Undead sense that kind. They watch over them, protect them. Where was her protector now? Stormy wondered.

She heard a shout, glimpsed a man on the opposite cliff. But it was too late for him to stop her.

"I'm finished," the tormented girl whispered. She opened her arms and rocked forward, just let go. Her body fell, and Stormy fell with it. The pounding foam and rocks below jetted toward her at dizzying speeds, and her stomach felt as if it had stayed behind on the ledge.

And then something was shooting toward her, a person, arrowing through the sky. His body hit hers, driving the breath from her lungs, and then he turned, putting himself beneath her. When they hit, she swore she felt his bones crack before the water swallowed them both. She heard his grunt of pain. He'd broken her fall. He'd kept her from dying. And then water embraced them, and for a moment everything was icy cold and pitch-black.

But then there was a shout.

"He's mine!" the tormented, grief-stricken young thing shouted, and in an instant it was as if Stormy was staring straight into Elisabeta's eyes. The woman spoke without moving her lips. He's mine, and I have nothing else. You will not keep me from him. *She closed her small hands on Stormy's throat and squeezed.*

When Stormy had woken that dark night so long ago, she'd found herself clawing at the hands on her throat and choking, struggling to breathe. But there were no hands there. She had gagged and struggled as the dream clung to her, then sat up and finally sucked in a desperate breath. The sensation of being strangled faded as if it had never been.

But she soon realized that she wasn't in the big, soft bed anymore. She wasn't even in the castle.

She was sitting up in a grassy field that stretched out forever and was bordered by distant forest. The wind was wafting over her, gentle, not harsh, but cold, and it carried a peculiar dampness that wet her skin. There was a roar in her ears, one that sent a chill to her bones. Slowly, she got to her feet and turned in a half circle, and then she went still and sucked in a breath.

Because there was nothing, just empty space at her

feet. Across the yawning, rocky chasm, a waterfall thundered and plummeted into the river below, and a huge cloud of wet mist rose up to engulf her.

"Oh, God. Oh, Jesus." She took a step backward, away from the edge, hugging herself and dragging in breath after breath of precious air. Her body was shaking. Her throat felt bruised, her lungs tight. God, it was so real! Elisabeta had been choking her. And somehow she'd made her way out here, to the very place she'd seen in her dreams.

Lifting her head, she shot a panicked glance at the night around her. But there was no one. She was alone.

Not alone, she thought. Not exactly. The enemy is inside me.

Pressing her hands to her head, she waited for her breathing to steady and her heart to stop racing. Gradually she recovered, and the dizziness—no doubt from being strangled half to death—faded.

Could she have died? Was it possible for an invasive presence to kill her from within her own body? It felt as if it was.

And she didn't feel alone, even now. She felt watched.

The sky was dark, and she was disoriented. She'd slept for what felt like hours in the cozy bed. Slept like the very dead. But she didn't know whether morning had simply not yet arrived, or whether the day had passed and it was night again.

She wanted to call out for Vlad. And even as she told herself how ridiculous a thought that was, she knew that didn't change it. She craved him like a drug. Or maybe Elisabeta did. She only knew she wanted him, there, with her, right then.

And then, suddenly, he was.

His hands closed on her shoulders from behind. He turned her slowly to face him as his probing, unreadable eyes searched her face. "Tempest?"

Her throat tightened. A sob tried to rise, and she clenched her jaw, closed her eyes tight to prevent the tears, and held her body stiffly.

"I woke to find you gone," he said softly. "What happened? How did you get here?"

"I don't know," she whispered, and it was an effort to get the words to pass through her constricted airways. "I just...I don't know." And then she lost it. She couldn't hold herself stiff and strong for another second. She let her body go, let it do what it was longing to do: fall against his strong chest, rest in his powerful arms while her own wrapped around him and held on hard. She lowered her face to his shoulder, and she let the tears come.

* * *

As the memory faded, Stormy struggled to wake up but found it impossible. She knew on some level that she wasn't really trapped in some dark nightmare in which she was imprisoned in a lightless, airless tomb.

The tomb was her own body. The cold stone walls were keeping her from the controls in her own mind. She couldn't hear or see or move. But she sensed that her body was moving, awake and walking around just as if everything were normal. Except someone else was behind the wheel.

Elisabeta.

Bitch. Give me back my mind!

She fought, strained against the darkness. And it seemed to give. Elisabeta must be weakening. But she was fighting, too, and she was stubborn. Stormy pushed harder, clasping a shred of control and then holding on for dear life.

The darkness gave way all at once.

It was like breaking through the surface of a mirror-still lake. First there was nothing, and then, everything. All her senses came to full, screaming life at once. She could suddenly see through her own eyes and feel her own limbs, and for a moment she had no balance or sense of orientation.

Stormy found herself standing near the windows

of her room in Athena House, wearing only her robe, her knees weak, her body lurching a little as she sought balance. She blinked her vision into focus. What she saw stunned her to the core.

The large, sparkling ruby ring. She held it in one hand, poised on the tip of her finger, and even as what she was seeing hit her, she was sliding the ring on farther.

She went motionless and stared at her hands, willing them to stop moving. She was holding the oversized ruby stone in her right and was about to slide it onto the forefinger of her left.

A scream was ripped from her chest as she flung the ring across the room. It hit the wall and then the floor, bouncing, tumbling, then coming to a stop, its red stone facing her like some demonic eye.

Her bedroom door crashed open. Melina lunged inside. "Stormy! What's wrong? What happened?" She scanned the room, wide eyed, as the sounds of others pounding down the hallway toward the room reached them.

Stormy gasped for breath, wondering what the hell to say, how to cover, when Melina spotted the ring and gasped. "Is that—"

"Jesus," Brooke muttered from the doorway. "Where the hell did that come from?"

"I don't know. I don't know!" Stormy's knees buckled, and then Lupe was beside her, sliding an arm around her waist before she could sink to the floor. Stormy hadn't even realized Lupe had come into the room. She was strong, way stronger than Stormy would have guessed from looking at her. She supported her firmly, and moved Stormy backward until her legs touched the bed. Stormy sank onto it gratefully, her entire body trembling. Lupe stayed close, her eyes sharp, missing nothing.

"Was it the Impaler?" Melina asked. She didn't look at Stormy as she spoke. Instead, her eyes remained riveted to the ring. "Has he been here?"

"No. Of course not," Stormy managed to mutter. It was a lie, but what was between her and Vlad was none of their business. She dragged her gaze away from Lupe's then and frowned as the raging waters of panic began to calm. "Why would you jump to that conclusion?"

She noticed Melina and Brooke and then Lupe looking toward the French doors, which were not quite closed. A breeze came through the gap, fresh and cold, pushing the curtains with its breath.

Slowly Melina turned to face Stormy. "It makes sense, doesn't it? Vlad needs a body for his dead bride to come into. Maybe he's chosen yours," she said. "Are you sure he wasn't here?"

"I think I'd know if Dracula had paid me a nocturnal visit, Melina. That's not the kind of thing that could exactly slip by me." She was careful to keep the left side of her throat away from their prying eyes. His marks would still be there, would remain until sunlight touched her skin.

"He's powerful enough to make you forget," Brooke said. "From what I've read, he can shapeshift, and his thrall is impossible to resist."

"Not for me. I've been working with his kind for sixteen years, don't forget."

"Where did the ring come from, then?" Brooke asked. "How did it get here?"

Stormy let the defensive attitude slide off her shoulders. "I...I don't know how the ring got here. I woke up and it was here, that's all."

"On the floor?" Melina asked. She was moving toward the ring now, reaching for it, and it took everything Stormy had not to knock her aside and snatch the ring before she could. She knew that urge wasn't coming from her own mind, not entirely. It was also coming from Elisabeta's. She flinched forward as Melina closed her hand around the ring and picked it up.

"In my hand," Stormy said. "I was sleepwalking or…or something."

Lupe's eyes narrowed at the "or something" part, but she didn't make any comment.

"When I woke, I was standing, and the ring was in my hand."

Lupe muttered in Spanish and crossed herself.

"That must have been terrifying," Melina said.

"Someone must have brought the ring," Brooke said slowly. "You didn't see anyone? Hear anything?"

"No. Nothing," Stormy insisted.

Brooke thinned her lips. "It didn't just appear here all by itself."

"I didn't say it had."

"Get off her, Brookie," Lupe snapped, stepping closer to Stormy in a way that was almost protective. "Maybe we should search the grounds," she said, possibly in an effort to change the subject. "We can check for signs, make sure whoever it was isn't still here. Give Stormy time to gather herself. I'll brew some tea. Chamomile, some valerian, maybe a little lavender, and we can talk."

Melina nodded. "You're very wise, Lupe. Safety first, analysis later." She turned to Brooke. "Rouse a handful of the girls and search the house, top to bottom. I'll take another group and search the grounds."

"I'll get started on the tea," Lupe said. And then she moved closer to Melina and held out her hand. "Maybe I should hold that for you until you get back. Just in case you run into…whoever."

Melina opened her palm and eyed the ring.

Brooke met her eyes. "I can hold it, if you want," she said.

Melina shook her head. "Lupe's right, it'll be safer here with her while we search. We'll decide what to do with it later." She handed the ring to Lupe, who closed her fist around it, nodded and dropped it into her bathrobe pocket. Then she turned to Stormy. "You should come to the kitchen with me. You shouldn't be alone right now."

"Thanks."

The four of them walked into the hallway. Melina and Brook headed down it in opposite directions, each intent on gathering troops to conduct a search. Stormy wasn't worried. Vlad was long gone by now.

But had he been the one to leave the ring with her? How else could it have ended up in her bedroom?

A voice inside asked if she needed to be hit over the head before she accepted the truth. He'd released her from his thrall and kept making love to her, knowing full well that would rouse Elisabeta to life. And then he'd given her the ring to put on. To drive Stormy out, to kill her.

He wanted her dead.

Why did she still want him so much?

She moved as if her legs were made of lead, down the stairs beside Lupe, who glanced nervously behind them and then said, "They know about you, Stormy."

She was so stunned she almost stumbled. Lupe's strong, tanned arm shot out to steady her. Stormy swallowed and gripped the railing. "They know what?"

"Come on." Lupe closed a hand around her forearm and picked up the pace, leading her to the bottom of the stairs, then through the mansion and into the oversized kitchen in the back. She ran water into a metal teapot and set it on a burner to heat. Then she reached into a glass cabinet and took out a china teapot, cups and saucers.

"What is it they supposedly know about me, Lupe?" Stormy asked.

"They know about you and Vlad. That he abducted you sixteen years ago, held you for a couple of weeks—time you don't remember. And…" She met Stormy's eyes, searching them and seeming hesitant. Then she gave her head a shake, went to a cabinet and flung open the doors. It was filled with jars, all of them labeled and packed with herbs. She scooped herbs from several of the jars and poured them into a cheesecloth sack with a drawstring closure.

"And what?"

"I'm getting to it, okay? This isn't easy. Saying it out loud sounds freakin' insane. But…they think you're the one. Elisabeta Dracula. Or her reincarnation or something."

"They think?" Stormy sank into a chair, shaking her head. "And what do *you* think, Lupe?"

"Damned if I know." She yanked the drawstring tight and dropped the sack of herbs into the china teapot. "I've seen the portrait—photos of it, at least. In our file on Dracula."

"You have a file on him?"

She shot Stormy a look that clearly said she wasn't supposed to have revealed that and wasn't going to elaborate. "It would make sense. Him abducting you, I mean. If he thought you were her."

Stormy lowered her head, shaking it.

"That's why Melina hired your firm to find the ring. She knew she would have a better chance of finding it if you were helping. You have a connection to it. A special interest in it. It's yours, if their theories are true."

"I promise you, Lupe. I am not Elisabeta Dracula. I'm Tempest Jones."

"Yeah?" She sighed. "So then how did you get the ring?"

"I don't know."

The teapot whistled. Lupe grabbed it and poured the steaming water into the china pot. The fragrance of the herbs wafted into the room with the steam. "Okay. So what's on the videotape?"

Stormy's head shot up, her gaze snapping to Lupe's.

"I saw it on the night stand. What is it, anyway? Did it get there the same way the ring did, or…?"

Stormy held up a hand. "I don't know if I want to discuss the tape. Not…yet, anyway."

"You don't trust me." Lupe shrugged. "Can't say I blame you. I mean, you don't know me. And you don't have any clue what I risked to tell you what I just did. If they find out…"

"They won't."

She smiled a little, lowered her head and put the china cover onto the teapot. "It needs to steep for a while." Then she met Stormy's eyes. "You've got more right to this than anyone else," she said, taking the ring out of her pocket and holding it up.

Stormy shook her head. "It's safer if you keep it away from me. At least until we destroy it."

"Oh, we can't destroy it," Melina said from the doorway.

Both women jerked in surprise and turned her way. Stormy had no idea how long she'd been standing there, how much she might have overheard, nor did Lupe, judging from the look on her face.

"But you told me the ring was dangerous," Stormy said. "That if it fell into the wrong hands…"

"It *is* dangerous. But legend has it Elisabeta's soul is somehow bound to that ring. If that's true, we have to set it free. With the ring, we can perform an exorcism. And then we can destroy the ring once and for all."

She reached out a hand, palm up and open. "Until we can do that, I think it best we put it into the vaults." She slid her gaze to Lupe's, then back to Stormy's, and it was open and reassuring. She fingered a chain she wore around her neck, tugging it from beneath her blouse. There was a silver key at the end. "I'm the only one with access, Stormy. Nothing will happen to the ring there. I promise."

Stormy thinned her lips, and finally she nodded. "All right."

"Good." Melina kept her hand out, and Lupe put the ring into it. "I'll take it to the vaults right after dawn."

"Why after dawn?" Stormy asked.

Melina licked her lips. "Just as a precaution."

That wasn't entirely true. Stormy knew it wasn't. Someone must have seen something. Someone knew Vlad had been there, or maybe Melina was as adept at spotting a lie as Stormy was. Either way, they knew there had been a vampire around, and they were not going to risk him seeing where they put the ring.

"Call us when the tea is ready," Melina said. "I need to check in with Brooke's group." She left them, taking the ring with her.

Stormy started to follow, but Lupe stopped her with a hand on her shoulder. "You have some time," she said. "There's a VCR in my room, if you'd like to use it. No one has to know."

"Thanks."

Lupe nodded, leaving Stormy to wonder why the girl was helping her, whether it was a trick, a trap or honest assistance. And then she knew it didn't matter. She was on a path here, and she wasn't going to get off until she found where it led.

Stormy thanked her and headed into the next room after Melina. "Melina, just one thing."

Melina turned to look at her.

"This…exorcism. Do you know how to perform it?"

Licking her lips, the other woman shook her head. "No."

"Do you know anyone who does?"

"No, not offhand. But I'm sure we can find someone."

"You don't need to. I...I know someone. Probably the best—maybe the only—person for the job."

7

Stormy returned to her room to make the call. Of all the vampires she'd ever encountered—and there had been many—Rhiannon was the one she was least fond of. She'd never been 100% certain just why. But there was something else. Rhiannon had helped her. She'd been there, in Romania. She'd been the one to return Stormy to her home, to Max and Lou and her old life. How it had happened, why, she didn't know. And maybe part of her was grateful while the rest of her resented being separated from Vlad. Even though staying with him would probably have killed her.

And still might.

Max liked to believe Stormy's dislike of Rhiannon was because she and Rhiannon were a lot alike, but Stormy didn't buy that. Sure, Rhiannon was tough, full of herself and fearless. But she was also,

Stormy knew, dangerous. More dangerous than the others she'd known. Except, perhaps, for Dracula himself.

She hated to bring the haughty vampiress into this mess, but there was no denying her powers or her skill. No one knew more about this type of thing than she did. She'd been a priestess of Isis. Besides, Rhiannon knew the backstory. More of it than Stormy did, at this point. And she knew Vlad, and for some reason she had tried to help before.

Stormy slid her PalmPilot from its case. The contact list was password protected, and she changed the password weekly. This week it was DRAC-2006. Yeah, he'd been on her mind big time even before she came here and ran into him again. Then again, he always was. Still, lately it had been worse.

She used the stylus to enter the password and opened her file of confidential contacts. She had a direct number for Rhiannon's cell phone, complete with voice mail. She never knew what time zone her vampire contacts might be in. Nor did they.

Stormy was taken by surprise when Rhiannon answered on the second ring.

"Well, well, well," she said when she picked up.

"If it isn't the spunkiest little mortal I know. It's been a long time, Stormy Jones."

"I'd be real impressed by your psychic skills, Rhiannon, if I didn't suspect you had caller ID."

Rhiannon laughed. It was slow and sexy. "Don't belittle my powers so quickly. I imagine I can tell you why you've phoned."

"Fine, I'll play." Stormy crossed the room, picking up her videotape on the way, and sank into the cushioned and elegant chair near the French doors. "Why am I calling?"

"Because the deadline is approaching. Time is running out."

She blinked, then frowned. "Deadline?"

Rhiannon was quiet for a moment.

"What deadline, Rhiannon? Does this have to do with that Red Star of Destiny shit?"

"I...I assumed you knew. Vlad hasn't contacted you by now to tell you?" she asked, her voice very low and way more gentle than Stormy had ever heard it. That alone was enough to shake her.

"No, Vlad didn't tell me about any deadline. But if it involves me, I think I have a right to know, don't you?"

"There's no question. I wouldn't even consider keeping this from you, though he, apparently, is foolish enough to see some benefit to it. Tell me this. Do you know the rest yet? That ring you're searching for, do you know what it is?"

"How do you know I'm searching for a ring?"

Rhiannon sighed. "I keep very close tabs on you—and on Vlad, as well. This situation—it's coming to a head, I'm afraid. Tell me, do you know about the ring?"

"Yes. I know that if it's put on my finger and some rite performed, Elisabeta will return, and it will probably cost me my life. That's what I'm trying to prevent."

"Good. It helps that you're aware of that much, at least. But there's more. Stormy, the magicians put a time limit on the magick they used to ensorcell the ring. If Elisabeta's soul hasn't been restored to life by the time the Red Star of Destiny eclipses Venus, they said, the magick would die. Elisabeta would be free."

"So I've heard." Stormy turned the video in her hand, wishing for a machine right now, here in her own room.

"They included all the women she had ever been or would ever be in the wording. If you *are* her reincarnation, Stormy, and the deadline passes, you, too, would be...set free."

"Meaning?"

"Dead."

Stormy went icy cold. She'd been afraid that was what the cryptic words in the journal had meant, but to hear them confirmed chilled her to the bone.

"Don't panic yet, child. There's still time to prevent it."

"I'm not prone to panic, Rhiannon. And I'm no child."

"Compared to me, you're a newborn."

Stormy lowered her head. "When is this Red Star of Fate—"

"Destiny."

"Whatever. When does it eclipse Venus?"

"Once every five and a half centuries or thereabouts."

"And that would be when?"

"Midnight on Tuesday," Rhiannon said.

"You're shitting me." Stormy closed her eyes, feeling as if the words had been a hammer blow to her gut. "Tomorrow's Monday," she whispered. "So I'm going to die in two days and Vlad didn't even bother to tell me?" She was going to kill that undead bastard herself.

"Apparently."

"What if we had the ring?" Stormy asked quickly. "Do you think you could exorcise her spirit from me if we had it?"

"Of course I could. There's no question."

Stormy nodded. "And would that prevent my untimely demise?"

"I can't be certain, Stormy, but I believe it would. Call it an educated guess, if you wish. But there is no one *more* educated in this area than I. Not alive, at least."

Stormy nodded, knowing it was true.

"You have the ring, then," Rhiannon said.

The woman never missed a thing, did she? "Yes."

"Does Vlad know?"

"He's in town," she said. "He knows the ring is here, that someone has it, but I have no idea if he knows it's me." *Yeah, I wish. I know damn well he's the one who brought that cursed thing here tonight.*

"Then you have nothing to worry about. It's too near dawn now, but I can leave at sunset and come to you. Where are you, Stormy?"

"Edmunstun," she said. "It's in—"

"New Brunswick. Canada. Gods, tell me you haven't got yourself entangled with that nest of Athena vipers."

Something cold seemed to waft from her words,

chilling the blood in Stormy's veins. "Why do you say that?"

"By the gods, you have, haven't you?"

"They're the ones who tipped me off that the ring was in town. They tried to hire me to steal it, actually, but someone beat me to the punch. I agreed to help them find it, and it turned up in my room."

"Your room where?"

Stormy swallowed, because her voice was getting hoarse. "Here at Athena House."

"Are you using their phone? By the gods, child, it's probably tapped."

"No. I'm using my cell." She was getting a very bad feeling, a dark foreboding in the pit of her stomach.

"They're not to be trusted, Stormy. Especially not one called Brooke, if she's still among them."

Stormy blinked, and her throat went utterly dry.

"Where is the ring now?"

She could barely move her lips. She glanced at the window, saw that the sun had risen. "By now Melina and Brooke are putting it in a vault for safekeeping."

"By the horns of Isis, Stormy, go after them! Now!"

Stormy snapped her cell phone closed and was halfway to the bedroom door before she realized she still had the videotape in her hand. Belatedly, she shoved it under the mattress, then headed back to the door and raced down the hall.

She met Lupe halfway down, gripped her arm. "Where are the vaults?"

Lupe's eyes widened. She shot a look down the stairs and then whispered emphatically, "I'm not allowed to tell you that. Only a handful of the women here know where they are, even fewer how to—"

"Don't give me that bullshit. You're third in command, after Brooke and Melina. I know you know. Get me there."

Lupe stiffened her spine, shook her head. "No."

"Dammit, Lupe, there might be a problem."

"Might be?"

"Just trust me on this. I have to—"

"I'll go. But I'm not taking you." She turned away.

"But—"

Lupe whirled to face her again. "Dammit, Stormy, do you have any idea what happens to women who betray the trust of the Sisterhood of Athena?"

Stormy went still, her eyes widening a little at the grim tone in Lupe's voice, the expression on her face. "No," she said. "I don't. What happens to them, Lupe?"

Lupe stared at her, and her eyes said volumes,

though her lips didn't speak a word. "Never mind. Come with me." She led Stormy down the stairs and through the mansion, into the library. "The phone in here has a two-way radio function. There's another in the vaults." She leaned over the phone, reaching out to hit a button, but before her finger touched down, a crackling sound came from the telephone's speaker.

Frowning, Lupe hit the "speak" button. "Melina? Brooke? Is that you?"

She released the button, her eyes seeking Stormy's. Stormy strained her ears to listen, and then the crackling came again, along with a single quiet word.

"Help."

"Melina?"

Stormy leaned past Lupe and hit the button herself. "Melina? What happened? Are you all right?"

She released the button, and when no answer came, she hit it again. "Melina, where is the ring?"

She waited. No reply. Then she shot a look at Lupe. "We have to go. And I think under the circumstances, you won't get into too much trouble for taking me with you."

"I could. But at this point, I'm willing to risk it. Come on."

8

Stormy followed Lupe through the mansion into the sunroom that had been added on at the rear, a room that was like a tropical rain forest. Enclosed in glass, filled with plants and trees, fountains and a bubbling hot tub, and paths that wound amid them all. She barely had time to appreciate the ingenious beauty of the indoor paradise before they were exiting through a glass door and heading along another path. This one led through an even larger paradise, an outdoor garden that seemed to cover acres.

The entire area was heady with the almost overpowering scent of countless flowers. Above them, between the colorful limbs of flowering trees, was a broad expanse of sky painted orange and pink by the sunrise. The path they took wound and branched until Stormy wasn't sure she could find her way again without an escort. At the center of the garden, or what Stormy presumed to be the center, stood a giant granite sculpture of the goddess Athena. She stood proudly, an owl on her shoulder, a staff in her hand and a crown of stars encircling her head. Her stone robe flowed from one shoulder to pool around her feet and drape in places over the square base on which she stood. The base had been chiseled with twisting vines, and a few real ones had begun to creep over it. The entire image was utterly amazing.

"My God," Stormy whispered.

"*Goddess*, you mean." Lupe knelt in front of the statue's base, which was at least four feet high, and touched one of the leaves that were carved there. Immediately a part of the base slid outward, along hidden tracks in the ground.

Stormy gasped, shocked. She hadn't even realized there were seams in the granite, they were so cleverly hidden by the pattern of the vines.

"This way," Lupe said, and she walked into the black void behind the chunk of stone.

Swallowing hard, Stormy followed, and as soon as she stepped inside, the stone slid home again, blocking out any light.

"Stay still a second," Lupe said. Stormy was surprised to feel Lupe's hand, palm flat against her shoulder, as if to ensure she obeyed.

Then there was light, and Stormy blinked in the sudden brightness before she realized Lupe was holding a glow-stick in one hand. Lupe held it out ahead of her, and Stormy saw that they were standing at the top of a set of stairs that vanished downward, into the darkness, plunging deep into the earth.

"You guys take this secrecy shit seriously, don't you?"

"We have to. Follow me." Lupe started down the stairs.

It was a long flight, with a hundred-yard tunnel at the end of it, and a door at the end of that. When they finally reached the door, Lupe punched a code into a numbered panel mounted to it, and the door opened.

She led Stormy inside, closed the door behind her and hit a switch. A light came on near them, then another and another, each one revealing more of the incredible room they had entered.

Room? It was more like a mini-stadium: huge and round with a concave ceiling. And the entire thing was lined in books. Hundreds—no, thousands—of them. Perhaps tens of thousands. She couldn't even begin to examine titles or subjects; she only got a sense of great age, and that could have come as much from the musty smells of old paper and leather as anything else.

"What *is* this place?" she asked in a whisper. Because it seemed appropriate to whisper in there.

"The Library of Athena," Lupe said. "There's barely a subject we can't research here. We have a hundred women employed at a separate facility, transcribing the books into computers, one by one. They don't know who they work for or why they're doing what they are. They just type and save, or scan the ones that are solid enough to withstand it."

"That's probably wise. If there were ever a fire—"

"There was, once. At our library in Alexandria."

Stormy blinked, stunned. "That was…?"

"This way," Lupe said. She crossed the vast room, and at the far end, she took a book from one of the shelves and reached into the space left behind. The shelf behind her swung open to reveal a hidden doorway. "Follow me."

Stormy followed her into the shadowy dimness, down another set of steps—a smaller one this time—and at the bottom there was a far smaller room. It was square, and its walls seemed to be made of rows upon rows of small doors in various sizes. One section held tiny doors, another slightly larger ones, and another, still larger ones. Some were tall and narrow, others short and wide. Each one of them had two things in common: a lock and a number.

Two of them were very different from the others. Both were tiny. And both stood wide open.

The room was dark and shadowy; the only light came from the still-open doorway into the stairway. But as Stormy stood there, staring at the two tiny open doors, her mind racing with the possibilities they suggested to her, she heard a moan and tore her eyes away from the little vaults.

"Melina!" Lupe shouted. And then she was darting into a dark corner of the room, falling to her knees beside the limp form that had to be Melina.

Stormy joined her there, kneeling on the other side of the fallen woman. She lay on her back, eyes closed, and the dark blotch on the right side of her forehead looked suspiciously like blood. Stormy touched her cheek, patted it. "Melina. Wake up, come on. Tell us what happened."

Melina's eyes fluttered. "The ring," she whispered.

"That's right, the ring. Where is the ring?"

Melina's eyes opened. She tried to focus on Stormy, then on Lupe. Her eyes grew wider. "Oh, God, the ring!" She sat up rapidly, then swayed to one side, but Lupe gripped her shoulders and held her upright.

"Easy, Melina. You're hurt. You're bleeding."

"Help me up. Hurry."

Lupe and Stormy flanked her and helped her to stand. As they did, she stumbled a few steps forward and stared at the open doors. Then her hand flew to her neck in search of something. A key, Stormy recalled. She'd worn it on a chain, but it wasn't there.

"The key. God, she took the key."

"No. Look, it's right here." Lupe bent and picked up the broken chain with the silver key still on it. "And here are the others." She scooped up another ring, this one huge, with more keys than Stormy could have counted.

"I don't get it. Look, someone better start explaining some things to me, and fast," Stormy said. "What happened down here, Melina? And where the hell is Brooke?"

"Brooke." Melina lowered her head. "Oh, God, Brooke. What the hell is she doing?"

"That's what I'd like to know," Stormy muttered.

Melina lifted her head, met Stormy's eyes and nodded slowly. "We came down here with the ring. I was going to use my key, the master key, to open vault number one." She nodded to the first tiny door that stood open. "That's where all the other keys are kept. I'm the only one with the master key."

As she said it, Lupe replaced the giant key ring in its vault and closed it. She used Melina's silver key to turn the lock, then handed it back to her. Melina eyed the broken chain. "She hit me with something," she said softly. And she lifted a hand to the back of her head. "I turned around to face her, and she hit me again. I went to my knees, felt her yanking the chain from my neck. She took the master key and...I don't know. I lost consciousness."

"Where was the ring at that point?" Stormy demanded.

"In my hand." Melina lifted her hand, opened her palm and blinked at its emptiness, her eyes wet. "I can't believe Brooke would betray me—betray the Sisterhood."

"She took the ring, didn't she?" Stormy asked.

"She...must have."

"But why? What the hell could she want with the ring? Unless it's just the value of it," Stormy said. "She could sell the stone. It's probably priceless."

"It's not money she's after," Lupe said softly. She was staring at the second of the two little doors, the one that still remained open.

"What was in that vault?" Stormy asked.

Lupe looked at Melina, who looked to the open door. Her face changed. It was overcome with something that looked a lot like fear. She moved closer and peered inside, but clearly there was nothing there.

"What was in that compartment?" Stormy demanded.

Melina pursed her lips.

"I can only guess," Lupe said. "But if it was what I think it was…" She turned to her mentor. "It was, wasn't it? We have to tell her, Melina."

Sighing, Melina lowered her head. "The rite."

"The…*rite?*" It took a moment for the meaning of the words to sink into Stormy's brain, and when they did, she damn near gaped. "The rite that's supposed to be used with the ring? The one that's supposed to restore Elisabeta to life? It's been here all along? And now Brooke has it?"

"It looks that way, yes." Melina closed the door. She didn't lock it.

"But why? Why the hell would you keep something like that from me?" Stormy demanded.

Melina averted her eyes. "You're an employee, hired to find the ring. You had no need to know—"

"Don't give me that bullshit, Melina. You knew about my connection to that ring and to Elisabeta. That's why you hired me. My fucking life is in the rifle sights here, and you had the only bullet. You should have told me."

"It wouldn't have mattered."

"No? You don't think so? It's my life, Melina. Shouldn't that have been my call?"

Melina sighed. "I'm sorry, Stormy. I did what I thought was best. I hope you can believe that."

"Yeah. What was best for you and your damned Sisterhood, maybe."

Melina only shook her head. "Let's get back to the manse. We've got to get to the bottom of this."

"You're damn right we do," Stormy said.

Brooke sat in a darkened room in an empty house a few miles away from Athena House. The torn, ragged remnants of curtains that remained in the windows were drawn as tightly as they could be, dimming the early morning light. The only other source of illumination came from the flickering candle that stood on the small round table before her. The other items on the table included a round slab of balsa wood, on which was painted a series of letters and numbers, an upside down wine glass, a pad and a pen.

Brooke had two more items to add. She took them from her pockets now and laid them within the pool of light at the base of the candle. The carefully rolled parchment, bound by a length a yellow ribbon, and the ruby ring. The Ring of the Impaler.

She took a few deep breaths and placed her fingertips on the bottom of the wineglass. "Elisabeta Dracula, I am calling you. Speak to me, Elisabeta. I've done as you asked the last time I contacted you. I have the ring and the scroll."

At first nothing happened. But Brooke was patient. The reward Elisabeta had promised her was enough to instill patience in her. She repeated her words and waited some more. Eventually she felt a breeze rush into the room. She saw it in the way the candle flame flickered, felt it icy cold on her face. She closed her eyes as was her custom. The wineglass began to move, only slightly at first, but then its motions grew stronger, until it was gliding over the smooth balsa wood in sweeping arcs and circles. When it stopped, Brooke opened her eyes to look and see what letter the glass covered, wrote it down and began again.

The spirit board spelled out: G-O-O-D.

"What do you want me to do now?"

G-E-T the spirit spelled. Brooke took one hand from the glass to jot down the letters of her target. The glass was moving quickly now, and in a far more agitated manner than it had before. T-E-M-P-E-S-T.

"And do what with her?"

P-U-T-R-I-

Brooke frowned at the letters and kept scribbling as fast as she could, even while keeping one hand on the glass, which was flying over the board now. It barely paused on one letter long enough for her to ascertain which one it indicated before sliding to the next.

N-G-O-N-H-E-R

Brooke's pencil fell from her hand and rolled to the floor. She bent to get it, removing her other hand from the wineglass to reach for it, snatched the pencil up and reached for the glass again.

And then she just sat there, staring. Because the wineglass was moving again, still spelling. All by itself—she wasn't even touching it.

A door slammed, but no one was there.

P-A-Y-A-T-T-E-N-T-I-O-N

"I'm sorry. You…go ahead." She looked at the notepad and read what she had written there. PUTRINGONHER. Put ring on her.

"You want me to get Stormy Jones and put the ring on her finger. Yes? But she's not going to let me do that, Elisabeta."

F-O-R-C-E

"Yes, yes, I understand."

P-E-R-F-O-R-M-R-I-T-E

Brooke nodded, but disappointment was rushing

through her now. There was still nothing about *her*, not a word about how Elisabeta would keep her promise to grant Brooke the gift of immortality in repayment for her help.

"I understand," Brooke repeated. "I take her, put the ring on her and perform the rite. By force, if necessary. It's very simple." She cleared her throat. "And after I do all this, assuming I can pull it off, what happens then?"

I-L-I-V-E

"I got that, Elisabeta, but what I want to know is, what happens to me? You promised me immortality. So when do I get it. And how?"

A-F-T-E-R

Brooke frowned, disappointment washing through her. She didn't trust this Elisabeta, had suspected a trick from the beginning. "No," she said slowly. "No, I don't think so. You need to tell me now. Tell me how it's going to work or the deal's off."

The icy wind returned, blowing harder now than before. It blew so hard that a shutter slammed outside the house and the door burst open. The candle went out, and the wind kept coming.

Brooke rose to her feet. "I'm not asking you to do anything. Just tell me, that's all. Tell me how it can happen!"

The wind increased. Her hair whipped, tugged against her scalp and tangled in the air. The candle tipped over and rolled across the floor. But there was no response from the board.

"You were one of The Chosen, Elisabeta. But I'm not. So how can I gain immortality? How is it possible?"

Still nothing.

"At least tell me this much, Elisabeta," Brooke shouted into the wind. "Why does it have to be Tempest's body? She's not one of The Chosen either. So why her? Why?"

The wineglass shattered, exploding outward as if some unseen force inside it had expanded all at once. Brooke jumped, emitting an abbreviated shriek of alarm. Then the wind died utterly. The entire house went silent, still as a tomb. Elisabeta was gone.

Brooke calmed herself and went through the house, opening the ragged curtains, putting everything back the way it had been before. "I don't think I trust this bitch," she said slowly, thinking aloud. "I think she's promising me the one thing she knows I want more than anything else just to get me to help her return to the land of the living.

"Well, I'll be damned if I'll let her give *my* reward

to Stormy Jones when I'm the one doing all the work to earn it."

As she picked up the pieces of the broken wine-glass, then tucked the spirit board, the candle and the scroll into the small bag she'd brought along, she mulled everything over in her mind. Clearly Elisabeta knew how to make an ordinary mortal immortal. She must know, because she would have to do that very thing to Tempest Jones once she took control of her body. Otherwise she would just end up dead again in a few years. But she'd been very clear about her goals. She wanted to return to life to reclaim the vampire she loved, and then to live with him forever.

Tempest did not have the Belladonna Antigen. She was not one of The Chosen.

So there had to be a way. But if Elisabeta succeeded, then what reason would she have to make Brooke immortal, as well, as she had promised to do? What was to stop her from using Brooke to get what she wanted and then just ditching her, leaving her high and dry?

Brooke wanted immortality for herself. She craved it. Sought it. Had risked everything to get it, and this was not the first time. She would do whatever it took.

There was one last item to put away. She picked the ring up from the small table and looked at it. Smiling slowly, she slid it onto her finger.

"Well, will you look at that?" she whispered. "It's a perfect fit. Maybe we'll just try doing this my way, Elisabeta. What do you think about that?"

Still wearing the ring, she took the scroll from the bag, carefully loosened the ribbon that bound it and unrolled it. She would perform the rite, just as Elisabeta demanded. She would just make one little substitution. "Now," she said as she read, "let's just see what we need for the ritual."

When they helped her back into the house, Melina refused to go to her room, heading instead toward the breakfast room, where a dozen or more women were sitting around, sipping coffee and munching fruit and pastries.

They went dead silent, every eye on Melina. And no wonder, Stormy thought. She was a mess. "We've been compromised by one of our own," Melina said. "That puts us all at risk. We're going to Plan Q. Immediately. Don't delay, unless you know something that might help me trace Brooke."

There was a collective gasp when she said Brooke's name. No wonder. She had been second in command here.

"Move," Melina said.

And the women scattered, just like that, head-

ing out of the room like a bunch of third graders in
a fire drill.

"So what's Plan Q?" Stormy asked.

"Quit the premises. They'll be cleared out of here
in twenty minutes, along with their notes, any personal items that might identify them as part of the
Sisterhood, their computers, every sign they were
ever here."

Stormy raised her brows. "Impressive."

"We drill for this," Melina said. "Though I never
thought it would happen for real. Never." She
blinked what might have been fresh tears from her
eyes. "Where's Lupe?"

As soon as she asked the question, Lupe appeared
with a first-aid kit in one hand and an ice pack in
the other. Melina held up a hand, shook her head.
"We don't have time for that."

"Yeah, we do. You'll be more useful without that
blood running in your eyes every time you frown too
hard. Sit down."

Melina sighed, but she sat. "We need to search
Brooke's room. And her laptop. We need to go over
it, as well. And—"

"And we will." Lupe handed Melina the ice pack.
"Press that to the lump on the back of your head.
I'll deal with the front." Melina obeyed as Lupe

opened the kit, took out a gauze pad and soaked it in antiseptic. Then she began dabbing at the wound on the front of Melina's head.

Stormy was still furious, but she needed action, not anger. For now. But she also needed reason. None of this made any sense. For a while she'd thought Brooke might be the one who stole the ring, but why would she leave it in Stormy's own room, only to steal it all over again?

She remembered the tape, the one Vlad had brought her. She had yet to view it. "I need to change clothes," she said. "And then I'll…meet you in Brooke's room."

"Wait for us in the hall," Melina said. "Don't go into her room on your own."

Stormy stared at her, not believing the woman was still issuing orders. But *she* was not one of the Sisterhood's devoted little robots. "I'm not waiting for anyone. If you're not there when I'm ready, I'll start without you. But before I go, there's something you probably should know. I put in a call this morning to a woman I thought could help us in exorcising Elisabeta's spirit and freeing it from the ring's hold over it. She'll be here tonight."

Lupe paused in dabbing at Melina's head and turned to search her face.

"Who?" Melina asked.

"A vampiress by the name of Rhiannon." Their eyes widened, and Stormy felt a rush of satisfaction. "Yeah, I thought you might know her. She sure as hell knows you. I have to say, I'm rather interested to hear *what* she knows."

She turned and left the room, then headed up the stairs against the tide of women coming down, bearing backpacks, suitcases, duffel bags. It was a mass exodus. And it was fast and orderly.

By the time she reached the second floor, the stairs were clear, and she could hear vehicles outside, doors and trunks slamming, gears shifting and motors humming.

Stormy went to her room, thrust her hand under the mattress and pulled out the videotape. Answers. She needed answers, and she needed them now. Privately. She was no longer so sure she could trust Melina and the Sisterhood. Certainly Rhiannon didn't. Maybe she had good reason. She'd certainly been right about Brooke.

She took the time to change her clothes, discarding the nightgown in favor of jeans, a T-shirt, a pair of ankle socks and her teal and green running shoes.

She took the tape with her to Lupe's room, and barely took time to notice the darkly stained woodwork and earthy green bedding and drapes, before she spotted the tiny, outdated TV-VCR combo on a stand in one corner. She closed the door and turned the lock—she wanted privacy for this. At least until she knew what she was going to find. She realized that she was trying to protect Vlad, even though he was most likely trying to help Elisabeta kill her. And that, more than anything else, told her what she was expecting to find on the tape.

She was a fool where he was concerned.

Stormy put the video into the slot, hit the Power button, pushed Play and watched as a slightly snowy image of the ring in its display case filled the screen. The time stamp in the lower right corner read nine p.m. According to the police reports, the alarms had sounded around 1 a.m., so she located a remote, sat on the bed, and hit the Fast Forward button. Then she waited and watched the time stamp until she got close.

Finally she hit Play again, set the remote aside and leaned forward on the bed, her eyes glued to the screen.

Right on cue, she saw something. Bits of something flying into the frame. Glass, she realized. The museum's window had just been broken. And a moment later, a small form stepped into reach of the camera's eye.

Not a vampire. Vampires didn't show up in photos or on videotape. This form was mortal, and clearly a woman. Small and slight. She wore a black turtleneck, with a little black knit cap covering her hair. She kept her face turned away from the camera, and she didn't waste any time. She yanked the plexiglass cube from the display, took the ring from its tiny pedestal, dropped it into her jeans pocket, and then turned right back toward the window and walked out of the frame. For just an instant, as she moved off the side of the television screen, Stormy glimpsed the full length of her, from her head to her teal and green running shoes.

She caught her breath. Groping for the remote, eyes still on the screen, she rewound, stopped, then played the tape again, but this time she hit the Pause button at the moment when those shoes appeared, ever so briefly.

Teal and green Nike Shocks.

She rose to her feet and stared down at her own shoes. Teal and green. Nike Shocks. She'd bought them for running.

"It's not possible," she whispered. "I *couldn't* have...."

But even as she said it, she remembered how she'd fallen asleep in the bathtub at the hotel that night but awakened in the bed. She remembered the clothes she didn't think she'd worn, littering the floor in the morning, and the way her car hadn't been in the garage where the valet had parked it.

She closed her eyes, disbelieving even now. But she knew she couldn't deny what was being shown to her in black and white. And as she watched the entire theft again, she recognized her own form, her own clothes. But not quite her own stance and stride and manner. She had taken the ring. But she hadn't been the one in control when it happened.

"Elisabeta," she whispered.

She pressed her hands to her head and fell back onto Lupe's bed, closing her eyes. And even as she did, a flood of memories came. Memories she had thought were lost to her forever.

"This is the place," Vlad said in a voice that was oddly hoarse. He'd taken her to the mouth of a cave near the edge of the falls, below the Romanian cliffs where Stormy had found herself only a short time ago, shown her the cave where Elisabeta had helped him find shelter for the night, and now he had brought her to the place where the two had consummated their love, all in an effort to make her remember. To become Elisabeta.

She only wanted to get to the truth and be rid of the woman.

"I had gone to the cliffs that night for the same reason Elisabeta had," Vlad told her. "To end my life. Oh, I wouldn't have flung myself from the top, as she did. I planned to await the sunrise there by the falls, the most powerful place I knew. But when I saw her, when she pitched herself from the brink, I felt compelled to save her."

"And so you did?" she asked.

He nodded. "I propelled myself like a missile, through the air, and wrapped myself around her to break her fall before we hit the rocks and water below."

Stormy didn't really look at the spot where he'd stopped walking. She was looking at him instead, and seeing what he tried to keep hidden: a pain that was almost beyond endurance. It was in everything about him. His walk had become less the powerful, confident stride she'd grown used to. His usual stance—shoulders broad, back straight and chin high—had softened, as if the steel inside him were gradually melting. And his eyes—the hurt that roiled in his eyes was something even he couldn't disguise.

"I was injured, broken. She helped me into the cave, stayed with me there, and I told her my secrets. Told her what I was, what she was. One of The Chosen. I told her I could cure the illness that was taking her life, but only if she would be mine forever. And she agreed."

"So two suicide cases meet one night and decide to get married? Vlad, don't you see how messed up that is? You didn't even know each other, and neither of you was in your right mind."

He glared at her. "No one has ever questioned my sanity, Tempest." The tone held a warning.

"Sane people don't kill themselves, Vlad."

"You have no idea what it's like to live for thousands of years. To live alone."

"No, I don't, that's true. But I know lots of vampires, Vlad, and most of them aren't walking into the sunrise, no matter how old they are."

Forcing herself to tear her gaze from him, she looked at where he'd brought her after the cave. It was a tiny grove of trees, with a circular patch of wildflowers and grasses amid them. It was private, quiet and beautiful. And she knew it was the place where he and Elisabeta had consummated their love.

One night. It was all they'd had.

Moved to tears herself, she put a hand on Vlad's shoulder. "I'm sorry this is so difficult for you."

He swung his gaze toward her. "Don't pity me, Tempest. I don't want that from you. All I want—"

"Is for me to remember. I know." She licked her lips and stared at the area around her, but no memories came. Nothing was familiar. "Has it changed much?"

"*The trees are bigger. Some have died.*" He nodded toward rotting black stumps amid the stand of hardwoods. "*Others have sprung up to take their place,*" he said, pointing out the spindly saplings that arched their backs as if standing up straight were too much of an effort. "*Other than that, no. It's almost exactly the same.*" He brought his gaze back to hers, searched her eyes. "*Don't you remember anything? Anything at all?*"

"*I'm sorry,*" she said. "*I don't.*"

"*You have to. You will.*"

She saw the desperation in his eyes just before he reached for her, and felt a quick jolt that might have been fear, or maybe desire. Or some twisted mix of the two. She didn't have time to analyze it, because he pulled her hard against his chest, snapped his arms around her, one hand going to the back of her head to keep her from turning away. And then he was kissing her.

And, God help her, she loved it. Wanted it—and more.

He opened his mouth over hers, then closed it slightly, as if he were devouring her taste. And when he used his tongue, she went hot right to her toes. Every coherent thought, every rational argument that this was a bad idea, fled her mind. The only thing that remained was sensation. The way he made her feel: wanted, desired beyond reason. It was heady, and it was too powerful to resist. That this man, who could have any woman he *wanted, wanted her. And she wanted him, too. Had, from the moment she'd set eyes on him, and maybe even before that.*

She twisted her arms around his neck and opened to him, kissed him as passionately, as hungrily, as he was kissing her. God, it was going to be so good. So incredibly, unbelievably good.

He laid her down in the grass, pushing the nightgown from her shoulders, baring her breasts to the night, to him. He slid a hand between her shoulder blades to hold her up to him. And then he kissed her breasts, suckled them, gently at first, but with growing hunger, until he was nipping and tugging, making her gasp and pant and arch her back.

Lowering her down, he slid over her, his mouth moving over her collarbones, his lips tasting her neck. She tipped her chin up to give him room and whispered, "God, Vlad, I want you so much."

"And I want you, Elisabeta."

It was like being doused in ice water. She went stiff, then drove her hands between them and shoved at his chest.

He stopped kissing her and lifted his head, his eyes glowing with passion and beginning to cloud with confusion. She could feel how aroused he was—he was hard and pressing against her thigh.

"Get off." She shoved him again.

"Tempest—"

"Exactly. I'm Tempest. I'm Stormy Jones. But that's not who you were making love to just now, is it, Vlad? That's not the woman you want. It's her. Elisabeta. Not me."

"You can be her. You will be. Don't you see that?"

"No. No, I'm not, never was and never will be. She's trying to take over my body without my permission, and just now, Vlad, you came damn close to doing the same thing. Using me so you could have her, or fool yourself into believing you had her. You don't want me at all, do you?"

He rose slowly, pushed a hand through his hair, paced away from her. "If I've hurt you, I'm sorry."

"No one hurts me," she said, sitting up and tugging her nightgown over her. "I'm way too tough for that, Vlad, so don't beat yourself up over it. I'm not some needy suicide case like your child bride was. Not even close." She got to her feet and started off through the forest.

"The castle is this way, Tempest."

Leave it to Dracula to ruin the perfect, pissed off, overly dramatic exit, she thought. Worst of all, if she turned around now, he was sure to see her tears. Because despite her denials, he had hurt her. Way more *than made any sense whatsoever. She was an idiot where he was concerned.*

"I need a minute. Go on ahead. I'll catch up."

"There are wolves."

"Yeah, well, I'm good and pissed off, so if they know what's good for them, they'll keep their distance." *She strode off into the trees, just far enough to give herself the privacy to wipe the tears away. She waved a hand to create what she hoped was a drying breeze and blinked to get rid of any residual moisture. And she breathed, deeply and slowly, to try to convince her tight airways to open up a bit.*

Finally she turned and, holding her head up, walked back to where she'd left him. And found him waiting there...with another woman.

She turned, and Stormy blinked as the question rolled from her lips. "Rhiannon?"

Rhiannon frowned at her, then shot her eyes back to Vlad. "You've made her cry already?"

"No one makes me cry," *Stormy denied.*

Rhiannon gave an exaggerated toss of her long, jet-black hair. She wore a floor-length dress that hugged her willowy form's every curve and might have been made of velvet. "This one could make the sphinx weep. There's no shame in it." *Then she dismissed Vlad with a wave of her hand and turned to face Stormy.* "I heard you'd been abducted by the Prince of Darkness himself. Thought I'd better...see for myself."

"I never knew you cared," Stormy muttered.

Rhiannon lifted her brows at the sarcasm in her voice. "I don't, particularly. But you happen to be one of those rare mortals I would, on occasion, lift a finger to help." She examined her own nails as she said it. They were long and bloodred. "Given that you're a friend of several of my dearest friends, I couldn't just leave you to fend for yourself."

"Fending for myself is what I do best."

"Maybe so. You do have a reputation for being tough—for a human. But be realistic, Stormy. It's not as if you could hold your own against Dracula."

"You might be surprised," Vlad said softly.

Rhiannon glanced his way, and when she looked at Stormy again, it was with speculation in her eyes. "Then perhaps I've come to rescue the wrong party? No matter. Vlad, could we please have this conversation in more appropriate surroundings? Traipsing through the wilds of Romania collecting nettles in the hem of my Givenchy gown is not my idea of a happy reunion."

"If I'd known you were coming—"

"Which begs the question, why didn't you? You're getting slow, Vlad. Not to sense another vampire making her way to you? It's disturbing. Makes me wonder just what has you so thoroughly...distracted."

He didn't reply, just began walking back toward the castle.

9

Footsteps in the hall let her know the others were on their way to begin the search. She was out of time to dwell on this, and she had to fight down the wave of nausea and the surreal feeling that made her dizzy. God, she'd been a fool sixteen years ago, to let herself fall in love with a man who didn't want her, except as a vessel for his dead lunatic of a wife.

But she'd been young then. She was older now, wiser, far stronger. And yet she was still a fool. She still wanted him. Still loved him.

She had never thought she would be one of those women she'd always secretly pitied. The type to fall for the wrong guy, to hold on to a man who didn't care a thing about her. Damn him, he was as stupid as she was, to cling for all these years to his obsession with a woman he'd barely even known.

She steadied herself, ejected the tape from the

machine, shut the power off and took the video back to her room before going to join Melina and Lupe in Brooke's room.

Her entire day was spent searching. They searched every nook and cranny of Athena House, searched the grounds and the basement, searched the nearby towns for any sign of Brooke. They started to examine Brooke's computer, but it proved to be no easy task, since the entire machine was password protected.

In fact, they were still trying to break into her files when the sun went down.

The three women were huddled around a desk in the mansion's library—not the secret, hidden one, but the one in the house itself. They were leaning over Brooke's laptop as Stormy tried keying in everything anyone could think of as a potential password. She looked up from her work to see that dusk was painting the sky beyond the windows in muted tones of plum and purple. She nodded stiffly, her decision made, got to her feet, and made a show of stretching the kinks from her back and shoulders.

"I need a break," she said.

Melina and Lupe frowned at her, but she stuck to her guns. "Keep trying if you want. I'm going to get some air."

She left them there, thinking they surely had as good a chance of breaking the code without her as they did with her. They knew Brooke, after all. Stormy walked tiredly through the mansion, toward the back doors and out them. Then she circled the house until she stood on the grassy lawn underneath the bedroom she'd been using. Because that was where Vlad would come tonight. To her window. As soon as he woke, she thought.

She needed to talk to him. She needed to tell him about Brooke, and the missing ring and the rite. She had accused him of stealing the ring. Had even believed he might have been the one to leave it in her room, somehow stirring Elisabeta to life, knowing she herself would try to put it on. And though she knew that was his ultimate goal, she also knew he hadn't done it.

She wanted to tell him she'd been wrong about that. Despite everything, she felt compelled to tell him. And even if that wasn't logical, the rest was. She needed all the help she could get to find Brooke, and she knew that, with his powers, he would be more help than anyone else. Once they found the ring, she would find a way to keep it from him, to remove its curse and render it harmless. Right. All in the minuscule amount of time remaining.

She could keep her heart out of this and use her head. She *could*. She had to. Her life depended on it.

She hadn't explored this part of the lawn before. It bordered the gardens and featured a mammoth weeping willow tree whose tendrils dragged the ground on all sides. Curious, she parted the veil and stepped inside.

"I knew you'd come," a voice whispered.

But it wasn't Vlad's voice. It wasn't the voice of a vampire, and it wasn't the voice of a man. It was a woman's voice.

She rose from the concrete bench that sat at the base of the tree. Around them, the tendrils of the willow moved with the breath of the wind, whispering their secrets, whispering a warning. It seemed to Stormy they were urging her to turn and run.

"Brooke?" she asked. But the woman who stood there wasn't Brooke, though it was Brooke's body. This woman didn't stand like Brooke, didn't hold herself the same way. And her eyes were black as jet.

"Not anymore," she said. "Don't you recognize me, Tempest? I was sure you'd know me. We've been so close for so long, after all."

Stormy felt a cold chill race down her spine, and her gaze slid down to the woman's hand, where the ruby ring glistened from her finger. She tried to swallow, but her throat was too dry and too tight. "Elisabeta?" she whispered. "But...how?"

"How is unimportant," she said with a bright smile. "Aren't you relieved, Tempest? I didn't have to take your body from you after all."

Stormy took a single step backward, sensing danger. "Yes. Very relieved."

"Well, you shouldn't be." Elisabeta took a step closer, and Stormy backed up again. "I'm going to kill you anyway, Tempest. You've been sleeping with my husband, after all. And I don't intend to let you continue being a distraction to him."

She reached behind her and, in a flash, brought a huge blade around in front of her, then lunged.

Stormy dodged the blow but tripped over a root that thrust upward from the ground and fell on her back. A second later the other woman was straddling her, raising the blade over her head to bring it down on a collision course with Stormy's chest.

Vlad couldn't believe what he was seeing. A woman was leaning over Tempest, bringing a knife down toward her with furious force. He lunged toward them, even as Tempest jammed the heel of her hand into the woman's chin, snapping her jaw closed and her head backward so hard she tumbled off, rolling onto the ground, face down. And then Tempest scrambled to her feet. She kicked the woman in the rib cage as hard as she could, so hard the woman's body rose from the ground. Tempest delivered a second kick, flipping the woman onto her back. This time the knife went sailing through the air to land in the grass several yards away.

Tempest advanced, and Vlad thought she intended to kill the stranger. And then the woman on the ground spotted him, frozen there, amazed and unable to look away. She lifted a hand toward him. "Help me, Vlad. Please, don't let her kill me."

That voice. And those eyes.

He blinked in shock; then, as Tempest surged forward, he gripped her shoulders from behind, stopping her.

Tempest whirled on him, her eyes blazing with anger. "She tried to kill me just now!"

"Who is she?" he asked, his voice a whisper.

The woman on the ground struggled to sit up. "It's me, Vlad. It's Elisabeta. Don't you know me? I'm your wife."

He narrowed his eyes. "How…how could this…?"

"Her name is Brooke," Tempest said, and she was a little breathless. "She's part of the Athena group. Vlad—"

His gaze was drawn to the woman, the stranger. His bride? Could it be?

Tempest gripped his shoulders and jerked him around to face her. "Listen to me, Vlad. I took the ring from the museum. It was me."

"You?"

"Yes, but only because she was in control. Elisabeta took over. I didn't even know until I woke this morning to find her running the show again. She was about to put it on me."

He frowned, searching her face.

"We were going to put it into the vault, where it would be safe. But Brooke stole it and also the rite, which was here all the time, locked away. Brooke thought somehow it could give her immortality for herself. She must have performed the rite."

He couldn't stop looking from her to the strange woman with the familiar voice and eyes. "So my Beta lives...in that body. Not in yours."

Tempest stared at him for a long, long moment. He felt her eyes on him but didn't meet them, because his gaze was focused on the other woman.

"Yeah, Vlad. She's not in my body anymore. She's not going to take over every time you get close to me."

Elisabeta sent him a watery smile, and his heart

contracted in his chest. It was a familiar smile. So much about her was familiar.

"It's been so long," she whispered. "I love you, Vlad. I've always loved you. I need you now, more than ever before. Please don't desert me, not now."

"I would never desert you, Beta."

"I'm hurt. *She* hurt me."

He moved forward, reaching out a hand, and Elisabeta took it and let him help her to her feet. She brushed herself off.

"Poor thing. I shouldn't have done that, huh, Vlad?" Stormy asked. The sarcasm in her tone was clear, and, finally, he looked her way. She was furious. "I suppose I should have just let her sink that blade into my heart." She shrugged. "Then again, you're doing a pretty decent job of that all by yourself."

She turned and started to walk away.

Vlad released Elisabeta's hand.

"Vlad!"

He glanced back to see his bride sinking to the ground again, bending nearly double and hugging her own middle, where Tempest had kicked her hard enough to fracture her ribs.

He looked to Tempest again, then back to Elisabeta.

"Go ahead," Tempest said. "Look, this is over as

far as I'm concerned. She's out of me. That's all I wanted. The rite has been performed—successfully, by the looks of things. I'm not going to die. What you do with her is totally up to you. I could care less." She sent a glare back at Elisabeta. "But if you come near me again, I'll fucking kill you. No question. And no one, not even Dracula himself, will stop me. Got that, bitch?"

Elisabeta didn't answer, just sank to her knees, weeping.

"Yeah, that's what I thought. Brooke would have decked me for that." She met Vlad's eyes. "Not that she doesn't deserve whatever your innocent little bride there did to her, Vlad, but you might want to find out what happened to Brooke before you two head off on your delayed honeymoon."

She spun on her heel and strode toward the house.

Vlad needed time to process what was happening here. How could Elisabeta be alive in the body of this woman, this Brooke?

But right then, he could only focus on one thing. His wife was hurt, and she needed him. He couldn't just walk away and leave her lying there in the grass, bleeding and broken. He *couldn't*.

He let Tempest go and turned to Beta. He slid his

arms beneath her, picked her up and carried her away, off the grounds of Athena House.

The pain lancing her heart was almost too much, Stormy thought, as she walked firmly and purposefully into the mansion. Just inside the doors, she stopped, then stood gripping the doorframe, waiting for the weakness to pass from her knees. She'd never wanted anything the way she wanted him. But she'd been deluding herself. For sixteen years she had hoped that Vlad would realize she was the one he wanted. That he would be with her if he could.

But now that he could, he had chosen to be with Elisabeta, instead.

"Fine," she said, lifting her head and swiping away the tears with an angry hand. "I hope they fucking rot together. I'm done with this."

"That's the tough little mortal I've grown to... tolerate."

She blinked past the hot moisture in her eyes to focus on Rhiannon. The vampiress stood halfway across the sunroom, between two tropical plants, with the steam from the hot tub forming a misty backdrop. A photographer couldn't have posed her more effectively, as she stood there in a dress of paper-thin red silk, draping from her shoulders to the floor.

"Now stop the weeping and tell me what's happened."

Stormy sniffed and shook her head. "It's over, that's all. I'm sorry you came all the way out here for nothing."

"Did I?"

Stormy nodded, stiffened her spine and lifted her chin. "Yeah. You were right about Brooke, Rhiannon. How did you know?"

"We'll get to that. What has the little traitor done this time?"

"Stolen the ring. And the scroll. Turns out the damned Sisterhood had it all along, locked up in a vault. I guess our pal Elisabeta decided Brooke was an easier mark, because she's taken over *her* body now."

Rhiannon's eyebrows arched. "Elisabeta is corporeal?"

"Sure as hell felt corporeal when she tried to kill me a few minutes ago."

Rhiannon gasped, but Stormy waved a hand. "Don't worry. I kicked her ass and sent her packing."

"Well, that goes without saying, doesn't it? And where is Vlad?" Rhiannon asked.

"Last I saw him, he was carrying her away. Probably helping her lick her wounds. I'm done with the both of them."

"I only wish that could be true. For your sake, if not for Vlad's."

Stormy shook her head. "It *is* true. I'm packing my shit and leaving. I no longer have any reason to stay involved in this mess. Let him deal with her."

"Stormy, it's not over." Rhiannon stopped speaking then and turned toward the doorway from the sunroom to the main part of the house. "We have company."

Before she finished speaking, Melina and Lupe appeared. They came to an abrupt halt when they spotted Rhiannon.

"Well," she said in her menacing purr—a purr that could become a growl without warning. "We meet again. Hello, Melina."

"Rhiannon."

Lupe just stared, her eyes wide but watchful. Finally she managed to tear her gaze from Rhiannon's to focus on Stormy. Then she frowned. "What happened to you?"

"Later. Did you manage to get into Brooke's computer files?"

"Yeah. The password was *immortality*."

Rhiannon sniffed. "Brooke has been obsessed with obtaining it for quite some time," she said. "And I suppose part of the blame for this mess belongs with my friends and I, for not telling you of her duplicity long ago."

"The Stiles incident," Melina said. "We found her notes in her computer, only a few minutes ago. She had planned to steal the formula Frank Stiles developed—the one he believed would make an ordinary mortal, immortal."

"Yes." Rhiannon waited, saying no more.

"Would it have worked?"

It *had* worked. Stormy knew that, because the vampires had used it to save the life of Willem Stone. And they'd learned how to recreate the formula, so that he could live as long as any of them. But she hadn't known the Athena group had been involved in any way with that case.

"Stiles is dead now, according to all reports," Rhiannon said. "So apparently his formula didn't work as he'd hoped."

Melina nodded slowly, sensing, perhaps, that there was more to the story than what she was being told. Stormy knew instinctively that Rhiannon would never reveal the secret of Willem Stone. And she thought she knew why. The Sisterhood would likely see him as a breach of their precious supernatural order. They might decide to do something about it.

"Why didn't your friends tell me, if they knew Brooke was trying to steal the formula? They must have known that was a betrayal of everything our order stands for."

Rhiannon shrugged. "You'd have to ask them."

"Why didn't *you* tell me, Rhiannon?"

She shrugged. "Because I don't trust any of you any more than I trust Brooke," Rhiannon said. "Besides, does it really matter at this point?"

"What else was in the files?" Stormy asked. "Anything about the ring or the scroll?" She told herself she no longer cared, but she thought a new topic might break some of the tension mounting in the room.

Melina nodded, allowing herself to be distracted for the moment. "Brooke believed that when Elisabeta returned to life, she would return with some means of gaining immortality. Speculated that she might somehow imbue the host body with the Belladonna antigen that Brooke believed Elisabeta had possessed during the course of her natural lifetime, enabling her to become a vampire."

"That wouldn't do Brooke any good, though," Stormy said.

"Brooke thought it would," Lupe said. "She was convinced Elisabeta could co-exist with another soul in the same body. She was willing to share her own body in exchange for eternal life." Lupe lowered her head. "My God, she intends to put on that ring and perform the rite. She means to bring Elisabeta into her own body."

"She's already done it," Stormy said.

The other two women gaped at her. She nodded and went on. "I just ran into her outside. Only she wasn't Brooke. She was one hundred percent Elisabeta. And I don't know about you, but I *know* that one. I've lived with her for a long time now, and I know damn well she has no intention of sharing that body with Brooke."

"She couldn't if she wanted to," Rhiannon said. "Two souls cannot long occupy the same body."

"Mine did," Stormy said. "She's been living in me for years."

"Yes, because the ring kept her from moving on. Brooke has no such anchor. She's surrendered her own body. In your body, Tempest, Elisabeta could only lurk and wait and occasionally take control. She wasn't strong enough to drive you out, and the power of the ring kept her from moving on. But Brooke has given herself over. Her own soul will shrivel, weaken and fade."

"How soon?" Melina asked.

"Melina?" Lupe was searching her mentor's eyes, her own huge and brown and full of questions.

"How soon?" Melina repeated, ignoring Lupe's unspoken question.

Rhiannon shrugged. "A few days, at most."

"Can we save her?"

"Why would we want to?" Lupe all but shouted her question. "Melina, she betrayed us. She betrayed the Sisterhood. She hit you over the head and left you lying there. Why would you want to help her now?"

Melina lowered her eyes. "I don't expect you to understand."

"No one could understand. It doesn't make any sense," Lupe said.

"To me it does." Melina looked to Rhiannon again. "Can we save Brooke?"

"Only by exorcising Elisabeta. And only after releasing the hold the ring has over her, so she can move on." Rhiannon lowered her head.

"I thought the ring's hold was dead, now that Brooke has performed the rite," Stormy said.

"Not entirely, I fear," Rhiannon replied. "If we free Elisabeta from Brooke's body, chances are the ring would still keep her from moving on as she should. She might very well return to your body,

Stormy. The ring's powers are that strong. We need to be sure."

"What if we can't do it?" Stormy asked.

Rhiannon bit her lip. "Then they'll both die. Brooke will move on, and Elisabeta will once again be trapped by the power of that ring. Stormy, it's your body Elisabeta needs. You are her spiritual descendant, I am convinced of this. You're spun from the same collective soul. What she's done, it's like…like performing an organ transplant between two incompatible patients. It cannot take. It cannot last."

Stormy lowered her head. "Well, good luck with that. I'm out of here. This no longer concerns me."

"I'm afraid it does, Stormy."

Stormy met Rhiannon's eyes, praying the vampiress had no rational argument to give.

"She'll realize soon enough that Brooke's body cannot hold her. And when she does, she'll come for yours. She still has the ring and the scroll."

And Vlad, Stormy thought. She has Vlad, too. And if he realized his precious wife was dying in Brooke's body, that she needed *hers* to survive, he might very well come for it himself.

Tough as she was, she knew she wouldn't stand a chance. Not against both of them.

"And there's the deadline. If her soul isn't at

peace, either fully re-established in a living body or fully relieved of the burden of physical life, she'll die. And so will you, Stormy. Tuesday. Midnight."

Stormy closed her eyes, lowered her head. "Fine. I'm in. But I'm not interested in saving Brooke. She got what she asked for, as far as I'm concerned." She recalled Lupe's words earlier, about her having no idea what would happen to her if Melina found out she had shared the Sisterhood's secrets with Stormy. "And from what I understand about the Sisterhood of Athena's rules and regs," she went on, "she's going to end up being executed anyway. Am I right about that?"

Melina gaped briefly, then looked away, refusing to answer.

"So I'm right on that one. There's no point. No one leaves this organization. And I'm not interested in freeing Elisabeta, so her soul can move on to eternal bliss. All I want to do is kill the bitch. Once and for all. I want her dead."

"It amounts to the same thing," Rhiannon said.

"Then let's do it."

"We're going to have to get her here," Rhiannon said. "We need to convince Vlad. And I think, Stormy, that you are the only one who can do that."

She lowered her head. "He won't listen to me."

"I think he will." The vampire shrugged. "I've been wondering, Stormy, why it is I like you, when I have little tolerance for most of your kind. And I've come to the reluctant conclusion that it's because you remind me of myself."

Stormy met the woman's dark eyes. "Is that a compliment?"

"Well, it was. But I'm wondering now if I was wrong about that. Because, frankly, I would never stand by and let some other woman walk away with the man I loved. I would fight."

Stormy sighed. "I've been fighting Elisabeta for sixteen years."

"Yes, you have. So what's one more night?"

She thought about that for a long moment; then, finally, she nodded, knowing Rhiannon was right. She was going to love Vlad forever, win or lose. She might as well give it one last try. Pride be damned. Her life was on the line here. "What do you want me to do?"

"Go to him. He's staying at a house, a vacant one, two miles north along this very road. I sensed his presence there when I arrived. Go to him, Stormy. Talk to him. Make him see that this is the only way."

She licked her lips, then nodded. "I think I'll walk. I could use the air."

10

As Stormy walked in the clear, warm night, she felt the rush in her mind as more of Vlad's blocks fell away and more memories of her time with him sixteen years ago returned.

She and Vlad had returned to the castle with Rhiannon, to find Rhiannon's mate, Roland, there waiting for them. Roland had, she recalled, coaxed Stormy into taking him for a drive into the local village for a proper meal. Partly to give Rhiannon time to speak to Vlad in private, Stormy suspected, and partly to give Roland time to speak to her; to ascertain for certain whether Vlad was holding her against her will. She had assured him that wasn't the case.

But as they'd driven back, along the winding road to the castle, she'd seen something that had hit her hard. A meadow, with an old foundation crumbling in one corner. She'd stopped the car and gotten out, compelled beyond reason. And then she'd blacked out.

When she roused again, Roland had been carrying her into Vlad's castle. And then...

She felt weak, sick, achy. Her body was limp, her head down, supported against Roland's shoulder, and her eyes refused to stay open for more than a heartbeat at a time.

"What the hell happened?" Vlad demanded.

"Damned if I know, my friend."

Vlad took her from Roland as he spoke, then turned and carried her into the castle. He laid her on the chaise, hands going to her cheeks as she felt his senses probing her mind. "Tell me everything, Roland."

"Of course. We had dinner, talked a bit. She seemed perfectly all right. Healthy, strong. But on the way back here..." *Roland paused, and Stormy forced her eyes open in time to see Vlad shoot him a look, one that begged the rest of the tale.*

Rhiannon sucked in a breath. "By the gods, Roland, what happened to your face?"

Roland touched his own face, and for the first time Stormy noted the four long scratches that ran from high on his cheek nearly to his jaw.

"Roland?" *Vlad prompted.*

"I don't know what happened, Vlad. She stopped the car and got out, hurrying into a meadow to examine an old foundation. I went after her, naturally. She seemed... distressed. Kept saying, 'She's coming.' And then...then she changed."

"In what way, Roland?" Rhiannon asked.

"In every way," Roland whispered. "Her voice, her stance, her scent. The color of her eyes turned to black, and she began speaking in a language I do not know. But I'm certain it was Italic."

"Romanian," Vlad said softly. He was stroking her hair now, leaning in close to watch her face, willing her to come more fully awake with his mind. She felt it but was too weak to obey. "It's happened before." Vlad looked away from Tempest only long enough to glance at the other man. "She put those scratches on your face?"

"Yes, when I tried to keep her from running off into the forest." He frowned. "She was strong, Vlad. Stronger than a mortal should be."

"It's exactly as Maxine described," Rhiannon said. "Is this an example of how your precious Elisabeta's spirit is melding with Stormy's own? By taking control from her? By attacking a friend?"

He continued stroking Stormy's face, her neck. "Wake up, Tempest. Wake now."

"Vlad, I do not remember your bride as being either violent or strong," Rhiannon said. "This is more like some kind of possession."

He shook his head. "Beta is confused and frustrated. Five hundred years she's been trying to find her way back to me. And now that she thinks she has, Tempest insists on fighting her."

"Perhaps for good reason."

Tempest blinked slowly and opened her eyes more fully. "I'm…I'm okay." She sat up slightly and pressed the heel of her hand to her forehead, closing her eyes tightly. "I remember seeing a foundation in a meadow and feeling compelled to explore it more closely. I pulled over, and Roland and I—" She stopped there and shot a look at Roland, then quickly lowered her head. "I did that to your face. I'm sorry."

"I don't believe it was you at all, Stormy," Roland said.

"It wasn't. Not really." She glanced at Vlad. "What made her come through so strongly?"

Vlad shook his head in apparent bewilderment, then glanced at Roland again. "Where was this foundation?"

"Off the main road, if you can call that dirt track a road," Roland said. "About a half mile down, where the forest ends, there's a large meadow with the foundation of a house in one corner."

Vlad closed his eyes and said nothing.

"The house," Tempest said softly. "It was her house. Elisabeta's."

"Yes, it was." Vlad looked at Rhiannon. "Do you still think I'm wrong?"

"In so many ways," she replied. "If this invading spirit is that of Elisabeta, Vlad, she is not the woman you remember. She has changed, warped, twisted."

"You're the one who is wrong."

She met his eyes, then moved closer to Tempest, leaned over her, clasped her hand. "Come back with us, Tempest. Let me find a way to exorcise this creature from you once and for all."

Tempest sat up and swung her legs around to put her feet on the floor. She looked at Vlad, searched his face. He couldn't seem to hold her gaze. Guilt? Did he know full well what he was doing to her? she wondered. Did he know Rhiannon was right?

"It will be dawn soon," he said softly. "There wouldn't be time to leave tonight, even if she wanted to."

"Dawn has no impact on her, Vlad," Roland said. "Our jet is waiting at the landing strip fifteen miles from here, with instructions to take her home should she show up asking to leave, with or without us." He looked at Tempest again. "You can go if you wish it, Stormy. We'll join you as soon as we can."

Vlad pushed his hands through his hair and paced away. "Dammit, why won't you stay out of this?"

"Because you'll destroy her, Vlad," Rhiannon said. "How many more of these episodes do you think she can withstand? Look at her!"

He whirled on her, his eyes blazing. "I'll destroy you if you continue to interfere!"

Roland stepped between the two, and Vlad hit him, a single, powerful blow that sent the man sailing across the room, where he hit a stone wall and sank to the floor. Rhiannon launched herself at Vlad then, growling like a wildcat as she swung both fists into his chest and put him flat on his back as surely as if he'd been hit by a wrecking ball.

She came on as he struggled to get upright. But then Tempest was on her feet, shouting, her voice deep and strong, despite the weakness still invading her body. "Stop it! Stop it now, all of you!"

Rhiannon froze and turned slowly to stare at her. Vlad remained where he was, on his back on the floor, and Roland lifted his head, but not his body, from where it had come to rest.

"Don't you think it should be up to me whether I leave or not? And how I decide to deal with this presence? It's my problem, after all. My life. Why are you all arguing over what I should do when the decision is no one's— no one's—but my own."

She crossed the room to where Vlad lay on the his back and extended a hand to him. He took it, searching her face. She knew full well he had no intention of letting her go, not yet. Not until she remembered. He was obsessed with his damned dead bride. But Stormy had her own reasons for staying. She needed to solve this thing.

And she hoped he would come to his senses and decide to let Elisabeta go at long last. That he would come to love her, instead.

She helped him to his feet, then turned to walk away from him, and knelt in front of Roland. "Are you all right?"

He nodded, and she helped him up, as well, frowning as she cocked her head to glance at the back of his. "He has a bit of a gash here, Rhiannon. You should bandage it before you rest. Do you two have a place to stay tonight?"

Her meaning was clear in her tone, she thought. They were not to stay here.

"We have accommodations on the jet. Quite luxurious ones, actually." Rhiannon came to check Roland's head wound as she spoke. She touched it, and Roland sucked air through his teeth. Rhiannon shot Vlad a narrow-eyed glare. "I should kill you for this."

"No one's killing anyone," Tempest said. "You two should go if you want to make it to the jet before sunrise."

"And you?" Roland asked.

Vlad watched her, awaiting her answer, and she knew damn well he would keep her with him by force if he had to. Or anyway he would try.

"I'm staying," she said. "One more night. I gave my word." She turned to Vlad. "Just as you gave yours that you'd see me safely back home after that. And I'm holding you to it, Vlad." She also knew he had no intention of letting her go until he was damn good and ready. But she had to at least pretend to believe. God forbid he should ever realize what a fool she was to have fallen for him so hard.

Stormy turned back to the others. "I'll be fine. You see?"

"Oh, I see, Stormy. But do you?" Rhiannon had her fingertips pressed to Roland's head to keep it from bleeding. "Do you understand who you're dealing with? This is Dracula, child. And if he decides to keep you here, no power on earth will set you free."

She blinked, then turned to Vlad, her eyes probing his. "I trust him," she lied. "He'll keep his word."

"And if he doesn't?"

She shrugged. "Then it'll be my mistake, won't it?"

Rhiannon scowled at her. "God save us from spunky mortals with more courage than brains," she muttered. "Courage won't help you in this, Stormy."

"It's never let me down before."

Sighing, Rhiannon seemed to give up. "If someone can locate a bandage, we'll be on our way."

Vlad nodded toward a cabinet visible just through an open door at one end of the room. "I always have a supply on hand."

"As do we," Rhiannon snapped. "But we left ours on the jet, never dreaming we'd have need of it here—in the home of my own sire."

"Sire?" Stormy asked with a gasp. "Vlad, you... you're the vampire who made Rhiannon?"

"I am. Though there are times when I sorely regret it."

Rhiannon left, then returned in a moment with adhesive strips and gauze, which she applied to Roland's head. Then she took his hand, and, without a goodbye, they headed for the door.

Rhiannon stopped there and turned briefly, but she spoke to Tempest, not to Vlad. "If you're not back in the States in a reasonable period, we'll be back." She slanted a look at Vlad. "And we won't be alone."

"Oh?" he asked, his tone sarcastic. "Bringing along an army of vampires, are you? Enough to set Dracula straight?"

"I won't need to bring them, Vlad. There are vampires everywhere. More than an antisocial creature like yourself could even imagine. And while they are different, there's one thing they pretty much have in common.

One value we all share, by unspoken mutual agreement. We don't do harm to mortals or meddle in their lives. And we don't tolerate rogues who do."

"You protect The Chosen. Isn't that meddling?"

"Tempest is not one of The Chosen."

"And yet you're here, meddling."

"I'm here to prevent you from destroying her. And in the process, yourself."

Vlad averted his eyes. "Doesn't matter."

"Yes, Vlad. It does." She sighed and opened the door, walked through and, without looking back, spoke to him one last time. "What you've done this night will not be undone. Goodbye, Vlad."

He didn't respond, only watched as the door banged closed, apparently on its own, and then turned to Tempest. "Thank you," he said.

"For what?"

"For trusting me."

"Do you think I'm an idiot?" she snapped. "Hell, Vlad, I don't trust you as far as I can throw you. Not when I know perfectly well whose side you're on in this…this war of mine. I just wanted to get rid of them so we could get on with this. I still think the answers to my issues might lie here, in this place and, maybe, in you."

His face turned angry. He took her arm and started for the stairs. "Tonight," he said, "we share the bed."

"Fine by me."

She knew he saw what she tried to hide. The flash of desire, of longing, of hunger in her eyes. She wanted him, even now.

She shuttered the desire, hid the ripple of delicious fear, buried them both in sarcasm. "You'll be dead to the world in twenty minutes, anyway."

"But very much alive again come sundown, Tempest."

She stopped halfway up the stairs, turning to spear him with her eyes. "Are you trying to frighten me into running away, Vlad? Into taking off as soon as you sleep, finding that jet and begging its pilot to take me home?"

He stared into her eyes. "Believe me when I tell you, frightening you away is not what I want."

"Then knock it off with the idle threats, okay?"

"My threats, Tempest, are far from idle. And I don't think you will mind at all when I carry them out."

Vlad carried Elisabeta, in Brooke's body, to the house a few miles away where he'd holed up for the night, and where he'd sensed the presence of a mortal upon waking this very evening. Even without his heightened senses he would have known that someone had been there. There had been shards of broken glass on the floor. Curved, as if from a wine glass. And the small rickety wooden table had been moved, and bore the soft drippings of a recently burned candle. A black candle. Which suggested workings of negative magick.

The scent that lingered was that of a woman.

This woman, he realized now. Though not precisely this one. She was different now. She was *Elisabeta* now.

He took her into the house, but not down the basement stairs to where he'd set up a secure haven. Instead, he carried Elisabeta into the back part of the house, where a sofa was covered in a filthy sheet. Then he yanked the sheet away, relieved that the fabric beneath it appeared far cleaner.

"Here now," he said, lowering her down onto the cushions. "Just rest. Are you still in pain?" He lifted her blouse to just below her breasts, to see the bruises already darkening the skin that covered her ribs.

"It's…it's better now," she said, her accent slighter than it had been. He supposed she'd had sixteen years of listening while she lived inside Tempest.

"I forgot how much it hurts to be…alive," Beta said.

He frowned as he drew his gaze from her bruised ribs to her face. Her meaning, he knew, went beyond the physical pain she had been dealt this night.

"Is it as bad for you?" she asked. "Pain, I mean. Hurting?"

"Worse."

"Worse?"

He nodded, lowering her shirt again. "In vampires, sensation is magnified. Pain included."

"God, how will I bear it?"

His eyes shot to hers. "How will you—"

"But you heal fast, don't you? Every ache and pain goes away as soon as the sun comes up. And when you wake again, you're as good as new. That's the way it works, isn't it?"

"Yes."

She nodded. "It's starting to feel better." She smiled at him and tried to sit up a little. "When will you do it?"

"Do what, Beta?"

"Change me, of course. I want you to make me immortal. A vampire, like you."

He stared at her, shook his head slowly as what she was saying became clear to him. And only then did he realize what he hadn't before. He smelled it on her, sensed it on her. The Belladonna Antigen. But it was different somehow. Weak. Thin. Altered in some way.

Brooke had not possessed it before. Of that he was certain. Had The Chosen been so close, he would have sensed it at once.

"It has to be done in just the right way, Beta. At just the right time."

She clasped his shoulder and drew herself nearer to him, brushing her lips over his jaw and cheek. "When will that be?"

"I don't know." Her mouth slid around to his, and for a moment he kissed her. But then he clasped her shoulders and held her while he tugged his mouth from hers. "Beta, we have to talk."

"But I've missed you so, Vlad. I don't want to wait."

"It won't be long. But if you want to be made over—"

"All right." She pursed her lips, then turned so that she was sitting up on the old sofa and leaned back against it. "What is it you need to know?"

He nearly sagged in relief. "Tell me about Brooke."

Her head came up, eyes narrow. *"Brooke?"*

"It's her body you're using, Beta. I need to know about it. She…wasn't one of The Chosen. I'd have known if one were that close."

"Oh, no. Do you mean…?"

"No, love, no. I sense the antigen in you." He stared at her. "I suppose you must have brought it with you somehow."

She smiled. "Maybe I did."

"But it's not full blown, Beta. It's not strong. I'm not sure it's quite the same. The transformation might not work."

"Or it might."

"If it fails, you'll die, Beta."

She blinked rapidly. "Well, we don't want that." Then she frowned at him. "Are you sure you're telling me the truth, Vlad?"

"Why would I lie?"

Shrugging, she watched his face carefully. "Because of her, of course."

"Who? Brooke?"

"Tempest."

He shook his head. "She no longer has anything to do with this."

"She does if you're in love with her. If you've decided you'd rather be with her than me. I've waited five hundred years, Vlad."

"You didn't wait at all, Elisabeta. Not even three days. You believed them when they told you I'd been killed on our wedding night, and you flung yourself to your death."

"A living death," she whispered. "Trapped, like being buried alive. You did that to me."

"I was trying to save you."

"You destroyed me. All so you could have me

back again. If you've decided you don't want me now, after all I've been through…"

"I haven't. I'm telling you the truth, Beta. We need to take some time, be sure you'll survive the change before we proceed." She didn't argue, so he pressed on. "Where is Brooke now?"

Beta sighed. "She's here, Vlad. Cowering inside this body. But she will not remain long. This I know."

"How do you know?"

"I simply do." She held his gaze; then, lowering her eyelids to half mast, she lay back on the sofa, her hands going to her blouse to open its buttons. "None of it matters. Not really. I'm here now. We can be together at last. The way we've both been waiting to be for all these years." She rose from the sofa, trailing her fingertips over his face. "Take me now, Vlad. Take my blood. Make me immortal."

He licked his lips, staring at her as she pushed the blouse apart, baring her breasts—no, some other woman's breasts. And he *did* want her. But he bent to snatch the sheet from the floor and draped it over her. "Not yet. You're not strong enough. There's something…not right."

Something changed then, in her eyes. Something dark came into them and shadowed her face. She backed away from him, and, moving so quickly he didn't seen it coming, she yanked out a blade she'd had hidden somewhere in the clothes she wore and drew it swiftly across her palm.

"Beta, don't!" He reached for her, but she danced away. Then she lifted her hand. Scarlet blood welled in her palm. His eyes fixed on it, and he couldn't look away as she moved closer again. And then she pressed her palm to his lips.

Hunger raged in him. He hadn't fed sufficiently in far too long. He had been obsessed with this situation to the exclusion of everything, including his own needs.

He closed his eyes, tasted the blood from Elisabeta's hand, and the bloodlust swelled in him. He gripped her wrist and licked a hot path over her palm, taking every droplet.

And then he drew away, his eyes narrow. "It's partly your blood, Beta. The Belladonna Antigen, the thing that made you one of The Chosen when you lived in your own body, it's there. But just barely. It's still partly Brooke's blood, coursing in your veins. She didn't have the antigen. You know this."

"How would I possibly know?"

He shook his head. "It doesn't matter. I know. She didn't have it, or I would have sensed it the moment I set foot in this town, much more so on the grounds of Athena House. She didn't have it, and now that you've taken possession of her body, she does. But only slightly."

"It's enough. It has to be enough. Make me over, Vlad. Make me what you are." She stared up at him, her eyes pleading.

"It wouldn't work. Not like this."

She lowered her head and turned away from him. "I don't believe you."

"Beta, I'm telling you the truth. If I try to change you now, this body you've stolen will simply die. I'm sure of it."

"I didn't steal it! It was given to me." Blinking, she turned and stared up at him. "Do you still love me, Vlad? Do you still love me at all?"

"I'll always love you."

"Then prove it to me." She moved closer, slid her hands, one of which was now wrapped in a handkerchief, up the front of his shirt, tugged at the buttons there. "Show me you love me and not her. Do it now." She reached up to kiss his neck, to bite it and tug at the skin there. "Prove it to me," she whispered, pressing her hips to his.

Vlad closed his eyes, his hands lowering to her shoulders and then to her waist.

She tipped her head up for a kiss, and he

couldn't refuse her, not with the longing and hope he saw in her eyes. He kissed her. Her fingers twisted in his hair. She sucked his tongue, drove hers into his mouth and kissed him with a fervor he'd never felt in her before. And when she broke the kiss, she pressed his head to her throat. "It *is* me you love. I knew it. Take me, darling. It's been so long."

Very gently, he pulled free of her.

"What's wrong, my love?" She blinked up at him, searching his face. "Is it this body? Is it not to your liking?"

"No, it's not that." There was nothing unattractive about the body Elisabeta occupied. Brooke's body.

"I can't do this. Not now, Beta. You're far too weak." And even as he said it, he felt like the worst kind of hypocrite. He'd taken women before. But not like this. In the past, when he'd needed to feed, he'd lured women to him, used the power of his mind to ease every inhibition in theirs and then ascertained the depths of their desire.

Sometimes he only drank. Other times, he took them in every imaginable way, but only if he sensed that, deep down, they wanted it. And always he left them with no memory of what had transpired.

This was different. He couldn't reach Brooke's

mind, because Elisabeta was in control of it. He couldn't test her desire, because Elisabeta was ruling her body. But she would be aware. A captive inside her own body. He'd heard Tempest describe it enough times. And even he, even Dracula, wouldn't stoop so low. He'd never needed to.

"I do not understand you. What could be wrong with—"

"It would be a rape, Elisabeta. It's not your body. Brooke—"

"Who cares about Brooke? She will be dead soon enough. She is not coming back, Vlad. It won't matter at all."

He frowned down at her.

"I have what I needed from her. A body. I would have preferred the other one but—"

"How can you sure Brooke's soul will leave this body?" he asked. Partly to change the topic, and partly because he needed to know exactly what was happening.

"I do not know *how* I know, only that my soul has taken this body, fully taken it. I can feel her weakening, even now. She will be dead in a few days. She will move on to some other realm. She cannot last."

"Why not?" Vlad asked. "You did. You lasted

years inside Tempest's body, even though she was in control."

"Yes, but I *could not* move on. I was bound, Vlad, by the power of the ring."

"I see."

"If that little bitch would simply have died as she ought to have… But I do not wish to talk about her. Or even to hear her name again."

He frowned. "She's a part of you. A part of all of this."

"I hate her," she said. "I wish her dead. When I am a vampire, she will be my first kill." As she said it, she smiled slowly, but her smile froze, perhaps at the look of surprise she must have seen in his eyes.

"Oh, Vlad, darling, don't look that way. Death is not horrible. I used to think it was, when I was young and naive. I howled in pain when my family died of the plague. My brothers. My baby sister. I wanted to die with them. But now I understand so much more. Death is…it's a lie. There is nothing to fear in it. When you kill someone, they do not stop existing. They only…move out of the way." She sighed, smiling wistfully. "To be a vampire—it must be like being a god," she whispered.

"No, Beta. It's not like being a god."

"Oh, but it is. I've been paying attention all these

years. Tempest, she deals with your kind all the time. You never die."

"We can die, just as anyone else can. Only the means are different. Fire, or loss of blood, or sunlight—"

"You can read minds. Influence the thoughts of mortals."

"So can some mortals," he said. "There's nothing so godlike about those skills."

"Vampires have the power of life and death in their hands."

"As does any criminal with a handgun," he told her. "We're not animals, Beta. We don't kill simply because we can."

She frowned up at him. "I do not remember this side of you."

"What side?"

She shrugged. "Vlad, this is not who you are."

"Not who I was, perhaps. But, Beta, it's been centuries. Perhaps I've changed."

"It's more than that. You refuse to make love to me, and it has nothing to do with the simpering ghost of a spirit still clinging by a strand to this body. It's *her*. It's Tempest."

"She has nothing to do with this. I told you, I've changed." He studied her. "You've changed, too."

"Yes, well, being imprisoned for a few centuries will do that to a person." She turned and started across the room toward the door.

Vlad gripped her shoulders to stop her. "Where are you going?"

"If you will not change me, Vlad, I'll find some other vampire who will. Trust me, I know where to find them. I learned a lot while I was trapped inside Tempest Jones."

She pulled free, but he gripped her arm again. "Dammit, Beta, don't leave like this."

She turned so fast that he didn't see it coming, didn't see her hand drawing the knife she'd tucked into the pants she wore. But he felt it. The blade sank deep into his belly.

Vlad's entire body erupted in pain. His eyes went wide, then bulged as he clutched his middle and fell to his knees.

"Well, what do you know? You were telling the truth about that much, at least. You *do* feel pain more intensely than mortals." She tipped her head to one side. "Is it true, what Tempest believes? That the older the vampire, the more heightened his senses? Because, if it is, that must *really* hurt."

She shrugged, then dropped to her knees so she

was at eye level with him again. He struggled to speak but couldn't form a word. The pain was too much.

"I can help you, Vlad. I can bandage that up for you and feed you from my own body. *If* you will transform me. Make me what you are, what I was born to be."

"It would kill you," he told her. "I can't be the cause of that, Beta."

She shrugged and got to her feet again. "Then… goodbye."

11

The front door slammed open, and Vlad lifted his head, trying to blink past the red haze of pain to see who was there. And then he knew, even before he saw her. He *felt* her.

Tempest. Her wide eyes swept the room, came to rest upon him, where he knelt on the floor, clutching his belly and bleeding, and then turned their full fury on Elisabeta.

"What the *hell* did you do?"

Elisabeta turned from where she'd been standing, and studying Vlad as if she'd never seen a bleeding man before. She faced Tempest, and her stance became stiffer. "Why are you here?" she asked. "Can't you see that my husband and I are having a long overdue reunion?"

"Yeah, I can see that."

"She has a knife, Tempest." Vlad managed to force out the words.

"I see that, too," she said. Then she stepped and turned, and lashed out with one foot, then the other. The two kicks were delivered powerfully, rapidly. The first sent the blade flying from Elisabeta's hand, and the second connected with her borrowed jaw.

Beta's head snapped back, and her body jerked before she hit the floor. Tempest didn't bother with her any further. Instead she turned and hurried to Vlad. Dropping to her knees, she gripped his blood-soaked shirt in her hands and ripped it open without taking time to unbutton it. He saw the way her lips thinned, the way her eyes flickered when they fixed on the wound in his gut. But she didn't give her reaction any more time than she'd given Beta. Instead, she tugged off the shirt she wore, revealing the T-shirt she had on underneath. She balled up her white button down shirt and held it to his belly.

"Press it to the wound. Press it *hard*, Vlad."

Behind her! He started to speak a warning, but before he made even a sound, Tempest sprang up, turned and slammed the heel of her hand to Beta's chin, then the other hand, then the first again, in a rapid fire assault that had Beta's head snapping like a punching bag. With the final blow, blood spurted from Beta's nose.

Beta shrieked, clutching her face and backing away. "*Tarva!* Bitch!" she cried as she blinked in shock at the pain and the blood on her hands. "I will kill you! I swear I will kill you if it's the last thing I do."

"Yeah, I'm worried about that. I couldn't fight you before, Elisabeta. You were inside me. But you made a big mistake getting out, getting a body, because I *can* fight you now, and I damn well intend to."

"You'll never win."

"I already have." Tempest reached for her, gripped her arm and tugged her away from the door.

"Tempest," Vlad managed. "What are you going to do with her?"

She looked down at him, her eyes filled with what looked like blatant disbelief, but before she could answer, Elisabeta bit her hand, and when she jerked it away with a gasp, Beta whirled and ran from the house as fast as Brooke's legs would carry her.

Tempest lunged as if to give chase, then stopped herself, turning slowly back to him. "I should let you bleed out, you know that?"

He nodded once, slowly. "Give me a few more minutes and I'll oblige you."

"Shit."

He fell backward, too dizzy to remain on his knees, as retaining consciousness became a struggle.

Stormy wished for her car and the heavy duty first-aid kit she kept in the trunk. In her line of work, it didn't pay to be without one. Vampires were bleeders. A lot of them were friends. And most of the people who knew of their existence would just as soon see them all dead.

But she'd decided to walk tonight, so she didn't have her car. She was just going to have to make do. She did have some supplies in her backpack.

She raced through the house in search of a kitchen or bathroom, glancing at her watch on the way. Not even eleven yet. There was a lot of time before dawn, when his wound would heal on its own. A lot of time—he could be dead before the sun rose.

Kitchen. Excellent, the water faucets worked. She peeled her T-shirt off over her head, and used her teeth to tear off the short sleeves. Then she put it back on, and soaked the sleeves in water.

Back in what she presumed to be the living room of the broken down house, she saw Vlad trying to get to his feet and shook her head. "Stay down. Just…stay down, or you'll make it worse."

"I thought…you'd gone after her."

"And leave you to die? I'm pretty pissed at you, but not quite that much." She sighed. "Sit down. Lean back against the wall there and let me see how bad it is."

He sank down, leaning back on the wall as she pushed his shirt off his shoulders and began wiping the blood away with the wet cloths. It didn't matter that she had no soap or antiseptic. It wasn't an infection that would kill him—it was the bleeding. But she had to be able to see the wound.

"Where did you learn to fight like that?"

"Hmm?" Kneeling, she straddled him and tried to quell the queasiness that washed over her at seeing so much blood coating his rippled abs.

"Martial arts moves," he said. "Flawlessly delivered."

"I'm a black belt in Tae Kwon Do."

Her hands were shaking as she continued to wash away the worst of the blood. It didn't do a lot of good, because there was more coming.

"I didn't know."

"I imagine there's a lot you don't know, Vlad. You couldn't possibly have watched my every move for the past sixteen years. Here," she said, pressing the wads of cloth to the wound. "Hold this tight."

He did, but she could see it was hurting him. As

old as he was, he probably felt a splinter in his finger the way she would feel a knife wound. God help him. It was nothing compared to what was coming.

She'd dropped her mini-backpack by the door when she'd come in, just before she'd dropped Elisabeta close beside it. She went for it now, brought it back to where he lay and dug around inside. She might not have a full blown first-aid kit, but she wasn't entirely without resources.

Being prepared had become a way of life for her.

She pulled out a small packet that contained curved needles and silk thread. Vlad spied the needle when she took it out of the pack, averted his eyes and swore.

"I know. It's going to hurt like hell, but if I don't stitch this up, you won't last until dawn. I don't see any other way to stop the bleeding."

He nodded. "I know. It's all right, go ahead."

"I intend to."

She bent closer, pinched the edges of the still-bleeding wound together and jabbed the needle through his skin. Vlad's entire body tensed, and he sucked air through his teeth.

"Sorry," she muttered and quickly knotted the silk and prepared to make a second stitch.

It would only take six. Three would be plenty for

a mortal, but this was a vampire. She couldn't leave any space between one thread and the next or the blood would just seep through.

"I wasn't going to hurt her, you know. I just wanted to take her back to the mansion."

"For what purpose?"

She jabbed the needle in. "Rhiannon's there. She says Brooke and Beta will both die if things aren't dealt with. She says Brooke's body is incompatible. That the soul won't *take*."

"She needs *your* body."

"Yeah. Fortunately, you're in no shape to deliver me to her right now."

He lifted his brows, forcing his eyes to focus on hers.

She averted hers, noting that he didn't deny that had been his intent all along. She put the stitches as close together as she could and tried her best to ignore the pain she was causing the man she loved beyond all reason.

By the time she finished, he was trembling. She cleaned the blood from his skin, watching the area she'd sewn up to see if the blood would still manage to escape. It didn't. She covered the wound with a gauze square from her purse and stuck it in place with the tiny roll of adhesive tape. Then she sat back on her heels. "Done."

She looked at his face when he didn't respond, and alarm shot through her. His eyes were closed. He lay still. The pain must have been tremendous to make him lose consciousness. Unless this was from the blood loss. Unless he was...

"Hey." She smacked his cheeks. "Come on, Vlad, talk to me."

He blinked but couldn't seem to stay focused, and his eyes fell closed again. "Sorry."

"Not your fault." She shrugged. "Well, actually, it's entirely your fault."

Barbs were lost on him at the moment, though. She slid an arm beneath his shoulders, raised him into a more upright position. "Come on, we need to get you off the floor and into your safe room, wherever that is."

"Safe room?"

"I know you have one. You people *always* have one. So where is it, Vlad? Where have you been spending your days?"

"Oh." He pressed his lips together, swallowed. "Downstairs. There's a room in the basement."

"Isn't there always?"

She stepped in front of him, sliding her hands underneath his arms. "I'm going to help you get up, okay?"

He bent a leg to press his foot flat to the floor and gripped her shoulders with his hands. "I'll try."

"Here we go." She lifted and pulled him forward, and he rose up, only to fall against her chest. She nearly went over backward but managed to keep her footing. She held him hard and told herself this was not the time to think about how much she wanted him pressed against her. Bare chested and needing her. Just not needing her quite like this.

"Easy. Okay, I've got you."

Vlad lifted his head, easing his body's weight from her, but she knew he wasn't strong enough to stand on his own. She pulled his arm around her shoulders. "Lean on me, Vlad. I'm stronger than I look."

"Stronger than I ever knew," he said.

"Stronger than I ever was. I've been working with people like you for the last sixteen years. Have to try to keep up."

He leaned on her, though not as much as she thought he should have, and pointed the way while she walked him to the stairs. She had to hold him close to fit them both down the basement stairs side by side, and he almost fell once. She gripped him hard, held him up with an arm locked around his waist, grunted with the effort.

Eventually they got to the bottom and through

the door into the private room. The room was small and Spartan. A king-size four-poster bed, neatly made, took up most of the space. No windows, of course, so it was dark as a dungeon. She supposed windowless rooms were a plus in the vamp real-estate market. She yanked back the bedcovers, then eased him down until he was sitting on the edge of the mattress.

"Can you manage to get the shirt off, Vlad? There's no point ruining the sheets."

"I can manage."

"All right. I'll be right back."

He held up a hand. "There's no need. I'll be fine here until morning. Just…lock the doors on your way out."

She scowled at him. The remark stung, but she told herself this was no time to let her hurt feelings interfere with what had to be done. "I said I'll be back." Then she hurried up the stairs into the main part of the house. She locked all the doors, checked the windows and commandeered a candle she found on a shelf. She always carried matches in her bag. On her way back down, she locked the cellar door, then returned to the hidden little room and locked its door, as well, after she entered.

And the entire time, she was still stinging over

his eagerness to get rid of her. But she congratulated herself on not stopping to cry or to lick her wounds. His were more serious right now. Besides, this wasn't about her broken heart. It was bigger. Elisabeta had to be stopped. Stormy's life depended on it.

"All secure," she said when she re-entered the saferoom and lit the candle.

He was still sitting on the edge of the bed. His shirt was pushed down off one incredible shoulder, and that was all. A small red stain showed through the bandage on his belly.

"Damn. It's bled a little more." She set the candle on a stand and moved close to him, stood between his thighs. "Don't move. Just let me do this."

Vlad closed his eyes and obeyed her, remaining motionless as she slid his shirt down the other shoulder, her hands running over him as she did. She couldn't quite deny herself this small pleasure. Her palm skimmed over his shoulder, down his arm, over the firm swell of his biceps and all the way to his wrist. She tried not to feel anything in reaction to the sensation of his skin sliding beneath her palm, her fingers, but she responded anyway.

She slid the shirt's one remaining sleeve over his hand and set it aside. "I'm going to ease you back now. I don't want you to try to do anything, Vlad.

You tense up your abs, and that's going to cause the bleeding to start again. All right?"

He nodded.

She got onto the bed behind him and put her arms around him. "Now just let your weight fall against me. No straining. Just relax against me."

She helped to guide him, and once she supported his upper body's weight in her arms, she lowered him slowly and slightly sideways, until his head rested on the pillows.

She got up then. His knees were bent, legs still over the side of the bed. She tugged off his shoes, peeled off the socks, tugged the covers back still farther, and then lifted his legs onto the bed. Finally she pulled the covers over him.

"There. Comfortable?"

He nodded. His eyes were closed again.

She moved up to stand beside the bed, lifted the covers to check the wound, but didn't see any sign of further bleeding. At least no more had seeped through the makeshift bandages. She walked to the other side of the bed, climbed up onto it, being careful not jostle it too much, and sat with her legs folded to one side.

He opened his eyes. "You don't have to stay."

She nodded. But she wasn't really listening to him. She was thinking and trying construct her argument. "I know your kind, Vlad. I know more about your kind than any mortal you've probably ever met. Some of my best friends are vampires. You understand?"

He nodded, though all she could see was the back of his head from her current vantage point.

"You're going to die before morning," she told him.

He rolled onto his back and blinked up at her. "I don't think—"

"You're going to die. You've lost too much blood. Look at you. You can barely keep your eyes open. I stopped the bleeding, but you don't have enough to keep you going until dawn. I can see that." She pursed her lips. "You won't make it unless you let me help you. Let me…do what needs to be done."

His eyes sharpened slightly, plumbing hers. "You would do that for me? Even after…?"

"After you chose her over me? Look, Vlad, I know you'd rather it was her, here with you, helping you right now."

"If it was, I'd be dead by now. She's…she's confused, Tempest."

"She's insane. As I've been trying to tell you all along." She closed her eyes, sighed. "We have to be practical. You need blood. I've got plenty. So let's just do this thing." She turned her arm, palm up, and stared at her wrist. Then, with a nod, she held it out to him. "Go on."

"It will…it will create a bond."

"You drank from me already, remember? And yeah, it did create a bond. It's how I knew you were in trouble when I got close to this place tonight. I felt it, your pain." She bit her lip for a moment, averting her eyes. "Frankly, I don't think what I feel could get much stronger, anyway. I'm like a fly in a spiderweb. But don't worry. I'm not going to let you destroy me." She lifted her wrist toward him. "Go on, do it."

Vlad ignored her proffered wrist, reaching up to cup her nape instead. He drew her downward, closer to him.

Halfway down, she resisted, and he stopped pulling her closer but didn't let her back away, either. Her face was only a few inches above his. And she wanted him so much it hurt. It hurt like nothing had ever hurt before.

"Not like this," she whispered.

"Like this, Tempest. *Just* like this."

Stormy closed her eyes and let him move her until her face was only a breath away from his. His lips brushed her cheek and then her jaw. She shivered in anticipation as his mouth slid to her neck. His fingers spread into her hair and caressed her there, his touch as soft as a breath. He kissed her neck, and she sighed, because it felt so damn good. She stretched out her legs and lay there beside him, her chest on his, her throat resting against his mouth. Involuntarily, she arched her neck, wanting him, *needing* him, to take her.

He whispered her name against her skin, and then she felt his mouth open to suckle her there. And finally there was the shock of pain as he bit down. She gasped, but the piercing hurt was brief and delicious in a forbidden way. And then he was drinking her, and her body shivered its response.

It was like sex—every part of her alive with pleasure at the sensations of his teeth sinking deeper into her flesh, of his tongue caressing, of the gentle and then more aggressive sucking of his mouth as he fed at her throat. She couldn't bear it. The sensations built, and every muscle in her body coiled and tightened as she yearned for release.

And then he was moving, rolling her onto her back, his own body moving over hers. He was still feeding from her while his hand shoved its way down the front of her jeans.

"Vlad…you shouldn't move or…oh, hell."

She stopped speaking, because his fingers were sliding into her. And he had to know then, if he hadn't before, what he was doing to her. How hot and wet and hungry she was. For him. Only for him. He worked her with his hand, and she spread her legs shamelessly, craving what only he could give her.

Then he found the nub that pulsed and cried for attention, and rubbed it with his thumb. He bit down harder at her throat, and pressed and rolled that tender, aching bud harder at the same time, as his fingers slid in and out of her. She climaxed in an orgasm so powerful she thought it would melt the flesh from her bones.

On and on it went. She went rigid, then began to shake and spasm and moan. She arched her pelvis to his hand and tipped her head back until her chin was pointing straight up at the ceiling. And he was merciless. He was inside her, owning her body, his teeth in her throat, his fingers in her vagina. And he wouldn't let go. He just kept working her, making her come, the sensations going on and on and on. The intensity didn't fade. Rather, it built, until her body was jerking and shivering so much it hurt. She was literally thrashing on the bed as he kept pushing her, forcing the pleasure that was almost beyond endurance. And even the pain was good. But it was too much. Too much.

Still, he kept on, until she screamed for mercy.

Finally, finally, the sensations peaked and began to ebb. He withdrew his fingers and then his fangs from her. He stopped drinking and instead kissed her neck in a way that was almost healing in its tenderness. And then he eased onto his back again, keeping one arm around her and drawing her onto her side, so that she snuggled against him.

She was weak from the power of that orgasm. And perhaps from the blood he'd taken, as well. And she was still feeling the shivery aftereffects of the climax. She'd never felt anything like that before. It was beyond human. They'd shared blood before, but Stormy knew, despite her denials, that each and every time it happened, the bond between them would become more potent, more powerful. She was making all of this harder on herself. Everything she did lately was self-destructive and stupid.

And yet she loved it. She loved *him*.

Lazily, Stormy reached down and drew the covers over them, and as she did, she checked the bandage. A little more blood stained it than had been there before. But not a lot, and she knew hers had replenished him. He would be all right.

But would *she*? Would she ever be all right again?

She felt dizzy, sated, weak and utterly compliant. He could do whatever he wanted to her tonight, and she knew she wouldn't resist, not after that. He'd devoured her will along with her blood. Not that she'd had a hell of a lot to begin with, where he was concerned.

She lowered her head to his shoulder. "Thank you, Vlad," she whispered. And then she fell asleep in his arms.

Elisabeta was confused and hurting when she left the house where Vlad was staying. She'd stabbed him—stabbed her beloved husband! She could hardly believe she'd done it. But he would be all right, surely. She had been angry, told him goodbye, but she hadn't meant it. And after all, he was immortal, a vampire. He would be all right.

She couldn't focus on any other alternative—she had more than she could deal with just...just *living*.

She wasn't used to the intricacies, much less the full blown sensations, of being incarnate again. And she'd lost touch with how fragile life could be. Oh, she had felt the stuff of living several times since her death, but only briefly, when she'd managed to take control of Tempest's body. Now she was inhabiting a body all her own. Brooke was trying to take it back, but her efforts were pathetic, at best. She was no threat. Already she was weakening.

But God, the sensations!

That *tarva* Tempest had *hurt* her. Blood had spurted from her nose, and pain had exploded in her face. It hurt for a long while after their fight. She was not accustomed to physical pain.

And there were other things. An unfamiliar pang in her stomach rumbled until she realized it was hunger. But she wasn't sure how to deal with that. She hadn't had to make her own way in the physical world in a very, very long time. More than five centuries. But she had found that if she searched her mind, she could access the knowledge Brooke had acquired during her lifetime, just as she had been able to access Tempest's storehouses of information.

There was *money* in her pocket, Brooke's memory told her. There was a twenty-four-hour grocery store a mere mile and a half away. She could purchase food there.

It seemed a very long walk to Elisabeta. She was tired long before she made it there, and by the time she did arrive, she was almost too tired to want to eat anymore. And another urge had made itself known, demanding to be dealt with. Fortunately Brooke's knowledge included the finer points of public restrooms, and Beta was able to find and use the one within the small grocery store. But it felt odd and disgusting. She'd forgotten some of the less pleasant aspects of physical existence.

She nearly jumped out of her skin when the porcelain bowl seemed to come to life all on its own the instant she rose from it. Water whooshed into the thing, then out the bottom with a rush of noise and pressure that left it as clean as it had been before she'd used it. She stared at the thing for a long moment, her hand pressed to her thundering heart.

And then she smiled, because she *had* a heart. A healthy, living, beating heart. And it was good. Surely she had experienced this kind of marvel before, while lurking inside Tempest's body. She simply hadn't paid attention.

Now she did. These bowls were called toilets, she knew that. And they were to be "flushed" after use. Apparently some of them flushed themselves. People today must be unbelievably lazy.

Finished with the nastiness of elimination, Beta washed her hands, enjoying the convenience and the feel of hot and cold running water, and the smell of the soap, which was nothing like any she'd smelled before. She even enjoyed seeing her reflection in the looking glass, after the shock of looking up to see a stranger's face. It wasn't a bad face. Attractive, in fact. She ran her hands through her auburn hair and over the trim figure. It was a good body.

But weak. She wondered why.

Finally she returned to the grocery store's aisles, and wandered up and down them, searching the shelves for something she could eat. Most of the items looked inadequate: cans and boxes with pretty pictures on them that didn't seem to match their size, shape or weight. Surely the large round can marked "Crisco" could not possibly contain the golden brown fried chicken depicted on its label. It didn't shake as if it had fried chicken inside.

Disappointed, she returned the heavy can to the shelf with a sigh. If only she were already a vampire, she thought sadly. She could just bite some stupid mortal and be done with it.

Like Tempest. She would *love* to drain the life out of that evil, husband-stealing wench. And she *would*.

For now, though, food.

She found some promising items behind a glass case in a section marked "Deli," and she eyed them. There were dishes of many sorts. Some salads, and piles of thinly sliced meats.

"May I help you?"

She looked up at the woman behind the counter. She wore a white hat and apron, and she smiled.

"I'm hungry," Elisabeta told her.

The woman's smile seemed to freeze, and her eyebrows rose a little. "We have sandwiches. They're pretty good. I have one myself most days, for lunch. Roast beef is my favorite. But the turkey's great, too, with provolone cheese and all the fixin's."

Elisabeta didn't know what "fixin's" were, but since they came highly recommended, she didn't suppose they could be bad. "Beef. I'd like that."

"Sandwich, sub or wrap?" the woman asked.

Beta frowned. "What's the difference?"

The woman tilted her head to one side. "Are you okay, hon?"

"Yes. I'm just…not from around here."

"You're foreign aren't you? I thought I caught a slight accent, but honestly, your English is almost perfect. Where you from, hon?"

"Romania," she answered, thinking it was really none of the woman's business, but deciding the salesperson was friendly, so she would try to be, as well.

"Romania! Imagine that. Well, don't you worry any. I'll help you out." She proceeded to explain the differences between sand-witches, subs and wraps; then she made a sand-witch for her, wrapped it in white paper, put it into a little basket, then added a bottle of something called "Coke" that looked like a very dark ale of some sort, and a shiny, small package of some kind of chipped potatoes. Then she led Beta to the front of the store, where another woman took her items from the basket and punched buttons on a machine.

Cash register, whispered the knowledge inside her mind.

The woman at the machine took her money. She gave Beta some coins in return and put her sandwich into a plastic bag.

She didn't need the bag, Beta thought. She was going to eat the thing right away. People today were not only lazy but terribly wasteful.

She left the store, painfully aware that she still had to walk all the way back to the house where Vlad was staying. Fervently, she hoped the other woman would be long gone by the time she returned. She needed to apologize to Vlad for hurting him the way she had. She needed to explain that he had made her angry, and that she had only reacted in response to that anger. He really shouldn't do that anymore—make her angry. And he needed to transform her into a vampire right away.

Brooke's body had seemed strong and fit when

she had first entered it. Why, then, did it get so tired and so sore from a simple walk?

Elisabeta unwrapped the sand-witch and ate it on the way. It was good. And eating was good, as well. The taste of the food on her tongue. The act of chewing. She almost choked several times before she mastered the rhythm of chewing and swallowing the food. But aside from that, eating was a pleasant experience. Only now did she realize how much she had missed it.

When she finished the sand-witch, she tossed the bag and white wrapper onto the roadside, and carried the package of chipped potatoes in one hand and the "Coke" in the other. She stopped long enough to open them both. The potatoes were terribly salty, but she enjoyed the crunch and flavor of them very much.

They made her thirsty, so she took her first large drink from the bottle, after a mighty struggle to remove its stubborn lid.

She drank, and then she choked. The fluid burst from her mouth, and shot from her nostrils. It was *strong!* And it *tickled!*

She caught her breath, wiped her face, swallowed hard. The inside of her mouth still tasted of the remnants of sweetness from the drink. Drawing a breath, she stared at the bottle and tried again, taking only a tiny sip this time.

Taken slowly, it wasn't so bad. She'd only been surprised. She supposed it took getting used to, and determined that it tasted better than the sour dark ale she'd mistaken it for. Each sip, though, made her belch. Disgusting. Why were the bubbles necessary at all? Surely the sweetness of the beverage would be as good without them.

When she finally made it back to the house where Vlad was staying, it was very, very late, or perhaps even very early—dawn might be near. She tried the door but found it locked tight, and a surge of anger rose up inside her, heating her face. How *dare* he lock her out? Didn't he know better than to make her angry again? Why on earth would Vlad push her to this extent?

She was tired and sore and thirsty, even though she'd drained the bottle of "Coke." Her legs hurt and her back ached. She felt heavy, and her head throbbed. She wanted a warm bed and Vlad's strong body wrapped around hers. But as it was, she settled for a comfortable patch of deep, dry grass off to the left of the house's front door, near a large maple tree. She curled up there to rest for a while. She would figure out what else to do later on. When daylight came, she thought, she would be able to find a way to get into the house. When the sun rose. She would be able to see then.

And he would be unable to stop her.

12

Stormy stayed with Vlad, wrapped in his arms and wondering where the hell this insanity could lead. Okay, maybe he still desired her to some extent, even though Elisabeta no longer lived in her body. But he felt no more than that. And in all likelihood, that desire had only been spurred by the blood lust. She knew his kind, knew sexual heat and hunger for blood were one and the same to them. Beyond that, there was the bond he'd created when he'd taken her blood before. He would feel that pull, just as she did, though maybe not to the same degree.

She was in love with him, after all.

As she lay there holding him, she searched her mind for more memories of the past they had shared. And she was surprised when she found them there, though she probably shouldn't be. Had he released her from the blocks he'd created in her mind deliberately? Or were they falling away on their own? Did he want her to remember, for some reason? Why had he wanted to make her forget in the first place?

It didn't matter. What did matter was that the memories were there, waiting for her to seek them out, retrieve them, relive them. And she needed them, needed to fill in the gaps in her past and to know what had really happened between them so long ago.

After Rhiannon and Roland had taken their leave from Vlad's castle, Tempest showered, put on a fresh nightgown and headed for the bed, to find Vlad already there, lying on his side facing her, his head propped up by one hand. He was undressed—from the waist up, at least. The rest of him was under the covers. But his shoulders and chest were unclothed, and the sight of him turned a switch in her that had no business being there. And the way he looked at her, his eyes moving up and down her and glowing with heat, didn't help matters a bit.

She didn't know why the hell she'd stayed. Being here wasn't helping her—if anything, it was only making matters worse. Elisabeta was stronger here, in her homeland. Taking over seemed to be getting easier for her here. Stormy felt almost sick, weak and achy, and she knew it was the constant fight for control that was to blame.

Rhiannon thought exorcism was the answer. And of all the vampires Stormy had ever known, none of them was more experienced or knowledgeable about matters of spirit and the occult than she. So why hadn't Stormy jumped at the chance to get out of here and let her try?

She thought she knew the reason. And she didn't like it, but she wasn't the type to hide behind self-delusion. Straight-up truth served her much better. And the truth was that she thought she might be falling in love. With Dracula. Which, to her mind, pretty much confirmed that her little red caboose was pretty close to chugging around the bend. She was freaking nuts. What kind of sense did it make for an ordinary mortal chick to fall in love with any vampire, much less Dracula himself?

Damn.

"Are you afraid to come to bed, Tempest?"

She shook free of her thoughts, realized she'd been standing there with her eyes glued to his powerful chest for a couple of minutes now, and forced herself to meet his steady gaze instead. "Should I be?"

"Given where you ended up last time you slept, yes, I would think you might be."

"Oh. That." *She shrugged and tried not to shiver at the memory of waking up on a cliff, so close to the edge.* "Not much that can be done about it."

"There is, actually." *He nodded toward the door.*

"I've locked it. And the windows. You won't be able to sleepwalk any farther than the confines of this room."

"Yeah? And suppose I decide I want to get out?"

"Why would you want that?"

She shrugged. "The castle could catch fire, I suppose."

"Then break a window."

"Lovely." She moved closer, and he flipped the covers back. The nightgown she wore was like all the others she'd found in the drawers. Flimsy and sheer, black this time rather than white, and shorter. She started to wonder if she should have just worn one of her T-shirts to bed.

She got into the bed, lay down on her back, not touching him, tugged the covers over her and stared at the ceiling. Vlad sat up long enough turn off the bedside lamp, then returned to his former position, on his side. It wasn't fair. The room was black as pitch now, and she couldn't see a thing, but he could. She knew all too well that he could.

"You were wrong before," he said. Something trailed over her face, down her cheek, then. She thought it was the backs of his fingers.

"About what?" She managed not to stammer, but the words emerged a little breathy.

"About me wanting her and not you."

"Was I?"

"Yes." Those fingers trailed over her jawline and then down her neck. "I was surrounded by memories of the past, Tempest. I misspoke when I said her name. It didn't mean anything."

"I doubt that very much." He was lying. He had to lie, to keep her here long enough for him to get what he wanted. His precious Elisabeta, in full control of Stormy's body.

"I only wish there was more time before dawn, so that I could prove it to you." His hand drifted across her chest, along her collarbone. Then his palm rested there. "As it is, though, we only have twenty minutes, give or take."

She shrugged. "Don't assume we'd be doing anything else, if we had longer. I do get a vote in that, you know."

"You wouldn't refuse me."

"That sure of yourself, are you?"

"I know when a woman wants me, Tempest."

She shrugged. "What I want and what's good for me are two different things, Vlad. In fact, in this case, I think they're polar opposites."

He said nothing, but his palm moved very slightly, a caress so light she could only barely detect it.

"Twenty minutes, huh? I suppose we could talk."

"Of course."

She nodded, rolled onto her side to face him, but kept enough space between them that he wouldn't get distracted from the subject. "Tell me about you and Rhiannon."

He was silent.

"You said you were her sire."

"How is this information going to help you remember your past life with me, Tempest?"

She shrugged. "It's not. I'm curious, is all."

He was quiet for so long that she thought he wouldn't reply at all. But then he did. "She was one of The Chosen. You know how powerfully vampires feel the instinct to protect and watch over them."

"Yes."

"And do you also know that for each vampire there is one of The Chosen with whom that bond is even stronger?"

She nodded in the darkness, knowing he could see it. "She was that one for you?"

"Yes. I sensed her need while traveling near Egypt and went there in response to it. She was the daughter of Pharaoh, but he'd wanted a son and considered her a curse from the gods, punishment for some crime, imagined or real. He'd sent her to be raised and trained by the priestesses at the Temple of Isis. She was never to be allowed to leave there, even when she fell ill. She was a virtual prisoner to them.

"The Chosen always die young, if they're not transformed," she muttered. "She must have been younger than most when the symptoms kicked in."

"Yes. At any rate, I went there, and I took her away. Not without effort. Both of us were nearly killed when another organization intervened on behalf of the priestesses. Still, we escaped with our lives. I told her what I was, what she could become, and she accepted the offer."

She wished to God she could see his face in the darkness, because she was sure there was more to the story. "I've seen the bond between vampires and their special Chosen ones. It's pretty intense."

"Yes."

"Even if they don't get involved sexually—"

"Are you asking, Tempest?"

She licked her lips, then lowered her eyes, because she could feel his probing them. "No. I only meant—you must have been close. Powerfully connected. It's a special and potent bond."

"It is."

"And yet you were willing to ruin it tonight. Because of Elisabeta."

He said nothing. And that told her as much as a full admission would have.

She licked her lips, focused on his face again, barely able to make out more than the shapes and lines of it in the darkness. She was quiet for a moment, as she lay there working up the nerve to ask the question that was burn-

*ing in her mind. Minutes ticked past. Finally she drew a
breath, closed her eyes and blurted it. "Are you going to
make love to me when the sun goes down tonight?"*

*She lay there, eyes still closed, awaiting his answer.
But it didn't come, and finally she rolled onto her side
and touched him. "Vlad?"*

*Nothing. She frowned and slid out of the bed, hur-
rying to the nearest window, which was heavily draped,
and shaded besides. Going to the side farthest from the
bed, she carefully lifted the drapes and saw the first rays
of morning sunlight, cool, dim and gray, slowly lighting
the sky beyond the thick old glass.*

*Sighing, she arranged the drape back in place again
and returned to the bed. He was at rest, then. Probably
hadn't even heard her question. And she wondered what
answer she'd wanted to hear that time. Because she
honestly didn't know.*

*Hell, maybe she did know. She wanted him. Burned
for him, and was growing increasingly frustrated with
having to wait and wonder.*

*Maybe she should stop waiting and wondering.
Maybe she should just give in to what she knew they both
wanted, get it over with and see what happened.*

*Maybe it was time she stopped trying to be smart and
logical, and just tried listening to the demands and hun-
gers of her own body.*

Yeah. It was time.

By the time the sun set and she hadn't slept a wink, she was ready. Her time with Vlad was coming to a close. This would be their last night together, assuming he kept his word and let her go. She wanted him. She could get through life without him, if she just had this one time with him to cling to, to remember.

He raised his head from the pillows and turned it her way. She lay on her back, the covers over her all the way to her shoulders, which were visible. His eyes moved over them, then over her neck, which seemed to tempt him. Swallowing hard and cursing herself for her own nervousness, she forced herself to lie still when he lifted the sheet and comforter as one and peered underneath.

She was naked. For him. And he knew that now, if he hadn't already sensed it.

He peeled the covers away, folding them back. She rolled onto her side, curling up a little in response to the chill in the room. He couldn't seem to take his eyes from her; they moved over the curve of her hip, the length of her thigh.

He put his hand on her shoulder and stroked a slow path down her upper arm, then slipped to her waist, and she shivered at his touch. Then he moved it lower, to cup her hip, slide his palm gently over her thigh.

He left his hand there, where it kneaded and caressed, but drew his gaze back to her breasts and finally to her face, staring into her eyes.

"Surprise," she whispered, her voice hoarse. She couldn't have spoken aloud had she wanted to.

He pushed with his hand until she rolled onto her back again, and his body moved with hers, his chest pressing her to the mattress as he finally took her mouth. She opened to his kiss, welcomed it and responded in kind. Their mouths locked, taking and releasing, suckling and freeing, over and over; a mimicry of the mating their bodies would be indulging in soon.

Soon.

He clasped her hip to hold her to him as he shifted his lower body over her, nestled himself between her legs. He moved against her there, rubbing her with his erection as he fed from her mouth. Then he slid one hand there, as well, and caressed her folds, felt the moisture, the dampness, there.

"Tempest," he whispered.

"Yeah. Tempest. Not Elisabeta. Remember that, Vlad. You're making love to me, not her."

His fingers moved inside her, and she sucked in a sharp breath. "I know who you are," he told her.

"It's been killing me to wait, to want you so badly, Vlad," she whispered. "Torture. Pure torture."

He delved more deeply with his fingers, kissed her

again, then moved lower to take a breast in his mouth and tease its peak until it went tight and hard. She arched her back to him and shivered with pleasure.

"Take me," she told him. "Do it now, Vlad."

"I want it to be good for you."

"I don't think that's going to be a problem." She moved her hips, rocking herself over his fingers, rubbing against them.

"I promise you, it won't be."

He taunted her breast again, then replaced his mouth with his hand and slid lower, until he could press his head between her legs and taste her there. He licked deep, and her entire body shuddered. Her hands closed on the back of his head, clasping his hair and holding him. He took that as consent to ravage her, not that he required it at that point. She thought he was beyond holding back, and he lapped and suckled and invaded her mind with his own. She felt him there, feeling every sensation he caused in her. He knew when she was on the brink of orgasm, and that was when he stopped, drew away, gave her a moment to come back down.

She growled in frustration and need.

"I want you to come with me inside you," he told her, and it sounded more like a command than a request. "I want you to know release only when I possess you, body, blood and soul."

She was panting, shaking.

He moved up her body and lowered himself again, and this time he slid into her. She tensed a little, unused to his size and shape. He was big and thick, and he filled her, stretched her. But he didn't change his pace. He pressed on, deeper and deeper still, and then he took her knees in his hands and lifted them, pressed them wide, and slid into her even farther than before.

She whimpered, close to asking for mercy. But if she felt full, it was a good fullness. If she felt stretched, then it was what he wanted, and that made her want it, too. And if she felt pain, it was the blissfully delicious pain that couldn't be distinguished from the most intense pleasure imaginable.

He withdrew then, slowly, and entered her again. A little faster this time. And again, still faster. His pace increased, but slowly, teasingly, and the force with which he drove into her increased, as well.

She moved her hips to accept him, to mesh with the rhythm he'd begun. She wanted more, but he wanted her to want. To crave. So he held back, damn him.

Her hands slid around him, gripped his backside and tugged him into her. And when he still didn't give her enough, she dug her nails into his flesh and flashed her eyes open, staring up into his. "Harder, Vlad. Faster."

It was almost a growl.

His control seemed to shatter. He drove into her, hard and fast.

She wrapped her legs around his waist, linked her ankles at the small of his back and snapped her hips up to meet his with every thrust. How she stood the force he was using she didn't know, but she did, and silently asked for more. He slid his hands beneath her backside, tipped her hips up so he could penetrate even more deeply, then held her to him to take every thrust, every inch, every ounce.

And just as she neared the precipice, he drove even harder and bent his head to her neck. He bit down, sinking his fangs through her jugular, shocking her, and sucking the lifeblood from her body as he plundered and took.

She shrieked his name as she came, and he drove into her twice more, and shot his seed into her body as he drank from her throat.

They clasped each other that way as the spasms of an endless orgasm ripped though them both, bodies straining, his rod piercing her to depths no man had ever touched, his mouth drinking at her throat. Her back was arched, her arms and legs locked around him, and she trembled with the force of the spasms.

It was only as her grip on him began to weaken that he seemed to realize he was still feeding, still sucking the blood from her throat, still spilling semen into her body. She was fading, fading fast.

He stopped drinking, withdrew his teeth. Beneath him, her body relaxed into the mattress. Carefully, he withdrew from her body and lay beside her, sliding his arms around her and drawing her into his embrace. His hands stroked her hair. "I own you now," he whispered.

She didn't reply. She couldn't. But she heard. As if from deep within a canyon, she heard. What did it mean? What had he done to her?

How long had that orgasm held him in its grip? How much of her blood had he taken? Was she dying? If felt as if she was.

He patted her cheek with his hand, softly, then with more force. "Tempest? Tempest, open your eyes. Look at me."

Her eyes did open. She felt them open, but she didn't open them. She was trapped inside, and suddenly she understood why. The climax, and maybe the blood loss, had weakened her grip. The other was in control now.

"Don't call me by that bitch's name," she whispered, her accent thick, her voice deeper than Tempest's had ever been. But Tempest, weak and trembling, trapped in her own body, heard it all.

"Elisabeta?" Vlad backed away slightly.

"Yes. It is me." She clasped his face between her palms, kissed his mouth. "Oh, Vlad, darling, do you still love me? Tell me you do."

"*Of course I do,*" *he whispered.*

Inside, Stormy felt her heart break.

"*Then find a way, Vlad. Find a way to let me stay. To let me have this body. You have to, Vlad. If you don't, I'll die.*"

He nodded. "*I'm trying, Beta. I'm trying.*"

"*You're the one who set this into motion, my love,*" *Elisabeta said, her tone harsh.* "*You with your sorcerers and magicians. They with their spells and charms. Do you know what it's been like for me? Trapped between the worlds all these years, with no way to come back and no way to move on?*"

He gasped.

"*You didn't know?*"

"*That wasn't how it was supposed to be, Beta. I vow to you, it was never my intent—*"

"*Your intent matters very little now. It is done. My suffering, being imprisoned as if buried alive, is done. So long as you follow through. You need to finish this, Vlad.*"

He met her eyes, shook his head slowly. "*I don't know where to find the ring and the scroll with the rite. I'm not sure I can finish this without those items.*"

She closed her eyes. "*Then I'll die.*"

"*I won't let that happen, little one.*"

A tear rolling down her cheek, she sniffled and said, "*Do you promise?*"

"I do. I'll make this right, I swear. Somehow."

"Thank you, Vlad. Thank you." She kissed him.

"Now I want you to rest. Go to sleep. Let Tempest return to her body, and wait for my call."

"Yes. Yes, Vlad, I will."

"Good. Good."

She faded off to sleep, or something like it, and Stormy felt her own control slowly returning. But she'd learned something tonight. Learned it beyond doubt.

Elisabeta was the woman Vlad loved. And he would say anything, do anything, even if it cost Stormy's own life, to get her back.

Stormy had tears dampening her cheeks as the memory faded. She knew now what it meant, what he'd done to her, so long ago. By taking her blood, he'd created a bond between them—one that could not be broken. He'd known that. He'd done it deliberately, probably to keep her vulnerable to his power, his control, for as long as it took to steal her body for his precious dead wife.

No wonder she loved him so much.

Part of her argued that she'd loved him even before that night. But she refused to listen to that part. He was using her, he cared nothing for her. Except that she provided a home for Elisabeta.

She remained with him until the sun rose. She couldn't see the sun, of course. The windowless room gave no hint what was happening in the skies beyond it. But she felt the change in him. He went very still. No sounds emerged, not even a breath, and his always cool skin went even colder. There was a different feeling to him once the sun came up. She imagined this must be what lying with a dead man would be like.

He didn't love her. He never would. She needed to get the hell out of here, get some perspective. But she sat there instead, looking at him as he slept. She still wanted him, although with her, want wasn't even close to a strong enough term. She craved him. Hungered for him. Ached and pined and bled for him. And why the hell wouldn't she? Even beyond the bond he'd deliberately created, then empowered again and again, now, she thought, she would want him. He was the sexiest man she had ever seen. God, he had the body of a twenty-year-old. A ripped twenty-year-old. And he played hers the way Santana played the guitar. He made it sing. There was no one who could make her feel the way he could.

But he'd commanded that, hadn't he? That she would know release only with him. Was that why she'd never gotten off with anyone else, not in all this time? The bastard.

He would still be with the other woman, the Elisabeta-Brooke creature, if she hadn't stabbed him in the belly. Stormy ought to hate him. Why the hell couldn't she?

She relit the candle. Then, carefully, she pulled back the covers and removed the bandage she'd placed over his wound. She pulled at the gauze, wincing at how it tugged the tender, wounded area. But he was beyond feeling any pain. And even when she bit her lip and ripped the bandage away, no fresh blood welled in the seam of the wound she'd painstakingly stitched up.

She sat on the edge of the bed, holding a blanket to her chest to fend off the early-morning chill, and kept her gaze riveted to the injured flesh. As she watched, the skin along the edges of the wound changed. It paled and it blended, the cut edges melding into each other by slow degrees. She was ready with the tiny scissors and tweezers from her purse. The stitches would be rejected by his body within a few days, but it would be irritating and perhaps painful. And she was fool enough to want to spare him that. So she waited until the skin had begun to knit itself together, then snipped each thread and tugged it free. The minuscule holes those threads left behind closed almost as soon as she pulled the threads from them.

When she finished, the wound was almost impossible to detect. A tiny red line marked its former position, and within a few more moments, even that was gone.

Sighing deeply, Stormy lingered a moment longer. She ran her hands over the beautiful shape of his chest, feeling every ripple of muscle beneath his smooth skin. She touched his belly and shivered at the feel of his abs. She traced his shoulders.

He was incredibly built, and that was far from the norm. Vampires tended to be lean and wiry. Sometimes even skinny. She supposed that was because the undead tended to keep the form they had at the moment of their transformation. Every vampire had the Belladonna Antigen as a mortal. And the antigen tended to make them weak and ill over time. Max's sister Morgan had been a shadow of herself from its effects. Had nearly died, in fact, before Dante had shared the dark gift with her. And so she would always be as she had been then. Painfully thin and slight, and though far stronger now, she would always be weak for a vampire.

Vlad must not have been feeling the effects of the

antigen yet when the vampire Anthar had transformed him.

Yes, Anthar. Another memory in the long list of them. He'd told her of his true origins. He'd been the helper of a Sumerian by the name of Utnapishtim, a man whose name was still known today. His story had been the precursor to that of the biblical Noah. Utnapishtim, it was said, had survived the great flood sent by the gods and had been given the gift of immortality. He'd been a relative of Vlad's. And Vlad had been sent to live with him as his servant and companion.

One day, the great king Gilgamesh himself had come, begging the old man for the secret of immortality. Vlad had been sent from the room, so he'd never seen what transpired, but he knew Utnapishtim had granted the king's request, in direct disobedience of the dictates of the gods.

Later, another man had come, an evil man, named Anthar. He was seeking Gilgamesh, and his intentions were dark. He, too, had demanded the gift, but the old man had refused. Anthar forced him at the point of a blade, then beheaded him, leaving him dead on the floor, and took young Vlad captive, to be his slave.

Vlad had been held by the dark vampire for years,

all the while working to grow stronger, so he could one day escape. By the time Anthar had decided he needed his slave to be like him, a vampire, in order to better serve his needs, and changed him over, Vlad was a powerful young man in the peak of health.

And so, by the time of his change, he'd looked... the way he looked now. Like a centerfold. A powerful, muscular, beautiful young man.

She lowered her head and pressed her lips to those rippling abs. God, she wanted to kiss every inch of him. But no. She had work to do. And she needed distance and perspective. She needed to find a way to be free of him, of the hold he had on her, the bond he'd made, the love that possessed her. Getting to her feet, Stormy tucked the covers back over him.

Her hand rose to press against her throat where Vlad had left his mark on her. She felt it clearly—two swollen, tender places. Tiny wounds. And her body heated all over again as she remembered the sensations he'd aroused.

She needed to remain aware of what he really wanted from her. She needed to make it very clear to her desire-glazed brain. She mustn't forget. He felt passion for her, a burning, nearly insatiable desire.

And yes, drinking from her again might have intensified it even more, on his side as well as her own.

But he didn't love her. He loved Elisabeta. He was willing to trade Stormy's life for hers. She mustn't forget that.

Carefully she unlocked the door, then turned the lock again before she pulled it closed. She did the same with the cellar door at the top of the stairs, and then exited the house through the front door, making sure it was locked, as well. She needed to get back to Athena House and formulate a plan to capture Elisabeta so Rhiannon could perform the ritual on her.

Vlad wasn't going to like it. In fact, he would probably never forgive her for it.

Elisabeta was still half-asleep in the grass when a sound brought her fully awake. Her first thought was that it was Vlad, coming out to get her, to apologize for his behavior, to bring her into the house and tell her how much he loved her.

But as she came fully awake, she realized it couldn't be Vlad. The sun had already cleared the horizon, and it beamed brightly down on her—so brightly that she had to shield her eyes to see who was coming out of the house.

And then she saw, and her anger burst into a full blown rage.

It was *her!* Tempest. She had spent the night with Elisabeta's husband. Dammit, she had known all along! He was infatuated with her. And too confused to realize that he'd only ever been drawn to her in the first place because she, Elisabeta, had been there, inside her.

"I am going to have to kill her," she said softly. "It's the only way."

She rose from the grass as the woman walked away from the house and along the side of the road. Elisabeta started to walk after her, her hands clenched, her rage burning. But before the second angry step, her head was spinning, her knees trembling.

She pressed a hand to her forehead, closed her eyes and braced her hand on a tree to keep from falling. What was this?

She stood there for a moment, holding her head, and waited for the dizziness to abate. When it did, she tested her footing and found her legs once again solid. Even so, she wasn't at her best. Perhaps it was the shock of adjusting to this new body. Or perhaps Brooke had some physical imperfection or illness that hadn't been apparent to Elisabeta until now.

Damn this body. She'd wanted a strong and healthy form, not this.

No matter. What needed to be done, needed to be done. Tempest was coming between Elisabeta and Vlad. That was the only reason he had refused to transform her. Beta had no choice but to remove Tempest from the equation. Vlad could not be distracted when she needed him to be focused only on her.

She was in no condition, however, to murder the woman with her hands alone. She remembered, with a flash of pain, the way Tempest had spun and kicked and hit her before. She was not experienced at physical combat. She would need an aid. A weapon.

She looked around and came upon a perfect one—a rock larger than a grapefruit, smooth and round. She picked it up and then hurried in the direction Tempest had gone. She must be heading back to Athena House. The road curved, looping around a stand of red pine forest. While Elisabeta was unfamiliar with the place, Brooke knew it well. And by now Beta had mastered the skill of probing Brooke's mind, mining it for information.

She veered off the road and into the pine forest, traveling through it unerringly. Its carpet of browning needles and fragrant pungence were soothing to her senses, and the pine cones that littered the ground only tripped her up once. After that she watched for them. She emerged on the far side of the woods, and the road was there, only a few feet from the edge of the trees. So she backed up a little, sheltered by the scented branches, and she waited.

Within a few minutes, Tempest came along the road. There was purpose in her step, a troubled, pensive look about her face. Was the contemplating the hopelessness of her future without Vlad? For she had to know his heart belonged to another. Was she in love with him?

Beta waited until Tempest had passed by her hiding place, so she wouldn't see movement from the corner of her eye and be warned. The attack had to be completely unexpected. A blow from the blue.

When Tempest had gone past her, Beta crept out of the trees, moving quickly and quietly up the grassy incline to the road. She raised the rock over her head, clasping it in both hands so she could bring it down *hard*, and she ran at Tempest's back.

Tempest spun around at the last possible moment and ducked to the side. The rock hit her shoulder instead of her skull, but it must have hurt her all the same. She grunted in pain and toppled over sideways, landing on the ground with a solid impact that must have hurt nearly as much as the blow had done.

Furious, Elisabeta lifted the rock again but even as she brought the rock down, Tempest swung her legs in a powerful arc that took Beta's feet right out from under her.

She went down hard, slamming her own head into the very rock she'd intended to use to crush Tempest's.

And then it was dark.

13

Stormy got to her feet, one hand on her shoulder, which felt as if it had been hit by a freaking freight train. "What the hell is the *matter* with you, you freaking maniac?"

There was no reply from the woman on the ground, and Stormy moved closer, cautious, but not too worried. "Damn sneak attack. That's not a very dignified way to fight, Elisabeta."

Still nothing. And, Stormy noted suddenly, a trickle of red marked the miniature boulder on the ground beside the fallen woman.

"Hell, you brained yourself with that thing, didn't you?"

She used her foot to turn Brooke's body—and it *was* Brooke's body, not Elisabeta's—over. Beta was unconscious. There was a little blood coming from a gash in her left temple, and Stormy figured there would be a goose egg damn near the size of that stupid rock later on.

Sighing, wanting to haul off and kick the bitch for the throbbing pain in her shoulder, she instead reached down and yanked the ruby ring from the other woman's limp finger. Then she searched her pockets and found the scroll. "I imagine we'll need these," she said. "And you never deserved them to begin with." She dropped the ring and scroll into her backpack, took out her cell phone, dialed Athena House and waited.

At sundown, Stormy was sitting watch over the unconscious woman in Brooke's bed at Athena House. She was sitting watch because it was her turn. She, Lupe and Melina had been taking shifts with the injured woman all day long. They couldn't do the ritual without Rhiannon. But if Beta's soul wasn't set free soon, Stormy would die with her. It was only now that the patient opened her eyes.

Stormy tensed in the chair beside the bed, then frowned. Because her eyes were pretty. And they were blue. *Brooke's* eyes, not Elisabeta's. Those eyes met Stormy's, and they were wet with unshed tears. And then Brooke said something so softly that Stormy couldn't hear her.

Her heart ached for the woman, despite the fact that she had brought all of this on herself with her foolish actions. She closed a hand around Brooke's and leaned closer. "I didn't hear."

"I didn't think…it would be…like this," Brooke whispered.

"I know. I know what you're going through, believe me. We're going to try everything we can to get her out of you, Brooke. I promise."

Brooke closed her eyes. "She…she wants…"

"What, Brooke? What does she want?"

"She wants you dead."

Stormy knew that already, but hearing it still sent a chill down her spine. Not, however, the same chill that came a split second later when Brooke's hand closed more tightly around Stormy's, and her other hand clamped to the back of Stormy's head and drew her face down even closer.

"And I will *see* you dead, too. I promise you that. Vlad is mine."

Her eyes, blazing into Stormy's, were black now, like glittering pieces of polished coal. Stormy jerked free of her. "Not having much success at that so far, are you, Elisabeta? Tried to brain me with a rock and wound up hurting yourself instead. And now you're here, and trust me on this one—you aren't going anywhere."

"He will save me. He loves me."

"Yeah, right, and you love him, too, don't you? That's why you tried to kill him last night."

"I did *not!*"

"No? Sinking a blade into his belly was what, then? Kind of like a little love bite?"

"He is *vampir*. He is immortal."

"There is no such thing as immortal, Beta. Everything that lives can die. Vamps just die a little harder than the rest of us." Stormy wrenched herself free of the clasping hands, twisted her own hand around and gripped Brooke's wrist hard. "If you hurt him again, I'll kill you. Do you understand me? I'll *kill* you, and damn the consequences."

Beta blinked, winced in pain and stared up at Stormy with a suddenly wide-eyed and child like expression. Utterly innocent and afraid. "You…you would really kill me?"

"Don't even doubt it. I should have picked up that rock and crushed your skull today. The only reason I didn't was because—"

"Because Melina came and stopped you," Beta said in a frightened little girl voice. And now there were tears rolling down her cheeks. "You're hurting my wrist."

Belatedly, the alarm bells sounded in Stormy's mind. That wasn't what had happened at all. She'd called Melina, asked her to bring a car to help her get Elisabeta back to the mansion. Why would the woman try to accuse her of something when they were alone in the room?

An instant later, she knew why, she heard Vlad's voice coming from behind her. "Let her go, Tempest."

She was already in the process of doing just that, and she rose from her chair and turned to face him. He held her eyes for a moment, then shifted them to the other women, when Beta spoke again.

"Thank goodness you've come, Vlad. Thank God."

Great. He'd been standing there long enough to hear what sounded like a threat, and maybe even a confession of attempted murder.

"She tried to kill me!" the bitch in the bed sobbed. "I tried to speak to her on the road this morning when she left you, Vlad, and she attacked me. She *hurt* me." The little phony lifted a trembling hand to the white bandages Melina had plastered to her head, her crocodile tears flowing like rivers.

Stormy let her head fall forward until her chin nearly touched her chest and expelled all her breath. Vlad was moving past her, making a beeline for the actress in the bed, and then he bent over her to peel up one corner of the bandage and peer underneath.

Straightening, then, he fixed his eyes on Stormy's. "Tempest? Is this true?"

She opened her mouth to supply a full blown denial and a long winded explanation, then stopped herself. She tipped her head to one side. "Why should I bother? You're going to believe the word of this psycho bitch from hell, even after she drove a knife into your gut and left you to die. Even after I gave my own blood to save your life. So why should I bother?"

"Tempest—"

She held up a hand, palm facing him, and smiled a bitter smile at the irony of the situation. "Fuck this. And fuck you, Vlad." Then she turned and left the room, slamming the door behind her. Let him care for his pathetic little murderess. Elisabeta would destroy him in the end, and it would be no less than he deserved.

She met Rhiannon partway down the hall but didn't even acknowledge her, just kept walking.

"Wait!" Rhiannon said.

Stormy didn't wait, so Rhiannon changed direction and caught up with her. "Stormy, where are you going?"

"To pack. I'm done with this. I got her here, all right? And I got the damn ring and the scroll." She turned, tugged the things out of her pocket and pressed them into Rhiannon's hand. "You can do your thing, exorcise her, send her to hell for all I care. And you can deal with Vlad, because he's not going to let her go without a fight, I guarantee you that. There's no longer any reason for me to be here. It's not my problem anymore. If I wake up tomorrow morning, I'll know it worked. And if I don't, well, then I guess I don't. I'm sure as hell not going to spend what might be the last several hours of my life watching him fawn over that bloodthirsty lunatic."

"Stormy, don't do this."

Stormy stopped walking. She was outside her own bedroom door. She forced herself to lift her gaze and meet Rhiannon's eyes, even though that meant revealing the unshed tears in her own. "Thanks for trying to help me. I owe you one."

"You can thank me when it's over, if I'm successful."

"I hope I get that chance, Rhiannon." She blinked her eyes dry and turned away. "This is getting disgustingly sappy. Go on, go to Brooke's room before Vlad has the chance to take his pathetic excuse for a bride out of here."

"She is pathetic, isn't she?"

"She's bloodthirsty, selfish, violent and insane. But worse than any of that, she's a whiner." She glanced at Rhiannon and saw a small smile appear on her lips.

"That was my first impression, as well. It hasn't changed. Goodbye, Stormy."

Then she turned and hurried back up the hall to Brooke's room.

Vlad sat beside Beta. The sight of her, lying in the bed, her tears, her pleas and the painful wound beneath the bandages, got to him. He wanted so much to heal her, to help her and make her well again. It killed him to see her suffering this way.

Rhiannon stepped into the room, took a seat on the opposite side of the bed. "Hello, Vlad. I'm surprised the Athena woman let you in."

He met her eyes, noting how stiff and guarded Beta had become the moment Rhiannon entered the room. "The one they call Lupe tried to forbid me from entering."

"Oh? Is she still alive?"

He noticed Rhiannon's smile, the touch of humor in her voice, and felt an answering smile tug at his own lips, in spite of his pain. "Of course." He rose to his feet, and went to her, wrapped his arms around her, half expecting her reaction to be cold. But it wasn't. Rhiannon hugged him in return. Whatever had happened between them, their bond was strong. Had always been. Would always be.

"It's been a long time," he told her.

"Too long. And I fear this embrace of yours will not last, Vlad. It's likely we'll end this thing on opposing sides."

"I wish that wasn't the case," he told her, stepping back to look into her eyes. "Regardless of what I say to you later, Rhiannon, even if I'm forced to destroy you, know that I love you."

"As I love you. I'll love you even when I'm killing you, Vlad."

He nodded. "Understood."

Rhiannon glanced at Beta. "Melina says the head wound isn't serious."

"Do not trust them, Vlad!" Elisabeta pleaded. "They are lying. They want me to die."

Rhiannon gave her a dismissive look, then focused on Vlad again. "She's right. We *do* want her to die. But we don't want Tempest to die, and we have no right to just execute Brooke, though her so-called sisters will likely do that in any event."

"You cannot save Brooke," Beta hissed. "This is *my* body now."

Rhiannon sighed and rolled her eyes. "Do you mind if we speak in the hallway, Vlad? This is growing tiresome, and my patience with this body thief is wearing thin."

He nodded and rose. Beta grabbed for his hand. "Vlad, no! Don't leave me!"

"You'll be fine," he promised her, patting her hand even as he pried loose her grip. "Beta, you've been here for the entire day. If anyone truly wanted to harm you, they would have done so by now. And you know now that I'm here, I won't let anyone hurt you. Don't you?"

She met his eyes, searched them, and finally nodded.

"Just rest. I'll keep you safe."

He went to the door, stepped into the hallway and pulled the door closed behind him.

"Did Stormy tell you what happened?" Rhiannon asked.

"No, but Beta did."

"Oh, did she." Sarcasm dripped from her words. "And what fiction did that little liar spin?"

He scowled at her. "Said she tried to speak to Tempest on the road, and that Tempest attacked her, would have killed her, if Melina hadn't arrived in time to prevent it."

Rhiannon just gazed at him, her eyes calling him an idiot. "And you believed that?"

"Tempest has felt attacked by Beta for sixteen years. Still, that doesn't justify—"

"Oh, for pity's sake, Vlad. You could put it together yourself if you were thinking clearly. I got the entire story from Melina. Stormy stayed with you in the house until sunrise. She watched over you until the knife wound your devoted little wife gave you had healed completely. And then she left. She was walking back here when Elisabeta ambushed her. Attacked her with a large rock. She'd have caved Stormy's skull in if Stormy hadn't glimpsed her shadow and spun around. The blow missed her head, thank the gods. Her shoulder took the brunt of it."

He didn't alter his expression in the least. "How bad is it?"

"She refused to let me see, though Lupe tells me it looks as if someone dumped blue and purple ink over her shoulder. She doesn't think anything is broken, however."

He nodded thoughtfully. "So Tempest was defending herself when she hit Elisabeta with the rock?"

Rhiannon frowned. "She didn't hit Elisabeta at all. Just kicked the madwoman's feet out from under her when she came at her again. Beta fell and hit her head on the rock with which she'd intended to crush Stormy's skull."

He closed his eyes. The other two women were coming along the hallway now, and they joined them there, outside the bedroom door.

"At least they're both all right," he said, glancing at the door, feeling with his senses.

"They're not all right," Melina said softly. "Brooke is in danger of dying, and Elisabeta…she's sick. It's not the head wound, it's…it's something else."

Vlad sighed, lowering his head. "Yes. I'm afraid I know what it is."

"As do I," Rhiannon said. "I can feel it from here. It's the antigen. Belladonna. It's killing her."

Melina frowned. "That can't be. Brooke wasn't one of The Chosen."

"No," Vlad said. "But Beta was."

"So she what?" Melina asked. "Brought it with her? Into another body? Is that even possible?"

Vlad started to speak, then narrowed his eyes and glanced at Rhiannon. "Why are we discussing this with them?"

"Believe me, I wouldn't be if I felt there were any

other way. However misguided, though, I've come to believe these two are, at their cores, decent. Though I'm more certain of Lupe than Melina."

Melina gasped.

"I don't like it. You know this group can't be trusted."

She shrugged. "What could they do to us, Vlad? We could snap them like twigs before they could blink."

"Hey, hey, hold up a sec," Lupe interrupted. "Just what is your problem with the Sisterhood of Athena?"

Rhiannon faced her. "If you really want to know, look it up. You keep scrupulous records. Cross reference Egypt and my original name, Rianikki, daughter of Pharoah, priestess of Isis—a group once tightly allied with your own." She shrugged. "When you have time. For now, let it go, and let us focus on the matter at hand. How did Beta bring the antigen into a body that did not formerly possess it?"

"I don't know how it happened, or why, but it has," Vlad said. "I'm not sure it even matters how or why. The antigen is different in her, altered somehow."

Rhiannon nodded. "It's taken up residence in a body never meant to house it," she said. "According to what I've read in the ancient texts the recipients of the antigen have a common ancestor. It's said to be you, Vlad. But I suspect it goes back further."

"To Utnapishtim," Vlad said softly. "The first immortal. I was his servant, but also a distant relation."

"I'm not sure it has to be a blood descendant, though," Rhiannon went on.

"What other sort of descendant could there be?" Melina asked.

Rhiannon met her eyes. "A future incarnation of the same soul," she said. "There is a master soul for each of us. Think of it as your higher self. It spins off parts of itself to come into each lifetime. When we die, we return to meld with that higher self, to share with it all of the wisdom and experience gained from our mortal lifetime. It grows wiser and stronger and more enlightened, and spins off another part to live another life."

"And what happens, Rhiannon, if that melding fails to come about?" Vlad asked.

Rhiannon shrugged. "I suspect each future incarnation is somehow less than complete, for it is missing a part of its spiritual ancestry that would make it whole."

He frowned deeply. "What do you suppose that means for our kind, Rhiannon? We never…meld."

"I have my theories," she whispered. "But I think it's a conclusion one needs to reach on one's own."

He lowered his head, shaking it slowly. "What are we going to do to help Elisabeta?"

"I think you already know that answer to that, Vlad." Rhiannon put both her hands on his shoulders. "We have to exorcise her. We must free her soul from the influence of that ring, so she can move on to the other side and meld with her higher self the way she was meant to do."

"It does seem to be the only way," Melina whispered.

"It *is* the only way," Lupe agreed. "Especially since she's going to die anyway."

"And if she does, she'll take Brooke with her," Melina said quickly.

Vlad remained stoic. "We could transform her."

"We'd still be condemning Brooke to death," Rhiannon said. "If Beta stays in her body, Brooke will die. And while I'm not certain she can escape that fate either way, Vlad, it is not our place to take her life."

"She asked for this. She invited Elisabeta in." He closed his eyes to keep his feelings hidden.

"Honestly, Vlad, you know perfectly well Beta is insane. You cannot tell me you would consider giving a lunatic the power of the Undead and turning her loose on the world of man. She would be a rogue. And a dangerous one. We would end up having to destroy her anyway."

She sighed, and when he said nothing, she went on. "And there's one more thing to consider. Unless Beta is set free, all of her spiritual descendants will die. That's the way your magicians worded the spell. And you know what that means, Vlad. Stormy, the only true innocent in all of this, will die. Tonight, Vlad. Midnight tonight."

He opened his eyes, parted his lips to speak, then closed them, rethinking his words. "Then I have to find a way to save Beta before then."

"Vlad? What ... what the hell is wrong with you?"

Rhiannon stared at him as if she'd never seen him before. And he couldn't speak to her, not even mentally, not without risk. "I wish to speak with Tempest now," he said instead. "Where is she?"

Lupe, who'd been mostly silent until then, looked at him with worry in her eyes. "Um, I thought you knew. She left."

He blinked, stunned. "Left?"

"She said this was no longer her problem, Vlad," Rhiannon said. "She was angry, furious—with you, I imagine."

Lupe added, "I saw her in her room, packing her stuff."

Vlad turned and ran down the hall to Tempest's room. He flung open the door, but it was empty. Then he opened the closet, the bathroom, but all were vacant, and every sign of her presence was missing—except the scent of her. That still lingered.

He went down the stairs and through the mansion to the front door, only to see that Tempest's car was gone. Only a trail of dust remained. She must have only just departed.

"Vlad!" Rhiannon shouted.

He returned to Brooke's bedroom door, which stood open. The others—Rhiannon, Melina and Lupe—were standing just inside.

He said, "You were right, Lupe. Tempest is gone."

"Yes, well, that might present a serious problem," Rhiannon said, and stepping aside, she gave him a view of the empty bed. "Because so is Elisabeta." She wrung her hands, closed her eyes.

"She was listening at the door only moments ago!" Vlad exploded.

Rhiannon lifted her brows and met his eyes. "Is *that* it? Is that why you—"

"Not now, Rhiannon." He closed his eyes. "We have to find them. And we don't have much time."

14

Elisabeta had dragged herself from the bed and across the room. She'd leaned close to the door to listen to what they were saying on the other side. And so she knew it was good that she had failed in her attempt to kill the feisty little blonde who was trying to steal her husband, because according to Rhiannon, Beta needed her.

She needed the woman's body. They'd still been talking outside her door when Elisabeta made her escape. The moment Rhiannon had stated that the only solution was to exorcise her, kill her, she had fled.

This body, the one she had taken from the foolish Brooke, was weakening, and at last she understood why. It was this Belladonna Antigen, yes. But it was more than just that. The body was wrong for her. A poor fit. She couldn't last in this home. She belonged in Tempest's body. It was the only way.

But how? Tempest had taken the ring and the scroll from her.

First, she knew, she had to get out of this place, before those fiends could send her to her death. Even if Vlad intended to protect her, as he'd promised, he was outnumbered. And the vampiress Rhiannon was, Beta sensed, a powerful foe. Escaping in her weakened state would have been more difficult had she not been able to plumb the depths of Brooke's memory for the solution. She knew this place. *She* knew everything about it—more than just how to get out. She knew where the weapons were kept.

And she would need weapons if she hoped to defeat Tempest. She took a change of clothing from the dresser and rapidly put the new outfit on. Then she grabbed a bag from Brooke's closet, one that contained all the items Beta would need to perform the ritual.

Her borrowed body was weak but not helpless. Not yet. Beta knew now that it was going to get a lot worse, and she might not have much time. She went to the window, and it opened easily. Then she climbed out and made her way down, finding every chink and bump in the stone outer walls, just as Brooke had done many times before.

Brooke. Elisabeta almost felt sorry for the woman. She understood, oh, so well, Brooke's hunger for immortality. It was what had driven her to risk her life by inviting Beta in. It was the same hunger that had driven Elisabeta herself all these long years. To live, to be immortal, to have limitless power and endless life. It was a dream, the one she craved beyond all others. Just as Brooke had.

She found another window, but it was locked. So she dropped the remaining distance to the ground, where a jarring landing subdued her, but only for a moment. She shook it off and hurried behind the massive house to the sunroom in the back, praying that door would be unlocked.

It was, and finally she was back inside the house. She crept through it, into the main parlor, listening. But there was no one. They were all still busy plotting her destruction upstairs. Bastards.

She made her way to the weapons room, quickly punching the code into the panel to unlock the door. Once inside, she armed herself, taking a sleek silver weapon Brooke thought of as a handgun, a supply of the "bullets" it would fire, and a deadly looking but small knife with a sheath that clipped onto the waistband of the jeans she wore, since that bitch Tempest had divested her of the blade she'd had before. She clipped the sheath in back, so that it hung down inside the jeans, rather than on the outside where it would be visible.

Would it be enough?

It would have to be—they would discover her missing soon.

She hurried to the front door and outside, then ducked behind a hedge when a shiny black car pulled swiftly up to a spot directly in front of the main entrance. Staying low, Elisabeta peered over the bush to watch. The car's trunk popped open, and a woman got out and hurried toward the front steps.

It was her. Tempest.

Beta's fingers itched to draw the handgun, even as she probed Brooke's stores of knowledge to learn how to use it. But she restrained herself. She needed Tempest alive.

She noticed, then, the small suitcase and duffle bag resting on the bottom step. Tempest was leaving? No. Beta couldn't lose her. What if she couldn't find her again in time?

Making a hasty decision, Beta leapt the hedge and ran to the car while Tempest's back was to it. The trunk would never do; she would be seen. Instead, Beta moved to the far side of the vehicle and got into the roomy back seat. She crouched on the floor and hoped the whore wouldn't look there before leaving.

Silently, she huddled there, not moving, barely breathing, as she waited.

She felt the car move when Tempest slung her bags into the trunk, and then the thud when she slammed the lid closed. Elisabeta tensed as the woman walked by the car, but she never looked inside. She just opened the driver's door and got in. And then they were in motion.

Elisabeta had no idea what to do next. Wait, she supposed, until they were in some secluded place. Tempest had the ring and the scroll. Surely if the ritual had worked once, it would work again. All she had to do was subdue the twit long enough to put the ring onto her finger and perform the rite the way it was meant to be performed. Her soul would be transferred into Tempest's body—this time, though, Tempest's would be evicted. She would be gone.

Beta would be strong again, and whole. And Vlad would be hers.

Carefully she settled into a more comfortable position on the cramped floor of the vehicle, leaned her head on the back of the front seat and closed her eyes.

* * *

As she drove, Stormy tried to put Vlad out of her mind, but she couldn't. The more she tried not to think of him, the more he invaded her soul. Memories of their past together, the one she'd forgotten for so long, those few forbidden days with him in Romania, lay waiting for her to find. So rather than dwell on her unrequited and hopeless love, not to mention her probably impending death, she let them come.

"*You're not well, are you?*" *Vlad asked as they drove along winding tracks through the Romanian countryside.*

"*I'm fine. It's probably jet-lag catching up with me.*" *She knew it wasn't that, though. It was Elisabeta. The woman's presence was stronger here, and the constant struggle for control of her own body was wearing Stormy down.*

"*You're pale,*" *Vlad said. More worried, Stormy thought, about Elisabeta than about her.*

"*So are you.*" *She sent him a sideways look, but he only scowled in response to her lame attempt at humor.*

"*Are you sure you're up to this excursion?*"

"*If not now, when?*" *she asked. Then she shrugged.* "*Keep driving, Vlad. Take me to Castle Dracula.*"

"I'm afraid this is as far as we can go by car." He pulled to a stop and got out. She got out, too, and looked in the same direction he was.

They stood at the foot of a peak, and the path up it was so steep, it was nearly vertical. At the top, shrouded in mist and darkness, she could barely make out a shape that might be a castle.

She sighed, unsure she had the strength to make the climb. But then Vlad turned to her. "Come to me, Tempest. Put your arms around my neck."

She frowned, told herself this wasn't the time or place—and complied anyway. Anytime she could put her arms around him was the right time. And she didn't think she had the will to refuse him, anyway. She slipped her arms around his neck. He quickly scooped her off her feet and whispered, "Hold on."

There was a rush of speed and motion too sudden and rapid to absorb, much less follow. Seconds later, he was lowering her to her feet again. He kept his hands on her waist, and it was a good thing, because her knees didn't want to hold her weight. They started to buckle as soon as she tried to stand, and her earlier dizziness was magnified a hundred times.

She let him hold her while she pressed her hands to either side of her head and tried to blink her vision into focus. "What the hell was that?"

"I didn't think you were up to hiking the distance. And really, there was no need. We're here."

Frowning, she searched his face briefly, then turned to follow his gaze. The castle wasn't a castle at all. It was a crumbling pile of ruins, ancient stone blocks piled atop one another to form walls, with little or no mortar left in between. A path wound amid them, and someone had put a modern railing along parts of it, to protect unwary tourists, she supposed, from what would be a deadly fall. "This is it? I thought Castle Dracula was big and white and fancy."

"That's Bran Castle. I was rarely there, but the tourists seem to like it. This…this was where I lived. Poenari Castle. There's…very little left to explore, I'm afraid."

"Is it safe?"

"Come." He took her hand—not because he cared, she reminded herself, but just to keep her from falling, and that only for Beta's sake—and led her closer. They moved past the walls toward the tallest section, a rounded portion. The top of it was long gone, and it was higher on either side, lower in the middle, where more stones had fallen away, so that its top formed a crescent. He led her all through the place, pointing out what used to be the keep, the courtyards and so on. But nothing was even vaguely familiar to her.

Finally she sighed and touched his shoulder. "Vlad, where is the tower? The place where she died?"

He stopped walking, stopped speaking, lowered his head.

"Is it going to be too hard for you? Seeing that spot again? Because I could go alone."

"No. It's fine. Come."

He took her hand again and led her along a twisting path through the crumbling stones, finally stopping to point at a cluster of other ruins, though they were in far better shape than the first one. "Do you see the tower down there?" he asked, pointing.

"Yes. Is that...?"

"No. That's where the legends say she died. They say she pitched herself from that tower as the Turks approached, in order to prevent herself being captured. But as you know, that's not precisely the way it happened."

"I suppose it makes her rather a heroic figure, to remember it that way."

"I suppose." He turned and looked at a narrow circle of stones, barely four feet high. "This was the actual tower. My chambers were near the top. I liked to be able to see all the way down the mountain as soon as I rose and before I slept."

He lifted his gaze, and she did, too, trying to picture the place before it had fallen to ruin. But what she saw in her mind's eye could have been more imagination than past life memory.

She moved to the far side of the circular base,

where it came within a few yards of a steep drop. She went to step closer to the edge, but Vlad gripped her shoulders. "Careful. The ground is no longer stable here."

Holding her, he moved a little nearer the edge, then stopped. Stormy stared down, such a very long way down, into a sea of mist. The rocky slope dropped straight out of sight beneath the glittering stars. And then, as if on cue, a wind came, and the mists below swirled and then dissipated, so she could see all the way to the bottom, where a narrow stream wound over jagged rocks and boulders far below.

She felt it, then: the powerful sensation of her body falling, plummeting. The sense of weightlessness, of flying. The deathly silence of her descent. Her hair was tugged tight by the force of the air through which she fell. The wind whistled past her ears and stung her face. Heartache pounded inside her chest, so large it felt she would split open and bleed. She felt the crushing impact, pain beyond human endurance exploding in every part of her, and then it vanished and there was nothing but blessed relief. Release. Her breath rushed out of her. Her final breath. And she smiled as she died. Finally, she thought. Peace. An end to this endless grief. Finally. Let me go.

"Tempest!"

She blinked slowly and found herself lying on the

ground, her upper body cradled in Vlad's arms as he smacked her cheeks and shook her shoulders.

"Tempest, talk to me. For the love of the gods…"

"Okay," she managed. "I'm…okay."

"Far from it, I think." He held her closer, folding her to his chest as he knelt there, stroking her hair. For that brief moment she could almost have let herself believe he really cared. Almost.

"What happened just now? What happened to you?"

She rested against him, closing her eyes, even though she knew this wasn't real, this show of affection. "I think it was her. Elisabeta. I felt what she felt as she plummeted to her death, Vlad. And it wasn't horrible. I mean, there was pain when she hit the rocks. But it was very brief, and it was nothing compared to the pain she was feeling beforehand. The emotional pain. God, it was killing her. But it left her, Vlad. As she died, there was this incredible feeling of relief—of release. She didn't want to hurt anymore."

He'd been rocking her in his arms, but he stopped then. "And yet, she did, didn't she?"

Stormy swallowed hard, lifted her head from his chest and tipped her chin up to stare into his eyes. "I think she still is. Vlad, the woman I feel in these memories or episodes of possession or whatever they are—she's sweet. She's innocent and naive, and very weak and needy. And in a lot of pain, almost all the time. But sweet. But *the one who comes in now, to take over the way she does, she's none of those things. She's cruel and angry and violent. I'm not sure she's the same woman at all."*

"Or perhaps she is. Perhaps this is what she has become, what my actions caused her to become." He lowered his head. "Perhaps Rhiannon was right. The ritual I had the sorcerers perform was a mistake."

"I think that might be true."

"God, what have I done to her?" He tipped his head back to stare up at the stars.

Stormy sat up, brushing her hair back from her face. "Maybe Rhiannon was right about that, too? Maybe we need to find a way to exorcise her? To set her free?"

His head came down, and his eyes locked onto hers, sparking with anger. "Kill her, you mean?"

"Vlad, she's not alive. Not really."

"Oh, she's very much alive. I see her in you. Even now, I see her. She's trying to come through, trying to speak to me through you, isn't she, Tempest?"

She set her jaw, stiffened her spine. "She has been, ever since we… I'm not sure how much longer I can keep on fighting her. It's…exhausting."

He averted his eyes quickly. "You, too, are suffering because of what I did."

She lowered her head then. "Guilt isn't going to solve this, Vlad."

"No. I'm not ready to give her up. Not yet, Tempest."

She lifted her head, met his eyes again. "I can't go on like this," she told him. "Not for much longer, Vlad. At least when I'm not with you, she stays…dormant. Asleep. But here…"

He sighed, impatient, angry perhaps and frustrated. He still expected her to suddenly remember and become the woman he longed for. All she wanted to do was figure out how to get rid of her.

And maybe convince him to love her, instead.

She swallowed hard. "Would you…take me to her grave?"

"Are you certain you're strong enough?"

"No. But I want to try. I feel as if I have to."

"Don't, not for my sake, Tempest."

"I'm not. It's for her sake, Vlad. Part of me…loves her as much as you do. I mean, the woman she was. Not the presence that haunts me now, but that girl. That innocent, grieving, heartbroken child who is, maybe, somehow, a part of me. I have to help her if I can."

"You're a generous woman."

She let her eyes go hard. "I want to help her by setting her free. Not by bringing her back."

His features hardened, but he got to his feet and held out a hand. She took it and let him draw her upright. "The night is aging."

"Yeah," *she said, and she slid her arms around his neck.* "So let's do this the fast way, all right?"

He nodded. She tightened her grip, and they whirled into the night.

Stormy resurfaced from her memories. She had recovered nearly all of them now, she sensed. She knew when she had fallen in love with him, and why he'd held her heart captive for so very long. Always it had been about Elisabeta. Never her. He'd never loved her.

He never would.

"There is no reason to believe anything dire has happened to either of them," Rhiannon said for the tenth time.

But that was exactly what Vlad believed, and he was kicking himself for his part in it. By the gods, if anything happened to prevent him doing what must be done in time...

Melina was on the telephone yet again, dialing Tempest's cell phone number. She met his eyes and shook her head. "I got her voice mail again. She must have the phone turned off, Vlad. If she doesn't want to hear from us, she's not going to pick up the messages I keep leaving."

Lowering his head, Vlad resumed his pacing. "This is my doing. All of it."

Rhiannon stepped into his path, blocking his progress. "Stop this. You can find her, Vlad. You, more than any of us, can find her."

He stared into Rhiannon's eyes, frowning. "I don't know. My bond with Elisabeta isn't as powerful as—"

"Not Beta, Vlad. For the love of the gods, would you stop focusing on her for one second? Are you that obsessed? It's Stormy. I'm talking about Stormy. Do you think I can't smell her on you?" Rhiannon snapped, looking as if she would like to knock him over the head with something heavy. "You drank from her, Vlad. And more than once. Her scent and her essence are still alive in you. The bond created by that act is a powerful one. You, more than any of us here, can sense her."

"You think I haven't tried?" He tipped his head back and pushed his hands through his hair in frustration.

"I think," Rhiannon said, "that you are trying too hard."

"I'm going after them," he said. "Tempest is likely going home, to her mansion in Easton. I'll go there and—"

"Not just yet." Rhiannon glanced at Melina and Lupe. "Does either of you have any skill at scrying?"

"I do," Lupe said.

"Then get a map, and a pendulum, and try to narrow the search. For both of them." Then she turned to Vlad. "Come with me, we have work to do."

He didn't want to go with Rhiannon. He wanted to be out hunting for the women. But Rhiannon was a wise woman. It wouldn't be smart to ignore the help she offered, though why she offered it, he couldn't fathom. He'd all but destroyed her trust in him. He went where she led him, into a room he'd never seen before—a room with sculptures and candles everywhere. It resembled a spiritual temple. There were huge satin pillows strewn about the floor, and she nodded at one, so he sat.

Then she closed the door behind them. She stood in the room's center and turned in a slow circle, waving her hand before her as she did. One by one, the candles came to life, flames leaping onto their wicks in obedience to her gesture and her will. He was impressed, in spite of himself.

"You're going to need to relax," she told him.

"Far easier said than done, Rhiannon."

"Lie back on the pillows, Vlad."

He did, pulling more of the cushions around behind him to make a bed of sorts.

"Listen only to my voice," Rhiannon said, and her tone had become deep and low, soft and, at the same time, commanding. "Thoughts will come. Just move them away and return your attention to my voice. Gently, steer your focus to my words. Only to my words."

"I'll try."

"You'll do it. Keep your eyes open. Choose a candle you see easily and focus on its flame. See the way it dances, the way its fire waxes and wanes like the tides. Like the moon."

He focused on a nearby candle flame.

"See how the wax heats and melts. Do you see it, Vlad?"

"I see it." He watched beads of wax roll slowly down the sides of the candle, pooling at the bottom.

"Feel your body heating and melting just as the wax does. Your feet are warming, melting. Feel the flame relaxing them into liquid."

He felt her words, her will, flowing into him. And he felt his feet grow warm until it seemed they were melting into the floor.

"And now your calves. Feel them pooling, like warm wax. Dripping, liquefying. And your knees, your thighs, warming, heating, melting."

He thought about the women as his body

obeyed, wondered what was happening between them right now.

"My words, Vlad. Listen to my voice. See the candle. Feel it heating you. Your groin and your hips. Your pelvis and your belly. Warming, melting, pooling."

She continued, and the thoughts that kept drawing him away seemed to come more slowly and to take longer to return each time he pushed them away.

When she had convinced him that his entire body was a puddle of hot wax on the pillows, she said, "Let your focus go soft. Let the candle flame split into two flames and become blurry. Relax your vision. See now, with your inner eye. See her. See Tempest. Taste her blood again. Feel it coursing through your body. She is inside you, Vlad. She's a part of you. You are bound. See through her eyes. See her."

His vision blurred, and in a moment his eyes fell closed.

"Where is she, Vlad?"

"She's…in her car. Belladonna, she calls it. She loves the thing." A smile tugged at his lips. "She's driving."

"Yes. Good. Don't strain, Vlad. Just let the images flow into you. Flowing like that warm, melting wax. Filling you. Warming you. What else do you see?"

He stopped trying and relaxed. Rhiannon's voice made resistance futile, even if he'd wanted to try. "She's...crying."

"That's all right. Don't let those tears distract you. They flow, warm and liquid, like the wax. They flow for you. They show you her heart. They are the waters of true emotion, and they are cleansing and healing to a woman's soul."

"She loves me," he whispered, feeling the emotion that filled her heart to bursting.

"Yes. And she wants you to know where she is. She wants you to come to her, Vlad. Listen to her thoughts now. Move gently into her mind and listen. Open to her. Let those thoughts roll like the melting wax. Let them seep into you. Let them...."

Her voice faded, replaced by the voice of Tempest's heart, of her thoughts.

He doesn't love me...never loved me. He loves her. I was just a means to get her back all along. He was using me. I've wasted my life, loving him, longing for him, waiting and hoping, when all the time he never...

Have to stop thinking about him. God, why can't I get him out of my mind? Have to go home. No, no, not home. Don't want to face Maxie and Lou, not now. Don't want to tell them what a fool I've been. Don't

*want to be around anyone, no one. Not now, not yet.
I need to be alone. I need to get past this.*

*I wonder if he'll let Rhiannon exorcise Elisabeta from
Brooke's body? He won't. I know he won't. I wish Rhiannon could exorcise him from my heart, though.
Maybe she can. Maybe I should ask her. Then again,
maybe it won't matter. I'll be dead anyway, if Rhiannon can't send Beta to the other side.*

She looked through the windshield of the car,
seeing darkness, a road and a sign. "Seaside, 80 km."
And she thought of the sea, the coast, a cozy inn
where she could rest and try to heal. *Far enough
away from him? Maybe. Maybe far enough. It's only
another hour. I'll go there. I love the ocean. If I'm going
to die tonight, it can be right there, on the shore, with
the waves rolling in around my feet. A good place to die.*

"Seaside," he said aloud, though even to his own
ears, his voice sounded a bit hoarse. "A town called
Seaside. She's going there."

"Good, Vlad," Rhiannon said softly. "Very good.
Now I want you to pull yourself out of her body, out
of her mind. I want you to see what's around her, in
the car. Is there anyone else there with her?"

"I am with her."

"Yes, but besides you."

He gently withdrew from Tempest's mind, the

voice of her thoughts fading away, until he was in the car, in the passenger seat. He felt something, a presence, a familiar one, and he frowned, guiding his attention toward it. And then he saw—

The door to the room burst open, jarring Vlad back into his own body, into the room, into reality, where he landed with as much impact as if he'd fallen from a tall building. The trance state shattered on impact, and he sat up so fast it made him dizzy. He had to press a hand to his head. Rhiannon's hands closed on his shoulders as she snapped, "Lupe, what are you thinking, barging in here during—"

Vlad growled an interruption. "When I can stand upright, you bungling mortal, I'll—"

"I've got her!" Lupe blurted almost at the same time. Then she looked at Vlad as his threat sunk in, and her face went tight with fear. "I'm sorry, I didn't mean—"

He held up a hand to shut her up.

"Ground yourself, Vlad. Here, hold this." Rhiannon handed him a large quartz crystal the size of his fist, and he took it and held it between his palms, trying to get his bearings again.

"We know where Tempest is going, Lupe," Rhiannon explained. "To a town called Seaside."

"I got the same thing. But not just for her," Lupe said, a little breathlessly. "I got the same results when I scried for Elisabeta. I think she's following her or—"

"She's not following her," Vlad said softly. Gripping the edge of a table, he got to his feet, still a bit shaky. "She's *with* her."

"With her?" Rhiannon searched his face.

"She's hiding in the back of Tempest's car."

A gasp came from the doorway, and they turned to see Melina standing there. Her fists clasped, she said, "The weapons room door was open, so I went in to check. There's a handgun missing."

Tempest pulled over and patted Belladonna's dashboard the way she would pat the neck of a sweaty horse, one that had just carried her away from trouble. "Thanks for taking me the hell out of there. You've been a pal. I'm gonna miss you."

She cut the engine, slid one arm through one of the straps of her backpack purse, and pulled it onto her shoulder as she got out of the car. Then she stood for a moment, looking down at the spot that had beckoned her. A rocky shoreline, choppy sea beyond, shallow waves rolling up and breaking over the stones and boulders. It appealed to her, this rough-faced beach. Not all smooth and sandy, but rugged and forbidding, harsh beneath the star speckled velvet black of the sky.

Stormy hitched her bag up higher onto her shoulder, walked down the little incline to the shore and stood for a moment, staring out at the sea. And even as she tried to find a positive spin to put on her heartache, warm tears welled in her eyes and rolled slowly down her cheeks.

"It's not entirely bad," she told herself. "At least I got rid of *her*."

She took a moment, then, to feel the lightness in her soul. No more was there that sense of something foreign, lurking and waiting to take over. Hating her from within.

It felt good. It was a huge relief.

And yet, there was another weight in her, this one crushing heavily down on her heart. She loved him. She loved him even now. And it was stupid— pathetic, really—to love a man who didn't love her back. She knew it. And yet there was nothing she could do about it. Pretty sad to think that she, the independent and notoriously feisty Stormy Jones, was going to die loving a man who cared nothing for her.

"Pathetic," she muttered, and bent to pick up a

small stone, then straightened and hurled it out into the waves.

"Yes. Terribly pathetic."

Stormy spun around at the voice coming from right behind her, knowing before she saw her, who it was. Elisabeta, in Brooke's body, holding a hand-gun and pointing it right at her chest. The wind blew in from the sea, tossing Brooke's normally sleek hair into a wild mass of auburn tangles as Elisabeta's black eyes glinted from her face.

Stormy stiffened, stifling the words that flew to her lips, realizing she was face to face with an armed lunatic who wanted her dead. Better to try to dif-fuse the situation.

"I left because I want no more to do with him, Beta," she said. "He's all yours. I won't be back."

"Sadly, that's not quite good enough."

Frowning, Stormy tried to size up her situation. She had no weapon. There was a cell phone in her bag, but Beta could squeeze that trigger before she would be able to take it out, much less dial 911. There was no one around. No one in sight. She tried to remember the last place she'd passed where there might have been people or even lights, and knew it had been a while.

"What do you want from me, then?" she asked.

"Not so much. Just your body."

Stormy went stiff. Could the bitch know, somehow, what was ailing her? Her face was drawn and pale, her eyes slightly sunken. Dark circles were beginning to form underneath them. "What's wrong with the one you've got?"

"It's dying," she said. "So I need yours."

"Sorry, but I'm using it right now." She could have kicked herself for letting the words out, heavy with sarcasm and impatience. She schooled herself to calm. "Maybe...there's some way I can help you, Elisabeta. Maybe—"

"Oh, there is. I need your body before midnight, or we'll both die. In order to do that, I must have my ring back. And the scroll. Give them to me."

She would need the ring and the scroll to perform the rite again. And this time, Stormy realized, she wanted to perform it on *her*. "I'm sorry. I can't—"

"Give them to me or I'll kill you!"

Stormy swallowed, held up a hand as if to calm the woman. "If you kill me, you'll never have my body."

"If you don't give them to me, I'll die anyway," Beta said. "Now give them to me."

Stormy waited a beat, trying to decide the best

answer to give, and finally decided not to push her luck. "I don't have them."

"You're lying!"

"No, I'm not. When I left, I washed my hands of this entire case. I wanted no more to do with you or with Vlad—*or* with that cursed ring. I'm telling you, Beta, I don't have them."

Beta closed her eyes, but popped them wide open again before Stormy could even think about going for the gun. "Who does?"

Stormy almost smiled. Almost. Because of all the lies she could think of, the truth was still the best option. "Rhiannon," she said. "Good luck getting them from her."

Beta was silent for a long moment, her eyes seeming to search inwardly. It was almost as if she were listening to something, or someone, and then she focused again, blinking and frowning. "You have a… *Celephone?* Yes?"

"A cell phone? Yes, I have one. It's in my bag here."

"Take it out."

Stormy started to take the bag from her shoulder, and Elisabeta wiggled the gun. "Slowly."

"All right. All right. Easy with that thing. If you shoot me by accident, we'll both be screwed." They were both screwed anyway, Stormy thought. Clearly

Beta had escaped before Rhiannon could exorcise her from Brooke's body. And time was ticking away. Slowly and carefully, Stormy slid the cell phone from its holder on the side of the backpack. "It's right here, okay?"

"Call her."

"Who? Rhiannon?"

Beta nodded, her gun hand starting to tremble. She was getting tired.

"Okay. Just…it's turned off. I have to turn it on." She flipped open the phone, and as soon as it powered up, the message signal sounded. No time now, though, for retrieving her voice mail. Instead, she located the number for Athena House in her phonebook and hit the call button.

It rang. And rang. And rang some more. She licked her lips, held the phone out so Beta could listen if she wanted. "No one's there," she said.

"Does she not have a…cell phone she carries with her. Like yours?"

"Yeah. You want me to try that number?"

Beta nodded, so Stormy placed the call. Rhiannon didn't pick up, though. Vlad did.

"Tempest?" he asked. And God, he sounded as if he really hoped it was her. Yeah, he probably did. He still needed her to save his lunatic bride.

"Yeah, it's me."

"Are you all right? Where are you?"

And now he sounded worried. *Really* worried. "I'm here with Beta. She has a gun on me."

"Give it to me!" Beta commanded.

"Hold on. Your wife wants to talk to you." Stormy held out the cell phone.

Beta snatched it from her, keeping the gun aimed, one handed now, and her eyes focused on Stormy. "Get the ring and the scroll from Rhiannon and bring them to me. If you want to save me, Vlad, do this for me. If you don't, Tempest and I will both be dead soon. And you know that's the truth. And if you come, Vlad, and you are not alone, I will shoot her, just to be sure you don't try to save the wrong woman."

Without waiting for a reply, she handed the phone back to Stormy. "Tell him where we are, so he can come to us."

Stormy nodded as she pressed the phone to her own ear again. "We're on a deserted stretch of beach off the Seaside exit. Take a right, about two miles down. You'll see my car along the roadside." She met Elisabeta's eyes and said, "She's going to try to take my body. If it were me, I'd let the bitch die, but I don't suppose you feel the same."

Beta snatched the phone from her hand and hurled it into the sea. "I should kill you right now."

"Go for it. I've got nothing pressing."

She swung. It came out of the blue; Stormy hadn't expected it. The gun hit her right in the side of the head, behind her left eye. There was a brief explosion of pain, and then the ground was rushing up to meet her as she went down for the count.

Her last thought was that her words to Vlad had been wasted and she'd taken the blow for nothing. There was no way he would let his precious Elisabeta die. He would probably bring the ring and the scroll and assist in Stormy's execution.

15

"She said to come alone. And that is *precisely* what I intend to do." Vlad hovered near the mansion's front door, addressing Rhiannon, while the other two mortal women stood a short distance behind her. They looked nervous, as if they expected a vampiric battle to break out at any moment and wished to avoid being caught in the crossfire. "And frankly, I'm growing weary of repeating myself. Give me the ring, Rhiannon. And the scroll."

He held out a hand, palm up, and looked into her eyes.

She held them in one hand but didn't offer them to him. He hoped to the gods she wasn't going to force him to take them from her.

"There is strength in numbers, Vlad. And she's not one of us. She'll never know if I'm lurking in the shadows nearby, ready to back you up, if needed."

"And since when does Dracula require backing up?" he asked. "Rhiannon, she's a mortal. A sick one, at that."

She pursed her full lips and stared at him, her eyes speaking volumes. "She's your wife," she said.

The words penetrated. The meaning clarified in his mind. "You don't trust me."

She averted her eyes. "I'm going with you. That's all and that's final. If you want to prevent it, Vlad, you'll have to kill me, and I don't think you're willing to do that." She shrugged and met his eyes again, hers less serious this time. "Moreover, I don't think you could best me even if you were willing to try."

"Don't bet your life on it."

Rhiannon locked her gaze on his. "I never thought it would come to this. The two of us on opposing sides. I'm going to Stormy, Vlad. And I'm going now." She moved toward the door, but she would have to pass him to get to it.

Vlad threw his will at her, hitting her squarely in the chest with a surge of energy that stopped her in her tracks and made her suck in a quick, sharp breath.

She glared at him. "You dare…"

"Give me the ring and the scroll, Rhiannon."

She flung out an arm in a powerful arc, sending a bolt of energy that knocked him backward until he hit the wall, hard. A nearby painting crashed to the floor.

He righted himself, shook off the pain and hurled his powerful will at her much harder than he had before. Rhiannon flew into the air as if hit in the gut by a wrecking ball, landed hard, on her back and struggled to suck in a breath of air.

Vlad lunged at her then, straddled her, and searched her until he found the items he needed in a deep pocket of her gown. He took them from her, paused only to gaze at her face, to touch her cheek as she blinked to clear her vision. "I'm sorry, Rhiannon. You left me no choice."

Then he turned from her and raced from the room, out through the front door and into the night. Regret gnawed at his soul. But he hadn't harmed her. Not truly. Hurt her, yes, but she would suffer no lasting effects. In fact, she would likely be strong enough to follow on his heels within the hour. So he'd best hurry.

He whirled, right there on the steps of Athena House. Spun like a top, gaining momentum and speed, and exerted his will to alter his form. As a giant raven, he flexed his wings, beat them once, twice, three times, as he pushed off with his legs and took to the starry sky. As he made his way to her, Vlad remembered the way their time together had ended in the past. He let the memories flow through him, hoping they would stiffen his resolve to do what he knew must be done.

He had been losing hope of ever finding a way to solve the riddle that had become his life. He stood beside Tempest at the site that had been his bride's grave, and he watched her stare at the ground that bore no marker, no memory. All had been lost to the ravages of time. Grasses and trees grew. The stream still bubbled and laughed its way past. The stars still shone down on her resting place.

Rest. That was a bitter joke, wasn't it? There had been no rest for his beloved. No peace, not in all this time. Why hadn't he had the strength to let her go?

Why couldn't he find it still?

Tempest looked ill. She was pale and trembling at intervals. She rubbed her arms with her hands as if she were cold, and he put an arm around her to warm her. "You haven't eaten all night," he said. "Perhaps we should go—"

She whirled on him, her hands fisting and rising, her eyes blazing into his. Black, black as coal. "Do not think to leave me here, Vlad! Do not dare think it!"

He recoiled, taken unaware by the sudden change in her. But he knew she was not Tempest any longer. He was staring into the eyes of his beloved, of his Elisabeta.

He lifted an unsteady hand, touched her face. "I wouldn't leave you."

"You have!" she accused. But she didn't pull away from his touch. Rather, she covered his hand on her cheek with her own, leaned into it, closed her eyes. "You've abandoned me to this existence, trapped, unable to return, unable to move on. I want to return, Vlad. I want to be with you. I will never give up."

Tears sprang into his eyes, though he fought them. "You shouldn't have taken your own life, Beta. You should have waited for me. Gods, if only you had waited."

"I have waited. All these centuries, I've waited. And now I've found you again. Don't let her come between us, Vlad. Don't let her take me away from you."

"I—" He searched her face, unable to speak, because it was as if she knew exactly what he'd been thinking.

"She wants to, you know. She wants to be force me back into that infernal netherworld that's neither life nor death. That limbo. That prison between the worlds. I cannot go back there, Vlad. I will not."

"I won't let that happen, Beta. Not if I can prevent it."

"She wants you for herself," she whispered.

He lowered his head.

"I'll never let her have you."

Vlad's head rose again at the venom in her tone. At

the hatred in her voice. She did not sound like the Elisabeta he had known.

"I'll kill her first, Vlad. I vow to you I will."

"Beta, don't think that way. It's not—" He broke off there, because she had whirled away from him and taken off running through the forest.

Vlad took off after her. "Wait! Beta, dammit, wait!" He poured on a burst of speed, even as the horrible scene unfolded before his eyes. Beta had flung herself— no, she had flung Tempest—into the stream at its deepest point, and she lay face down in the water. Her arms flailed as if she were trying to get up, as if something were holding her down. She was drowning!

Vlad gripped her around her waist and chest, and hauled her, dripping, out of the water. Then, turning, he took her to the grassy bank and laid her down on her back. He pressed his ear to her chest to listen to her breaths and heard none. But then, suddenly, her head came up and she began choking, water spewing from her nose and mouth.

"Thank the gods," he muttered, and rolled her onto her side, to help her eliminate the icy water from her lungs.

Leaning over, weak, and shaking now from head to toe, she gagged and spat and gasped, until, finally, she managed to empty the water from her lungs. As she sucked in breath after breath of air, he took off his coat and wrapped it around her shoulders.

"Tempest?" he asked.

She lifted her head, eyes tired and unfocused. "What…happened?"

"I…I don't know."

A twig snapped behind him, and Vlad whirled to see Rhiannon standing there, Roland at her side. She looked furious. "You know exactly what happened, Vlad. Elisabeta just attempted to murder Tempest. You saw it. You know it's the truth."

He closed his eyes, lowered his head.

Rhiannon moved closer, knelt beside Tempest. "Has this happened before, Stormy?"

Still shaking, she tugged the coat closer around her shoulders and nodded, the movement jerky. "Yes. I think so. I mean, I wasn't sure until now, but—"

Her words were cut off by another round of coughing.

"We have to get her back to the castle," Roland said. "She needs to get warm and dry. Mortal bodies can't tolerate this sort of trauma easily."

Nodding, Vlad got to his feet, reached to gather Tempest into his arms, but Roland stopped him with a hand to his shoulder. "Let me, my friend. I'll get her there quickly, bundle her by the fire and care for her until you arrive."

"But why?" he asked, searching the man's face.

It was Rhiannon who answered him. "I think you

know why. You know what must be done, Vlad. There are things we'll need, for the rite of exorcism."

Vlad gasped, and his gaze shot from Rhiannon's to Tempest as Roland gathered her weakened, battered body into his arms. She was not doing well. She couldn't take much more of this attack—and he knew now that she was indeed under attack. Without the ring and the scroll, he couldn't hope to help her find union and harmony with the soul he believed to be her former self, a part of her own. But she couldn't go on like this, either. Not and survive.

His tears spilling over, he no longer tried to control them as he whispered, "So be it, then."

By the time Rhiannon and Vlad arrived back at the castle, Tempest was warm and dry, as Roland had promised she would be. She'd changed clothes, and now wore a nightgown and a heavy velvet robe, and had a blanket wrapped around her shoulders besides. She was sipping hot soup from a large mug, and sitting with her legs curled beneath her in front of a roaring fire. Her hair was beginning to dry, its tendrils springing into their natural curls around her face. She looked exhausted, drained, as she stared into the fire.

Rhiannon had explained that she and Roland, knowing full well Vlad's folly could only lead to disaster, had decided to stay on another day, another night, in case *they were needed. Rhiannon had deliberately tuned into Tempest's mind, and had picked up on her distress and located her easily.*

Just as well.

His quest was at an end. And yet a spark of hope remained. He had to say goodbye to his goal of almost six hundred years. He had to say goodbye to Elisabeta. But perhaps something of a chance would remain for himself and Tempest. He didn't know. He didn't know if her feelings for him were her own or a part of the possession of her body by his long dead wife. In fact, he wasn't even certain his own feelings were truly for her or for the woman she had been in another time, another place.

And even if it turned out they did still care for one another, there was the inevitable end they both must face. She was mortal. She was not one of The Chosen. She would die. He would live on.

But one thing was certain. She couldn't go on this way.

"*Are we ready to do this?*" *Rhiannon asked.*

Vlad looked at Tempest. "*Are you certain she can withstand it?*"

"*It shouldn't be too trying, Vlad. It's only a ritual.*"

He nodded. Tempest turned to face him. "*I'm ready,*" *she said, her voice soft.* "*I'm sorry, Vlad. I'm sorry I wasn't strong enough to give her a chance.*"

He moved closer, touched her hand. "*Perhaps this*

was the way it was meant to be, Tempest. She needs to be at peace. We can give her that, if nothing more."

She nodded, then looked to Rhiannon. "What should I do?"

"Just lie down. Relax." She nodded toward the chaise that stood a few feet from the fire, and Tempest rose unsteadily. Roland gripped one arm, Vlad the other, and they helped her to the chaise. She slid the blanket from her shoulders as she lay down and pulled it over her instead.

"Very good." Rhiannon slid a pack from her shoulder, and opened it began taking items from it one by one. Weeds she'd gathered from the forest. A handful of dirt from Elisabeta's grave, a stone from the stream where her body had landed, a vial of water she'd provided herself, and salt and candles, black ones. A bell. She gathered candles from around the castle and brought them to place with the rest of her items.

She pulled a small table closer and began laying the items out one by one. Then she carried the black candles to the extreme directions of the room. One on the mantle by the fire in the south, another on a table in the west, where she poured the water into a bowl. A third rested in a spot she cleared on the bookshelf in the north, the fourth beside a dish of herbs in the east.

She stared at the candles, and one by one they burst into flames at the sheer power of her will. Then she touched one burning wick to the herbs, until they began to blaze. After a moment the died flames out and left the herbs to smoulder in a silver dish. The spiraling smoke they emitted was pungent and strong.

"You two sit on either side of her. If Elisabeta realizes what we're doing, there's a chance she could come through and try to prevent us from completing the ritual, or if that fails, to try again to harm her. You'll need to hold her to prevent that."

Vlad looked down at Tempest, the way her eyes widened at Rhiannon's words, and he stroked her forehead. "I won't let that happen. I promise you."

When she nodded, he turned to Rhiannon. "Proceed."

Rhiannon stood still for a long moment, as if gathering her thoughts, but Vlad thought she was doing something far deeper than that. She was connecting to some force within her, or perhaps beyond herself. When she opened her eyes again, she looked different, more powerful than she ever had—and that was saying a lot.

She moved as if floating, lifting a hand and tracing the shape of a circle around the room, encompassing all of them as she muttered words in what he thought was Egyptian. And Vlad swore he could see an ether forming a sphere around them. Thin, barely visible, it wavered and danced, and he had the odd sensation of being contained within a bubble of power.

Then she moved to the westernmost part of the circle and moved her arms as if parting a curtain. And he glimpsed a darkness there, a dark portal within the bubble's wall.

Finally she moved to Tempest and began her work. She chanted over her body, and used her fingers to sprinkle it with water from the bowl. Then she returned the bowl to its place and came back to take up the incense, and again using her hands, she wafted the smoke over Tempest, from her head to her feet.

She continued chanting haunting, mesmerizing words in a melodic, hypnotic tone. Deep and rich and commanding yet gentle.

Tempest's eyes fell closed. Her breathing grew shallow, and she began to turn her head to the left and right.

Vlad held her shoulders, wanting to speak to her, to comfort her, but Rhiannon caught that urge and then his eyes, and told him without speaking to remain silent. She kept chanting.

She put the smouldering herbs back in their spot and took up the bell, ringing it over Tempest, over her head, her chest, her belly, her hips, her knees, her feet. And now her chanting took on a more urgent tone. It was louder, more commanding.

Tempest twisted her head harder. Her breaths came short and sharp and fast, and she started to move her body, twisting and writhing from side to side.

Rhiannon slipped into English. "Leave this body, Elisabeta. Go, through the western gate and on to your reward, to rest. To peace. Go, Elisabeta. Release this woman and go!"

Tempest's eyes opened wide and blue. She shrieked as if in agony, and her body lifted from the chaise as her back arched nearly double.

Roland and Vlad gripped her, and to his amazement, it took all their strength to press her down again.

"Go," Rhiannon commanded. "You do not belong to this plane! Go, Elisabeta!"

Tempest's entire body began to spasm, as if she were having a seizure of some sort. The men struggled to hold her, and Vlad shot a panicked look at Rhiannon. "I don't think she's breathing. She's not breathing, Rhiannon!"

Her face turned red, and then her lips turned blue, and the rest of her skin tone followed.

"It's killing her, my love," Roland said. "This isn't going to work. Elisabeta will not leave her alive."

Rhiannon hesitated only a moment as the spasming continued. But then she ran to Tempest and gripped her shoulders. "It's ended," she said. "It's over. Breathe again, child. Breathe."

Immediately Tempest's body relaxed and stopped shaking. But it was a long, long moment before she sucked in a breath so powerful Vlad wondered that it didn't burst her lungs.

Rhiannon sagged in relief. "See to her. I must attend the circle."

"Did it work?" Vlad asked. "Is Beta gone?"

Rhiannon met his eyes and shook her head sadly. "Her grip on our little mortal is more powerful than I could have imagined, Vlad. If I'd forced her out, she would have taken Tempest's soul with her. I'm sorry."

Vlad sighed. He wasn't certain if it was in disappointment or relief. Perhaps both. He gathered Tempest into his arms, carried her to the chair nearest the fire and sat there, holding her in his lap, her body resting against his chest. He held her and pondered what on earth he could do now that the exorcism had failed.

Rhiannon had taken away the sphere of energy, extinguished the candles and poured the smoking herbs into the fireplace. She turned to him then, her face grim as she moved closer, her hands going to his shoulders. "We cannot exorcise the trespassing soul from her body. But we can minimize its strength and power over her. That power, Vlad, is at its peak when she is near you. You know that. You've seen it." She closed her eyes, and Vlad thought he glimpsed a tear on those thick lashes before she spoke again. "You have to let her go, love. For her sake, you have to let her go."

Vlad stared down at the beautiful woman in his arms. Her eyes were closed, her breathing deep and regular at last. He stroked her hair away from her face. "It won't be forever, Tempest. Only until I can locate the ring and the scroll. Only until then. I promise you." He bent to press a kiss on her lips, committing their softness to memory. "It will be easier for her if I can make her forget," he said. "Give me just a few more moments with her. I'll erase her memory, and then you can take her away."

"Rhiannon?"

Melina and Lupe knelt on either side of her as Rhiannon regained her senses and struggled to sit up.

"Are you all right?" Melina asked.

"Of course I'm all right." She gathered the shreds of her dignity and pushed her hands against the floor in an effort to rise. To her utter humiliation, the two mortals helped her, gripping her arms and tugging until she was upright again. As soon as she had her footing, Rhiannon shook their hands away. "I don't desire your help."

"I don't blame you," Lupe said. Melina shot her a look, but the younger woman ignored it. "I looked in the archives, as you suggested, Rhiannon. I know that members of our order assisted the priestesses who tried to hold you against your will, so long ago."

"What they tried, mortal, was to kill me. Had Vlad not taken me from that place, not transformed me when he did, I would have died. And that was precisely what they wanted. They nearly killed both of us in trying to prevent my escape."

Lupe lowered her head. "It was wrong, what they did. I'm sorry."

Rhiannon lifted her brows.

"Rhiannon," Melina said. "You have to know those women were not acting in accordance with the laws of the Sisterhood. They took it upon themselves to align with the priestesses of Isis to act against you in exchange for the reams of wisdom those priestesses promised them in return."

"Of course. And I suppose the Sisterhood punished them for it. Or were they given some sort of medal, instead?"

Melina glanced at Lupe and said nothing. Lupe frowned and returned her gaze to Rhiannon's. "I couldn't find any mention of what action was taken against them, if any," she said.

"We don't keep written records of that sort of thing," Melina said.

"What sort of thing?" Lupe asked.

Melina licked her lips. "They were executed. Hanged, both of them, for betraying the laws of the order." She met Rhiannon's eyes. "Read my mind if you don't believe that's the truth, Rhiannon. I'm not proud of what they did, and I'm not proud of what was done to them as a result. But I suppose you have a right to know. You *can* trust us."

She was skeptical. "An order is only as trustworthy as its members, Melina. And this order seems to me to be lousy with traitors. Take Brooke, for example."

"Three, in all these centuries," Melina countered.

"Three that I know of. I have no doubt there have been more. You don't exactly choose wisely when you recruit these women."

"I've made mistakes, that's true. I'm only human."

"Precisely."

Lupe licked her lips nervously. "We're wasting time. We need to go after him if we want to have any hope of saving Stormy."

"We?" Rhiannon cocked one brow as she speared the woman with her eyes.

Melina stepped closer, clearing her throat nervously. "We…need to go along, Rhiannon. And I'm afraid I can't take no for an answer. If Brooke survives, she'll need us there. We need to bring her home."

Rhiannon rolled her eyes. "Where she'll no doubt

be tried, convicted and executed for betraying the order."

"Don't pretend to understand our ways, Rhiannon. You're making assumptions. If there's a way I can save her, I will. But she has to face the repercussions of her actions."

Lupe came up to stand beside Melina. "I don't want to tell you guys your business, but it seems to me we also need a plan."

She had a point, Rhiannon thought, though she hated to admit it. With a deep sigh, she said, "If you mortals are coming along, I suppose we'd best travel by car. I have copied the rite we'll need to exorcise Beta from Brooke's body, to set her free of the power of the ring. It's right—" She dipped a hand into her pocket, but it came up empty. She frowned.

"I have the copy you gave me," Melina said.

Rhiannon swallowed hard. "There's one thing I must tell you, and on this I am adamant," she said. "We do not intervene until we are certain of Vlad's intentions."

"We already know his intentions," Melina said. "He's going to help Elisabeta take Stormy's body. He's going to kill her, Rhiannon."

"Perhaps," Rhiannon said. But deep down, she hoped she was wrong. Vlad had made the right decision once before. She had to believe he would do so again, despite the fact that his obsession for Elisabeta seemed only to have worsened over the past sixteen years. For his sake, she had to give him the chance to do the right thing.

And then she was going to kick his ass for what he'd done to her tonight.

"We do not intervene," Rhiannon said again, "until I am certain. If either of you tries to step in before I give the word, I promise you, you will not see the sunrise. Is that understood?"

The woman looked at each other, fear wide in their eyes. "Understood," Melina said softly.

As she lay there, drifting in and out of consciousness, Stormy was flooded with memories, the missing pieces of her time with Vlad, sixteen years ago. The memories Vlad had erased from her mind for so long.

He'd tried to save her. He'd tried to let Rhiannon exorcise Elisabeta from her body. He'd been forced to choose between them...and he'd chosen her.

The knowledge made her heart sing, gave her a surge of strength, enough to bring her back from the stupor into which Elisabeta's blow had plunged her. But the moment she did so, her joy faded and her doubts returned. Just because he had chosen her in the past, that didn't mean he would make the same choice again. He'd shown no hint of his feelings for her since their reunion. He'd given her no reason to believe he would act against his bride to save her.

Would he?

Stormy forced her questions to the back of her mind and tried to take stock of her current situation. She found herself paralyzed. Panic at being unable to move her limbs hit her like a blast of ice water in the face, and she came fully awake, eyes flying wide as the instinctive need to move surged through her. She strained and pulled.

Something hit her, a hard, stinging smack across her face.

She went still, blinking through the surge of hot tears that sprang into her eyes and tried to focus.

Brooke—no, not Brooke, Elisabeta—stood before her, silhouetted by the moon against darkness, the pounding sea at her back. There was something different about the beach. And slowly as her mind cleared, Stormy became aware of several things all at once. First, she wasn't paralyzed at all, but bound by lengths of rope that had been in the trunk of her own car. They held her immobile. She lay on her back, her arms outspread and staked to the ground on either side of her. She felt the ropes chafing her skin. Her ankles were bound together, and staked, as well. And she had been moved. She was no longer on that gorgeous stretch of rocky shore where she had stopped to work through her feelings and her pain and, perhaps, to die.

No, this spot was different. There were trees and brush around, and the ground was just as rocky here, but amid the rocks was soil, not sand. The waves crashed to the shore beyond Elisabeta, but that shore was farther away than it had been before.

Finally she drew her gaze back to the woman who stood before her. And the cold breath of panic crept into her veins as it fully hit her—she was bound. Completely vulnerable to the whims of this insane, unnatural being. A being who wanted nothing more than to see her dead.

Hell.

Elisabeta seemed satisfied that Stormy had stopped her struggling, and she turned and resumed what she had been doing. What she had been doing, it turned out, was placing candles on the ground. And as Stormy slid her gaze back along those she had already set out, she saw that they would form a complete circle around her staked body. A circle in which she lay not in the center, but toward one side. There was room for another to lie within the ring beside her, and she had no doubt Elisabeta intended to be that other.

At four equally spaced points around the circle, censers were at the ready, heaped high with herbs that would burn to surround her in clouds of fragrance and power; herbs that would help Beta in her purposes. No herb had the power to eject a soul from its body. But the right ones would grease the wheels, so to speak. And though Stormy had no idea where the insane woman had located the candles and herbs, she had little doubt that Beta knew what she was doing.

She had to get the hell out of this. She resumed tugging at the ropes that held her. Elisabeta paused with the lighted match in her hand, poised at the wick of one of the candles, and sent her a scowl. "Stop it. It's no use, anyway. You're only wasting your energy."

Stormy stopped but not because of what Beta had said. She stopped because of the way the other woman looked there in the light of that tiny flame. Her eyes were even more deeply sunken than before, and rested atop giant, dark brown half moons. Her face was gaunt and pale in the flickering matchlight, and her skin seemed papery and loose. Dry to the point of peeling, and hanging from the bones of her face as if it were no longer attached.

"My God, how long have we been here?"

Beta shrugged. "A couple of hours. Why?"

Clearly Beta didn't know about the drastic and rapid changes in her appearance. But as Stormy watched her, she could tell the woman didn't feel a hell of a lot better than she looked. She walked in tiny, weak steps, feet barely leaving the ground, back bent, head low. She was out of breath, it seemed. She had aged fifty years in the space of a few hours.

"Where did you get the candles?"

"They were in Brooke's bag. She saved them from last time."

"And the herbs?"

"The same. I only wish Brooke had memorized the rite itself, but she didn't." She shrugged. "It doesn't matter, I suppose. I need to wait for the ring."

"I see. And, uh, what are you doing now?" Stormy asked.

"Lighting the candles." Her voice was hoarse.

"Well, yeah, I can see that. But could you elaborate?"

"For the ritual," Beta said. "Vlad is coming. He's bringing the ring and the scroll."

Stormy would have liked to think he wouldn't go through with it. That he would arrive like some kind of a dark knight in onyx armor and save her from the madwoman. But the madwoman was his wife. The love of his life. That was fact. Anything else she might come up with was guesswork. Hell, he'd never told Stormy how he felt about her. Not even in the past. Maybe if Beta had never been squatting inside her body, he never would have felt a damn thing to begin with.

And yet he tried to save me from her, all those years ago. Maybe he would again.

No, she couldn't count on him to get her out of this mess. She had to save herself.

She tugged, pulling her right arm, but not jerking it as she had before. Best to keep her efforts hidden. She exerted steady pressure and hoped to feel the stake in the ground give a little.

It didn't.

Perhaps sensing something, Beta turned to study her. "What are you doing?" She had lit half the candles by now.

"I can see why you moved us to a different spot," Stormy said. "The wind isn't even touching the flames, is it?"

"No. We're sheltered here by the trees and those bigger boulders over there," she replied, nodding toward the giant rocks that flanked their spot. So dark, the boulders. They blended into the night; Stormy hadn't seen them there behind the trees before.

Elisabeta resumed lighting the candles.

"You don't look so good," Stormy said. Making conversation, hoping to mask her movements by keeping Beta distracted. She'd had no luck with the stake at her left arm and so was tugging surreptitiously on the right one now. One at a time, she thought, would let her exert more strength on a single goal. But so far this stake wasn't moving any more than the first one had.

"It doesn't matter. I'll be out of this body soon enough."

"Yeah, it looks like any minute now."

She felt the glare Beta shot her and stopped tugging on the right stake. No progress at all. Okay, maybe the one at her feet. She tugged hard, bending her knees upward a minuscule amount.

"Ahh, he's coming," Beta said, straightening from the final candle and turning slowly. Her form was bowed, as if she were very old or very tired. The change in her from only a few hours earlier was astounding.

Stormy twisted her head to look in the direction the other woman was staring, and she saw a giant raven, as large as an eagle, easily, land heavily on the ground nearby. And then it opened its wings and seemed to stand straighter, stretch higher, and right before her eyes it changed until it became a man, all dressed in black.

Dracula.

Smiling, an expression that was downright frightening to behold, Beta called out, "Here, Vlad. I'm here."

Stormy closed her eyes and tugged harder against the ropes holding her ankles. They burned, scraping her skin. It didn't matter. She had to get away. Dracula had arrived. To kill her or to save her? There was no way to know. She kept her eyes trained on his approach and struggled against her bonds, no longer trying to be quiet or still.

And then he stepped into the light cast by all those dancing candles. His eyes sought her out, found her, but gave nothing away. No sign of affection. No hidden, reassuring smile. Nothing. He just looked at her, his eyes skimming her face, then the stakes that held her arms and her ankles. She stopped straining to pull free while his attention was on her.

Then he looked at Elisabeta, and this time his face *did* change. He couldn't hide his shock and horror at the way she looked.

"By the gods, Beta—"

"I know," she said. "I know how I look. I'm dying, Vlad."

He nodded, moved closer, and lifted a hand to touch her hideous face. Damn him.

Stormy tried not to see the tenderness in his eyes, but she saw it anyway. He was here, and his mission might very well be to take her life.

And yet she loved him.

God, she was sick. Hopeless. Possibly helpless. And love him or not, she wouldn't hesitate to slit his throat and let him bleed if it meant the difference between her own living and dying. Not for a second. Maybe she wasn't totally hopeless after all.

She tugged harder. And the stake at her feet moved just a little.

Vlad couldn't believe the change in Beta. Though he supposed, logically, the changes were happening in Brooke's body, not in Beta at all. Just to the body she happened to be occupying at the moment. She looked weak. And in pain. She was suffering, and it hurt him to see it.

Tempest, on the other hand, seemed fine. Her eyes flashed the same fire as always, and though there was a swollen, purplish lump on one side of her head, she was well. Strong. Whole. Frightened, though. And angry, too.

He'd felt her eyes searching his, probing, as if for some sign of his intent. She didn't trust him, then. No. Why would she?

"Did you bring the ring and the scroll?" Beta asked.

"Yes."

"Give them to me."

He glanced at Tempest. Her eyes pleaded with him, but he tore his gaze away, and took the ring and the scroll from his pocket.

Elisabeta snatched the scroll from his hand, unrolled it and bent to set it on the ground, using small rocks at the top and bottom to keep it from rolling up again. She positioned it between two candles, so she could see to read it; then, as her eyes raced over the lines, she spoke to him without looking up. "Put the ring on her, Vlad."

He looked at Tempest again.

She stared back at him, her eyes holding his powerfully as she shook her head slowly left, then right, then left again.

He hadn't moved. Beta swung her head toward him. "Do it, Vlad. We haven't much time. I...am weakening, even now." Then she moved to the first pot of herbs and touched one of the candles to the pile until it caught and blazed. She let it burn a moment, then bent close and blew it out. Smoke wafted then, thick and fragrant. And Beta moved on to the next pot, and the next.

Vlad forced himself to step past the ring of blazing candles. To kneel beside Tempest, between her outstretched arm and her legs. He held the ring in his fingers, and he moved it toward her hand.

She bent her wrist, flinching from his touch. "Don't do this, Vlad."

He looked at her, and saw the mistrust and hurt in her eyes. "I'm doing what I have to do." The smoke from the herbs was increasing, growing thick, swirling around them.

"Look, I get that you love her and not me, okay? I totally get that. You want to be with her, and you'll do whatever it takes to be with her."

"Stop it, Tempest."

"No, I won't stop it. This is my *life*. I don't blame you for wanting to be with the woman you love, Vlad, but it's not fair that I should have to surrender my life to make it happen."

He hesitated, the ring near the tip of her finger. He had to put it on her, but his hand was shaking.

From beyond him, Beta said, "And is it fair that I should have to die? Was it fair to keep me trapped between life and death for the past five hundred years?" She paused to draw a breath, exhausted, it seemed, just by the act of speaking. "One of us has to die, Tempest."

"One of us already did, Elisabeta. One of us *chose* to die, by her own hand. You made that decision. Be woman enough to deal with the consequences."

"Enough," Vlad said. But his voice was choked and shaky, even to his own ears. "It's enough. There's no point in arguing. The decision is made. What must be done, must be done." He clasped Tempest's wrist in his hand to hold it still.

She clamped her hand into a tight fist. "No! I won't let you do it."

"Open your hand, Tempest."

"No!"

Gods, he hated this. If emotional pain could kill, this would surely be the end of him. He stared into her eyes through the smoke that made his own water, and for one brief moment he let his heart show through. "Please, Tempest. Open your hand."

She held his eyes, tears pooling in her own. "Vlad?"

Trust me, just this one more time.

He didn't know if their bond was powerful enough to allow her to hear his thoughts. But he thought it must be, when slowly, her fist unclenched, her fingers unbending slowly. "Damn you for this, Vlad," she whispered. "Damn you. I love you."

"I'm sorry." He slid the ring onto her finger, then turned away, unable to meet her eyes for even a moment longer.

Elisabeta took his hand in hers and tugged him to the spot at the top of the circle of candles. "Here. You can read from the scroll here. Follow each instruction precisely."

Nodding, he knelt and bent to look at the words on the scroll, then turned to observe what Elisabeta was doing.

She was lying down, taking a position beside Tempest.

"Begin," she said.

"Don't do this to me, Vlad," Tempest begged.

Vlad ignored her, though it wasn't easy. Not when there were tears sliding from the corners of her eyes and down her face. "Beta, this ritual isn't going to work."

"Of course it will. Just begin, for the love of the gods. We haven't much time."

She lay there, eyes closed. He slid a look toward Tempest but didn't dare let his eyes linger on her. "No. It's worded in a way designed to release you from the bonds of the ring, into the body of the one who wears it. But you've already been released from the bonds of the ring into Brooke's body."

"We have to try, Vlad."

"I didn't come unprepared," he said. "I was afraid of exactly this problem, in fact. But I located another ritual, this one designed to do specifically what we need it to do."

Beta opened her eyes but didn't look at him. "And what is it that we need it to do?"

"Free your spirit from Brooke's body." He said it slowly. "Once we do that, *then* we can proceed with the original rite, the one to take you into Tempest's body."

Beta drew a deep and stammering breath. "I... see. And where did you get this ritual?" She tried to sit up, struggled, and Vlad quickly went to her side, gripped her shoulders and helped her.

"I stole it from the files of the Sisterhood of Athena. No one knows I have it." It was a lie. He'd stolen it not from the Sisterhood's files but from Rhiannon's pocket.

Once sitting upright, Beta leaned forward, bending over herself, hugging her waist. "Thank you, Vlad. I just...I'm not sure I—"

And before he knew what she had intended— the very instant the alarm in his mind began to warn him, in fact—he heard the explosion and felt the red-heat impale him. The gun barrel stabbed into his chest at the same moment she pulled the trigger, sending the bullet straight through him. The pain was blinding, and he sank to his knees to the sounds of Tempest's screams, blood gushing from his body.

Beta tore the ritual from his hand and moved toward the candlelight to read it. "I knew it," she rasped. "I knew it was a trick. This ritual would exorcise me! You...you were going to kill me!"

"No. Beta, no," Vlad said through clenched teeth. "I was going to free you."

"You were going to save me," Stormy whispered. "You...you chose me."

He met her eyes, though his vision was beginning to blur. "I made that choice long ago, Tempest. I love you. All this time, I have loved you."

"Bastard!" Beta shouted.

She crumpled the ritual Rhiannon had copied down for him, then held it to the flame of a candle until it caught and burned. Then she bent over the original sheet, the one with the ancient rite that would condemn Tempest to death, and she began to read the words. "Powers of the ancients and of the Underworld Gods, open the gates between life and death. Open the gates and take this one, this Tempest Jones. For her body belongs to me—Elisabeta Dracula."

Vlad lifted his head, knew he was growing weaker by the second. "It won't work, Beta. It won't work, not this way."

She paused to send him a hate filled glare. "How do I know you are not lying to me yet again, *print, ul meu?*"

"I swear it. I swear it on…on her life."

"Her life? Yes. She matters that much to you, doesn't she? That the most meaningful vow you can imagine is to swear on her life. It does not matter, Vlad. Her life is about to end."

"It won't work, I tell you. You'll both die if you go through with this."

"I am dead either way," she said. "Better I die trying to save myself than to simply give up. Better she die with me than I should die alone. She will never have you, Vlad."

"I have him now, Elisabeta," Stormy told her. "I've had him for sixteen years. Only I didn't know. I'm sorry I didn't trust you, Vlad."

"I gave you no reason to trust me. And yet you did, in spite of everything, when you let me put that ring on your finger."

"Shut up, both of you! You're making me sick!" Beta turned and moved to where Tempest lay, bending to clasp her ankles in a brutal grasp. *"Sînge la sînge! Minte la minte! Corp la suflet! Al t u la al meu!"* She shouted the words, and then she shouted them again and again.

Around her hands at Tempest's ankles, a silvery mist seemed to take shape.

"It is working," Beta whispered.

"No!" Vlad cried. "Stop this, Beta! I beg of you, stop it now!"

"Soul to soul. Mind to mind. Body to body. Yours to mine," she chanted. "Tempest, out! Elisabeta, in! By the powers of the Underworld, I will it so. Tempest, out! Go! Cross the veil! Do it now!"

The mist around Tempest's body began to spread up her legs, over her torso. It was like a thin shadow of Tempest, rising from her form as she lay there, wide eyed, thrashing and fighting to hold on. And now there was a similar shroud around Elisabeta.

"Hang on, Tempest!" Vlad cried. "Beta, don't do this! I beg of you!"

"Out, out, out!" Beta cried, her head tipping back now, her voice growing softer, her eyes taking on a glow not unlike that of a hungry vampire about to feed. "Guardians of the Underworld, take her now!"

Vlad used his remaining strength to rush at her, hitting her body and knocking her over onto her side. Her hands were wrenched free of Tempest's ankles, her chanting silenced. But as he lay there, struggling with the blinding, crippling pain, she wrestled free of him, got to her feet and, drawing the gun once more, pointed it at him.

Vlad felt hope desert him, and then it returned in a rush as he sensed Rhiannon's presence. She had followed him. Just as he had known she would. He turned his gaze toward where he sensed his dearest friend stood, just beyond the shadows. He felt her there, felt her waiting. He found her mind with his, nodded once. "Do what must be done."

And she spoke. "Now, Melina."

There was no sound other than Elisabeta's sudden shriek as her body jerked backward, away from Tempest. Stumbling, she landed on her side on the ground, gazing, stunned, at the dart that was embedded in her chest. She lifted trembling hands, grasped it and tore it free with a whimper of pain; then she tossed it angrily aside.

Melina stepped out of the shadows, a weapon in her hand. A gun made to shoot tranquilizer darts. Lupe stood beside with a gun of her own. A real one. It was Rhiannon who rushed forward, bending over

Vlad, pressing a large piece of cloth to the wound in his chest.

"Don't waste time with me. It's Tempest you should be attending," he cried. He stared at Stormy even as the mist that had been rising seemed to settle into her body once more. "Please, Rhiannon. Is she all right?"

Reluctantly, Rhiannon left him to crouch over Tempest, touching her, sensing her. She stroked a hand over her brow, then rose with a nod and returned to Vlad's side. "She'll survive. I'm not so certain about you." She lifted her eyes and looked at Melina, who was kneeling now beside Elisabeta. "What about her?"

Leaning close, Melina spoke softly. "Brooke? Brooke, are you there?"

A clawed hand shot upward and raked Melina's face. She rocked backward. Lupe jerked her weapon into position and fired a shot at Brooke's body, but the bullet only hit the ground beside her, spitting sand and soil with its impact. Beta jerked at the sound, then went still.

"Are you trying to kill her?" Melina shouted. She whirled on Lupe, snatching the weapon from her hands.

"Elisabeta is still inside her," Rhiannon said.

"It doesn't matter. We have the rite we need now, Rhiannon," Melina said softly. "The one you wrote for us. We know how to set Elisabeta free."

Vlad closed his eyes, moaned.

"What is it, Vlad?"

"I took the rite. I tried to use it myself, but Beta caught on. She burned it."

"No matter," Rhiannon said. "I knew it went missing—and hoped to the gods my guess that you had taken it was correct." She glanced at Melina. "You'll find another copy of the rite in the library desk at the manse. Use it."

"We will," Melina said. "Tonight. There's still plenty of time to get Brooke back to Athena House and perform the ritual. We'll take care of it. I promise you that." She got to her feet, and brushed herself off, then moved closer to Vlad, while Lupe removed handcuffs and shackles from a bag, and snapped them around Elisabeta's wrists and ankles.

Melina knelt beside him. "If you don't make it, I promise you, your love will be awaiting you on the other side. I'll see to it."

Vlad shook his head, glancing toward Tempest, who lay still, barely conscious now, her eyes unfocused and wet. "No," he said. "The one I love is here."

Melina nodded and turned to Rhiannon.

"Take her and be done with it," Rhiannon said. "I've work to do here."

"I hope…I hope we're okay now. You and me," Melina said to her.

"My issue has been with your organization, not with you, Melina. And that remains the case." She thinned her lips. "However, I will concede that the Sisterhood of Athena has a few…worthy members." Quickly Rhiannon gathered Brooke's ravaged body up into her arms. "I'll take her to the car for you." She shot a look back at Vlad. "Don't move. And for the sake of the gods, don't bleed out."

Vlad wished he could promise not to. Instead, he waited until she was out of sight and then dragged himself toward where Tempest lay. He pulled himself alongside her and then lay still, his head close to hers, one hand in her hair. He used what strength remained in him to free her hand from the rope that held it.

"Vlad?" she whispered. Her newly freed hand came up to cup his cheek.

"It's you, Tempest," he told her. "Not her. It's been you all along. I'm sorry it took me so long to tell you. But if I had revealed my heart, she would have known. I had to make her trust me in order to save you."

"Vlad, you're bleeding again." She turned to the side, rapidly freeing her other hand; then she sat up, untied her ankles and cradled his head in her lap.

"Please, just listen to me," he said. "There may not be much time. You were right all along. I barely knew Elisabeta. We met at a time of crisis, when neither of us had anything to live for. We clung to each other. But I didn't know her. You—I know you, Tempest. I knew you sixteen years ago. You are the woman I love. There can be no other. Nor has there ever been. Not really. Perhaps the reason I was drawn to Elisabeta so long ago was because she was foreshadowing of her spiritual descendant. Of you, Tempest. Only you."

"Vlad, we have to help you. You're…you're…"

"No, love. There's nothing you can do. Just tell me, please. Tell me you believe me this time. I came here to save you, not to hurt you."

"I believe you. And I love you, too, Vlad. I have all along. I've loved you for sixteen years."

He felt as if a weight had been lifted from his soul, and he smiled. "Thank you, Tempest." And then his eyes fell closed.

16

Rhiannon dropped to her knees beside Vlad, who lay still in Stormy's lap. She touched his face, and tears rained from her eyes. "My sire," she whispered. "My beloved friend, my preternatural father. Gods, how I hate to see you go."

"No!" Stormy shrieked the word, clutching Vlad's shoulders, shaking him. "He can't die. You can't just let him die. Rhiannon, we have to *do something!*"

"I…it's too late."

"No. No, it's not. Give him blood. Give him mine, and then we'll patch the wound and keep him alive until dawn comes and—"

"I'm sorry," Rhiannon said softly. A sob seemed to catch in her throat, and she averted her face. "You've no idea how sorry."

"Step aside, Rhiannon."

Stormy gasped at the deep voice that came from

the darkness. She'd heard no one approach, but then, she'd been entirely focused on Vlad. The man who stood there was dark, and exuded a palpable aura of strength and power. Stormy had seen him only once before, but she knew him. He was Damien—the once great king, Gilgmesh. He was the oldest, most powerful of them all. The only vampire alive older than Vlad himself. The first.

"Damien," Rhiannon whispered, rising to her feet. "How did you know?"

Stormy stared at the man. He looked stricken and went immediately to Vlad's side, kneeling there and clasping his hand. "Though it's been years since I've seen him, Iskur is my brother, in a way. Our connection is powerful."

"Iskur?" Stormy whispered.

"That was his name, before he adopted his new identity. It's the name of—"

"The Sumerian Stormy God," Stormy filled in. Tears filled her eyes to brimming as she gazed at Damien. "Can you help him, Damien?"

"I don't know. If I can't, there's no one who can." Damien rolled back his shirt sleeve, unfolded the pocketknife he carried and swiftly drew the blade across his wrist. Even as the blood pulsed from the wound, he moved lower.

"What are you doing? Aren't you going to…?"

"He's too far gone to drink, Stormy," Damien muttered. "I only hope my blood is powerful enough to reach him this way."

He held his wrist, wounded side down, over the wound in Vlad's belly. Stormy scrambled over the ground to tear the shirt away, giving him better access. But that gave her a horrifying glimpse of the bullet wound, and she had to close her eyes. It was too much. Too much.

"By the gods," Rhiannon whispered. "Stormy, look. Open your eyes and look."

Forcing herself to obey, Stormy opened her eyes and focused on Vlad again.

"Oh, God, what's happening?" There was mist, or steam of some kind, hissing and rising from the bullet wound as the blood trickled down into it. She'd never seen anything like this. Never even heard of anything like it. "What's happening, Damien?" she whispered.

"I'm unsure. I've never done this before, but it's the very method by which Utnapishtim gave me the gift of immortality. He was no vampire. His immortality was bestowed by the gods. He had no fangs, could walk about by daylight, exist on meat and vegetables. When he agreed to make me immortal, he sliced me open, right across the chest, then slit his own wrist and poured his blood into the wound." Damien's gaze was riveted to Vlad's face.

"And created a whole new race."

"I only hope…" He lowered his head, then lifted it again and shook it as if trying to shake away sleep.

"Enough, Damien," Rhiannon whispered. "You're weakening."

"Just a bit more," he said.

"You've given all you can," she told him, clutching his shoulder. "It will either work or it won't. Bleeding yourself dry won't make the difference."

He sank back onto his heels, head falling forward, a lock of his hair slipping over his eyes. Rhiannon gripped his arm, rapidly twisting a length of fabric around it and yanking the knot so tight that Stormy thought she would break his wrist. She realized a second later that the cloth had been torn from the hem of Rhiannon's own gown.

Vlad's wound was still hissing, steam still emanating from it, but dissipating now, until it finally vanished altogether. She stared at Vlad, watching his face, praying, hoping, *willing* him to live.

And then he moaned and blinked his eyes open. He was alive!

Vlad lay there, blinking and unfocused, clearly

confused. Stormy leaned over him, barely able to believe what she had just witnessed. "Vlad?"

He stared at her. "I didn't expect to be seeing you again, my love."

He lifted a hand, cupped her cheek, and she fell against him, sobbing in relief and holding him. "You're alive. God, Vlad, I thought I'd lost you."

"So did I." His arms came around her, and he held her close. "Perhaps...there's a chance for us after all, Tempest."

"There is," she whispered. "There has to be."

Then Vlad's gaze shifted to Damien's and widened. "My king," he whispered.

"Your brother and friend," Damien corrected. "I'm glad you have survived, Iskur."

"Survived?" Vlad's gaze turned inward for a moment. "I feel...empowered beyond reason. Something new is burning through my veins." He blinked as he took stock and sat up to stare at Damien. "You gave me your blood."

"And it did the job," Rhiannon said, reaching down to clasp Vlad's hand and draw him to his feet. "I suppose now that you have the blood of the first running in your veins, you really will be able to best me in a fight."

"I already bested you with my own, don't forget."

"Don't fool yourself, Vlad. I let you win that little battle."

He crooked a brow.

"You two fought?" Stormy asked.

"He demanded the ring and the scroll," Rhiannon said. "I wasn't sure whether he intended to use them to save you or to kill you."

"And you fought him? For my sake?"

"Briefly," Rhiannon said. "But don't get a swollen head, little mortal. In the end I decided to risk your life by trusting in my friend." She smiled very slightly and turned to Vlad. "I'm very glad you didn't let me down."

"I'm very glad you didn't fight too hard. I would have hated to have to hurt you."

"You'd have hated more what I would have done to you, had I truly had the will."

They held gazes for a moment, then Vlad shifted his to Stormy again. His eyes met hers and stayed.

Damien cleared his throat. "We should take our leave, Rhiannon. These two have things they need to…discuss."

Rhiannon nodded, reached up to hug Vlad, kissed his cheek, then released him. "There's a boat docked a mile back that way," she told him. "We'll take shelter there before sunrise." She looked at the sky. "You have several hours."

"Is it midnight yet?" Stormy asked. She'd let herself forget for a little while how limited her own time might be.

"Eleven-thirty," Damien told her. "Why?"

"We should leave them," Rhiannon said. "I'll explain on the way."

She sent Stormy a look of sympathy, encouragement and hope. Clearly she realized that if Melina and Lupe failed to free Elisabeta's soul from Brooke's body, Stormy might have only thirty minutes left to live. Then Rhiannon hooked her arm through Damien's and raced away, vanishing in a blur of darkness.

"Did you mean what you said?" Stormy asked Vlad. "That you feel more powerful then ever? You're really all right?"

His smile was slow and full of all sorts of promises. He cupped her face in his hands and kissed her mouth tenderly, but deeply and long. "Shall I show you?"

"Yes. Yes, Vlad. And hurry. Because if Melina and Lupe—"

"Shhh. They're not going to fail. We couldn't have triumphed over all of this only to lose everything now."

His fingertips brushed over her cheek, then her neck, and her tummy tightened in pure sexual need. She vowed not to think about what might happen when midnight came. She wouldn't ruin what might be her last time with Vlad by letting herself be distracted. If she had to die, she would die in his arms. And die happy.

He loved her.

He closed his arms around her, bending her backward and kissing her as if he would devour her whole.

"Vlad," she whispered. He was kissing her neck now.

"Don't tell me to stop."

"If you stop I'll stake you." She smiled up at him. "I was just wondering if we could relocate."

He lifted his head, his eyes glowing with passion and hunger. "Where do you want to be, Tempest?"

"The beach. The shore. In the sand. Not here, where—ugly things happened."

He nodded, and before she could stop him, he scooped her off her feet and began striding away from the trees and boulders toward the beach. "No more delays, Tempest. You're about to be ravaged by a vampire."

"By *the* vampire. Dracula himself. And not for the first time," she said, gasping as he bent his head to nuzzle her breasts right through the fabric of her blouse.

"Nor the last," he promised.

He carried her down onto the beach, but they didn't get very far. Just beyond an outcropping of rock that gave them a little privacy from the vantage point of the road.

Vlad lowered her to the grassy, stony ground, laying her there on her back. Then he darted away from her, into the surf, where the washed the remnants of Damien's blood from his belly. It took him only a moment. He was back at her side a heartbeat later, sinking to his knees in the sand beside where she lay.

"I love you," he told her.

"You'd have been stupid not to," she told him with a teasing smile.

"The stupidest vampire in history." Then he pushed her blouse up and attacked her breasts as if he couldn't wait for them. It was almost too much, too fast, the suckling and biting. She moved to push at his head, but he kept on, and she didn't want him to stop. Not really. So he didn't. He pushed her jeans down and impatiently removed his own.

She couldn't get enough of running her hands and then her lips over his chest. Oh, God, and his belly. Washboard abs she couldn't stop touching. It amazed her to see no wound where the bullet had torn through him. Only a small pink scar remained. "You're the most beautiful man I've ever seen," she whispered.

"Then no wonder I chose the most beautiful woman. I've waited for you, Tempest. Centuries, I've waited."

Vlad pushed her knees up and outward as he lowered himself between them, and he slid into her so naturally she knew he belonged inside her, so deeply he felt like a part of her.

Her brought her to screaming climax twice there on the beach before he let himself achieve release. And afterward he lay beside her, cradling her in his arms as if she were the most precious, most cherished, thing he'd ever held.

Stormy lay there in bliss. But it was still bittersweet. She knew they were both thinking about her mortality, though neither of them had spoken of it. Not yet. It wasn't yet midnight. Only a few ticks of the clock remained. But even if she didn't die tonight, there was still a dark future looming ahead of them, and she thought it was time, now, to bring it up.

"Vlad?"

"Hmm?"

"You know...even if Lupe and Melina are successful tonight, this can't last. I don't have the antigen. I can't become what you are. There is a formula that could extend my life...but there's no way to be sure it would work on me, or that I could even get hold of it."

He was quiet for a moment, and she felt his arms tighten a little, as if in response to the thought of ever letting her go. "I'll love you for your entire life. And even after that."

She let her head rest on his powerful chest, felt his fingers trailing in her hair. "I'll grow old, but you'll stay young."

"Not young, Tempest. The body doesn't age, but everything else does. I'm already old inside, though my body remains the age it was when I was changed over."

"And how old is that?"

He smiled at her. "Twenty."

Stormy closed her eyes fast and tight. "My God, I'm thirty-six. I'm robbing the cradle."

"I've been alive for thousands of years, Tempest. I'm the one robbing the cradle."

"Oh, I know that. But...physically, I mean, I'll age. And that's important, too."

"Not to me. I've spent the last few centuries believing myself in love with a dead woman, one who had no body at all, don't forget."

"I'll get wrinkles," she whispered.

"And I'll love you."

"My hair will go gray."

"And still I'll love you."

"My body will get flabby and saggy and—"

"And I'll love you all the more," he told her, kissing the top of her head.

She drew a deep breath, lifting her head a little so she could see into his eyes. "I'll die, Vlad."

He held her gaze steadily, intently. "Then maybe I'll know it's time for me to move on, as well."

"Vlad!"

He cupped her cheeks. "I don't want to talk about this now, Tempest. Not now. There will be time enough for all that later. Now, I just want to be with you. To experience the joy you've brought into my life. By the gods, do you have any idea how long it's been since I've felt this way?"

"What...way?"

"Happy, Tempest. Truly happy." He looked skyward and shook his head. "It's heaven. I'm in paradise because of you."

He kept on speaking, but Stormy stopped listening, because there was a sudden buzzing in her ears. In her head.

Frowning, she sat up and pulled her shirt on. It was long enough to cover her, so she didn't bother with the jeans, just got to her feet and looked around.

Vlad rose, his expression puzzled. He searched her face, spoke her name, but she could barely hear him because of the buzzing.

And then her vision started to close in, darkness surrounding her from all sides.

"What…?" she muttered, unsure if she said the word out loud, losing the rest of her question before she spoke it.

She saw a woman—and she recognized her. Elisabeta, looking the way she had in the portrait. It startled Stormy terribly at first. My God, had she come back to finish what she'd tried to begin?

But no, she didn't look menacing, or cruel. There was something frail about her, and fear in her eyes. And it hit Stormy all over again how much the young woman's face resembled her own. They could have been sisters. Maybe they were, in a way.

"Beta?" Stormy whispered.

"They're making me go!" Beta cried. "I don't want to go!"

The pain in her voice gripped Stormy's heart and

twisted, and in that moment she realized this Beta she was seeing wasn't physical. She was opaque, nearly transparent. Melina and Lupe must be performing the rite.

Stormy felt her throat tighten, her eyes well in empathy. "It's what we all do when we die, Beta," she told the frightened girl—for she was that, once again. Just a girl. Afraid and confused. "It's what we're supposed to do. Look, look behind you."

Beta turned slowly and saw what Stormy did. Beyond her, resting on the water, was a glowing, golden light. It had a texture to it like liquid gold, and it pulsed and called to her. There was something incredibly beautiful about it, something magnetic. It drew Stormy. She moved closer, involuntarily, and yet she wasn't afraid.

"It's beautiful," Beta whispered.

"Yes."

Beta paused, swallowed hard; then she closed her hand around Stormy's. "Will you walk with me?"

Stormy nodded and found she wanted to move closer to the glow. And as they drew near, something became visible within the light: a woman. She might have been a goddess or an angel, or the blessed virgin. But she felt much more personal than any of those. And she looked…

"She looks like us," Stormy whispered, glancing at her companion.

Beta had tears streaming down her cheeks. The woman seemed to be speaking to her, but Stormy couldn't hear. The golden woman's expression was incredible; serene and loving and transcendent.

"I know," Beta said to her in reply. "I know I was supposed to come sooner. But I was trapped. And then I was afraid."

The woman lifted a hand, holding it out to Elisabeta.

Beta turned to Stormy and blinked back her tears. "I understand now," she said softly.

"I don't. Who is she, Beta?"

"She's…she's us. She's you and me and all the women we've ever been. She's all of us. Everyone we ever were or will be. She's…our higher self."

Stormy looked at the beautiful woman standing within the golden light with her arms reaching out, and she heard herself whisper, "I love her."

As she watched, Elisabeta pulled free of her hand and moved forward. And then the woman opened her arms and embraced her, and it seemed that Elisabeta was absorbed into the light.

Stormy was awestruck, and then she moved closer, too, reaching out her hands.

The woman met her eyes. "Not you, Tempest. Not yet. Not for a long, long time. But at least now you will be complete. The parts of you that were missing, shall now be restored."

She held out her hands, and a beam of that golden light surged from her palms and hit Stormy square in the chest. It was like being hammered by heat and light. It knocked her backward as surely as a speeding train would have done. And then the light faded, and she was alone in the dark, yet unafraid. And she felt…wonderful.

Vlad carried Tempest aboard the yacht in a state of panic. "Rhiannon! Damien! Help her!" he shouted.

Rhiannon raced forward, meeting him at the hatch that led below, Damien close behind her. "What happened?" Rhiannon demanded. She took his arm and tugged him through the hatch, down the stairs and into one of the cabins. She led him to a small sofa, where he laid Tempest down and bent over her. He stroked her hair, her face.

"I don't know," Vlad said quickly. "She was fine—and then she just suddenly started walking toward the sea. She was…talking to someone—Elisabeta, I think. She kept saying her name. And then she just flew backward, landing on her back on the ground." He pressed his hands to his head. "Gods, is it past midnight? Did those Athena women fail to set Beta free? Is she dying now?" He closed his eyes. "It can't be. Gods, I can't lose her now."

Rhiannon bent closer, touching Stormy, seeking, Vlad knew, for signs of life in her. She was alive, he knew that. But when Rhiannon stood rigid and wide eyed and whispered "By the gods!" he was frightened, even more than he had been.

"What, Rhiannon? What is it? By the gods, tell me I haven't waited all this time for her only to lose her again so soon."

"Lose her?" Rhiannon blinked her long lashes several times. "Don't you feel it? Vlad, don't you smell it on her?"

Damien moved closer and whispered, "The antigen. Belladonna."

Rhiannon met his eyes and nodded, then shifted her focus to Vlad.

And he felt it. He sensed it the way a vampire could always sense one of The Chosen. That energy was coming from *her*—from Tempest.

He lifted his eyes to those of the vampiress he'd made. "But…how can it be?"

Even as he asked the question, Tempest blinked her eyes open and whispered his name, drawing his gaze back to her. She smiled at him. "She's all right," Tempest said. "Elisabeta is all right."

He could only frown at her, searching her face.

"Melina and Lupe must have done the ritual. They must have freed her. I saw her, Vlad. I walked with her. God, it was so beautiful. There was this woman, all clothed in golden light. Or maybe she *was* the light. And Beta went into her arms and they just…they sort of melded."

Vlad sank onto the sofa to gather her gently into his arms. "I'm glad if Beta has found peace. But, Tempest, are *you* all right?"

Her smile grew brighter. "I'm wonderful. Better than ever. That woman, she…gave me something. She filled me with…something."

Rhiannon put a hand on Vlad's shoulder, repeating slowly what she had told him before. "When we die, our souls merge with our collective soul, our higher self. That being is our source. All that we are melds and combines to generate the next soul and the next, and the one after that. Stormy has been missing a part of herself. The part that was Elisabeta. The part that had never melded with her source. She has that part now."

"And that part includes…?" he asked.

"The Belladonna Antigen," Rhiannon whispered.

Stormy shifted her gaze from Vlad's—though it seemed to take a great effort—to Rhiannon's. "What?"

"You're one of The Chosen now, Stormy," Rhiannon told her. "You can become one of us, if and when you choose it."

She shot her eyes back to Vlad's. "Is it true?"

He nodded. "I don't pretend to understand it the way a priestess of Isis does," he said. "But yes—you have the antigen now. And it's not weakened or diluted or different in you the way it was in Brooke's body. Perhaps because it was meant to be in you as it was never meant to be there."

"Then…" She blinked and searched his eyes. "Then we can be together? Forever?"

"If you want it, Tempest."

She slid her arms around his neck and hugged him close. "I do. You know I do."

Rhiannon smiled slowly. "Oh, may the gods have mercy on us all."

Stormy shot her a questioning look.

"Well, do you blame me? As a mortal you're almost unbearably full of yourself and…*feisty*. I detest feisty."

"You *exemplify* it," Damien said with a chuckle.

"No, I exemplify arrogance," she said. "And with good reason. It's not the same thing."

"I stand corrected."

"She'll drive us all mad," she said, turning as she and Damien walked to the cabin door. But she glanced back, caught Stormy's eye and winked.

Stormy took it as a "welcome to the family" sort of gesture.

Vlad walked her to the upper deck, where the full moon hung very low in the sky. It would set before too long, and the sun would rise. Vlad removed all her clothing, and all his own, and then he brought her legs around his waist and entered her. And while she moved over him, he sank his teeth into her throat and drank her very essence into him. He drank until she trembled, until she weakened, until she sank so completely into his arms that it was if they were one. And then he jabbed a blade into his own neck, gently, just piercing the jugular with the tip, and he brought her face to him there.

She didn't move until the blood touched her lips. And then she did. She parted her lips and tasted, and then she latched on and drank, and drank, and drank. He moved inside her as she did, and he bent his head to drink more of her.

They were locked that way, mouths to throats, bodies mated, straining and moving and striving. And he thought that by the time he released his seed into her that their blood had mingled several times over.

She went limp in his arms, and he picked her up, and carried her below into the cabin again. A bed and blankets waited. He lowered her into the bed and climbed in beside her.

"Listen!" she said suddenly. "Do you hear it?"

"What, my love?"

"The ocean! I can hear it…."

"Well, we are in a boat," he said with a smile, though he knew exactly what she meant.

"Oh, it's different. I can hear…the fish swimming past. And I can smell it—not like before—I can taste it, but it's…"

He nodded. "I know. Your senses are heightened, all of them, a hundred times what they were before. And soon, perhaps, a thousand times. You'll be powerful, Tempest. As strong as Rhiannon. Perhaps stronger."

"Stronger than Rhiannon?"

He nodded. "Perhaps. In time. My blood is old. Only one vampire lives who's blood is older, and you've got his running in your veins, too, just as I do."

"Damien," she whispered.

"Gilgamesh," he confirmed.

She sighed and snuggled close to him. "I don't care how strong I am, Vlad."

"You're a terrible liar, Tempest."

She smiled and kissed his chest. "All right, I care. I'm going to love being powerful. And I'll taunt Rhiannon about that for the rest of our lives and enjoy every minute of it." She almost laughed at the notion. She liked the teasing, almost friendly relationship she seemed to have developed with the vampiress she'd once considered the haughtiest bitch of the bunch. "But more than that," she whispered, returning her attention to where it belonged, "more than anything else, Vlad, I'm going to love being with you."

"You'll be with me," he promised her. "Forever."

He kissed her deeply, and when he broke the kiss, she curled into his arms and knew she would still be there when they awoke. And she would be again and again, every sunset, for the rest of eternity.